PORTRAITS OF POWER

PORTRAITS OF POWER

An Introduction to Twentieth-Century History

Through the Lives of Seventeen Great Political Leaders

by

S. E. AYLING

NEW   YORK

BARNES & NOBLE, INC.

PUBLISHERS · BOOKSELLERS · SINCE 1873

First published in Great Britain, 1961
under the title *Twelve Portraits of Power*

New edition with five additional chapters
Published, 1963, by BARNES & NOBLE, INC.
by special arrangement with George G. Harrap & Co., Ltd.

Introduction © 1963 by BARNES & NOBLE, INC.

L. C. Catalogue Card Number: 63–20011

Printed in the United States of America

Preface to the Second Edition

This book, in a shorter version, first appeared in 1961 under the title *Twelve Portraits of Power,* being an attempt to convey to non-specialist students a picture of some vital chapters of the history of the twentieth century through brief biographies of twelve of its leading figures. The period it spanned was largely the no-man's-land between the 'modern history' of the examination syllabuses and the current events of the newspapers.

The hope expressed in the original preface that the book might appeal to readers outside school or college has apparently to some extent been realized. A second edition has been made the occasion to bring some of the chapters more nearly up to date, and to include five further portraits—of Nehru, Khrushchev, de Gaulle, Salazar, and Franco. Of the twelve statesmen of the original book, only three were still in active politics; but all the five now added are currently prominent figures on the international scene. Such close following upon the heels of history has, I well know, its dangers; and I cannot hope altogether to escape a kick or two from the hoofs of controversy—any more than I can expect to avoid being here and there left behind by the gallop of events. But these are risks that must be taken, unless we are to sit down until the dust has quite settled. I wonder, in any case, if historians are further away from a 'final,' 'objective' judgment upon Stalin, or Hitler, or even a still living figure such as Salazar, than upon Napoleon, or Cromwell, or King John.

Acknowledgment is due to the following authors and publishers for permission to quote from the works stated: Frances Perkins and Hammond, Hammond and Co. (*The Roosevelt I Knew*); John Gunther and Hamish Hamilton (*Roosevelt in Retrospect*); Sir Fitzroy Maclean, Peter Townsend, and Jonathan Cape (*Eastern Approaches* and *China Phoenix*); Alan Bullock and Odhams Press (*Hitler, a Study in Tyranny*); André Deutsch (Von Papen's *Memoirs*); B. R. Nanda and Allen and Unwin (*Mahatma Gandhi*); Irfan Orga and Robert Hale (*Phoenix Ascendant*); Robert Guillain and Secker and Warburg (*The Blue Ants*); Wolfgang Leonhard and William

Collins, Sons and Co. (*Child of the Revolution*); Hollis and Carter (*Stalin*, by L. Trotsky); Isaac Deutscher and the Oxford University Press (*Stalin*); Sir Winston Churchill and Cassell and Co. (*Into Battle*); Lawrence and Wishart (*Ten Days That Shook the World*, by John Reed). Attempts made to locate the copyright holders of Count Ciano's *Diary* proved unsuccessful. My more general debt to these books and many others will be apparent. Perhaps I should specially mention *Tito of Yugoslavia*, by K. Zilliacus; *Winston Churchill*, by Virginia Cowles; *Roosevelt: the Lion and the Fox*, by J. M. Burns; *Nehru, a Political Biography*, by M. Brecher; *Mahatma Gandhi*, by H. L. S. Polak, H. N. Brailsford, and Lord Pethick-Lawrence; *The Spanish Labyrinth*, by Gerald Brenan; and *The Spanish Civil War*, by Hugh Thomas.

I should like to thank Mr L. M. Wallace for reading proofs, and Mr L. R. Fennelly for much valuable advice and criticism.

S. E. A.

Contents

Maps

PORTRAITS OF POWER

Introduction

On the last page of the last portrait in this book, Mr. Ayling reveals his personal judgment. Of Nehru he writes: "Few other great national leaders have sat in the seat of power so long, or enjoyed such undisputed supremacy; perhaps, even now, few combine so many impressive qualities. In an intolerable and ranting world, his, on the whole, has been the cool voice of sanity." This is the cool voice of the sane Englishman talking, as it talks throughout the book. Although the author has not attempted to draw lessons from the lives of the seventeen twentieth-century political leaders whose portraits he paints, he has selected his details with great care for the light that they throw on each character. The book is therefore extremely informative. The writing is always clear, incisive, selective and—one must repeat—eminently sane.

One might add that after the passionately partisan writing of some authors when dealing with "the other side" in international affairs, the pre-eminent fairness of Mr. Ayling is a refreshing tonic. Not that he lacks moral convictions. But these are based not on emotional patriotism or consciousness of rectitude but rather on a judicious appreciation of the aims and deeds of his protagonists. Stalin, for example, comes off noticeably better than Hitler (although due account is taken of Stalin's crimes and cruelty) mainly because of his undoubted courage and leadership during the war. Even Hitler is conceded political genius, though Mr. Ayling views this genius, which consisted of a devilish ability to take advantage of his opponents' weaknesses, as wholly evil. For Mussolini, on the contrary, he has nothing but contempt as a "Sawdust Caesar," with no relieving human virtues, and neither genius nor courage.

All of Mr. Ayling's readers would probably have liked to see others in his gallery, although these are a good selection. I myself could have wished that he had included even one of the Latin American leaders of lesser magnitude, but as powerful in his own domain as any of the seventeen. Trujillo, for example, would be a most instructive character to place beside them, or Gomez of

Venezuela, or even Batista. Such a portrait might have served to illuminate the world of Latin America, and its essential difference from Europe or North America. Also valuable would be a sketch of Canada's Mackenzie King, that too little-known figure who held power longer than any other English-speaking statesman in this century. Only Franklin D. Roosevelt is here from this side of the Atlantic, a good solid portrait which includes the essentials, but perhaps is more useful for Europeans, who did not know him as well as we. However, there must be few Americans who are familiar with the remaining sixteen. Even for those who are, it is salutary to be given a view at one time of all these men, allowing us to see for ourselves what kind of qualities have been needed to rule in our twentieth-century world.

The pre-eminent quality common to the best and worst of these men, the "strong men" and the democrats, was the ability to seize an opportunity. Without this it is certain that they would have formed the debris of history, not been its masters. Some played a large part in creating the opportunity; others grasped it when it was presented. Some came to power legally, and their rule was, at least in a narrow sense, legitimate. It is well to be reminded that not only the statesmen in the democracies belong to this category, but also Adolf Hitler and Benito Mussolini, though both employed violence and threats to persuade existing authority that they must be allowed to rule. Lenin, Mao Tse-tung, Kemal Atatürk, Nasser, and Franco won their power through revolution and civil war; Salazar, as the result of a military coup planned and executed by others. Tito earned his right to rule by his effective resistance to the Germans, as well as by eliminating his competitors in their joint struggle. Stalin and Khrushchev succeeded their predecessors under a system which did not permit of an orderly transfer of power; they won power by intrigue and violence and continued to hold it by the same means.

The great majority of these leaders came from humble beginnings and were self-made. The exceptions were Roosevelt, Churchill, and Nehru, all of whom came from wealthy and distinguished families. Gandhi's father and grandfather, though not wealthy, had both been chief ministers of their tiny unimportant state of Porbandar. For India this background constituted at least some privilege. De Gaulle, whose father was a professor, and whose forebears were military men, was able to go to military school and make a career in the army, as did Kemal Atatürk and Nasser (the son of a peasant who rose to the position of postmaster). Lloyd George and Lenin were the sons of village schoolmasters; Mussolini was the son of a blacksmith, Stalin of a bootmaker, Hitler of a minor customs official, Mao Tse-tung of a rice farmer. Tito, Salazar, and Khrushchev were sons of peasants. Among these it may be noted that only Lloyd George reached his position of power because his neighbors chose him as their spokesman and representative. The others, with the exception of Salazar (who was chosen as a civilian efficiency expert by the incompetent military) all imposed themselves on their contemporaries by intrigue and violence.

This predominance of self-made men who came to power by illegal means serves to point the contrast between our century and those that preceded it. In earlier centuries some Chinese revolutionaries rose from the ranks of the common people and founded their own dynasties; the Mameluke sultans of Egypt were descendants of Turkish slaves; here and there an occasional adventurer established himself as ruler. Common soldiers in the later centuries of the Roman Empire could aspire to the purple and occasionally won it. But throughout Western civilization until Napoleon, only in the Church could the self-made man hope to achieve power—in spite of the fact that violence and warfare have been endemic in Western civilization from its beginning.

A study of the men who have come to power in this century not only confirms the general belief that ours is a revolutionary age but also raises the natural question: Why is it revolutionary? It would seem to emerge from this study that the major causes are the weakening of previously stable institutions and the widespread refusal of ordinary men to be bound by a tradition which to them does not appear to meet the needs of the time. The violence generally characteristic of these new leaders has been engendered by the failure of the upholders of tradition to move forward with the changing times and by what Toynbee calls the "intractability of institutions."

Faced by the array of self-made rulers presented to us in this book, we Americans may naturally wonder why it is that we have hitherto been free from them. The mobility of our own social and political life contrasts strongly with the relative immobility in most other countries. The type of "strong man" who has succeeded elsewhere has surely not been missing in our own society. Is there something in our own institutions—and perhaps in the institutions of the other democratic nations—that has in our case saved us from having other revolutions than our first? Or has the "log cabin to president" tradition, though seldom observed in practice, taken care of our potential revolutionaries? It remains not impossible for a son of sharecroppers to reach the summit of power, though it becomes increasingly unlikely. Our last contender from this class was Huey Long, the "Kingfish" of Louisiana. But if he had not been assassinated could he ever have hoped to become president? (Could Joseph McCarthy if he had not been cut down at the height of his power?)

The answer seems to be No—though if there had been no New Deal and if the Great Depression had deepened further instead of slowly righting itself, Huey Long might have widened his circle of admirers. But it remains true that our institutions would not have presented an insuperable obstacle to his presidential ambitions. If then he had been elected president, could he have acted as a dictator, European style? Here, and the answer is of supreme relevance to this inquiry, the answer must surely be No. The built-in checks and balances of the Constitution would have prevented him from working his will. Only one-third of the Senate would have been elected in the year he became president, and it would have been extremely unlikely that *all* of that third would have been his supporters. His presidential program could have been blocked at every turn. Congress, for example, has the power to hamstring the President's program by withholding funds. Indeed, it may be argued that Huey Long enjoyed more power as a senator than he would have had available as president. Roosevelt was elected president four times in succession; but he never wielded a tithe of the power of, say, Stalin, Mao Tse-tung, or even Franco or Salazar. A revolution of the dimensions of the Turkish revolution under Kemal Atatürk would be quite impossible in this country by *legal* means. It would be at least as difficult by illegal means. Though the president is commander in chief it is difficult to believe that the armed forces, made up not of professional soldiers, but mostly of ordinary citizens, would continue to obey him against the wishes of Congress and the courts. As long as the United States is at peace, or engaged in the kind of war we have known hitherto, there is almost no chance that a dictator could come to power, or an armed uprising succeed.

But it is far from difficult to imagine that in the event of a nuclear holocaust this situation would change. Or if we were losing a war, were invaded, or were in danger of invasion, the armed forces might come to regard themselves as the only group capable of winning a war being bungled by civilian leadership. In such circumstances even the common conscript soldier might come to trust his officers more than he trusted his civilian leaders. The president and Congress might be physically powerless against weapons in the hands of determined soldiers. If confidence were lost in the ability of president, Congress, and the courts to protect us from military or economic disaster, then a more radical leadership might be demanded.

Such conditions were present in almost every country where the self-made rulers whose lives are described in this book prevailed. Hitler and Mussolini rose to power because the governments that they replaced could neither govern effectively nor solve economic problems—the Great Depression in Germany and the post World War I depression in Italy. The regular armed forces could have destroyed these men and suppressed their extra-legal militia—if they had wished. But they distrusted their own civilian leaders and were not entirely unsympathetic to the aspirations and professed purposes of the would-be leaders.

Franco in Spain and Salazar in Portugal likewise became rulers as the result of the weakness of the governments that they succeeded. In Spain the republican government had been in existence for only five years, had established no traditions, and commanded support only from the least powerful sector of the population. The Portuguese republican government had ruled so feebly during its sixteen years of life that there also no stable institutions existed to overcome. (Portugal was spared a civil war like Spain's because she had at the time no classes willing to fight for the deposed government.)

Other leaders came to power as the result of losing wars and foreign domination. Kemal Atatürk in Turkey, Lenin in Russia, and Tito in Yugoslavia took over authority following the defeat of their countries in warfare. In China, Chiang Kai-shek's government had not been able to recover sovereignty over the whole country since the years of warfare against the Japanese and Mao Tse-tung took advantage of the government's weakness following this long, largely losing war. In the Middle East, Nasser headed a movement against a corrupt monarchy, established by foreigners, which had little support inside Egypt.

It can therefore be seen that the two major conditions for the establishment of "strong-man" rule are: (1) the failure of a legitimate civil government to cope with its problems, above all its failure to govern; and (2) the collapse of all civil government, as in a losing war.

In France when de Gaulle came to power the conditions were subtly different, and for this reason the case is especially instructive. France, it is true, had been compelled to submit to dictatorial rule during World War II. However, this change was not a true revolution but the result of military defeat by the Germans. The democracy had been restored after the war, but the constitution of the Fourth Republic had been so framed that the executive lacked power to govern effectively. As a consequence by 1958 the French had lost confidence in the ability of their leaders to bring the Algerian war to an end. The military coup that brought de Gaulle to power in that year resulted in the establishment of the Fifth Republic under a constitution that gave much, perhaps overmuch, power to the executive. It also placed the power to change the constitution itself in the hands of the executive, as well as the legislature. It is therefore not impossible that a kind of dictatorship could be established in France by legal means. Nevertheless de Gaulle came to power by impeccably legal means, and he has since ruled legally—though the legality of a recent change in the constitution providing for the direct election of the president has been widely questioned. The major consequence of the military coup and the threats of violence that persuaded the civil authorities to recall de Gaulle from his self-imposed retirement has been the establishment of a government that can really govern—thus in effect obviating the need for an extra-legal dictatorship.

If we range further and consider other "strong-man" governments elsewhere the evidence of basic economic and political causes is even clearer. In an earlier century Napoleon came to power because of the weakness of the government of the Directory, and the French Revolution itself was in large measure due to the bankruptcy of the royal government and its failure to cope with its problems. Few Latin American governments today have seriously begun to solve their problems; in the absence of any tradition, civil government has always been at the mercy of the military. But even military rulers cannot govern exclusively by force; and either a military man, or a leader put in power and supported by the military, has been the norm for Latin American governments ever since they freed themselves from Spain. In the East, Ngo Dinh Diem became the ruler of South Viet-Nam as the result of a prolonged war with the French, while Ayub Khan became ruler of Pakistan and Ne Win of Burma because of the failure and corruption of the civilian governments.

The rise of strong-man governments in our day is thus to be viewed as the reaction of a determined group of dissidents under a strong leader to a set of circumstances which were none of their making, but which they had the ability to exploit to their own advantage—and sometimes to the advantage of their country. The set of circumstances may include unsolved economic problems, the result of the world-wide economic revolution which has been in progress since the eighteenth century, and which in our own century has been making its effects felt far beyond the countries of its gestation. Whether or not economics is involved—and the case of France, which was economically booming when de Gaulle came to power, suggests that economic failures are not necessarily present—there is governmental weakness which the dissidents find, or pretend to find, intolerable. They begin by conspiracy and intrigue, win allies who are of the same mind, then by their determination succeed in overthrowing a government already in the process of disintegration. Not one of these strong men overthrew a stable government with a tradition of legitimate rule. Indeed, I find it difficult to discover a single case in all history of a successful conspiracy to overthrow such a government. Usurpers have ousted legitimate governments in palace conspiracies but thereafter have continued the traditions of government established by their predecessors. In such cases there has been no revolutionary change— only a change in governing personnel.

These reflections suggest that in our age too few of the world's governments have established any tradition, that too few of the newly established governments have been able to cope with their economic and political problems, and that wars have brought to ruin many of the traditional and long-lived forms of government. On the other hand, those governments which have established a tradition and are making a serious effort to cope with their problems may have little to fear from conspiracies designed to overthrow them.

All the strong men described in this book provided a more stable and efficient government for their countries on coming to power— or they would have been long forgotten and found no place in these pages. But it is also noteworthy that only one, Kemal Atatürk, has so far handed over power peaceably to a successor and begun what may prove to be a tradition. Hitler's and Mussolini's regimes died with them; Franco, Salazar, Tito, and Mao Tse-tung are all over seventy and are reluctant to retire. In the Soviet Union a new system was indeed created, but it did not include any provision for a smooth and peaceable succession. At the death of Lenin the government was still far from stable. His successors, Stalin and Khrushchev, reached supreme power by triumphing over their competitors through intrigue followed by violence. This pattern is brought out clearly in the book in three of its best portraits. It is difficult indeed to see how Khrushchev, who is now in power, if less securely than his predecessors, can hand it over peaceably, without the development of the customary lethal competition. If he can create a tradition by the manner in which he finally quits office he may have done his country a greater service—and perhaps even a greater service to the world—than any he performed in his lifetime. But the very nature of the Soviet system, and especially its secretiveness, militates against the possibility. Kemal Atatürk achieved his success by permitting the existence of real political parties, including an opposition. After his death the parties were allowed to vote for their candidates, thus at least beginning a tradition of democracy. And in spite of a recent interlude of military rule during which the former prime minister was hanged for "violating the constitution," the system has hitherto proved to be durable.

A study of the book along the lines I have suggested in this introduction will lead inevitably, in my opinion, to the recognition of the superiority of the democratic system as the only truly stable *form* of government, even though under the system individual governments may be weak and unstable and hence achieve less at a particular period than the rule of a strong man might have done. However, the book reminds us, though this warning is never made explicit by the author, that in the wings may be waiting the strong man ready to take over if the democratic governments are unable to govern. I think it salutary for all democratic governments to be aware of this possibility—especially the more conservative and tradition-bound among them.

The supreme virtue of the democratic system is that it makes possible the transfer of power to younger and more effective hands without a coup d'etat and without civil war. The three great democratic leaders in the book, David Lloyd George, Winston Churchill, and Franklin Delano Roosevelt, were all cast up by the democratic process at a time of crisis. Lloyd George at a crucial moment abandoned his party leader and joined with those who were ready to unite with him in fighting the war according to his own ideas. There was a Cabinet reshuffle, and he replaced his former prime minister, all well within the limits of legality. Neville Chamberlain's failures had been such that in 1940 he was impelled to resign, to be replaced by his strongest critic, Churchill, without even the necessity of a new election. Roosevelt, who had won a reputation as governor of New York, was chosen president in the ordinary course of events at a time when his capacity was still largely untested. He rose to the occasion during the Depression and again during World War II and was thereafter invincible in presidential elections. Perhaps this was good luck for America; it was certainly a triumph for our democratic system. If he had failed from 1933 to 1936 the electorate could have chosen another leader and won another chance to solve urgent problems.

I have left Gandhi and Nehru to the last, since the conditions for their rise to power were exceptional and are unlikely to be repeated. Though Gandhi, for reasons which are very well explained in this book in what I regard as the best of Mr. Ayling's portraits, never himself became the leader of his country after independence, his chosen friend and collaborator Jawaharlal Nehru became prime minister under a system inherited from the British. In a curious way Gandhi's life also demonstrated the strength not of Indian democracy but of British. From the beginning of his agitation for self-government he always had supporters in England. It was humanly and politically impossible for the British to execute him, as he would no doubt have been executed by a Hitler or a Stalin, or perhaps by any of the violent strong men discussed in this book, if they had ruled an Indian empire. Gandhi had the remarkable faculty of being able to place the British in the position either of behaving like tyrants—which they did not wish to appear, even to themselves—or of giving in to him against their own better judgment. In 1920 the British had no intention of yielding up the "brightest jewel in their Crown." When General Dyer fired on the unarmed Indians at Amritsar in 1919 he intended to teach the "natives" a lesson they would not quickly forget. But it was he who was dismissed from the service, and his victims and their compatriots who triumphed, compelling the British to change their mind about the future of India. The real hero was the British conscience, which Gandhi thereafter never permitted to sleep. And when the British left, they bequeathed to the Indians a parliamentary democratic system which the English-educated Nehru has managed so long that he has perhaps begun a tradition in India which he in turn can bequeath to his successors.

Few of us will be familiar with all these men of power. We may know vaguely of the lives of most of them. Mr. Ayling has performed a service in bringing them all before us in this gallery, in a book which is still of manageable size. Here we have in a small compass much of the raw material for reflections on the nature of power and leadership in the modern world, though we need to fill in much from our own knowledge, especially of the full political circumstances which it was impossible to record in the book.

The author's interest is in the lives of these men; and in telling us of their lives, he has, I hope, stimulated us to think of what they had in common and what made it possible for them to rule in the twentieth century. This is the work we have to do for ourselves, each according to his own knowledge and understanding.

STEWART C. EASTON
Former Associate Professor of History
City College, New York

1

David Lloyd George
(1863–1945)

Lloyd George was the first son of a humble home to become Prime
Minister of Britain. He was, with Churchill, one of the two
foremost British statesmen of this century; Churchill, the duke's
grandson, Lloyd George, the poor Welsh orphan. Both of them were
war leaders of sterling energy and courage, but of the two Lloyd
George's impact was greater on the purely domestic scene. Between
1900 and 1914 he pioneered a new radicalism that laid the foundations of the Welfare State, defied the power of the aristocracy, vanquished the House of Lords, completed the parliamentary enfran-
chisement of men, and for the first time gave women the vote. Yet
this man who entered Parliament under Gladstone's leadership in the
high summer of Liberalism, and remained to perform for it so many
notable tasks in its fruitful autumn, proved to be the last Liberal
Prime Minister. He left a Party split and exhausted, ground between
the upper millstone of the Conservative Party—which had good
reason to dislike him—and the nether millstone of the Labour Party,
emerging as the champion of the working classes, which found no
reason to like him. Lloyd George's talents were not without flaw,
nor was his record without reproach, but no British statesman of
this century has left a greater mark on the fortunes of his country.

He may be thought of both as the product of the social ferment of
his age and as part-producer of it—for history makes men, but men
too make history. It was an age when old conceptions were giving
place to new at an ever-increasing pace. Trade unions were thrusting forward the claims of the working class to higher wages and
better conditions. New elementary and secondary schools were for
the first time providing universal education. New modes of travel
like the bicycle, the cheap omnibus, and (soon) the motor-car were
rapidly widening the horizons of ordinary men and women—women
especially, and for the first time they began effectively to demand
equality with men in legal, political, and even economic status. The
age of the landed aristocrat was dying. Ever since the first Industrial
Revolution and the early agitation for the reform of Parliament it

had been increasingly challenged by the trading and working classes, but it had lingered powerfully, especially away from the towns. Now it was facing the final assault, which Lloyd George led.

He was a Welshman, and he was brought up among the poor; and these two facts governed all his early actions and accounted for his early reputation: the champion of the little man and of the little nation. His father, an elementary schoolmaster, had died when young David was only eighteen months old, and his mother had sold up and gone off to live with her younger brother, Richard Lloyd, a shoemaker, who was also pastor of a minority Baptist community known as the Disciples of Christ; a hero of an uncle, a more-than-father to the growing and gifted child. The workshop adjoining his grey stone cottage in the little village of Llanystumdwy (a few miles from Criccieth) was much more than a workshop; it was a kind of village debating society, a social and political club—one might almost say a village university, for the Welsh were less afraid of learning than the English, and labourers were not ashamed even of recitals of Welsh poetry. Richard Lloyd, being an ardent Liberal, a passionate Nonconformist, and a man of proud and bold indepen‐dence, was inevitably something of a rebel in the Llanystumdwy of those days; for the village, like most of the villages of Wales, was mainly Liberal in politics and overwhelmingly Nonconformist in religion, while the men of authority were Conservative and Anglican. Young David read Macaulay, Gibbon, Carlyle, and the Bible from his uncle's shelves; he was well taught at the village school, which, however, belonged to the enemy, the Anglicans; he was baptized in the stream beside the chapel at the age of twelve; he played with the sons of farmers who were evicted by the Tory squires for voting Liberal in the election of 1868—the last before the secret ballot; he even organized an unsuccessful schoolboy rebellion against reciting the Creed and Catechism before the squire and parson on Ash Wednesday. How could such a boy, with such an uncle, in such a village, grow up other than a Radical Liberal, a rebel against the Tory-Anglican powers, and a passionate complainant against the wrongs of Wales?

A career had to be found worthy of him. Doctoring did not attract him, and in any case involved too much expense; the ministry of the Church of England was unthinkable, and that of the Baptists largely unpaid. There remained the law. So Richard Lloyd coached his brilliant young nephew in all the subjects necessary for the Pre-liminary Law Examinations, even where (as in French and Latin) this meant learning them simultaneously himself by dictionary and primer—a touching instance of devotion. Together mentor and pupil fought their way up the tangled slopes of learning; Richard Lloyd paced anxiously round Liverpool while young David took his examinations. A Portmadoc firm of solicitors found him a place while he worked for his final Law Society examination, but when in 1884 he passed it, he refused their offer to put him in charge of their Criccieth branch; instead he set up for himself. Within a year or so he was locally famous as the champion of poachers and small farmers in the courts, and of Welsh rights on the political platforms. One story from those days shows his impudent fearlessness in dealing with magistrates whom he saw, not as dispensers of the law, but as the entrenched enemy wielding their power. An angry chairman of the magistrates reprimanded him for implying bias in the court (it was a case of poaching) and continued, "A more insulting remark to the Bench I have never heard during all my experience as a magistrate."

LLOYD GEORGE: But a more just remark was never made in court.
CHAIRMAN: Tell me, to whom are you referring?
LLOYD GEORGE: I was referring in particular to you, sir.

He was quick-witted; he was eloquent; he was successful. Soon he was thinking of a seat in Parliament, the best place after all to carry on the Nonconformist struggle against Church of England privileges in education and finance, and to fight the landlords at the centre of their power. Perhaps (since at this time English politics were so full of Home Rule for Ireland) he might even dare to demand Home Rule for Wales; as he himself put it, "a free religion and a free people in a free land." By 1890, when he was twenty-seven, he had made a great name for himself in Caernarvonshire as an audacious champion of popular causes, and that year he captured the Conservative seat of Caernarvon Boroughs by the exciting majority of eighteen. He was to hold it for the next fifty-five years, the idol of the men of North Wales. The story is told of an Englishman, exasperated by a North Welshman's extravagant praise of Lloyd George, bursting in, "You talk as if your Lloyd George could do everything. He's not God Almighty!" "Ah," replied the Welshman, "but he's young yet."

Churchill once said of Lloyd George that his talk would "charm a bird out of a tree." In Parliament, a natural orator with the musical lilt of a Welsh preacher in his phrases, he showed every sign of independence, vigorously attacking, if his convictions so guided him, even a Liberal Bill that had the strong backing of Gladstone himself. He never missed a chance of speaking against landlordism, against the Tory brewing interest (as a Welsh Nonconformist temperance reform was very near to him), against the House of Lords veto, against the undue financial power of the Church of England in education, and its superior social status over the Nonconformists in Wales. Above all, Anglican bishops pricked spurs into his scornful eloquence. One of these had foolishly set the social world of the Church above that of the Chapel, and Lloyd George rode into him. "What is this social paradise? ... It is a close corporation which slams the door in the face of honest toil, where idleness is regarded as a badge of nobility, and where the highest prizes are given to him who can count the longest lineage of ancestors who have continued to live luxuriously upon the labour of others." But it was the Education Acts of 1897 and of 1902 ("Balfour's Education Act") that did most to reveal him as the Parliamentary champion of Welsh Nonconformity. These measures, by relieving church schools of the burden of local rates and extending their financial grants from public funds, confirmed the supremacy of the Anglican schools, especially in those villages (like Llanystumdwy) where they provided the only school. All Wales was indignant, and some Councils flatly refused to work the 1902 Act. Lloyd George even had visions of a united Welsh party pressing for Disestablishment and Home Rule, but greater issues were soon to push these into the background, and the men of South Wales were soon to find other leaders than Lloyd George among the new Labour Party.

One such greater issue had already arisen—the Boer War of 1899–1902, when long-standing hostility had at last exploded between on the one side an expanding, imperialist Britain, anxious to exploit the rich gold and diamond resources of South Africa without hindrance from the conservative Dutch boers, or farmers, and on the other side the two independent republics of Transvaal and the Orange Free State representing those farmers who put every obstacle in the path of British political and commercial expansion. Joseph Chamberlain, the ex-Radical turned Conservative, was the champion of British expansion and the most prominent Government spokesman for the war; Lloyd George, the Radical champion of the rights of little nations, anti-imperialist, anti-jingo, could not forgive Chamberlain or the Conservative Government he had come to represent. All wars were expensive; this war was in addition unjust and unnecessary. "There is not a lyddite shell which burst on the African hills that did not carry away an old-age pension. ... The money that would have built comfortable homes for hundreds of thousands of our fellow-men has gone to dig graves in South Africa."

"We shall miss many a gallant name from the roll-call of our warriors. But there is something infinitely more precious to every true lover of Britain that we shall miss, and that is the distinction of being the hope and shield of the weak in all lands, which was once the brightest gem of Britain's glory. No Liberal would have bartered that for all the gold of the Rand." It was the voice of the old Radical-Liberal tradition, the voice of Fox and Bright and Gladstone; and it was not welcome to a country that was intoxicated by patriotic fervour and at the same time exasperated by unexpected defeats. Lloyd George became the most unpopular man in England —and even Wales had doubts of him. He was saved from serious head injury in Bangor only by his bowler hat; and although the old magic was strong enough to get him re-elected for Caernarvon, in London his solicitor's practice dwindled almost to nothing. He was the arch 'pro-Boer' and therefore taboo. The climax of this phase of his career came in Chamberlain's own Birmingham, where he dared to address an anti-war meeting in the Town Hall. Brass bands played *Rule Britannia* from the body of the hall; seven thousand infuriated patriots waved Union Jacks and called for his blood; half-bricks were sold at three a penny to throw at him, and he at last narrowly escaped with his life, disguised as a policeman, and marching two miles in file to Ladywood Police-station. In the riot that followed his escape one man was killed and forty injured. It was a strange episode in the career of a man destined to be the greatest British war leader for a century and a half.

In 1906 was fought one of the most famous general elections in British history; it resulted in a sweeping triumph both for the Liberal Party, standing for free trade and cheap food against the Tariff Reform proposals of Chamberlain's Conservatives, and for Lloyd George himself—"the best fighting general in the Liberal army," as Winston Churchill called him. He had not been content merely to attack the Conservatives on their proposed policy of protecting British industries by tariff duties; he had stressed the necessity of redistributing some of the great wealth of Britain, of protecting the poor and aged against the harshness of their days and of reducing the great burden of expenditure on armaments—three or four hundred millions a year being spent on "machines of murder." In short, he stood for social revolution—old-age pensions; an end to sweated labour; an end to the tyranny of squire and employer; a tax on land values whose automatic increase flowed into the bank balances of idle ground-landlords; fair rents and security of tenure for those who paid them; rehousing of slum inhabitants; "above all,

I would have a fuller, freer, and better education. . . . That is where Germany is beating us, if she is beating us at all. . . . No poor man can afford to be ignorant—leave that to the rich." Always his attack was on the rich, in those Edwardian days when the rich were still really rich and relatively untaxed, and when every big town contained in its slums "the submerged tenth" of the destitute and the grossly undernourished, and perhaps a further quarter or so on the fringes of poverty and malnutrition.

In Campbell-Bannerman's new Liberal Government of 1906 he was President of the Board of Trade and a great success. Showing unexpected gifts for negotiation and tact, he averted a major railway strike, reformed the laws relating to merchant shipping and patents, set up the Port of London Authority, and even planned to nationalize the railways. On Campbell-Bannerman's death in 1908 and Asquith's succession to the Premiership, Lloyd George stepped up to the Chancellorship of the Exchequer, where his first achievement was to pilot through Parliament the Old Age Pensions Bill that Asquith had been preparing.

Then came the explosion of his 1909 Budget. Pensions had to be paid for, and so did the new Navy to meet Germany's challenge. Taxes therefore had to rise. But Lloyd George determined to kill two or three birds with one stone. He would finance battleships and social reforms—sickness insurance, unemployment insurance, old-age pensions, and pit-head baths for miners among them; he would aim the new taxes specifically at the wealthy and above all at the landowning class; and thus he would, given luck, provide a battle, on favourable terms, with the ancient enemy that had consistently opposed Liberal reforms for years—the House of Lords. His greatest struggle was to get his aristocratic Liberal colleagues in the Cabinet first to accept his proposals. When at last they had, he rode out to battle. To begin with, conventional taxes were raised: income tax, death duties, tobacco and drink duties. But the two new classes of tax that raised the great hubbub were, first, a small super-tax on all incomes over £5000 a year and, second, a set of land taxes and taxes on mining royalties aimed at the 'unearned' wealth of the aristocracy. In the old-established income tax too (still, by modern standards, at the very low rate of 1s. 2d. in the pound) the distinction was made for the first time between 'earned' and 'unearned' (i.e., investment) income, the latter being charged at a higher rate. All through 1909 battle raged round the new proposals, and Lloyd George was in his element defending his "People's Budget" and attacking the "idle rich" in such venomous terms that Edward VII sent him a measured reproof. In due course the House of Lords did swallow his bait and reject his Budget, defying the old tradition that precluded them from discussing money bills. "Their greed," said Lloyd George, "has overcome their craft, and we have got them at last."

Before the issue was settled, the Liberals appealed to the verdict of two general elections—two of the most excitable of this century —in which no Conservative language was too strong for Lloyd George, and Lloyd George's own attacks on "the dukes" hit them above and below the belt as the heat of the moment determined. A month or two previously the Duke of Beaufort had expressed the wish "to see Winston Churchill and Lloyd George between twenty couple of dog hounds," and Lloyd George was not above sneering at "the first of the litter" of the aristocracy who had the right to sit in the Lords. In this sort of free-for-all controversy, with the gloves off, he was supreme. "I would dearly like a rest," he said, "but I would rather have a fight." When Lord Curzon asserted that the best work in the world had always been done by the aristocracy Lloyd George leaped to the reply, "He evidently doesn't think much of the Christian religion. No doubt he would have rated it higher had it been propagated, not by twelve Galilean fishermen, but by a dozen dukes." Emotional Welshman that he was, his attack was also serious and rational. Placing rank before ability had destroyed Spain, and it would destroy Britain. "The brilliance of the sunshine of their lives blinds them to the squalor around them." "Who ordained that a few should have the land of Britain as their perquisite? Who made ten thousand people owners of the soil and the rest of us trespassers in the land of our birth? . . . Where did the table of the law come from? Who inscribed it?"

The Liberals survived the two 1910 elections, but with a majority dependent on the support of Irish and Labour members; this was sufficient to force the Budget through and, following it, the Parliament Act of 1911 that took away from the House of Lords its absolute right of rejection. Instead they might merely delay legislation for two years; and as for money bills, they were altogether forbidden to discuss them. It was a famous victory, ranking with the Reform Acts of 1832 and 1867; and, like the 1832 Reform Act, it was not won without the threat of the creation of enough new Liberal peers to swamp the opposition. It was perhaps fitting that one of the first reforms to be forced through against the two-year veto of the Lords was the Disestablishment of the Welsh Church—a measure dear to Lloyd George's heart.

Further domestic reforms followed. The Budget of 1911 provided a salary of £400 a year to members of Parliament, to enable others than the rich to maintain themselves there. The same year he introduced perhaps his greatest measure of social welfare—the ambitious health and unemployment scheme that laid the foundations of modern national insurance. Not every one was covered by it; the doctors, the employing classes, and the *Daily Mail* all indignantly attacked it; but it was a major victory in the war against poverty. Before it the poor had seldom been able to afford a doctor; now every manual worker between sixteen and seventy earning under £160 a year was insured against sickness by weekly contributions to be provided by themselves, by their employers, and by the State, and two million workers were grouped into an unemployment scheme to provide out-of-work benefit of seven shillings a week.

These were big strides into the twentieth century; but the equally big stride of land reform which Lloyd George now planned was frustrated by events. "Do you know what is in front of you?" he asked one of his audiences. "A bigger task than democracy has ever undertaken in this land! You have got to free the land, to free the land that is to this very hour shackled with the chains of feudalism." Both in town and country, he claimed, the landlord had pocketed his rents at the expense of agricultural improvement and commercial enterprise. Rural workers still lived in 'pretty' slums, and earned near-starvation wages. The land produced not more than half of what it was capable. Shopkeepers were exploited by ground landlords whose unearned rent overflowed in the ostentation of Cowes and Monte Carlo. The land reforms, however, did not command universal support even among Liberals. Asquith's Government became caught up in a host of pressing problems—the Ulster revolt against Home Rule in Ireland, industrial strife at home, the suffragette disturbances, the German menace—and Lloyd George himself was the victim of a 'smear' campaign arising out of the 'Marconi affair,' in which Ministers were accused of profiting on the Stock Exchange from inside knowledge of the award of Government contracts. So land reform sailed into the doldrums and was becalmed; and a similar fate overtook it when Lloyd George revived the idea twelve years later.

During these years just before the First World War, Lloyd George, realizing how the bitter party battles were tearing the nation in two, on several occasions made overtures to responsible Conservative leaders for a party truce, a coalition to work out an agreed progressive policy, with each side making concessions to the other. He was never a rigid party man, and Balfour, the Conservative leader till 1911, paid him the compliment of taking him seriously. So too did Churchill, though Asquith remained amused and sceptical. And of course it all came to nothing. The bulk of the Conservative Party would have nothing of the idea, until war, the great maker of coalitions, forced them to reconsider it.

Ever since the Boer War Lloyd George had been looked upon as a member of the 'pacifist' wing of his Party, one of those who would preserve peace at almost any price, and resent the cost of every new battleship built that meant a thousand pensions lost. He had never in fact been a true pacifist; and as the European war clouds gathered a very different Lloyd George began to appear. A visit to Germany in 1908 had opened his eyes to the frenzied quality of German patriotism: he had watched an almost hysterical crowd sing *Deutschland über Alles* after a Zeppelin crash. Yet as late as 1910 he had scoffed at the building of Dreadnoughts "against nightmares." Now, in 1911, the Government of the German Kaiser, William II, chose to make a challenge to the French colonization of Morocco by sending a cruiser to the Moroccan town of Agadir, and there was a serious risk of war. British diplomatic support for their new French allies can hardly have surprised the Germans; but what did surprise and incense them was the vigorous declaration of the 'pacifist' Lloyd George at a Mansion House banquet that Britain would not be treated "as if she were of no account in the cabinet of nations. . . . Peace at that price would be a humiliation intolerable for a great country like ours to endure." The Kaiser instructed his Ambassador in London to press for Lloyd George's dismissal, but the speech had had the effect intended. The Germans withdrew from Agadir, and the war-clouds looked a little lighter for a short space.

Lloyd George's attitude to Germany and the threat of war at this time shows a perhaps understandable confusion of judgment. As late as 1910 he scoffed at the building of battleships; but he did now favour (in theory) a build-up of British military strength, and even seriously contemplated conscription. One of his reasons for favouring a coalition was to put over to the British people so unpopular a possibility; and he strongly supported the appointment of the militant Churchill to the Admiralty. Yet whenever Churchill wanted money for armaments Lloyd George, as Chancellor of the Exchequer, stood against him, and whittled down his demands. Wishing for peace and improvement, he was deluded into thinking he saw them: eleven days *after* the fateful murder of the Austrian Archduke at Sarajevo, from which the war was to spring, he committed himself to the opinion, "In the matter of external affairs the sky has never been more perfectly blue," and, between Britain and Germany, "the feeling is better altogether." And when war was already declared between Austria and Germany on the one side, and Serbia, Russia, and France on the other, still Lloyd George favoured British neutrality, at least for a time. The callous German invasion of Belgium decided him: Britain was "in honour bound" to fight. Once Britain and Germany were at war, all hesitations and reservations vanished, and all Lloyd George's dynamic energy was channelled into the one supreme task of winning the war. He threw all his Welsh preacher's eloquence into the recruiting campaign (conscription was still in the future), confounding his enemies, and disappointing some of his late friends, by the lyrical passion of his warlike strain. He hammered away at the sleepy hidebound War Office in an attempt to galvanize it into effective action to produce more, and more modern, armaments—shells in particular. He put a stiff tax on beer to discourage the drunkenness that was so severe a brake on industrial production. (George V, to set an example, went teetotal for the duration of the war.) He even entered the fields of diplomacy and strategy, trying to persuade the generals that, in view of the bloody stalemate in France and Belgium, a blow should be launched from south-eastern Europe through the port of Salonika and elsewhere, to arouse the Balkans and the subject peoples of Austria against her, and so to economize in casualties and bring the war to a quick end.

For terrible things were happening in Flanders. After the first menacing German advance, checked by the French on the river Marne and by the British in Belgium, the hostile armies had become locked in a deadly clinch which permitted advances to be counted only in hundreds of yards, while casualties mounted by hundreds of thousands. Worst of all, the British Army was catered for by a War Office that had not realized that this was a new sort of war—the first mass war of industrial civilization, where victory would go to the side that produced most shells, machine-guns, barbed-wire, lorries, locomotives, mines, grenades, mortars, howitzers, trenching-tools, signal-flares. In 1914 Kitchener, the War Minister, suggested four as a suitable maximum number of machine-guns per battalion—a figure he raised, with an appearance almost of reluctance, to sixteen at the end of 1915. The fact that by 1918 it was eighty per battalion is a measure of Lloyd George's later achievement.

He had within him, as the American Colonel House wrote home to the President, "something dynamic which his colleagues have not." He fumed at the delays of red tape. He hammered away inside the Cabinet at the more leisurely figures such as Asquith (the Prime Minister) and McKenna (the new Chancellor of the Exchequer when Lloyd George was appointed Minister of Munitions). He toured the chief engineering centres, trying to get the workmen to give up their restrictive practices, reminding them at Manchester, "The soldier cannot say, 'I have been in the trenches eight-and-a-half hours, and my trade union won't allow me to work more than eight hours.'" (In Glasgow they howled him down.) He laboured to persuade armaments manufacturers to share their carefully guarded trade secrets. He used every chance of influencing great newspaper magnates like Lord Riddell and, more indirectly, Northcliffe of *The Times* and the *Daily Mail*. In the key posts of the Ministry of Munitions he employed, not civil servants, but the best business brains that he could find—Eric Geddes most notably; and for the first time, though there were frequently deficiencies of quality, the shells began to flow to the military front in quantities to match the weight of bombardment thrown against the British trenches. As another of his 'discoveries,' William Beveridge, wrote of him, "Lloyd George had a passion to win the war which none of the other members of the Cabinet seemed even to understand."

The others (perhaps Churchill excepted) did not understand. So, at least, Lloyd George thought. Asquith was "hopeless," he confided to Riddell. Kitchener made him want to scream; McKenna was "in blinkers"; Balfour was "a dawdler." And the war was going badly. 1915 saw the defeat at the Dardanelles, 1916 a rebellion in Ireland, and then in the summer the horror of the great offensive on the river Somme, when on the first day alone the British dead and wounded numbered 57,000, and in four-and-a-half months of largely fruitless mass murder 400,000 British casualties were suffered—a greater number than in the whole course of the Second World War. (It was little comfort that the Germans suffered a similar number.) Such a holocaust the world had never before seen or thought possible. And all the British dead were volunteers—the cream of the nation. "The battlefields of the Somme," wrote Churchill, "were the graveyards of Kitchener's army." At sea too things were going unsatisfactorily: Jutland was a battle of missed opportunities, and the submarine menace grew monthly. "We are going to lose this war," said Lloyd George, and pleaded with Asquith for a change of strategy, for full conscription (which was duly introduced), and for better public relations at home. "Nothing can save us," he wrote to Asquith, "but the nation itself. The people do not realize how grave the situation is. I feel they ought to be told. They ought to have a chance of saving themselves." As for the military High Command (directed by Kitchener at the War Office and by Haig and Robertson in the field), "there has not been a plan conceived and carried out by them which has not ended a bloody failure."

The nation should have a chance of saving itself—but he himself should have a chance too of saving the nation. With the justifiable egotism of a Pitt or a Churchill Lloyd George knew that he, and only he, was the man for the task. He was War Minister now, following Kitchener's death by drowning on the way to Russia in June 1916, but in his new post he met nothing but frustration. He despised the judgment of the leading generals, Haig and Robertson; and, although he respected Asquith as a leader in peace, he considered him hesitant, unimaginative, and ineffective in war. He therefore asked Asquith to retain the Prime Ministership but to hand over the direction of the war to a small committee presided over by Lloyd George. On Asquith's refusal, Lloyd George, with the support of many Conservatives and some Labour members, forced his resignation; and Lloyd George accordingly took over the leadership of the war coalition in December 1916. He was the first British Prime Minister to emerge from humble stock and it was fitting that his bootmaker-preacher-uncle, Richard Lloyd—the saintly old man to whom he owed so much, and to whom he still wrote almost daily —lived just long enough to see the impossible dream come true.

The split with Asquith was the beginning of the end of the Liberals as a major Party. For Asquith never forgot or forgave what had been done, and half the Party sided with him. Divided into two hostile groups, and, after the war, ever losing votes to the rising young Labour Party, the Liberals dwindled to a shadow—a feeble double-shadow—of their former selves. Within thirteen years of the split of 1916 they were a spent parliamentary force.

Meanwhile there was a war to win, and never did the omens seem so grim. But Lloyd George now proved his greatness. He concentrated power in the hands of a small War Cabinet of five, which, unlike Asquith's Cabinet, met daily. He radiated energy and authority. He galvanized his subordinates. Waking early to read the telegrams and dispatches, cross-examining the experts over breakfast, picking the brains of soldiers, civil servants, industrialists, trade unionists, cutting through the red tape of procedures, nursing his at times precarious majority in Parliament, making the sort of public speeches which could rouse and sustain a nation shaken by the war's disasters, always driving, driving, driving (himself hardest of all)—he was the spirit of the nation at war.

One of his first tasks was to persuade—and finally almost to command—a reluctant Admiralty to introduce the convoy system. The Germans had now begun their campaign of unrestricted submarine warfare, sinking merchantmen at sight without warning; and the shipping losses, both of British and neutrals, mounted so alarmingly that if they had thus continued the war would have been lost. The Lords of the Admiralty said an efficient system of convoying warships was impracticable. Lloyd George directed that one must be found, and announced that he would be arriving to inspect their plans. Convoys *were* introduced, and they did work. The submarine menace was defeated.

The generals proved more intractable. They naturally resented the amateur interference of politicians in their professional operations, and if the Prime Minister had dictated to them he might very soon have lost those Conservative supporters in the House of Commons upon whom his whole position depended. He argued and pleaded with them for a new strategical approach to win the war without a repetition of the ghastly slaughter of 1916. But Sir William Robertson considered there was no escape from the Western slogging match, and Sir Douglas Haig was full of confidence and optimism concerning the forthcoming campaign in Flanders. In any case, the plans for 1917 were already made. So again there was enacted a bloody full-scale offensive with terrifying British casualties (about 400,000)—the "murder in the mud" of Passchendaele. Haig's object was to exhaust the resources of the enemy, to make him fight until he could fight no more; in such a war of attrition the superior resources of the Allies must prevail. Perhaps he was right, and there was no other way but through the hell of Passchendaele; but Lloyd George did not think so. One hundred and forty pages of his *Memoirs* are given over to a bitter attack on Haig and Robertson, for their egotism, their lack of imagination, their brutal waste of precious lives. On their side, they resented his interference, and especially they mistrusted his apparent readiness to submit all British armies to the supreme command of the French General Nivelle. It has been told that when Haig's Chief of Staff paid his first visit to the front line of Passchendaele when the fighting was over "he grew more and more unhappy as his car approached this desolation. At last, he broke down, and wept. 'Good God,' he sobbed. 'Did we really send men to fight in that?' His companion, who had fought there, replied stonily, 'It's worse farther on up.'"

Lloyd George's long struggle with Haig and Robertson culminated in the appointment—at last—in April 1918 of a Supreme Allied War Commander, the French Marshal Foch. At last the vast resources of the Allies could be used intelligently, and one great army could fight the Germans instead of three or four independent and mutually suspicious armies: a reform all the more necessary after the retirement of Russia from the war, following the Communist revolution of November 1917. The Supreme Command decision was a famous victory for Lloyd George, and involved the supersession of Robertson. Even as it was, it came almost too late. The last great German offensives had been launched in March in an attempt to push the British and Belgian Armies into the sea before American aid could become effective. Terrible fighting again resulted in monster casualties—about a third of a million on each side —before the offensives were halted. It was a desperate moment: Haig's armies with their backs to the wall of the Channel; Lloyd George exerting superhuman efforts to transport over the Atlantic the vital American divisions; reserves of manpower becoming exhausted, with the age-limit for military service raised to fifty. In Churchill's words, Lloyd George "concentrated his whole being upon meeting the new situation. . . . The resolution of the Prime Minister was unshaken under his truly awful responsibilities." Sometimes he worked twenty-one hours a day, and the Conservative leader, Lloyd George's one-time enemy, Bonar Law, said, "He thought of nothing and aimed at nothing, and hoped for nothing, except the successful end of the war. . . . We saw what courage meant."

The German offensives continued until the beginning of August. This time, however, Haig's confidence was justified: as he had forecast, they proved to be the gambler's last throws. Allied desperation was great, but the German was greater: once checked, Ludendorff's armies were beaten. Foch's counter-offensive rolled up the exhausted German divisions; the new tanks came into their own; the war was over.

The victorious Coalition Government immediately held a walkover general election to confirm themselves in office, and proceeded to the more difficult tasks of making peace. These had not been simplified by the hysterical atmosphere of the election campaign, with Northcliffe's *Daily Mail* shouting for the German Kaiser to be hanged, and Sir Eric Geddes promising that Britain would "squeeze the German lemon until the pips squeak"—and Lloyd George himself did his ultimate reputation little good by the cheap tone of many of his election speeches and the opportunism of his tactics. He was dragged down by his audiences too often to their own level of revenge and pettiness: the statesman temporarily disappeared beneath the vote-catcher.

It was an exhausted, sick Europe that had to be settled, almost prostrate with its troubles: the Western Powers bitterly licking their wounds, the defeated Central Powers torn by revolution and the threat of famine, the East sucked into the maelstrom of the Communist revolution, the whole Continent (and Asia beyond) suffering the greatest influenza epidemic of history (killing more than the war itself). The statesmen who worked at Versailles from January to June 1919, and laboured to produce the peace treaty, were not likely to receive much praise—and they have not received it. Yet the Treaty of Versailles had many virtues. It left only 2 per cent. of the people of Europe within national boundaries that they disapproved of; no other treaty has ever done half so well. It created the League of Nations, which, with all its imperfections, was the best attempt up to its time to lay a foundation for international law; and it treated Germany much less harshly than Germany had treated vanquished Russia in mid-1918.

It was, like all major settlements, a compromise, and Lloyd George himself well represents the spirit of that compromise. For he stood midway between the idealism of the American President Wilson and the tough realism of the French Premier Clemenceau. Of Wilson, the Princeton government professor who came to Europe in 1919 like another Moses to present the tables of the law, Lloyd George wrote that "spiritually he dwelt beyond the snowline, in an atmosphere pure, glistening, and bracing—but cold." He wished to make the League of Nations the foundation-stone of the new order, and to sign a peace devoid of bitterness, revenge, or injustice. Of Clemenceau, the "Tiger," the embodiment of French hatred of the brutal German barbarians—the "Boches"—one need only quote from his many tart answers to the holier-than-thou Wilson. "Pray, M. Clemenceau, have you ever been to Germany?" "No, sir! But twice in my lifetime Germans have been to France." Lloyd George's task was to arrive at some acceptable synthesis of the two apparently irreconcilable worlds of Wilson and Clemenceau, and on the whole that is what he succeeded in doing. He opposed the French plan to place her frontiers upon the Rhine, but accepted the demilitarization of the Rhineland and the temporary use by France of the Saar coalmines. As for "making Germany pay," yes, so she must—but not so much that collapse would follow (with Bolshevism round the corner) and not in such a way—in goods, for instance—that damage would result to the receiver country's own industries; reparations must be substantial but tolerable. France similarly must be secured against future German aggression, yes; but not so radically as to make that aggression actually more likely, in a war of revenge. Poland must be re-created on Germany's eastern borders, yes (the French wanted her as a future ally); but to place more than two million Germans in the "Polish Corridor" under the Poles would "sooner or later, lead to a new war in the East of Europe." Lloyd George's approach was much the same as he had learned years before at the Board of Trade in disputes between employers and workmen: compromise, conciliation, opportunism, refusal to admit that a settlement could not be reached. His attitudes pleased neither side, and Clemenceau once said that "Wilson talked like Jesus Christ—and acted like Lloyd George"; but after a hectic five months of crisis, squabble, and 'temperament,' with the plight of central Europe deteriorating towards starvation and revolution all the time, peace was eventually signed, and the "war to end war" was formally concluded.

Over Versailles lay the shadow of Russia. The Allied interventions there had begun as anti-German interventions, to keep the struggle going when the Communists made peace, but they had by now become anti-Communist campaigns, to stamp out the dangerous disease of revolution that might so easily spread all over Europe. It was no idle fear. Even in comparatively comfortable England—and even at the great crisis of the war in 1918—there had been severe strikes. At the 1918 election the Labour Party (still pledged to full Socialism) ousted Asquith's Liberals as the main opposition, and there were not a few who talked of the "coming revolution," and "planting the red flag on Buckingham Palace." On the Continent of Europe the threat was much more severe; and in Hungary and parts of Germany there were temporarily successful Communist revolutions at this time. Some, like Winston Churchill, wished to turn the Allied intervention into a great anti-Communist crusade; but Lloyd George would have none of it. It was not that he did not abhor what was happening in Russia; but, as he pointed out to Churchill, begging him to rid himself of this "obsession," intervention had already cost £100—£150 million in a year and led nowhere. Accordingly the British Expeditionary Force was withdrawn from Archangel, bringing seven thousand refugees with it; and the local White Russian contingents were left to the vengeance of the Reds.

There was to be no such violent revolution in Britain, for all the cheers that the inaugural Labour Party election meeting gave for Lenin and Trotsky, and all the fervent singing of *The Red Flag*. Yet in a sense a revolution had already occurred in Britain. It was not merely that the war had vastly accelerated social change; Parliament had achieved quietly and almost unnoticed, amid the very thunder of the guns, two major reforms that it had stubbornly resisted in peace-time: the extension of the vote to all men over twenty-one and to most women over thirty. This Act added more voters to the electoral roll than any of the great nineteenth-century reform Acts; with it, Lloyd George practically rounded off the British system of parlia-mentary democracy, and took the critical step towards the political emancipation of women. Between that moment early in 1918 and the shrill antics of the suffragette martyrs five short years before lay the immense work done by women in the hospitals and munition factories. The door that the suffragettes had fruitlessly and painfully hurled themselves against opened at the touch of a little finger.

In his Irish policy Lloyd George at last obtained a statesman's settlement, but before reaching it he employed shifts that have left a slur upon his reputation. For decades—indeed for centuries—before Lloyd George was in power, Ireland had been the skeleton in the cupboard of English statesmanship. After long and bitter years of religious discrimination, economic exploitation, and political sub-jection, during which the Irish were in a condition of chronic revolt and semi-starvation, British Governments since the rise of Glad-stone (1868) had wrestled with the complicated problems of Ireland. Religious reforms and land reforms having failed to satisfy, at last Asquith's Government had passed a Home Rule Bill, in 1912—but the Protestants of Ulster, backed by English Conservatives and armed with German rifles, had threatened revolt if the Bill became law. Then, in 1916, in the middle of the war, there was an unsuccess-ful rising in Dublin, which the Asquith Government treated with perhaps unwise severity: fourteen of the rebel leaders were executed. From that moment, for the next five years, the whole of Catholic Ireland was in growing rebellion against British rule. Voluntary Irish enlistment in the British Army fell away; and when in the dark days of early 1918 Lloyd George tried to introduce conscription, Irish anger was so bitter that the attempt had to be abandoned. The 'troubles' multiplied, and in the 1918 election the nationalist "Sinn Fein" party swept the board everywhere but in Ulster, returning seventy-three out of seventy-seven members—thirty-six of them in prison! During a six-month period in 1919 there were 1500 political offences, including eighteen murders and seventy-seven armed attacks. It was, in effect, guerrilla war.

Lloyd George's Government decided to meet violence with violence, ambush with ambush, murder with murder; and they enlisted two forces of special 'police,' one known as the Auxiliaries, and the other as the "Black-and-Tans" from their khaki uniforms and black caps; their joint mission was to strike at the Irish Republican Army before the Irish Republican Army could strike back—and rapidly Ireland slid down the slippery and brutal slope to civil war. Lloyd George, busy with Versailles, with strikes at home, with the problems of Russia and a dozen other matters, was slow to realize that Britain had in fact lost control of Ireland; the Sinn Feiners' self-constituted Republic was increasingly becoming the Government of the southern and western districts. Lloyd George, proclaiming that he would not "negotiate with assassins," had failed to realize that he had himself promoted assassination. The ex-champion of little nations (Wales, the Transvaal, Belgium), he had failed also to realize that world opinion, and especially American opinion, now saw David Lloyd George in this respect not as David but as Goliath.

In 1921 he redeemed his reputation, achieving a peace treaty with the rebels that established Southern Ireland (Eire) as a Free State while allowing the six counties of Ulster to remain within the United Kingdom. It was the fruit of months of patient bargaining whose success hung by a thread till the end. When at the end the Irish representatives seemed to be about to refuse to remain within the Empire, Lloyd George, holding up two letters addressed to the Ulster leader, Craig, in Belfast, forced the Sinn Feiners to choose.

> If I send this letter it is war, and war within three days. Which letter am I to send? Whichever letter you choose travels by special train to Holyhead, and by destroyer to Belfast. The train is waiting with steam up, at Euston. . . . We must know your answer by 10 P.M. to-night. You can have till then, but no longer, to decide whether you will bring Peace or War to your country.

By 2.30 A.M. the unhappy and divided Irish delegation had signed.

The 'troubles' were far from over. Of the two principal Irish signatories, Michael Collins was ambushed and shot five months later; Arthur Griffith died of strain the same year; the Ulsterman Field-Marshal Wilson was shot down by gunmen in Westminster; in the streets of Belfast Catholic continued to murder Protestant and Protestant Catholic; and throughout Southern Ireland the intricate clockwork of revenge took many months to run itself down.

For one more year Lloyd George was to remain in power, travelling from conference to conference in an attempt to settle the tangled affairs of a Europe torn by war and revolution, and trying constantly to soften the rigour of France's demands on Germany. While France pressed for the payment of every mark of reparations demanded of Germany by the Versailles Treaty, Lloyd George was all for concession and compromise: the Germans must be nursed back into the civilized community of nations, not ground down into economic breakdown and Communism. Perhaps even Russia might be "brought back into the world," and this he tried to do at the Genoa conference, in 1922. He even claimed to have succeeded; but the wish was father to the thought.

At home too there was little good to report. During 1921 the number of unemployed reached two million. The dreams of "an England fit for heroes" faded as the boom of 1919–20 stumbled into the long slump of the twenties. There was a major coal strike, with the threat of a general strike; all-round economy cuts in Government expenditure and protective tariffs on foreign goods to bolster declining British trade. The nation began to be impatient with the Coalition; and the Conservatives in the Coalition, by far the most numerous element, began to be impatient with their Liberal leader. He was said to be absent too much from the House; he was too clever by half; he dictatorially thwarted the policies of his Conservative Foreign Ministers; he was accused of selling honours—£15,000 for a knighthood, £50,000 for a barony—to swell the Liberal Party funds—and he had been cynical and unscrupulous; and he finally was held to have brought Britain to the brink of war with Kemal Atatürk[1] over the Chanak crisis. He himself reasonably claimed that his firmness had checked Kemal and preserved peace—but in October 1922 his Conservative supporters threw him over. It was the end of Lloyd George as a dominant political force.

He was by no means ready to retire. He had become accustomed to the driver's wheel, and did not take kindly to a back seat. And although he had by now become a landowner and farmer at Churt, among the heathlands of Surrey, and was about to make very large sums of money from the publication, in Britain and abroad, of newspaper articles and war memoirs, he constantly strove to play a leading rôle in the nation's affairs for another twenty years or so.

For him to do this, however, the Liberal Party must be welded together again—and this task proved too much for him. The Asquith Liberals never forgave him: he had torpedoed the Party in 1916; he had secured their defeat in the 1918 election; he had gathered to him-

[1] See Chapter 2.

self (possibly by improper means) the very large Party funds, which he controlled quite autocratically. In the 1923 election the Liberals still returned 149 members—enough, voting with Labour, to outnumber the Conservatives and permit for the first time the uneasy experiment of a Labour Government. In the 1924 election they were down to forty-two, but Lloyd George campaigned vigorously for five years in books and speeches to present the image of a Liberal Party full of up-to-date ideas for reforming the land system, reviving the coal industry, and above all for conquering unemployment by a vast and imaginative programme of public works. Alas, at the election of 1929 the reward of all this was sixteen more seats only—fifty-eight in all. Again Lloyd George maintained a Labour Government in Office with the votes of his small group. But the world economic disasters of 1929–32 that swept Hitler into power in Germany and Roosevelt in America, and in Britain produced the financial crisis of 1931, administered the final blow to Lloyd George's fortunes. The bulk of his Liberal supporters supported the "National" crisis Government of that year, and left the opposition Liberals numbering just four—Lloyd George himself, his son Gwilym, his daughter Megan, and a relation by marriage. The "National" Liberals became eventually as indistinguishable from the Conservatives as earlier the Irish "Unionists" had become; Gwilym himself became one after his father's death, while Megan later joined the Labour Party; and —a final irony—when the Liberal Party at last showed some signs of revival in the later nineteen-fifties, it was under the enemy banner, the Asquith family connexions of Bonham-Carter and Grimond.

In the last dozen years of his life Lloyd George was a sadly diminished figure. Still physically vigorous, and still prepared to offer opinions on all political matters foreign or domestic, his judgment often deserted him. So anxious was he for reconciliation with Germany that he made every excuse for Hitler and his revolution, which he took to be a bulwark against Communism; and on a visit to Hitler at Berchtesgaden, in 1936, he appears to have been completely hoodwinked by that consummate actor and liar. His disillusionment with the Nazis in the years immediately preceding the Second World War never brought any acknowledgment of his previous misjudgment. For Lloyd George never took kindly to admitting an error, and his castigations of Baldwin and Chamberlain would have carried more weight if they had shown more modesty. He advocated firmness against Mussolini and (at last) against Hitler; yet when war arrived in 1939 he was full of nervousness, almost of defeatism. Constantly listening to the Hamburg propaganda broadcasts, he would mutter,

"I don't like the look of things," and, when Hitler turned his armies eastward, "Russia will be defeated." He constantly compared Churchill's running of the second war with his own running of the first—always to his own credit. At the dark crisis of June 1940 Churchill had in fact invited the old warrior to join the War Cabinet, and he had refused—as he said later, because it was too much of "a Churchill Cabinet"; but almost to the end he indulged the daydream that they would invite him again.

He was alert and lively on occasions, especially back home among his fellow-Welshmen, or experimenting with a new strain of wheat on his Surrey farm, or admiring the fruit in his apple-orchard—but on the whole he dwindled. In 1941 his wife died, and he was married in 1943, at the age of eighty, to his secretary. He had now been member for Caernarvon Boroughs for well over half a century, and the question arose: Could he possibly stand again? And if he did, and if he were defeated—? He could not bear the thought of being cut off from Parliament even though he seldom visited it now. Partly to avoid the awkward issue, Churchill offered him an earldom, and he accepted. The war was patently ending, and he wished, he said, to make a contribution to the debates on the peace. Perhaps it was a mistake to have accepted; perhaps it was irrelevant. No one would ever remember Earl Lloyd-George of Dwyfor. He died less than three months after that strange contradiction was created.

But men would long remember David Lloyd George of Llany-stumdwy, the bootmaker's nephew who took to the law: terror of Tories, scourge of squires, champion of poachers and chapelgoers against magistrate and parson; the man who had the courage to denounce the vanity of the Boer War; the greatest radical reformer of his generation; the tamer of the House of Lords; above all, the "man who won the war"; and, after it, the man who laboured to lay, however shakily, the foundations of the peace. He was never an intellectual; he was far from being a saint. In beliefs and morals he was a pagan; indeed, his sexual life was persistently scandalous. He could be ruthless and, on occasions, cheap; he had about as much gentleness and humility as a dynamo. Pugnacity was perhaps his outstanding quality. "He is a man," said Clemenceau, "who thrives on fighting." Lenin thought him the greatest of all British political leaders. And his colleague of many years, his peer in war leadership, Winston Churchill, wrote of him, "When the English history of the first quarter of the twentieth century is written, it will be seen that the greater part of our fortunes in peace and in war were shaped by this one man."

Table of Events

1899–1902. Boer War.
            Big Navy policy in Germany.
1901.   Death of Victoria, accession of Edward VII.
1902.   Balfour's Education Act.
1903–6.   Chamberlain's Tariff Reform campaign.
1906.   Liberal free-trade triumph in election.
            Lloyd George President of Board of Trade.
1908.   Asquith Prime Minister, Lloyd George Chancellor of the
              Exchequer.
            Old-age Pensions.
1909.   Lloyd George's Budget rejected by House of Lords.
1910.   Two general elections.
            Death of Edward VII, accession of George V.
1911.   Health and Unemployment Insurance.
            Parliament Act lessens Lords' powers.
            Agadir crisis.
1912.   Asquith's Home Rule Bill.
1913.   Ulster revolt.
            Suffragette movement at peak.
            Industrial strife.
1914.   First World War begins.
1915.   Lloyd George Minister of Munitions.
            Dardanelles Campaign.
1916.   Easter rising in Dublin.
            Lloyd George War Minister, then Prime Minister.
            Battle of Jutland.
            Battle of the Somme.
1917.   Height of submarine attacks: convoys introduced.
            Battle of Passchendaele.
            America enters the war.
            Russian Revolutions (March and November).
1918.   Ludendorff's offensive broken.
            Foch generalissimo of Allied armies.
            Allied victory: Armistice ends war (November).
            Votes for all men and many women.
            "Khaki" ("Hang the Kaiser" or "Coupon") Election confirms
              Lloyd George coalition in office.
1919.   Treaty of Versailles.
            Lloyd George ends British intervention in Russia.
1920.   "Black-and-Tans" in Ireland.
1921.   Irish Treaty.
            Strikes, unrest, and unemployment in Britain.
1922.   Collapse of the Lloyd George coalition.
1923–29.   Liberal electoral decline.
            Lloyd George schemes for industrial and agricultural revival.
1931.   Economic crisis, "National" Government. Lloyd George
              Liberals almost annihilated.

2

Kemal Atatürk
(1881–1938)

The Ottoman Turks had come originally from as far east as the fringe of the Gobi Desert. Driven by drought and the Mongols, they moved rapidly westward in the thirteenth and fourteenth centuries, conquering as they went the Arab Empire of Baghdad and the Turkish Empire of their kinsmen, the Seljuks, and threatening the Byzantine Empire itself. Then in 1356—about the time of the arrival of that other unwelcome invader, the Black Death —three thousand of them forced the passage of the Dardanelles, and menaced the great Christian capital of Byzantium (Constantinople). A century afterwards Byzantium itself fell to the Sultan, and a century or two later the Turkish tide had lapped westward over the whole Balkans, to the very walls of Vienna. In the Near East the Ottoman power ruled directly from Albania to Persia, from Egypt to the Caucasus; it controlled the Arab lands of Syria, Palestine, and Iraq, and the islands of the Eastern Mediterranean; the sheikhs of Arabia and the rulers of Hungary and the Crimea owed it tribute, and in Africa it claimed overlordship over the whole immense north coastal area. It dominated the great land and sea links between Europe, Asia, and Africa: Suez, the Dardanelles, and the Damascus route from the Mediterranean to the Persian Gulf. The Ottomans governed by their Janissaries—Christian children taken from their families at a tender age, nurtured intensively in the faith of Islam, and educated to be either civil servants or the finest and most fanatical soldiers of Europe. In Constantinople itself the Sultans lived in Byzantine splendour; but, growing more effete as the years went by, surrendered increasing power to the Janissaries and the pashas (lords) of outlying provinces. With the eighteenth century came the beginnings of decline: southern Russia was lost to Catherine the Great. The Balkans began their many wars of liberation with the Greeks' achievement of independence, in 1829. Serbs, Rumanians, Bulgarians, and others were swift to follow. Egypt could not be held against mighty pashas like Mohammed Ali, so powerful that he overran Syria and threatened the Sultan himself in Constantinople.

By 1850 the Sultan was indeed "the sick man of Europe," and even his friends (like Britain) supported him only at the price of heavy concessions (like Cyprus, leased to the British in 1878).

Within Ottoman territory lay not only Jerusalem and Bethlehem but also Mecca, the birthplace of Mohammed and the holy city of Islam; and of course Turkey was a Muslim power. If Mecca was the Bethlehem of the Muslim world, Constantinople was its Rome, and in Constantinople was the Sultan, who was also the Caliph, the spiritual head of Islam, and 'successor' of Mohammed—a kind of Islamic Pope and Emperor rolled into one.

Mustafa Kemal was destined to sweep all this away. By 1881, when he was born in the Turkish quarter of Salonika—a big, mainly Greek seaport at the head of the Aegean Sea—the Sultan was Abdul Hamid II. He was anti-British, pro-German, tyrannical, stubborn, haunted by a constant fear of spies and rebels, refusing all the reforms which the Western countries urged on him; he massacred his Armenian Christian subjects in huge numbers; he imprisoned anyone under the vaguest suspicion of liberal intentions. It was said that wherever three Turks talked together there was a fourth listening in order to report to the secret police. The rotten fabric of his Government was apparent to all who were educated enough to compare it with Western Governments. In particular the Army, upon which it finally depended, was officered by men among whom few were not to a greater or lesser degree rebels at heart.

The young Mustafa was sent to the military school in Salonika, where he acquired a second name, Kemal (meaning "perfection"), to distinguish him from another Mustafa. He was a precocious pupil, hard-working, ambitious, unpopular, scornful. His father died and his mother remarried; the young Mustafa quarrelled with her, and refused to speak to his stepfather. At seventeen he was sent to the senior military school at Monastir, in Northern Macedonia, where he revelled in his studies—but more especially in the banned writings of the English and French philosophers of liberalism and enlightenment—Locke, Voltaire, Rousseau, John Stuart Mill: all the more so because they were forbidden fruit. He became in fact an unbeliever and a rebel—but he was a good enough cadet to be selected for Harbiye, Turkey's Sandhurst, where he found himself at twenty within easy—too easy—reach of the maelstrom of Constantinople. Here he learned dissolute habits, which he never lost, and which in due course killed him. He drank immoderately and chased women indiscriminately—but he worked too, was gazetted out, and promoted rapidly to the rank of captain: a man to watch.

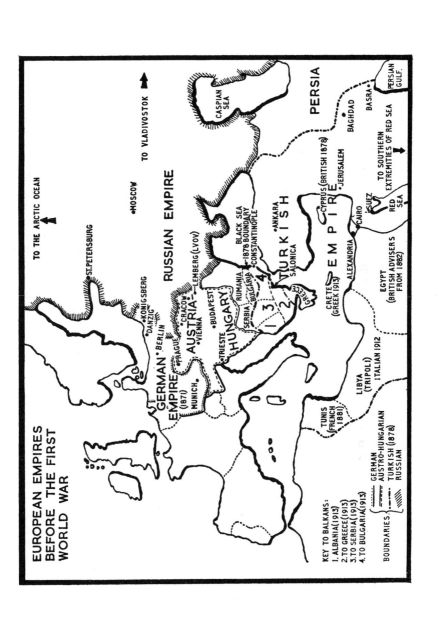

EUROPEAN EMPIRES
BEFORE THE FIRST
WORLD WAR

TO THE ARCTIC OCEAN

TO VLADIVOSTOK

ST.PETERSBURG

•MOSCOW

RUSSIAN EMPIRE

KONIGSBERG
•DANZIG
BERLIN
GERMAN •PRAGUE
CRACOW•
EMPIRE •VIENNA
(1871) MUNICH• AUSTRIA• •BUDAPEST
TRIESTE• HUNGARY

EMBERG(LVOV)

RUMANIA
SERBIA BULGARIA
GREECE

CASPIAN
SEA

PERSIA

BAGHDAD

BASRA

PERSIAN
GULF.

BLACK SEA
1878 BOUNDARY
CONSTANTINOPLE
•ANKARA
T U R K I S H
SALONICA
E M P I R E
CRETE
(GREEK 1913)

CYPRUS(BRITISH 1878)
•JERUSALEM

•SUEZ

TO SOUTHERN
EXTREMITIES OF RED SEA

RED
SEA

ALEXANDRIA
•CAIRO

EGYPT
(BRITISH ADVISERS
FROM 1882)

TUNIS
(FRENCH
1881)

LIBYA
(TRIPOLI)
ITALIAN 1912

KEY TO BALKANS:
1. ALBANIA(1913)
2.TO GREECE(1913)
3.TO SERBIA(1913)
4.TO BULGARIA(1913)

BOUNDARIES:⎰ GERMAN
⎱ AUSTRO-HUNGARIAN
⎰ TURKISH (1878)
⎱ RUSSIAN

The Harbiye Staff College harboured a revolutionary society, the Vatan, or Fatherland, which was fiercely hostile to the Sultan's regime and to the dead hand of the Islamic priesthood. The college tutors knew of it but pretended not to; and of course Mustafa joined it, spoke violently at its debates, and wrote articles and poems for its journal. When the Sultan forced the authorities to ban it, it continued in secret, with all the exhilaration of codes and passwords, secret handshakes and oaths. Soon Mustafa took over the society's direction, editing its broadsheet from a back-street office; but, denounced by spies, he was arrested, imprisoned, cautioned—and posted to Damascus. Unimpressed by this leniency, he first organized a branch of the Vatan among his Damascus fellow-officers; then, tired of this Syrian backwater, faked false papers and returned to Salonika in disguise—for Salonika, he felt, was the most likely centre of revolution. Lying low in his mother's house, he was eventually smelled out by the Sultan's police, but again escaped—this time back to Syria, with the aid of sympathizers in the Army—and among the police officers themselves. Ordered to arrest Mustafa, his superior replied that there must be some mistake—he had never in fact left Syria at all. For a year he had to wait, kicking his heels, waiting for time to heal the damage to his reputation in Constantinople, pulling every string to get back to the centre of things. At last it came: transfer, and to Salonika!

But he found the rebels of Salonika dominated by a new secret society: the days of Vatan were over. Instead there was the Union and Progress Party, led by Enver Pasha, but containing many Jews, and using the organization of freemasonry and of international nihilism. In this atmosphere Mustafa cut no ice. He had not the charm of Enver. He had little use for Jews, freemasons, or nihilists. Turkish revolution should be by Turks for Turks, he thought; and in any case he had little use for any organization that he could not dominate. So when the big moment came, and suddenly, in 1908, the Young Turks, as they came to be called, proclaimed the revolution from the balcony of the Olympus Palace Hotel, in Salonika, Mustafa Kemal, though he was there all right, was in the background, taciturn, envious, sardonic, while Enver Pasha—gay, dashing, glamorous —took all the limelight and the applause. Abdul Hamid first accepted the revolution, then roused an ultra-Muslim counter-revolution; but the Army, Enver and Mustafa among them, smashed the counter-revolution, deposed the Sultan, and installed his feeble cousin. Mustafa, back at his soldiering, consumed himself with envy and impotence. The real reason that moved him to sneers against Enver's

Government was that he, Mustafa, was treated by it as an outsider. So he invented for himself more respectable reasons: they governed the country as inefficiently as Abdul Hamid himself; the Minister of Finance was a Jew; above all they were slaves of the Germans, who were treating Turkey more like a colony every day. The German Ambassador was running the country; German advisers were organizing the Army; German financiers were buying up concessions; German engineers supervising the railway to Baghdad. "Turkey for the Turks!" became Mustafa Kemal's slogan. At the moment he was impotent, snarling his contempt for the world in general, intriguing with other dissatisfied politicians whom he privately despised, drinking his black moods away in savage frustration. But with his slogan lay the future.

From 1911 till 1922 Turkey was to be involved almost continuously in war and revolution. At the end the Ottoman Empire was destroyed, the Islamic religion toppled from its age-old pedestal, Mustafa Kemal was dictator, and Turkey was for the Turks alone.

War began in Tripoli when Italy suddenly judged the time propitious for an attack on the Turkish position in North Africa. Mustafa, first and foremost a soldier, got himself somehow to Libya through Egypt, though the neutral British there tried to stop him, and for a year fought inconclusively against the Italians. In 1912, however, worse came: the Balkan Christian states banded together to make a joint onslaught on Turkey in her weakness. Something near panic reigned in Constantinople. The Bulgarians were within fifteen miles of the city. In the Army and the refugee camps raged dysentery, typhus, cholera. Hospitals, mosques, private houses were full of the wounded. Salonika fell to the Greeks, and among the refugees were Mustafa's mother and his cousin Fikriye, later for a time to be his mistress. Returning to Constantinople, he searched long for them in the refugee camps before at last finding them. Meanwhile Enver too had returned, and had taken control of the Cabinet (shooting the War Minister dead and hanging mutineers); but his attempt to outflank the Bulgarians failed, and Turkey was forced into a humiliating peace. Historians know this as the First Balkan War. The second followed rapidly in 1913, when the victorious Balkan powers fell inevitably to squabbling over the spoils, and Enver swiftly and shrewdly took the opportunity to reconquer Adrianople. Again Enver was the great man, marrying a princess, and living in magnificence in a palace overlooking the Bosphorus. Mustafa growled and snarled from a distance, a mere lieutenant-colonel. Worst of all, Enver, full of grandiose plans for a greater Ottoman Empire, decided that the Army must be re-organized—and by the Prussian, Liman von Sanders. Growling once too often and too bitterly, Mustafa was 'banished' to Sofia, the Bulgarian capital, as military attaché; and while he was here—kicking his heels, gambling, drinking, frequenting the dens of a variety of vices—over the border the Austrian Archduke was murdered, and yet another Balkan War began that was this time soon to become the Great War. Turkey ought to remain neutral, he thought; but Enver Pasha's Government and Army were already half-Prussianized, and straightway entered the war on Germany's side.

At least life now offered something more purposeful than the cafés and prostitutes of Sofia. War; war was his true element. His touchiness disappeared in the stress of action. He became cool, fearless, shrewd, efficient, ruthless; a great leader. Appointed to serve under Liman von Sanders, anti-German that he was, he soon came to be valued at his true worth. Twice von Sanders intervened on his behalf when Enver would have transferred Mustafa or vetoed his plans. When the British leaders, Lloyd George and Churchill, conceived the grand plan for forcing the Dardanelles and linking hands with their Russian allies through the Black Sea it was Mustafa Kemal's troops that took the main brunt of the Australian and New Zealander attack upon Gallipoli. From April to December 1915 he was in bitter and bloody fighting to prevent the "Anzac" and British troops from breaking through over the mountains to Gallipoli—taking every necessary risk, and some unnecessary ones, inspiring his hard-tried men, never happier than when the position was desperate—as it frequently was. In August he led his men in a formidable bayonet charge, the Turks yelling "Allah! Allah!" as they charged, until the British broke and ran. That day the Wiltshire Regiment was practically wiped out. Then the Turks in their turn took fearful punishment from the guns of the British ships standing off shore. For three more months the troops fought a stubborn trench war until, in December, the Dominion and British troops were quietly taken off: the Dardanelles Campaign had failed.

Back in Constantinople, he continued to preach hatred of the Germans and distrust of Enver. Indeed Enver had cause to fear lest Mustafa Kemal be involved in plots to assassinate him, and again was relieved to get rid of him on a distant front—the Caucasus, where, in the mountains between the Black and Caspian Seas, the Turkish armies had just suffered a great disaster. Sixty thousand men had frozen to death in the mountain blizzards, and of an army of nearly a hundred thousand men, twelve thousand only had returned. These, with reinforcements, were put under Mustafa Kemal's command. The year was 1916, and he was, as always, lucky. The Russians were unable to press their advantage, for their own discipline was cracking, their spirit ebbing. The revolution of March 1917 was on the way, and Mustafa (after he had harried a few inefficient officers and hanged a few corrupt contractors from the nearest tree) found little difficulty in thrusting back the numerically superior Russian forces.

Promoted general, he was brought back to another theatre of war: the south, where British armies and Arab revolts were threatening the Turkish hold on Arabia, Palestine, Syria, and Iraq. He regarded this (and told Enver so, insolently, in public) as a device to get him discredited, for here it was the Turkish position that was crumbling. Medina, second only to Mecca among the sacred places of Islam, was evacuated amid the general mourning of the faithful. Baghdad fell in April 1917. Mustafa Kemal quarrelled so violently and persistently with his German 'adviser,' von Falkenhayn, that he resigned his command, told Enver that von Falkenhayn would sacrifice the last Turkish soldier for German interests, and wrote in a passionate letter, "We must defend, and defend *Turkey*. Not one single soldier must be sacrificed for the Empire but saved for Turkey." Refusing an order to take up his command again, he was put on indefinite 'sick leave'—which did not prevent him from carrying on vociferous opposition in Constantinople to Enver Pasha and the Germans. In 1918, however, he was once more in command on the southern front, this time in Palestine, but nothing now could stop the British advance. Planes and machine-guns caused panic among his retreating troops; Lawrence with his Arabs fell upon any units unlucky enough to straggle. From Jordan they retreated to Damascus, to Beirut, to Aleppo. All Syria was lost. He despatched a telegram to the Sultan demanding the dismissal of Enver, and his own appointment as Minister of War. This remained unanswered, but in Constantinople the game was up. The Turkish Government fell on November 1, 1918; Enver and his associates fled in a German torpedo-boat; an armistice was signed; the Ottoman Empire was shattered. Mustafa, omitted from the new Government as from the old, flatly disobeyed orders to disband his troops, and refused to allow the English to occupy Alexandretta; but returning to Constantinople, he found British ships in the Bosphorus, British troops in the capital, Indian troops, French troops, Italian troops everywhere. To Mustafa Kemal's fury, a French general chose to make a ceremonial entry into the city on a white horse (the Turkish cere-

mony of 1453 in reverse). Again he made himself such a nuisance in
the city, intriguing with politicians, and building up a nucleus of
diehard resistance, that yet once more he was 'banished.' The
British would have liked to have him arrested and under their eye in
Malta, but the Sultan sent him to Central Turkey (Anatolia) to act
as his 'representative'—an ironical but, for Mustafa Kemal, a lucky
choice. (The consistency of his luck was amazing.) In May 1919 he
got his chance to organize defiance, revolution, and revival out of
chaos and defeat.

In Anatolia he gathered to himself all the forces of resistance:
generals who resented the disbanding of the Army; nationalists who
chafed at the submission of the Sultan to the British, and at the
manner the country was being overrun by French, British, and,
above all, Greek troops; intellectuals, ex-soldiers, young cadets, seeing in Constantinople nothing but helplessness and corruption; politicians retaining some trace of idealism or ambition. All these were
drawn first to Anatolia, where Mustafa Kemal, now in flat defiance
of the Sultan, proclaimed the national revolution. "I shall stay in
Anatolia until the nation has won its independence." The Sultan
tried to raise the Kurds against him, and a price was put on his
head. When the Constantinople Parliament showed sympathy with
him the Allies closed it down and deported some deputies—but
others, dodging the police, travelling secretly by night, fled to
Anatolia to swell the rebels. Yet their position was desperately precarious. Hostile Armenians and Kurds to the east, hostile French to
the south, hostile Greeks, in large numbers, to the west, moving
against them, with Allied support, from Smyrna (Izmir) and the coast.
Mustafa Kemal had by now taken up his headquarters at Ankara,
destined to be the new capital of the new Turkey. A bloody civil and
religious war complicated the fighting—and, like all civil wars, it
was full of atrocity and bitterness: floggings, tortures, hangings,
crucifixions. The Sultan-Caliph had called on the priests to rouse the
people. Mustafa Kemal had called on the nation to defy the priests,
the Sultan, the foreigners. Every village and every family was
divided against itself.

In Ankara there followed an extraordinary tug-of-war between
Mustafa Kemal and the Assembly, which had now constituted itself
a "National Assembly," and declared the Sultan to be "a prisoner
in the hands of the Allies." Mustafa heartily despised politicians, and
had no intention of sharing authority with anyone; yet he needed
the backing of civilians as well as soldiers. Hence he was persuasive
and dictatorial by turns, sometimes all sweetness and light, some-

times roaring his contempt at the infuriated Assembly. His tongue was savage, and his malicious irony made him scores of enemies. His life constantly in danger, he surrounded himself with a villainous bodyguard of black-eyed, moustached tribesmen. He sent men to their death as a matter of routine, but wept for his horse dying of tetanus. Passionate in argument, drinking too much, carousing his nights away in orgies which rumour magnified—though they were wild enough—deriding and debunking Islam in language many took to be plain blasphemy, he was nevertheless fanatically serious where Turkey's independence and honour were concerned. Then he became once more the inevitable leader, the personification of the national revolution. The treaty of Sèvres would have neutralized the Dardanelles and held Constantinople in ransom for good Turkish behaviour to her non-Turkish minorities—a humiliation that few Turks could stomach. More than ever Mustafa Kemal appeared as the only possible saviour. With strengthened authority he attacked the British forces shielding Constantinople and brushed them aside. The dilemma of the Allies was acute, and Lloyd George in particular had far too much on his hands to contemplate another war with Turkey: trouble in Ireland, in India, in Iraq, industrial troubles at home. The Allies turned, therefore, with relief to the Greeks, always ready to strike at their ancient masters, and eager for a new empire along the Turkish Aegean coastline. A large Greek army advanced to the rescue of Constantinople and the invasion of Anatolia. The Turks fell back. Mustafa Kemal shot the deserters and breathed fire back at the Greeks. "We are Turks; we will never be the subjects of a people who only yesterday were our slaves." But despite a victory won by Ismet (eventually Mustafa Kemal's successor) at Inönü, in January 1921, the Greeks continued to advance inland towards Ankara. The Turkish Army appeared to be at its last gasp, and a resentful Assembly reluctantly gave Mustafa Kemal supreme power to deal with the supreme crisis. But the very violence of his fanaticism betrayed how near he was at this moment to despair. "Not one inch of Turkish soil will be surrendered until it is drenched in Turkish blood." A big battle raged at the Sakarya River, thirty-two miles from Ankara, and the Greeks seemed to be winning it, when the scales were turned, and gradually the Greeks were driven back towards the coast. In the winter that followed (1921–22), although Mustafa lorded it as the hero in Ankara and was officially proclaimed Ghazi, or Destroyer of Christians, he still had many enemies and intrigues to cope with. He was merciless: twenty-five insubordinate officers were hanged; struggling to reassert itself, the Assembly was told curtly that he was Generalissimo and would remain so. In 1922 he moved once more against the Greeks, surprising and routing them, and driving them back towards the sea. They took with them such Christians as could keep pace with them, murdering what Turks they could on the way, being themselves cut down by the pursuing Turkish cavalry: a grim nightmare of hatred and revenge. Mustafa revelled in it, pitiless and savage, yet sardonic and objective in his contemplation of the horror. Looking round upon a group of ragged Greek wretches, "Here," he said, "in these prisoners you see the centuries, and the progress made by that wonderful animal, man." But still he urged pursuit and slaughter. The main Greek Army escaped to its ships, but tens of thousands of helpless Greek civilians, caught in Smyrna, were murdered in cold blood. The town was looted and fired, the charred corpses pitched into the harbour.

The French and Italians at this stage prudently withdrew their troops, but the British left a small force at Chanak, barring the Turkish Army's advance into Europe. To the anxiety of many Englishmen, Lloyd George and Churchill actually reinforced this British contingent, and issued a bellicose warning to Mustafa Kemal; and behind the British troops, re-forming in European Turkey, were the Greeks who had escaped from Smyrna. Mustafa Kemal was prudent. He ordered his men to advance with reversed arms. But the danger of war with Britain was acute, when, thanks to French mediation, an armistice was arranged. In London the Lloyd George coalition fell, largely because of its risky Turkish policy; and in due course the British agreed to evacuate Turkey, and to see that the Greeks did likewise. Mustafa Kemal had achieved his first ambition: Turkey was independent, and free of the foreigner.

In the middle of all this he had married. When originally he had set up his establishment at Chan Kaya, outside Ankara, his formidable mother followed him there—she was blind now—and was set up in state. To Chan Kaya also had come Fikriye, his cousin, a delicate, attractive, sensitive girl whom he established as his mistress. Pleasure-loving and quarrelsome as they both were, there were fearful scenes; and when he made advances to a respectable 'Europeanized' daughter of a Smyrna shipowner and she demanded marriage as her price, Mustafa Kemal, to the surprise of many—perhaps including himself—agreed. So Latife became his wife; but the rake did not stay reformed for very long. The drinking orgies and the painted women returned to Chan Kaya very soon. Mustafa Kemal was a strange mixture of the hectic and the clear-eyed, the foul and the idealistic, the destructive and the creative: he would suddenly sicken of his drunken party, take a cold shower and a fast car, and drive at dawn to inspect a model farm or a new building project—or perhaps just to get away, to drive fast to nowhere in particular, to be away from the follies of the world, or simply to indulge the mood of despair.

Fikriye, his ex-mistress, declined into a consumption, and had to be sent away for two years (perhaps to his relief) to a Munich sanatorium. At the end of that time she returned, begged to see Mustafa, was turned away by the bodyguard, and shot herself in the gardens of Chan Kaya. By that time he had also quarrelled with his wife, Latife, authorized his own deed of divorce, and sent her packing. He returned to ever more shameless living with every fresh personal disaster.

This was in 1924—and by this time Mustafa Kemal, the Ghazi, the hero of Smyrna, was so bitterly unpopular that he dared drive nowhere unguarded along a public highway. There had in fact been two attempts on his life and others were to follow. Armed motorcycle escorts screened him, all traffic was cleared off the road before he could make the simple journey from Chan Kaya to the Parliament house in Ankara. This extreme unpopularity was due to his ruthless and radical reforms. First, surrounded by his armed supporters, he forced the Assembly, under threats, to abolish the Sultanate. "I am sure the Assembly will be unanimous," he said with menace. A few hands went up. "Carried unanimously," announced the President. Mustafa Kemal's men had their hands on their revolvers. Pandemonium broke out. There was no shooting. Mustafa Kemal left the Chamber. The Sultan, five days later, fled from Constantinople in a British battleship, a frightened old man carrying a few jewels and a set of Imperial coffee cups of gold, attended by one eunuch. So vanished into the drizzle of the Bosphorus the last of the Ottoman Sultans, the Emperor of All the Turks. His spiritual powers as Caliph were assumed by his nephew.

Mustafa Kemal proceeded the next year to proclaim Ankara the capital of Turkey and to force the Assembly, by a combination of shock tactics and intrigue, to declare Turkey a Republic and Mustafa Kemal its President. Yet he would rage at being called a dictator or compared with Mussolini—that "hyena in jackboots," that "bull-frog of the Pontine Marshes." The facts remained: he was President of the Republic, with power to appoint the Prime Minister; he was President too of the Cabinet, of the Assembly, and of the People's Party. He was also Commander-in-Chief of the Army.

He turned next, in a frenzy of reform like that of the French Revolutionaries, to a frontal attack on religion. Islam was suitable for nomad Arabs, but not for a modern civilized people. "Islam is a dead thing." As for the Caliph, "Was it not for the Caliphate, for Islam, for the priests and such-like cattle, that for centuries the Turkish peasant has fought and died in every climate? ... The Caliphate has bled us white for centuries." Such blasphemy from a professed atheist could only mean that the priests would rouse the faithful against him and that his political opponents would run to Constantinople to rally round the Caliph. Certainly they dared not oppose him with safety in Ankara. One night a deputy who spoke against him was murdered on the way home; others could take a hint.

For months he hesitated before the vital dangerous move. Then in 1924, in one hour, he presented a Bill to the Assembly, and had it passed, for the abolition of the Caliphate. "The Ottoman Empire was a crazy structure based on broken religious foundations. The new Republic must have good foundations and a well-made scientific structure. The Caliph and the remains of the house of Osman must go. The antiquated religious courts and codes must be replaced by modern scientific civil codes. The schools of the priests must give way to secular Government schools. State and religion must be separated. The Republic must finally become a secular State." Orders were sent to the local Governor to see the Caliph despatched out of Turkey. He obeyed. Police and troops unceremoniously ejected him. He was driven away in a car. Two days later all the remaining Ottoman princes and princesses followed: a clean sweep. There was no immediate revolt, though later the Kurds rose; but hostility to this brutal and ruthless revolutionary growled underground. It was at this time that he dared not show his face unguarded in public. It was at this time too that Fikriye committed suicide and he divorced Latife. The countryside was impoverished after years of war and revolution. The people were not far from starvation. In Chan Kaya Mustafa alternated between violence and fear, between debauch and despair.

The attack on Islam can be seen as one aspect of the work for which he is most famous: the westernization of Turkey. Mustafa Kemal was an implacable enemy of European powers, such as Germany or Britain, who attempted to treat Turkey as a colony or a second-rate power; but he had a fanatical respect for what had made these powers great—their scientific and technical achievements. In fact, material progress came to represent to him almost a religion. Turkey must be driven to transform itself into a modern

Western power. This meant education, inspiration, coercion: those who could not be persuaded must be compelled. So his slow-moving, priest-ridden, medieval land was struck by a tornado of new legislation. English and French replaced Persian and Arabic as foreign languages to be taught in the military schools. The Koran was translated from the sacred Arabic to modern Turkish. The Gregorian Calendar of the West ousted the old Turkish calendar. Thursday and Friday lost their status as special days, and the Western 'week-end' was introduced. Two million acres of Church land were redistributed. The Prime Minister, as head of religious affairs, could now dismiss priests who made difficulties; in 1934 a law was passed forbidding the wearing of religious clothes in public. The Roman alphabet of the Western World was adopted, and all Members of Parliament, civil servants, and professional men were required to master it. The metric system was introduced. Surnames in the European manner were made obligatory, and Mustafa Kemal himself took the name of "Atatürk" (literally "Father of the Turks"). Islamic law was abandoned in favour of the Swiss Civil Code, the Italian Penal Code, and the German Commercial Code. Education was made universally free, and all university graduates were compelled to teach for three years. Western music was introduced. Schools of forestry, agriculture, and veterinary studies were instituted. Vaccination was made compulsory. Swamps were drained, and a centre for the study and treatment of malaria set up. A big campaign was launched for building up a nursing profession.

The most famous and difficult of his struggles to change age-old customs related to an apparent triviality: costume, and above all hats. The Turkish fez and kalpak were the result of an adaptation to two necessities: to protect the head from the heat of the sun, and to permit the faithful Muslim actually to touch the ground with his forehead during the obeisance of prayer. Mustafa wished to sweep away this medievalism together with all the others; accordingly, after the abolition of the Caliphate, his officers were instructed to wear peaked caps. He himself appeared in public in a Panama hat, to the scandal of the devout. "We must dress," he declared, "like a civilized people." But conservatism and fear of sin combined to make progress so slow that, as usual, he took the bull by the horns and in 1925 banned the fez. The police had precise instructions how to deal with backsliders, and those who could not bring themselves to wear their compulsory 'Christian' hat next to their Muslim skin —and therefore insulated it by means of a handkerchief—found the handkerchief stripped away, and the bowler or trilby firmly banged back by the police. For formal wear—for example, inside Parliament—it was not the trilby but the top-hat, with morning-suit, that Kemal Atatürk insisted on.

As for women, "let them show their faces to the world." His wife, Latife, never wore the veil, and in 1923 the two of them carried on a big campaign to ridicule this age-old Muslim custom. "Do the wives and daughters of civilized countries behave like this?" he demanded. And it was not only the veil that he attacked but the whole conception of the lower status of women. Women were persuaded into the professions—law, medicine, teaching, nursing; two women judges were appointed; "a nation cannot progress without its women." 'Smart' Western clothes were encouraged, the hideous smartness of the twenties—short skirts, low waists, flat chests, and pudding-basin hats; high heels and Hollywood glamour were all part of the necessity of being 'civilized,' 'emancipated,' 'modern,' though of course only a small proportion of Turkish women were affected by such novelties. More important, polygamy was declared illegal, and divorce made more difficult; and in 1934 women were actually given the vote. The cynic might interpose that these admirable reforms were undertaken by a man who had driven his mistress to suicide and summarily divorced his own wife when he tired of her; and who treated women like so many bottles of champagne to be enjoyed and forgotten. Perhaps, however, no one should expect reformers to practise what they preach; neither is simple consistency to be looked for in complex characters, and Kemal Atatürk was a whirlwind of conflicts and cross-currents. The schoolmaster in him was very strong. When the Roman alphabet was a novelty he toured the country with a blackboard and a box of coloured chalks, personally demonstrating the new medium.

Emphatically, however, he was the sort of schoolmaster who carries a stick. Opposition to his policies was met by the bastinado and the hangman's noose. When, in 1926, resistance to his dictatorship crystallized round a group calling themselves the Progressive Republican Party, and yet another plot to murder him was discovered, he struck viciously at any politician thought to be a danger. A large number of prominent men—including one of his closest associates, Colonel Arif—were hanged with little pretence of justice. Many more were imprisoned. Popular resentment was not sufficient to save them, though it did force him to release four leading generals, fellow-heroes of the war of national liberation.

Yet one of the most important decisions ever made by this most incalculable of dictators was that it would in fact be a good idea to have an opposition—a legalized and official second party to criticize, on the British pattern. This experiment arose in the following manner. Since 1925 the Prime Minister of Turkey (under Mustafa Kemal's Presidency) had been Ismet, one of the victorious generals in the Greek war. Ismet and his Ministers were responsible for the day-to-day conduct of the nation's affairs. Mustafa Kemal, especially during his periods of dissipation or gloom, liked to preserve a certain aloofness from the affairs of the Assembly, and Ismet liked to consider himself sometimes as the real ruler of Turkey. By 1930 the country was seething with discontent, and some of this was expressed by critical deputies. Mustafa Kemal himself was often contemptuous of the precise and dogmatic Ismet. Perhaps it would be a good idea to encourage criticism of Ismet and the Government; this would perform the double function of safety valve and corrective for Ismet's self-importance. So the Turkish Ambassador in Paris, Fethi, was brought back specially to lead a British-style Opposition. But as with the Khrushchev 'thaw' of 1956, in Russia, the intended manageable trickle of criticism turned rapidly into an unmanageable torrent. Newspaper offices were stoned. Revolvers were drawn inside the Assembly. Throughout the country everybody's pent-up resentment became vocal against tax-collectors, the cost of living, interfering officials, shortages, State monopolies; a host of grumbles. Shipowners, bankers, civil servants, farmers, above all faithful Muslims —every one had grievances, and the novelty of being able to air them proved too strong. Strikes and rioting were followed by another Kurdish rising. Then, near Smyrna, a dervish proclaimed himself the Mahdi, or Messiah, destined to destroy the atheist republic.

It was the end of the Opposition, at least for the time being. Mustafa Kemal packed off Fethi, sent an army to defeat the Kurds, and hanged twenty-eight of the Mahdi rebels. It was not, however, the end of the idea. Turkey was spared from developing into a totalitarian one-party dictatorship. Later on a genuine opposition was permitted to operate. Side by side with the Kemalist People's Party there grew up the Democratic Party, and under Ismet, who became Kemal Atatürk's successor, the Democratic Party grew in strength until in 1950, in free elections, they won the election—and again in 1954. This would have delighted Atatürk, who always declared that his dictatorship was merely a transitional phase. Adult countries became democratic—Turkey must become an adult country. The events of 1960–61—mass arrests and trials, military rule, and the execution of corrupt politicians—showed she still has a long way to go.

Atatürk lived long enough to see some at least of his dreams come true, and certainly to be venerated by his countrymen, despite everything. He drove them unmercifully to the end, with high taxation and state planning almost as ruthless as that of his northern neighbour, Stalin. Himself too he drove mercilessly to the inevitable end. In 1938, a few weeks after the Munich settlement, worn out at last by his excesses, he died at the age of fifty-seven, leaving a world plunging downhill into war.

How far had he succeeded? He could not of course transform Turkey in a decade or so to become one of the great and powerful nations of the world. Many of his domestic schemes were defeated or slowed down—by lack of technicians, or by shortage of water (a chronic problem in Anatolia), or by failure to mine enough of the coal that lay plentifully below the surface. Turkey was not economically a giant, and her material progress could not match the giant strides made by Britain or Germany or America or Russia in their heyday. But very great material advances were made; and above all political stability was achieved in an area of the world, the Middle East, that has seen continuous intrigue, upheaval, and war. Turkey became a moderately prospering haven of calm in a storm-tossed world. It is in the religious sphere that his reforms seem most precarious. When Prime Minister Menderes returned to Turkey in 1959, after narrowly escaping death in an air crash on the way to sign the Cyprus agreement in England, fifteen thousand animals were sacrificed in the streets of Istanbul in thanksgiving, and six hundred more in Ankara. Menderes was hailed as a great religious leader saved by Allah's direct intervention. The modern Turkey is building mosques faster than schools. One can imagine Atatürk's disappointed contempt.

That Turkey has survived the past generation so well is due largely to the shrewd and cautious foreign policy pursued by Kemal and his successors. Contemptuous of the European dictators, Mustafa was hardly likely to be drawn into the orbit of the Axis Powers. He had fought the Italians as enemies and the Germans as allies, and he had no liking at all for foreigners. He had fought against the British and French too; but in the 1930's it seemed to him, and to Ismet, that there was less to lose (and indeed financial credits to gain) from an understanding with a Britain that had by that time been taught to respect the new Turkey. In 1939, therefore, a month after the war began and a year after Atatürk's death, a defensive treaty of alliance was signed with Britain; and although the disasters of 1940 made Turkey think again, Atatürk's old mistrust of the foreigner was strong enough in his successors to keep Turkey from going over to an apparently all-conquering Hitler. Turkey, wooed by both sides, surrendered to neither, and maintained her neutrality unviolated.

After the war vigorous hostile pressure was put on her by Russia for the surrender of territory, but the Turks again, conscious of their own importance in the world and of their own considerable military strength, maintained a calm defiance, later joining both the NATO and CENTO alliances in hostility to Soviet expansion. Eighteen thousand Turks fought in the United Nations army in Korea against the Communists, in 1952–53. And how it would have pleased Kemal Atatürk to learn that those troops were accounted among the best and toughest there—and when taken prisoner proved utterly resistant to brain-washing and torture.

For it is as a soldier that Mustafa Kemal would have chosen to judge himself, and would have liked to judge his compatriots. As one of his Turkish biographers, Irfan Orga, has written, he was a soldier first and last—"blazing a trail of fire through the nation's mind . . . and from the ashes of the past arose the tremulous shape of his civilized dream: Turkey—the modern phoenix bird who consumed herself in the fire of revolution in order to live again. The dying Ottoman Empire produced him, the man of strength and vision with the hour of the twentieth century chiming in his blood."

Table of Events

1356.   Ottoman Turks force the Dardanelles.
1453.   Turks capture Constantinople.
1683.   Turks at the gates of Vienna.
18th–19th centuries: Steady decline in Turkish power.
1881.   Mustafa Kemal born in Salonika.
1908.   "Young Turk" Revolution.
1911.   Italo-Turkish War.
1912–13. Balkan Wars.
1914–18. Turkey ally of Germany in First World War.
1915.   Gallipoli (Dardanelles) Campaign.
1917–18. Total defeat of Turkey.
1919.   Mustafa Kemal proclaims national revolution.
1921.   Assumes supreme power.
1923–25. End of the Ottoman Empire and the Caliphate.
          Turkey a republic, Ankara the new capital.
1924 onward: Westernizing reforms.
1938.   Death of Kemal Atatürk.
1939–45. Turkey maintains neutrality in Second World War.
1951.   Turkey a member of NATO.

3

Vladimir Ilyich Lenin
(1870–1924)

Vladimir Ilyich Ulyanov (who is known to history as Lenin) was born at a time when Russia was seething with talk of revolution. He grew up breathing its atmosphere, and it was his destiny to be the most daring and successful of all modern revolutionaries.

When he was born in 1870 Russia was a vast backward State where serfdom had only just been abolished by Alexander II. This liberation had come disastrously late, and a Russian educated middle class had grown up, completely devoid of practical political experience, strongly critical of the Tsar's Government and the landed gentry, and steeped in sundry revolutionary doctrines of a most violent nature. Terrorism and violence among the revolutionaries inevitably bred repression and counter-terror in the Tsar's Government, who acted with the greatest sternness, not only against bomb-throwers and assassins, but often against those very Liberals who urged a break in the vicious circle by the grant of greater freedom.

When Lenin was a schoolboy of eleven an event occurred that confirmed the pattern of violence and extremism in Russia: at last, after repeated attempts, Nihilist conspirators succeeded in assassinating the Tsar, Alexander II, the "Liberator." The bomb that killed him killed also all hope of moderation; under his son, Alexander III (1881–94), a narrow, courageous, obstinate, honest ox of a man, Tsarist repression was firmly in the saddle; and it continued so under the next and last of the Tsars, Nicholas II (1894–1917). By 1905 it was impossible for students to walk down the street together; the universities were honeycombed with spies; police permission was necessary before a private party could be held in St Petersburg; pogroms against the Jews, arbitrary floggings of discontented peasants, imprisonment of strikers, were frequent. Russia was the complete Police State. Siberia was full of exiles—all potential revolutionaries; but every new violence against the revolutionaries, every new blind restriction, produced ten more revolutionaries. An explosion was sooner or later inevitable.

This conspiratorial world was the world in which the Ulyanov children grew up. The father was an educated man, a teacher of physics and mathematics, and the six children all took as naturally to revolutionary activity as ducks to water. One of them, indeed—the eldest boy, Alexander—was involved in a St Petersburg students' bomb plot against Alexander III, and was hanged in 1887; and Vladimir Ilyich himself was expelled from Kazan University within three months of entering it for taking part in a student demonstration. Eventually, however, he was allowed to complete his legal studies as an external student, driving the powerful engine of his brain to do four years' work in one. He even practised for a short time as a barrister's assistant, but his talents were to lead him to defy, break, and remake the law, not to practise its administration. He was soon travelling Europe to interview the leading revolutionary exiles, returning with a false-bottomed suitcase full of explosive literature. He joined Marxist study circles and urged them to make contact with the factory workers; and he began preparations for launching an illegal newspaper.

Marx had died about the time Lenin was born, and although it is impossible to summarize his complex work in a paragraph, some understanding of his main conclusions is essential to appreciating the work of Lenin. The idea of Socialism is much older than Marx, but it was he who claimed to have made of it a 'scientific' theory. By appearing to show the inevitability of Socialism in the evolution of civilization, he transformed the socialist idea from a vague Utopian *ideal*, of which every man's notion was as good as the next man's, to a *doctrine*. He appeared to show that Capitalism would follow Feudalism, and Socialism Capitalism, as inevitably as the chrysalis follows the caterpillar and the butterfly the chrysalis. This is what gave—and gives—his followers such certitude, however much they squabbled, and still squabble, over points of interpretation: the main body of doctrine is, to them, unchallengeable. Embedded in that doctrine are, first, the theory of the class struggle—especially in modern conditions the struggle between the *bourgeoisie*, or employer class, and the proletariat, or working class; second, the materialist conception of history—the idea that basic to all the ideals and systems of law and notions of right and wrong that man develops are the varying material conditions under which he lives: alter his mode of life and you will alter his ideas of right and justice; and third, the belief that Capitalism contains within itself essential 'contradictions' which inevitably lead to its violent overthrow by the socialist working class.

Marx had asserted that the capitalist (or *bourgeois*) phase of society was a necessary preliminary to Socialism. Capitalism was in fact making considerable strides in Russia in Lenin's youth, as Anglo-French money earning high dividends poured in for the construction of railways, mines, metal industries, textiles, and other industries. There was an enormous fund of ex-peasant cheap labour, and these were the new factory workers that Lenin was out to convert; but just as his newspaper was about to print its first number, he was arrested, given a fourteen months' preliminary detention, and then sentenced to three years' deportation to Siberia. In prison he studied hard, methodically apportioning the hours of his day; he wrote letters and pamphlets in milk (which could be made visible by being dipped in tea and warmed!); his mother sent him parcels and winter clothing, and a certain Nadezhda Krupskaya, a fellow-Socialist, waited outside the prison at a certain point so that he could glimpse her from the exercise yard. In Siberia he shot snipe, visited, and argued with, his fellow-exiles, translated Sidney and Beatrice Webb's *History of Trade Unionism*, wrote a book on the development of Russian Capitalism, and married Krupskaya, exiled to the same village. Compared with life for one of Stalin's political prisoners forty years later, it was humane and civilized.

In 1900 he returned to Europe, and soon settled down to the life that he pursued for the next seventeen years. He shabby, prematurely bald, with a reddish beard and quick small eyes; she strong-faced, austere and calm-eyed, utterly devoted to him; the two of them moving from one pair of unfurnished rooms to another, from lodgings off the Tottenham Court Road to Munich, from Geneva to Brussels, from Paris to Stockholm, from Copenhagen to Zürich. Shabby boarding-houses, conference meetings in the Brotherhood Church; comrades appearing at all hours in every possible disguise or alias; three knocks on the door in the middle of the night; weeks of study in the British Museum; illnesses without the money to afford a doctor; long rucksacked trudges through English meadows or German forests or Swiss valleys to shake off the latest Party wrangle; cycle-rides down rough Finnish roads, mending the many punctures with pieces of old goloshes; endless reading, endless writing of pamphlets, of illegal news-sheets, of books on political economy, of long letters refuting the arguments of a comrade at the other end of Europe, or trying to rig the voting at the next Congress.

During these seventeen years Lenin and his associates, in their various and ever-changing exiles, built up the technique and theory of socialist revolution that in 1917 altered the course of world history. Arguing like theologians, spitting venom at one another in the name of universal brotherhood, peppering Europe with seditious printing-presses and pamphlets on the tactics of revolution, they present an extraordinary picture of devotion, fanaticism, and intrigue; a picture of organized bank robberies back in Russia, mail-train hold-ups, and even guerrilla warfare to raise funds for the movement; of endless police-dodging, convictions, and deportations to Siberia, secret journeys by reindeer sleighs to Party meetings in the remote tundra; escapes, re-deportations, and more escapes; conferences, charges of treason to the working-class movement, counter-accusations; expulsions, more conferences, more arrests: the Party was being created. In the intervals between one Finland conference the delegates retired to the woods to do target-practice with their revolvers.

From the beginning, immediately after his release from Siberia, Lenin began to take the lead, challenging the older socialist exiles by the ruthless novelty of his ideas. Broadly speaking, Lenin stood for unrelenting hostility to all other reformist groups; revolution must come from the uncompromising leadership of a solid group of Socialists, disciplined to think alike and act together. In 1900 the older Marxists had joined forces with Lenin and his younger associates in the production of *Iskra* (the Spark), which was printed in Switzerland, and smuggled into Russia by a network of underground agents. In fact, it was in *Iskra* that V. I. Ulyanov first became Lenin, and soon this Lenin became the most formidable force both in the paper and the Party. On one point they were all agreed: terrorism of the sort that had murdered Alexander II or brought Lenin's brother to the scaffold was ineffective.

In 1903 a conference was held first in Brussels and later in London to sort out the differences that had arisen. Nearly sixty Russian Socialists, overwhelmingly intellectuals, came from all over Europe —even some from Russia. After getting into trouble with the Belgian police they adjourned to London, "arguing fiercely on the boat all the way over," and continuing to argue on arrival. Lenin, finding more opposition than he expected, worked feverishly behind the scenes to get a majority, but succeeded only when his tactics so infuriated the Jewish group that they walked out. Thus at last Lenin obtained his fleeting majority (*bolshinstvo*) of two, and his followers came to be called Bolsheviks. In effect they were a new Party; they broke in 1903 with the 'minority' of Mensheviks (in fact, the true majority), who wished to work in collaboration with the Liberals.

Then, in 1905, revolution came to Russia, touched off by the national humiliation in the war with Japan (1904). On Bloody Sunday (January 1905) a procession of 200,000 men, women, and children, moving towards the Winter Palace of the Tsar, in St Petersburg, bearing a petition, singing hymns, and holding images of the saints, was fired on by troops at point-blank range, hundreds being killed and thousands injured. There followed more rioting, strikes, and naval mutinies, with protracted unrest and bloodshed in many parts of Russia throughout 1905 and 1906—continuing in places even into 1907. In October Nicholas II was actually forced to grant a constitution, though the Duma, or Parliament, he set up possessed but feeble powers. In St Petersburg the striking factory workers elected delegates to a worker's Council, or Soviet, which directed revolutionary activity in the city. It was a significant rehearsal for 1917. But in 1905 the Cadets,[1] or Constitutional Democrats, withdrew their support for the Soviet directly the Tsar granted a constitution, and slowly the Tsar's Government regained control.

Revolution had come to Russia, but where were the revolutionaries? With few exceptions, they remained abroad, pursuing their doctrinal differences, offering tactical advice, and even sending in supplies of firearms (though Lenin's supply from Britain failed to arrive); but of the leading socialist revolutionaries, only Trotsky distinguished himself in the 1905 risings. Lev Bronstein, the adventurous young Jew who took the name Trotsky from one of his Odessa prison warders, although an admirer of Lenin, had taken the other side in the wrangle of the past few years; however, the fact that he was at this time a Menshevik made him no less radical or fiery. He had smuggled himself out of Russia in a farm-cart; now he smuggled himself back again, and soon took the lead among the Socialists in St Petersburg. Forced temporarily to flee into Finland, he was back in October to direct the very thorough general strike and the Soviet of Workers' Deputies. Meanwhile Lenin had spent ten precious months merely offering advice from Switzerland and Britain—and organizing another congress to decide what to do. It was not until late October that he left Switzerland, and made a leisurely journey to St Petersburg *via* Stockholm. Disguised, he attended a few of the meetings of the predominantly Menshevik Petersburg Soviet. He led a largely underground existence both in the capital and in Moscow, where there was heavy street fighting—though he played a prominent part in the journalism of the struggle. Within a few weeks of his arrival, however, the Tsar's Government was well on the way to regaining its grip. Trotsky and his chief

[1] So called from the initials of their Party.

associates were arrested, and Lenin was forced to flee to the safe haven of Finland. A favourable explanation of his comparative inactivity in 1905 is that he did not believe in the possibility of a socialist revolution at that stage. First, there had to come the *bourgeois* democratic revolution, an affair of western-style Liberals and Parliaments. Only later could come the planned seizure of power by the socialist working class; and this could not arrive by pious unarmed processions to the kind Tsar in his Winter Palace, or through sham Dumas where one landed aristocrat had as much voting power as five hundred peasants. It would arrive later, in Lenin's way and Lenin's time, by disciplined Communists seizing the keys of power at the vital moment. But perhaps this explanation is a little too kind in its assessment of his analysis and vision. Perhaps he miscalculated; it is at least arguable that he would have had a better chance of influencing the course of history in 1905 if he had sized up events more quickly and returned at the first opportunity. In 1917 he was to make no such mistake.

In the years following the 1905 revolution Lenin was the object of growing resentment from other members of the Party. They objected to his unscrupulous attempts to steal the Party for his group, and to his support for fund-raising terrorist raids which, they thought, had proceeded past the stage of honest bank robberies and train hold-ups to the point of systematic banditry and murder. They resented his uncompromising pugnacity and his refusal to accept the will of the majority, and eventually they made him give up the editorship of his latest paper, *Proletarii*. By 1909 Krupskaya was writing, "We have no Party at all," and many times Lenin himself said that he did not expect to live to see the revolution.

Part of the reason for this slump in the fortunes of the Bolsheviks lay in the relative prosperity of Russia in the years 1906–12. Some of the worst grievances of the peasants had been remedied as a result of the rising of 1905; a Duma was now in existence, even though it had little real power; and for a few years Russia was under the stern but constructive premiership of Stolypin, who, while hanging 3500 persons in one year alone, and flogging in some villages every tenth man, at the same time instituted land reforms that set up a new class of peasant landowners, and gave the Russian peasant a goal worth working for at last. Industry, too, prospered, and the number of men taking part in strikes fell steadily from over two million in 1905 to forty-six thousand in 1910. All these were factors weakening the Bolsheviks; and yet another one was their systematic penetration by police spies. They, like all the other revolutionary groups, became eventually worm-eaten by agents of the Okhrana, the Tsarist secret police, an organization twenty thousand strong, whose members stirred up antagonisms within the revolutionary groups, and betrayed their members to the authorities. Sometimes it was more complicated: rival groups within the Okhrana spied on one another; there were some spies who ended by being genuine revolutionaries and others whose loyalties became so confused that sometimes they were police agents spying on the Bolsheviks and sometimes Bolsheviks spying on the police agents. A certain Malinovsky was so trusted by Lenin that he became leader of the small group of Bolsheviks in the Duma, but even he proved eventually to be an Okhrana man.

Had Stolypin been given proper support from Nicholas II, the continued success of his policy might have been disastrous for the Bolsheviks—if Russia could also have stayed out of the war. Lenin seriously feared such a success. But in 1911, in the Kiev Opera House, with the Tsar as a witness of the crime, Stolypin was assassinated. The next year two hundred strikers in the Lena goldfields were shot down by police; more strikes and riots followed, until by 1914 industrial conditions were approaching those of 1905: between January and July over a million men went on strike, and there was open fighting in the Caucasus oil town of Baku. Lenin's hopes revived, and he moved to a resort in the Carpathian mountains near Cracow, so that a moderate walk would take him to the frontier; but there is nothing in his writings to suggest that he expected war.

For his plans to mature in his lifetime he needed unrest and he needed war; but he did not think that the rulers of the shaky East European Empires would be foolish enough to engage in a struggle that would provide the necessary yeast for his revolution. Yet now this was precisely what they did. In the Balkans, Austria and Russia had been manœuvring for power for fifty years, using the Balkan nationalities (Serbs, Bulgars, Rumanians, and so forth) as pawns in the great game of chess where the King was Constantinople. In this contest Russia, the largest Slav state, regarded herself as the champion of the minor Slav peoples, such as the Serbs, struggling for their freedom against the Teutonic (and in particular, Austrian) enemy. In 1908 war had come very near, and over the next six years the Balkan pot was constantly on the boil. Now at last, in July 1914, with the murder by Serb terrorists of the Austrian Archduke who was heir to the imperial throne, the pot boiled over. Russia supported Serbia; Germany supported Austro-Hungary; France supported Russia; Britain supported France and Belgium. The lunatic logic worked itself fully out.

Lenin had expected that war, if it came, would be a signal for the European working class to revolt, and now he was both amazed and downcast. At first he refused to believe the report that the German Parliamentary Socialists had voted for the Kaiser's imperialist war; but it was so, and all over Europe Socialists proved to be as patriotic as anyone else. In Russia, as everywhere else, there was a great surge of national emotion in the early days. The churches were full; crowds in the streets sang *God Save the Tsar*; the German Embassy was sacked, and the capital rid itself of its German name to become "Petrograd" for a decade; strikes were things of the past; young men, rich and poor alike, sprang to the colours; and in the first weeks of the war big Russian armies rumbled into Austria and over the Baltic lands into the forest and lake country of East Prussia. Talk of revolution was as out of date as last year's fashions, and the few Bolsheviks in the Duma who criticized the war were soon bundled off to Siberia.

Lenin, in Austrian territory, found himself an enemy alien, and suspected of espionage, but, after a short imprisonment, was permitted to go to Switzerland, where he spent the next two-and-a-half years before the revolution, often in considerable poverty, for his income as a professional agitator was shrunken with the fortunes of the Party that provided it. Here, in Berne, he helped to bury the Second Socialist International that the war had killed, and to bring to birth the Third, and here he wrote his work on *Imperialism as the Last Phase of Capitalism*. He was out to "wage war on the war," not as a humanitarian, still less as a pacifist; but the only good that could come out of the 'imperialist' war was through its being turned into civil war. He was content to be called a revolutionary defeatist: he worked for the defeat of his country, because only out of defeat could come the end of Tsardom and the beginning of Socialism. The German Government was accordingly only too pleased to give him facilities for distributing his propaganda among their Russian prisoners-of-war.

The war would no doubt have put an impossible strain even upon a Russia that had efficient men at the heart of things; but the figures who came to dominate Russia in these critical years were grotesquely ill-equipped for the situation. There was, first, the Tsar Nicholas II himself, intellectually naïve, hesitant, a devout son of the Orthodox Church, believing that he was responsible only to God in the rule of his vast Empire, a weak, decent man torn hither and thither in the

tempest. Then there was his wife, the Tsarina Alix, a grand-daughter
of Queen Victoria, obsessed with the well-being of her family, and
especially of her young son, the Tsarevich, who suffered from
haemophilia—uncontrollable bleeding—and was not expected to
live; devotedly religious, but superstitious and gullible to an
extreme degree; intense in both love and hatred, and hating blindly
any critic of the Tsar and his God-given autocracy; forever goading
her husband into strong, and usually unwise, action ("Be strong, my
sweetheart." "Russia loves the whip"); in short, petticoat government
at its most disastrous. But the Tsar and Tsarina were figures of drab
normality compared with the fantastic figure who became the real
power behind the Tsarina, and therefore the Tsar, during the last
years of the monarchy—Rasputin, the ex-peasant 'holy man' of
immense strength and sensational sexual and alcoholic reputation;
greasily shrewd; dirty-bearded and tangle-haired; claiming clair-
voyant powers and gifts of healing. It was these last that gave him
a special power over the Tsarina: when the doctors despaired only
Rasputin (if necessary by telegram) could stop the bleeding that
might any day be fatal to the Tsarevich. So it was "our Friend"
who in the end really ruled Russia; it was "our Friend" who, after
sleeping off his stupors, awoke in the morning to advise the dismissal
of Ministers and generals, and the appointment of his own protégés
and cronies: in particular, the husbands of his mistresses (and woe
betide the husbands of those who refused him). Thus by 1916 Russia
—in the midst of disastrous military defeats—was in the power of an
Emperor who was in the power of an Empress who was in the
power of a monstrous charlatan.

Meanwhile Russians died in their millions. In the first ten months
alone they lost 3,800,000 men, and the untrained and often unarmed
peasants that were rushed into the gaps suffered desperate losses and
privations. Artillery and ammunition were short, equipment inadequate; and the communications broke under the strain. By 1916 there
were mutinies, punished by the firing-squad. By the autumn there
was open talk of revolution, and bold men even spoke against
Rasputin in the Duma. Then, at the very end of the year, he was
assassinated by patriotic aristocrats, being at last shot and battered,
and shot again to death, after apparently thriving on cakes injected
with cyanide of potassium. The Tsarina knelt for hours before his
tomb, shattered but inflexible. Protopopov, one of the chief Ministers, a protégé of Rasputin and a dabbler in spiritualism, fed her
regularly with faked telegrams of loyalty. The Tsar, who would
permit no one to offer him, the Agent of God, advice, had ceased to

count. Everywhere men discussed who would succeed after his abdication. Queues outside the bakers' shops; soldiers among the crowds demonstrating in the streets; news of more defeats on the military fronts; strikes, and the closing of schools; rumours of the forcible dispersal of the Duma—such was the picture in Petrograd by the beginning of March 1917.

On March 8 Nicholas, who was Commander-in-Chief of the armies in the field, left his palace near Petrograd for the Army Headquarters at Mogilev. He was tired and dazed; he hoped that events would appear less complicated away from the buzzing capital, and was looking forward to some respite, a little leisure, a few games of dominoes in the evenings. That day the revolution began. It was not organized by any revolutionary group as the Bolshevik revolution of November 1917 was; it was a culmination of popular hunger, discontent, cold, and resentment. It began quietly with protest marches and strikes; soon the workers were on the streets in their hundreds of thousands, overwhelming the police barriers; first, a few troops fired into the air instead of into the crowd, as ordered; next day sixty were killed when other troops obeyed their orders—but the revulsion sent first one, then another, regiment over to join their civilian brothers, until almost all the 160,000 of the Petrograd division had to be written off as unreliable. Railway workers prevented the train bringing Nicholas back to the city from arriving; and he finished his reign willy-nilly where his train took him. His abdication, at Pskov, left Russia with two rival groups struggling to control events, both meeting in the same Tauride Palace, in Petrograd: one a group of Duma politicians who became eventually the Provisional Government, under the nominal leadership of Prince Lvov, and the other the Executive Committee of the Petrograd Soviet. The only man who was a member of both groups, the moderate Socialist, Kerensky, soon emerged as the most important and energetic member of the Government.

The so-called February Revolution (March 8–15; typically, the Russian calendar had 'got slow') was greeted with enthusiasm throughout Russia and beyond. The American President, Wilson, called it "wonderful and heartening"; Moscow and the other provincial centres rushed to set up their own Soviets; a million soldiers within the first month simply made off for their villages to share in the redistribution of land. Another million orderly citizens of Petrograd, filing past the common grave of those who had died in the shooting (while the fortress guns boomed out their tribute) might reasonably have concluded that the revolution was all over.

But there were those who thought otherwise. Lenin, unable at first to get out of his "damned Switzerland," spat forth contempt for "the Kerenskys and Co." "Our tactics," he telegraphed to Party members, "absolute distrust, no support of new Government. Kerensky particularly suspect; to arm proletariat only guarantee..." He would not even give two cheers for the revolution. The Provisional Government was capitalist; its policy was to continue "the imperialist slaughter." Indeed, he suspected that the February Revolution had been engineered by the British and French Ambassadors to prevent a separate Russo-German peace. Directed as it was, moreover, by aristocrats like Lvov and *bourgeois* Liberals like Milyukov, it would never undertake radically revolutionary reforms. It was a sham.

This attitude might have remained the tiresome pose of an uncharitable and extreme doctrinaire, and history might by this time have forgotten the agitator, Ulyanov-Lenin, had not the German High Command now (April 1917) seen the military advantage of allowing this uncompromising defeatist to travel through its territory to the Russian border. During the war Lenin had had frequent contacts with the German authorities, who were willing to use all possible means to defeat Tsarist Russia—including the encouragement of socialist revolution; and now he and thirty-one others, including Krupskaya, Zinoviev, and Radek, were shunted across Germany in a sealed railway-coach, and enabled to proceed *via* Sweden and Finland to Petrograd. So the Germans, as Churchill put it, loosed upon Russia the most grisly of all their weapons, the "plague bacillus" Lenin; and it was not surprising that when he and his group arrived they were widely regarded as German tools. Indeed, in one sense this is precisely what they were.

In the short view the German generals had made a clever move. Driven from the Petrograd railway-station by an armoured convoy of Bolshevik admirers, fretting with boredom at the speeches of welcome, Lenin suddenly scorched his supporters with the fire of his criticism. Why were they co-operating with Mensheviks and Liberals? Why were they merely playing at revolution? Socialism had been betrayed by "defensists"—that is, by those willing to continue the war—so deeply betrayed that he proposed a new name for the party of true International Socialists: the Communist Party. "We have got to take off our dirty shirt and put on a clean one." They must realize that the *bourgeois* revolution was ending: the revolution was "entering its socialist phase." Banking and industry must be brought under Soviet control, and the troops must be taught to fraternize with their German and Austrian brothers.

There was a fiery certainty about him, and his shock tactics succeeded. Kamenev and Kalinin and a few others dissented, but the bulk of the Bolsheviks (including the editor of *Pravda*, a certain Stalin) were fired by the flame of his conviction and leadership. Trotsky, returned from his Canadian internment, flew eloquently to his support. From the day of Lenin's return, the Bolshevik Party was committed to overturn the Provisional Government, and to carry through a new revolution; and from the day of his return the fortunes of the Party began to improve. His slogan of "Peace, Bread, and Land" carried more and more weight. In municipal elections during the summer Milyukov's Cadet Party (Constitutional Democrats, or Liberals), the nucleus of the Provisional Government, lost ground; by June the Bolsheviks were the biggest single party in the Moscow Soviet; and although that month Lenin was shouted down at the first All-Russian Congress of Soviets, which gave its support to a new offensive against the German and Austrian armies, the disastrous failure of that offensive strengthened his position and weakened that of Kerensky, who had gone personally to the front to launch it and to raise the morale of the troops.

Just before the rout of the offensive, however, there was an unsuccessful Bolshevik rising in Petrograd that might well have been fatal to Lenin's cause. The Bolsheviks had worked hard to spread their seditious ideas among the Army (in particular, the Petrograd garrison among the naval forces near the capital at Kronstadt, and among the factory workers). Their paper, *Pravda*, was constantly hammering away at "Peace, Bread, and Land" (the bread ration was still very low) and "All Power to the Soviets"—in other words, "Down with the Provisional Government." Their agents honeycombed barracks and factories—in particular, the great organizations like the Putilov Metal-works. All this propaganda produced in mid-July a series of 'spontaneous' demonstrations by half a million workers, soldiers, and sailors that caught the Bolshevik Party organization in two minds. They were loath to damp down the revolutionary ardour of the working class, but they were loath to be caught heading a premature rebellion that could not assert its authority throughout the country. Meanwhile the mob took command; confused street fighting lasted two days and caused four hundred casualties; the Kronstadt sailors seized the Fortress of St Peter and St Paul; and Lenin, Zinoviev, Trotsky, and Stalin had the unusual task of trying to moisten the fire of Bolshevik crowds without actually quenching it. These "July Days" did Lenin and his associates much harm. They coincided with terrible news from the front, and the

Government seized the opportunity to publish papers which claimed to establish Lenin as a German agent. A howl of patriotic fury rose against him. Right-wing groups and Cossacks paraded through Petrograd, occupying the Bolshevik headquarters (the commandeered palace of the ballerina, Kshesinskaya), and wrecking the offices of their paper, *Pravda*; and the 'middling' citizens of the capital were incensed against the Bolsheviks in general and him in particular. Trotsky gave himself up, boldly facing the charges against him, and being imprisoned with Kamenev, but it was decided by the Party Committee that Lenin and Zinoviev should again go into hiding, since in the prevalent hysteria they could not possibly expect a fair trial. The warrant for his arrest named as his offence, not his revolutionary or seditious activities, but simply treason. Hence once more Lenin slipped into Finland, that only partly Russianized state so luckily situated to provide a refuge for Bolsheviks within convenient striking distance of Petrograd. From here till his return in October he still dominated the Party by post: the old slogan, "All Power to the Soviets," should be shelved, he wrote, until such time as the Bolsheviks could dominate the Soviets. Yet that time was approaching, perhaps rapidly; membership of the Party was rising steadily as the nation sickened more and more of the hopeless war and its endless slaughter. Were the members of the Central Committee in Petrograd sufficiently in tune with the situation? Were they not too casual, too convinced that the pear would fall into their hand when it was ripe? Perhaps Kamenev in particular might be suspected on this count. Yet he wrote in friendly enough fashion to Kamenev. "Strictly *entre nous*: if I am done in, please publish my book"—for he was, inevitably, writing a book as well as a dozen or so letters a day. This one was eventually called *The State and Revolution*, and laid down the necessary prerequisites of a successful revolution, namely:

(1) the support *either* of a majority of the peasantry *or* of a majority of the revolutionary vanguard in the towns; (2) "the incoming revolutionary tide" must be flowing over the whole country; (3) the existing Government must be in a state of moral and political bankruptcy; (4) the "irresolute elements" must be in a state of insecurity.

Lenin was essentially a theorist and systematizer; he thought in '-isms,' to an extent indeed which repels most Western readers. What makes him pre-eminent among revolutionaries is his simultaneous combination of this intellectual's pursuit of the theoretical with his uncanny sense of the practical, his ability mentally to take the temperature of events as they actually happened. One does not after all expect the violinist to write a book on Beethoven while actually performing the Violin Concerto.

While Lenin was in Finland events occurred in and around Petrograd that greatly strengthened the Bolsheviks' hand. A day or so after the "July Days" Kerensky had become Prime Minister, replacing Prince Lvov; and he had appointed a new Commander-in-Chief in General Kornilov. But the General, a tough, courageous, Cossack from Asia, and politically a simpleton, soon began to challenge the authority of the Prime Minister. Conservative patriots began to see him as the strong man who would call a halt to the revolution and restore discipline; there was no secrecy about it, the beginning of September being freely forecast as the date of the proposed coup. As Kornilov advanced on the capital, however, the power of the organized working class was revealed. Railwaymen tore up the tracks; telegraphists ignored his messages; factory workers took to the barricades; the Petrograd Soviet formed a military committee independent of Kerensky's official Government, and Bolsheviks and Mensheviks worked together in support of it. The Kronstadt sailors again were ready to fight; the Red Guards mobilized ("Red" at this time did not necessarily mean Bolshevik only), and even Kornilov's own troops were penetrated with Soviet sympathizers. Lenin saw every advantage, for once, in co-operation: not only must Kornilov be stopped, but everything was to be gained by the Bolsheviks taking the lead in stopping him—not least important, by a free distribution of arms to the civilian volunteers, who retained them against Kerensky's orders when the Kornilov threat melted away. When the general was arrested Kerensky was by no means the victor, although he assumed the office of generalissimo; the real victor was Lenin and the Bolshevik group, who had done most to paralyse Kornilov.

Kerensky had been "caught between two fires." The Bolsheviks, whose leaders he had imprisoned, were now the dominant socialist group in both Petrograd and Moscow, their Party membership increasing daily; and Lenin now offered an alliance to the Mensheviks and Social Revolutionary groups if they would break with the Liberal-Democrats (Cadets) in the Governments. They refused, but pressure was brought to bear on the weakened Kerensky to release Trotsky and Kamenev. So strongly was Lenin's "revolutionary tide" flowing in favour of the Bolsheviks that a group grew up among them, led by Kamenev and Zinoviev, hostile to armed revolt, and favouring the gradual peaceful winning of power through democratic means. An armed insurrection, they considered, might risk the defeat and ruin of the Party.

Against this view Lenin thundered from his Finnish exile. Armed revolution was imperative, and it must be planned to the smallest detail. "The crisis is here. It is criminal to delay." "Delay means death." He was in a fury when they appeared to be listening to Zinoviev and Kamenev rather than to him, and kept up a running fire of violent agitation in the papers. Now that the moment was approaching which his life had been a preparation for, it was a torture to him that waverers should be prepared to throw it away. He reprimanded the Central Committee; he jeered at them; he *instructed* them. By October 22 he could bear it no longer: he acquired a wig, shaved off his beard, and suddenly (although still 'wanted' for treason) turned up in their midst.

A day or so later the vital meeting of the Bolshevik Central Committee, after a ten-hour discussion, decided in his favour, but it was not the end of the struggle: Kamenev and Zinoviev, deliberately indiscreet, attacked the proposed uprising in newspaper articles. A furious Lenin in return denounced them as "traitors to the revolution." Meanwhile Trotsky, the ex-Menshevik who was now a passionate Leninist, was completing his own preparations: all but two regiments in the Petrograd garrison were won over in advance, and when the Government tried to switch these 'rotten' regiments for loyal ones, orders were simply ignored. The Bolsheviks now had their own headquarters in the big Smolny Institute, until the Revolution a convent school for young ladies; from here they prepared for battle —as it were in full view. Outside the Institute Red Guards controlled ingress and egress (so well that a rather too well-disguised Lenin had difficulty himself in passing them); inside were the Military Revolutionary Committee, with Trotsky in his bare attic working like one possessed, planning every man's task when the sign should be given. Some thousands of men filled the hundred rooms of the Institute— as John Reed, the American journalist present among them, described,

> burly, bearded soldiers, workmen in black blouses, a few long-haired peasants.... The depths of Russia had been stirred, and it was the bottom which came uppermost now.... The benches along the wooden tables were packed with hungry proletarians, wolfing their food, plotting, shouting rough jokes across the room ... The committee rooms buzzed and hummed all day and all night, hundreds of soldiers and workmen slept on the floor, wherever they could find room. Upstairs in the great hall a thousand people crowded to the uproarious sessions of the Petrograd Soviet.... Downstairs in the office of the Factory Shop Committees sat

Seratov, signing orders on the Government Arsenal for arms—one hundred and fifty rifles for each factory . . . Delegates waited in line, forty of them . . . Towards four in the morning I met Zorin in the outer hall, a rifle slung from his shoulder. "We're moving!" said he. "We pinched the Assistant Minister of Justice and the Minister of Religions. They're down the cellar now. One regiment is on the march to capture the Telephone Exchange, another the Telegraph Agency, another the State Bank. The Red Guard is out" . . . On the steps of the Smolny, in the chill dark, we first saw the Red Guard—a huddled group of boys in workmen's clothes, carrying guns with bayonets, talking nervously together . . . Far over the still roofs westward came the sound of scattered rifle fire . . . Behind us great Smolny, bright with lights, hummed like a gigantic hive.

In some such manner the most momentous revolution in modern history proceeded—in a turbulence of talk and counter-talk, "roaring," as Reed says, "like the sea"; a confusion of accusation and counter-accusation, of mass-meetings, of plots and rumours, of arrests and counter-arrests, of small, apparently isolated, shootings; the strangest mixture of careful planning and hour-to-hour improvisation. But it was Trotsky's Military Committee that was calling the tune, "throwing off orders like sparks"; the railway-stations, power-stations, bridges over the Neva, the bank and telephone exchange were theirs by November 7; the guns of the cruiser *Aurora* in the river were Bolshevik guns. Kerensky left the city in a desperate effort to find loyal troops, leaving his fellow-Ministers in the Winter Palace. They waited. Bolshevik troops surrounded them; their protecting garrison melted gradually away to only a thousand or so; the *Aurora*'s guns were trained upon them. Kerensky did not return, and the Ministers awaited their downfall with dignity. With the merest dozen or so casualties, the Winter Palace fell. The city was Lenin's and Trotsky's, victors in a largely bloodless revolution. Within the next week Moscow followed; Kerensky had been defeated and had fled; the "ten days that shook the world" were over.

The day after the fall of the Winter Palace, writes John Reed, Lenin took the platform at the Smolny meeting. "He stood there, gripping the edge of the reading-stand, letting his little winking eyes travel over the crowd." When they had roared themselves short of breath "he said simply, 'We shall now proceed to construct the Socialist order.'"

Never have so many reforms of such sensational radicalism been propounded within so short a period. All land remaining in landlords' hands was to go to the peasants (but not yet to be nationalized); production in the factories and distribution of goods was to be

E

in the hands of the workers' soviets; all banks, all railways, all foreign trade, and some major industries were nationalized; all inequalities based on class, sex, nationality, or religion were abolished. All existing legal institutions were abolished and replaced by "people's courts." In the Army officers were to be elected. All citizens between eight and fifty who could not read or write were to attend "literacy schools." And above all, the war was to be ended immediately.

In the peace negotiations with the Germans that followed at Brest Litovsk Trotsky was the main Bolshevik representative, and he was offered terms so crushing that even he could not stomach them. Lenin's defeatism, however, went to extreme lengths; no price in surrendered territory was too high to pay. In any case, two factors outweighed all others: first, the Russian soldiers were already, as Lenin said, "voting with their feet" for peace—deserting to get back to their villages in time for the share-out of the remaining lands; and, second, the treaty of peace, however brutal, he thought, was bound to be a temporary settlement, lasting only until the day of the great Communist revolution in other lands—Germany in particular. By the Treaty of Brest-Litovsk (1918) Lenin "yielded space to gain time": the space amounted to a quarter of the territory of the Russian Empire, with a third of its population and three-quarters of its coal and iron. Lenin signed the treaty but would not read it. He had not the slightest intention of respecting it; and of course the Allied victory in the West a few months later made it a dead letter.

The new reforms inside Russia—the remaining three-quarters of it—sounded magnificent but were largely unpractical, and indeed Lenin frankly admitted as much. Laws, he said, were intended as programmes for action, general indications of policy, means of propaganda. Even so, much of the early law-making was preposterous. None of the Bolshevik leaders had had any experience of industry or business, and when the factories were handed over to the workers, with pay irrespective of work, naturally work practically ceased: production fell to one-seventh of the previously already low level. The railways were run simply in the interests of the railway-men, which meant that most trains did not run at all. As for the abolition of private trade, which made all shopkeepers outlaws overnight, this led directly to starvation in the towns, and indirectly to a fantastic system of barter, by which the town populations sallied forth into the surrounding countryside to exchange their valuables—furniture, cutlery, jewellery, anything—for the peasants' produce.

Thereby, of course, they practised 'private trade,' itself illegal. Money ceased to have any value.

These wild experiments of the early days of Communism completed the ruin of Russia that had begun during the war and continued between the two 1917 revolutions. In order to get work restarted Lenin's Government introduced the conscription of labour, and put the whole working of the nation's farms and industries under the direction of Communist Commissars. Already the country was in the steel grip of Communist Party dictatorship: when the Bolsheviks found themselves in a minority in the constituent assembly they simply got rid of it, and of all other parties in the State. In the countryside the commissars had the task of forcing the surrender of crops to provide food for the towns—to which the peasants replied simply by producing enough for themselves and no more. When the Communists established State farms these were ignorantly run, against the non-co-operation and often the armed revolt of the peasants, to whom the land meant much but Communism meant nothing. The towns, hungry in 1918, grew steadily hungrier, until by 1920–21 the famine had reached catastrophic proportions. Nobody knows how many died—several millions. Still larger numbers suffered from the grim diseases that always march with famine, malaria especially. Many thousands abandoned their towns, searching for food; even cannibalism was reported.

All this, terrible enough, was rendered doubly terrible by the continuation of war, or rather of many small wars, throughout the country. Although Petrograd fell bloodlessly to the Communists in November 1917, there were many places where Tsarist officers rallied enough support for some months to resist the local Soviets and Red troops. But this purely Russian civil war would have collapsed early in 1918 had not the Allied countries, seeing with alarm the impending withdrawal of Lenin's Russia from the war against Germany, decided to give aid to the White (anti-Bolshevik) forces wherever they were to be found. Hence British troops landed in the north at Archangel; Japanese, American, British, and other forces (in particular Czech prisoners-of-war) gave notable help to Admiral Kolchak in the east; Denikin in the south, Yudenich in Estonia, a Polish army attacking in White Russia and the Ukraine, all had assistance from the French and British. So civil wars became merged in wars of intervention to plague Russia for three years. By the end of 1918 the area controlled by the Red Army—which was brilliantly led by Trotsky—had shrunk to an area of a few hundred miles around Moscow. Allied support dwindled after the war in the West ended in

November 1918; and little as most Russians liked their Red commissars, they liked the White Guards less. Many districts changed hands several times—each time to the terrible tune of new atrocities. Red guerrillas operated in White areas, White guerrillas in Red—savage barbarities being practised on both sides. At last, by 1921, the Red Army was triumphant over the last of the White Russian armies (Wrangel's in the Crimea)—but peace returned to a Russia that had almost bled to death. Famine and terror were the masters. Ever since an attempt on Lenin's life in 1918 the Bolsheviks' dictatorship and terror had grown in ferocity, until some even of their own supporters found them intolerable. In March 1921 the very Kronstadt sailors who had been Communist stalwarts in 1917 rose in revolt; "this was the flash," as Lenin himself said, "that lit up reality better than anything else."

Lenin and his close associates were not monsters of cruelty; they were ruthless and dedicated men consumed by an idea and passionately certain of their own rightness. And since the end of Communism was to them so patently right, any means seemed justified that led to that end. Even so, Lenin should not be held responsible for all the crimes committed by his followers between 1918 and 1921. The butchering of the Tsar and his entire family, for instance, at Ekaterinburg, in 1918, he disapproved of—though he considered the Tsar himself capitally guilty. Maxim Gorky, the writer and friend of Lenin, was probably right in claiming that Lenin "hated suffering"; he reports him as saying, after listening to a Beethoven sonata, that it made him "want to say stupid, nice things, and stroke the heads of people who could create such beauty while living in this vile hell. And now you mustn't stroke anyone's head—you might get your hand bitten off. You have to hit them on the head, without any mercy . . ." And on another occasion, "The cruelty, which the conditions of our life made necessary, will in the future be understood and vindicated." Neither was Lenin the sort of dictator that Stalin later became. As President, and as chief architect of the revolution, he was accorded immense respect; but he always expected criticism and opposition from other members of his Government, and when he received it he did not treat his critics in Stalin's way, as dangerous rivals to be eliminated. Lenin, while forced to use the state machine, remained still critical of it. In 1921 Trotsky wanted to make the trade unions part of that state machine, to be directed from above, but Lenin opposed him; he saw in them a counterpoise to the otherwise too powerful commissars and bureaucrats. He was constantly aiming at the successful exercise of power "from below" (it was in theory the whole basis of a 'soviet' state); and he constantly worked towards the ideal of a genuine "workers' and peasants' state," where the underdog was not in danger of constant kicks from state police and state officials. The powerful, oppressive, and privileged bureaucracy that Stalin took refuge in later would have horrified him. As for the Party purges of Lenin's later years, these were child's play compared with Stalin's wholesale brutalities. Unlike Stalin, he was never in love with tyranny.

The shock of the Kronstadt rising, on top of the economic breakdown of Russia, forced Lenin to reconsider his whole policy. He concluded that the Bolsheviks' first attempt to create a socialist Russia in one great leap had failed. They must go back in order to go forward more slowly. Accordingly he promulgated the New Economic Policy of 1921, or, as it came to be called, NEP: a great retreat, but a realistic one. Only Lenin had the prestige to carry through so humiliating a policy. Communism was retained as the basic principle of Soviet Russian law, but only in the sense of an ideal to work towards. The major industries remained nationalized and foreign trade remained a State monopoly; but in other respects Lenin was forced to return to private trade and private peasant enterprise—in short to Capitalism. So Russia developed what is known as a "mixed economy," with some state and some private enterprise. The peasant had first to pay the state a tax in goods; but for the rest his profits were his own. Again it became worth working hard on the land for private gain, and a new class of kulak, or prosperous peasant employing labour, grew up—later to be cruelly exterminated under Stalin. A new trading middle class grew up too, the "Nepmen," sometimes liable to be pounced upon with their profits, and always hampered by Government restriction, but basically similar to the ordinary businessmen of *bourgeois* countries. All this was gall and wormwood to the stern, uncompromising Communist, and Lenin met much opposition. His statesmanship and his ruthlessness were equal to it; the opposition was purged, and gradually Russia began to climb out of the depths.

She even deliberately cultivated relations with foreign countries —Britain first of all (March 1921)—though these were always bedevilled by intense mutual suspicion and a stream of irritant and abusive propaganda from the Russian side. For though they needed the trade of the capitalist countries, the men ruling Russia could never forget that all this was, like NEP, a temporary expedient. The time must come (for had not Marx proved it?) when the capitalist countries must have their Communist revolution, and Russia must work to speed the day, partly on general grounds, and partly because her own position in the world would until that day be shaky. Hence the dilemma of all Russo-Western foreign policy from then till now: how to co-exist with a world whose death one must welcome and therefore work for—yet how to work for that death when one needs both trade and peace.

But these problems, internal and external, were for a Russia where Lenin was no more. The New Economic Policy was his last great contribution to Russia's future; for in the spring of 1922 he was struck down by the first of three paralytic strokes that in rather less than two years killed him, a middle-aged man of fifty-three.

He could not be happy, lying largely helpless through 1923, mentally still alert and able to dictate notes, conscious that the triumphs of the revolution were still insecure. Worse, there was obviously the risk—even the likelihood—of a split in the Party once he was dead. The story of the struggles between Trotsky and Stalin for the succession are told more fully in the chapter on Stalin; the dying Lenin was only too acutely aware of "obscure happenings behind his back," and the dangers of men coming to the top who might forget his ideals for which the revolution had stood. From his deathbed he strove to prevent Stalin's triumph, but the crafty Georgian was already too well dug in. When Lenin died, in January 1924, at the town renamed after his friend Gorky, it was Stalin who stage-managed the funeral, the pomp and ritual of the Oath to Lenin, and all the religious incantation of the Lenin-worship that set in from that day. "In leaving us, Comrade Lenin ordained us to guard the unity of our Party like the apple of our eye. We vow to thee, Comrade Lenin, that we shall fulfil honourably this thy commandment . . ."; all this, and a great deal more that would have made Comrade Lenin, who loathed humbug, sick and angry.

For a week he lay in state, while hundreds of thousands queued patiently in the bitter cold to spend a few seconds filing past his bier. Later a great mausoleum was built to house his embalmed corpse on Red Square, against the advice of Trotsky; but Stalin knew well the power of the legend and the popular value of such a cult. By now Moscow was the new capital of Soviet Russia; but away on the Baltic the old capital city that had seen his bitterest fights and greatest triumphs was renamed, in his honour, Leningrad. Leninism became at once a science and a religion; his most casual utterances, as well as his weighty works of political economy, were quoted, with those of Marx, to provide yardsticks of wisdom and standards of correct thinking. They still are so quoted, over perhaps one-third of the modern world; and it is reasonable to suppose that he would be more shocked than flattered by this cult of his memory.

Lenin was an unscrupulous and merciless fighter, a dominating public speaker (though never an orator of the stamp of Trotsky), a powerful controversialist both in print and on the platform, a matchless opportunist in the field of action. An opponent once came out of a political argument with him saying that he felt as though he had been hit over the head with a flail. Gorky said of him, "His words always brought to my mind the glitter of steel shavings"; and a famous historian lamented, "What a professor lost to the world!" Lenin is one of those very rare men in history, the original thinker who was also the steel-spirited man of action. Personally he was without pretension. As President of the Republic after 1917 he accepted the wage of a skilled worker. His tastes were simple, and he slept in the Kremlin on an iron bedstead in an uncarpeted room. He lacked charity for his enemies, but he did not lack humanity. He disliked tyranny and he despised cant and verbiage. He did not suffer fools gladly. A measure of his stature is perhaps the unquestioning attitude of subordinacy that the brilliant Trotsky always preserved before him; and so indeed did all that considerably gifted band who helped to "give history a shove" in 1917.

Table of Events

1861.	Emancipation of serfs in Russia.
1867.	Karl Marx begins publication of *Das Kapital*.
1870.	Birth of Vladimir Ulyanov (Lenin).
1881.	Assassination of Alexander II.
1894.	Accession of Nicholas II.
1900.	Lenin returns from Siberian exile: his seventeen-year European exile begins.
1903.	Bolshevik-Menshevik split.
1904.	Russo-Japanese War.
1905.	Revolution. Trotsky heads Petersburg Soviet.
1906–11.	Reforms of Stolypin.
1914.	Russia enters First World War. Battle of Tannenberg.
1916.	Mutinies in Army. Murder of Rasputin.
1917.	Revolution (March). Nicholas II abdicates.
	Lenin returns from Switzerland.
	Bolshevik Revolution (November).
1918.	Treaty of Brest-Litovsk.
	Wars of intervention and civil wars.
1920–21.	Famine and breakdown.
1921.	Lenin's New Economic Policy.
1923.	Struggle between Stalin and Trotsky begins.
1924.	Death of Lenin.

4

Mahatma Gandhi
(1869–1948)

Of all the remarkable men who have guided the twentieth century on its swift and startling course, perhaps the most remarkable of all was Gandhi. At his birth Britain was approaching the peak of her imperial power both in India and the world. The great Indian Mutiny had been suppressed twelve years earlier; when he was a boy of seven Queen Victoria, to her own gratification and the delight of the British public, assumed the title of Empress of India. Even those parts of the great sub-continent that were not under British rule were drawn into the web of her imperial influence—and that influence was largely admirable. For the first time in centuries India began to achieve a certain unity of law and administration, and even language, for English provided an extra official and universal language; railways and telegraphs helped to bind India together; Britain, who had earlier used the weapon of war to gain control of India, now used her sovereign position to give India peace. Some schools and universities were started, and benefited a minority of more fortunate Indians. The British Government had worked conscientiously to put down what they took to be law-·less and cruel practices (such as *sati,* the burning of Hindu widows); some progress was made in agriculture and medicine. All this was achieved by a few thousand British scattered over India, from the Viceroy in his magnificence at Delhi to the humblest missionary in his country district: the Indian Army and police were officered by the British; the civil service was dominated by them. Above all, the presence of the British merchant and planter reminds us of the basic reason that had taken the white man to India: trade and profit. Gandhi himself estimated that there were perhaps 100,000 Englishmen in India.

In Gandhi's youth there grew up in India a nationalist movement that he himself was destined eventually to lead and inspire, whose criticism of Britain may be summarized somewhat as follows:

First, the British were taking out of India far more than they were putting in. Vast fortunes had been made, and were still being made, by British companies in India, and only a small portion of this money was spent in India for the good of Indians, who remained wretchedly poor; by far the greatest part of it was spent in England by the English, who were thus sucking the Indians dry, and using them as cheap labour. All the colleges and irrigation schemes and hospitals and law-courts only added up to a contemptible fraction of the monetary value of India to the British.

Secondly, the British in India behaved as a master race, whose spiritual arrogance and automatic assumption of superiority over the 'natives' engendered among Indians of all castes and classes a resentment which was slow to mature but in the long run was irresistible. However just the British district magistrate, however brave the British officer, however valuable the employment afforded by the British planter, however impartial the British missionary, they all at bottom constituted a tiny aristocracy, different people of a different colour and a different continent, with different ways and a different language, born (and educated in their public schools) to *rule*, just as the Indian, they assumed, was born to obey. There was perhaps one Englishman to every three or four thousand Indians. He lived his own life largely apart from the 'natives'; his society revolved around the white man's club, a little oasis of comfortable 'Englishness' in a vast, profitable, servile world. To rich and educated Indians, above all, this assumption of superiority was intolerable. However good the British Government (and they admitted that, though selfish, it was not tyrannical) "good government was no substitute for self-government": Indians must govern themselves, and the British must leave India.

Mohandas Karamchand Gandhi was born in 1869, in Porbandar, just one tiny British-protected state of the three hundred that went to make up Kathiawar, in the Gujerat area of Western India. His family, which was of the third great Indian caste group of traders and agriculturists, was of some importance in the little state, for both his grandfather and his father too, for a short time, had been chief minister. Thus government and trade were both 'in the family' —the very name of Gandhi means grocer. The religious influence in his upbringing was very strong: his mother, although she was illiterate, lived a strenuous life of prayer, fasting, and self-purification, and enormously affected her son's outlook; the Hinduism of that part of India where Gandhi grew up was much influenced by severe puritanical sects who, strict vegetarians, regarded all life as sacred. The adolescent Gandhi's excursions into 'sin' took him into the forbidden land of meat-eating and smoking: but later in life (a married man in his 'teens), though he was never an orthodox Hindu, he took an oath that he would never touch wine, women, or meat. He had married, like so many Indians, at an extremely early age, while still a schoolboy of thirteen years. His child-wife, Kasturba, a merchant's daughter, was a few months younger. India was a country where life was cheap (an average life might be twenty to twenty-five years), so early marriages and maximum propagation of children to support the parents' declining years had always been accepted as part of the Hindu way of life. To Gandhi later it was one of the many evils that he fought. It distracted his mind; it interfered with his schooling; it put altogether too great a responsibility on him and his child-wife-mother. It confirmed his shrinking from sex that later led him at the age of thirty-eight to take a vow of complete celibacy.

He was altogether a shy, unimpressive youth, but his studies had advanced far enough by his nineteenth birthday for him to leave his family and come to London to study law. His father was by now dead, and his mother had been very reluctant to agree to his going, especially as the caste leaders had refused to sanction his departure; in fact, his disobedience rendered him an outcaste; the elders 'excommunicated' him.

Gandhi presents a rather strange and lonely figure at this time, conscientiously learning British ways, studying (as well as his law) dancing, French, elocution, the violin, joining the London Vegetarian Society, hating the strange London food, and living cheaply on one-and-threepence-worth a day, tongue-tied, sensitive, but struggling so hard, with his shiny top-hat, flashy tie, morning coat, striped trousers, spats, and silver-topped stick, to be a pukka English gentleman.

He was a conscientious but not a brilliant student; he passed his barrister's examination in 1891, and the very next day set out for India, ignorant still of Hindu or Muslim law, still 'excommunicated,' his legal prospects not very bright. He soon made them even worse by falling foul of the local British political agent, who had him turned out of his house. Insulted, humiliated, resentful, he jumped at an opportunity that presented itself of going to South Africa to fight a civil suit. The arrogance of the British official had important consequences for the Empire he represented, for Gandhi stayed in South Africa for twenty-one years, and it was there that he learned both to know his own capabilities and to lead his fellow-Indians in their fight for justice.

There were many Indians in South Africa—they had been introduced in large numbers since 1860 as indentured labourers—*i.e.,* labourers bound under contract; and following upon the Indian labourer had come the Indian merchant. They were of all castes of Hinduism, and there were many non-Hindus (Muslims and Parsees in particular). Gandhi soon found a degree of racial intolerance in South Africa far worse than anything he had experienced in England or India. Often he was treated as a 'coolie'; forced to remove his turban in court, forcibly removed from first-class railway-compartments, refused accommodation at hotels, violently pushed and kicked by watchmen. His lawsuit having ended, he stayed on as the champion of the Indian labourers of Natal and Transvaal, who were being deprived of the right to own land except in restricted areas, and robbed of the right to vote. He addressed a letter at this time to all prominent Europeans in Natal. "It is for you," he wrote, "to treat Indians as dogs or fellow-beings demanding your sympathy in the cruel persecution that they are put to." After three years of work he returned briefly to India, wrote a pamphlet there on the conditions under which Indians suffered in South Africa, and returned in 1897, bringing this time his wife and four children, to continue the fight. A garbled version of his pamphlet had preceded him, and when he arrived back in Natal he was nearly lynched by an angry mob of whites who assailed him with abuse, rotten eggs, and brickbats. He was saved by the courage of a white woman, the wife of the local police superintendent, who walked by his side with her sunshade up to help keep off some of the missiles. The mob might well have killed Gandhi; they dared not attack a white woman in the streets. The Natal Prime Minister and the Press apologized to him, and Gandhi typically refused to hate his enemies or to seek personal redress against them in a court of law. In the Boer War that soon followed he was active in organizing an Indian Ambulance Corps that worked for the British armies.

The violence against Gandhi shows just how strong feeling was in South Africa against the Indians, who were still emigrating to the country. Even moderate men like General Smuts referred to the "Asiatic cancer" which must be eradicated, and the Transvaal Government insisted now, against the advice from the British Government, on a compulsory re-registration of all Asiatics and an Act to restrict any further immigration of Indians.

The situation produced a famous reaction. At a meeting in the Empire Theatre in Johannesburg Gandhi boldly invited his fellow-countrymen to take a solemn oath of peaceful resistance, even if it were to mean imprisonment, flogging, or even death. They would not re-register. Gandhi had hit upon a technique of revolution that was to be his peculiar contribution to history: he had also invented a name for it—*satyagraha*; which means 'firmness in truth.' It was not a sudden flash of insight, for Gandhi had been moving towards this spiritual decision for years. "I remember," he said in 1908, "how one verse of a Gujerati poem which, as a child, I learned at school clung to me. In substance it was this: If a man gives you a drink of water and you give him a drink in return, that is nothing; real beauty consists in doing good against evil.... Then came the Sermon on the Mount.... It was the New Testament which really awakened me to the rightness and value of Passive Resistance." It is not difficult to see what Gandhi meant when he said much later, "I am a Christian and a Hindu and a Muslim and a Jew."

Meanwhile the Bill limiting the civic rights of Asiatics was passed in 1907. When ordered to leave the country Gandhi and his companions refused. When prosecuted for their defiance Gandhi asked for the heaviest penalty and received two months—the first of many terms of imprisonment.

Well before this his life was becoming more and more austere. His diet, always strict, became stricter still, until it consisted largely of wholemeal bread, peanut butter, and fruit. Later, under the stress of possible death, he took to goat's milk, but cow's milk was a "stimulant of animal passions," and he would never touch it! He did his own laundry, and cut his own hair. Reading as he did a great deal of the Hindu and Christian scriptures, and Ruskin and Tolstoy among nineteenth-century writers, he more and more became a rebel against our complicated modern machine society. The machine was the "monstrous idol" of our civilization. Tolstoy himself expressed interest in this Natal *satyagraha* that was so close to his own later ideas, and Gandhi named a settlement near Johannesburg Tolstoy Farm. In 1904 a Ruskin community settlement of one hundred acres near Durban was founded by Gandhi and his followers, called the Phoenix Settlement. Manual labour, they claimed, had equal value with mental; the shoemaker was the equal of the doctor; the barber was the equal of the lawyer. Indeed (following Ruskin) the farmer's and the craftsman's were the most enviable of all callings. And the individual ought not to strive for riches against his fellows; the best life was in a community. "I want to find God," Gandhi said; and nobody could find God alone—only by working with *people*. This community of men, women, and children was the prototype of the *ashram*, or retreat, in which Gandhi was to spend many of his remaining years both in South Africa and in India. In 1906 he entered the Phoenix Community with his family, taking the oath of celibacy at the same time. Life in these settlements was hard: if you wished to go from Tolstoy Farm to Johannesburg you must walk there and back, forty-two miles; the food was strictly limited; only 'nature cures' were allowed, Gandhi having a horror of drugs; all must share the dirtiest tasks, and material comforts were shunned. Prayer and dedication and discipline went hand in hand with a good deal of gaiety: Gandhi was always a merry man, combining prodigious seriousness with a quick humour. Disciples of his brought up in the atmosphere of Tolstoy Farm or the later *ashrams* had no need to fear jail: they had been schooled in hardship, devotion, and self-knowledge. Above all they practised the art of *satyagraha*; for Gandhi was not merely a religious oddity or a vegetarian crank— he was a revolutionary in the making, and it was South Africa that made him.

It was almost impossible for Gandhi to be hated by moderate men. When he was taken from prison in 1908 to see General Smuts he greatly impressed him, and it appeared for a time that a compromise had been agreed. When later it seemed to the Indians that they had been tricked Gandhi was temporarily in real physical danger from the Pathans, the most violent among the Indian Muslims. He himself accused Smuts of foul play. Smuts called Gandhi a "cunning fellow"—but thought kindly enough of him to send him a parcel of books to relieve the prison monotony, and when Gandhi at last left South Africa he sent Smuts a pair of sandals made by the shoemakers of Tolstoy Farm. Gandhi, said Smuts much later, "even then was a man for whom I had the highest respect." There was a liberality of heart and mind about him that was very attractive. "I want the culture of all lands to be blown about my house as freely as possible," he said—though he did add, "But I refuse to be blown off my feet by any of them."

All this time the *satyagraha* movement was growing. When the Government declared all marriages illegal other than those according to Christian ceremonial many indignant Indian women (including Mrs Gandhi herself) joined. Yet when there was a strike of white workers in that same year Gandhi suspended the passive-resistance campaign for a time: he did not wish to embarrass his enemies!

The climax of Gandhi's South African career came in this year 1913. A handful of *satyagraha* women from Tolstoy Farm, in Transvaal, illegally crossed the frontier into Natal, went to Newcastle, and persuaded the Indian coalminers to strike in protest against the Government's Asiatic policy. Almost starving, six thousand men eventually marched thirty-six miles to cross the Transvaal border—an illegal act deliberately courting arrest. Possibly the "cunning fellow," Gandhi (and he *was* cunning), calculated that in prison his strikers at least would not starve. But the authorities too were cunning: the sentence involved hard labour *in the mines*. Those who refused to go down were flogged and eventually forced down by mounted military police. A few were shot. Gandhi himself was given a sentence of a year's imprisonment; he felt "as if bullets had passed through his heart." But he had not entirely failed. Imperial opinion, especially in India and Britain, was on his side; and the South African Government was forced to compromise and reverse for a time some of its more extreme policies.

Back in India, in 1915, Gandhi set about re-settling his large 'family' from Phoenix and Tolstoy Farm on a new *ashram* at Sabarmati, near Ahmedabad, the Manchester of India. When to its original twenty-five members Gandhi admitted an 'Untouchable' teacher, his wife, and baby daughter, a storm broke. An 'Untouchable' was one of India's forty to fifty million casteless people, mainly (but not necessarily) poor, and to have contact with them meant, for a caste Hindu, pollution and dishonour. Strict Hindus, the merchants of Ahmedabad who had been financially supporting the *ashram*, even some inside the *ashram* itself, even Gandhi's own wife, Kasturba, were shocked. But Gandhi stood firm. To him Untouchability was India's shame, and he offered his wife the alternative: accept the teacher's family, or quit the *ashram*. Kasturba, deeply torn, submitted, and the other members became gradually accustomed even to an 'Untouchable' serving food and drink to them, though "they risked Hell at every sip." Again he horrified devout Hindus when he ordered that a calf in the *ashram*, in its dying agony, should be killed to save it further suffering. Killing a cow or calf, sacred animals, was to a Hindu a serious sin, and many never forgave him.

In the *ashram* life went on as in Tolstoy or Phoenix, under the vows that all members had to adopt: to tell the whole truth always; to return love for hatred, and to abjure violence; to renounce sexual indulgence; to be sparing of food and drink; to give away your wealth if you were rich (we have no right to riches, said Gandhi, until the poor are clothed and fed—"*all* self-denial is good for the soul"); to use only the goods made in one's own country (part of his belief in valuing one's own immediate heritage—the *Hindu* religion, the *Indian* community, the *village* of your birth); to spin one's clothes with one's own hands (the spinning-wheel became Gandhi's symbol, and he had a horror of a machine-ridden westernized

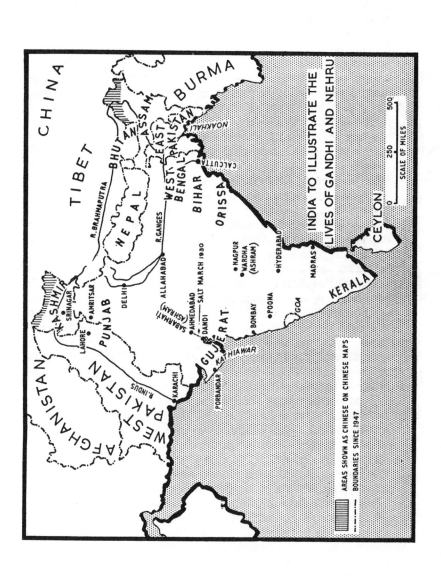

INDIA TO ILLUSTRATE THE LIVES OF GANDHI AND NEHRU

India); to be fearless; to work to end 'Untouchability'; these and more. As for himself, he always observed a vow of silence every Monday—even when his political campaign was at its height later on. Yet he was never a fanatic: when one visitor, noticing that he was not always *entirely* austere in his meals and seemed to be doing himself well with his orange juice and small choice titbits, twitted him on his little luxuries, Gandhi paused, laughed, and with his quick twinkle said, "God is good, God is all-forgiving, He will forgive us."

When he returned to India he decided to keep out of politics for a year, and in any case not to press Britain too hard during its hard struggle in the First World War. To the founder of the Indian Home Rule movement, Mrs Annie Besant, an Englishwoman, he said, "Mrs Besant, you are distrustful of the British; I am not, and I will not help in any agitation against them during the war." In fact, in 1918 he even acted as recruiting-sergeant for the British, though how this fitted in with his creed of non-violence is not clear. There was, quite apart from the war, much other work to do. For instance, the labourers on the indigo plantations of Champaran, in Bihar, were shamefully exploited by their white employers, and Gandhi appeared among them as their champion. Ordered to leave the district by the British district commissioner, he refused on grounds of conscience. His arrest was ordered, but the Lieutenant-Governor of Bihar intervened, released him, and actually appointed him to a committee of inquiry that eventually came down heavily on the side of the indigo-workers. Such decisions as this confirmed Gandhi's respect for many aspects of British rule.

Then in Ahmedabad there was severe labour trouble between the Indian cotton-mill owners and their underpaid employees. The local British official asked Gandhi to arbitrate, and he eventually 'awarded' a 35 per cent. pay increase to the men. Tempers were very high when the employers, refusing to pay more, locked the men out; and Gandhi had his work cut out to prevent violence. When some hungry workmen grumbled that Gandhi was not himself likely to suffer he began one of his many fasts. He would not eat food until 35 per cent. was granted; but on the fourth day a compromise settlement was reached, favourable enough to the strikers for him to feel justified in breaking the fast. The millowners had at least been forced to accept arbitration.

After the First World War there was much unrest in India, and the atmosphere was not improved by the ravages of the world-wide influenza epidemic that killed thirteen million Indians. When the

British Government took a firm line, tried political cases without a jury, and suspended *habeas corpus*, Gandhi was stung into rebellion. He toured the country to teach the principles of passive resistance (*satyagraha*), and called for a twenty-four-hour "day of mourning," to be combined with a general strike. In some parts—Bombay, for instance—this went off peacefully, but in the Punjab the situation was very tense and explosive. In Amritsar, in the Punjab, some Europeans were killed, and an Englishwoman beaten up. Gandhi was anxious to go there, but was arrested near Delhi. The rioting spread, and on April 13, 1919, the British General Dyer decided to break up a nationalist meeting by gunfire: in ten minutes 379 persons were killed and twelve hundred wounded. Admittedly General Dyer was recalled and dismissed, but the Tory *Morning Post* collected £30,000 for him, and his admirers presented a sword of honour. Indian opinion was appalled and bitter at this "Amritsar Massacre," but it was typical of Gandhi that when later that year the Indian National Congress Party met in Amritsar, he succeeded in persuading them to condemn also the *Indian* violence. "I say, do not return madness with madness, but return madness with sanity."

By the next year, 1920, Gandhi's breach with Britain was complete. The moderate reforms offered by the British Government seemed inadequate; the Amritsar bitterness lingered on; and the whole Muslim world was boiling with indignation at Britain's treatment of the ex-Turkish Empire. Gandhi, always a shrewd opportunist as well as a holy man, thought a perfect chance had arrived to unite Hindu and Muslim, those ancient enemies, in a common national bond of non-violent rebellion. That year, 1920, the Congress meetings in Calcutta and Nagpur were dominated by him: the revolutionary struggle was launched. For nearly thirty years more Gandhi was India's outstanding man. For the first time the Indian masses were a force to be reckoned with, and Gandhi had won them. His programme of "non-co-operation," or "civil disobedience," was, briefly, the boycott of British courts, schools, councils, and cloth. If successful it would plainly paralyse the whole British administration. A great surge of optimism, buoyed up on the new-found Hindu-Muslim unity, promoted the wild hope that Indian Home Rule, *swaraj*, might come quickly—perhaps inside a year. Wherever Gandhi went, travelling always by train, third class, he was greeted by crowds of enthusiasts—to such an extent, indeed, that he himself became sickened by "the adoration of the unthinking multitude," as he described it. Constantly his words to the idolizing vil-

lagers who greeted him on the railway-stations became sermons—
"Independence is a state of mind." They would only win self-rule if
they *deserved* it; they must purify themselves, throw away hatred
but regain a just pride, *feel* themselves to be the equal of the British.
Gone was the old softness and affection for British rule: it was a
"satanic system" of "imperialistic greed"; but even when speaking
of the "iron heels" of Britain that stamped upon India he spoke
gently, often sitting, in a calm, precise voice.

At this period he distributed two million spinning-wheels, although the campaign for home-spinning earned him much criticism
even from Indians; and indeed the Indian National Congress was
largely dependent on the contributions of rich Indian millowners
who stood to lose heavily if Gandhi should succeed. But he firmly
held that for the Indian peasant, always unemployed for four months
in the year, the spinning-wheel offered a supplementary source of
wealth, of self-respect, and of independence from Western domination. In 1921, in Bombay, Gandhi presided over a great bonfire of
foreign cloth, and when his friend C. F. Andrews protested at this
wanton waste, often of very valuable materials, and asked why they
could not be given to the poor, Gandhi was firm that this must not
be. The materials were poisonous, and "the poor too have a sense
of honour."

Yet, at this very moment of power and popularity, Gandhi's
leadership faltered. In 1921 the Prince of Wales (later Edward VIII)
visited India, and was greeted by another *hartal*, or day of mourning; but in Bombay the Parsees, out of step with Hindus and
Muslims, welcomed him, and were set upon by murderous mobs.
Fifty-three had been killed and four hundred injured when a five-
day fast by Gandhi helped to put an end to the bloodshed. But further massacres followed. In United Provinces twenty-two police
were murdered. Again Gandhi fasted in protest and repentance for
his followers' sins. The violence shook his confidence so fundamentally that suddenly, to the consternation of the other Congress
leaders, he called off the campaign of *mass* non-co-operation, though
individual disobedience might continue under certain conditions.
Gandhi fully admitted it was a humiliation, but, he said, they had
made errors and must pause to confess them, for confession was
"like a broom to sweep away dirt." Fifty thousand of his supporters
were in prison (one of them, Subhas Chandra Bose, "beside himself
with sorrow and anger" at the decision; another, the young Jawaharlal Nehru, hearing it "with amazement and consternation"); now
the British authorities arrested Gandhi himself, at the moment when

his star seemed to be sinking. In Ahmedabad, in 1922, Gandhi pleaded guilty to sedition, submitted a dignified statement of his position, and asked for the maximum sentence. "No jugglery in figures can explain away the evidence the skeletons in many villages present. . . . I have no doubt whatsoever that both England and the town-dwellers of India will have to answer, if there is a God above, for this crime against humanity." When the judge sentenced him to six years' imprisonment, paying tribute to Gandhi's idealism, Gandhi smilingly and serenely thanked him. "I must say that I could not have expected greater courtesy." The Frenchman Romain Rolland wrote of this episode as "a manifestation of rare nobility and high-mindedness. . . . Never in the struggle did England rise to more magnanimous impartiality."

After a harsh start his treatment in prison was not severe. He read widely—the Koran, the Bible, Sir Walter Scott, Emerson, Ruskin, Tolstoy, George Bernard Shaw (*Saint Joan*, which delighted him); above all, the Hindu scriptures and legends. He wrote many letters, he dictated his autobiography; he learned Tamil, one of the languages of the South; he refused privileges, and would not have collections organized to improve his amenities, for ultimately it would have to come from the poor of India. He declared himself "as happy as a bird." He refused a sedative from a doctor who wanted "to make him sleep," and successfully demonstrated that if he wished he could be asleep in two minutes—and was. But a new and grudging respect for Western surgery came when he had perforce to be operated on for acute appendicitis by a British doctor. (Half-way through the lights failed—and then the pocket torch too by which the surgeon was working!) In February 1924 the Viceroy, Lord Reading, released him on medical grounds, and he emerged into a political scene embittered by communal strife between Hindu and Muslim and by quarrels inside his own Congress Party. Gandhi might be a saint (he again entered a prolonged fast in September 1924 when murderous rioting occurred in Frontier Province), but some thought him too much of a dreamer to be a successful political leader. After presiding over the 1924 Congress he resigned from the leadership in 1925 and devoted the next three years to influencing the movement "from the bottom up," touring the villages again (India has seven hundred thousand of them), popularizing spinning, addressing meetings—often of tens of thousands—coping as well as he could with the tide, again rising, of Gandhi-worship. In one village his speech consisted of one sentence—"Empty your pockets for the poor." When villagers brought him garlands they received polite reproof—"For every rupee saved on these garlands you should give sixteen women one meal." Everywhere he campaigned against Untouchability.

Meanwhile the political campaign was developing strength again after the collapse of 1922. There was a great and successful campaign in Gujerat against an increase in the land tax, led by Patel along the lines of Gandhi's *satyagraha*; an all-India trade-union movement was set in motion, and strikes were numerous; and when a British Parliamentary Commission visited India in 1927–28 to report on its fitness for self-government the Indian National Congress boycotted it, on the grounds that it contained no Indian members. (One of its junior members was Clement Attlee, twenty years later destined to take the historic step of granting Indian independence.) Congress instead served notice on the British Government that they would give it cne year to realize independence; and when the year was up, in December 1929, "declared war." There were hundreds of ceremonies round a flagstaff; and the flag of independent India was raised. Gandhi himself issued a manifesto, typical both in what it included and in what it omitted. Prohibition of alcohol, a tariff against foreign cloth, the reduction of the land tax and abolition of the salt tax, the halving of military expenditure and of the upper range of official salaries, were among his demands—but there was no mention of schools or hospitals or of any measures to raise industrial production. The year was 1930. The world was reeling from the effects of the economic slump that had gone from Wall Street round the globe. And in India not less than in Britain or Germany its effects were tremendous not only in human suffering but in political upheaval. If revolution was in the Indian air at this time perhaps only Gandhi could keep it from murderous violence. As it was a bomb was exploded, under the Viceroy's train—a new and important Viceroy, Lord Irwin (later Lord Halifax), an earnest Christian, with whom Gandhi had something in common. He began by congratulating him on his escape from the bomb.

The situation eventually produced his most sensational demonstration of the power of *satyagraha*. When opinion in Britain would not support Lord Irwin's known desire for a conference between the British Government and the Indian Congress Gandhi and the Congress (led now, at Gandhi's insistence, by the forty-year-old Nehru) again inaugurated a campaign of civil disobedience, and Gandhi himself decided on a spectacular gesture. The salt tax was not heavy, but it was universal: it hit the poorest in the land; so Gandhi would organize a march of his disciples from Ahmedabad to the coast at

Dandi, and there they would solemnly break the law by collecting salt from the sea. He first wrote to Irwin ("Dear Friend . . .") announcing his intention, and at the same time pointing out that Irwin's salary was about five thousand times that of an Indian peasant. Then with seventy-eight followers, all hardened to the severe *ashram* discipline, and keeping a spiritual diary as they went, Gandhi marched for twenty-four days through the three hundred villages that stood between Ahmedabad and the coast. Every evening the disciples recounted to Gandhi their innermost thoughts before composing themselves to sleep on mats, usually in the open. Up at four o'clock, he conducted his usual prayer-meeting, wrote articles and letters *en route*, and always did his daily quota of spinning. Arriving at Dandi, by now in the full light of national publicity, they took first a ceremonial bath of purification, and then a symbolic pinch of the forbidden salt from the beach. The Government, as in 1922, was forced to take notice, and Gandhi was duly arrested and imprisoned; so, altogether, were about sixty thousand of his followers, some of them after much police brutality. The discipline of non-violence was never put to sterner test than in these months: kicked, beaten, charged down, writhing and blood-stained, the staunchest of the *satyagrahis* succeeded in not even raising a hand against the rain of blows from the *lathis* of the police. Several died, many hundreds were seriously hurt. Two devoted men in Frontier Province even broke open the door of a blazing school, where an infuriated mob, after just such a *lathi* charge, had shut in the police, intending to let them burn to death. Newsreels and reports of these *lathi* charges shown in the U.S.A. at this time did nothing to decrease existing American distrust of British imperialism.

Gandhi was imprisoned but Congress stepped up their campaign. They made salt, they picketed clothiers selling British cloth and 'toddy shops' selling alcoholic drink (forbidden to both Hindus and Muslims); their big demonstrations often fetched out twenty thousand sympathizers, including many women bright in their orange-coloured saris; when they called a *hartal* nearly everybody obeyed the call. Even in prison Gandhi was the King of Bombay.

Lord Irwin was not content to let him remain in prison. He not only released him, but invited him to Delhi for talks, out of which came eventually a suspension of civil disobedience and the 1931 Round Table Conference in London. Some Indians criticized Gandhi for being "taken in" by Irwin, and some English criticized Irwin for being "soft" with Gandhi. Winston Churchill, against 'appeasement' here as later with Hitler, said, "It is alarming and also nauseating to see Mr Gandhi, a seditious Middle Temple lawyer, now posing as a fakir of a type well known in the East, striding half-naked up the steps of the Viceregal Palace, while he is still reorganizing and conducting a defiant campaign of civil disobedience, to parley on equal terms with the representative of the King-Emperor." When Gandhi came to London a few months later Churchill would not meet him, though George V did.

Out of the talks with Irwin came the London Round Table Conference of 1931. It was held in St James's Palace, and representatives of every conceivable Indian interest were there—except, as Gandhi pointed out, of the peasants who *were* India. They were an unwieldy assembly—princes, landowners, industrialists, trade unionists, Hindus, Muslims, Sikhs, Parsees, Christians, Untouchables—a hundred and twelve of them in all. Gandhi himself, an odd figure among so much magnificence, travelling *second* class on the liner, sleeping on the roof of an East End settlement despite the winter cold, provided endless interest for gaping Londoners and feature-reporters—Gandhi with his bare limbs in shivering England, with his goat's milk, his spectacles low on his nose, his toothy smile. He thought that if he stayed among the poor he would reach more of Britain's heart than if he mixed with fashionable or intellectual folk, and certainly he provided Bow and Stepney (and the scholars of Eton) with a curiosity; but he hardly "won the workers" as he hoped. In Lancashire certainly he was a hit with the millgirls. He went there partly to try to explain why India boycotted Lancashire cotton and thereby caused unemployment; but he did not go to apologize. "You have three million unemployed, but we have nearly three hundred million unemployed for half the year. Your average unemployment dole is seventy shillings a month. Our average *income* is seven shillings and sixpence a month." His impact in the conference-room was negative. He was so intent on repeating his two or three essential principles—endlessly, boringly—that he became an irritant. Muslims, Sikhs, and even the Untouchables' representative opposed him. The princes were, he said, merely "British officers in Indian dress." The conference achieved hardly anything. He admitted the sincerity of many Englishmen and the many kindnesses that met him, and still protested that he wished to be a citizen of the Commonwealth; but not of the *Empire*. Indians must be treated as equals. They must control foreign policy, defence; the Army must be gradually transformed to be *India's* Army. The Congress, which he claimed, with doubtful accuracy, to represent 85 per cent. of Indians, should become the Government of India.

These things the British Government was not yet ready for. He met
George Bernard Shaw, who claimed him, a little surprisingly, as "a
kindred spirit." He had long talks with Charlie Chaplin. He went
several times to Oxford, where Gilbert Murray thought him a great
man, but essentially a wily politician. He saw Lloyd George. He met
the bishops of the Church of England (and was worried it might
involve his missing his seven o'clock prayer—but it was all right:
he said it in the car on the way). And then he met the King.
George V, conscientious as ever, expressed a wish to see him. But
what dress would it be correct for Gandhi to wear, Buckingham
Palace wondered. The naked knees, the loin-cloth and sandals, inspired misgivings. Gandhi, unperturbed, arrived in his customary
simplicity; questioned later, "Oh," he said, "it was perfectly all
right. The King wore enough for the two of us." When George V
had observed, "I can have no attacks on my Indian Empire,"
Gandhi had been too much the polite, and perhaps overawed, guest
to broach an argument.

On his return home he visited the Sistine Chapel in Rome, and
gazed spellbound at a figure there of Christ crucified. Many times
afterwards he referred to it. "It was wonderful. I could not tear
myself away. The tears sprang to my eyes as I gazed." Though
Mussolini saw him, the Pope did not grant an audience.

The civil disobedience campaign shrank in effectiveness after the
failure of the Round Table Conference. The new Viceroy, Lord
Willingdon, severely controlled the Press; he even banned the
Congress and denied it the use of postal facilities. Eventually Gandhi
wound up the campaign (to the distress, as in 1922, of many followers), and in 1935 actually resigned membership of Congress—
though before then he, like Nehru and many other leaders, had again
spent a considerable time in prison; he was arrested three times in
1933 alone. The paradoxical situation later arose that, although not
strictly a member, he continued to lead the Party from the outside
by the force of his personality.

But the bulk of Gandhi's work in the 'thirties was done in other
ways. These were the great days of his campaign for the Untouchables, whom he would not call Untouchables but rechristened the
Harijans, the Children of God. "Should we Hindus not wash our
bloodstained hands before we ask the English to wash theirs?" he
had written. "Untouchability has degraded us." He differed strongly
with Dr Ambedkar, their leader, over the question whether in the
new Indian constitution these wretched outcastes should be treated

as a separate community with a separate voting-list (though in a sense this was intended to give them *double* representation as an extra privilege). Gandhi, from his prison near Poona, in September 1932, suddenly threw down a sensational challenge to Indian and British authority alike: if the scheme of separate voting-lists were not abandoned he would embark on "a perpetual fast unto death." To the British this was hitting morally below the belt—the fast was a form of blackmail. For the Hindus it pushed everything else out of the picture. As Gandhi lay under his mango-tree in Yeravda jail near his wife, specially released from another prison, all the Hindu world was in ferment over this challenge to its conscience. Untouchability was in the scriptures, said the orthodox. (So much the worse for the scriptures, Gandhi had said.) Not only Untouchability but caste itself must disappear, said Ambedkar. (Gandhi had disagreed, for in many ways he was deeply conservative; yet in due course he did come to agree. "Caste must go," he wrote, in 1935.) Weakening daily, Gandhi argued with Ambedkar in the jail garden, until at last the "Poona Pact" was agreed both by them and the British Government. "Henceforth among Hindus no one shall be regarded as an Untouchable by reason of his birth," said Gandhi. His fast was ended; but the battle against Untouchability was only beginning. Such battles are not won in a day or in a decade. Many high-caste Hindus remained resentful of the undue weight given to the votes of these latrine-emptiers and scavengers, this submerged sixth of society who must not use the wells, the schools, above all the temples, of the other five-sixths. When Gandhi undertook a "Harijan tour" in 1934 he was met by a good deal of stone-throwing and black-flag demonstrations—even once by a bomb. When a fearful earthquake hit Bihar that year he was sure it was God's judgment on Hindu wickedness; and, challenged by more modern minds on this concept of a vengeful "Old Testament" God, he stuck to his opinion. "I believe literally that not a leaf moves but by His will. ... The knowledge of the tallest scientist is like a particle of dust." Everywhere on his tour he campaigned against even modest luxuries; he bartered his autograph for bangles—and gave the proceeds to the Harijan fund. In nine months he and his begging-bowl travelled 12,500 miles. In Delhi he even organized the *students* to clean out the latrines of the Harijans. And everywhere with him went the spinning-wheel and his other enthusiasms—for *unpolished* rice, for the soya bean ("the perfect food"), for native *gur*, so much better than grocer's sugar; for the idea that all school subjects should be taught through crafts. Children might pay for schooling through

selling the products of their spinning—and of the seven hours of a
school day, *four* should be spent in spinning! To parents he preached
an end of child-marriages; to Hindu widows he preached their
undoubted right to remarry. To Muslims he argued against the
seclusion of their womenfolk (*purdah*). He was saint, crank, and
social reformer in one; a dozen movements working through one
frail frame: a triumph of mind over matter, of personality over
malaria, malnutrition, high blood pressure, and hookworm.

He was both the inspiration and despair of his fellow Congress
nationalists, for the Untouchability campaign had taken men's
minds off the main target of independence. But the British Government, with Sir Samuel Hoare at the India Office, was not sitting
still. In 1935 Parliament passed an Act designed to give India independence by stages—against the powerful opposition of Winston
Churchill. "It was as if a motor vehicle had been set in motion in
low gear with the brakes on," but at least it was moving. Congress
could now rule the provincial governments—even though the British
retained power at the centre. "A charter of slavery," said Nehru;
"responsibility without power." But thirty million Indians received
a vote. Congress ministries arose in many parts of India; British
officials gradually learned to be servants as well as masters; there
was an uneasy period of brief partnership between Congress and the
British, though a powerful enemy of Congress was arising in the
Muslim areas with the growth of Jinnah's demand for Pakistan, a
second independent, Muslim, India.

Many events conspired in the late 'thirties to confuse the politics
of India. Not least of these was the tide of events in Europe. While
Gandhi was in Yeravda jail Hitler was gaining power in Germany.
While he was campaigning for the Untouchables, those other untouchables, the Jews of Germany, were suffering the Nazi Terror.
'Non-violence' was not fashionable in the Europe of Mussolini,
Hitler, Franco, and Stalin. And now, in 1939, came the war. What
were the Indians to do, when, much as they hated British rule, they
recognized that it was mildness itself against the injustice and brutality of the European tyrannies? Gandhi himself was in a quan-
dary. He could never support war—any war. Yet he thought that it
would be inconceivable to organize mass civil disobedience against
an England fighting to some extent for civilization. On the first day
of war the Viceroy, without consultation, declared India at war with
Germany. "One man, and he a foreigner," complained Nehru,
"plunged four hundred millions of human beings into war without
the slightest reference to them." Gandhi, sent for by the Viceroy,

promised his moral support for Britain, but declared that even if India were threatened herself by armed attack (as she later was by Japan), the answer must be non-violence, charity, love. His was a sad, lone, disconsolate voice. He well realized that most of the Congress Party were not with him in this extreme pacifism.

A half-hearted Congress campaign against Britain continued between 1939 and 1941. Then came Pearl Harbour, and the war was suddenly on India's doorstep. The British Government tried the gesture of releasing political prisoners. This did not, said Gandhi, evoke in him "a single responsive or appreciative chord," but in many Congressmen it did. Why not join with Britain to fight Japan, at a price—the price of independence? The Churchill Government grasped at the chance, and sent out Sir Stafford Cripps, a well-known friend of Indian independence, to negotiate with Gandhi, Nehru, and the other Indian leaders. Briefly, he brought the offer of dominion status for those parts of India that wanted it *after the war*. To Gandhi and Nehru that offer seemed to contain far too much encouragement both to the Muslims to break away in a new separate "Pakistan" and to the Princes to retain their own rights outside the Indian Union. To them it seemed a 'take it or leave it' offer, only offered because of American pressure and the desperate state of the war: a 'post-dated cheque.' Nothing could produce enthusiasm for India's defence but an immediate declaration of India's independence; and Churchill was hardly likely to promote "such an act of madness" (his own phrase). So the Congress committee launched its famous "Quit India" campaign, and prepared, even in the face of the imminent Japanese invasion, yet another programme of civil disobedience. In Churchill's words, they had "come into the open as a revolutionary movement," and in August 1942, Nehru, Gandhi, and the other leaders were all arrested.

Non-violence was no more. Mobs rioted. The authorities struck back with arrests, machine-guns, even aircraft. Both sides were desperate—and some indication of the British grimness is shown by their decision not to interfere when Gandhi announced in February 1943 his expected twenty-one-day fast. If Gandhi was to die, die he must. "Political blackmail," said the Viceroy (Lord Linlithgow), and opinion in Britain thought him right. It needed Smuts, his old South African enemy, to remind the British that Gandhi was no pro-Japanese traitor, but "one of the great men of the world." Gandhi survived his fast, but remained a prisoner for two years—this time in the Aga Khan Palace. Here his beloved secretary died; here his wife died, in his arms, in 1944 (she was cremated in a sari spun by

Gandhi); here Gandhi himself grew seriously ill of malaria, hookworm, and anaemia. The war began to go against Japan and Germany, and the Government once again judged it safe to release him.

He now met Jinnah, the leader of the Muslims, to discuss their
demand for "Pakistan"—a prospect that depressed Gandhi greatly.
No progress was made. In Europe the war ended with the defeat of
Germany. The atomic bombs were dropped on Hiroshima and
Nagasaki. Japan surrendered. Meanwhile in Britain an event of
great significance for India had taken place: Churchill had lost the
election of 1945, and a Labour Government led by Attlee came to
office. In this Government were men like Pethick Lawrence, Stafford
Cripps, Aneurin Bevan, Ernest Bevin, Attlee himself, who were
much more friendly than most Conservatives to the idea of rapid
independence—however sceptical the Congress leaders were of their
intentions. Besides, many (perhaps most) Englishmen were anxious
to end a situation where they could govern only by imprisonment
and coercion. In India there was pessimism; after all, Britain had
won the war and victorious powers do not give away empires. There
were sad signs, too, of intolerance and division between Indians
themselves: serious and repeated Hindu-Muslim riots, looting, arson
—as well as famine and unemployment. The Hindus blamed the
Muslims; the Muslims blamed the Hindus; both blamed the hooligans—and ultimately they could all blame the British officials. The
Attlee Government first sent out a Cabinet Mission to collect facts;
they repeatedly met Gandhi, and convinced him that they meant
business. But things were rapidly getting out of the control both
of the British and responsible Indians; the country was sliding, as
Churchill had always said it would if Britain went, into anarchy and
murder—multiple civil war. On August 16, 1946, Calcutta lived
through a fearful day of butchery, when gangs of Muslim hooligans
roamed the streets at will, killed five thousand, and injured fifteen
thousand. The Hindus replied with counter-savagery. The Muslims
struck back again in East Bengal, systematically destroying Hindu
crops, murdering those who did not flee, burning temples; terror ran
riot.

To Gandhi this was terrible news; and, despite illness, he decided
again on a spectacular gesture. He would himself go into the worst
riot area of East Bengal, the remote Noakhali district, a thousand
miles from Delhi, where he lived for six weeks in a Muslim-
dominated village from which all but three of the two hundred Hindu
families had lately fled in terror. He received some slight military
protection, but asked that this should be discontinued. From the hut

of a village washerwoman—his office, bedroom, and living-room—he tried to calm the passions of both Noakhali and India at large. But his success was only relative. "I have been awake since 2 A.M.," he wrote in his diary on January 2, 1947. "God's grace alone is sustaining me. . . . All round me is utter darkness." Around him indeed were the evidences of hatred and frenzy: ruined huts, charred bones, the jeers of the still unrepentant Muslims. Two months later, in Bihar, the same story was unfolded in reverse: a huge Hindu slaughter of the Muslim minority. "Bihar of my dreams has falsified them," he wrote, and hurried away the long journey to Bihar to urge peace, repentance, and forgiveness.

By this time the Attlee Government had made one of the great decisions of world history. India must be shocked out of her irresponsibility: a definite date was fixed by which Britain would have "quit India." In Gandhi's words India was to be "jerked into independence." It was, perhaps, a gamble; Churchill professed no surprise at the massacres and expected worse. Attlee himself feared a total collapse of order, and thought that he knew only one man with just the right qualities to be Viceroy for these last few vital months. Lord Mountbatten, he wrote, "might pull it off," and in March 1947 he replaced Lord Wavell.

It was a happy inspiration. Mountbatten, tactful, charming, tireless, did magnificent work in steering a battered India towards her goal. Six times he saw Gandhi, and six times Jinnah; and he managed to bring them to a joint meeting from which they issued a condemnation of their followers' violence. Nehru had been won over to the inevitability of Pakistan, but Gandhi was known to regard it as a betrayal of what they had fought for—a united India and the fellowship of all the communities. Would he upset everything by condemning the partition of India? He was sad. On the day the partition decision was taken he observed a day of silence (communicating to Mountbatten by pencil-stub scribbles on the back of envelopes); but he would not sabotage the agreement. "Support your leaders," he told the anxious crowds.

On August 15, 1947, India and Pakistan became independent powers. A life's work was culminated; but Gandhi could feel no elation. His fears for the immediate future were too strong. In Calcutta, especially, fears for August 15 were very serious; hence two days earlier Gandhi himself moved into a Muslim workman's house there in a *Hindu* quarter, and prevailed on Suhrawardy, the Muslim leader, to live there with him peaceably under one roof. Temporarily the 'miracle' worked: Hindus and Muslims even danced together in

the streets. Then a fortnight later a Hindu mob, worked up by news
of massacres in the Punjab, invaded his house, and roughly handled
him; and he began yet another fast, to be continued till peace returned. Once again the old weapon was effective: the two communities in Calcutta were shocked or shamed into observing the peace.

Away in Punjab it was not so: five million Sikhs and Hindus were
fleeing from West to East Punjab; a similar number of Muslims were
going the other way—terror-stricken minorities dragging their
scanty possessions down the long weary roads to where their communities were a majority, but where, at the end of the road, there
was only hunger and homelessness, and the bitter memories of
bereavement. These people did not readily listen to Gandhi's "forgive and forget." But this was his message, and he came at last to
India's capital, Delhi, to preach it. There conditions were very bad,
with overflowing refugee camps of both Hindus and Muslims.
Boldly visiting one for the Muslims, he was greeted by howls and
catcalls, but he persisted in speaking to them, and later attended one
of the great Muslim festivals. Many Hindus, too, regarded the old
man with exasperation. When he fasted again (for self-purification,
he said, and an end to violence in Delhi), a hostile Hindu crowd
gathered beneath his window and chanted, "Let Gandhi die": he had
been too 'soft' with the Muslims. It was to be his greatest fast, he
wrote; but it was not thus that he was to die. Delhi quietened again,
and the fast was broken. But on January 20, 1948, as he was addressing his daily prayer-meeting, a Hindu youth threw a bomb that
exploded in his vicinity. He was unhurt, asked the police not to
molest "the misguided youth," and refused police protection at the
prayer-meetings. Ten days later he made his way as usual on the
arms of his grand-nieces, his "walking-sticks," over the lawns of
Birla House to the little pavilion round which several hundred had
as usual gathered to pay reverence to him, and join him in prayer. A
young man edged his way to the front of the crowd, bent down as
though in reverence, suddenly whipped out a revolver, and fired
three shots at point-blank range.

It was a violent death after all. But, as one of Gandhi's best
biographers, B. R. Nanda, writes, his very death achieved a victory.

The bullets which passed through Gandhi's chest reverberated in millions of hearts. The very wickedness of the crime exposed, as if in a flash
of lightning, the fatuity and futility of communal fanaticism. The flames
which reduced the Mahatma's body to ashes on the banks of the Yamuna
on the evening of 31st January, 1948, proved to be the last flicker of that
conflagration which had enveloped the Indo-Pakistan sub-continent since

August 1946. Gandhi had fought this fire with all his strength while he lived. His death was to finally quench it.

Whether in the long run his gospel of *ahimsa*—love and peace —will triumph is another and a bigger matter. Gandhi's attitudes were too spiritual, and many of his ideas too eccentric, to be generally adopted in India or any other country. Under Nehru, since 1947, India has championed 'neutralism' between the West and the Communist East, but hardly 'non-violence' in a Gandhian sense. She has welcomed foreign capital, and vigorously pursued five-year plans of industrialization very far from Gandhi's spinning-wheel. Yet Gandhi's influence and importance were enormous. First, it is very doubtful if without him the transfer of power could have been effected without a breakdown into a prolonged civil war on a vast scale. Second, the example of India's emancipation from Britain, which he led, acted as a powerful stimulus to the other peoples of Asia and Africa to demand freedom from "Colonialism"—one of the most vital and revolutionary movements of our time. Third, inside India, great social reforms, and above all the decline of Untouchability, stem directly from Gandhi's campaigns. No other statesman of this century has left behind him such a weight of love and respect. His name in India is a legend, and outside India his greatness (not always perceived in his lifetime through his undoubted wiliness and crankiness) grows as the years recede. He loved India, and he called himself a nationalist; but, more important, he loved God and man; and, most surprising, really did forgive his enemies. The twentieth century has seen many successful revolutionaries and many great men. It has not seen many who were, in addition, simply and powerfully good.

Table of Events

1600.	English East India Company founded.
18th–19th centuries.	Steady advance of British power in India.
1857.	Indian Mutiny.
1869.	Birth of Gandhi.
1876.	Disraeli makes Queen Victoria Empress of India.
1891.	Gandhi completes legal studies in London.
1893–1914.	Gandhi champion of Indian rights in South Africa.
1897.	Victoria's Diamond Jubilee.
1899–1902.	The Boer War.
1904.	Gandhi founds Phoenix Community, and enters it (1906).
1915.	Gandhi, back in India, founds Sabarmati "Ashram."
1919.	Amritsar Massacre.

1920.	Civil disobedience begins.
1922–24.	Gandhi in prison.
1930.	The Salt March. Arrests throughout India.
1931.	Gandhi in London for Round Table Conference; re-arrested on return.
1935.	Government of India Act.
	Poona Fast and Pact ("Untouchables").
1941.	Japanese armies approach India.
1942.	"Quit India" campaign.
1946–47.	Savage Hindu-Muslim rioting.
1947.	Gandhi at Noakhali (February).
	Mountbatten becomes Viceroy (March).
	Independent States of India and Pakistan (August)
	Gandhi's fast to end riots.
1948.	Assassination of Gandhi.
1950's	Nehru's India promotes industrialization at home and neutralism abroad.

5

Benito Mussolini

(1883–1945)

The Italians, one could hardly deny, have given European civilization much more than their share of its great achievements: in religion, in painting, in architecture, in science, in literature, in music. It is the more surprising, then, that for twenty-one years of the twentieth century, from 1922 to 1943, this great people permitted themselves to be governed by a dictator in whom there was no shred of greatness: a caricature figure, perhaps the least considerable of all the statesmen in this book. One account of his life is entitled *Sawdust Caesar*: it is a fair assessment. The most that one can say for him is that he was a less evil man than Hitler. But Mussolini was vain, pompous, brutal, mean, gross; a liar, a sensualist, and a tub-thumper; a dummy hero lacking courage, originality, or intelligence—in short, a sham. His one gift was in showmanship, and here lay the secret of his long success.

He was born at Predappio, near Forli, among the vineyards and foothills of the Romagna, in 1883. Later, Fascists boasted of his peasant origins, but in fact his father was a blacksmith and his mother kept a school. The young Benito grew up a rather aggressive child at the Catholic school to which his mother had persuaded his socialist-atheist father to send him. Twice he just escaped expulsion. Eventually he went away to train as a teacher; he read widely, began his long catalogue of affairs with women, wore a flowing black bow tie, and thought of himself as a socialist revolutionary. This violent young man with the piercing eyes began his career as a teacher at the age of eighteen. At nineteen he abandoned it, preferring the livelier pursuits of hooliganism, journalism, and women. He ran off to Switzerland, where he was imprisoned as an agitator, and remained there after his release to escape military service. He went about unkempt, looking like a desperado, but earning enough to live on as secretary of a bricklayers' union, private teacher of Italian, and journalist. He loved violent phrases—"Religion is a disease of the mind" ... "Christ was a small, mean man," His disciples "the scum of Palestine." He derided uniforms and military glitter. He played at reading philosophy, but failed to understand it very well. His head became a rag-bag of revolutionary ideas—Socialism, Syndicalism, Anarchism, Nihilism—the current -ism depended on the trend of the latest book he had read. In 1904 he was expelled from Geneva and later that year took advantage of an amnesty for deserters to return to Italy; by 1906 he had fulfilled his patriotic duties as a national-service man, and was back in the revolutionary swim as a bohemian-desperado in Northern Italy, writing articles for Left-wing papers, spending another spell in prison, falling ferociously in love with half a dozen girls, but especially with one, Augusta, who refused to marry him—so he set up house instead with her young sister Rachele, who bore him a daughter, Edda, in 1910. Six years later he married Rachele, who became the mother of his five legitimate children. At his birthplace near Forli, where he settled at this time, men nicknamed him "the lunatic," from his staring eyes, unshaven beard, violent speeches, and a certain tendency towards being discovered drunk in the cemetery declaiming poetry. Five more months in prison followed for leading riots in Forli intended to be part of a revolutionary general strike against Italy's declaration of war on Turkey (1911). His reputation as an extreme anti-militarist, anti-Catholic revolutionary grew as his platform oratory gained in experience and his newspaper articles in violence; and in 1912 he was appointed editor of the Milan Socialist paper *Avanti* (*Forward*). Even before the outbreak of war in 1914 he had been concerned in an excitable but half-hearted republican revolt in Milan and other northern centres.

The war of 1914 brought a complete change of tune in Mussolini that earned him the hatred of many, a general notoriety, and the applause of many more. Suddenly he announced—to the hisses and catcalls of a Socialist meeting—that he was in favour of Italy's entry into the war. A supporter set him up with a new paper, *Il Popolo d'Italia*, whose soaring circulation proved the popularity of the new line; but his patriotism, vociferous in print, was not so ardent as to prompt his joining the colours. In due course he was conscripted, and, like Hitler, proved a satisfactory corporal. His talent for bombast and self-dramatization continued to develop. Just as in 1914 he claimed to fear no one so long as he had a pen in his hand and a revolver in his pocket, so in 1917, being (as soldiers often are) wounded, he dictated a message to his comrades. "I am proud to have reddened the road to Trieste with my own blood in the fulfilment of my dangerous duty." It was the first and only road that was reddened with his blood until his squalid end in 1945, but it qualified him to talk in later years of the nobility of sacrifice, and the tough character-school of war, and to redden many other roads with blood.

The peace of 1918, and still more the Versailles peace treaty of 1919, left Italy in a state of revolutionary ferment. Economic hardships, strikes aimed at political control, patriotic resentment at the shabby treatment Italy received at Versailles (where President Wilson refused to consider her claims to the Tyrol and Dalmatia), combined to produce the sort of excitable atmosphere in which Mussolini could flourish. By now he no longer called himself a Socialist; the word was contaminated by Pacifism and Bolshevism. He gathered round him a new group of patriotic and revolutionary fire-eaters: young men disgusted by stay-at-home war-profiteers; ex-soldiers yearning for violence and adventure; unemployed, angry young students contemptuous of the old gang of politicians; romantic patriots anxious to emulate d'Annunzio, who had just defied Europe and President Wilson by leading a sudden successful swoop on Fiume. The situation matched very closely that in Germany, where Hitler's little group of disgruntled violent men was busy taking shape. A new name too was on men's lips—the Fascisti, the men of the 'fascio,' or fighters' club, whose symbol came to be the Roman fasces, the bundle of rods carried by the lictors of old as an emblem of authority and discipline. These gangs of Fascists set up as rivals of the Socialists and Syndicalists and Anarchists; they paraded in semi-military fashion; they wore black shirts and berets; they carried a black flag with a white skull; they beat up their enemies or dosed them with castor oil—a cheap and convenient form of torture; they prepared for revolution.

The whole atmosphere in Italy in 1920–22 was revolutionary. Prices had doubled; there was a large budget deficit; postal workers struck; trains ran only when the railway workers cared, as unpunctually as they cared, and for whom they cared—notably not for troop movements aimed at putting down disorder; eventually the railwaymen staged their own triumphant strike; trouble at the Romeo works at Milan spread to the whole metal-working industry, and many workers seized their factories, sometimes breaking open the safes and distributing the findings; in Mantua, Bologna, Turin, Milan, Florence, Ancona, and many more places there were outbreaks of terrorism, bomb-throwing, Communist murder, and Fascist counter-murder. Five people were killed in anti-Fascist riots in Rome, in November 1921. Even the peasants of Sicily, Tuscany, and the Veneto organized themselves against the landlords—and then the Fascists organized against the peasant societies. In August 1922 a general strike was called throughout Italy by the Socialists "to assert the authority of the State against the Fascists."

Just as in the late 1930's Mussolini was for war one day and for peace the next, and had to be pitchforked into his destiny by events, so in 1921 and 1922 he was for violence one day, for restraint the next. It was young firebrands like Balbo and Grandi, both afterwards regarded by Mussolini as potential rivals to be kept in their place, who roused the Fascist squads to smash up the trade unions and the co-operative societies, and eventually to demand a march on Rome and the seizure of power. Balbo did in fact organize a Fascist coup in Bologna against the Communist-dominated council, and by October 1922 Mussolini was swept forward by the enthusiasm of his hotheads to demand office of the King, although the number of Fascist Members of Parliament was insignificant. The blackshirts marched on Rome; Mussolini stayed behind in a tense Milan at his newspaper-office, and informed the King that if he was sent for to come to Rome it would have to be as head of the Government. The King (Victor Emmanuel III) accepted, scared as he was, and as most of the more prosperous and conservative elements were, by the prospect of chaos or Socialist revolution; and Mussolini, some hours after the famous march, "followed in the train." His jubilant supporters gave him a great welcome at the Rome railway-station; friends lent him the necessary top-hat and morning coat to go to the Quirinale, the royal palace—and dissuaded him from wearing the white spats that he had come to affect. The Fascist dictatorship had arrived. It was to last twenty-one years, and the decent but undignified little King who helped to make it lived long enough to play a significant part in at last unmaking it in 1943.

The Fascists had claimed that they would put down strikes and lawlessness, and restore order in Italy—and this they did. Their own methods were sometimes lawless, it is true, and even brutal, yet they never developed the organized devilishness of the Nazi gangs in Germany later. Most Italians were indeed delighted with the new regime. Mussolini was cautious at first, and Parliament continued to function for a time. The Fascist marchers, the squadristi, were sent home from Rome. There was as yet nothing in Italy to parallel the wicked campaign against the Jews in Nazi Germany. Catholics and Liberals were for a time even included in the Cabinet. Industrial production revived. The eight-hour day was restored; it had been whittled down previously to four or five. Thefts on the railway declined, and trains even began to run on time, despite a cut of fifty-five thousand in the swollen railway staffs. The value of the lira, after dipping to 150, went up to 120 to the pound sterling; the budget achieved a handsome surplus; by 1925 the wheat crop was over 30 per cent. up on the pre-war average. Visitors such as Winston Churchill praised Mussolini's achievements, while the American bank of Morgan viewed him favourably enough to float a loan, heavily oversubscribed, of 100,000,000 dollars to help stabilize the economy. The fear of Bolshevism receded, and Mussolini was hailed as the saviour of Italy.

At the election of 1924 the Government received over 65 per cent. of the total votes cast, a sufficient testimony to its popularity—but in June 1924 a crime was committed which was also a blunder: Matteotti, a leading Socialist deputy, was kidnapped by Fascists, driven off in a car, and murdered. The indignation and horror felt by all decent men for this deed, and the suspicion that Mussolini was himself implicated, suddenly gave new life to the Opposition; and for a time the new regime hung by a hair. Mussolini himself was tortured with anxiety and indecision, and again had to be galvanized by tougher men into action; there was a genuine fear among the Fascists that their leader was about to resign because he could not rule "with a corpse under his feet." Later he was not to be so squeamish. By 1925 he had gathered enough determination to proceed against the Opposition, who had kept up a constant pressure of newspaper abuse, and not to proceed against the known murderers of Matteotti.

The Fascist dictatorship now really took hold. Step by step Parliament was weakened and power concentrated in the Fascist Grand Council, which had the right to 'ratify' the list of Parliamentary candidates, to decide the prerogatives of the Crown, and to formulate policy. By 1929 electors were merely required to vote "yes" or "no," *en bloc*, for a Government list of four hundred Parliamentary candidates. Opposition was at an end. Eventually the powers of Parliament were altogether superseded by the National Council of Corporations, a body composed of twenty-two syndicates or corporations representing employers, workmen, and professions. Arbitration in labour disputes was compulsory, and strikes became illegal. Needless to say, Mussolini was head of both the Fascist Grand Council and the Ministry of Corporations, and power was entirely centred in his hands.

"Power tends to corrupt and absolute power corrupts absolutely." Of no one is the famous epigram more devastatingly true than Mussolini. He was hoodwinked by his propaganda into thinking himself a great man, and began to see himself as the new Augustus

or the new Napoleon, as the occasion suited. He learned to thrust
forward his already over-large chin, and to stand strut-legged and
scowling, as one who was brooding huge Napoleonic thoughts.
Thousands of portraits of him found their way on to the walls of
schools, public buildings, and private houses, his short stature art-
fully concealed, his heroic ferocity carefully suggested: Mussolini
giving the Roman salute, Mussolini towering on a noble horse,
Mussolini fencing, Mussolini driving the latest racing-car, Mussolini at the cockpit of his aeroplane, even Mussolini relaxing with
his violin (so much was conceded to the arts of peace, and he could
in fact play just a little). Mussolini's own greatness had to symbolize the greatness of the Italian people; so the image of Il
Duce, the Leader, was scientifically built up by every device of
modern showmanship. Uniforms, parades, the glamour of the
grand occasion—all the things that the youthful Mussolini had
been most eager to ridicule he now took delight in; even schoolmasters and civil servants had eventually to wear uniforms; even
tennis players competing in international matches had to wear black
shirts. As for hand-shaking, it was soft and *bourgeois*; so men must
give the Roman salute, as in the brave days of old. Mussolini
was a vain man corrupted by the limelight, without the strength of
character to laugh at his own foibles, and eventually accepting as
real the fabricated mask of pomposity and play-acting originally
intended to impress the simple contemptible public.

The textbooks and curricula cf the nation's schools were adapted
to sustain the legend. Spelling was learned, much as in China to-day,
from such sentences as "Mussolini has made Italy the first nation
in the world." The very calendar was altered, as it was during the
French Revolution, and 1922 became the Year One of the Fascist
era. Mussolini himself, by trade a journalist, sent endless hand-outs
and instructions to the Press to ensure his presentation in an inspiring or heroic light. Every day he attended a private view of the latest
films of his own appearances and watched the crowds' reactions, and
once a week he regularly wrote his anonymous full-length article for
the Press.

It is often said that statesmen must not be too aware of their own
faults, or self-criticism paralyses leadership. Mussolini suffered the
reverse danger: he totally lacked self-analysis. He could not even
laugh at his own cynicism—for there was much cynicism in his cult
of the new warlike Italy. He knew very well that modern Italians were
not a great military nation; on the contrary, as he was constantly
grumbling, they were too civilized—or, as he put it, soft, pleasure-

loving, lazy, "made flabby by art." Italians must be made to *feel*
that they were men of martial valour; they must be kicked into
performing great deeds. The *bourgeoisie*, he once said, must be
"kicked in the behind and chased into war"; and again, "The
Italians must learn to grow less likeable and to become hard, implacable, and full of hatred." "War is to man as maternity to
women." He delighted in making his personal staff perform harsh
and tough deeds—run, for instance, in the hot sunshine, in their
heavy uniforms with a breastful of medals, at the famous Bersa-
glieri trot. It was "virile," and therefore befitted Italians. He was
proud to do it with them to demonstrate his own virility, though he
would carefully edit and censor the film-reels before releasing them.
Virility was in fact his key-word, both in public propaganda and
private life: he enjoyed a long succession of casual and crude
amours, rumours of which were not resented because they were all
consistent with the image of the fiery red-blooded man of action,
Mars to a formidable string of Venuses. Preferring women to be
plump, he began a Press campaign against the fashion of slimness;
artists and fashion-designers were not permitted to glamorize what
he called "crisis women." Women, moreover, should have many
babies: five he stipulated a satisfactory target for an Italian mother,
and made a point of his own family by Rachele reaching the required
figure. Birth-control was anti-social, and liable to work against
Italy's military greatness; propaganda for it was consequently made
illegal.

In this last respect at least the State saw eye to eye with the
Church, and as time progressed Mussolini realized more and more
the desirability of a general agreement with Catholicism. No genuine
national unity could exist in Italy until the Government had come
to terms with this supreme institution in the country. Since 1870,
when the Kingdom of Italy occupied Rome by force and made the
city its new capital, the Popes had lived in self-imposed imprisonment within the palace and grounds of the Vatican—a protest
against the seizure by the Kingdom of Italy of the old papal lands
and authority. Now, in 1929, Mussolini, the anti-Catholic, made
Italy's peace with the Vatican at last. The Church was compensated
for its properties seized in 1870; Vatican City was constituted a tiny
independent State with the Pope its temporal ruler; and the rights of
Catholicism were recognized in an important Concordat between
Church and State. The Fascist State was "integrated by Catholicism." It was an achievement to parallel Napoleon's similar Concordat of 1801—a point which publicity did not allow to escape.

About this time Mussolini devoted much of his energy to schemes of public works with which his propaganda made great play. Although these hardly revolutionized the face of Italy, they were planned on a considerable scale, and they did have some effect in softening the impact in Italy of the world economic depression. Even as it was, unemployment rose and wages fell; exports sagged and budget deficits soared once more. There was a big scheme of re-afforestation; development of highways and ports; a programme of school and hospital building; some attempts to improve irrigation; the electrification of railways; the partial draining of the Pontine Marshes near Rome, from time immemorial a malarial swamp; and the 'rebuilding' of Rome. "In five years," he had said as early as 1923, "Rome must appear wonderful to the whole world, enormous, orderly, and powerful, as she was in the days of the first Empire of Augustus." Everything between Augustus and Mussolini he tended to think of as "the decadent centuries," and consequently Fascist town-planners had no hesitation in destroying much of the old medieval and Renaissance city. Mussolini himself delighted in inaugurating these public-works schemes personally, delivering the first blow of the demolition hammer, digging the first sod, planting the first tree—and with no short symbolic gesture suitable for a monarch of a *bourgeois* country, but a full sweating enthusiastic job of work. He was liberally attended, not only by Press cameras, but by plain-clothes police disguised variously as peasants or workmen, or what best suited the occasion—a precaution made more pressing by four early attempts on his life. One policeman would always be detailed to follow him at public functions distributing largesse.

In 1932 Fascism celebrated its tenth birthday with rather more than the customary flourish of trumpets; in 1933 the Duce, as it was now compulsory to address him, reached his fiftieth birthday and refused to celebrate it. All mention of it was censored in the Press; the Duce must be ever young, ever virile. Although he now suffered with recurrent stomach trouble from an ulcer, and needed glasses to correct his long sight, such things must never be made public. He was never photographed wearing glasses. Even his incipient baldness was put to good effect: he shaved his head close to resemble a Roman emperor.

The world picture in 1933 was gloomy in the extreme. Everywhere trade had contracted and wages fallen; the world economic conference called in London that year failed dismally; the disarmament conference that had been in session for years staggered from frustration to frustration; in the Far East Japan had defied the League of Nations and occupied Manchuria; in Germany a new dictator, modelled somewhat after Mussolini's Fascist model, had emerged in the sinister person of Adolf Hitler; France was torn asunder by political divisions and her own Fascist and Communist threats; the whole of south-eastern Europe was rent by national jealousies, Communist subversion and bankruptcy; in particular Austria, saved once by the League of Nations, appeared to be developing as a battleground for Socialists and Fascists, including Nazis anxious to link with the new Germany. There was hardly a nation of Europe, America, or Asia unaffected by the world-wide political and economic crises.

In this shaky world Mussolini grew increasingly belligerent and unco-operative. The League of Nations was publicly derided, and the Fascist Grand Council pronounced in 1933 that Italy's further participation in its affairs would depend on its being radically reformed. The next year rearmament was intensified, two new battleships were laid down, and a new air programme was initiated which was to make "the skies dark" with Italian planes. Military training was to begin for all boys in the Fascist youth organization at the tender age of six.

Mussolini was looking in two directions: to the north he needed security; to the south he dreamed of glory. To the north, in Europe, at this time (1934) his main preoccupations were with Austria; to the south, in Africa, he dreamed of a new Fascist Empire in the vast lands of Ethiopia.

Post-war Austria, all that was left in 1919 of the great Austrian Empire, had led for fifteen years a precarious existence, navigating awkwardly between Berlin, Moscow, and Rome. Many Austrians looked to union with Germany, because the little republic of 1919 was quite unable to feed itself or remain solvent on its own resources. Many looked to Moscow, and the Marxist parties were strong in Vienna and the industrial centres. But most of all Austrians looked to Rome, the centre of their Catholic world, for support against the rival magnets of Berlin and Moscow. Loans from the League of Nations kept Austria on its feet for twelve years, but in 1931 it was bankruptcy in Vienna that combined with the effects of the American crash to touch off the world economic depression. Dollfuss, dictator in Vienna from 1932, represented primarily the Catholic peasantry, and looked therefore to Mussolini for support; and the independence of Austria was indeed a cardinal point in Mussolini's foreign policy at this time. But in 1934 the first great challenge to his power came from the Nazis, when Dollfuss (who had just suppressed a 'red' rising in Vienna) was murdered by brownshirt gangsters simultaneously with a Nazi attempt, fomented from Germany, to seize power throughout the Austrian republic.

Mussolini regarded Hitler at this time as a natural rival and enemy. Most Italians had an age-old contempt for the northern barbarians, and Mussolini was no exception. "They are Germans, and so will end by ruining our idea. They are still the barbarians of Tacitus and the Reformation, in eternal conflict with Rome. I don't trust them." And despite all the later ballyhoo and parade of undying friendship, he never did trust them, or they him. The time was to come when he was entirely at Hitler's mercy, but in 1934, when they first met, it was Mussolini who was still the bigger international figure. "What a clown this Hitler is," he remarked to his staff; and pointing his thumb towards his Teutonic guest—"he's quite mad."

When Dollfuss was murdered by Hitler's supporters in July 1934 Mussolini reacted for once swiftly and effectively. Troops were immediately dispatched to the Brenner Pass to threaten Hitler and safeguard Austria's independence. It was sufficient: Hitler was forced to wait until he was stronger. Mussolini was hailed throughout Europe as the saviour of peace, and two years later Hitler, while still glorifying the name of the murderers of Dollfuss, had the effrontery himself to guarantee the independence of Austria. Meanwhile a still confident Mussolini had met British and French Ministers at Stresa, in North Italy, and formed an anti-German peace front despite his contempt for the French and the English as potential allies. The French were riddled, he thought, with intellectuals and pacifists, while the British——; but what could one expect of a nation who (he understood) changed into dinner jackets every afternoon to drink tea? In September 1934 a cock-a-hoop Mussolini was publicly proclaiming his "majestic pity" for the Germans, "the descendants of people who were illiterate in the days when Rome boasted a Caesar, a Vergil, and an Augustus."

He did not think it worth while to tell his new 'allies' that he was contemplating glory in the south—a war on Ethiopia (Abyssinia), the only large African State still free of colonial influence; but he was in fact planning this aggression during 1934. It was likely to be swift, all over in a year, so that the troops could be safely back on the Brenner Pass to put down any German nonsense in Austria. By the summer of 1936 he would be crowing on another dunghill: Addis Ababa, where Haile Selassie had his throne. The Emperor of Ethiopia, the "Lion of Judah," could soon be tamed. His people still fought with spears. Some of them still practised slavery. It would be both simple and glorious to raise the Italian tricolour in Addis

Ababa, to make Victor Emmanuel III (whom he privately detested) an Italian Emperor, to send the eagles of conquest flapping over Africa.

Troops were accordingly concentrated in Italian Somaliland and Eritrea. France and Britain, Mussolini calculated, would be too pre-occupied with German threats to interfere seriously with so distant and harmless a project. By October 1935 he had 250,000 troops ready for the campaign, and that month they struck. Mussolini (in Rome) was determined to run the war himself, although his military knowledge was negligible, and it says much for the independent-mindedness and good sense of his commanders, De Bono and Badoglio, that they decided to ignore his telegrams.

In Geneva the League of Nations faced its second crucial crisis within four years. It had failed to stop the Japanese invasion of Manchuria, in 1931; if it now failed again to stop the Italian in-vasion of Ethiopia its days were clearly numbered. Accordingly Italy was declared the aggressor, and financial and trade 'sanctions' imposed on her within a few weeks of the war's beginning; in other words, an economic blockade, voted by fifty-two nations. A great hope surged up among peaceful liberal opinion in the West that the League would measure up to its chances, champion the weak, stop Mussolini, and thus teach all aggressors a lesson. But, alas, soon the doubts began to arise. Should Mussolini be weakened and humili-ated? Was he not a champion of anti-Communism and anti-Nazism? Would not trade decline if 'sanctions' were seriously applied? Could Ethiopia hope to survive independently anyway in the twentieth century? Even so staunch a foe of dictators as Winston Churchill considered Mussolini should not be humiliated to the point where he might seek to ally with Hitler instead of the democracies. The French Government felt similarly, and their Foreign Minister, Laval, persuaded the British Foreign Minister, Hoare, to agree to a com-promise suggestion: Ethiopia to be partly Italianized, partly inter-nationalized. But when this proposal was made public there was such an outcry against it at Geneva and in the British Press that Baldwin was forced to accept Hoare's resignation and put in his place Eden, who was a strong League of Nations man. Eden had even supported an oil blockade of Italy, which was not included in the 'sanctions' policy so far adopted. So the League of Nations had the worst of both worlds. It imposed sanctions, but not severely enough. It offended Mussolini without seriously impeding him, and did in fact thrust him into the arms of Germany. It buoyed up hope for a brief period only to accentuate the cynicism and despair that followed failure. In short, Mussolini won Ethiopia and the League committed suicide.

In May 1936 Badoglio entered Addis Ababa; in Rome, from the balcony of the Venetian Palace, Mussolini proclaimed Victor Emmanuel Emperor of Ethiopia. Fewer than five thousand Italians had died in the campaign; and aeroplanes and poison gas had, not surprisingly, prevailed over rifles and spears. "One day," said Mussolini after stepping in from the balcony, "the part I have played in the technical direction of the war will be known." The wedding-rings that Italian wives had gladly surrendered in reply to the sanctions campaign had not been in vain. The victory had been won, and the solidarity between dictator and people cemented.

No sooner was the Abyssinian war over than the Spanish Civil War began—the revolt of the Spanish Army, Church, and propertied classes against the Left-wing anti-clerical "Popular Front" coalition of parties that formed the official Government of Spain. Like all civil wars, it was fought on both sides with heroism and tenacity; like all Spanish wars, it was fought with fanaticism and bitter ruthlessness. But it was more than a civil war; it was a symbol and a prologue. It was a symbol of the war of ideologies, of Right versus Left, Fascism versus Communism, Catholicism versus its enemies; and it was a prologue to the Second World War that so closely trod on its heels. For immediately the smouldering extremism of both sides burst into flame in July 1936 foreign intervention began. Money, war material, and volunteers flowed in to the Spanish Government from Russia, Mexico, and an international host of idealistic Left-wingers who saw in its cause the cause of civilization against Fascism and barbarism; and the Fascist states of Italy and Germany poured in men and munitions to help General Franco, the rebel leader, destroy in Spain the menaces of Communism and militant Liberalism. Many brave young Socialists and Liberals from many countries fought and died with the International Brigade in Spain; but as the war progressed the brigade became increasingly under the domination of its most fanatical and illiberal element, the Communists. It was in Spain that George Orwell, an International Brigade volunteer, learned for the first time the disillusionment with Communist methods that led eventually to *Animal Farm*: but had a Fascist bullet strayed a fraction of an inch from its course, that satirical masterpiece would never have been written. And it was in Spain that the Fascist dictators, Hitler and Mussolini, made the preliminary strategic moves and tactical experiments that preceded the war they knew their policies must lead to. It was over Spanish villages such as Guernica that Hitler's dive-bombers showed their devilish paces, and it was ships bound for Spanish ports that Mussolini's submarines attacked and sank. All this was unofficial; a façade was maintained of 'non-intervention,' so that when a British or French merchant ship was damaged by German bombs or sunk by Italian torpedoes it had to be pretended that the attacker was 'unidentified.' For these were the years of appeasement, when Hitler and Mussolini scoffed at Chamberlain's "pluto-democratic" England that was too soft to fight, having, as Mussolini asserted, "made a religion of eating and of games." (In Mussolini's view the Italian middle classes were little better. They must be kept up to the mark constantly. "When the war in Spain is over I shall find something else; the Italian character has to be formed through fighting. . . . I shall not leave the Italians in peace until I have six feet of earth over my head.")

In 1936 Mussolini appointed a new Foreign Minister, his own son-in-law, Count Ciano, a rich, naïve, bumptious, unprincipled, but more good-natured echo of Mussolini himself. The best thing about Ciano was that he kept a diary, in which from August 1937 to December 1943, a few days before his execution by a firing-squad, he noted down his little triumphs, disappointments, suspicions, and trickeries. He is a sort of Boswell to Mussolini's Dr Johnson, repeating casual remarks of his master and father-in-law, portraying for posterity the astonishing mixture of corruption, power-lust, cynicism, vanity, inconsistency, shallowness, bombast and sheer muddle that lay behind Mussolini's Empire. Of these piratical episodes off the coast of Spain in 1937 he writes, "The navy is very active—three torpedoings and one prize. But international opinion is getting worked up. Particularly in England, as a result of the attack on the destroyer *Havock*, fortunately not hit. It was the *Iride*.[1] The row has already started. . . . Full orchestra—France, Russia, Britain . . . The Duce is very calm. He looks in the direction of London and he doesn't believe the English want a collision with us." The next year, after Italian planes had bombed Barcelona (without Franco's knowledge or approval), Ciano wrote, "Mussolini believes that these air-raids are an admirable way of weakening the morale of the Reds, while the troops are advancing in Aragon. . . . He was delighted that the Italians should be horrifying the world by their aggressiveness for a change, instead of charming it by their skill in playing the guitar. In his opinion this will send up our stock in

[1] An Italian submarine.

Germany too, where they love total and ruthless war. In Spain the offensive is making good progress—heroic and victorious."

This theme of "keeping up with the Germans" constantly recurs with Mussolini and Ciano—though it was the last thing wanted by the average Italian, who became heartily sick of the Spanish War and these closer bonds with Hitler. But Mussolini was more and more casting his lot with the Germans over the years 1936–39, the years of the Spanish War. In 1936 he first used the expression, "The Axis," meaning the imaginary line connecting Berlin and Rome around which the world was learning to revolve, and the next year he travelled to Munich to meet Hitler. Ciano wrote (August 1937), "I am personally making arrangements for the Duce's visit to Germany.... Pay attention to the uniforms. We must appear more Prussian than the Prussians." Mussolini, prodigiously impressed by the power and ruthlessness of what he saw in Germany, made a public speech (in his rather bad German) in which he proclaimed that Fascism had found a friend with whom it would march side by side to the end. The Germans continued to despise the Italians, and the Italians continued to resent the Germans, but the fatal alliance was sealed; and the more often pompous rhetoric on both sides of the Alps talked of marching side by side to glory and a new world order the more difficult it became for Mussolini to follow rational policies. The Germans passed the time of day or concluded their speeches and letters with "Heil Hitler." So Italians must be made to do similarly with "Viva il Duce." The Germans persecuted the Jews, so the Italians must be made to do likewise—although King Victor Emmanuel protested, and Mussolini himself had earlier given anti-Semitism as a sign of Hitler's stupidity. The Germans were past-masters in the art of public military display; so the Italians must learn the goose-step too, despite widespread ridicule and public disgust. The goose, after all, said Mussolini, was "a Roman animal. It saved the Capitol. Its place is with the eagle and the she-wolf." The goose-step, the passo Romano, was a sign of virility. "Clearly that wretched little King could never do this on parade; but it doesn't matter. I shall get rid of him. The course of history can be changed in a night." Absolute power had corrupted absolutely. Mussolini was now hell-bent; he had sold what was left of his soul to Hitler.

All the same, his policies now took on a terrifying wobble. One day he would be presented with a report revealing the disastrous failure of his armaments plans and would rage at the Italians' un-worthiness of him ("even Michelangelo had need of marble to make statues"); the next he would agree to Ciano's plans for invading Albania "even if it should set the European powder-barrel alight." One day he would press forward with plans for an Anglo-Italian settlement; the next he would proclaim war between the two countries to be inevitable and indeed desirable—and then he would indulge his daydream of a sudden raid on the British Fleet in Alexandria ("history can be made in a night"). One day he would bitterly complain of German arrogance; the next (at a Florence railway-station in May 1938, when, says Ciano, "the Führer's eyes were full of tears") he would shout—and mean it—"Henceforth nothing can separate us." The only consistent thing about Mussolini in his later years was the steady growth of a kind of insane rage; only the objects of this rage shifted from day to day or hour to hour. It might be the King, or President Roosevelt, or the Pope, or the Jews, or the conductor Toscanini for befriending the Jews, or the British newspapers, or Starace (Fascist Party boss), or Anthony Eden, or the soft Italian middle classes, or the French—he was perpetually furious with something or somebody. Partly perhaps it was his stomach ulcer and the after-effects of disease; partly it was a measure of his own indecision; partly it was his essential nature—he had, after all, begun life as an anarchist. During these years the only point of rest in Mussolini's life seems to have been his affair with Claretta Petacci, a doctor's daughter thirty years his junior, attractive, romantic, hero-worshipping, entirely devoted to her lord and master, the only woman among Mussolini's very numerous and mostly casual mistresses who was capable of retaining her hold on him for any time. She was to stay by him through his later defeats and humiliations until they shared the final savage ignominy.

Humiliation began in 1938, and it came from his ally, Hitler. In 1934 Mussolini had threatened war when the Nazis looked like taking Austria. Now Hitler took it, and waited anxiously for Mussolini's reaction. He did not stir a finger, so hypnotized was he by the Nazi spell. "Tell Mussolini I will never forget him for this; never, never," reiterated a relieved Führer down the phone to his Ambassador in Rome. The words were easily said. The world knew, and most Italians feared, from that moment that Mussolini was in Hitler's pocket.

Later that year and early in 1939 he scored his last, fleeting triumphs before he began reaping his harvest of dragon's teeth. As the Czech crisis of 1938 approached its height, and he realized that this was no matter of speeches and propaganda, but that the Germans really meant war, Mussolini, who one day in every three seemed to relish the prospect, began to see more and more on the other two days the deplorable military and strategic weaknesses of Italy. Consequently he threw his weight on the side of those like Chamberlain who strove for peace, and consented to Chamberlain's last-minute request that he, Mussolini, should act as mediator with Hitler. Undoubtedly Mussolini was one of the architects of the Munich settlement that bought peace at Czechoslovakia's expense, and on his return to Italy he was greeted with wild enthusiasm by a relieved Italian public. In Rome the crowds hailed him as "angel of peace"—at which the Muse of History, one imagines, allowed herself one of her rare smiles. The other peacemaker-hero of those days, Neville Chamberlain, came to Rome soon after with Lord Halifax, and moved Mussolini to one of his few understatements. "These men," he said, "are not of the same stuff as Francis Drake." A little later Chamberlain actually submitted to Mussolini for approval the draft of a speech he proposed to make in the Commons —a unique gesture of English self-abasement.

While he treated Chamberlain and Halifax with condescension and contempt, against France he unleashed a furious campaign of envy and hatred. The Italians must be made to loathe the French: they must be drilled into demanding back Corsica and Nice; they must be bludgeoned into yelling for Tunisia. The French must be convinced beyond a doubt that if they lifted a finger to save the Spanish Left-wing Government he, Mussolini, would march against them even if it meant a world war. In fact, a Franco-Italian war was positively desirable; this "mean people" must be taught a lesson. After their defeat the French would learn how a European peace should be made. He would not ask for reparations, but would go in for wholesale destruction. Many cities would be levelled to the ground. So the angel of peace daydreamed to Ciano, who faithfully recorded it. Into the hands of such men had the destinies of Europe fallen in an evil hour.

Meanwhile he played at soldiers.

> The Duce has a terrible cold: he is very much concerned about the preparation of the militia for the parade of February 1 [1939]. He concerns himself personally with the most minute details. He spends many a half-hour at his office window, concealed behind the blue curtains, watching the movements of the various units. It was his order that the drums and trumpets should be used at the same time. [Later that year Ciano, facing the realities of serious Italian arms deficiencies, becomes exasperated.] But what is the Duce doing? His attention seems to be devoted mostly to matters of drill; there is trouble if the "present arms"

is not done correctly, or if an officer doesn't know how to do the goose-step, but he seems very little concerned about the real weaknesses. . . .

Despite seventeen years of drum-banging, the military weaknesses were in fact desperate. As Ciano discovered, "the ammunition depots are short of ammunition. Artillery is outmoded. Our anti-aircraft and anti-tank weapons are altogether lacking. There has been a good deal of bluffing in the military sphere, and even the Duce himself has been deceived—a tragic bluff." When war actually came between Germany and the Western Powers in September the Italian Minister of War Production said that he would be glad if Italy's stocks allowed her to fight for three months.

The Germans now treated Mussolini with the contempt he merited. When Hitler tore up the Munich agreement in March 1939, occupied Czechoslovakia, and so made a war virtually inevitable, he again (as with the occupation of Austria) failed even to inform his brother dictator until after the event. Mussolini was depressed. "Every time Hitler occupies a country he sends me a message," he complained. He suddenly seemed to be showing his age; events had shaken him, and his illnesses were wearing him down. But he would show Hitler that he could occupy countries too; accordingly on Good Friday 1939 Italian troops moved into Albania and incorporated it into the Italian Empire. "If the Germans think they can stop us we shall fire on them," wrote Ciano; yet two days later he was praising Mussolini's "marvellous speech" to the Fascist Grand Council on the necessity of absolute loyalty to the Axis. Whom God wishes to destroy he first drives mad.

By August 1939 Ciano at least had lost any remaining illusions about the Germans, and by August 15 thought he had convinced his father-in-law that Italy must keep out of the coming war. But Mussolini continued to vacillate alarmingly. One day he decided on peace; the next he yearned for war to ensure his share of the booty (preferably part of Yugoslavia). Then he would read an article in an English newspaper suggesting likely Italian neutrality and instantly wanted to make war. His instincts led him towards war; prudence drew him back. Eventually he settled for delay, and when war at last broke out in September 1939 Italy was not 'neutral' but 'non-belligerent'; it was a nice distinction. When the Nazis overran Poland so soon and ruthlessly he was tormented with jealousy; why were the Germans so efficient and strong and brutal, while he had to hold back for weakness? It was a humiliation. His hands itched to strike at Yugoslavia (the phrase is Ciano's) or to launch some swift revenge against the British fleet in return for their intolerable blockade. When May came and Hitler's tanks swept through the Low Countries and France, he could restrain himself no longer. His hope was that the French would not collapse *too* soon, which would permit the Germans to "reach the end of the war too fresh and too strong." On June 10, at long last, with the war apparently all but won by Germany and the French Army apparently in tatters, Italy declared war, and proceeded immediately to run into trouble against the French troops in the Alps. A humiliated Duce resumed his rage against the unmilitary Italians and the cowardly middle class; after the war he would "destroy it, or save perhaps twenty per cent."! When Hitler failed to invade England he was glad: for one thing, it was a check to Hitler, and for another, it would enable Italy to make greater sacrifices and himself more strongly to assert her rights.

In October 1940 he decided once more to show Hitler that the Italians too could conquer, and from his base in Albania launched a sudden unprovoked attack on Greece. "This time I am going to pay him back in his own coin. He will find out from the papers that I have occupied Greece." But what his sober military leaders, Graziani and Badoglio, had told him proved disastrously right. The wretched Italian Army was routed by the Greeks, and the Duce's impotent fury mounted. He ordered Graziani to attack the British defending Egypt. Graziani begged for more supplies and for time to ensure success. Mussolini, a complete ignoramus in military matters, refused, and the hapless Graziani launched his offensive, which soon lost momentum. By January the British counter-offensive, directed by Wavell, had rounded up over 100,000 Italian prisoners and swept the Italians out of Egypt. "It will take at least a week for this washing to dry," said Mussolini.

But his washing never dried. Catastrophe followed catastrophe now until the ultimate collapse. The British captured Somaliland by February 1941; by April their forces entered Addis Ababa. Only a tiny number of Italian casualties were suffered; for the troops simply surrendered, preferring to play football behind British barbed-wire rather than to die for Fascism and glory. Mussolini had lost an Empire and bitterly resented it; even the vanquished French had managed to keep theirs! At sea things were no better; the Italian Navy proved no match for the British, and suffered very heavily in convoying supplies to Africa. Back in port too they proved very vulnerable to attack from bombs and torpedoes. The big cities of Italy themselves suffered—but when British bombers did heavy damage at Naples, destroying six thousand tons of precious oil,

Mussolini professed himself pleased. "I am glad that Naples is having such severe nights. The breed will harden. . . ." In June Hitler peremptorily phoned for him to come to an immediate meeting, and, fuming, he had to go and listen to what he called "a five-hour monologue." He was "sick and tired of being rung for"—but he had not the spirit to disobey. He was now (as Churchill put it) Hitler's "tattered lackey," a "whipped jackal frisking at the side of the German tiger." He loathed those "dirty dogs" of Germans—yet when a few days later Hitler launched the great war against Russia he longed to send twenty divisions to help him, and was nettled when the Germans made it clear they would rather do without. He had no ears for his economics Minister, Riccardi, who tried to ram home to him the grievous situation of food and supplies.

Ciano's diary shows the progressive decay during the next year or so of Mussolini's mind and body and of Italy's situation in general.

December 14, 1941: The fact is that in these days the people feel the lack of food more than ever, and complain, but Mussolini, as is his custom, takes it out even on the Almighty when things go wrong.

December 22, 1941: Mussolini has again attacked Christmas. He is surprised that the Germans have not yet abolished this holiday, which "only reminds one of the birth of a Jew who gave the world debilitating and devitalizing theories, and who especially contrived to trick Italy through the disintegrating power of the Popes."

February 24, 1942: Mussolini expounds one of his new theories on war. Wars are necessary in order to see and appraise the true internal composition of a people, because during a war the various classes are revealed: the heroes, the profiteers, and the indolent.

June 9, 1942: On Mussolini's order the newspapers have for some days tried to show that during the 1914–18 War the food situation in the country was worse than it is to-day. It is a sort of propaganda that produces the opposite effect to that intended.

August 8, 1942: His stomach pains have returned; the old ulcer has come to life again. This means that he is worrying. . . . This year there will be suffering because of the cold. There is no coal, and wood will be rationed.

September 2, 1942: Rommel is halted in Egypt for lack of fuel. Three of our oil tankers have been sunk in two days.

September 26, 1942 [letter from his wife, Edda, Mussolini's daughter]: My father is not well. Stomach pains, irritability, depression, etc. . . . In my opinion it's the old ulcer again. (His private life of the last few years gives us much to think about, its effects, etc. . . . Well, let's not talk about it.)

November 5, 1942: The Libyan front collapses [*i.e.*, the British victory at El Alamein] . . . I see the Duce at the Palazzo Venezia. He is pale. His face is drawn; he is tired. . . .

November 6, 1942: The Libyan retreat is assuming more and more the character of a rout.

November 7, 1942: To-day the Duce sees the situation favourably.

November 8, 1942: At five-thirty in the morning von Ribbentrop telephoned to inform me of American landings in Algerian and Moroccan ports. . . . The Duce's reaction was lively as usual.

December 13, 1942: Mussolini is calm. This morning he came to very pessimistic conclusions about humanity. Two things, he believes, have really eternal value, "bread and guts." The rest are dreams, ideals, sacrifices—nothing.

December 26, 1942: To-day Princess di Gangi opened her heart to me about the Petacci affair. . . . According to her, Mussolini has had enough of Claretta, her brother, her sister, and all of them, but he can't get rid of them because they are bad people, ready to blackmail and create a scandal. . . . The Duce is supposed to have said that he once loved this girl [Claretta Petacci] but that now she is "revolting" to him. . . . The Gangi woman blames the Petaccis for everything that is going badly in Italy, including the Duce's ailments, which seems to me, frankly, a bit exaggerated.

During 1943 the downward slide gathered momentum. The Italo-German Armies under Rommel were completely cleared from Africa. In June the Allied Armies landed in Sicily. Now at last the twenty-year dictatorship was crumbling to ruin. Ciano had been transferred from the Foreign Ministry in February, and was growing more and more critical of a Mussolini who seemed incapable of even trying to break free of the German toils. Grandi and other important Fascists, who had always had reservations about the Duce, now began to concert plans against him. Badoglio, Ambrosio, Castellano —all generals and anti-German—went further, plotting to arrest him, and overthrow the regime. Mussolini begged Hitler "to end the Russian episode"—which after the Stalingrad disaster now seemed further than ever from victory; but Hitler would not listen to such a suggestion. In mid-July 1943 he suddenly sent for Mussolini to fly to yet another (their thirteenth) meeting, and many Italian politicians and high-ranking soldiers hoped Mussolini would have the courage either to demand of Hitler much more assistance or to threaten him with Italy's defection from the war. In the event, to the despair of his advisers, Mussolini did neither. As usual, Hitler hypnotized him, and he sat, hour after hour, cross-legged on the edge of his armchair, occasionally putting his left hand behind his back, and pressing it against the spot where his ulcer was paining him, while Hitler, "in a voice that grew more strident every minute, continued imperturbably to pour forth a stream of reproaches and recriminations." The scene was described by the Italian Ambassador to Berlin: as he put it, it was Mussolini's last card and he refused to play it.

A week later the inevitable, the incredible, happened. The world suddenly learned that the Duce had been voted down in his own Fascist Grand Council, that the King had placed him under arrest, and that Badoglio was head of a new Government. It later transpired that the initiative against him was first taken at the meeting by Grandi, that his own son-in-law, Ciano, had helped to vote him down, that Mussolini himself had submitted almost feebly. He had been driven off in an ambulance, at first querulous and fearful, then apathetic and resigned, with sudden brief outbreaks of petulance. The Germans, rightly mistrusting Badoglio when he announced that the war would continue, proceeded to occupy Rome and take over the defence of Italy. Badoglio, the King, and the Government moved south to Brindisi.

Any jubilation experienced by the Italians at their liberation from a tyrant was short-lived, since now, for five or six weeks, their cities felt the full fury of Anglo-American air attack. They were now made to understand what Churchill meant when he said that British policy was adapted to both ends of the Italian donkey—carrot for the front end and stick for the back. The carrot was the hope of peace, but this was the stick. Genoa, Turin, Naples, Milan, Rome itself (earlier spared), all suffered, until the Badoglio Government in September signed an armistice taking Italy out of the war. A month later she completed her about-turn and declared war on Germany.

By that time, however, had occurred the astonishing incident of Mussolini's kidnapping. He was in a hotel in the Gran Sasso district, over six thousand feet up in the Apennines, when one day in September eleven German gliders and a small Stork plane appeared out of the blue. They were under the command of Otto Skorzeny, who specialized in the performance of the impossible, and they found Mussolini listless, unkempt, and ill-looking, caring little for the 'rescue' they proposed to him. But he consented to be carried off, perilously, in the Stork to Munich, where he was greeted by his family and by Hitler, proclaimed head of the new Republican Italy, and made to go through the motions of Axis solidarity. In a diary that he kept in these last years he gives his own version of these events, with a whole section (entitled *Hard to Kill*) showing how he had always borne a charmed life. "The Greek philosopher, Thales, thanked the gods for creating him a man and not a beast, a male and not a female, a Greek and not a barbarian. I thank the gods for having spared me the farce of a vociferous trial in Madison Square,

New York—to which I should infinitely prefer a regular hanging
in the Tower of London. . . ." The same diary contains bitter attacks
on all his enemies and the so-called traitors, chief among them
Grandi, Badoglio, and the King. He lamented that Fascism had
failed to be sufficiently totalitarian; it should have declared a republic much earlier.

It is impossible entirely to resist some sympathy even for Mussolini in these last eighteen months of his life. He was allowed to go
to his country home, officially Duce of Republican Italy, but not, of
course, to Rome. The Germans treated him with contempt, posted
S.S. troops to guard him against counter-kidnapping, used him
simply as a political puppet, and got on with the main business of
using Italy to keep the Allied troops at arm's length from their
homeland. They did this brilliantly, fighting a dogged, skilful, and
very slow retreat up the mountainous peninsula. But slow as it was,
it was a retreat, and Mussolini was again moved, far to the north,
to Gargnano on the shores of Lake Garda. Here he grew thinner,
more querulous, and more pathetic than ever. His grandchildren
squealing round him merely irritated him. His eyes troubled him
severely as well as his other ailments; it is probable that he was
going blind. He regarded his S.S. guards as his jailers. Visitors were
treated to a farrago of historical, philosophical, and political vapour-
ings. When he wrote to Hitler he did not even get an answer.

The men who had 'betrayed' him at the Fascist Grand Council
meeting of July 1943 were now tried by the Germans, the luckier
among them in their absence; and Mussolini's 'consent,' the merest
formality, was obtained to the proceedings. Among the five executed,
bound astride chairs with their backs to the firing-squad, was Ciano,
whose life his wife Edda begged for in vain. But she had managed
to smuggle the famous Diary out of the Verona prison where the
Gestapo were holding him, and from where the last entry is dated,
December 23, 1943. ". . . I accept calmly what is to be my infamous
destiny. . . . The treatment inflicted upon me during these months of
imprisonment has been shameful and inhuman . . . I am preparing
myself for the Supreme Judgment . . ." He had been more an accessory than a principal war criminal—often a half-unwilling accessory.
He had wanted only the wars that would bring easy victories to
Italy and a glorious sunlight for Mussolini that would permit his
moon to shine a bright reflected glory. He came to hate the Germans
(above all Ribbentrop) and to despair of his father-in-law's follies
—which he had earlier helped to promote. He died calmly.

Mussolini had not long to survive him. Claretta came to live near him at Gargnano, and he even enjoyed a few fleeting triumphs in 1944, visiting the German troops, and being cheered in a public appearance at Milan; but all around him, and around Hitler and the Nazis, retribution was closing in. It was 1944–45, perhaps the most terrible year in modern history—all over Europe slaughter, murder of prisoners, destruction of cities, revenge of the subject peoples; a crescendo of blood, hunger, despair, and horror, the wicked harvest of the hatred that Mussolini, Hitler, and their followers had sown. Gradually Eastern Europe, France, Belgium, Holland, Italy were liberated, and rejoicing mingled with the horror. North Italy was full of partisan bands, many of them Communist, operating against the rear of the retreating Germans. With the spring of 1945, and defeat imminent, nobody had time any more to worry about Mussolini. After days of indecision and brave talk of a last-ditch resistance in the mountains, he left for the Swiss border with a small German escort—though nobody knew whether the frontier guards were hostile or not. The last stages of the journey he spent in a German greatcoat, with dark glasses over his eyes, crouched in the driver's cabin of a German lorry. Accompanying it was a car containing a "Spanish diplomatic party"—in fact, Claretta and others of the Petacci family. They were stopped near Lake Como by partisans, and taken prisoner. Driven off in cars, Mussolini and Claretta were taken to a house and allowed a night's rest. The next morning they were taken on to a place called the Villa Belmonte, where in front of the entrance gate, they were 'tried' and shot. Together with fifteen other Fascist corpses they were bundled back to Milan by lorry. The news spreading, a crowd gathered in the Piazza Loreto. Some one thought of hanging the bodies from a roof-coping either to save them from the mob or to enable them to be better seen; so they were strung up by the ankles, grotesque in the attitudes and grimaces of death, to the hideous glee of the good folk of Milan. Mussolini, the master showman, was making his final appearance. It was a starker, more impromptu, and more suitable finale than he would have made at Madison Square, the Tower of London, or among his fellow-criminals at Nuremberg.

Table of Events

1914.	Abandons pacifism, advocates war.
1919.	Treaty of Versailles embitters Italy.
1920–22.	Italy in grip of strikes and lawlessness.
1922.	The Fascist March on Rome.
1924.	Murder of Matteotti.
1929.	Concordat with the Vatican (Lateran Treaty).
1934.	Murder of Dollfuss: Mussolini preserves Austrian independence.
1935–36.	Abyssinian War.
1937–39.	Mussolini aids Franco in Spanish Civil War. "The Axis" created.
1938.	Mussolini accepts Nazification of Austria, helps to promote Munich Pact.
1939.	Mussolini remains 'non-belligerent.'
1940.	Enters war on Hitler's defeat of France, attacks Greece but is defeated. Italian defeat in Egypt.
1941.	Loss of African empire.
1943.	Invasion of Italy by Anglo-American forces. Fall of Mussolini.
1944–45.	Mussolini a 'prisoner' of the Nazis in North Italy.
1945.	Death of Mussolini.
1946.	End of Italian monarchy.

6

Adolf Hitler
(1889–1945)

All the evil fairies were present at Adolf Hitler's birth; all the witches of Europe danced round his cradle, brewing the fatal mixture that boiled over in the nineteen-thirties and forties: German nationalism, German militarism, German self-pity; worship of the state, false theories of blood purity, hatred of the Jews; economic disturbance, social turbulence, political disaster. And never had the hour been so propitious for such a brew to ferment—an age of mass communication to spread lunacy rapidly, of modern propaganda techniques of Press and radio, of universal semi-literacy quick to absorb half-baked ideas; a war-racked age steeped in hatred; a time when change ran along so fast that the whole of society was subject to immense psychological strain; the Age of Hysteria. In some times and places that hysteria produced merely the idolatry of an athlete, a film star, a transatlantic airman, a 'pop' singer. The evil Teutonic fairies conjured up Adolf Hitler.

He first thrust his way into an unwary world in the town of Braunau, Upper Austria, in 1889, the third child of his father's third marriage. Nothing in his ancestry, his environment, or his early record promised distinction. He found little to love in his father, an ageing minor customs official who nevertheless afforded the cost of a secondary education for him; but he was closer to his mother, and it was her death when he was adolescent that helped to turn him into a drifter. Failing twice to get entrance to art school, he gravitated to Vienna, and for five years moved from one lowly job to another—copying and peddling picture-postcards, drawing up advertisements for back-street shops, painting and decorating houses, and spending his nights in a working-men's hostel, or doss-house, where a few of the other inmates later remembered this strange, ill-dressed, staring-eyed misfit, always ready for a political argument over the dying early morning fire.

The Austro-Hungarian Empire before 1919 was a land of many nationalities, and it was perhaps natural for the Germans of Austria proper, rulers of the Empire for many centuries, to regard them-

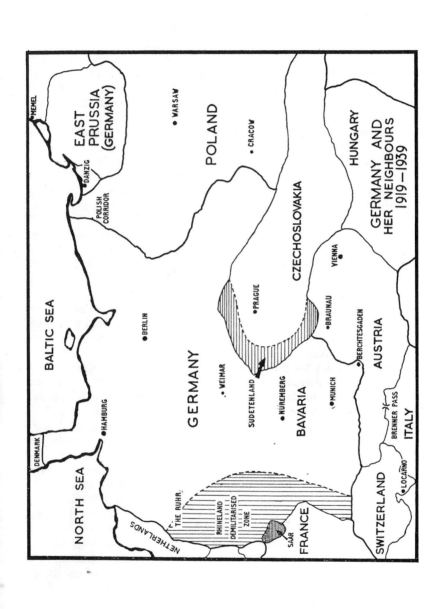

GERMANY AND HER NEIGHBOURS 1919–1939

NORTH SEA

BALTIC SEA

DENMARK

NETHERLANDS

HAMBURG

●BERLIN

GERMANY

THE RUHR

RHINELAND DEMILITARISED ZONE

SAAR

FRANCE

●WEIMAR

SUDETENLAND

●NÜREMBERG

BAVARIA

●MUNICH

SWITZERLAND

LOCARNO●

ITALY

BRENNER PASS

AUSTRIA

BERCHTESGADEN●

BRAUNAU●

●PRAGUE

CZECHOSLOVAKIA

VIENNA●

HUNGARY

POLAND

MEMEL

EAST PRUSSIA (GERMANY)

DANZIG

POLISH CORRIDOR

WARSAW●

CRACOW●

selves as representatives of a superior people, guarding the sacred traditions of Germanic civilization. Hitler was a German, and he was a failure in a Vienna that was full of Slavs and Jews, many of them not failures. Jealousy, resentment, frustration, and rage combined in the young Hitler to produce an insane fanaticism concentrated against the 'lesser breeds,' and above all against the Jews.

In 1913 he moved to Munich, over the frontier in the German Empire ("A German city! I said to myself. How different from Vienna"); and here he continued his life of petty casual jobs and gutter politics until the outbreak of the First World War. The enlarged detail of a bystander's photograph of the Munich crowd cheering the announcement of the declaration on August 1, 1914, shows by a freak of coincidence Hitler's face, transfixed with joy. He had something to live for; the garish lights of patriotism had come to supplant the drab frustrations of his early years.

He was a devoted soldier, aloof from grumblers, a message-runner always near the thick of the fighting, promoted to the rank of corporal, and decorated with the Iron Cross (First Class) in 1918. Just before the armistice of November he was temporarily blinded by a British gas attack near Ypres, and the German collapse found him in hospital near Stettin, shocked, and living intensely the humiliations of his country. Demobilized and unemployed, he drifted back to Munich, as loath as ever to look for steady work, and there, in the political melting-pot of the Bavarian capital, he found his mission. In a tragic day for Europe he became a professional politician.

In 1918 a defeated Germany had overthrown the monarchy and established a moderate republican regime (the Weimar Republic), based on reluctant acceptance of the Versailles Treaty, and on democratic Parliamentary institutions. From the start it faced every conceivable difficulty—a half-starving population, serious epidemics, partial occupation by Allied troops, strikes, riots, but above all attempts both by Right-wing extremists and by Communists to overthrow it. Lenin had always assumed that a German soviet revolution would follow hard upon the Russian, and although it did not, it nearly did; and in Hitler's Bavaria, in 1919, there actually was a Communist republic for nearly a month. But, as things turned out, the most powerful enemies of the Weimar Republic were not the Communists but those conservative and ex-military elements who could not bring themselves to accept the humiliation of defeat, the "dictated peace" of Versailles, with its virtual abolition of the German Army, and the heavy demands for reparations to make good the damage of a war whose guilt they refused to accept. In

Berlin, in 1920, these elements unsuccessfully attempted to over-throw the Social Democratic Government (by the Kapp Putsch), but in Munich they succeeded, and a Right-wing regime was set up which excluded all Socialists and Communists. (It must be remem-bered that in Germany, as in America, though not Britain, the indi-vidual states have their Parliaments and Governments.) Hitler's Munich, then, was a favourable soil for his particular views and ambitions to flourish. The city was full of Army politicians and conspirators like von Epp and Röhm; and of uniformed patriotic leagues and Free Corps volunteers, who played a part similar to that being played in Italy at this time by Mussolini's blackshirts. As in Italy, murder was not excluded; among the German victims of these 'patriots' was Erzberger, who had signed the peace treaty, and Rathenau, Germany's Foreign Minister from 1922, a Socialist and a Jew. In Munich too, or near it, were Ludendorff, the war-time head of the German Army, a man of stubborn personal courage, to whom the Army was God and the Weimar Government a kind of blasphemy; Göring, an ace ex-fighter pilot; Hess, a fanatical young student and ex-airman, weak of intellect but dog-like in his devo-tion; and Rosenberg, a failed architect, who elaborated solemn and nonsensical theories of the superiority of the German Race. It was among men like these that Hitler found his first supporters when he joined, and soon came to lead, the small National Socialist Ger-man Workers' Party, in 1919–20; a Party of a few dozens, then a few hundreds, meeting mainly in Munich beer-halls. Soon they were augmented by Free Corps ex-Service men, encouraged to join by Major Röhm and Lieutenant-General von Epp. When the Free Corps were disbanded by Government decree in 1921, it proved convenient to defeat the decree by forming a Sports and Gymnastic Section of the Party, soon to be conveniently re-christened the Storm Section (Sturmabteilung, or S.A.)—the original Storm-troopers, who specialized in gang-fights with Communists, and whose numbers grew so promisingly that as early as 1922 eight hundred of them could defy the police at a Coburg political meeting. Already the swastika was their badge and symbol. That same year Hitler was saying, "The Marxists taught—If you will not be my brother I will bash your skull in. Our motto shall be—If you will not be a German I will bash your skull in." Soon the 'Socialist' factor in the Party's name and policies became entirely ridiculous, and the few men in it of genuinely socialist ideas left; nobody called it by its original long name—it became shortened simply to the National Socialist, or Nazi, Party. It was dedicated to the destruction of the Weimar

Republic, revenge on the 'traitors' of 1918, and above all revenge on the Jews, liquidation of the Treaty of Versailles, and the revival of a powerful and united Germany. It despised parliamentary democracy, it promoted a cult of violence, and it aimed at total power. Few people outside Bavaria knew anything of it or of the ill-bred stump-orator who led it, the strange fanatic with the shabby mackintosh, the straying forelock, and the madman's eyes.

Two linked events of national and international importance hastened its ominous rise—the French occupation of the Ruhr, and the collapse of the German currency. Both arose out of the terms of the Treaty of Versailles, which, in addition to depriving Germany of all her colonies and of European territories containing seven million people, reducing her Army and Navy to nominal forces only, demilitarizing the Rhineland, and making her sign a declaration of war guilt, also asserted her obligation to pay substantial war reparations both in money and in goods. The commission appointed to determine the sums to be paid failed to agree, the Germans claiming that their impoverished state made payments impossible; and consequently the French Government, against British advice, advanced its troops to occupy the Ruhr basin, the seat of four-fifths of Germany's coal, pig-iron, and steel production. The German mark had been worth a little under a shilling or between four and five to the dollar, before the war; by 1921 it was about a hundred to the dollar, a year later four hundred. The French invasion of the Ruhr, which promoted hatred and resentment throughout Germany, with passive resistance, strikes, sabotage, and rioting, speeded the economic disorganization and financial ruin of Germany. The mark no longer slid down the hill; it tumbled over the cliff to destruction: on November 15, 1923, a dollar was worth two and a half thousand million marks. The effects of all this were uneven: the great landowners were relatively unaffected, while some big-business men and clever manipulators even managed to make money out of the affair —but the great bulk of Germans, and above all the solid middle classes who had saved money, suffered seriously. There was unemployment, bankruptcy, and destitution, and the soberest, thriftiest, and normally most cautious sections of the community were hit hardest of all. A lifetime's savings disappeared in a few months. It was this inflation, coming at the same time as the wave of anti-French bitterness, that fertilized the soil for the growing seeds of Nazism. The lower middle class had by 1923 lost any faith they might have had in their leaders, and Hitler, as Schacht said—the banker who built up the mark again after 1924—"could play like a virtuoso on the keyboard of lower middle-class hearts." *Some one* must be to blame for such disasters—the French, of course, and international financiers, but who else? The Jews, screamed Hitler; the "November criminals" who had signed the armistice; the politicians who had "stabbed Germany in the back" before she was defeated in the field; the pacifists, and the filthy Marxists. The distorted fantasy world constructed in the gutters of Vienna and Munich was beginning, incredibly, to come true, and sober German shopkeepers and housewives began to take Hitler seriously.

Even his first major setback he turned to some advantage. When a premature attempt to seize power in Munich in 1923 failed—a Nazi "march on Munich" rather in the manner of the previous year's Fascist "March on Rome"—Hitler was able to gain nationwide publicity from the trial where he and others were accused of high treason. The court allowed him to make outrageous propaganda speeches from the dock—"there is no such thing as treason against the traitors of 1918"—and to mouth his rhetoric unchecked, save when applause from the public benches became too enthusiastic. He was finally sentenced to five years' imprisonment, only nine months of which he was made to serve, in comfortable quarters, on excellent food, and surrounded by books, flowers, and visitors. He grew temporarily plump on the treatment, and spent his time writing an autobiography (he was thirty-five), entitled *Mein Kampf* (*My Struggle*), a mixture of rambling narrative and half-chewed, high-falutin ideas. In later years a whole legend was built up round the sixteen Nazis who died in the march (or Munich Putsch), and round the heroic deeds of November 1923; in fact, the march would not have been attempted at all if Hitler had not thought that he had the Bavarian authorities in his pocket. He *almost* had.

In the five years 1924–28 Germany made an excellent recovery from the disasters of 1918–23, and Nazi fortunes correspondingly failed to prosper. Prices became steady, wages advanced by 10 to 20 per cent., production doubled, unemployment fell to 650,000; on the reparations issue the Dawes Plan compromise extracted payments averaging about £80 million a year while granting Germany very substantial loans to re-establish her industries. The French withdrew from the Ruhr, and by the Locarno Pact of 1925 the main Western Powers guaranteed each other's frontiers. For a few deceitful years world prospects looked bright; Germany even entered the League of Nations, and in 1928 the Great Powers solemnly 'outlawed' war in the Kellogg Pact. All this did not suit Hitler at all, and although Party numbers began increasing after 1926, the recruits were largely from the lunatic fringe; in the summer of 1928 it would have taken either a great pessimist or an unusually shrewd observer to forecast serious trouble from this strange and unbalanced Austrian agitator. In the election of that year the Nazis won only twelve out of the 491 seats in the Chamber.

But after the Dawes Plan for reparations came the Young Plan, and after the recovery of 1924–28 came the economic slump of 1930–33. These two developments made Hitler and unmade democracy in Germany.

The new plan for reparations envisaged further German payments at a level slightly lower than the average of 1924–28, for another fifty-nine years, and, as a reward for German acceptance, the departure from Germany of French and British troops in 1930, five years ahead of the date fixed at Versailles. Opposition to this scheme gave the Right-wing die-hards like Hitler their golden chance. For it perpetuated what they called the "lie" of German guilt for the 1914 war, and it fixed a lifetime before the slate could be wiped clean. In the tremendous campaign waged against its acceptance the two wildest and most prominent leaders were Hitler and Alfred Hugenberg, steel and film boss who had made a fortune out of the Inflation and bought a vast chain of newspapers. But even the unholy alliance between these two men—Hitler with his S.A. and S.S. gangs, his wild oratory, and his propaganda now under the control of a certain Joseph Goebbels, and Hugenberg with his big-business friends, and his influential nationalist newspapers—did not move more than a minority of Germans. The Young Plan was accepted, though of course never fulfilled; the Reichstag (Parliament) voted it, and President Hindenburg signed it (1930). During the agitation against this reparations scheme Nazi Party membership doubled, and Party funds were swelled handsomely by donations from big business; but it was the Great Depression, hitting Germany in 1930, that presented Hitler with the keys to the castle. What the Inflation had begun the Depression completed. American bankers, hit by the Wall Street crash, withdrew their loans from Germany; production lagged, prices fell, wages fell; everywhere there were bankruptcies and closed factories; and the numbers of unemployed grew and grew until by 1932–33 they exceeded six million—perhaps one in every three workers. A similar situation produced in the U.S.A. a Roosevelt, in Britain a coalition 'National' Government; in Germany the strain proved too great for the young and perhaps fatally diseased democracy. The Weimar Republic foundered without a fight, and by January 1933 Hitler was in possession.

It was not a revolution in the usual sense. There was no storming of any Bastilles or Winter Palaces, though there was continual violence in the streets of the big cities as Communists and Nazi gangs shot and beat one another up. Perhaps the worst incident of all was at Hamburg, in 1932, when Nazi formations parading through the strongly Communist working-class district of Altona were fired on from rooftops and returned the fire; over three hundred were left killed and wounded. There were perhaps as many as a thousand similar, but smaller, incidents, and by 1932 riot and murder were normal features of city life.

Yet the real revolution came by 'correct' procedures—by elections, by parliamentary intrigues and alliances, by well-calculated political poker-playing. In five elections held during 1932 the Nazis polled between 30 and 37·3 per cent. of the total vote—and in the last of them their proportion dropped back to 33; so the central problem remained—how to gain power without an all-out armed rising, which might well fail and ruin everything. Hitler absolutely refused to *share* power with anybody; he would be Chancellor or nothing, so even when the Nazis polled more votes than any other party he still would not accept a coalition that tied his hands. Meanwhile the months went by and the S.A., above all, were restive. These uniformed ruffians could not understand what they were being made to wait for; their trigger-fingers were itching. Five of them had just kicked a Communist to death in front of his mother, and the whole movement was outraged when they were condemned to death. (In fact, Hitler's influence procured first the reduction of their sentence and eventually their glorification as heroes.)

Goebbels, the Nazi propaganda chief, wrote in his diary, "A premature Putsch would nullify our whole future.... The feeling in the Party is still divided ..."; and then, after the electoral setback, "The future looks dark and gloomy; all chances and hopes have quite disappeared." But, unluckily for mankind, they had not. At last the long intrigues, the hard bargains, the calculated gambles behind the scenes bore fruit. Von Papen and General von Schleicher, Hitler's two chief rivals for the Chancellorship, were ready to take desperate measures to exclude one another. So at last Hitler, von Papen, and Hugenberg made their pact, and secured the backing of the President (the aged Hindenburg) and of the Army, without which no German Government would live long. Thus Hitler came to power finally as a consequence of his acceptance by the Right-wing politicians and the generals. They thought they could harness this Nazi tornado.

Von Papen, in his *Memoirs*, later made his own apologia for these events, protesting his own "deep-seated Conservative convictions, based on Christian conceptions of the social order."

Hitler took me for an opportunist, which is what he was in essence himself, and I misunderstood his character in return, assuming that his political ideas were based on fundamental principles ... I am accused of having betrayed the Weimar Republic, and of having hoisted Hitler into the saddle under a secret pact ... The legend that Hitler came to power through the help of a small group of Junkers, generals, and industrialists is pure fantasy. He derived his momentum from a heterogeneous mass of support ... It had no clear idea of how its aims were to be achieved, but only an instinctive and elementary feeling that "there has got to be change. Things cannot go on as they are" ... The Weimar conception of democracy had failed to solve the problems of the post-war world. A large number of people had lost faith in the political parties ... Marxist conceptions of materialism had broken the moral resistance of whole sections of the population. Christian ideals, which alone could counterbalance this threat, had lost their appeal. The younger generation ... sought and found a substitute in Hitler and his programme. His mixture of social and nationalist catch-phrases filled the vacuum. ... The Germans are blamed for failing to recognize where Hitler's ideas would lead them. It is easy to forget that Communism was regarded as the principal enemy, and that many people saw in Hitler's movement the best, and probably, the only, defence. ... A high proportion of the nation—and by no means the worst elements—regarded 1933 as the year of national rebirth. ... A nation's pride had been wounded and was now on the way to being healed. My own fundamental error was to underrate the dynamic power which had awakened the national and social instincts of the masses. ... We were convinced, foolishly perhaps, that the good elements would triumph. ... We underrated Hitler's insatiable lust for power as an end in itself ...

"Foolishly perhaps." To have imported Hitler as the saviour of Christian values: it would seem sober to describe such folly as criminal. But political judgment is normally offered a choice of evils, and hindsight is always easy. Hindsight shows us—and von Papen himself too, with reservations—that he was wrong; Hindenburg was wrong; the generals were wrong—for Hitler eventually destroyed them and their beloved Army; the trade unionists were wrong not to fight Hitler with an immediate general strike (as they had the Kapp Putsch, in 1920); the defenders of Christian values were wrong; the German people were wrong, taking the easy way to salve their wounded pride. Everybody was wrong. Only the lucky ones, like von Papen, lived to make their excuses.

There was no doubt that the revolution had arrived. Suddenly the streets were full of swastika flags, of torchlight processions to rouse the people's sense of power and drama, of marching squads of S.A.

and S.S. men, or of gangs of them going the rounds in tradesmen's vans to pick up their victims. Now the police merely stood by while the brownshirts beat up Jewish shopkeepers, or Communist shop stewards, or broke into private houses and hanged their enemies in their own kitchens. And those enemies were not only Jews and Communists. A Catholic who spoke up at a meeting against the Nazi tyranny, or a journalist who ventured some mild criticism in his paper, might be the next victim; he might be simply shot, or he might be taken off to one of the new concentration camps for enemies of the regime, at Dachau, Oranienburg, or elsewhere. Any civil servant failing to register sufficient enthusiasm for the new masters of Germany simply lost his job, and Göring supplemented his own cowed and subservient civil police with the special secret police, the "Gestapo," who were to earn in frightful measure their own special distinctions of infamy in the following twelve years. The 'ordinary' Germans? Perhaps two-fifths of them accepted the revolution with enthusiasm, and perhaps another half accepted it simply as inevitable. Only one-tenth had the courage to vote against Hitler in August 1934, when he asked for public confirmation of his succession to the Presidency on the death of Hindenburg.

Most of Hitler's early troubles came not from the docile bulk of the German people but from his own ranks. He played his cards very astutely, and one of the tricks he had to win and keep was the confidence of the Army. He could not both do this and satisfy the demands of Röhm and his S.A. brownshirts, by now numbering over two million, who saw themselves as the new military force in Germany, destined to oust the professional old guard. Further, Himmler's blackshirted S.S. (Schutzstaffel, or Protection Brigades) were jealous of their brownshirt rivals, and Himmler had secured from Göring the key appointment of head of the Prussian Gestapo. Thus Göring, Himmler, the S.S., and the professional generals would all be glad to see the S.A. toppled from its pedestal; and in June 1934 they took their chance. The Army leaders (headed by von Blomberg, a member of Hitler's Cabinet) gave their approval; so did Hitler himself; but the actual killings were organized by Göring, Himmler, and their men. On "the night of the long knives," Röhm and the other S.A. leaders were taken from their beds and murdered; General von Schleicher and his wife were shot as they answered the bell at their villa in Berlin; some leaders of Catholic Action and friends of von Papen were conveniently disposed of at the same time, together with an unknown number of other enemies of the regime —several hundreds: a neat, economical week-end's work. The Army proceeded to acquiesce in Hitler's presidency on Hindenburg's death, and 38,000,000 Germans voted *Ja* at the ensuing plebiscite. A little before this the Reichstag had performed its own death ceremonies by passing a bill to enable Hitler to enact laws for four years without its consent. The Reichstag building had already disappeared in a fire which the Nazis wrongly claimed was lit by Communists—and this provided them with a further excuse to arrest four thousand of them, including most of the Communist members of the Reichstag. (It was believed for many years that the Reichstag was in fact fired by the Nazis themselves, but this too has proved to be a lie—a Communist lie.) So the funeral rites of the Weimar Parliament were conducted appropriately in an opera house, in an atmosphere heavy with intimidation, upon a stage dominated by an immense swastika. Every avenue to the building, every corridor and gangway inside it, bristled with S.S. brigades. To the ninety-four brave men about to vote against him, Hitler ranted, "The star of Germany is rising. . . . Your death-knell has sounded." The menacing roar of the S.S. troops sent a chill down the spine of sanity. By 1934 Hitler was Führer, a leader as 'divine' as any Roman emperor, and wielding an apparatus of might ten times as thorough. All power had come into his malevolent hands: ignorance, vengeance, hatred, and tyranny were supreme; and, worst of all, he was mad.

All parties other than the Nazi Party were dissolved or banned. The trade unions were tamed. All the von Papens, Hugenbergs, and the rest were kicked contemptuously out of office. All newspapers and broadcasting services came under the control of Goebbels. Anti-Nazi teachers were dismissed, and the whole educational system was impregnated with the new poison. *Mein Kampf* became compulsory school reading. The independent rights of the federal states disappeared; and the new German Reich was created, the Third Reich, that was to last for a thousand years. The Nazis specialized in the spectacular, the theatrical, the breath-catching. Huge bonfires were made of all the books they disapproved of. Great torchlight processions glorified the Führer and the power of the new Germany. (It is interesting to ponder the use made by Hitler of the symbol of *fire*, and its fascination for him; and it is not surprising that his favourite opera was Wagner's grandiose *Ring of the Nibelungs*, with the potent mystery of its Fire Music and the dramatic conflagration of its climax, when Valhalla itself takes fire. A day was to come when a few cans of petrol would serve to light another fire, for the remains of Hitler.) The garish, the grandiose, the barbaric, the mysterious: Hitler touched many of the primitive springs of poetry and religion which move the emotions of men, and which the older regime had neglected. "We have no scruples," he shouted. "Yes, we are barbarians. We want to be barbarians. It is an honourable title."

Hitler's 'madness' was unfortunately the madness of brilliance. The cunning ability he displayed in the conduct of affairs, especially foreign affairs, over the years 1933–39, was astonishing: it amounted to genius. He had the three immense advantages of being a law to himself, completely unprincipled, and, in the last resort, ready to make war—while his diplomatic opponents in the Western democracies were tied to Parliaments and electorates, and were prepared to cede almost anything rather than risk the end of civilization in war. Hitler, a supreme actor, was able to convince his chosen audience in almost any of his rôles; he could command the roar of the lion (for home consumption), the subtlety of the fox (for soothing the fears, say, of the Poles, or for contriving always to put the French in the wrong), the wickedness of the serpent (inciting assassins, for instance, to murder the Austrian Chancellor and then disowning them), and the mildness of the dove (as when he cooed to the British his horror of war, and his profound longing for peace—once certain wrongs had been righted).

He began by withdrawing from the League of Nations and obtaining for his gesture a 95 per cent. vote of approval in an all-German plebiscite. He then signed a non-aggression pact with Poland. When Austrian Nazis murdered Chancellor Dollfuss in 1934 he was quick —once the coup was seen to have failed—to repudiate its perpetrators. He gave numerous interviews protesting his love of peace and the honour of his word. "What I sign I will stand by," he said to the *Daily Mail*. "You and I know too well the uselessness and horror of war," he declared to a visiting French Member of Parliament. "No problems remained" between France and Germany now that the Saar, with its coalmines, returned to Germany (again by overwhelming plebiscite) in 1935. That year he introduced military conscription, but only *after* France had doubled its period of military service; a huge ceremony in the Berlin State Opera House promoted the event almost to a religious celebration. But still he talked peace. As Alan Bullock writes, "He understood intuitively the longing for peace [of the Western democracies], the idealism of the pacifists, the uneasy conscience of the liberals, the reluctance of the great mass of their peoples to look beyond their private affairs." Public alarm in France was now reflected in the Franco-Soviet Treaty of 1935—an alliance that came to nothing, but an excellent pretext for another move by Hitler. He took his most desperate step so far—a gambler's throw against his generals' advice: he launched his troops over the bridges of the Rhine, against the ban of the Treaty of Versailles, to occupy and refortify the Rhineland. The joy of the honest Rhinelanders was ecstatic. The embarrassed consternation of the British and French was increased by German peace offers timed to coincide with the march; but if only the British and French Governments and peoples had then been prepared to meet march with counter-march there is no doubt that the Germans would have had to withdraw with their tails between their legs. (They are Hitler's own words.) But his intuitive diagnosis of the democracies' paralysis was again right: only the Polish Government was ready to fight!

By 1936 the Italians had succeeded in conquering Ethiopia notwithstanding the condemnation of the League of Nations; but that condemnation, and the angry hostility of Western public opinion, had made the sensitive patriotism of the Italians, and of Mussolini in particular, very susceptible to suggestions from Germany of an Italo-German alliance—foreshadowed a dozen years earlier in *Mein Kampf*. So the idea was born of the Rome-Berlin Axis round which the great globe itself should rotate; and Mussolini was now from time to time imported into the Nazi propaganda circus, out-saluting and out-dressing and out-acting Göring and Hitler themselves at the monster political carnivals that were such a feature of Fascist showmanship—but being left by Hitler in no doubt of his junior position in the new partnership.

By 1937 Hitler's success and the progress of his rearmament (which, moreover, had cured unemployment inside Germany) had reached a pitch where he could risk bigger stakes. Ultimately his eyes were set on a vast eastward empire (Lebensraum—living-space for German civilization), which he planned to achieve by 1943–45, the years when his arms supply would reach maximum power; but his objective for 1938–39, to be achieved by war if necessary, was the creation of a new Great Germany—a State to unite in one whole Germany itself, Hitler's own Austria, and the German-speaking areas of Czechoslovakia and the Baltic. The German generals who had helped to put him in power now began to have grave doubts of him —but the more independent of them were systematically besmirched, and replaced either by Nazis themselves (such as Göring, whose medals encroached daily over his considerable frame), or by 'yes-men' such as Keitel and Brauchitsch, who had a due sense of the Führer's flair. When General von Fritsch, the Commander-in-Chief, was 'framed,' and removed early in 1938, some bold spirits among the officers, led by General Beck, tried to persuade von Fritsch to lead a *coup d'état* against Hitler, but upon his refusal the last hopes of removing the tyrant dwindled, until the ill-starred bomb plot of Beck and his fellow-conspirators in July 1944. Raging and roaring against all "fine gentlemen," and generals in particular, Hitler himself became the new Commander-in-Chief; Göring, of all people, was made supreme economic director, and the disastrous von Ribbentrop, the ex-champagne-salesman and ex-ambassador to Britain, who had offended all sections of British society, was made Foreign Minister. The last feeble brakes were off: Germany, and with her Europe, was signposted to catastrophe.

The immediate consequence was the union of Austria with Germany, achieved by summoning Schuschnigg, the Austrian Chancellor, to Hitler's mountain retreat at Berchtesgaden, and submitting him to insults, sneers, and threats until he capitulated. Meanwhile Hitler ordered his generals to keep up "military pressure shamming military action." The method was blackmail: the heat was on. Göring shouted hour-by-hour orders down the phone to the Nazi chief in Vienna, and when the Austrian Chancellor, back home again and recovered from his pummelling, tried to organize a plebiscite, these phoned orders became urgent and explicit: "The troops already stationed at the frontier will move in to-night"—if Nazi terms were not accepted.... "Call out the National Socialists all over the country. They should now be in the streets...." There was no resistance; the luckier Jews and anti-Nazis fled; 76,000 of the unluckier ones were arrested; and Hitler, returned thus incredibly to his homeland in triumph, publicly wept tears of joy and pride. A majority of Austrians—if not the 99·75 per cent. claimed by the Nazis—shared, for a brief period, his emotions.

The unfortunate Czechs were now all but encircled by German might, and immediately the heat was transferred to them: the Czechs, typical of those lesser breeds given the status of nationhood by the Treaty of Versailles, and, worst of all, accommodating within their frontiers three and a quarter million Germans. Worst of all, yet best of all; for it provided the perfect justification, the perfect net with which to ensnare Western public opinion. Soon the Goebbels lie-factory was turning out enough atrocity-stories to embitter the mildest German bosom—villages fired, refugees on the roads, pregnant women kicked in the stomach by brutal Czechs, and so forth; soon Hitler was screaming his terrible rage over microphone and at monster meeting—and now all Europe was listening awestruck over its radio to this inspired man. For inspired he was: by insane patriotism; by personal glory; by venomous personal hatred of the Czech

President Beneš; by all the eloquent devils of hell. His performances at the Nuremberg Rally, at the Berlin Sports Palace, were both repulsive and brilliant. Every sentence was an explosion. Every inflection of the strange, harsh, exalted barking sent a thrill or a chill down the spine. He was, of all moderns, the supreme mass-orator. He felt the mood of the crowd with mysterious antennae: he made it and it made him; they were one. His power seemed almost hypnotic. He appeared as one possessed. "Sieg Heil!" he would cry at the end, "Hail Victory!"—and the other participants in this strange and terrifying performance would roar back in disciplined exaltation, "Sieg Heil! Sieg Heil! Sieg Heil!" But even on such occasions he would say neither more nor less than he had exactly calculated.

There was another Germany, of course, but it was silent. The time had gone by for protest; the few brave resisters were rotting, alive or dead, in the concentration camps. And the time had not yet come to discover that one had never really been hypnotized by it all, that all the time the Nazis were *the others*.

Hitler played his cards against the Czechs soberly enough. He watched with satisfaction the efforts of the British and French Governments to bring pressure to bear on their Czech friends to be 'reasonable.' He was convinced that neither Britain nor France would fight. He knew that the Poles would not allow Russian troops to cross their country to assist the Czechs. He knew that both Poland and Hungary also had territorial grudges against Czechoslovakia, which he could make use of. The moment was ripe for war, and he gave orders for war to be ready by September 30. His whole attitude was remarkably parallel to that of Frederick the Great planning a similar aggression against Silesia two hundred years earlier—"It is up to you to discover the [pretexts]; the orders to the troops are given." Twice Chamberlain flew to see him in an effort to bring him to reason, but his word was slippery, and his price went up between meetings. Finally Mussolini helped to achieve what the British and French could not: he persuaded the Führer to call a third meeting, at Munich, in the last days of September; and there Hitler gathered without a blow the fruits of a successful war. Peace was 'saved'; the Czechs were deserted by their friends, all their fine fortifications captured, and their natural geographical frontiers destroyed. Three-and-a-quarter more millions of happy Germans "came home to the Reich," and in Britain Chamberlain foresaw "peace in our time." "Our enemies are little worms," said Hitler to his generals; "I saw them at Munich."

Six months later he repeated upon the Czech President (Beneš's successor) the gangster's interview that he had used on the Austrian Chancellor Schuschnigg: give your country up to us or see it destroyed by bombs and gunfire. The Nazis marched into Prague on March 15, 1939. Again Hitler could not contain himself for joy; running into the room where his secretaries were working, he bubbled over. "Children, kiss me, this is the greatest day of my life. I shall go down in history as the greatest of Germans."

He had won big victories, but at a price. After the seizure of Czechoslovakia never again could he expect to be trusted even by the blindest of men. Never again could he say that when all the Germans were united in a Greater Germany his ambitions were complete. ("I want no Czechs!" he had rasped in 1938.) Never again would he have sympathizers in Britain prepared to listen to his claims for a return of the old German colonies. The brutality of his power-lust stood naked after March 1939. In Britain his treachery and aggression had united all parties to face war, if necessary, rather than repeat the fruitless humiliations of Munich. Conscription was accepted that summer; an angry Chamberlain grimly offered British guarantees against further Nazi aggression, and even began military conversations with the Russians. In America, similarly, public sympathy shifted heavily against Hitler, especially after a hideous state-organized pogrom against the Jews at the end of 1938. Most thinking men and women, though they might not say it aloud, knew in their bones that war was inevitable; few but Americans thought they could avoid involvement.

Hitler continued to move forward on the impetus of triumph, and now it was the Poles' turn to feel the pressure. A Polish Corridor (giving access to the sea down the Vistula) had since 1919 separated the main territories of Germany from East Prussia on the Baltic coast; and along that Baltic coast lay cities like Danzig and Memel, German—but set amid the non-German lands of Poland and Lithuania. But the old techniques would work no more. As the vicious anti-Polish propaganda campaign spat its way through the summer of 1939, and the now formidable German forces lay poised to strike, men gritted their teeth, shrugged their shoulders, tried to imagine how bad the worst could be—and more and more felt, as the French said, "il faut en finir."

If only an alliance could be brought off between Russia and the Western Powers all might yet be saved. But Hitler was about to pull the most brilliant of his diplomatic rabbits out of the hat. In August 1939, while British, French, and Russian staff officers were still in stodgy session, Stalin and Hitler jointly announced the incredible:

the Nazi-Soviet Pact of Non-Aggression. Now the British guarantee of Polish boundaries looked the merest gesture, for what could Britain or France do to preserve them if war should come? The two dictators had given one another the green light to achieve their ambitions at Poland's expense. War became inevitable, unless—as Hitler still hoped, as Mussolini still strongly hoped—the feeble democracies of Britain and France would sign another Munich settlement, and accept their diplomatic and strategic defeat.

In any case Poland was done for. "The destruction of Poland stands in the foreground," said Hitler to his generals that week; "I shall give a good propaganda reason for starting the war, whether plausible or not. The victor will not be asked later on whether he told the truth or not." Some condemned criminals were accordingly shot and dressed up in Polish uniforms; their bodies were then strewn inside the German frontier near a radio station, and correspondents invited to witness and photograph "the proof of Polish aggression." The lies having prepared the way, punctually on September 1 the tanks and dive-bombers followed. The era of bloodless diplomatic victories was over; that of easy military victories had begun. Britain and France declared war, but it was only two or three weeks before Western Poland was Hitler's, and Eastern Poland Stalin's. When heavily publicized 'peace offers' were then rejected by the Western Powers the Nazis made great play with the theme of the responsibility of Britain and France for continuing the war.

There followed the autumn and winter of the 'phony war,' with a faked 'attempt' on Hitler's life, organized by the Gestapo, a time-bomb in a beer-cellar Nazi meeting causing several deaths—but miraculously the Führer's intuition had prompted him to leave early. The more gullible among the German people, uneasy at the outbreak of hostilities in September, were reassured by the blitz-krieg in Poland, soothed by Hitler's repeated efforts to effect peace with Britain and France, and now comforted by a further demonstration of his providential luck—his 'star.'

It was on the whole to shine benevolently upon him for another two years yet. At the close of 1939 the Russians attacked Finland to protect their northern flank, and in consequence both Germany and Britain became acutely aware of the strategic value of Scandinavia —especially the Norwegian coast-line with its ports and fjords. Again trusting his star, Hitler achieved what cautious advisers told him was desperately risky—an overseas expedition to capture Norway against the opposition of the Power with naval mastery of the North Sea, Great Britain. Then, in May 1940, came the great hammer-blows in the West that in the short space of a few weeks prostrated the resistance of Holland, Belgium, and France: prodigious successes that lacked only the annihilation of the Franco-British Army at Dunkirk to make them complete and overwhelming. This failure to destroy the Dunkirk armies was one of the many military misjudgments that the German generals later blamed on their amateur Commander-in-Chief. By June 1940, however, the amateur seemed to have done brilliantly enough, beyond all reasonable Germans' dreams; and in a clearing in that same forest of Compiègne where Foch had received the surrender of the Kaiser's army in 1918, Hitler staged his most impressive ceremony yet—the formal surrender of France, in the very same railway restaurant-car that Foch had used. The official film-camera that day vividly revealed his complicated mood of vindictiveness, contempt, and elation: the cameras clicked and the bands played; the arm rose up in the familiar tense salute, but the feet could barely resist their little jig of triumph.

Again came a volley of peace suggestions. The war, after all, was won; Britain's position hopeless. Surely even the "warmonger Churchill" would not force Hitler to destroy her by the ordeals of air attack and military invasion. So ran the propaganda; but its authors knew better. The invasion of Britain would be a much more desperate undertaking than that of Norway. Admiral Raeder, in charge of the German Navy, advised against it, preferring to starve Britain out by aeroplane and submarine, and Göring, in charge of the German Air Force, seemed unable to master the English skies as he had promised. Delay followed delay, as Churchill hurled his own mixture of sober challenge and taunting defiance back over the Channel. More and more, as the months went by, Hitler strengthened in the resolve that was half-formed as early as August 1940: to leave Britain helpless on her island and turn eastward to the destruction of Russia, or, in the words of his own directive to the Army, the establishment of "a defence line against Asiatic Russia from a line running approximately from the Volga River to Archangel."

Göring and Admiral Raeder tried to persuade him first to clear the British at least from the Mediterranean and the Middle East, but Hitler would not be deterred from his grandiose plan by considerations of prudent strategy. In the West, since the collapse of France, things had not gone well, and in the south things had gone even less well, with Spain refusing to attack Gibraltar, Mussolini running into defeats in North Africa and Greece, and the British Navy still mistress of the Mediterranean. But now, if only the grandest gamble of all succeeded and Soviet power were overthrown, he could afford to smile at such trifles.

The Nazis did not go into the great adventure unprepared. Quite apart from the huge military machine itself, which at this time represented perhaps the most terrible and efficient engine of power that the world had ever known, every other Nazi department was prepared, psychologically and administratively, for the new conquests. It was essential to wipe out large sections of the enemy, and not put them to flight, said Hitler. Many tens of millions of people in the industrial areas would become redundant, said Göring, and would either die or retreat to Siberia. Famine was inevitable, and measures to relieve it must not stand in the way of building the new Nazi order; Russia must be bled white to feed the rest of Europe. Himmler and his S.S. battalions would be given a free hand, announced Hitler to his generals, to wipe out traces of the Soviet system; Communist officials were to be liquidated. Himmler's own technical department was investigating the relative efficiency of various methods of mass extermination of "the racially impure"; mobile vans and gas-chambers were being objectively tested with Teutonic thoroughness. The experts on manpower requirements were investigating the likely demand for agricultural and factory slave-labour. It could not be said that the Nazis approached the Russian campaign in any mood of careless improvidence; they prepared realistically and ruthlessly to translate their fantasy world into reality. A few of the old-style generals blinked and grumbled, but by now it was much too late to grumble, and even blinking was a little dangerous.

At midsummer the great attack began, and for a month the German armies drove forward at over a hundred miles a week. Even when differences arose between Hitler and the professional generals very great successes continued to be won. The generals wanted an all-out thrust towards Moscow, Hitler triple thrusts towards Leningrad, Moscow, and Stalingrad—three towns that he saw as symbols of Bolshevik power. As it turned out, the greatest victory was won in the Ukraine, where 600,000 Russians were captured near Kiev, in September. But to encircle them men had been taken from the Moscow front; October came before the Nazi tanks reached Mozhaisk, eighty miles from Moscow. Another 600,000 Russians were taken prisoner behind them—and Hitler's Press chief in fact announced "the end of the war in the East"—but Moscow was not taken; Leningrad was not taken; and the Russian manpower reserves seemed inexhaustible. When, on December 6, a hundred fresh Russian divisions launched a winter counter-offensive the shadow of Napoleon must have lain heavy over Hitler's head-quarters. His ill-clothed and bitterly suffering troops fought with traditional German tenacity, and there was no rout. But things were never quite the same again. Hitler had been proved a bungler. His propaganda was exposed to ridicule. His great gamble had failed, and the failure was underlined that very week by the sensational events at Pearl Harbour. "A historical revision on a unique scale has been imposed on us by the Creator," he announced, as he rushed with sublime casualness into war with the U.S.A. Although in the summer of 1942 German advances began again both in Russia and in North Africa, the high tide of Nazi fortunes had already been reached, even though their actual armies would penetrate deeper yet—to the Volga, to the Caucasus, to El Alamein at the gates of Alexandria; and for a few more months yet their submarines would maintain their toll of merchant shipping in the Atlantic.

By the close of 1942 the first major disasters had shaken the Nazi Empire, and the glaring incompetence of Hitler's personal conduct of the war had been revealed. Threatened both at Stalingrad on the Volga, and at El Alamein in Egypt, with annihilation of his over-stretched forces, he refused to countenance retirement. To Rommel, possibly his most brilliant general, in command of the Afrika Korps, he telegraphed, "No retreat, not so much as one millimetre. Victory or death!"—melodramatic nonsense which Rommel sensibly ignored. To von Paulus, in command at Stalingrad, where a vast battle raged for three months, he telegraphed similar instructions, and when the Russians drew round the shrinking German perimeter a thickening circle of steel until flesh and blood could stand no more—and Paulus surrendered—Hitler's megalomaniac rage boiled over. Every German should have been ready to suffer agony and death for Him, the Führer of the Reich that was to last a thousand years, and these cowards had let him, and Germany, down.

After the effective entry of America into the war the decline in submarine sinkings, the battle of Stalingrad, and the expulsion of Axis forces from Africa, it was apparent to most non-Germans and to an increasing number of Germans that Hitler could not reason-ably hope to win the war. It was all the more vital, therefore, to the Nazis—after shutting their own minds to all such ideas of defeat—to organize their Empire in the most efficient and ruthless manner possible. Vast populations and areas had been overrun; now they must be consolidated, and exploited to the greater efficiency and glory of the master-people and its "new European order." The lesser breeds could be divided into three classes. There were the natural slaves—Czechs, Poles, Russians, Hungarians, Lithuanians, Estonians, and the rest, necessary labourers in the building of the new order. There were Nordic peoples and other civilized Western nations such as Danes, Norwegians, Dutch, Italians, French, who might qualify, as it were, for associate membership of the German Empire. And there were the "racially impure"—especially Jews and partial Jews, to be made at best to wear their leper's badge of contamination, the Star of David, or, better, to be confined to ghetto or concentration camp, or, perhaps best of all, to be exterminated.

A post-war world, sick of horrors, eventually grew tired of hearing of the wickedness of the Nazi concentration and extermination camps; and some Germans in particular, in a sort of wishful disbelief, shut their eyes and ears to the accumulated evidence of flogging, working to death, slow starvation, death from disease, torture, human guinea-pig experimentation in the cause of "medical science," and finally mass execution in the gas-chamber, that make this the most revolting chapter in the whole of modern history. But the bleak statistics are inescapable. At Mauthausen, in Austria, two million were exterminated; at Auschwitz, in Poland, three million—in both cases mainly Jews; through Buchenwald, in Thuringia, a quarter of a million victims passed; in the second half of 1942 alone 70,000 out of 136,000 new arrivals at concentration (as distinct from extermination) camps arrived already dead of their brutal transit treatment; altogether a total of about six million Jews were killed by shooting or gassing. All these are German figures. The S.S. commandant at Auschwitz, in a sworn statement after the war, coldly testified, "I estimate that at least two-and-a-half million victims were executed and exterminated at Auschwitz by gassing and burning, and that at least another half-million succumbed to starvation and disease, making a total of about three million dead. This figure represents about seventy to eighty per cent. of all persons sent to Auschwitz as prisoners, the remainder having been selected and used for slave-labour in the concentration camp industries." He had visited another camp, at Treblinka, to study their extermination methods (based on monoxide) but found these inefficient. "So at Auschwitz I used Cyclon B, which was a crystallized prussic acid dropped into the death chamber. It took from three to fifteen minutes to kill the people in the chamber, according to climatic conditions. We knew when the people were dead because their screaming stopped. . . . Another improvement that we made over Treblinka was that we built our gas-chamber to accommodate two thousand people at one time." Such was the type of work carried on by the S.S. under Heinrich Himmler, an idealist striving for a better world free of racial and political impurities. The imagination cannot long stomach a contemplation of these vast iniquities.

As for the slave-labour upon which the German war effort came increasingly to rely, again the S.S. themselves offer the best commentary. The Hitlerian approach is well-illustrated from a speech of Himmler to his group leaders in 1943.

> ... We must be honest, decent, loyal, and comradely to members of our own blood and nobody else. What happens to a Russian or a Czech does not interest me in the slightest. What the nations can offer in the way of good blood of our type we will take, if necessary, by kidnapping their children, and raising them here with us. Whether nations live in prosperity or starve to death interests me only in so far as we need them as slaves for our "Kultur." Whether ten thousand Russian females fall down from exhaustion while digging an anti-tank ditch interests me only in so far as the anti-tank ditch for Germany is finished.... Our concern, our duty, is our people and our blood. We can be indifferent to everything else....

Such was the spirit in which five million foreign workers, male and female, were recruited to work for Germany, the luckier ones on farms, the unluckier ones in industry, after they had suffered the miseries of kidnap, transport by cattle-truck, and all the brutalities of Nazi hospitality. Some of these industrial slave-workers were housed in camps only a little better than concentration camps, and subject to the maximum hazards of Allied bombing.

Through 1943 and 1944 the disasters accumulated. In Italy Mussolini was overthrown; in the Atlantic the submarines were more hunted than hunting; Anglo-American armies at last landed in France, and advanced rapidly to Paris and beyond; and on the Russian front overwhelming strength was pushing the Germans relentlessly back through White Russia, through the Ukraine to the borders of Rumania, Poland, and East Prussia. Hitler, directing the war from his East Prussian bomb-proof bunker, seldom appearing in public either personally or on radio, was an unrepentant but declining figure. Ageing rapidly, and suffering from stomach pains, fits of giddiness, and a convulsive twitching of the left arm and leg, he became more and more addicted to drugs, more and more hysterical, more and more liable to fits of insane rage. He gradually relinquished the few contacts with civilization and humanity that had graced his life in the days of success. He even abandoned listening to the music of Wagner, whose sensuous Germanic grandiosity had always appealed to him; he saw little of such friends as he had, and nothing of his faithful empty-headed mistress, Eva Braun; his company, apart from his secretaries and the generals, consisted now mainly of his few fellow-fanatics such as Himmler, Bormann (his new deputy), occasionally Goebbels—never Göring, who was now critical of him, and out of favour. There was also Dr Morell, his personal physician, whom many considered a quack; and there was Blondi, his Alsatian bitch. In this lonely, world-hating isolation his illnesses multiplied and his depression grew; so too did his dream-like view of the events around him. Always a builder of fantasies, he more and more saw the history of his time not as flesh-and-blood reality, but as a sort of Wagnerian music-drama, with himself and the other faithful as heroes and demi-gods circled by the mists and fires of wider visions. And in the culmination of Wagner's epic was not Valhalla itself, were not the gods themselves, destroyed in the last fateful conflagration? Hitler's *Twilight of the Gods* began with Stalingrad. It would almost have been inartistic to tamper with the splendours of the tragic myth. Was not a man like von Paulus, surrendering at Stalingrad, a traitor to the heroic theme?

Among his fellow-generals, however, Paulus was no traitor; it was Hitler's incompetence, rather, that had prevented Paulus's retreat. And at last in 1943–44 a courageous group of anti-Nazi officers, led by Beck and others, plotted to assassinate Hitler and seize power. Several projected attempts dissolved before, in July 1944, a certain Colonel von Stauffenberg carried his brief-case containing a time-bomb into Hitler's military conference, duly made his apologies, retired "to make a phone call," heard the explosion, assumed success, and phoned up Beck in Berlin, who proclaimed Hitler's death and an Army coup. But the bomb, though it had shaken Hitler, had not killed him. Goebbels acted with promptitude in Berlin, a patched-up Führer broadcast to his people, Beck committed suicide, and a brutal vengeance was taken, not only on those involved in the plot, but on those like Rommel (many thousands of them), who were not immediately implicated. Most perished by slow hanging; Rommel, a national hero, was offered at a few minutes' notice the choice: either such a death, after trial by People's Court, or an immediate farewell to wife and family, a phial of instantaneous poison, and a hero's funeral to follow. Choosing the second, he was proudly laid to rest—a victim, so it was announced, of heart failure; a heart, it was declared, that "belonged to the Führer."

The next month Field-Marshal von Kluge, in command in France, also committed suicide, advising Hitler in a farewell message to sue for peace. Hitler, however, was still borne aloft on phantoms. "Secret weapons" were to finish the war in his favour: the "V" weapons—flying-bombs and the long-range rockets—were to work miracles. But the Allied armies overran these weapons' launching-bases in France and the Low Countries before their effect could be fully exploited. Moreover, day by day and night by night now, through 1944 and 1945, fleets of American and British bombers wreaked unprecedented havoc on German cities, and the German people were paying heavily for the political folly and ineptitude that had saddled them with such a load of guilt and vengeance.

Extreme powers were taken after the bomb-plot to squeeze out the last drops of manpower for the depleted German Armies. Every man and boy between sixteen and sixty was now conscripted to plug the gaps in the Armies so dangerously scattered over the fronts in Russia, in the West, in Italy, in Scandinavia, in Yugoslavia, in Hungary. And all over occupied Europe the partisans and resistance groups increased the pressure on their hated masters, risking torture and death from the Gestapo or the military authorities if they were captured, as many tens of thousands were. Even now the skilful German Armies could pull off temporary successes, like the offensive of late 1944 against the Americans in the Ardennes, but the writing was plain on the wall.

The beginning of 1945 brought Hitler back from his various field headquarters, where since the bomb-plot he had been a near-invalid, to the Chancellery in Berlin that was to be the setting of the final chapter. The city was already pulverized by Anglo-American bombing. The Russians were massing for the last brutal punch while Hitler and his staff moved between the richly furnished Chancellery itself and the fifty-foot-deep concrete air-raid shelter in the garden. He entirely depended now on drugs and injections. A shaking old man of fifty-five, he had to have a chair pushed under him to sit down. From time to time he would rage against the "fine gentlemen," against the generals, against Göring who wished to betray him, or the latest subordinate who had happened to cross his will. Guderian, the tank expert, describes one such scene. "His fists raised, his cheeks flushed with rage, his whole body trembling... He was almost screaming, his eyes seemed about to pop out of his head, and the veins stood out of his temples." By the spring he was losing control entirely of events: he simply did not know what was happening on the various fronts. The wonderful German military machine was seizing up.

Early in April Eva Braun arrived at the Chancellery to share his twilight and the eventual dark. The position was by then utterly hopeless, but young lads newly trained were still flung to their death. The Americans reached the Elbe. The Russians blasted their way through the suburbs of Berlin. Roosevelt died (a moment to celebrate with champagne). Himmler opened negotiations for peace. Only Goebbels, Bormann, and a very few others of the leading Nazis remained with their Führer, apart from the secretarial and domestic staff—and of course Eva Braun, and Blondi, the Alsatian, who chose the moment to have puppies.

Plainly the end was fast approaching. The Russians began shelling the Chancellery a little before the news came of Mussolini's death; at least Hitler determined to avoid so sordid an end. He made his "political testament," blaming the war on the Jews. He went through a ceremony of marriage with Eva Braun. He put a bullet through Blondi. He named his "successor," Admiral Doenitz—a surprising and in any case pointless choice. He ordered the petrol for the cremation. He shook hands with the staff. On April 30, 1945, in a room to themselves, Eva Braun took poison, and Hitler shot himself through the mouth. Amid the explosion of Russian shells the bodies were quickly disposed of. Goebbels followed suit, poisoning his children, and shooting his wife and himself. Of the other leading Nazis, most either committed suicide or were hanged as war criminals by the victors after public trial at Nuremberg.

They left Eastern Europe at the mercy of that same Russian Communism that—next to Jewry—they had represented to be man's worst enemy. They left Germany battered and bleeding, her roads creeping with the millionfold tragedy of the refugees, her cities gaping to the sky, her territory divided between East and West. The European victors were little better off, drained of resources, and dependent on American aid for survival. That aid, and their own efforts, did at last permit a revival of prosperity—and Western Germany too staged a remarkably rapid recovery—but the wounds of war, human and political, were enormous and permanent.

Was Hitler a cause or an effect? Was he merely the expression of the twentieth-century disease, and if there had not been Hitler would there have been another such? Was he a specifically German phenomenon, or merely the German expression of a hysterical Nationalism, a revolt against reason, a contempt for democracy, a reaction against Christianity common to the time? If there had been no slump in 1930 would he have died, as he deserved to die, a rather contemptible agitator of shabby intellect, who strutted his short ridiculous hour, and was forgotten? Certainly the man without the situation would have been nothing—but then much the same could be said of any great political figure. If there had been no 1940 who would now think Churchill the greatest Englishman of the century or de Gaulle the greatest Frenchman? Hitler represented, alas, sufficient of the spirit of the age in Germany for him to come to dominate both Germany itself and, for a brief, disastrous period, the fortunes of Europe. The crowning misfortune for both Germany and Europe was that he was, however contemptible, a man of narrow but definite genius: treacherous, irrational, strident, mentally diseased—but as actor, as orator, as intriguing politician, as practical psychologist, a most extraordinary man. No one else in modern history has equalled his subtle mastery of crowd emotion; no one has matched his instinctive grasp of the application of modern advertising methods to politics or of modern techniques of mass communication. Moreover, in the early days, until megalomania and impotent fury clouded his judgment, he showed a brilliant touch in the niceties of political manœuvre at home and the calculated gamble abroad. After his defeat and the full revelation of his military blunders after 1940 there was a tendency, encouraged by the now self-justifying German generals, to write him off as a bungling amateur, but time and again in the period of the achievement of power, in the diplomatic game of the thirties, and in the military triumphs of 1936–40 he behaved with shrewd cunning—like a crook of genius. Even to the end he could switch from apparently infantile rages to sudden charming smiles; there was a time to roar and a time to consider words and action. "He never let slip an unconsidered word," said Schacht, his financial expert; "... he never blurted out a secret. Everything was the result of cold calculation."

But his rôle in history was entirely evil. He and his fellow-Nazis bewitched Germany and bedevilled all Europe. Six million Jews and tens of millions of other Europeans died because of his swollen ambitions and twisted dreams. A whole continent was crippled, widowed, orphaned, tortured. Serious historians may long argue the precise assessment of blame for the First World War; they will not fail to agree that the Second was Hitler's War.

Table of Events

1871.	German Empire proclaimed at Versailles.
1889.	Hitler born at Braunau.
1913.	Hitler goes to Munich and serves in German Army (1914–18).
1918.	Defeat of Germany. Revolution.

1919.	Weimar Republic established.
	Treaty of Versailles imposes severe terms on Germany.
1920.	Beginnings of Nazi Party.
1922.	Breakdown of reparations payments; French invade Ruhr.
1923.	Collapse of German currency.
	Failure of Hitler's Munich Putsch.
1924.	Hitler writes *Mein Kampf* in prison.
	Dawes Plan for German reparations.
1925.	Locarno Pact improves international situation.
1929–30.	Young Plan for German reparations.
1932–33.	Six million unemployed in Germany.
	Disorders throughout Germany.
1933.	Hitler Chancellor. Full Nazi terror begins.
1934.	Hitler President, Third Reich created.
	Purge of Röhm and others.
	Murder of Dollfuss by Austrian Nazis.
1936.	Rhineland re-entered by German troops.
1937.	The Axis.
1939.	Nazis occupy Czechoslovakia.
	Danzig crisis, Nazi-Soviet Pact, partition of Poland.
1940.	German Armies occupy Denmark, Norway, Holland, Belgium, France, Hungary, Rumania; but fail to invade Britain.
1941.	German Armies occupy Bulgaria, Yugoslavia, Greece.
	Hitler attacks Russia and scores great victories.
1942.	Germans defeated at Stalingrad and El Alamein.
1940–45.	Slave-labour, concentration camps, Gestapo tyranny, extermination of Jews.
1943–45.	Anglo-American air-raids; Russians defeat Hitler's forces.
1944.	Unsuccessful bomb-plot on Hitler's life.
	Anglo-American forces land in Normandy and advance into Germany.
1945.	Russians reach Berlin; suicide of Hitler and others.
	Nuremberg Trials of remaining major war criminals.

7

Winston Churchill
(1874–   )

Winston Churchill, whom many consider the greatest Englishman of the century, began life as the disappointing son of a famous father. Lord Randolph Churchill, third son of the seventh Duke of Marlborough, had had a brilliant, though short, career in the House of Commons, in the course of which he had tried to push the Conservative Party farther and faster than most Conservatives wanted down the path of 'Tory democracy' where Disraeli had led. A small but brilliant handful, led by Lord Randolph, had come to be known as the Fourth Party. They made many enemies, Lord Randolph in particular being regarded as a dangerous and ambitious man. To many he seemed, as Winston himself later wrote, "an intruder, an upstart, a mutineer who flouted venerable leaders and mocked at constituted authority with a mixture of aristocratic insolence and dramatic brutality." But although the boy worshipped his father with a blind loyalty, father and son could make no contact. The brilliant father was also strange and intimidating, and even shy; and to him the son seemed dull—he was singularly unable to make progress at school. Indeed so stupid did he seem that it appeared he would have to go into the Army.

Winston was not stupid; it was just that he thought Latin stupid, and was firm-minded enough to resist all attempts to teach it to him. And in 1885 not to know Latin was to be uneducated. He hated his preparatory school, where the discipline was cruel and the headmaster such a bad headmaster that young Winston was once moved to kick his straw hat to pieces. This made him a hero but did not improve his Latin, and when he sat his Harrow entrance examination it was lucky for him that he was the son of his father, for the all-important Latin prose paper was handed in containing—apart from his name, W. L. Spencer-Churchill—a figure (1), two smudges, and one blot.

At Harrow, on the whole, he was unpopular and undistinguished, a rather aggressive boy who answered his betters back. Yet thanks to his own passion for great words and great deeds, and to the able teaching of two masters, he did learn to love English—the language, the literature, the roll and flow of its poetry and rhetoric. Many years later he wrote, "Naturally I am biased in favour of making boys learn English: and then I would let the clever ones learn Latin as an honour, and Greek as a treat." And with his own brand of sedate irony he sums up, "I am all for the Public Schools but I do not want to go there again."

He eventually passed into Sandhurst and found his way into the cavalry—the traditional destination of the gallant but less intelligent sons of the wealthy—just before the death of his father, in 1895. Lord Randolph left little money, and Winston found himself insufficiently wealthy to maintain the ardours of a cavalry officer's winter, which meant five months' expensive hunting and shooting. He therefore looked around for adventure, for fame—and for a living.

The year was 1895, and Britain lay in the warm glow of the Victorian sunset. There had been no great war for eighty years, for the Crimean could hardly count as such. Trading activity, industrial power, peaceful penetration, and an occasional punitive war against natives slow to accept the blessings of British rule had carried the Empire round the world. The British Navy steamed majestic and unrivalled over the oceans. At home, certainly, there was still much poverty and ignorance, but less of both than there had ever been before. Science was blazing new trails all the time; in that very year of 1895 an Englishman, Ross, tracked down the mosquito parasite that caused malaria, and an Italian, Marconi, sent a radio message near Bologna a distance of over a mile. Hope and Glory were the keynotes of the era, soon to reach its climax in the celebration of the great little Queen's Diamond Jubilee. "Wider still and wider" were the bounds being set, not only of the British Empire, but of the Englishman's belief in himself and in the future.

For the young impoverished cavalryman, hungry for glory and a war to occupy an idle winter, there was hardly enough trouble about. But luckily (even inevitably) there was a small revolution in Cuba which he 'covered' for the *Graphic* at £5 per dispatch. The exciting outing also introduced him to Havana cigars, an event of significance for the trade. Lieutenant Churchill was then posted to Southern India, where he played polo, and for the first time began seriously to apply himself to self-education; he devoured Plato and Aristotle, Malthus on Population, and Darwin on the Origin of Species, but above all the great English historians—Gibbon and Macaulay and Lecky. On Gibbon above all he began part consciously, part unconsciously, to model his weighty prose style. A short interlude on the North-West Frontier produced his first book; and then, in 1898, came the chance, which he had to fight hard for with General Kitchener, to go on the Sudan campaign as correspondent for the *Morning Post*. This was the life for an adventurous young writer of a military turn of mind, and he seized it, both in his share of the big battle of Omdurman, one of the last great 'set-piece' cavalry-charge battles, and in his book that followed, which is full of vigour and characteristic Churchillian touches. ("The Egyptians came, they saw, they ran away.")

It was the Boer War that brought him fame. For the first time he achieved the headlines. Securely placed now as a successful war correspondent, to whom the *Morning Post* was glad to pay £250 a month, he was determined to do or die, with a strong preference for doing, and determined thereby to become a national figure, enter Parliament, and emerge a great man. Events were not lacking. He was captured by the Boers after showing "magnificent bravery and coolness" attempting to free an ambushed armoured train; he escaped, and arrived in Portuguese territory by lying concealed for three days in a goods-wagon. He arrived home in a blaze of Fleet Street ballyhoo, stood immediately as Conservative candidate for Oldham in an aura of anti-Boer patriotism, narrowly won the seat, and proceeded to secure his finances by a short burst of Anglo-American lecture-touring, which netted over £14,000. He had arrived.

To arrive, however, was not necessarily to be loved. Many, both in Westminster and out of it, thought that Randolph's son was even more of a bounder than Randolph: an egotistical publicity-hunter with too much bounce. Moreover, he was not a good Party man, and criticized his own leaders in Parliament almost as frequently as the Liberals—the true son of his father. He had the habit of nagging away at Ministers on detail which he had taken great pains to master —and then (since he was no natural orator) he took further pains to memorize and rehearse every telling word and oratorical trick in his speeches. A wit (F. E. Smith) once said of him that he devoted the best years of his life to preparing his impromptu speeches. He was, like his father, ambitious, unconventional, impish, assured, unpredictable; indeed, his dead father was his only political hero, and to emphasize his filial devotion he wrote in these years a full-length biography of him.

He grew more and more critical of Balfour's Government, and by 1903 was ready for his first crossing of the floor of the House. The writer W. S. Blunt, who knew both Randolph and Winston, thought that the change of allegiance was due to a desire for "full vengeance on those who caused his father's death." Lady Warwick wrote that it was because, wanting power, he saw the Tory road blocked "by the Cecils and other brilliant young Conservatives, whereas the Liberal path was open." Both these reasons stand; but the third and ostensible reason was that the Conservative Party was, during 1903, converted by Joseph Chamberlain to a policy of Protection—duties on foreign imports and preference for colonial goods—whereas Churchill remained a free-trader of the old school. As such he became a Liberal in 1904, and remained one for nearly twenty years.

The Liberal Governments that exercised power for a decade as a result of the landslide victory of December 1905 were some of the most famous and distinguished in English history. In them Churchill held four different offices: Under-Secretary at the Colonial Office (1906–8), President of the Board of Trade (1908–10), Home Secretary (1910–11) and First Lord of the Admiralty (1911–15). In these posts he had a big part to play in most of the events and issues of these vital years—the settlement with South Africa, the first major steps towards the creation of the Welfare State, the suffragette agitation for the woman's vote, the struggle between the Lords and the Commons that led to two more elections in 1910 and the Lords defeat of 1911, the industrial troubles of the same year, the threat of rebellion in Ireland, the German naval challenge to Britain, and the great war that arose largely out of it. During these years Churchill learned to change his views on many matters: the duke's grandson found it almost too easy, some people thought, to adapt his ideas to the new Radicalism of Lloyd George and the small but important Labour Group. But although Churchill took a leading part in labour legislation and the fight against the House of Lords, and although his reforming energy was genuine enough, he was never a thoroughgoing Radical as Lloyd George instinctively was. Churchill always had behind him a sense of the majesty of Britain and her great military and aristocratic tradition, and he moved increasingly towards the Conservative-imperialist wing of the Liberal Party. Then the First World War and the Russian Revolution confirmed his instinctive patriotic toryism, his respect for the bulldog breed that he more and more came physically to resemble, his passionate attachment to the romance and drama of British history, in which he was determined himself to play a significant part.

These were the days when the Welfare State was born, when its pioneer thinking was being done by social writers and reformers, and above all by the group of socialist intellectuals known as the

Fabians. George Bernard Shaw was one of the more colourful of them, and, for a time, H. G. Wells; they were led by the remarkable and formidable Sidney and Beatrice Webb, the godfather and god-mother of the British Labour Party. The Webbs advocated not a sudden revolution but "Fabian tactics," a slow penetration and transformation of capitalist society by socialist ideas—municipal housing, municipal libraries, parks, schools, a national scheme of labour exchanges, unemployment insurance, health insurance, poor assistance, old-age pensions. These were the ideas that the more radical Liberal politicians of 1906 were beginning to grasp, and in the course of the next half-century politicians of all parties have assisted in putting them into operation. Churchill was considered in 1908—by the new Prime Minister, Asquith—for the post of head of the Local Government Board, but declined, as he said, "to be shut up in a soup kitchen with Mrs Sidney Webb." He instead accepted the Presidency of the Board of Trade, where, however, he found no refuge from Mrs Webb. She judged him at first, she writes, "ego-tistical, bumptious, shallow-minded, and reactionary." This was a common reaction. His own private secretary once wrote, "The first time you meet Winston you see all his faults, and the rest of your life you spend in discovering his virtues." Soon Beatrice Webb con-ceded that he was "brilliantly able"; from which one may rightly assume that Churchill had been a good pupil.

Churchill's achievements at the Board of Trade and the Home Office justified this Fabian praise. His Trade Boards Act of 1909 set up impartial committees to determine minimum wages and maximum hours in the 'sweated' industries—a crying need; and his Labour Exchanges Act (1909), a Fabian project, did much to help unemployed workers to find new work. At the Home Office he instituted or greatly extended the scope of libraries, entertainments, and lectures in prisons.

The Home Secretaryship, however, brought him about once a fortnight a task which he came to dread: the necessity of confirming the death sentence on condemned murderers; he told Wilfrid Blunt it was "a nightmare" to him. The Home Office brought him, too, some unpopularity; for instance, when he sent London police, with troops in reserve, to quell rioting following a strike of coalminers at Tonypandy in South Wales and, paying no heed to working-class protests, again called out troops in the dock and railway strikes of 1911. Then there was his escapade in the Sidney Street affair. Some armed burglars, thought mistakenly by the police to be anarchists, had barricaded themselves in a house in the East End of London and killed several policemen. Churchill, hot for any fray, could not resist personally taking charge of the 'siege,' hiding in doorways, conspicuous in top-hat and fur-lined astrakhan overcoat. It was as exciting as Omdurman or the veldt; but it earned him some ridicule and much criticism in high quarters (including some from the recently acceded George V). All the old charges of irresponsibility and publicity-hunting were revived. Rebukes, however, were pointless; as some one said of him about this time, "one might as well try to rebuke a brass band."

In the great affair of "the People versus the Peers" (1909–11) Churchill, in the early stages, was vociferously on the side of "the People." No landowner himself, and poor for an aristocrat, he had no compunction in flaying the House of Lords, an institution (he said) "absolutely foreign to the spirit of the age." And although his invective was not as powerful or bitter as Lloyd George's, he succeeded in arousing equal resentment among the aristocracy; for whereas Lloyd George was low-born, Churchill was himself the grandson of a Duke of Marlborough, and was widely regarded as a traitor to his class. He publicly supported all the measures taken in the Parliament Act of 1911 to draw the teeth of the House of Lords, but his heart had gone out of the fight long before the end, and he grew increasingly critical in private of Lloyd George.

The quarrel with the Lords had arisen out of the high taxes proposed in the Budget of 1909, and those high taxes in their turn stemmed from two main roots—the welfare legislation already noticed, and the rising expenditure on naval armaments. The surprising thing is that Churchill took so long to recognize the menace of the new German fleet which had by 1909 been building for nine years. In the Cabinet he had taken Lloyd George's side against the Right Wing, who had wished to spend more lavishly on battleships. During 1910–11, however, he convinced himself of the reality of the threat from the Kaiser and Admiral von Tirpitz, and, once he was convinced, the shadow over the North Sea dominated his political thoughts. In 1911, to his delight, Asquith appointed him to be First Lord, the civilian head of the Admiralty; and during the next four years he found himself in the rôle the world was to know him in— strategist, patriot, champion of the free civilizations of Britain and the world against the insolent tyranny of the Germans. On our score or so of great ships, he considered, "floated the might, majesty, dominion, and power of the British Empire."

> All our long history built up century after century, all our great affairs in every part of the globe, all the means of livelihood and safety for our

faithful, industrious, active population depended upon them. Open the sea-cocks and let them sink beneath the surface ... and the whole outlook of the world would be changed. The British Empire would dissolve like a dream; each isolated community struggling forward by itself; the central power of union broken: mighty provinces, whole Empires in themselves, drifting hopelessly out of control, and falling a prey to strangers; and Europe after one sudden convulsion passing into the iron grip of the Teuton and all that the Teutonic system meant.

This was the Churchillian vision; this was what inspired him and obsessed him. What were trade boards and Mrs Sidney Webb against this? Who could be bothered with suffragettes when beyond the horizon, ever growing, lay the shadow of German ambition, tyranny, and ill-will? In a speech which gave great offence in Germany he summed up what many Englishmen thought—"There is this difference between the British naval power and the naval power of . . . Germany. The British Navy is to us a necessity, and the German Navy is to them more in the nature of a luxury. Our naval power involves British existence. It is existence to us; it is expansion to them . . ."

If indeed it was "existence" it must be safeguarded—and paid for. The big ships were refitted with fifteen-inch guns. The whole Navy changed over from coal to oil during 1912 and 1913. The naval estimates for 1914 involved £51 million, and Lloyd George all but resigned in protest; for those days it was a huge sum. Admiral Fisher, the tough old eccentric who was Churchill's collaborator in all this, had forecast October 1914 as the month when Germany would launch a war; Churchill was determined not to be caught napping. When the Grand Review of the Fleet in Spithead by George V ended on July 18 the Admiralty ordered the fleets not to disperse. There had been a murder at Sarajevo, an obscure provincial capital in the Austrian Empire, and the Balkans were restless. When Austria attacked Serbia the following week Churchill gave orders for the fleet to move secretly through the Channel at night and take up stations in Scottish waters opposite the main German fleet. On August 4, 1914, the terrible die was cast, Churchill was happy, and the Fleet was fighting-fit and ready for action.

Churchill threw himself into the war with his customary gusto, but some people reacted against a First Lord of the Admiralty who spent half his time dashing over to Dunkirk directing the still-primitive air operations, conducting experiments with steam-rollers that would crush enemy trenches (the tank was on its way), and helping to direct the last-ditch but unsuccessful defence of Antwerp. Naturally when things went wrong at sea this "showman," this

"Jack of all trades," took the blame. In truth, he needed three bodies, one for the First Lord, one for the impetuous man of action, one for the inventive tactician and strategist.

In the end it was the last of these that destroyed his war-time career. He conceived the dangerous idea of forcing the Dardanelles, capturing Constantinople, making contact with Russia, neutralizing the Balkans, and advancing on Germany and Austria-Hungary from the east. Such schemes as these had been forced on humane and imaginative strategists by the murderous trench stalemate on the Western Front, with hundreds of thousands of casualties piling up month after month—a fearful slaughter. The Dardanelles, or Gallipoli, campaign which Churchill championed, and which cost many lives, was conceived to save lives and to shorten the war.

If the campaign had succeeded it is indeed true that the war might have been over two years earlier, the Russian revolution might have been a fundamentally different affair, and the whole course of world history changed. Could it have succeeded? The answer seems undoubtedly yes, if only from the beginning it had been planned, by people who believed in it, as a major combined sea-and-land operation. It was not. Churchill, knowing the opposition of Kitchener, the War Minister, and many other experts, agreed to plan it as a purely naval assault. Even this might have succeeded but for one of its commanders falling sick and another not honestly believing in it. (Admiral Fisher himself did not believe in it.) When at last Kitchener agreed to commit troops to the project fatal delays enabled the Turks, with German assistance, to fortify their defences. Daunting naval losses from mines were followed by heart-rending losses on the beaches of Gallipoli: British, French, and above all Australian and New Zealand (ANZAC) forces suffered between them a quarter of a million killed, wounded, and sick, and at the end of 1915 the survivors evacuated the beaches. All Churchill's enemies shouted for his dismissal, for it was his scheme, and it had disastrously failed. Turks and Germans both later attested the soundness of the strategic idea and their surprised relief at its abandonment. The Conservatives under Bonar Law insisted on his dismissal as the price of their co-operation with Asquith, and Churchill went off to the Western Front as a major of the Grenadier Guards, where he received more evidence, in the shape of narrow escapes, that destiny was reserving him for future greatness. About this time he took up painting: partly as a relief, a means of releasing thwarted energy ("Anyone could see that the canvas could not hit back"); and he became rapidly proficient in the style of the French Impressionists.

By the end of 1916 Asquith too had fallen, and Lloyd George was Prime Minister. Although Churchill now re-entered the Government, he was a minor figure; it was Lloyd George's hour. Churchill had not yet recovered from the Gallipoli disaster; many thought he never would.

In one aspect of policy he was even then the leader. His mind had grasped powerfully and passionately the German menace to civilization. Now the German menace, it was reasonable to suppose, was dead; but there had arisen what seemed to him an even greater menace—International Communism. The Tsar had been overthrown; the moderate revolutionaries had, in their turn, been overthrown by the violent and ruthless Bolsheviks, and chaos reigned in Russia. The Communists, said Churchill, "have given vast regions which a little while ago were smiling villages and prosperous townships back to the wolves and the bears." In these years (1919–21) he came to be the leader of that section of British opinion that favoured intervention to crush this Bolshevik revolution that might infect all Europe. Consequently he remained for many years after, to the Russians, the arch-enemy, and to the Left Wing in Britain the arch-reactionary. Military help for the "Whites" in Russia had originated naturally in 1918 as an attempt to preserve the Eastern Front from total collapse; it had seemed both prudent and reasonable to support those forces—Czech, Cossack, or White Russian—that proposed to remain allies of the West, especially since at this time (May 1918), as Churchill himself put it, "the training of the Red Army had not progressed beyond a knowledge of Communism, the execution of prisoners, and ordinary acts of brigandage and murder." But subsequently he supported intervention on wider grounds: the "foul baboonery" of Bolshevism, the "hideous atrocities" of Trotsky and Lenin (those "deadly snakes"), who had set up the worst tyranny in history—these were so destructive and degrading that they must be fought on general grounds. Communism was a disease that might well be catching. Hence during 1919 Winston moved heaven and earth to get arms and supplies sent to Admiral Kolchak, the White Russian leader, even though the British troops themselves were withdrawn. Lloyd George did not mince his words: he wrote later of Churchill as "a formidable and irresponsible protagonist of an anti-Bolshevik war." In 1920 indeed Churchill was begging Lloyd George to rebuild Germany as a bulwark against the Russian giant—for he thought Europe and Asia might well be in immediate danger of "universal collapse and anarchy." To most Englishmen this sort of thing sounded hysterical; to the working class, and to a great majority of the educated young, it sounded aggressively mischievous. It is not easy even forty years later to say who was right.

All this was frustration: but when Lloyd George transferred him to the Colonial Office he found himself with more practicable tasks to perform. There had been revolutions in Egypt and Iraq, and in both countries large British forces were stationed. Churchill's best achievement as Colonial Minister, and one of which he himself was legitimately proud, was to arrive at an arrangement with the new Iraqi State by which the Emir Feisal, who had fought alongside Lawrence of Arabia in the war, was recognized as King and his brother Abdullah as King of Transjordan (Jordan). The British Army was withdrawn, but the right to maintain air bases retained. The British taxpayer was relieved of a costly military burden; a friendly Iraqi regime was installed that survived the Second World War, and lasted, albeit shakily, until Feisal's grandson was murdered in the Baghdad revolution of 1958. This settlement was in 1921; the next year Egypt too was granted her independence.

That same year of 1922 produced also the delicate and dangerous negotiations surrounding the granting of independence to Southern Ireland, in which Churchill played a considerable part; and then came the last straw that broke the back of the Lloyd George coalition which had governed Britain since the fall of Asquith in 1916. Again it was Churchill who found himself cast as the unpopular "strong man" who was leading Britain to the verge of yet another precipice. There had been the Dardanelles, then the intervention in Russia. Now it was Turkey. Mustafa Kemal's victorious revolutionary armies had defeated the Greeks, and were now threatening British troops at Chanak—again near the Dardanelles. It fell to Churchill to draft the ultimatum to Mustafa: to withdraw from the neutral zone of the Dardanelles or face a war with the British Empire. The ultimatum had its effect; and although Mustafa was soon to get his way, temporarily he saw the prudence of the soft pedal. But again Winston was seen as the bellicose adventurer. It was enough to produce the puff of wind that blew away the coalition Government.

Three times between 1922 and 1924 Churchill was defeated in Parliamentary elections, so that for a time he was politically unemployed. This gave him time to paint, to write, to learn bricklaying, and to think. The painting produced some fine, sensitive landscapes. The writing produced an enormous book on the First World War and its aftermath, entitled *The World Crisis*, whose substantial profits enabled him to buy Chartwell, near Westerham, in Kent.

This led indirectly to the bricklaying; for now that he was at last a landowner it was like him both to want to improve his estate and to want to do it at least partly himself. Here his four children grew up in a true family atmosphere, with Winston himself revelling in tree-top houses and home-made waterfalls, goldfish ponds and bathing-pools. The thinking led him away from Liberalism, and in 1924 he all but won a hectic by-election at Westminster as an Independent—he was forty votes short. Slowly he returned to the fold. The ample bosom of the Conservative Party received him back in time for the 1924 general election and the Chancellorship of the Exchequer.

There was plenty for cynics to talk about. Most Liberals, all Socialists, and many Conservatives mistrusted or hated him. But Churchill always had to have two causes to serve at a time. One of them was consistent and ever-present—it was the cause of Winston Churchill, great man. The other was equally powerful but changed from year to year, or decade to decade. Once it was his father's memory, then social reform, then the fight against Germany, then the fight against Russian Bolshevism. By 1924 it was Socialism in Britain that occupied all his contempt and hostile energy; and it was the Conservative Party that appeared to offer the most substantial opposition to that Socialism. Thus ambition and reason combined to make it natural enough that he should make his peace with his old Party. His five years at the Treasury, however (1924–29), are the least distinguished period of his whole career.

It was a time of protracted business depression and industrial strife. Many of Britain's basic industries and services—in particular her railways and coalmines—were antiquated and grinding towards breakdown. Others, like cotton and steel, were in the middle of stiff difficulties. In 1921 there had been a national coal strike, and the consequent threat of a general strike had forced the Government to mobilize the armed forces in readiness. Next year there was an engineers' strike—a failure like that of the miners—and wage reduction had to be accepted by dockworkers, railwaymen, cotton opera-tives, printers, and many others. Unemployment rose alarmingly; the "dole" was born; tariffs were imposed on many foreign im-ports; cuts and economies were the order of the day. All these events were prime causes of the sudden rise to importance of the Labour Party that so alarmed Churchill.

The exchange value of the pound against the dollar had fallen by 1924 to 4.40 against its pre-war rate of 4.86. The City of London, anxious to preserve its prestige and profits as the centre of the world's banking and exchange, was determined to restore the value of the pound to its pre-war level. Churchill's first important false step as Chancellor of the Exchequer was to accept this 'City' view, urged on him in particular by the board of the Bank of England, and re-establish the pre-war rate of 4.86. This in effect was a 10 per cent. over-valuation of the pound sterling, which in turn produced a situation where our exports were 10 per cent. too dear to sell abroad, and the only remedy for that was to lower costs by a reduction in wages at home. The miners were sacrificed, and their wages were forced down.

British coalmines were the oldest in the world, and for generations the coal-owners had taken their profits and spent them without ploughing them back into the industry to provide the new capital, new machinery, and new amenities which could have helped the British mines to survive in the twentieth century. As it was, by 1925 they could not make a profit without a Government subsidy, and this the Baldwin-Churchill Government was not prepared to pay. The miners, faced with wage reductions, struck; and the rest of British labour prepared to strike in sympathy with them. Many trade-unionists felt that the time had come for a 'show-down' with both masters and Government, while undoubtedly many Conservative M.P.'s were similarly anxious to take the gloves off. Strike votes multiplied all over England, and on May 4, 1926, the General Strike began.

Churchill threw himself into the struggle like a buccaneer. Among Treasury statistics he was never quite at home; but this was a straight fight of the sort that he relished—honest patriotism versus socialist revolution, St George versus the dragon. He revelled in the measures which soon made the strike an expensive and pathetic failure. He published and edited an official Government paper, the *British Gazette* ("For King and Country"), and was selling at the end two million copies a day. When the battle had been won he pressed forward with support of an act to make any such 'political' strikes illegal in future. Fear of Socialism led him on to actions which caused him to be regarded by the working class as their most militant and powerful enemy, and the natural generosity of his nature was forgotten. As for the coal strike, it went on and on until the miners crawled back to work from sheer necessity—totally defeated, and carrying a store of anger in their hearts that lasted for perhaps another thirty years. Their strike, it has been estimated, cost the nation perhaps £800 million, and it is impossible to acquit Churchill of responsibility for the monetary policy that helped to cause it. Yet it is equally impossible wholly to resist a man who afterwards related at a dinner-party, "Everybody said I was the worst Chancellor of the Exchequer that ever was. And now I'm inclined to agree with them."

Certainly in 1929 few people had a good word to say for Winston Churchill; and when the Conservatives lost the election of that year he was out of office, and remained so for ten years. Most people regarded his political career as finished. He was a might-have-been; a potentially great man flawed by flashiness, irresponsibility, unreliability, and inconsistency; a born leader but a poor member of a team. Well before 1929 Baldwin, the Conservative Prime Minister, had had enough of him. "He is often right," Baldwin once said, "but when he is wrong—my God!" And as for Churchill, he had had enough of Baldwin too, with his lazy good-nature, and his talent for evading difficulties.

1929 saw the Wall Street crash, whose repercussions intensified the depression in Britain. The dole queues lengthened. The Labour Government staggered helplessly onward, and were eventually sucked down into the same whirlpool that destroyed civilization in Germany and permitted the emergence of Hitler. In 1931 there was a financial crisis in Britain; the 'National' Government took over, first under Ramsay MacDonald, and later under Baldwin. Unemployment figures reached peaks of approximately fifteen million in the U.S.A., six million in Germany, and three million in Britain. Among all these disastrous events Churchill could play the rôle only of observer and critic; and even as critic he was acutely isolated. His major achievement over these years is his monumental life of his great ancestor, the Duke of Marlborough.

On no matter was Churchill more isolated than on India. All parties in England were agreed that India must eventually be given a form of independence; the main arguments turned on how soon, and in what form. Churchill, however, would have none of it. He strenuously opposed the Conservative Bill of 1935 that gave India a federal constitution and the promise of dominion status. Any weakening of British authority would result in chaos and bloodshed throughout the sub-continent to which the British had brought unity and peace. To Churchill's romantic but powerful imagination "India" conjured up a vision of imperial greatness, of high mercantile adventure, "that most truly bright and precious gem" in the King-Emperor's crown (it was his father's phrase). India was, too, a source of military strength and economic prosperity for Britain, and none of all this—neither the romantic vision nor the realistic calculation—should be lightly squandered. The verdict of historians is likely to be against him.

Churchill's 'wrongness' over India throws into relief his brilliant 'rightness' over the rise of the European dictators, and in particular of Hitler. Admittedly he had paid a visit to Italy in the 'twenties, and reported very kindly on Mussolini; but so soon as it was apparent that the new totalitarian rulers, especially of Germany, stood for tyranny, for anti-civilization, and for war, Churchill was pre-eminent among British politicians of the Right in the consistency and force of his condemnation. Session after session in the House of Commons he challenged the official Government figures of German rearmament, and set against them his own more alarming and more realistic figures. In 1934 Baldwin affirmed that we had a 50 per cent. margin over Germany in air-power. A few months later he disarmingly confessed that he had been wrong: the two air fleets were level. By 1939 it was two to one in Germany's favour. Yet it was Baldwin who maintained his popularity to the end (1937), and Winston who remained unpopular (a situation accentuated by the Edward VIII abdication, where Churchill rushed impetuously to the defence of his King, while Baldwin, in masterly fashion, piloted through the abdication). The truth was that the British people, little as they loved Hitler, could not bring themselves to face the possibility of war or to credit that a great nation like Germany could, when it came to it, initiate cold-blooded aggression. Therefore they shied away from a tough 'risky' policy such as Churchill represented—and in so doing drifted into the still more risky policy of appeasement, peace at almost any price. Tolerant, pleasure-loving, escapist, they voted Baldwin back into power in 1935—and Baldwin appointed as his Minister of Defence (a new office), not Churchill, who still hoped for a Government post, but an expert on the Prayer Book. So Hitler continued to bluff, bully, and rant his way to the top. He had remilitarized the Rhineland; he now seized Austria, and in 1938, after a disgraceful campaign of lies and intimidation, held the big stick over Czechoslovakia. To all this Churchill reacted with a single-minded toughness entirely justified by subsequent events. Hitler meant war; he must therefore be faced with overwhelming force by Britain, France, and such other powers as could be attracted to their support; all concessions were weakness. Churchill's realism even led him to be unenthusiastic when the League of Nations seemed to be trying to stand up to Mussolini early in the Abyssinian war; he argued that the prime enemy was Hitler, and it was folly by antagonizing Mussolini to throw him into the arms of Hitler.

By 1938 Neville Chamberlain had succeeded Baldwin, and was

aiming at a business deal with the dictators. Chamberlain, an honest man, but with no great knowledge of foreign affairs, lacked until too late the appreciation that he was dealing, not with shrewd business-men, but with gangsters led by a near-maniac. He drove his own Foreign Secretary, Eden, to resign. Having failed in the summer of 1938 to persuade the Czechs to make sufficient concessions to Hitler, he flew self-invited to talk with Hitler in his mountain lair at Berchtesgaden. Returning to Germany after consultations in Lon-don, he found that Hitler had put up the price of a settlement. After days of anguish in London and sinister war preparations in Ger-many, Chamberlain flew out a third time to see Hitler, with Musso-lini and the French Prime Minister; and Hitler succeeded in obtain-ing nine-tenths of what he was asking for. Czechoslovakia was not even allowed to negotiate. Back in England, Chamberlain pro-claimed from his balcony in Downing Street that it was an honour-able "peace in our time." A frightened Europe heard him with joy and relief; and for a fortnight he was the most popular man in the entire Continent.

Churchill's reactions were far different. In the debate following the Munich agreement, to a House of Commons already half ashamed of what had happened, he foretold doom. "All is over. Silent, mournful, abandoned, broken, Czechoslovakia recedes into the darkness. . . . We have sustained a total and unmitigated de-feat. . . . And do not suppose that this is the end. This is only the beginning of the reckoning. This is only the first sip, the first fore-taste of a bitter cup which will be proffered to us year by year unless, by a supreme recovery of moral health and martial vigour, we arise again and take our stand for freedom as in the olden times." The events that followed rubbed home the dismal truth. Hitler pro-ceeded cynically to break the agreement and occupy Prague, and in September 1939 the Second World War began.

In its early months Britain was still led by Chamberlain, a sad, fish-out-of-water Chamberlain; but back at the Admiralty, as in 1914, was Churchill, in his element again, aggressive, bounding with energy (he was sixty-five), broadcasting to the nation with relish the details of the sinking of the German pocket battleship *Graf Spee*, chiding the neutrals for being neutral ("Each one hopes that if he feeds the crocodile enough the crocodile will eat him last")—plainly *enjoying* the challenge of the war. Yet the fall of Chamberlain in May 1940, following Hitler's successful invasion of Norway and the failure of the British attempt to assist the Norwegians, was, ironi-cally enough, brought about by a decision of Churchill's which some

regarded as timid: the failure to launch an all-out frontal assault on
the German-held Norwegian port of Trondhjem. The decision was
Churchill's, but the failure was the failure of the Chamberlain
Government. "In the name of God, go," said a Conservative,
Amery, to his own leader. Faced by a revolt, Chamberlain resigned,
advising George VI to appoint Churchill as his successor. "I have
nothing to offer," said Churchill to the House of Commons, "but
blood, toil, tears, and sweat."

That very week Hitler's armies struck in the West; and stagger-
ing, unimagined disasters followed. In quick succession Holland,
Belgium, and France were struck down and Britain isolated, her
Army barely escaping from Dunkirk by the mercy of a week of fine
weather and the enterprise of hundreds of little rescue-craft. Let
Churchill himself summarize the story in a speech he made to the
House of Commons in August 1940:

> Rather more than a quarter of a year has passed since the new Govern-
> ment came into power in this country. What a cataract of disaster has
> poured out upon us since then. The trustful Dutch overwhelmed; their
> beloved and respected Sovereign driven into exile; the peaceful city of
> Rotterdam the scene of a massacre as hideous and brutal as anything in
> the Thirty Years War. Belgium invaded and beaten down; our own fine
> Expeditionary Force, which King Leopold called to his rescue, cut off
> and almost captured, escaping, as it seemed, only by a miracle, and with
> the loss of all its equipment; our ally, France, out; Italy in against us; all
> France in the power of the enemy, all its arsenals and vast masses of
> military material converted or convertible to the enemy's use; a puppet
> Government set up at Vichy which may at any moment be forced to
> become our foe; the whole Western seaboard of Europe from the North
> Cape to the Spanish frontier in German hands; all the ports, all the air-
> fields on this immense front, employed against us as potential spring-
> boards of invasion. . . .

Britain had indeed met catastrophe, but it had found a leader of a
mettle unsurpassed in all her long history. Defiant, rugged, tough; the
spoken tones of his voice rasping with contempt for the unspeak-
able "Narzies," or vibrant with pride in the exploits of the fighter
pilots or of the little ships of Dunkirk; sombre and measured in
defeat, neither minimizing the losses nor over-estimating them;
ironical and eloquent; impish and deadly earnest; prodigious in his
own efforts, and expecting prodigies of everybody around him—he
galvanized the nation in its extreme peril to an almost unanimous
resolve to resist. To work; to survive; to have faith in a victory that
reason could not at that moment support—this was what he inspired
in the British of 1940. "He was a man, take him for all in all . . ."
He was a man even in his foibles. His language was not always lady-

like. He loved good food and good liquor ("This war will be won by carnivores"); his smoking of cigars was prodigious—but he throve wonderfully. "If I had not smoked so much," he said, "I might have been bad-tempered at the wrong time." As for liquor, "all I can say is, I have taken more out of alcohol than alcohol has taken out of me." Englishmen do not like their heroes to be saints. They prefer a common, even a vulgar, touch. Churchill had it.

An iron constitution was necessary to perform all that he did perform, and luckily he had that too. Waking at eight, he read all the overnight telegrams, dictated from his bed (sitting up in his Chinese-dragon dressing-gown, smoking endlessly) dozens of orders and memoranda for the military and civilian chiefs, planning, goading, reprimanding, suggesting, seeking expert opinion: after lunch he would sleep for an hour; there followed Cabinet meetings, speeches, or answers to questions in the House of Commons; visits to airfields, to coast defences, to civil-defence units, to wherever the fighting was thickest and the danger most acute. After dinner he worked regularly till two or three in the morning, exhausting many secretaries, and reducing many thousands of cigars to ash. Not only to the British, but to the world, he became a symbol of resistance and courage. In June 1940 many foreigners expected a speedy British move for peace; in August they waited and wondered—and friends in America held their breath; in October, when still no invasion came, and London survived under the air-raids bloody but unbowed, free men all over the world, and some who had lost their freedom, dared to hope that Britain might again "save herself by her exertions and Europe by her example." When in December it was realized that he had actually given orders at the height of the danger for precious tanks to be sent to Cairo so that General Wavell could win his neat victory over the Italians, every one applauded his coolness and sagacity. (The Italian Army, unenthusiastic for the war, was cleared entirely out of Egypt, and over a hundred thousand prisoners taken.) Englishmen, used to seeing Fascist cartoons of the fat flea-bitten lion, delightedly saw again one that could spring—and in Churchill they heard one that could roar too.

In a broadcast on June 4, 1940, after three hundred and thirty-five thousand men (but no equipment) had been ferried back from the beaches of Dunkirk, he did not attempt to disguise the "colossal military disaster," but after urging upon his listeners that a few months' hard work could replace the loss of equipment, he ended:

Even though large tracts of Europe and many old and famous states have fallen, or may fall, into the grip of the Gestapo and all the odious

apparatus of Nazi rule, we shall not flag or fail. We shall go on to the
end; we shall fight in France, we shall fight on the seas and oceans, we
shall fight with growing confidence and growing strength in the air, we
shall defend our island, whatever the cost may be: we shall fight on the
beaches, we shall fight on the landing-grounds, we shall fight in the fields
and in the streets, we shall fight in the hills; we shall never surrender; and
even if, which I do not for a moment believe, this island or a large part
of it were subjugated and starving, then our Empire beyond the seas,
armed and guarded by the British Fleet, would carry on the struggle,
until, in God's good time, the new world, with all its power and might,
steps forth to the rescue and the liberation of the old.

A fortnight later France had sued for peace, those in the French
Cabinet like Paul Reynaud, or in the Army like General de Gaulle,
who wished to continue the fight from overseas, being overruled.
Churchill had already pledged Britain would. Again he broadcast to
Britain and the world, striking precisely the right combination of
realism and idealism.

> What General Weygand called the Battle of France is over. I expect
> that the Battle of Britain is about to begin. Upon this battle depends the
> future of Christian civilization. Upon it depends our own British life
> and the long continuity of our institutions and our Empire. The whole
> fury and might of the enemy must very soon be turned on us. Hitler
> knows that he will have to break us in this island or lose the war. If we
> can stand up to him all Europe may be free, and the life of the world may
> move forward into broad, sunlit uplands. But if we fail, then the whole
> world, including the United States, including all that we have known and
> cared for, will sink into the abyss of a new Dark Age made more sinister,
> and perhaps more protracted, by the lights of perverted science. Let us
> therefore brace ourselves to our duties, and so bear ourselves that, if the
> British Empire and its Commonwealth last for a thousand years, men will
> still say, "This was their finest hour."

The Battle of Britain was indeed about to begin: but first came the
melancholy necessity of putting the French Fleet out of action—or'
all those of its units that failed to co-operate with the British Navy.
The big ships in Oran harbour, in Algeria, were sunk or seriously
damaged; few actions could have better shown the grim resolve of
Britain to continue the struggle (as many thought she would not,
despite Churchill's brave words). On July 4, in the House of Commons, he spoke again, deploring the necessity of attacking former
allies, who had fought with "characteristic courage. . . . A large proportion of the French Fleet has, therefore, passed into our hands or
has been put out of action . . . by yesterday's events. . . . I leave the
judgment of our action, with confidence, to Parliament. I leave it to
the nation, and I leave it to the United States. I leave it to the world

and history." Darkness sank over defeated France, divided between
the Gestapo, the German Army, and the "men of Vichy" who collaborated with the Germans. In England General de Gaulle set up
his command; in France millions of radios tuned in to London
despite fearful penalties. One night in November 1940 they might
have picked up Churchill himself speaking in his fluent but uniquely
mispronounced French. "Allons, bonne nuit, dormez bien, rassem-
blez vos forces pour l'aube—car l'aube viendra. Elle se lèvera bril-
lante pour les braves, douce pour les fidèles qui auront souffert,
glorieuse sur les tombeaux des héros. Vive la France!..."

A month or two before this, in August and September 1940, the
Battle of Britain was at its height. The advantage of radar, the technical excellence of the Hurricane and Spitfire fighters, and the skill
and courage of their pilots, took so heavy a toll of the raiding
German planes that by September 7 Hitler was forced to switch to
night bombing; the "Blitz" began that was to continue for many
months. Four days later Churchill broadcast again, assessing the
advantages so far won, and Hitler's motives in the new civilian
terror-bombing. "This wicked man, the repository and embodiment
of many forms of soul-destroying hatred...has kindled a fire in
British hearts, here and all over the world, which will glow long
after all traces of the conflagration he has caused in London have
been removed." A few months later he stood amid the smoking ruins
of what had been the House of Commons, the tears streaming unchecked down his cheeks.

The determination and the tears were both typical of Churchill,
an emotional and sensitive man for all his bulldog toughness. Virginia Cowles (one of his best biographers) narrates how he wept
throughout the christening about this time of his grandson Winston,
and murmured, "Poor infant, to be born into such a world as this"
—and many other witnesses testify to this Elizabethan proneness
to tears. He could be glum and temperamental; he could be masterful and dictatorial; he could be scathing, especially to pompous and
long-winded subordinates; he could be suddenly considerate, for
instance, to an overworked secretary; an essential humanity and
humour were always round the corner. Nearly all his great speeches,
however solemn or eloquent, are shot through with humour. ("We
are waiting for the invasion. So are the fishes.")

His fertility of invention astonished those around him. He had
ideas on everything, and for eighteen hours a day threw them at his
perspiring advisers—on tanks, on submarine detection, flat-bottomed
boats, commando raids, amphibious craft, artificial islands, concrete

harbours, a thousand and one devices for winning the war. Roosevelt is reported as saying of him, "He has a hundred brilliant ideas a day, and about four of them are good"; and sometimes, as General Sir Alan Brooke found, it was very difficult to talk him out of those that were not good. He would growl about the Air Force chiefs and the generals who were there just to obstruct him; for his whole make-up led him to the daring and the unexpected. "Great fellow, that Churchill," said Roosevelt, "if you can keep up with him."

The personal friendship achieved between Roosevelt and Churchill proved of immense value. Indeed, it was the faith that one day "the new world would step forth to the rescue and liberation of the old" that buttressed Churchill's courage in 1940 and 1941. At first Roosevelt could give only moral support and arms in return for cash; then came the deal by which Britain received superannuated U.S.A. destroyers in return for a lease of British possessions, expanded later into Lend-Lease. Churchill's own reputation in America soared as Britain stood battered but inviolate against the Nazis, until he became—and ever after remained—America's favourite foreigner. At last, at the end of 1941, came the Japanese attack at Pearl Harbour, and America herself was in the war. Many times Churchill and Roosevelt met in the next three-and-a-half years; and although they frequently disagreed, and even suffered mutual irritation, the friendship was never broken; "anything like a serious difference with you would break my heart," wrote Churchill; and never did Churchill in his great public pronouncements fail to underline the basic necessity of Anglo-American understanding. It was the foundation on which man's hopes for the future were built; break it, and civilization as we understood it would perish.

Just after Pearl Harbour followed another succession of shattering disasters that rocked even Churchill's pre-eminent position in Britain, so that he had to call for a vote of confidence in the House of Commons to silence his critics: there were terrible losses in the never-ending war at sea, including the two new battleships, *Prince of Wales* and *Repulse*, sunk by the Japanese; Malaya lost; Singapore lost, with seventy thousand prisoners; the Japanese at the threshold of India and Australia; a severe defeat by Rommel in the North African desert—another great catalogue of catastrophe. "England," said Goebbels, "is on the toboggan."

In the midst of all this Churchill was subjected to constant pressure from his new allies, the Russians, for a second front in Western Europe to relieve the terrible and almost mortal Nazi threat to the Soviet Union. When on June 22, 1941, Hitler attacked Russia and the most terrible operation of war in the whole of human history was launched, Churchill had been ready with his policy. Churchill, the arch anti-Communist, had no hesitation in proclaiming a common cause with the Soviet Union. "Now this bloodthirsty guttersnipe must launch his mechanized armies upon new fields of slaughter, pillage, and devastation . . . Can you doubt what our policy will be? We have but one aim and one single irrevocable purpose. We are resolved to destroy Hitler and every vestige of the Nazi regime. Any man or state who fights against Nazidom will have our aid. Any man or state who marches with Hitler is our foe. . . ."

By 1942 the Russians were reeling from the second great Nazi summer offensive, and their cry for more help was shrill and bad-tempered. In August 1942 Churchill flew to Moscow to see Stalin for the first time. Telling him that a second front in the West was at that time out of the question, he was upbraided by Stalin, and replied angrily, "You of all people have no right to make reproaches to us." Relations with the Russians remained uneasy and bitter below the surface, though publicly Churchill made constant and handsome references to their achievements and spent many British lives in bringing military aid to Russia's northern ports.

In the autumn of 1942 came the turning-point. The Russians won the battle of Stalingrad; in Egypt the British won the battle of Alamein; Americans landed in Algeria; the Australians held the Japanese in New Guinea; the American Fleet fought its way back through the islands of the Pacific; in the Atlantic the U-boats were destroyed at an ever-increasing pace; armadas of American bombers began to appear in the skies of Western Europe—a terrible omen for the towns of Germany.

Churchill's plan to finish the war was to strike hard and swiftly at Germany through Italy, using North Africa as a springboard. Certainly Italy was 'soft' in the sense that she collapsed rapidly in 1943; Mussolini was overthrown, and Italian forces were soon fighting on the Anglo-American side. But Italy was not 'soft' in any other sense, and her mountains (notably Monte Cassino) provided formidable defensive positions for the skilful German Armies to fight in. The 'underbelly' proved disappointingly tough meat. Still Churchill wished to deploy stronger forces in this southern battlefield than the Americans agreed to. Churchill was for pushing up through Northern Italy to Vienna and Budapest; already visualizing the post-war situation, and with reason mistrustful of the Communists, he stressed to Roosevelt the desirability of arriving in south-central Europe before the Russians. But Roosevelt, in some respects an old-fashioned American, smelt "British Imperialism," and preferred to think he could trust Stalin. Hence the southern war never became more than a prologue and a sideshow. Everything was to be concentrated on a massive hammer blow in the West, with an auxiliary thrust up the Rhône Valley.

When D-Day at last came, in June 1944, it took an 'order' from George VI to stop Churchill from accompanying the assault troops to the beaches of Normandy—just as later Eisenhower had to issue a command forbidding him to cross the Rhine. The famous Mulberry Harbour, the system of prefabricated concrete landing quays towed from Britain in sections, and assembled off the Normandy coast, owed much to the Prime Minister's own ideas. Churchill was, of course, thrilled with the great prize of victory that was palpably coming within grasp during these months; but his mind was preoccupied with a fear and a resentment at Roosevelt's patent readiness to trust Stalin rather than Churchill. In Roosevelt's defence it must be seen that he was aiming at a world in which his own country and Russia, the post-war giants, were in accord. But Churchill was deeply hurt at not being invited to Russo-American parleys, and angry at seeing the sick (and, in fact, dying) Roosevelt waste his charm on a shrewd and ruthless Stalin. At the Teheran and Yalta conferences (1943–45) there was little fun in watching Roosevelt and the Americans treat Britain as the potential aggressor in post-war Italy, Yugoslavia, and Greece, while Stalin happily signed such agreements as that to respect "a free and independent Poland" without the intention of honouring them. Churchill was at least determined that Italy and Greece should not fall into Communist hands, and, against some furious opposition in America, went on Christmas Day 1944 to Athens to prevent a Communist seizure of power, and to supervise the setting up of a new Greek Government. A little later Eisenhower and Marshall, the American military leaders, allowed their victorious forces to stop short at the Czech border, despite calls for help from the partisans in Prague, because they were "loath to hazard American lives for purely political purposes." So the Russians occupied Prague instead. Czechoslovakia soon afterwards fell to Communism; Greece did not: and few in Britain or America subsequently doubted the rightness of Churchill's, or the wrongness of the Americans', policies. Even Berlin itself might have been liberated by Western troops—but Eisenhower regarded it as "militarily unsound."

In May 1945 it was all over; for a few halcyon days Churchill was bathed in the glow of triumph and congratulation, the chief architect of Western victory, the toughest warrior of them all. Yet at this very moment this undeniably great man exhibited the flaws that flecked his greatness. In the election campaign that followed the achievement of victory in Europe the tone he adopted towards his opponents, so recently his loyal colleagues in the war-time coalition, was unworthy and unwise. It was childish of him to talk of mild Labour leaders like Attlee, Cripps, and Bevin as a potential "Gestapo"; it was ludicrous to hold up Professor Laski, Chairman of the Party Executive, as a future "boss" of a Labour Government. Moreover, he now had to speak, not as a national leader, but as a Conservative leader, and to many Englishmen, rightly or wrongly, the Conservatives were associated with the unemployment of the 'twenties and the appeasement of the 'thirties—the very party that had cold-shouldered Winston in the old days; and the British public was ready for a leap forward in "social justice," which it thought, again, rightly or wrongly, the Labour Party was more likely than the Conservatives to provide. Hence came a resounding defeat for Churchill immediately after his heroic achievements of 1940–45. He took his humiliation hard. He had not thought such ingratitude or blindness possible.

In opposition again, he was derisive and contemptuous of the Labour Government, but not always very effective; and when he attacked the Government for "equalizing misery and organizing scarcity," many felt that this was merely playing a political party game. On world affairs, however, he always commanded, if not agreement, at least attention—as at Fulton in the U.S.A., when he first used the "iron curtain" metaphor, and called for a "fraternal association" between America and Western Europe to resist the Communist tide that had lapped all over Eastern Europe. And although political opponents in Britain attacked him on party issues, there were few who failed to hail him as a great man on the countless public occasions when he cast aside party differences, and was honoured for his war-time services.

His energy was still prodigious for a septuagenarian. He extended his farm at Chartwell; he travelled endlessly, receiving honours, and returning his famous V-for-Victory sign, with the two upraised fingers, over half Europe and America; he became a racehorse owner; he painted, and exhibited regularly at the Royal Academy; and above all he dictated his vast *History of the Second World War*, in six great volumes: all this on top of leading His Majesty's Opposition in the House of Commons.

The political pendulum swung back as it was bound to do. By

1951 Churchill, at the age of seventy-seven, was back in office as Prime Minister: leader of a purely Conservative Government for the first time. But there were no surprises—indeed, no major changes of policy. Rationing at home was ended rather more speedily than it would have been under the Labour Government. More freedom was allowed to private industry; inflation continued at much the same rate as before. In foreign policy there was the same attempt to cement a great Atlantic alliance of American and Western European powers—the NATO group; the same support for the United Nations force fighting Communism in Korea; the same promotion of independence among the colonial peoples of the Commonwealth. Many times in his life he had been accused of being a warmonger, an imperialist, an adventurer: he now showed none of these qualities. All his efforts were bent towards an understanding with Russia that would end the 'cold war' before the hydrogen bomb put an end to civilization. He was the first Western statesman to campaign for a 'summit' meeting—but by now neither the Americans, under the stampede of anti-Communist McCarthyism, nor the Russians, in the last years of Stalin's stranglehold, were willing to retreat from their rigid positions of hostility.

In 1952 George VI, his loyal friend, died; and at the coronation of the new Queen he at last accepted the knighthood of the Garter that he had earlier refused. Some regretted that he had at last ceased to be *Mr Churchill*; but he himself entered into the coronation pageantry of 1953 with all the patriotic-romantic enthusiasm so natural to him. That year even his oaken frame began to show signs of wear. He suffered a stroke, but recovered to linger on as Prime Minister for another year or so: a year devoted to a last passionate exploration of the chances of peace before Russia too should have the hydrogen bomb, and the dangers of a new war, already hideous, should become too ghoulish for contemplation. He did not succeed. He retired, in 1955, from a political scene still tense and deadlocked —and soon to be lit by the glares of the Hungarian revolt and the Suez crisis. His last message as Prime Minister was of calculated hope that the new weapons would be too frightful to use, that "safety would be the sturdy child of terror and survival the twin brother of annihilation."

Then he added an exhortation that he of all Englishmen was most qualified to utter—"Never flinch, never weary, never despair." For of his many virtues courage had always been the greatest. He had been rash on occasions, and self-willed. He had had blind spots. But he possessed a breadth of mind, a restless inventiveness, and a largeness of vision supreme among Western leaders. He combined sardonic humour with impressive seriousness. He made countless enemies, but was without rancour. He was the most lovable and the most loved of modern English statesmen.

Table of Events

1874.	Winston Churchill born at Blenheim Palace.
1895.	Death of Lord Randolph Churchill.
1898.	Battle of Omdurman.
1899–1902.	The Boer War.
1906–15.	Churchill a Liberal Minister, promotes social legislation and builds up the Navy.
1915.	Failure of his Dardanelles Campaign.
1918–19.	Promotes anti-Communist intervention in Russia.
1924.	Rejoins Conservative Party as Chancellor of the Exchequer.
1926.	The General Strike.
1931.	Financial crisis, 'National' Government, Churchill "in the wilderness."
1935.	Opposes Government of India Act.
1936.	Abdication of Edward VIII.
1936–39.	Churchill intensifies attacks on the dictators and castigates weakness of British policy.
1938.	Criticizes Munich agreement.
1939.	War: Churchill First Lord of the Admiralty.
1940.	Loss of Norway brings fall of Chamberlain and Premiership of Churchill.
	Hitler conquers Western Europe.
	Dunkirk and the Battle of Britain.
	Churchill leads Britain in defiance of Hitler.
1941.	Lend-Lease Act.
	Churchill proclaims common cause with Russia.
1942.	Japanese triumphs. Loss of Singapore.
	Battle of El Alamein.
1943.	Fall of Mussolini.
1944.	Anglo-American forces land in Normandy.
	Churchill aids Tito and prevents Communist revolution in Greece.
1945.	Victory in Europe and Asia.
	Labour victory in elections, Churchill leader of the Opposition.
1946 onward:	Churchill demands alliance between U.S.A. and Western Europe, writes *History of the Second World War*.
1951.	Prime Minister again.
1955.	Retires: Eden Prime Minister.

8

Franklin D. Roosevelt
(1882–1945)

In 1952 Eisenhower won his presidential election on the slogan,
"I like Ike"; he was the man *everybody* liked. Franklin Roosevelt could never have campaigned on such a phrase. People
loved Roosevelt or they hated him; they did not 'like' him. The
magazine *Esquire*, in 1938, showed a cartoon of a child drawing the
word Roosevelt on a pavement; his brother is shouting to their
mother at the door, "Mother, Wilfred wrote a bad word!" Roosevelt appreciated the cartoon so keenly that he had a framed copy
hung outside his bedroom door at the White House. Yet after his
death in 1945 this most hated President was mourned as a personal
friend by countless millions of Americans.

It fell to Roosevelt to be President of the greatest Power in the
world during, first, the greatest of trade depressions, and second, the
greatest of wars. Dying at the moment of victory, he left his country
overwhelmingly the richest and most powerful state that the world
had ever seen. Such a position is not gained by leadership alone; but
it is not gained without leadership, and for a dozen vital years the
United States had a leader of rare gifts.

In some ways he strongly resembled Lloyd George. Both personified the liberal spirit of their age; both championed the 'common
man' and, attacking the seats of power, earned the hatred of the
ruling class; both laid the foundation in their country of social
insurance and welfare; both combined idealism and courage with a
shrewd opportunism; both were essentially charmers and maintained
their power by consummate exploitation of their personal magnetism; unintellectual themselves, both were superb pickers of other
men's brains; both coming to prominence on domestic issues were
destined to lead their countries to victory in war.

In the circumstances of their birth, however, the difference could
hardly be more striking: Roosevelt was born in the comfortable
family residence of Hyde Park, a Georgian-style mansion with lawns
running down to the Hudson River, eighty miles above that New
York that had begun its life two-and-a-half centuries earlier as New

Amsterdam. Here the Roosevelts were old-established Dutch aristocrats in old-established Dutch country—benevolent squires of a smiling countryside. Franklin's mother, a millionairess in her own right, a beauty, and a formidable personality, was a Delano, and traced her descent from a Pilgrim Father of 1620. It was under her eye and that of his rather elderly father that the young Franklin Delano Roosevelt grew up, in the happiest of boyhoods, privately tutored up to the age of fourteen, learning to ride, to swim, to play tennis and polo, to shoot, and above all to sail; travelling in Europe; proceeding at fifteen to Groton (the approximate American equivalent of Eton or Winchester) and at eighteen to Harvard University, where he studied history and government. Summers were spent at another Roosevelt property, Campobello, on the distant New Brunswick coast, bathing, boating, hitting the trail. Nothing in this handsome, 'social,' athletic youth suggested more than a conventional distinction: a letter written to his mother seems to sum up his college career—"... am doing a little studying, a little riding, and a few party calls." The *name* Roosevelt was certainly of world-wide fame at this period—but that was because Theodore Roosevelt, a distant relation of Franklin's, had been elected Vice-President of the United States in 1900, and then, when President McKinley was assassinated the next year, succeeded to the Presidency. "Uncle Ted" was a force (more than a force, an explosion) to be reckoned with, and, although a Republican, he provided something of an idol for the young Franklin: one-time cowboy, rough-rider, and war hero in the Spanish-American War of 1898, a crusading reformer in the war against graft (he first invented the phrase "vested interests")—a real buccaneer of a president, "strong as a bull-moose." He too was a rich Roosevelt, had been to Groton, to Harvard, to the Columbia Law School, where Franklin proceeded in 1904; he too had been a dark horse. Consciously or unconsciously, how could Franklin avoid a degree of emulation? Even closer links were forged between Roosevelt and Roosevelt when Franklin married his own distant cousin, Eleanor, the President's niece, in 1905. For a time he worked, without much promise or distinction, in a law office, and in 1909 surprised everybody by getting elected for his own home county to the State legislature of New York. Some said it was the Roosevelt name elected him, and there was very likely truth in that, though he was of the *other* party: Theodore was a Republican, Franklin a Democrat. As State Senator he showed courage and ability in defying the powerful party bosses of Tammany Hall, and winning his fight with them; and in 1913 the newly elected President Wilson offered him

the Under-Secretaryship of the Navy; again it was an office that
Theodore had held. Tenure of it put him into the Federal (all-
American) Government at Washington. He had arrived, the big
young athlete with the explosive name, the confident vigour, the
already uptilted jaw, and the gold pince-nez spectacles through
which he appeared to look *down* at people. Gay, rich, and agreeable,
he still had not developed much of that sympathy with the common
man that made him the great Roosevelt. Much later he said to his
friend Frances Perkins, the first American woman Cabinet Minister,
"You know, I was an awfully mean cuss when I first went into
politics."

He was, however, quick to learn (it was always his most brilliant
asset); and Wilson, the liberal idealist, taught him much. He caught
from him and others of his new colleagues and associates a sense of
moral drive and reforming earnestness. Poverty might perhaps be
prevented, slums might be cleared, child labour legislated away,
women's labour prohibited on night shifts, men's hours shortened,
and their wages improved. America was no working-man's paradise
in 1913, and Wilson's Government did a good deal to eradicate ugly
social and industrial evils; his very slogan of the "New Freedom"
sounds like the parent of Roosevelt's "New Deal" of the 1930's.
Something else, too, Roosevelt learned from Wilson: a respect for
intellectuals and for ideas; the projects of the New Deal that twenty
years later were the salvation of the U.S.A. after the disasters of the
Great Depression were mainly the brain-children of university dons
and their like.

For seven years Roosevelt was Assistant Secretary to the Navy,
very much at home in nautical affairs (he loved the sea), increasingly
confident and efficient in administration, cutting red tape, campaigning for submarine chasers, and pioneering new techniques for defeating the German submarines in the First World War. Roosevelt
was an enthusiastic pro-war and pro-ally man, and when Wilson
launched his great project of the League of Nations in 1918 Roosevelt was an outright internationalist like his chief. But America, tired
of Europe's quarrels, withdrew into isolationism and rejected
Wilson, whose health gave way. The Senate threw out the Versailles
Treaty. The Democratic Party was torn between League of Nations
men and isolationists, and by 1920, when Roosevelt was adopted as
Democratic candidate for Vice-President, Wilson was a dying man,
and the League of Nations, in America, a dying cause. So the Republicans came to power, and remained there through the golden
'twenties and the disasters of 1929–32.

In the San Francisco Convention of August 1920, when Roosevelt was adopted as vice-presidential candidate, he was, as Frances Perkins relates, "tall, strong, handsome, and popular, one of the stars of the show. I recall how he displayed his athletic ability by vaulting over a row of chairs to get to the platform in a hurry." Exactly one year later, when he was thirty-nine, he was struck down by the crippling disease that almost destroyed him, yet in some way helped to make the mature Roosevelt. Holidaying at his beloved Campobello with the family, swimming and sailing, he was suddenly smitten with severe polio, which all but killed him, and left him totally paralysed below the waist. For a long time it was feared that he would be permanently unable even to sit up; as it was, he never walked again unaided; he could never be left alone except in sleep; he never could stand to make a speech without his steel leg-braces and a strong lectern to rest upon; he could not even bear fast travel by car or train, lacking the muscular ability to compensate for swerves and bends. His recovery, such as it was, was slow and initially very painful, though in 1924 he discovered the wonderful curative power of Warm Springs, Georgia, and the underwater exercises that later became a standard form of treatment for this sinister and, in 1921, little understood disease. Then, finding the warm water his own salvation, he poured out his wealth in turning the place into a polio spa for other sufferers. Never for a moment did he abandon the fight to defeat his handicap; indeed, some have said that his wonderful victory over it strengthened in him the conviction that almost any problem was soluble given the resolution: "the only thing we have to fear is fear itself." Others said that his plumbing of the depths of his illness, his very physical helplessness, sharpened his appetite for power. Certainly it rubbed constantly home to him the interdependence of mankind. "Without the help of thousands of others every one of us would die, naked and starved." Certainly, too, his sufferings gave a new depth to his nature and increased his already growing sympathy for other unfortunates—the poor, the sick, the unemployed, the exploited. And certainly in one respect his achievement was unique: no one else crippled to the extent that he was ever reached the foremost position of power in any country or period.

Paralysis did not keep him from politics even in the mid-'twenties. He took a prominent part in the 1924 election; he was popular; he bore a magic name; even then such men as Louis Howe (later his campaign manager) believed in his star. Meanwhile he spent much of his time at Warm Springs, talking politics and swimming back to health; and he was still there in 1928 when a surprise invitation came for him to run for the Governorship of New York State. He refused on grounds of health, was eventually persuaded to change his mind, and narrowly won the election for the Democrats in a year when forty out of forty-eight states carried the Republican Hoover to the White House: a dismal day for the Democrats but a triumph for Roosevelt.

In 1928 the economic climate was still sunny in America. The 'twenties were an era of vast technological and material progress, the age of the first Ford moving assembly lines—and as early as 1923 over two million Fords flowed off them to speed the new automobile age, the age when all America was on the move, spending its bright new money; the age of Hollywood and the new cinema industry that revolutionized the habits and manners of the country, and indeed of much of the world; the age of the new electrical gadgets, cookers, toasters, irons, refrigerators, stoves, washing-machines; of the telephone in every home, the bath and shower in every home, the still novel radio in every home. In the words of President Coolidge (1923–29), the business of America was *business*, and until 1929 business had never been better. By that year nearly 70 per cent. of American manufacturing was done by electric power, which not only speeded production but promoted a big expansion of industry in hitherto little-industrialized areas of the Middle West, West, and South. An enormous new oil industry accompanied the boom in automobiles; synthetic plastics began their far-reaching and beneficent revolution in domestic habits, and stimulated the already booming chemical industry. The aircraft industry was another rapidly growing child. The new machines in the tobacco factories turned out one thousand cigarettes a minute. The building industry had never seen such activity; housing was doubly stimulated by the new wealth and the new cars which enabled the cities to expand into ever more distant suburbs; in one generation the numbers of Americans in schools and universities was more than quintupled. Only agriculture, mining, and textiles fell somewhat behind in the race of prosperity.

In so dynamic an economic situation it was only to be expected that there should be rapid changes in manners. But it is more difficult to generalize of the temper of the 'twenties than of its bulging pockets. It was the decade of women's emancipation: American women got the vote; they 'bobbed' their hair; they smoked in public; they wore their skirts short, and affected hideously 'boyish' fashions. It was the decade of the 'prohibition' of alcoholic liquor—

which meant in fact the decade of the speakeasy (or illicit bar) and the bootlegger (or smuggler of illicit drink). It was the heyday of the racketeer and the gangster. It saw the sinister revival of the hooded Ku Klux Klan—anti-negro, anti-Catholic, anti-Jew, anti-foreign— with four million members in 1924. It saw the first million-dollar gate for a sporting event; the shimmy and the "Charleston"; the mass popularization of jazz; a falling church attendance and a rising divorce-rate. It became fashionable to talk of the late war as Wilson's war, something a foolish President had been tricked into by clever British politicians; and when various European nations fell behind in their debt repayments (the U.S.A. had lent 10 billion dollars, mostly at 5 per cent.), President Coolidge hit off the typical American reaction: "They hired the money, didn't they?"

Europe was a puzzling and distasteful subject; but Europe was a long way off, and meanwhile prosperity was 'permanent.' Stocks and shares were booming even faster than business; on Wall Street the prices of shares mounted and mounted, and expert after expert predicted that further rises were inevitable. The business tycoon was the man of the hour; one dollar-drunk observer even committed himself to the opinion that the captains of industry would "finish the work that religion, government, and war have failed to do."

In such an atmosphere Herbert Hoover was elected President in 1928 to succeed Coolidge, in the year when Roosevelt won his lonely Democrat victory in New York. Hoover and his advisers knew the dangers of the swelling bubble of financial speculation, but they did not know how to control its size: it is easy enough to prick a bubble, but how gently to deflate it without bursting it was a tricky problem. Meanwhile the index of prices for the high-grade industrial stocks mounted from 110 in 1924 to 338 at the beginning of 1929. By July it had reached 394, by September 452. Then suddenly the bubble did burst. Prices had advanced unrealistically beyond the true rate of industrial expansion; a little selling was enough to prompt a rush to 'unload' while profits could still be realized. Five days of panic selling sank the share index to 275 (and this related to the 'sound' shares only); by November 13 the figure was 224. Slowly but steadily share prices sank lower still, and by July 1932 the index had fallen to 58.

The Wall Street Crash was not the only cause of the depression. Another significant cause was the post-war poverty of Europeans and their inability to buy the over-expanded American products; in this sense the depression began in Europe and was only 'exported' to America in 1929. American prosperity had advanced too far ahead of the rest of the world, and the very gold that in European hands might have bought American products was languishing uselessly in American vaults.

Americans thus learned the bitter way that prosperity, like peace, was 'indivisible.' The depression snowballed along through the three remaining years of Hoover's administration. Farmers could not pay their debts. Hire-purchase commitments caught their makers out on a limb. The new car was not bought that year or the next. One bank after another was forced to close its doors; and Hoover was obliged to grant Government loans to keep others afloat. By 1932 production was down 40 per cent. and wages down 60 per cent. At least fifteen million were unemployed, representing perhaps one American family in three; many of them were destitute, for America had no national unemployment insurance as Britain had. Hence many Americans lived by grace of the bread line, the soup kitchen, and the garbage bin. Some did not manage even that; they starved.

This was the situation that brought Roosevelt to the helm in 1933. Throughout the Hoover period he had been Governor of New York—a good governor, who among much else had introduced old-age pensions and unemployment relief into the state of New York, and raised income tax 50 per cent. to help meet the bill. His energy, ambition, magnetism, confidence, popularity all pointed to his winning the next Democratic nomination, and the staggering disasters of the Hoover term then pointed to his safe election. Thus he sailed into power on an overwhelming Democrat victory: a new captain at the helm, and one who had a horror of drifting. The great thing was to be sailing *somewhere*—and by 1932 Roosevelt had a shrewd general idea of the direction he was going in.

Hoover and the Republicans, while ministering charitably to the worst distress, stood basically for *laissez-faire*: the depression would work itself out; the temporary 'interruption' to the immutable processes of economic progress could not last much longer. Roosevelt, on the other hand, had been worrying his way towards (for most Americans) a new conception of the State's duty. In a Governor's message to the New York legislature he had said, in 1931: "The duty of the State towards the citizens is the duty of the servant to its master.... One of the duties of the State is that of caring for its citizens who find themselves the victims of adverse circumstances.... To these unfortunate citizens aid must be extended by Government, not as a matter of charity, but as a matter of *social duty*." To provide work for the New York unemployed he had proposed new taxes to the tune of twenty million dollars to give work where possible, and elsewhere "to provide them with food against starvation and with clothing and shelter against suffering." Such social-welfare sentiments were bold enough for America in 1931; but some of his later speeches became almost socialist in tone. "I do not believe that in the name of that sacred word, individualism, a few powerful interests should be permitted to make industrial cannon-fodder of the lives of half the population of the United States"... "Our industrial and agricultural mechanism can produce enough and to spare. Our Government ... owes to every one an avenue to possess himself of a portion of that plenty sufficient for his needs, through his own work."

He did not entirely write these ringing speeches himself. Already the American politician of those days employed his staff of speechwriters. But the point about Roosevelt was the *quality* of his speechwriters; already he was gathering round himself that group of able idealists that later grew into the famous Brain Trust—and some one once said of Roosevelt that every pore in his body was an ear. Judge Rosenman, one of his closest advisers, has told how Roosevelt wished to improve on the usual routine advice—from industrialists, financiers, political experts; instead, he asked, "Why not go to the universities of the country? You have been having some good experiences with college professors. I think they wouldn't be afraid to strike out on new paths just because the paths are new. They would get away from all the old fuzzy thinking..." These men (Rosenman, Moley, Berle, Tugwell, Johnson, and many others) did more than write speeches for him, of course; they propounded policies. And even the speeches that men like Rosenman concocted with such passion and such care, Roosevelt worked over and edited, sometimes through half a dozen drafts, and made thoroughly his own. His was the warm smile, the confident jaw, the ringing voice, but also the sincere conviction behind the famous phrases that soon became historic. "Plans ... must put their faith once more in the *forgotten man* at the bottom of the economic pyramid"... "The country needs *bold, persistent experimentation.*" "Above all, *try something*"... "I pledge you, I pledge myself, to a *new deal* for the American people"... "*Action, and action now*"; and, most famous of all—it was an echo from the nineteenth-century writer, Thoreau —"*The only thing we have to fear is fear itself.*"

This last was said at the ceremony of his Inauguration as President, on March 4, 1933, three weeks after a maniac's attempt on his life, in Miami. America was sliding down the slippery slope to bankruptcy at a breakneck speed. In February the Michigan and Maryland banks closed; on the day of the Inauguration those of New York, Illinois, Massachusetts, New Jersey, and Pennsylvania followed suit: ruin was staring Uncle Sam in the face. It is one of the coincidences of history that the very next day, March 5, Adolf Hitler, facing a situation of parallel economic ruin, assumed full powers in Germany.

The phrase, the "New Deal," was an accidental creation. Judge Rosenman had used the expression in his draft of Roosevelt's acceptance speech at the Democratic Party Convention in 1932 without any intention of creating a label or slogan; but it did become a label for the astonishing avalanche of new measures that emanated from the President and his advisers in 1933. First, to avoid immediate destitution and starvation, they gave sums eventually totalling three billion dollars of federal money—that is, money from central Government resources—to the almost bankrupt State treasuries. But such direct relief was only a beginning: the Federal Government proceeded to establish a large number of agencies (the most important was the Works Progress Administration, or W.P.A.) to provide jobs for the jobless, to set men to build roads, bridges, dams, parks, schools, and women to make clothing or to teach in nursery schools. Youngsters who had just left school drained swamps, cleared trails, planted trees and otherwise fought soil erosion in the Civilian Conservation Corps, or C.C.C. Musicians were set to give concerts, artists to paint pictures, actors to put on plays, authors to write books. Many an American farmer had already lost his land in the depression, having been unable to keep up his mortgage payments; to help those who were still struggling, Roosevelt rushed through a Bill a fortnight after his inauguration to relieve the pressure of mortgages and to increase the value of bank loans to farmers. A similar Bill protected house-purchasers, whose hire-purchase payments were collapsing in April 1933 at the rate of a thousand a day; they were given lower interest rates, and protection against forfeiting their houses. An Emergency Banking Act guaranteed bank deposits up to 5000 dollars (later 10,000) for each account, and kept the banks themselves afloat with Federal loans. Agencies were set up to make it easier to obtain credit. By the National Industrial Recovery Act (N.I.R.A) a huge attempt was begun to stabilize production, maintain wages, and regulate conditions and hours of labour. Within two years it had set up five hundred industrial codes under the stamp of the N.R.A. "Blue Eagle." Again, within a few weeks of inauguration Roosevelt and his "ginger groups" had launched the huge Tennessee Valley Authority (T.V.A.), which provided perhaps the most permanent of all the New Deal's monuments; as John Gunther wrote:

> It was a project for harnessing a hitherto savage and obstreperous river in seven states and developing its valley for the people as a whole. It . . . touched everything in its watershed from reforestation and reclamation to cheap electric power, from flood control and rural education to the most advanced techniques in agriculture. Its real essence, which F.D.R. seized at once, was its attempt to get man and nature working together to restore life to the land.

"Pure socialism," objected Roosevelt's enemies—as indeed it largely was—but the farmers, industrialists, and housewives from the basin of the Tennessee, six hundred miles of it, with their secure flood control, cheap power, and flourishing new industries, did not press the political objection over-hard.

Not that the President had to meet much opposition in the first honeymoon period of the New Deal—the Hundred Days from March to June 1933. He was an idol, a national saviour. His consummate radio technique brought him, a live, sympathetic, vigorous man, into every home in the country. With his gift of explaining things simply but without 'talking down,' his "fireside chats" remained for many years among the strongest weapons in his armoury. Congressmen too were temporarily mesmerized by him into nearly unanimous enthusiasm, and one major Act after another went through with bumper majorities. The new men in his Cabinet, and the chiefs of the dozens of new agencies that he called into existence to operate his programmes, caught his infectious zest. Nothing of the invalid about him beyond his wheel-chair, he was persuasive, indefatigable, gay, and, when necessary, masterful. When committees disagreed he told them to lock themselves up until a solution was reached. "No lunch till they agree!" He frankly advertised his lack of political philosophy or theoretical consistency; every crisis was treated on its merits, one snap judgment following another. He was "playing the situation by ear," happy, he said, if he were right 75 per cent. of the time. But this laughing, red-blooded invalid commanded the sort of admiration which made one Agency chief declare, "After spending an hour with the President I could eat nails for lunch."

It is not in the nature of honeymoons to last, and during 1934 and 1935 Roosevelt began to encounter more opposition. But he pushed ahead with New Deal legislation at a still rapid rate. Some of it, like his agricultural programme, was indeed open to obvious criticism, for in fact, in order to prevent the over-production that had flattened prices in the depression the Federal Government paid farmers money *not* to raise crops, "to kill every third pig, and plough every third row under," as some put it. The Government also rented land from farmers to keep it out of production. In a world where famine was chronic this seemed to many a sad proceeding, but it was not so foolish or wicked as it sounded. Many millions of American acres had been destroyed by over-production of wheat, maize, and cotton, and if now Government subsidies paid the farmer to plant other crops that would hold and reconstitute the soil there might well be smaller yields in the short run but the long-term benefit remained. Even in the short run smaller crops meant higher prices and happier farmers—and consequently happier farmers' wives to spend more in the shops, and hence happier shopkeepers to make happier industrialists and bankers, and fewer unemployed. Recovery was slow and erratic, but it proceeded; the Blue Eagle of the N.R.A. was on every magazine and cover-girl and shop-window through the country; six million were back in jobs by the beginning of 1936. The Social Security Act of 1935 made general for the whole U.S.A. those measures of relief for unemployment, old age, blindness, crippledom, and poverty that some states had already pioneered—though possibly 'pioneered' is hardly the word for a department of political action in which individualist America was notably behind Britain and many other Commonwealth and European countries. (National Health insurance she continues to resist.) In the same year, 1935, there was a tax bill in the Lloyd George manner, with supertax, estate and inheritance taxes, and company and dividend taxes, all designed, as Roosevelt himself put it, to "share the wealth." He might disclaim sympathy with Socialism, but such a Robin Hood of a President could hardly hope to go on being loved by the wealthy, the successful, or the conservative. The Wagner Act of 1935 tended in the same radical direction, encouraging as it did the organization and development of trade unions, and guaranteeing their bargaining rights. If a majority of workers in a factory voted by secret ballot to be represented by a union the employer was now forced to recognize that union; and largely as a result of the Wagner Act, the number of trade unionists in the U.S.A. doubled.

Nobody could do so much so fast and remain every American's hero. Businessmen in particular growled against him and joined the new Liberty Leagues organized against him. Some of his own advisers broke with him. The Hearst Press chain flayed him, and the *Chicago Tribune* roared, "Turn the rascals out!" Al Smith, Roosevelt's predecessor both as Governor of New York and Democratic candidate for the Presidency, accused him of Socialism. Demagogues like Huey Long, the boss of Louisiana, and Father Coughlin, the radio priest of Detroit, who had earlier supported him ("the New Deal is Christ's Deal," said Coughlin), now turned violently against him. Perhaps of many reasons for this sourness developing by late 1935 the most interesting is Roosevelt's attack on the rich; Americans had been accustomed to venerating the winning of wealth, and Roosevelt's bitterness against the "economic royalists" the "gentlemen in well-warmed and well-stocked clubs," shocked many conventional Americans' ideas—even those who could never belong to those clubs.

Another typically American reaction against Roosevelt came from the vastly increased power his New Deal legislation gave to the Federal Government of Washington as against the jealously guarded rights of the forty-eight states of the Union. The founding fathers of that Union in the eighteenth century had established what they understood to be a necessary and delicate balance both between Federal and states' rights, and between the powers of the Federal Executive (the President), the legislature (the Congress), and the judiciary (the Supreme Court). It was this old and respected constitutional balance that Roosevelt now seemed to be upsetting: Washington was wielding too much power over the individual states, and the Presidential executive was tending to over-balance the other two partners in the constitutional equilibrium. The first whispers against Roosevelt's 'dictatorial' tendencies began to circulate, and indeed he did play heavily on his personal 'image' as the Presidential election of 1936 approached. "There's one issue in this campaign," he told Moley, one of his Brain Trust who had now quarrelled with him. "It's myself, and people must be either for me or against me."

He was re-elected by 523 electoral votes to 8; but the Congress was now by no means willing to eat out of his hand, and, worse still, the Supreme Court of nine Federal judges pledged to uphold the United States Constitution had begun finding his measures illegal. During 1935 one after another of them had been invalidated—including the National Recovery (Blue Eagle) Act—and in January 1936 the great A.A.A. (Agricultural Adjustment Act) had itself been declared unconstitutional. On his re-election Roosevelt proposed to Congress a plan by which for every Supreme Court justice who failed to quit the Bench at the age of seventy, the President could appoint one new judge (up to a total of six). These "Nine Old Men" —their average age was seventy-one—were, he declared, not the guardians but the "sappers and miners" of the Constitution, the friends of privilege, and foes of progress. Again the parallel is there (and Roosevelt realized it) with Lloyd George and the Liberal attempt to force the creation of sympathetic peers in the struggle of 1911. But the British House of Lords, though an ancient institution, was never sacred. Roosevelt found to his cost that the American Constitution was. His proposal looked too much like 'packing' the Court; it was too clever by half; it smelled of dictatorship. In 1937, however, one of the nine judges transferred his vote in favour of further New Deal bills, so that 5-4 against became 5-4 in favour; this was the "switch in time that saved nine." The Wagner Act and the Social Security Act were both accepted; but now, more than ever, Congress would not have Roosevelt's judicial reform, and the episode closed with a curious balance for the President of victory and defeat. Democratic Congress had defied him; but as several of the judges soon retired he was in fact able to replace them with New Dealers.

It was not only on the Supreme Court issue that Roosevelt ran into difficulties. The heroic days of 1933 would never come again. Then the nation would welcome any actions, even contradictory actions as many of Roosevelt's were, so long as they *were actions*. But when a trade recession again hit the U.S.A. in 1937–38, the old magic seemed to have deserted the President: one day he talked as in 1933 of vast spending programmes, the next of economies to balance the budget. Again he listened to the rival experts, but the old intuitive decisions were not there. Congress growled critically; the Press, "all the fat-cat newspapers—85 per cent. of the whole," as he himself grumbled, were against him. John L. Lewis, the most powerful of trade union bosses, attacked him for remaining neutral in the strikes of 1938; in view of Lewis's electoral support in 1936 he regarded such neutrality as ingratitude. Businessmen by now regarded him as the devil's agent. Unemployment reached nine to ten million by 1938, and even the New Dealers had doubts of him, sensing his shifts and hesitations. Only the ordinary, and especially the poor, Americans never swayed in their allegiance. Still he was the master of the mass audience, the fireside radio chat, the cross-country tour. When in Marietta, Ohio, a little old woman knelt down and patted the dust of his footprints, the gesture symbolized the reverence of the many. Newspapermen, Congressmen, union leaders, businessmen might assail him—but the American people would never fail to vote for him.

By these domestically troubled years of 1937 and 1938 foreign affairs were beginning for the first time to challenge for a leading place among America's and Roosevelt's worries. In a sense they were easier than economic affairs. Good and wise men might have opposite theories of how to fight a trade recession, but no good or wise American could sympathize with Nazi persecution or with Japanese aggressions in China. In a vital sense, however, it was more difficult for Roosevelt to give leadership in foreign than domestic affairs. To the average American Hitler and Mussolini were deplorable but they were distant; the Japanese were wicked to attack the Chinese, but it was inconceivable that they would ever attack the Americans. Hence war was something that happened to other nations. Once before, certainly, through the folly of American leaders, the U.S.A. had sent its boys over to fight a European war; but that could never happen again: America lay secure and militarily invulnerable behind her two oceans. Hence when Roosevelt followed up earlier warnings to the Americans that they could not "hide their heads in the sand" with a strong anti-Axis speech in 1937 demanding that the aggressors should be "put in quarantine," the outburst against him was so loud that he was forced to soft-pedal. He was a wily enough campaigner not to fall into Woodrow Wilson's error of getting too far in advance of popular opinion. A great mountain of Isolationism had first to be nibbled and scratched away before America could begin to think of taking sides in foreign quarrels. It is easy now to accuse Roosevelt of timidity, compromise, and 'double-talk' in these years when the nations were rushing downhill to ruin, but, conscious as he was of Wilson's shadow ever behind him, he had to make haste slowly and with infinite subtlety. As for himself, he had few doubts after early 1937, still fewer after Hitler's seizure of Austria. About that time he said to Admiral Leahy, "Bill, there is going to be a war, and I am going to need you."

Most Republicans, and many Democrats, were determined to tie his hands so that he *could* not drag America into the coming war. In 1937 Congress voted for a Neutrality Act banning trade with, or loans to, any nation at war (not merely *aggressor* nations, as Roosevelt proposed); and three times they reaffirmed this policy. In the Far East Roosevelt contented himself with subsidies to Chiang Kai-shek in return for promises of continuing resistance to the Japanese. As for Europe, Roosevelt and his Secretary of State, Hull, could do little more than issue a series of moral protests against the enormities of Hitler. "No risks, no commitments," was still the order of the day—though Roosevelt and Hull both knew that these were mere politicians' phrases, and some critics were furious with the President for his caution and lack of leadership. One wrote, "Why

don't you tell our idol F.D.R. to quit beating around the bush, get
on the radio, and be honest with his people?. . . *Of course* we cannot
afford to let France and England get licked. *Of course* we should
prepare to help them. . . . Why stall around? Why let these pussy-
footing Senators kid the American public into the belief that we could
stay out of another war? Why not talk brutal realism to the American people *before* it is too late?" But this was not the Roosevelt
way at all. "Thank him very much," he told his secretary. "Say
delighted to get it, and it came just before I left for the cruise."
Secretly he facilitated Anglo-French purchase of American planes;
and when the secret leaked out the isolationists raised the inevitable
hullabaloo. When a Senator reported him as privately giving the
opinion that the frontier of the U.S.A. lay on the Rhine he denied it,
all the same knowing that it was true. He seriously considered raising the embargo on arms to the anti-fascist forces in the Spanish
Civil War, but the threatened loss of Catholic votes, Hull's opposition, and his own indecision held him back. In the Munich crisis he
could do little more than issue naïve appeals for peace, repeated
again as the stormclouds gathered again in the summer of 1939.
Then, at 2.50 A.M. on September 1, 1939, a phone call from Bullitt,
his Ambassador in Paris, awoke him to report, "Tony Biddle has
just got through from Warsaw, Mr President. Several German divisions are deep in Polish territory and fighting is heavy. Tony said
there were reports of bombers over the city. Then he was cut off. . . ."
"Well, Bill," said Roosevelt, "it's come at last. God help us all."

Could Roosevelt have prevented the war by bolder leadership of
peace-loving nations in 1937–39? Many have said yes, but perhaps
it is not an answerable question. Roosevelt was not a Stalin who
could manipulate his public opinion by the flick of a propaganda
switch. True, he failed to bring his people along fast enough—but
politics is the art of the possible, and perhaps it was not possible
for the elephant of American public opinion to learn to jump
through unaccustomed hoops so quickly. It is a weakness of democracies that they cannot always move fast in the right direction—but
then it is a worse weakness of dictatorships that they *can* move fast
in the wrong direction.

In a radio fireside chat he immediately notified the Axis that they
must not expect neutrality of thought. Then at last the Neutrality
Act was amended, but only to permit "cash and carry"—that is,
permission for British and French ships to come to the U.S.A. to
purchase arms for cash. Two Republicans, Stimson and Knox, were
taken into his Cabinet to be in charge of the War and Navy depart-

ments. He set his country the target of 50,000 military planes a year, and promised the Allies every "aid short of war."

Meantime came the 1940 thunderbolts, the collapse of Western Allies, Dunkirk, the fall of France, the siege of Britain. All this plunged Americans into acute psychological crisis, which helps to explain their almost hysterical admiration for the British stand of 1940–41. What in fact was the U.S.A. to do, faced by a world dominated everywhere but in America by totalitarian tyranny? How resist a breathless, fearful hope for the one small remaining bastion of "Christian civilization," Britain? How keep admiration and relief within reasonable bounds when the Nazi trumpets sounded but the walls of Jericho, the cliffs of Dover, held firm? The President acted with increasing boldness, as always a modest way, but not too far, ahead of the nation: knowing that Congress would "raise hell about this," but knowing equally that delay might be fatal, he gave Britain, without Congress's permission, fifty over-age destroyers in return for the use of British bases in the Western Atlantic; "of all the real-estate deals in history," said the St Louis *Post-Dispatch*, "this is the worst.... Mr Roosevelt to-day became America's first dictator." Next he persuaded Congress (but only just) to pass a Selective Service Act, introducing a form of military conscription; on the very day of the first great fire-raid on the City of London he broadcast the famous fireside chat to persuade the American people that they must become "the arsenal of democracy." By this time (December 1940) his attitude was, on the opposing side, very similar to Mussolini's active non-belligerent support. The isolationists roared their disapproval: he was dragging America into the slaughter. An America First Committee was organized; Senators Borah, Johnson, and Wheeler denounced him fiercely and persistently; Colonel McCormick's chronically anti-British *Chicago Tribune* screamed at him daily; and, perhaps most influential of all, Colonel Lindbergh, ex-hero of the first lone transatlantic flight, and a legend in his own way as potent as Roosevelt himself, said, early in 1941, "This war is lost..." and again, only "the British, the Jews, and the Roosevelt administration" wanted war.

Between 1936 and 1939 it had been assumed that Roosevelt would respect the old tradition that forbade an American president to run for more than two terms. Roosevelt himself had signed a contract to become an editor of *Collier's* magazine at 75,000 dollars a year on his retirement, in 1941. The war, however, changed everything, and he did not need much persuading to run for a third term, loving power as he did, and rightly convinced, as he was, of his own abilities—although his acceptance lost him many friends, and confirmed the old fears of a would-be dictator. The Republicans, after a bitter struggle within the Party, nominated Wendell Willkie to fight him, a big-business man but another pro-Allied anti-isolationist. A current Bob Hope joke was, "Willkie has his eye on the Presidential chair, but look what Roosevelt has on it!" As it happened, Willkie did better in the election than any other of Roosevelt's opponents, polling over 22 million votes against Roosevelt's 27¼ million. This third-term campaign, begun during the Battle of Britain, culminated during the London blitz; and although Englishmen had taken to Willkie, they did not bother to conceal their relief at the return of Roosevelt, whom they felt now to be a trusty friend—and never had there been such another hour of need. Although it was probably true that Roosevelt's continuing electoral success was due rather to working-class support for the New Deal tradition than to the President's foreign policy, it is equally true that after 1940 the New Deal remained *only* a tradition. No new domestic legislation of any importance was to follow now; Roosevelt had now to conciliate the big-business men, without whom he could not get the necessary productivity to win the war. As he himself put it a little later, "Dr New Deal," the old family physician, had to call in a new partner, "an orthopaedic surgeon named Dr Win the War."

Still in 1941 it was to be won by foreigners, not Americans. "Your boys are not going to be sent into any foreign wars," proclaimed Roosevelt during the election campaign (perhaps a little equivocally, for just what was a *foreign* war?). Still America was only to be the "arsenal of democracy," and Churchill was proclaiming, "Give us the tools and we will finish the job," while Roosevelt's emissary in London, Harry Hopkins, was telling Churchill, "Roosevelt sent me here to tell you that at all costs and by all means he will carry you through." In January 1941 the President enunciated what he considered to be America's aims in aiding the Allies: to ensure in the post-war world the Four Freedoms—freedom of speech, freedom of religion, freedom from want, freedom from fear; and he followed this up with the Lend-Lease proposal—the daring suggestion that American supplies should be made freely available to all nations fighting against aggression, regardless of whether they could afford to pay for them. The matter had become urgent since British gold and dollar reserves were becoming exhausted. Churchill, with his mouth ever at Roosevelt's sympathetic ear, had put the stark facts before him in the bluntest terms, and having placed the ball at the President's feet, waited for the President to kick it. Roosevelt knew Congress would not repeal the Neutrality Act outright, but hit upon the brilliant brain-wave of Lend-Lease; the ball was indeed kicked to some purpose. If comparison is made with Coolidge's classical comment about the American loans during the First World War—"They hired the money, didn't they?"—the difference of approach is highlighted. Roosevelt's innovation marked the beginning of a series of imaginative American moves—Lend-Lease, Marshall Aid, the Point Four programme of aid to underdeveloped lands—to use their vast wealth and resources to hold disaster at bay by the exercise of generosity that was also enlightened self-interest. The enemy varied—Nazism, Communism, Malnutrition—but the principle remained constant, and although many factors bedevilled post-war politics, bitterness over debt repayments was, thanks to Lend-Lease, not one of them. An immediate advantage to America of sending abroad foodstuffs, lorries, jeeps, aeroplanes, and so forth instead of mere loans was that this helped to promote a rapid and vital expansion of American production, which was going to be essential to the winning of the "shooting war" that Roosevelt now knew must come. He proceeded to act more and more toughly, occupying bases in Greenland and Iceland, giving orders to American destroyers to convoy Allied merchant ships (it was the heyday of the submarines' triumph, and they were sinking British merchant ships three times as fast as we could build them), seizing German and Japanese ships in American ports, bringing all trade with Japan to an end, and extending Lend-Lease aid to Russia when Hitler attacked her at midsummer. On October 31 a German submarine sank the U.S. destroyer *Reuben James*, and Roosevelt went on the air to announce, "America has been attacked. ... The shooting has started."

But all this was soon to be forgotten amid the earthquake shock of Pearl Harbour. At the very moment when two Japanese representatives were in Washington going through the motions of trade negotiations with the Secretary of State, Hull, powerful forces of Japanese carrier-borne aircraft moved in to strike suddenly and overwhelmingly at the main U.S. Pacific fleet in Pearl Harbour, Hawaii. In a few minutes five battleships were destroyed and three more damaged, as well as a number of smaller ships—a temporarily paralysing blow, and easily the greatest the American Navy ever suffered. But even the events of December 7, 1941, did not rob Roosevelt of his sleep; this imperturbably confident man, wrote Harry Hopkins, "as ever, had a good night's sleep." He arose to go down to the Congress, and make a six-minute speech to the effect that since "yesterday, December 7, 1941, a day that will live in infamy," the United States of America was in a state of war with Japan.

A braced and united people was reflected in the reactions of a united Congress—united at last by the folly and perfidy of the Japanese blow: Isolationists and New Dealers cheered the President together. Three days later Germany and Italy declared war on the United States.

For about another year the disasters multiplied. Japan's treacherous gamble had given her for a time control of the Pacific, and she proceeded to consolidate huge conquests: Hongkong, Indo-China, Burma, Thailand (Siam), Malaya, Singapore, Sumatra, Java, Borneo, Celebes, Timor, the Philippines, northern New Guinea and New Britain, and countless island bases in the southern Pacific, including Wake and Midway Islands and the Gilberts and Solomons. By the end of 1942 the Japanese were at the gates of India and Australia. In the Philippines American Marines under General MacArthur put up tough, devoted, and skilful resistance until Roosevelt *ordered* MacArthur to escape from Corregidor. A hero in adversity, MacArthur survived to lead the great come-back of United States forces in 1943–45, and was perhaps the supreme American idol of the war. As an example of the skill and punch of Roosevelt's radio propaganda, his broadcast after Corregidor may testify:

> ... From Berlin, Rome, and Tokyo we have been described as a nation of weaklings—"playboys"—who would hire British soldiers, or Russian soldiers, or Chinese soldiers to do our fighting for us.
> Let them repeat that now!
> Let them tell that to General MacArthur and his men.
> Let them tell that to the sailors who to-day are hitting hard in the far waters of the Pacific.
> Let them tell that to the boys in the Flying Fortresses.
> Let them *tell that to the Marines!*

That last line (originating from Robert Sherwood, the dramatist, now among his top speech-drafters) was surely ideally calculated to rouse the patriotic scorn of a now very angry America: rather in the vein of Churchill's "We are waiting for the invasion. So are the fishes."

The two great men saw a good deal of one another during the last four years of the war, and corresponded endlessly, with mutual friendliness and respect, on a baffling array of strategic problems. In general, Roosevelt left military matters to the experts; but frequently the experts did not agree, and Roosevelt had to become mediator and arbiter. Frequently, too, Churchill and he did not see eye to eye

—though on the most important issue of priorities they did agree within a week or two of Pearl Harbour: Germany must come first and Japan second, which must mean the continuing humiliation of American pride in the Pacific area through long and anxious months. On the question of an Allied landing in France (Operation Overlord), Roosevelt brought constant pressure to bear on Churchill, as did Stalin; but Churchill was adamant, and persuaded Roosevelt that 1943 would be premature and disastrous for such an immense task. The President agreed with Churchill, however, against some of his own advisers (including General Marshall), that 1942–43 should see the American landings in North Africa, the squeeze on Axis North Africa, and the southern attack on the "soft underbelly" of Hitler's Europe.

He worked prodigiously hard, taxing to the utmost the vigour of his great frame (great from the waist up). He was Commander-in-Chief of the armed forces, Chief Executive of civilian administration, including the vast industrial apparatus of war-time America, and ornamental Head of State: a staggering concentration of work and responsibility. But above all this, like Wilson before him, he always kept before him the problem of what was to happen when peace arrived. The high principles of the Atlantic Charter may have been casually drawn up by Roosevelt and Churchill aboard their mid-Atlantic warship and scribbled down on scraps of paper, but it was like Roosevelt to think such a statement of war aims necessary at all. It was like him also to get all the Allies (even Russia!) to subscribe to them, and form themselves into the United Nations (1942). His mind was always looking forward to the urgent, immediate post-war task of getting food, and especially fats, to the people of Axis-occupied lands. Flying low over Arabia to the Teheran conference in 1943, he catechized an army engineer in the plane with him on the subject of the land's poverty and lack of water. "They really ought to be able to raise food," he said. "There must be a way if there is water underneath the soil. . . . Look what the Jews have done in Palestine. . . ." Then, after a pause, "When I get through being President of the U.S., and this damn' war is over, I think Eleanor and I will go to the Near East and see if we can manage to put over an operation like the Tennessee Valley system that will really make something of that country. . . ." Naïve comment, no doubt, and typical of his boundless self-confidence; but typical too of his endless quest for betterment, his passion for the big, beneficent idea.

Frances Perkins, his Labour Minister, who tells this story, tells also another that shines a light through the man.

At the Teheran conference Roosevelt first met Stalin. He had conferred with Churchill many times by now, in mid-Atlantic, at Quebec, Washington, Casablanca, and Cairo; at Cairo too he conferred with Chiang Kai-shek. But now, in 1943, with North Africa conquered, Italy in dissolution, and Stalingrad won, the time had come to get to grips with the other giant, Stalin's Russia, that Roosevelt (like Churchill) had supported directly she was at war with Hitler—on the principle of supporting the lesser to drive out the greater evil. Roosevelt told Frances Perkins how discouraged he felt at first, not being able to cut any ice with Stalin, who was "correct, stiff, solemn, not smiling." Was it, perhaps, thought Roosevelt, because Stalin considered that Churchill and Roosevelt, so easy together with their common language and traditions, were 'ganging up' on him? In fact, Roosevelt, though he liked and admired Churchill, was always teasing and jollying him, in Christian-name terms, about his Toryism and Imperialism; and he genuinely considered—pro-British as his policy had been—that the British lion should be kept firmly within its cage. But perhaps Stalin might not understand this? Perhaps the Roosevelt charm could melt that Russian ice?

> On my way to the conference-room [he told Miss Perkins], we caught up with Winston, and I just had a moment to say to him, "Winston, I hope you won't be sore at me for what I am going to do." Winston just shifted his cigar and grunted. I must say he behaved very decently afterwards. I began almost as soon as we got into the conference-room. I talked privately with Stalin . . . quite chummy and confidential, enough so that the other Russians joined us to listen. Still no smile. Then I said, lifting my hand up to cover a whisper (which of course had to be interpreted), "Winston is cranky this morning, he got up on the wrong side of the bed." A vague smile passed over Stalin's eyes, and I decided I was on the right track. As soon as I sat down at the conference-table I began to tease Churchill about his Britishness, about John Bull, about his cigars, about his habits. It began to register with Stalin. Winston got red and scowled, and the more he did so, the more Stalin smiled. Finally Stalin broke out into a deep, hearty guffaw, and for the first time in three days I saw light. . . . It was then that I called him "Uncle Joe" . . . The ice was broken and we talked like men and brothers.

In all this his motives were admirable; the two post-war giants must learn to live together if the world were to have peace. But his words do betray a certain intellectual simplicity, a failure to comprehend the Russian's methods, ambitions, and preconceptions. Roosevelt may have melted a little superficial ice upon this Soviet iceberg, but how deep was the solid matter below sea-level! And Churchill, however "decently" he behaved, was offended and furious; he surmised that one could not circumvent Soviet designs by "chumminess." Even Roosevelt was not entirely complacent about his conquest. "I wish somebody would tell me about the Russians, I don't know a good Russian from a bad Russian . . . I just don't know what makes them tick. I wish I could study them. Frances, see if you can find what makes them tick." And she did, giving him a little digest of some good books. He read them and was fascinated.

The next conference was at Yalta, in the Crimea, early in 1945. American naval forces, with their Commonwealth allies, were fighting their way back across the Pacific, island-hopping their air and sea bases ever nearer the Japanese homeland. The battle of Leyte Gulf, perhaps the greatest sea battle of all history, a struggle of giants between the two great fleets of aircraft carriers, had brought MacArthur to the point of re-occupying the Philippines. From Iwojima, captured in February, and Okinawa, captured after savage fighting in March 1945, it was only a few hundred miles by bomber to Tokyo—or to Hiroshima. In Europe Hitler's monstrous edifice was visibly crumbling to ruin, with Stalin's forces on the Oder and Eisenhower's on the Rhine; the main question was, what was to happen after the final crash? Roosevelt, just re-elected for a fourth term, was nevertheless a sadly declining man. He had been warned by doctors to take more rest, but he had worn himself out in his superhuman tasks. "One man simply could not do it all," said one of his Cabinet, "and Franklin Roosevelt killed himself trying." At Yalta he shocked friends who had not recently seen him by his sunken face, his trembling hands, and, as Churchill put it, "a transparency . . . a far-away look in his eyes." He was still as charming as ever, and gay despite his frailty. He was full of the conviction that he had put into his fourth Inaugural speech—"We can gain no lasting peace if we approach it with suspicion and with mistrust—or with fear." But Stalin was full of suspicion; Churchill was heavy with mistrust; and the many people whose future these men were ratifying had good reason to fear their decisions, for the Red Army had already occupied Poland, and was wreaking its terrible vengeance through East Germany. An Iron Curtain was already a fact, and no friendly words could dispel it. Compromises were certainly reached, but Stalin gained most of the advantages; and to some extent he had to be appeased, for his promise of help was still thought necessary to finish off the still undefeated Japan. At this moment the shattering finale of the atomic bombs could hardly be anticipated. "Stalin? I can handle that old buzzard!" said Roosevelt. But he was too optimistic, too confident that he could win the co-operation that all humane and liberal men in the West assumed to be the only sanity. He made a generous, and, as it turned out, a bad bargain: Stalin ended with control of Poland, Hungary, the Balkans, Germany east of the Elbe (apart from the West's precarious foothold in Berlin), with effective occupation of Czechoslovakia at a crucial time, with the Kurile Islands and half of Sakhalin in the Far East—in return for less than a week of nominal war against Japan. The return was to be goodwill. It was not there.

Roosevelt returned a dying man. He went down to his beloved Warm Springs, in Georgia, and there died, on April 12, 1945, a few weeks before Hitler destroyed himself in the Berlin bunker. Their careers had been strangely contemporary, parallel—and opposite. Perhaps nations get the saviours they deserve.

More than three years after his death, when all the world expected a Republican victory in the 1948 elections—for all the Gallup polls chorused together—and Harry Truman, Roosevelt's second-in-command, won his sensational and undreamed-of victory (undreamed-of, that is, except by Truman), the London *Times* headed its leading article, "Roosevelt's Fifth Term." It was a comment that would have delighted the old campaigner, the idealist whose explicit ambition was, as his wife wrote, "to make life better for the average man, woman, and child," but who was also the greatest vote-winner in the whole of American history.

Table of Events

1901–9.   Theodore Roosevelt President.
1913.   Wilson President; Franklin Roosevelt Under Secretary for the Navy.
1917.   U.S.A. enters First World War.
1920.   Wilson, the League of Nations, and Treaty of Versailles rejected by U.S.A.
1921.   Roosevelt crippled by polio.
1924.   Roosevelt at Warm Springs, Georgia.
1921–29. Republican administrations of Harding and Coolidge.
1929.   Wall Street Crash.
1929–33. Hoover President.
          Roosevelt Governor of New York State.
1932.   Roosevelt elected President.
1933.   Lowest point of the Great Depression.
          Roosevelt's Hundred Days: the New Deal begun.
          Agricultural Adjustment Act (A.A.A.).
          Works Progress Administration (W.P.A.).

National Industrial Recovery Act (N.I.R.A., N.R.A.).
Civilian Conservation Corps (C.C.C.).
Tennessee Valley Authority (T.V.A.).
1935. Social Security Act.
Wagner Act.
Neutrality Act.
1936. Roosevelt re-elected for second term.
1937. Battle with the Supreme Court.
1940. Destroyers-for-bases deal.
"Arsenal of democracy" broadcast.
Roosevelt re-elected for third term.
1941. Atlantic Charter.
Lend-Lease Act.
American destroyers operating in Atlantic.
(December) Japanese attack Pearl Harbour.
U.S.A. at war with Japan, Germany, and Italy.
1942. Loss of the Philippines.
Casablanca conference.
American forces land in North Africa.
1943. Teheran conference.
Anglo-American forces invade Italy.
1944. Air-sea battle of Leyte Gulf.
Americans return to Philippines.
Anglo-American landings in Normandy.
Roosevelt re-elected for fourth term.
1945. Yalta conference.
Russian and American forces meet on river Elbe.
(April) Death of Roosevelt, Truman President.

9

Joseph Stalin

(1879–1953)

Joseph Djugashvili, who later used many names, among them that of Stalin, was not a true Russian, but a Caucasian from the province of Georgia, the son of a bootmaker of a small town near Tiflis. Georgia boasted an honourable ancient civilization, but by the nineteenth century was so backward that the Russians came to it as colonists and civilizers. They built roads and railways; they brought their language and literature; they brought, not least, their fermenting social and revolutionary theories, and even their political prisoners—for distant Georgia, like Siberia or Australia, did very well for a land of exile. The young Joseph Djugashvili was lucky to pick up the Russian tongue at a very tender age, but his parental language was Georgian. His appearance too, especially in youth, was Middle-Eastern rather than European. He grew up in a half-tribal, half-feudal atmosphere, where mountain gang warfare still flourished, and serfdom was still normal. Russia in 1879, the year of Stalin's birth, was backward enough, but Georgia was centuries behind even Russia.

One institution the Georgians had long shared with the Russians: the Christian Orthodox Church, and it was to the seminary in Tiflis, conducted by Orthodox monks—the best school in Georgia—that Djugashvili went at the age of fifteen. The seminary was in fact the only advanced school in Georgia—strict, in the manner of monastic schools, austere, almost military in atmosphere. One of the pre-occupations of the monks was the task of suppressing the enthusiasm of the boys for banned literature and Georgian nationalism. Just before Djugashvili's arrival a headmaster had been assassinated; it is perhaps not surprising that the monks systematically spied on their pupils just as the secret police spied on Russians in general, both in Tsarist days and under Stalin's own rule. It was, after all, the atmosphere in which he, even more than most Russian citizens, had been brought up. When a search of Joseph Djugashvili's belongings disclosed a public-library book and ticket he was duly reported and confined to the punishment cell. He himself later wrote of the school's "harsh intolerance and Jesuitical discipline," and of the atmosphere that was "saturated with hatred of Tsarist oppression"; but he perhaps was not conscious of the invaluable training that the Tiflis seminary gave him in cunning and deceit.

By the time he was nineteen he had moved beyond the patriotic Georgian revolutionary movement to a socialist secret society that met in the town of Tiflis. He was reported upon as being argumentative and disrespectful; and finally, failing to present himself for his examinations, he was expelled in 1899 at the age of twenty.

Now his whole energies were directed towards the work of the Socialist underground movement; it organized a railway strike; it held secret meetings; it celebrated May Day; it dodged the secret police. But in 1901 Djugashvili's share in all this was discovered; and though he managed to escape arrest, he had to leave Tiflis and adopt the rôle which was to be his for the next sixteen years: that of the hunted, anonymous, professional agitator and revolutionary journalist, moving from Tiflis to Batum to Baku, from the Caucasus to St Petersburg, to Finland, to Vienna, to wherever the latest Socialist conference was being held, repeatedly being deported to Siberia and repeatedly escaping, adopting one *nom de guerre* after another—first Koba, after a legendary Georgian hero, then Ivanovich, and a dozen others, and at last Stalin, the man of steel. It was a strange, dedicated existence, as dedicated as any priest's. As much as with a monk, it meant the abandonment of domestic life and the pleasures of the world. It is true that Stalin married early in life, but his wife died early, and not until 1918, after the revolution, when he was nearly forty, did Stalin marry again.

In the great arguments and quarrels among the Socialist exiles in the early years of the century Stalin was the devoted supporter and protégé of Lenin. Stalin was a strong Bolshevik in the quarrel with the Mensheviks; he was more Leninist than Lenin himself in the insistence upon doctrinal uniformity: he had not been to theological college for nothing. He who fights for the Party must accept one hundred per cent. of the Party's rulings. In the matter of bank and train robberies to raise funds for the Party, Stalin played a part typical of his character and career. He was early on made provincial organizer in the Caucasus of the armed raiders, the squads of robbers who entered so enthusiastically into the business of building up the Party's treasury that many members protested against their criminal activities. Stalin, however, was the organizer of his local branch, never the actual raider: in a position of secrecy, control, and authority; wielder of power from a position of obscurity. These were the days when the sporadic Revolution of 1905 was rumbling on in the aftermath of 1906 and 1907. To historians it is "the Revolution of 1905"; to Stalin, in Georgia, it was a protracted three-year campaign of raids, strikes and above all of illegal journalism, to keep the flames of revolt alight. He wholeheartedly defended "arming the proletariat," and using all necessary violence when his "explosives department" was expanding its activities in 1905–6 to real guerrilla warfare—"only on the bones of the oppressors can the people's freedom be founded—only the blood of the oppressors can fertilize the soil for the people's self-rule." Before a Party congress finally condemned the "fighting squads" of the Caucasus and elsewhere they had carried out some thousands of raids—over a thousand in Stalin's Caucasus alone between 1905 and 1908, including the most famous coup of all—the seizure in a Tiflis square of a quarter of a million Government roubles.

Seven of the next ten years before the 1917 Revolution were to be spent in, or escaping from, prison and internment. For a time he carried on his underground agitation in the Caucasus (the very printing-press had been raided from a newspaper office); he was writing in Russian now, not Georgian, and his was one of the few resident Communist voices reaching Lenin and his fellow-leaders in distant exile; and although they could hardly have regarded this Koba-Ivanovich-Stalin as a 'big gun' of their heavily intellectual revolutionary Party, he had this and other advantages to bring him to notice. Not only was he resident in Russia, but he was a genuine proletarian, a son of parents who had been born serfs (unlike nearly all the other leaders). Further, this Georgian was more and more being regarded by Lenin as an expert on the problem of minority national groups, and it was in due course as Commissar for Nationalities that Stalin took his place in 1917 in Lenin's first revolutionary Government.

He was arrested, in 1907, in the town of Baku. Still regarded as only a minor trouble-maker, from his skill in remaining obscure, he received a comparatively mild sentence of deportation to Vologda province—cold and inhospitable, but after all not Siberia. He caught typhus, recovered, escaped after four months, and duly reappeared in Baku. He had a further run for his money before being re-sentenced—but again only lightly. A third time in due course Stalin was arrested, in St Petersburg, on the very day that the first number appeared of the famous paper of which he was the first editor: *Pravda* (*Truth*). This time his exile was to Western Siberia, but he stayed only two months before escaping, and was soon back among the faithful in Cracow and Vienna. Returning to St Petersburg, he was betrayed by a police spy, yet once more arrested (disguised as a woman), and this time paid the compliment of a full four years' sentence in the grimmest far north of Siberia. Here he lived among the settlers and the native hunters, and managed to survive the long bitter Arctic winters. He hunted and he fished; he read such books as were available; he received every few months a batch of letters and newspapers or a parcel. Early on came news of the outbreak of the First World War, and sometimes he would go by dog-sleigh many miles over the stark tundra to a Socialist convicts' meeting to discuss the opportunities the war offered. But mainly he was a recluse. He wrote little and brooded much. He survived.

Then came the dazzling news of the February Revolution of 1917, and the overthrow of the Tsar's Government; and Stalin was one of the first Communist leaders to arrive back in St Petersburg—three weeks ahead of Lenin. He resumed the editorship of *Pravda*, assumed temporary chairmanship of the Central Committee, and was careful to adopt a middle-of-the-road attitude between the two bickering wings of the Party. When Lenin returned from exile, however, in April, and launched his furious, uncompromising revolutionary line, Stalin faithfully followed his leader; yet when after the abortive Bolshevik rising of July (the July Days), Lenin and the other principal leaders were forced yet once more to go to ground (this time in Finland), Stalin, the relatively unknown, again emerged temporarily as the leader of the Party. Again his very lack of brilliance served him well, while Lenin, Zinoviev, Kamenev, Lunarcharsky, Trotsky, and the others who were his apparent betters and seniors all were forced into exile or thrust into prison. A month later he presided at a Party congress that re-admitted the Menshevik Trotsky and his supporters to the Bolshevik fold. In October Stalin once more supported Lenin, Trotsky, and the other seven members who voted (against Kamenev and Zinoviev) for armed insurrection. This backsliding and timidity on the part of Zinoviev and Kamenev, although they later backed Stalin in his great struggle against Trotsky, they were to pay dearly for. It was to prove in the ripeness of time a powerful lever against them, and Stalin was a man who knew how levers worked.

Although he voted for the uprising and supported its preparation both by speech and in his newspaper, Stalin took very little active part in those "ten days that shook the world." He attacked the timid ones—especially the writer, Maxim Gorky—who sided with

Zinoviev and Kamenev, but he played in the revolution itself a small part compared with Lenin's and Trotsky's. In Trotsky's own words, "He waited for others to take the initiative, took note of their weaknesses and mistakes, and himself lagged behind developments. . . . He listened and observed with malevolence, but sharply and vigilantly." Trotsky, who had reason to be bitter by the time he wrote these words, even accuses Stalin of sitting on the fence through the days of the revolution and re-insuring himself against its failure. "In the event of failure he could tell Lenin and me and our adherents, 'It's all your fault.'"

But the revolution was a brilliant success, at least to begin with. Lenin could take off his make-up and his wig. Kamenev, the doubter, could preside over the Congress of Soviets that approved the first Council of People's Commissars, among them Stalin as Chief Commissar for Nationalities. It was all, as Lenin said, "easier than lifting a feather." In the councils of the Party Stalin was now advanced above Kamenev and Zinoviev, and inferior only to Lenin, Trotsky, and Sverdlov.

In the brief period before the Treaty of Brest-Litovsk (March 1918) Stalin had an important rôle as Commissar for Nationalities, for he was responsible, under Lenin, for the future status of the one hundred and eighty non-Russian nationalities that made up half the population of the old Russian Empire; but when the Bolsheviks, as the price of peace with Germany, had to surrender all the non-Russian border-lands on the west his job was somewhat cut from under his feet. While it lasted his policy was remarkably liberal. The man who ended his career as tyrant over all the peoples of Eastern Europe began it as the champion of national self-determination. It was he who gave the Finns their independence. It was he who proclaimed the right of Ukrainians and Georgians to secede from Soviet Russia if they wished—and in this Lenin backed him against the criticism of other Communists. "It is unthinkable," Stalin said, "that we should acquiesce in the forcible keeping of any nation within the framework of any state." If they did they would be themselves "the continuers of Tsarist policy." The time had not yet come when it was to be 'revolutionary' for Irish and Indians to wish to break with the British Empire but 'reactionary' for Yugoslavs and Ukrainians and Poles to wish to break with the Russian. By 1921–22 Stalin was already dealing firmly with Georgians and Ukrainians who wished to secede from the Russian State. Indeed, in Tiflis, in 1921, his own home district, he incurred much hostility when he went down and lectured the Georgians on the wicked stupidity of their local Nationalism. But his manipulation of the Georgian Communists was successful; the opposition was bloodlessly purged, and the Caucasus was duly federated within the U.S.S.R. So were many even more backward Asiatic areas, with major economic and social benefit to them all—Tartars, Kirghiz, Daghestanis, Uzbeks, Turkmens, Kazaks, Tajiks. Huge areas previously tribal and primitive began to feel for the first time the breath of an expanding and vigorous civilization—schools, irrigation schemes, ideas of man's equality, and of women's equality with men. Stalin, the "Asiatic," in his time undoubtedly depressed the level of freedom in Europe; but no man did more to transmit Western ideas to the remote vastnesses of Asia.

The revolution was "easier than lifting a feather"; but the civil wars and wars of intervention that followed proved burdens so heavy that the revolution almost broke under their weight. In a sense it did so break: never after 1921—certainly never after the death of Lenin in 1924—did the regime recapture its first flush of idealism. In the civil war Stalin went as political commissar to Tsaritsyn, on the Volga—the city soon to be renamed Stalingrad—where he launched, in his own words, "systematic mass terror against the *bourgeoisie* and its agents." Originally sent to ensure the dispatch of grain supplies from the south to the starving cities—in Moscow and St Petersburg the bread ration was about half a pound a week—Stalin soon became involved in the whole direction of the war in the south, and indirectly in his first big quarrel with Trotsky. Trotsky had convinced Lenin that the Red Army must continue to employ ex-Tsarist officers (despite the dangers of desertion) if it were to maintain any effective military power. Proletarians like Stalin and ex-N.C.O.'s like his friends Budienny and Voroshilov disliked this policy intensely, and instructed Trotsky, the War Minister, to the point of countermanding his orders. The situation in Tsaritsyn was desperate; the city was ringed round with counter-revolutionary Cossacks. Trotsky accused Voroshilov of incompetence and Stalin of exceeding his authority. The ultimate freeing of the city was claimed by Trotsky as a victory for his Red Army command despite the men on the spot, and by Stalin (and all the writers of the Stalin era) as a triumph for Voroshilov and Budienny—and of course Stalin—over the "military gentlemen." The same contempt for the "fine, educated, professional gentlemen" appears with Stalin, the bootmaker's son, as with Hitler, the no-good son of the minor official. The Tsaritsyn legend grew and grew, until Tsaritsyn became Stalingrad, and the huge struggle of 1942, when the city became the scene of the greatest battle in world history, confirmed the old legend and created a new one.

The civil war lasted throughout 1919 and into 1920, piling chaos upon ruin, starvation upon atrocity, nightmare upon horror. Stalin, after the Tsaritsyn episode, went to St Petersburg, to the Caucasus, and many other places threatened by White forces. Although a lesser figure than Trotsky—who was all fire and steel—he played an important part in many local decisions; and Lenin, if not Trotsky, came more and more to value his shrewd judgment, his ability in summing up an awkward situation and acting quickly, his powers of organization and improvisation. For his part in the defence of St Petersburg he was, with Trotsky, awarded the order of the Red Banner. In the Russo-Polish War of 1919 he was at least partly responsible for the disastrous Russian defeat; Trotsky accuses him in his life of Stalin of "waging his own war" and thinking it more important to gain glory for himself by taking Lvov than to help others to capture Warsaw. In the final southern campaign against Wrangel that freed the Crimea and ended the civil wars in 1920 Stalin certainly played an important part in the general direction of strategy, though Trotsky insists that even there he was a "third-rate figure."

Whatever his military stature in the civil wars, he was certainly beginning to gather to himself those diverse civilian powers that were to carry him so soon, upon the death of Lenin, to the dictatorship of the U.S.S.R. In 1919 he became Commissar of the Workers' and Peasants' Inspectorate, an organization set up by Lenin to maintain Party control of the inefficient and by no means Communist civil service. So Stalin controlled the police who spied on the civil service who mismanaged Russia: the system hardly made for simplicity, mutual trust, or efficiency—but it certainly made for Stalin's importance. He was already, of course, a member of the Central Committee of the Party. Now he was, in addition, one of the Polit- bureau of seven—the inner Cabinet; he was also the link between the Politbureau and the Organization Bureau, a kind of Ministry of Labour, with total powers to conscript and direct workers anywhere in Russia; he was in charge of the Control Commission in Moscow that became the supreme arbiter in the purges of corrupt or ineffi- cient local Communist officials—a sort of supreme Party appeal court; and above all, from April 1922, he was General Secretary of the Central Committee of the Communist Party itself, and as such at the very nerve-centre of the great Party web that was being spun all over Russia. Thus, even though perhaps a hundred had heard of

Lenin and Trotsky for every one who had heard of Stalin, already before the death of Lenin the reins of power were slipping quietly into his hands. Had Lenin been an old man, Stalin's rivals for the succession might have been more wary. As it was, when Lenin was struck down it was too late for them to manœuvre; they proved to be themselves flies caught in the web.

The dying Lenin diagnosed the trouble without prescribing a remedy for it. In his "testament," dictated after his second cerebral seizure in December 1922, he forecast the Stalin-Trotsky feud. Trotsky was "personally the most able" of the Central Committee, Stalin the most powerful. "Comrade Stalin, having become General Secretary, has concentrated an enormous power in his hands; and I am not sure that he always knows how to use that power with sufficient caution." Ten days later Lenin added the famous postscript, or codicil, "Stalin is too rude, and this fault ... becomes unbearable in the office of General Secretary. Therefore I propose to the comrades to find a way to remove Stalin from that position and appoint to it another man more loyal, more courteous, and more considerate." The testament was duly read before the Central Committee with Stalin himself sitting on the steps of the rostrum; but the Committee did not remove him from his secretaryship. Lenin then publicly attacked Stalin and his associates for their "arrogance" in Georgia; he dictated a final letter to him, breaking off relations, on March 6, 1923. Three days later he had his third and fatal stroke, and his power to demote Stalin was gone. Trotsky (admittedly a hostile witness) even suggests that when the dying Lenin asked for poison to hasten his inevitable end, Stalin was all too eager to allow him to have it against the judgment of the rest of them. "Ever since, each time I mentally review this scene, I cannot help repeating to myself: Stalin's behaviour, his whole manner, was baffling and sinister. What does the man want? And why doesn't he take that insidious smile off his mask?"

Even while Lenin lay on his death-bed the knives were out and the fight on. Trotsky demanded a relaxation of the bureaucratic machine, a greater degree of freedom. Stalin, supported by Kamenev and Zinoviev, insisted that Russia was no debating society and must have discipline and organization from above; the Party must be "of one piece, a party of steel, monolithic." Further, Stalin and his supporters accused the too-brilliant Trotsky of wishing to be the Bonaparte of his day. They raked up his Menshevik past and his ancient hostility to Lenin, long forgotten in the heat of battle. When Trotsky replied with reminders of the hesitations of Zinoviev and Kamenev in October 1917, although these two may have been singed by such talk, Stalin remained unscathed. Then came the great doctrinal argument over "Socialism in one country," which reverberated round the Soviet Union for two decades. The great "heretic" was Trotsky, and in good time he suffered the excommunication and execution reserved for heretics; though there are many who consider his version of the Marxist-Leninist gospel sounder and purer than that of Pope Stalin. To an outsider the doctrine in debate seems dry, almost academic: must Russian Communists work for world revolution, the so-called "permanent revolution," or could they hope to make their own Russian revolution a success *on its own*, in an isolated Communist Russia? Trotsky stood for the necessity of world revolution as a safeguard for the Russian revolution. But Stalin, in putting forward the slogan "Socialism in one country," gave Russians a sense of something immediate to fight for that was within their grasp. By their own efforts they could build a new and great Russia regardless of what happened in Germany, or Britain, or China. So Trotsky, the theoretician, in the stress of debate forced out of the slow intellect of Stalin, the practical man, its one original contribution to Marxist doctrine.

Trotsky's fall was gradual between the years 1923 and 1929, and it was accomplished with the aid, to begin with, of Zinoviev and Kamenev. By January 1925 Trotsky was forced to resign as War Minister, in October 1926 he was expelled from the Politbureau, and by the close of 1927 he had been expelled from the Party and sent to Alma Ata, in Southern Siberia. He was finally exiled in 1929, to the Turkish island of Prinkipo, and the Comintern (Communist International Organization), to whose authority he had tried to appeal over the head of Stalin, was closed down for six years. But already by 1925 Zinoviev and Kamenev were denouncing "Socialism in one country"; the next year they were siding with the Trotsky that they had helped to pull down, and in 1927 they shared his expulsion and disgrace. By now Stalin had packed the Politbureau (where originally he had been dependent on the support of Zinoviev and Kamenev) with Molotov, Voroshilov, and Kalinin—all good Stalinist yes-men, and he was in a position to oust the remaining old members of the Politbureau who had helped him to get the better of first Trotsky and then Zinoviev and Kamenev. So by 1929 Bukharin, Tomsky, and Rykov (the Premier) were all subject to Stalin's will; and it profited them little that they repudiated their own views and prostrated themselves before the new master. They bought a little time—but they all went down in the grand final settlement, when the knife that had been held at their throat was at last plunged home.

These mortal personal struggles, though they were associated with greed for power, were not quite so sordid as their bare recital suggests. The personal struggles arose out of the desperation of Russia's own struggles—to avert starvation, to achieve industrial independence and expansion, to socialize industry and (much more difficult) agriculture. It was the hectic nature of the prolonged crisis that heightened and embittered the parallel struggle for power.

First, there was the problem of farming. Was the Government again to attempt the nationalization (or collectivization) of the land, after the disastrous failures of 1919–21—or would this again produce a peasants' revolt and starvation? By 1927 Russian farming was in a bad way; food production had never recovered from the shocks of the revolution and war, and the splitting up of the great estates of Tsarist days had merely reduced efficiency. The town populations, hungry and dissatisfied, were grumbling. The peasants were failing to deliver their quotas. It looked as if Russia was caught in a vicious circle of hunger, inefficiency, and unrest. Without food, no tractors; without tractors, no food. Thus, in 1928, Stalin began to take steps which led him personally to extremes of ruthlessness and Russia to a prodigious and tragic crisis. First, he waged war against the kulaks, the small minority of comparatively prosperous farmers who hired the labour of others: the 'capitalists.'

These were to be expropriated—that is, their land, dwellings, and implements were simply to be taken from them without compensation. Further, they were to be scattered and, as a class, exterminated. Excluded from the new collective farms in their own districts, they were herded off to Kazakhstan or Siberia, often simply dumped down at rail-head in the remote wildernesses of the U.S.S.R., and left either to starve or scratch out a new subsistence with their hands. Altogether there were perhaps six millions of kulaks, counting women and children. Very large numbers of them perished. Some survived by digging themselves holes in the ground, and later mud-huts, in the wilderness in which they had been dumped, where the winter temperature sank to forty degrees below zero. And these were the *successful* farmers of the 'twenties. It was the crime of success that made them kulaks, and it was being kulaks that made them enemies of the regime.

Stalin had hoped to win over the poorest peasants to his schemes of collectivization by holding out to them the promise of a share of the kulaks' land and implements, and to begin with, in 1929, things seemed to be going well; so well, that he expanded his plans to embrace the total forced collectivization of all farms. Middle peasants were to be included as well as the nearly destitute muzhiks. This meant the colossal undertaking of depriving twenty to thirty millions of peasants—with their families well over a hundred million people—of their holdings, and forcing them to take their own labour, their beasts and their tools, to the new collective farms. There was rebellion. All over Russia desperate and disillusioned men slaughtered their cattle and horses rather than 'lose' them in the collective farms. At least they could eat a dead cow—even a dead horse. Stalin, meeting resistance with force, mobilized troops and police to terrorize the rebels into accepting their lot, while famine swept through the Ukraine and the great industrial centres. Isaac Deutscher, the best of the biographers of Stalin, relates how he talked at this time to a colonel in the train from Moscow to Kharkov, in the Ukraine. The man was "broken in spirit by his recent experiences in the countryside. 'I am an old Bolshevik,' he said, almost sobbing. 'I worked in the underground against the Tsar, and then I fought in the civil war. Did I do all that in order that I should now surround villages with machine-guns, and order my men to fire indiscriminately into crowds of peasants?' " It is not known how many human beings died of starvation or were killed in the punitive expeditions, but about half the total population of horses, cattle, sheep, and goats were slaughtered. Vast numbers of rebellious peasants were taken into forced labour, where they worked as convicts in timber-felling, mining, navvying, and other heavy pursuits. As they worked (or until they died under the strain) they were 're-educated' in the principles of Stalinist Communism. Temporarily, in 1930, Stalin, faced with total breakdown, called for a slower tempo in collectivization, and even managed to shift some of the blame for the disasters on to his colleagues and subordinates; and when the drive was taken up again it was more cautiously, and with some regard for peasants' human weaknesses—they were allowed inside the collective farm to own their private allotments, up to three cows, and as many pigs and poultry as they could manage.

The huge agricultural battle could not be won without tractors and electricity, without oil and steel; so side by side with this struggle went another—the attempt to revolutionize industry in five years, by means of the first famous Five Year Plan. Here again Stalin had begun as a moderate; but suddenly, in 1929, he became obsessed with giant dreams and ambitions, and then there was no holding him. The Russian people must be harried and bullied and cajoled into superhuman efforts to build "Socialism in one country," and to make the U.S.S.R. another U.S.A., an industrial giant capable of leading or defying the world.

The Five Year Plan was envisaged and prosecuted as a military operation. Its casualties were as prodigious as its scope. The morale of the workers was maintained at concert-pitch by the never-ending barrage of propaganda, itself with a military ring—"shock troops," "workers' brigades," "youth pioneers," the "iron-and-steel front"; and in this large imaginative effort Stalin did undoubtedly capture the idealism and energy of a whole generation of young Russians, especially in the towns. This was something that united and inspired, despite (or because of) the great hazards of moving large forces to work in often empty lands in the rigours of the Russian climate. Frequently food supplies broke down and the workers starved. An American who helped in the building of Magnitogorsk, the big iron-and-steel town beyond the Urals, reckoned that more lives were lost in that battle than in the Battle of the Marne, in the First World War. Thousands perished in tents in the Siberian winter; riveters froze to death high up on the scaffolding; riggers fell to their death; the slack or incompetent were court-martialled and shot.

The targets of the first Five Year Plan were set high and were seldom fully attained; but very great rises in production took place in each of the years 1929 to 1932, when the rest of the world was facing a severe contraction of trade and output. Thousands of tractors (though still not enough) poured into the collective farms, and muzhiks who had never progressed beyond a wooden plough learned in their hundreds of thousands how to drive the new wonder. Great new tractor-works rose like mushrooms, in particular those at Kharkov and Stalingrad (lately Tsaritsyn). Ninety new towns were built, largely beyond the Urals, far from the bombers of a potential enemy. The furnaces of Magnitogorsk were linked to those of Kuznetsk, in Turkestan, by the big new Turk-Sib railway. A new canal built by convict labour joined the White and Baltic seas. A great dam for hydro-electricity was built across the river Dnieper, at Dnieprostroy, which was now made a dramatic symbol of Soviet triumph. Where Russian 'know-how' was inadequate, high salaries were offered to American, British, or German engineers and technicians to train Russian workers. Complete automobile plants were imported from America, and often grossly mishandled by raw and ignorant Russians fresh from the farm and the wooden plough. Like children they learned, wastefully but rapidly, by making mistakes.

The Russians were not allowed to forget the siege atmosphere.

Stalin and the immense apparatus of his propaganda constantly reminded them of their foreign enemies. "We are fifty or a hundred
years behind the advanced countries. We must make good this lag
in ten years. Either we do it or they crush us." It had proved difficult
to appeal to a sense of universal brotherhood, even the limited
brotherhood of the "workers of the world"; how much easier to
arouse Russian pride in Russian achievement, and hatred of the
"capitalist jackals" abroad! So Stalin turned out to be as great a
nationalist as Hitler or Mussolini. He filled his Politbureau with
home-bred Communists who had seldom been abroad. Red Army
officers became as privileged and honoured a caste as those of the
German Army, and ever larger military parades each anniversary of
the October Revolution underlined Russian glory and Russian
might. Soldiers were no longer required to take an oath to the
International Workers of the World, but instead to the Defence of
the Soviet Fatherland; and when the Comintern was revived in
1935, after its six years' eclipse, it was as an agent not so much of
the world revolution for the good of mankind as of Communist
intrigue for the dominance of Moscow—and death to the Trotskyists. Stalin, in short, came to speak a language that Lenin would
have found distasteful and reactionary.

Meanwhile the political world was full of his enemies and victims, and the Communist Party lived in a constant atmosphere of
suspicion and purges. Schools and colleges lost their last vestiges of
freedom, and all scholars of individual thought were ruthlessly expelled, imprisoned, or simply shot. The two-hundred-year-old
Academy of Sciences became merely a place of Stalinist incanta-
tions. History became merely a tool to justify the policies of Stalin,
and any teacher who failed to press home in his lessons the correct
political instruction simply disappeared. Stalin himself, the practical
man, the bootmaker's son, had always resented the clever intellectuals who formed so strong an element among the old Bolsheviks.
He was now in a position to show them what constituted wisdom and truth. Wisdom and truth were what suited Stalin's policies.
Stalin was planning the greatness of Russia and a new Socialist
society, and anyone who opposed it in any way, whether he were
Platonov, the historian, or the defeated members of the Politbureau,
or Trotsky from his various exiles, or critics of the latest iron-and-
steel target, or stubborn Christians who resisted his new drive
towards atheism, or fifty million peasants who resisted his farming
revolution—anyone at all who resisted was a "wrecker" or "saboteur"
or "distortionist" or "capitalist hireling" or "leftist blockhead" or

"rightist blockhead" or any one of a score or so such categories of villain, deserving punishment or death. Perhaps the most telling of all the pointers to what life in Russia had become by 1932 was provided by the fate of Stalin's second wife. The daughter of an old Bolshevik, she had followed faithfully behind her husband in his climb to power. One evening at Voroshilov's, with Stalin himself and many leading Communists present, she suddenly spoke up, voicing her horror at the bloodshed, the famine, the atmosphere of tyranny and hatred. Stalin broke out against her in noisy anger. She went home and committed suicide.

The tyranny tightened in 1932 and 1933. Factory workers could henceforth be expelled for one day's unexplained absence—and expulsion meant loss of a food ration card and of a room to live in. All movement was controlled by a system of internal passports, and food rations were distributed not from the stores but direct from the factories themselves. But temporarily the worst was over by 1933. By then the first Five Year Plan had been wound up, according to Stalin, 90 per cent. successfully, and a second one inaugurated, of somewhat less heroic and punishing proportions. But even this one continued to force up production at the pace of 13 to 14 per cent. per year. Grain production in the compromise collective farms rose so that by 1935 bread rationing could be abolished. Big red posters announced to the Muscovites, "Now, comrades, life is better." A sense of pride and achievement was in the air: Russians, and especially young Russians in the towns, rightly felt that they were taking part in the building of a new sort of civilization, based on planning, Socialism, welfare, and communal effort. Education was free and compulsory, and taking great strides forward, especially in the sciences. The health service similarly was open to all, and the number and quality of the young Soviet doctors represented sensational progress: there were five times as many doctors in 1936 as in 1916. Conditions of housing were still abominable by Western standards— about one room per family. Clothing was wretched, and food still poor compared with that of most of Europe. An Englishman or American of 1936 would have found Moscow drab and cheerless; but at least the danger of starvation seemed to be over.

The new society that Russia was building under Stalin was a planned welfare society, and despite its tyranny wielded by Government, by party officials and by political police, it could lay claims to be a largely Socialist society. But many aspects of that society would have puzzled and distressed Lenin, and did distress the comparatively few surviving old Bolsheviks. Attention has already been directed to its highly nationalist flavour; and in other respects, too, Stalinist society represented an about-turn. The older Communists had stood on the whole for economic and social equality (Lenin accepted the wage of a skilled worker), for free discipline in both school and family, and for loose marriage ties. But under Stalin all this was changed. Much stronger discipline was enforced in schools, and strong measures taken against juvenile delinquency. (The up-rooting of society had meant that very large numbers of tough, pathetic orphans roamed the streets in lawless gangs.) Co-education, which had been encouraged, was discarded in favour of single-sex schooling. Divorce, which had been easy in the early days of the revolution, was made difficult, and expensive to obtain. Bolshevism had been attacked in Western countries for its pagan attitude to sex, and its godless disregard of the family. Stalin restored the prestige of the family, though he continued to attack the churches. For all the ultra-radicalism of his economic drive, he proved in many ways so-cially a conservative. Artistically even more so: here his attitude was as reactionary as that of Hitler or any retired Cheltenham brigadier. His Ministers of Culture banned (through the managed votes of the suitable academies) all 'ultra-modern' art and music. Architecture was rich and Victorian-looking; composers were made to apologize for writing *bourgeois* (over-academic) music. "Socialist realism" was to be the official prescription for all art, literature, and music. The fine arts were to exist not for the artist, or the composer, or the select intelligentsia, but for the common man, and the glorification of Socialism. Some of the rubbish which even 'good' writers poured forth under these directives brings a blush to the *bourgeois* cheek, even allowing for the losses of translation. Alexis Tolstoy, a descen-dant of the great Leo, wrote this sort of thing:

> We receive our sun from Stalin
> We receive our prosperous life from Stalin. . . .
> Even the good life in the tundras filled with
>   snowstorms
> We made together with him,
> With the Son of Lenin,
> With Stalin the Wise.

The most significant of all Stalin's about-turns was his campaign against economic equality. It had always been assumed that the Communists, as the enemies of privilege, stood for a rough equality of reward. The Stalin system re-created great differences, which Lenin's had tried to abolish, between the rich and the poor; and this was not accidental: it was a piece of cool policy. First, it was necessary to offer workpeople incentives for working hard, and during the Five Year Plans a system of bonus pay was developed, named after a certain Stakhanov, a Donets miner of prodigious output. By hard work a labourer might well earn more than his foreman; by very hard work he might become really rich. No trade unions (in the Western sense) being allowed to say him nay, Stalin was thus able to create at the same time an aristocracy of labour and a great surge of productivity. Had this been all, there might have been few grounds for serious criticism. However, as the years proceeded, Stalin saw the advantages to his system and to his personal position of having a large privileged caste whose interests were deeply involved in his own. Only the members of this caste—Red Army officers, Communist Party officials, civil servants, police officers, technicians, teachers, and intellectuals of all kinds—were paid the sort of salaries and given the sort of privileges that went with being a member of the governmental 'apparatus.' These were the 'apparatchiks' who effectively ran the Soviet State under Stalin. As Trotsky put it:

> When there are few goods the purchasers are compelled to stand in line. When the lines are very long it is necessary to appoint a policeman to keep order. Such is the starting-point of the power of the Soviet bureaucracy. It "knows" who is to get something and who has to wait. . . .
> Qualifications, wages, employment, number of chevrons on the military uniform, are acquiring more and more significance, for with them are bound up questions of shoes, and fur coats, and apartments, and bathrooms, and—the ultimate dream—motor-cars. The mere struggle for a room unites and divorces no small number of couples every year in Moscow. The question of relatives has acquired exceptional significance. It is useful to have as a father-in-law a military commander or an influential Communist, as a mother-in-law the sister of a high dignitary.

Wolfgang Leonhard, the Russified German "child of the revolution," saw at its most glaring the contrast between the privileged rich and the wretchedly poor in his visit to Karaganda, in Kazakhstan. (This was somewhat later, in 1941.) After seeing the holes in the ground and the mud huts of ex-kulaks he came upon some large, fine modern buildings—the local Party headquarters, the secret police (N.K.V.D.) headquarters, a cinema, and a hotel.

> The hotel . . . was very comfortably furnished: carpets, flowers, well-dressed people going about without a care in the world . . . It seemed almost incredible, after the ordeal of the last four weeks, to be able to sleep in a real bed in a real hotel! A few minutes later . . . I was shown into a restaurant, which at that time seemed to me the height of elegance, with a little orchestra, and an elaborate menu . . . The contrast with the old town of Karaganda and the mud huts of the deported kulaks was simply beyond belief.

Russia was indeed a Socialist State, in that the means of production belonged to the State, but there was much truth in Trotsky's accusation that the state 'belonged' to the bureaucracy.

Stalin's dictatorship had survived the terrible years 1928 to 1933, and emerged into a slightly more relaxed period between 1934 and 1936. But only now, between 1936 and 1938, was a world already staring in dazed horror at Hitler's tyranny to witness another exercise of tyrannical power as ruthless and far-reaching as anything in the long history of mankind. Stalin's prestige in the West had been rising rapidly during the years 1933 to 1936; the prodigies of the Five Year Plans had captured the world's imagination. The Dnieprostroy dam, the tractors flocding from the factories to the collective farms, the Stakhanov heroes of labour, the opening-up of the Russian East—every bit as exciting and tremendous as the nineteenth-century conquest of the American West: all this was powerful and inspiring. The new Soviet constitution of 1936 even claimed to be "the most democratic in the world"—while still permitting one party only. Yet at this very moment there came out of Russia such a nightmare story of persecution and slaughter that Stalin's reputation, despite all the Western will to be friendly during the war years 1941–45, never recovered. Stalin the Builder was submerged under Stalin the Monster, who in these years, 1936–38, destroyed every surviving old colleague and every conceivable future rival—and in the process—to make fifty times sure—imprisoned and banished and tortured and executed hundreds of thousands of innocent men and women.

There had been a preliminary outbreak of persecution even in the kindlier year of 1935–36. Kirov, a good Stalin man at least until early in 1934, had been sent to Leningrad to wipe out Zinoviev's great influence there; in December 1934 he was murdered. Even now the precise circumstances of his death are unknown, *all* his associates being later liquidated. Khrushchev and others have strongly suggested that Stalin himself ordered the murder, being afraid that even Kirov was turning against him. Certainly Stalin was frightened, conscious of the hatred of innumerable enemies, and the assassins were tried secretly, and executed. Forty of Stalin's own bodyguard, too, were tried, and either imprisoned or executed; and tens of thousands of Leningrad Communists purged and deported to Siberia, to live in conditions infinitely more harsh and degrading than those Stalin had himself suffered twenty years earlier. Zinoviev and Kamenev saved their skins temporarily by a further admission of errors, but were held in prison. There was indeed opposition to

Stalin, as well there might be. Trotsky, from his exiles in Norway
and Mexico, fulminated against Stalin's betrayal of the Revolution
and the "leaden rump of the bureaucracy," and as the great purges
proceeded conspirators like Marshal Tukhachevsky did plot (as the
German generals eventually did against Hitler) the overthrow of the
tyrant. But the overwhelming mass of the victims of 1936–38 were
good Party men, Communists whose crime was that they were the
friend of *x*, who was known to be a friend of *y*, who was thought
possibly to be a secret supporter of Zinoviev, or Kamenev, or
Bukharin, or any of the other leading men who could conceivably
rival Stalin—or, worst of all, of Trotsky, the arch-plotter, the un-
speakable. At school one day the mathematics teacher would simply
not be there; the next week the history teacher; a day or two later,
perhaps, the headmaster. One would not hear of them again, and
would learn not to ask questions. One's father, brother, husband, was
simply called for 'questioning' at 4 A.M. by the secret police. Most of
the 'trials' were secret, but there were three great show-pieces, public
trials of famous men: in the first were condemned Zinoviev,
Kamenev, and fourteen others (August 1936); in the second Radek
and sixteen others (January 1937); in the third Bukharin, Rykov,
Yagoda (himself the chief witness against Zinoviev and Kamenev)
and eighteen others (June 1937); and in addition Marshal Tukhachevsky, the great Red Army hero of the Civil War, together with other
high-ranking officers, was tried secretly, and shot on June 12, 1937.
That day five out of six pages of *Pravda* were given over to the trials,
and every page carried a banner headline: *Spies, Despicable Hire-
lings of Fascism, Traitors to Their Country—Shoot Them! Spies,
Mutineers, Traitors to Their Country and the Red Army—Shoot
Them! Spies sought to break up our Country and re-establish Power
of Landowners and Capitalists in U.S.S.R.—Shoot Them! Spies
carried out Sabotage to undermine Might of Red Army—Shoot
Them! Spies worked for Defeat of Red Army—Shoot them!*
    At every one of these public mass trials, to which foreign Press
reporters were invited, the Chief Prosecutor, Vishinsky, closed his
accusations with "*Shoot the mad dogs!*" Bukharin, whom Lenin
called "the favourite son of the Party," became to Vishinsky "a
loathsome hybrid of fox and swine," his fellow-victims "a putre-
fying heap of human scum." Party officials were required to hold
meetings demanding their blood; school-teachers had to make their
classes "formulate their attitude"; people generally were divided
between indignation, horror, suspicion, and fear. The very agents of
the terror were least safe: both Yagoda and Yezhov, the two chiefs

of the political police over these years, were in succession executed. At the end of it all, of the seven members of Lenin's original Polit-bureau, only one, Stalin, was left; of the twenty-one members of Lenin's Central Committee, only two survived—Stalin and the sole woman member; of the five Marshals of the Red Army, two sur-vived; and more officials of the Comintern were arrested at this time by the Soviet authorities than by all the capitalist Governments during the previous twenty years. No "old Bolsheviks" survived—except Stalin; Stalin who throughout it all stayed in the background, allowing his creatures Vishinsky, Yagoda, Yezhov, and the rest to take the publicity. Only Trotsky appeared to be beyond his reach; but the arm of the political police was long, and one day in Mexico, in the eventful summer of 1940, Trotsky, in the middle of his *Stalin*, was done to death with an ice pick. Blood, suitably, spatters the unfinished page.

The most sensational aspect of these gruesome purges was to set a pattern for many subsequent political trials in police states. Nearly all the prisoners—the Red Army men excepted—prostrated them-selves in making confession of their imaginary sins and wickedness. The world, amazed at the unreality of the charges against con-vinced Communists of plotting on behalf of Hitler and Western Capitalism, rubbed its eyes as one after the other of them grovelled in penitent self-criticism. Even now it is not easy to assess the exact combination of explanations for these false confessions. 'Self-criticism' was in any case a well-established Soviet technique. The prisoners had probably been given false hopes of a reduced sen-tence, and perhaps hoped to save their families, who were being held as weapons against them. They had certainly been subjected to end-less pressure akin to brain-washing, and had been systematically deprived of sleep. Above all, their own moral resistance was under-mined by their past acceptance of the need for a united Communist front and iron Party discipline. None of them gained by their confes-sions; none lived to tell the tale. A few were given a mere twenty years in jail. The rest faced the firing-squad, to obedient howls of popular execration.

The great purges did surprisingly little damage to the progress of the new industrialized Russia of the Five Year Plans. New bureau-crats and technicians, mostly young and ignorant of any civilization but Stalin's, took the place of the old. In the Red Army, however, serious weakness arose out of the liquidation of so many of the leaders, with grave consequences to Russia's safety in a world where Hitler was already coiled to spring eastward.

Ever since Stalin's rise to power his foreign policy had been marked by extreme caution and suspicion: a sort of Balance of Fear policy. Which was he to fear most, the dominant Anglo-French League of Nations Powers, with their Eastern partners such as Poland and Czechoslovakia, or the defeated but resurgent Germany, Russia's traditional enemy, and after 1933 dominated by Hitler, who openly advocated war against Bolshevism and a German Empire in the Ukraine and Siberia? He oscillated craftily between the two. On the whole, until 1933, he sided with Germany against Versailles Powers; on the whole, after Hitler's rise he tended towards a suspicious co-operation with Britain and France. He joined the League of Nations; he signed a treaty with the French; he even invited Anthony Eden to Moscow, and played *God Save the King* in his honour. But he never trusted the 'capitalist' West any more than he trusted Fascist Hitler. Convinced that the 'appeasers' in Britain and France were trying to divert Hitler's war eastward, he set his policies towards diverting it westward. He needed peace, peace for his great internal work to mature, peace above all after the domestic earthquake of the purges, for Russia to recover her sense of unity and her military poise.

Stalin regarded the Munich settlement of 1938, when Hitler won his bloodless triumph over the Czechs, as confirmation of his conviction that Britain and France would not fight Germany so long as Hitler's eyes were fixed eastward. When, therefore, after the cynical German occupation of Prague (March 1939), the British made overtures to Stalin for a guarantee of the Polish and Rumanian frontiers, he refused unless a full military alliance were undertaken. Chamberlain, the British Prime Minister, would not consider this; the Poles and Rumanians flatly refused to allow Russian troops or planes within their borders; and Stalin was generally treated (perhaps understandably) as a powerful crook whose assistance in dealing with the German lunatic-at-large would be very valuable but who could not really expect to be dressed up as an honest policeman. And when at last, at "one minute to twelve" (August 1939), an Anglo-French military mission went to talk with the Russians, they were comparatively junior officers; they delayed their departure for eleven days, and then went, not by plane, but by five-day boat journey. Stalin may perhaps therefore be understood for thinking that the British and French Governments did not really mean business in building an alliance against Hitler.

He had, true to his nature, craftily re-insured his hand. While appearing to negotiate with the British and French, he had secretly approached Hitler to do a deal: no Russo-German war over Poland but an agreed partition of that country. If there was to be a major war let it be between Germany and the West—if indeed the West would fight, which he doubted. At the very least he would gain time: a few more years to build up the bomber-proof industries of the far Urals, Siberia, and Central Asia, and to re-establish the cohesion of the Red Army. So the famous Hitler-Stalin Pact of August 1939 broke like a bombshell upon the world, and made Hitler's attack on Poland doubly certain. To the West it looked a dirty double-cross. In the Soviet Union it produced a momentary bewilderment, while the propaganda machinery was being sent into reverse. To the non-Russian Communists of Europe it presented a startling exercise in standing on their heads, a situation in which they stayed for two years, and soon found quite natural. To Stalin it was a calculated risk and the lesser of two evils—but it was still a blunder. It earned him the ill-will and ridicule of thoughtful men; it failed to stave off the war for long; and it ensured that when that war came in 1941 his potential allies were all defeated and either mobilized against him or, like Britain, helplessly isolated from the Continental struggle.

During 1939–40 Stalin attempted to build up a 'cushion' of defence on his Western borders while being very careful not to give unnecessary offence to Hitler. His forces occupied eastern Poland; he made war on Finland to give himself more elbow-room; and he staged Soviet revolutions in the Baltic States of Latvia, Lithuania, and Estonia—with bogus pro-Russian plebiscites to follow. He appeared unmoved by the collapse of the West in 1940. He spent the year 1940–41 unsuccessfully jockeying for position in the Balkan States and signing a treaty of neutrality with Germany's ally, Japan, to secure his back door.

As Hitler occupied the Balkan States in the spring of 1941, Stalin switched from a show of friendship for Hitler to public protest and private alarm. But he was still confident that Hitler would not risk a military conflict, and showed nothing but aloof hostility when Sir Stafford Cripps, the British Ambassador in Moscow, brought him Churchill's straight warning of imminent German attack. The immense German bombardment of June 22, 1941, caught hundreds of Russian planes uncamouflaged and unalerted on their aero-dromes, and hundreds of Russian divisions only half ready for the assault. For a fortnight Stalin remained silent, and during that time Russian troops were sent reeling back along the whole vast front.

They continued to retreat for five more months, often a hundred miles or more a week; a terrible destruction was wreaked upon the Red Army, upon the civilian population, upon the farms and factories, the villages and towns of Western Russia and the Ukraine. In the battle of the Dnieper alone over half a million Russian prisoners were taken. From the lands conquered by Hitler's armies in those five months came 40 per cent. of the Soviet population, 65 per cent. of the coal production, 68 per cent. of the pig iron, 58 per cent. of the steel, 60 per cent. of the aluminium, 95 per cent. of the ball-bearings, 38 per cent. of the grain, 84 per cent. of the sugar. Well might Stalin have moments of despair, for this was no planned retreat to lure the over-extended Germans into the trap of the Russian winter. This was an unlooked-for disaster, partly occasioned by his own blunders and those of his old comrades in command of the Army—Budienny and Voroshilov in particular.

However, he had never lacked courage, tenacity, and ruthlessness; and now these qualities made of him a war leader of the mettle of Churchill, and superior in every respect to Hitler or Mussolini. First, he ordered a policy of 'scorched earth'; what could not be evacuated eastward must be burned. The Germans were to inherit an empty land—and so, too, those wretched Russian survivors who were left behind in it when the tide of destruction had rolled past them.

> The enemy must not be left a single engine, a single railway-car, a single pound of grain or gallon of fuel.... In areas occupied by the enemy guerrillas must be formed; sabotage groups must be organized to combat the enemy, to foment guerrilla warfare everywhere, to blow up bridges and roads, damage telephone and telegraph lines, set fire to forests, stores, and transport. The enemy ... must be hounded and annihilated at every step, and all their measures frustrated.

Well and bitterly were his instructions obeyed, except in a few areas of the Ukraine and the Caucasus where anti-Russian and anti-Stalinist sentiments persisted. For this was a genuine patriotic war, wholly unprovoked; and Stalin was now a genuine patriotic leader. The whole past of Russia rose up to fight with him, and he became one with Alexander Nevsky and Peter the Great, Suvorov and Kutuzov, and the heroes of 1812. And the future too; if Soviet Russia were to have a future she must work and fight for it now. Millions of families accordingly were moved eastward ahead of the advancing Germans, and 1360 plants and factories transported to the other side of the Volga and the Urals. When the Germans reached the suburbs of Moscow and the Russian Government was forced to evacuate he stayed on, no figurehead, but the effective commander-in-chief, steadying the panic which was to some extent inevitable. The old divisions inside the country were melted in the furnace of war, and the Man of Steel, tempered in the furnace, justified his *nom de guerre* before the nation and the world. When his war bulletins ended, as they regularly did, with "*Death to the German invader!*" he voiced the hatred and indomitability of a grimly united people.

In December 1941 he launched the first Russian winter counter-offensive, and its successes heartened both him and his people. America had just entered the war after the Japanese attack on Pearl Harbour, and Stalin pressed both Churchill and Roosevelt for sorely needed help, and especially for the re-opening of that Western front in Europe that Stalin's own policies had helped to destroy in 1940. Churchill and Roosevelt did in fact promise such a front, but in 1942, and again in 1943, had to disappoint Stalin by failing to open it. Stalin, ever suspicious, was certain that he was being tricked, and that the U.S.S.R. was being deliberately made to bleed to death: the old fears of Munich made more bitter by the terrible sufferings of war.

For Russia continued to bleed. Again the Red Armies fell back in the summer of 1942, at the very moment when Stalin was upbraiding the visiting Churchill in the Kremlin. Starving Leningrad had held heroically out; Moscow was partially surrounded, and in the south the Nazi armies were moving swiftly towards the Volga and the oil of the Caucasus. But to the forces defending Stalingrad, the old Tsaritsyn, on the great bend of the Volga, the City of Stalin that symbolized the achievements of the new Russia and its leader, he issued a 'no-retreat' order. Here, between August 1942 and January 1943, was fought the greatest battle in the history of the world. To both sides, and especially to both dictators, it became the crucial test, a matter of life and death to their prestige and their cause. This industrial city was fought for street by street, factory by factory, house by house, until it was an enormous graveyard of rubble. At four points the Nazis actually reached the great river, after savage losses, while the defenders under General Chuikov were deliberately starved of reserves, and the Germans threw in more and more men. The Russians then achieved their master-stroke. The reserves Chuikov had been denied had been drafted to two other armies under Generals Rokossovsky and Malinovsky. These now struck from north and south to cut off the besieging Germans, themselves in turn besieged; and by February 1, 1943, the entire German Sixth Army of 300,000 men under von Paulus was destroyed, half of them killed, the rest captured. The stretched elastic of the German offensive snapped, and for the next two-and-a-quarter years they were, with short exceptions, in steady and ever more hopeless retreat. As their forces dwindled, the Russians' grew. Now Stalin's technical and educational revolution came into its own. Despite prodigious losses that would have brought any other power to its knees, the iron and steel, the oil and synthetic rubber, the tanks and guns and tractors, and—most important of all —the men and women educated to produce and operate all these things, were there in a sufficiency to roll back the invader through the lands that he had laid waste, exploited and tortured. Every few nights the fanfare on Moscow Radio was prelude to a further victory; a wave of patriotic triumph carried Stalin upon its crest. Old enmities were apparently laid aside, and in 1943 he not only abolished the Comintern, as a gesture to his allies abroad, but in Russia actually restored the Greek Orthodox Church, with a Patriarch independent for the first time since Peter the Great.

The leopard, however, had not really changed his spots. It was not long before the Comintern was to be resurrected in the guise of the "Cominform." Moreover, it was not inconvenient to have made peace with Orthodox Christianity at the moment when the Red Army was poised for an invasion of the largely Orthodox Balkans. And although inside Russia all the emphasis was on the liberation of the Fatherland and the patriotic triumphs of the Red Army, Stalin never forgot that, although he might be Father of All the Russias like the Tsars of old, he was also Pope of All the Communists. Meanwhile he regarded Roosevelt and Churchill, his capitalist allies, with ingrained suspicion, and Churchill at least, for all his public praise of Russia's "rugged war chief," reciprocated the mistrust.

The story of the meetings between the Allied leaders at Teheran (November 1943), Yalta (February 1945), and Potsdam (August 1945) is told to some extent in the chapters on Roosevelt and Churchill. Churchill, bent on an Anglo-American offensive in the Balkans to forestall the Russians, was overruled by the other two. He then concentrated on pinning Stalin down to "spheres of influence": Russia to be predominant in Rumania and Bulgaria, Britain in Greece, 'fifty-fifty' in Yugoslavia; and, to begin with, Stalin, who understood old-fashioned power politics, seemed content to play this game. He soft-pedalled support for the French and Italian Communist Parties and for Tito, and he was apparently happy to see a world dominated by the Big Three. He raised no objection when Britain helped the anti-Communists to defeat the Communists in the civil war in Greece.

But as the Russian triumphs of 1944–45 unfolded, and the Red Army drove bitterly across the ruined lands of White Russia and the Ukraine, and then into Poland, Hungary, and the Balkans, Stalin's attitude stiffened, and his suspicions deepened. The very hatred of the Russians for their German tormentors, and the tales of ferocity and rape that moved ahead of the avenging Red Army, generated a fanatical German resistance and a corresponding eagerness to surrender to the 'civilized' British and Americans. Stalin constantly feared that a forgiven Germany would 'gang up' with the West against the old Communist enemy, and altogether under-estimated the genuine willingness both of the common man and the official Governments of Britain and America to build a new world in company with the U.S.S.R. For idealism in 1945, albeit a wary idealism, was strong. The United Nations Organization was being born, but from the start that too ran into the ditch of suspicion dug by the history of the previous thirty years—or even of the previous century-and-a-half, for it was only too easy now to see Stalin as the new Red Tsar, aiming at Constantinople, a Balkan Empire, and the subjection of Poland.

The stronger Western suspicions grew, the more Stalin acted to deserve them. It was over Poland that the ditch became a chasm. In 1939 Britain had originally made war as *Poland*'s ally, and she could hardly stand by without protest as Catholic Poland, whose exiled Government was centred in London, fell under Communist domination. But Russia too was Britain's ally, and Churchill at the Teheran conference had compromised so far as to admit her claims to the old Curzon Line boundary of 1920, incorporating Eastern Poland. Then the Red Army swept through Poland in 1944, and by the end of July approached the tragic city of Warsaw, already victim of enough slaughter and torture from bomber and Gestapo, from slave-labour, concentration camp, and the iron hand of war. Inside Warsaw on August 1 the 'resistance' rose against the Nazis—heroically, rashly, without the co-operation of the advancing Russians. Whether because of a military check, or by malevolent design, or something of both, the Red Army halted (the controversy is still a lingering sore); and systematically the Germans took their panicky revenge. The Polish resistance fighters, men and women, were exterminated, fighting it out at last in the city's sewers. What was left of the town of Warsaw itself was wantonly burned and blasted to cinder and rubble. The Poles may have been rash, and they were certainly almost as hostile to the Russians as to the Germans; their Government in London undeniably so. But it is difficult to resist the conclu-

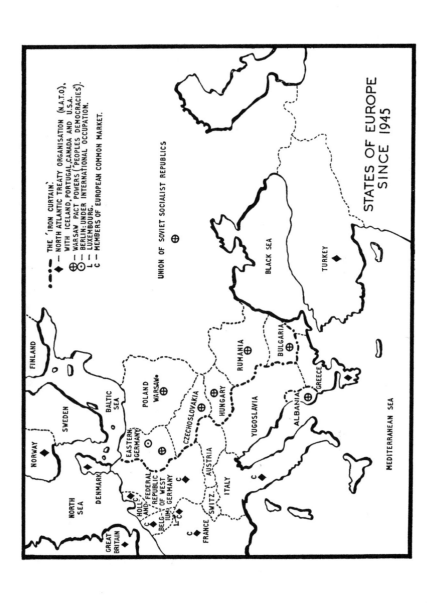

THE 'IRON CURTAIN'.
◆ — NORTH ATLANTIC TREATY ORGANISATION (N.A.T.O),
   WITH ICELAND, PORTUGAL, CANADA AND U.S.A.
⊕ — WARSAW PACT POWERS ('PEOPLES DEMOCRACIES').
○ — BERLIN: UNDER INTERNATIONAL OCCUPATION.
L — LUXEMBOURG.
C — MEMBERS OF EUROPEAN COMMON MARKET.

STATES OF EUROPE
SINCE 1945

UNION OF SOVIET SOCIALIST REPUBLICS

FINLAND

NORWAY

SWEDEN

BALTIC SEA

NORTH SEA

DENMARK

GREAT BRITAIN

HOLL- AND
BELG- IUM

FEDERAL REPUBLIC OF WEST GERMANY

EASTERN GERMANY

POLAND
WARSAW•

CZECHOSLOVAKIA

FRANCE

SWITZ.

AUSTRIA

HUNGARY

ITALY

YUGOSLAVIA

RUMANIA

BULGARIA

ALBANIA

GREECE

TURKEY

BLACK SEA

MEDITERRANEAN SEA

sion that Stalin delayed the Russian advance while the pro-Western Poles in Warsaw destroyed themselves; he even denied permission for British planes (proposing to drop supplies and medicines to the Warsaw resistance) to land for refuelling on Russian aerodromes— a refusal which made the use of planes from distant bases impracticable. The old malevolent Stalin, the monster of the Kremlin, did much to resurrect himself by these actions, even on the most generous interpretation.

Now he went ahead with a full revolutionary policy. A satellite Communist Government was set up in Warsaw; and in all the other countries of Eastern Europe, except Greece, Turkey, and Yugoslavia, he prompted a Communist "revolution from above," by the device of promoting 'popular' coalition Governments in which Communists manœuvred to hold the key Ministries of War and Police, and then gradually ousted the other elements in the coalition until a full Communist dictatorship emerged. In 1917 the Russian revolution had sprung genuinely out of the popular ferment, however small a minority the active Bolsheviks were; but these revolutions of 1944–48 in Poland, Rumania, Bulgaria, Hungary, Albania, Eastern Germany, and Czechoslovakia were engineered and imposed; they did not arise from a spontaneous people's uprising. So the satellite empire of East Europe was built, and the Iron Curtain drawn across Europe. The ugly Stalinist pattern of police torture and tyranny, of one-party rule, and liquidation of political enemies, of forced indoctrination, and the denial of intellectual freedom ran eastward from the Elbe to the far Pacific, with only West Berlin as an oasis of freedom. It was a sombre conclusion to a war fought, in the eyes of most Westerners, to free the world from totalitarian tyranny.

Poland was eventually 'awarded' by Stalin the line of the Oder and Neisse rivers as her western frontier, to compensate her for the loss of her eastern lands to Russia—though none of the Western Powers would be bound by this decision, which brought 'Poland' to within a few miles of Berlin. In Russian-occupied Germany, as in all the other satellite states, the old landlord class was destroyed, and its estates divided. So ended the rule of the Prussian Junkers, the landlords and soldiers who had been for so long the strongest pillars of the Prussian military tradition. Industries were nationalized. Soviet-style planning was the order of the day, with an inevitable tightening of belts. Some reparation was enforced for German war guilt by a massive transportation to the Soviet Union of factories and equipment. The old East Prussia was annexed by the Russians while

Danzig became a Polish town, Gdansk. Millions were uprooted from their homes, destitute and helpless. Millions more fled blindly westward, from the Red Army, from the Communist-dominated Governments, from the bleak unknown. Europe, and Eastern Europe in particular, was full of displaced persons, ex-slave-labourers, children seeking parents, parents seeking children, political refugees; a whole civilization was in the melting-pot. Stalin seized eagerly what was there for the taking, and in so doing he both enormously extended his Empire and held the hostile West a long arm's length from his Russian homeland.

In the Far East too he went as far as he could towards regaining all the territory that had been Russian in the last days of the Tsars; this was the price which he claimed for the few days of war that he eventually waged against Japan, and for which he was prepared to renounce at the Potsdam conference all support for Mao Tse-tung's Communists. In the Middle East, upon the war's conclusion, he brought immediate pressure to bear on both Persia and Turkey, renewing the old Tsarist claims to share in the garrisoning of the Dardanelles. All this helped to lay bare to a depressed world the raw wounds that had been long festering under the bandages of the war-time Grand Alliance. The hostility between East and West was now total; the era of the Cold War had arrived. The world was hence-forth to live in a long twilight between peace and war. There was a diplomatic and military stalemate, with a roughly even balance held between on the one side the power of Russia and her satellites, with the huge Red Army capable of overrunning the whole of Con-tinental Europe in a few weeks, and on the other the power of the U.S.A., based on (at that time) sole ownership of atomic bombs. Perhaps the last hope of genuine partnership in rebuilding Europe dis-appeared in 1947 when Russia declined—and forced her satellites to decline—America's offer of aid known as the Marshall Plan. It was true that America had good economic reasons for wanting a prosperous Europe, and it was true that the aid was intended to stop the spread of Communism, but there was genuine generosity in the offer, and Stalin's brusque rejection of it built the Iron Curtain doubly high and strong.

The very successes of Stalin in spreading the power and influence of the U.S.S.R. during the years 1944–48 brought their own antidote. As one attempt after another to co-operate with Stalin and his Foreign Minister, Molotov, broke down, as one more country after another was subjected to Moscow, almost all parties in the states of West Europe and America saw the necessity of economic and military co-operation against Russia, even of reviving Germany (and in the Far East Japan) to play their part against the new menace.

The year of decision was 1948. In that year occurred a succession of significant events: the seizure of power by the Czechoslovak Communists, with the sinister death (by murder or suicide) of Jan Masaryk, the highly respected Foreign Minister; the sensational defiance of Stalin by Tito; the Brussels Pact of five Western Powers, morally backed by the U.S.A. and Canada; the victory of the Catholic Democrats over the Communists in Italy; and, most decisive of all, the Berlin Blockade.

Berlin had been declared at the Potsdam conference to be an inter-Allied responsibility, though it was deep inside the zone of Soviet occupation (Eastern Germany); hence American, British, and French zones in Berlin existed as a Western 'island' in the great Soviet 'ocean,' and in 1948 Stalin attempted, by denying the Western Powers acccess, to starve them out. By risking war the West avoided it; they kept Berlin supplied for a year by air-lift, until Stalin was forced to admit defeat. For the last five years of his life[1] he accepted the Cold War, the twilight, the stalemate, waging a ruthless battle against Titoists within his sphere, ever seeking in the West for cracks, such as Anglo-American or Franco-American quarrels, into which he could drive a wedge, ever strengthening behind the Iron Curtain the industrial might and political discipline of his Empire.

Stalin died in March 1953, and was laid beside Lenin in the Red Square Mausoleum that is the greatest of Communist shrines. He had been in the saddle just thirty years, and in that time had perhaps wielded more power in the world, for good and evil, than any other figure. His achievements were immense: modern Russia, the industrial and military giant, was largely his creation. Her survival in the war, after initial mistakes, was dependent on his leadership. As the world's leading Communist, for a generation he organized the only new mass religion of modern times, and side by side with it a new type of civilization. He died in an odour of Communist sanctity, amid a deafening chorus of obituary adulation. But already, so to speak over his coffin, the new purges were beginning, and the candidates for the vacant throne manœuvring and jockeying for place: Beria, Malenkov, Khrushchev—or would it be Zhukov, the honest soldier? It was left to the successful candidate, Khrushchev, to admit to the Communist world what the so-called free world had known all along—that there was another Stalin, with what Khrushchev described as "negative characteristics.... He abused his power, bru-

[1] See also Chapter 15.

tally violated Leninist principles, and indulged in administrative violence, mass repressions, and terror... with monstrously falsified fabrications he killed thousands of Communists... and ordered the mass deportations of whole nations.... He was capricious, irritable, and brutal... a very distrustful man, diseased with suspicion... His military ignorance cost us much blood... His rule was one of torture and oppression." It is still difficult to penetrate to the true Stalin, wrapped as he is in the monstrous cocoons of his own and his enemies' lies. Or rather one should say that there is no 'true' Stalin at all, only a complex of contradictory Stalins: the far-sighted planner, the bloody tyrant, the revolutionary, the Great Russian traditionalist, the greatest of Communists after Lenin, the betrayer of the Revolution. Comparing him with Hitler, his equal in ruthlessness, one may say that over the corpses of Hitler's innumerable victims arises only the stench of corruption; over those of Stalin, innumerable too, there stands a giant edifice—modern Russia.

Table of Events

1879.	Joseph Djugashvili (Stalin) born near Tiflis.
1905–7.	Stalin active in Georgian revolutionary activity, and
1907–17.	serves various sentences of deportation.
1917.	Revolution. Stalin Commissar of Nationalities.
1919–20.	Civil Wars. Stalin at Tsaritsyn (Stalingrad).
1922–23.	Stalin General Secretary of Communist Party, accumulating influence against Trotsky.
1924.	Death of Lenin.
1927.	Trotsky expelled from the Party, and exiled (1929).
1928–32.	First Five Year Plan.
1930.	Forced collectivization of farms.
1933–38.	Second Five Year Plan.
1936–38.	The Great Purges.
1939.	Stalin-Hitler Pact. Partition of Poland, Finnish War.
1940.	Murder of Trotsky.
1941.	Hitler attacks Russia, reaches outskirts of Leningrad and Moscow.
1942.	Battle of Stalingrad.
1943–45.	Russians defeat Hitler's armies. Teheran, Yalta, and Potsdam conferences.
1944–48.	Stalinist revolutions throughout Eastern Europe.
1948.	Berlin air-lift, Tito's defiance of Stalin.
1950.	Treaty with Chinese Communists. Korean War begins.
1953.	Death of Stalin.
1956.	Khrushchev attacks memory of Stalin.

10

President Tito

(1892–   )

Joseph Broz, whom the world knows better by his *nom de guerre* of "Tito," was born into a typical provincial area of the great Habsburg Empire—that Austro-Hungarian Empire in which the First World War was to originate, and which was itself to crumble into ruin at the end of the war. Adolf Hitler was another subject of the same Empire—away to the north in Braunau, three years old when Joseph Broz was born, in 1892, seventh of the fifteen children of Croat-Slovene peasants living near Zagreb, among the high hills of the Zagorje district.

The Austrian Empire, over which the ancient house of Habsburg still ruled, was a unique institution. Its capital, Vienna, was one of the great cultural centres of Europe, a city basically German, a bastion which the ocean of barbarian or Turkish invaders had beaten against through the centuries, but had never submerged. It was the Paris of central Europe, a gay and civilized city, the city of Haydn and Schubert, with a great wealth of theatres, concert-halls, colleges, palaces, churches: abounding in monuments of 'Western,' Catholic culture—though in addition a strong Jewish strain had been introduced in later years. But Vienna was more than this. It was the centre of a very large, and mainly rather primitive, rural empire, partly Magyar (Hungarian), partly Slav (Slavonic), partly Muslim, covering an area where races, languages, and religions were more mixed than anywhere else in Europe. It stretched from Trieste, in the south-west (a largely Italian city and the one great sea-port), to Galicia, on the borders of Poland, in the north-east; from the Sudetenland of Bohemia, in the north-west, to distant Transylvania, to the east of Hungary. The Hungarians had been given, since 1867, a position of equality with the German-speaking Austrians; the Czechs and Italians were felt by the Austrians to be peoples only slightly less civilized; but the other peoples of the Habsburg Empire —Slovaks, Ruthenians, Serbs, Croats, Slovenes, Montenegrins, Albanians, Macedonians, Poles, and the rest—were largely living in extreme poverty, and tended to be regarded (emphatically so by Hitler) as Untermenschen—lesser breeds.

These lesser breeds, however, were not content to be so regarded. Each had its own distinct passionate nationalism; and in this many among the Slavonic peoples had a sense of kinship, of common language and common destiny, which historians call pan-Slavism. Before 1914 the most vocal of all the national groups was the Serbian, and it was Serb terrorists who threw the bomb that killed the Austrian archduke at Sarajevo, in 1914. In the First World War that grew out of the tension between Austrians and Serbs all the subject peoples of the Habsburg Empire demanded liberation, and in 1919 that Empire was no more. Austria became a small, mainly pastoral mountain land, surrounding a large capital city, Vienna; a tourists' paradise, but heading for bankruptcy and revolution. Hungary became independent, and the bulk of the rest of the Empire was made into two new states: in the north, Czechoslovakia, the land of the Czechs, Slovaks, and Ruthenians; and Yugoslavia, the land of the South Slavs—that is, Serbs, Croats, Slovenes, and many more.

But by 1919 Tito was twenty-seven years old, and had already known excitement enough to fill ten ordinary lives. We must return to his childhood in the Zagorje mountains of Croatia, in the Habsburg Empire that still had a score of years to run.

His father was a Croat, his mother a Slovene; they were 'middle' peasants, enjoying the produce of ten acres and a garden, and living in half a house that gave them two rooms and half a kitchen. Of the fifteen children, seven lived. The elder ones shared an upstairs garret, the smaller ones slept on rags on the floor. Maize bread was their staple food, though they were frequently short of it. Joseph's father eked out his farming with blacksmith's work, wood-hauling and carrying. His grandfather was a charcoal-burner up in the mountains. His mother was a strict and pious Catholic; over-strict, thought Joseph quite early on, and overmuch under the influence of the priests. Neither parent thought much of school; and the time came when Joseph had to play *truant from home* to get the education he wanted. Not that he was over-studious: he appears to have been a normal country child, strong and active, loving horse-riding and swimming and climbing, raiding orchards, and even leading the gang: a tough, wiry, intelligent boy. When he was fourteen he left home intending to become an apprentice-waiter in the town of Sisak; but instead he became apprenticed to a locksmith, and for the first time was introduced to the fascinating new world of machinery, of railways, and of politics.

Young Joseph Broz was quick to learn—about precision tools,

about the German language, about chess, about Socialism, about the iniquities of the Austrians, about the ignorance and superstition of the priests. In 1908 every Slav in Sisak was indignant at the Austrian seizure of the provinces of Bosnia and Hercegovina. For thirty years the Austrian Government, anxious to extend its power southward and south-eastward against both the decaying Turkish power and the rising Slav nationalism, had possessed an 'overlordship' over these two important provinces, but now they annexed them outright. There was a big European crisis and a war scare, for the Russians reacted almost as strongly as the Serbs and Croats; but it died down, and the cracks were papered over for another six years until 1914. Such events hastened on Joseph's nationalism. His contacts with workmates, and especially with a Croat foreman called Schmidt (who wore a red tie and damned the capitalists and the priests), nourished his growing Socialism. Joseph was an avid reader, even at the work-bench; once he was caught red-handed, three months from the end of his apprenticeship period. In sudden anger or shame at his exposure, he foolishly ran away; but he was captured, spent a short time in the local jail, and returned to complete his apprenticeship. By 1910 he was a fully qualified engineering-worker, and by 1912 a fully paid-up trade-union member, and also a member of the Croat Social Democrat Party—both the latter involving secret, illegal, or semi-legal activities.

It was not a time of prosperity. Work was short in Sisak. He went off to Ljubljana, then to Trieste—both big towns—seeking work unsuccessfully. For a time he found it at Zagreb, though not for long. He travelled through Vienna northward, worked for a time in Chenkov (in what is now Czechoslovakia) in a hardware factory; then on through Bavaria, to Mannheim, eventually to the Ruhr. It was a priceless experience. His German became fluent; he obtained a wealth of diverse factory training; he knew, from working in them, what German railway-works and shipyards were like. Above all, on his return, such an experience, with such a knowledge of German to add to it, was bound to make a man of his qualities a natural leader among the poor and often illiterate Croats and Slovenes.

In June 1914 his period of conscript military service was still not finished when the Archduke Francis Ferdinand, nephew of the Habsburg Emperor and heir to the thrones of Austria and Hungary, was assassinated, together with his wife, in the Bosnian town of Sarajevo, by a band of nationalist Serbs who belonged to the secret terrorist society of the Black Hand. It is fairly certain now that the Serbian Prime Minister and some Serb generals and officials were

privy to the plot. This murder was the match that ignited the dry bonfire of the Balkans, and in due course made the forest fire of the First
World War. Austria made war on Serbia; Germany supported Austria but tried to keep the quarrel from spreading; the Russians
stumbled into support of their fellow-Slavs, the Serbs; Germany
declared war on Russia; France mobilized her Army, so Germany
forestalled her by declaring war on her too. To attack France, she
sent her army the 'easy' way, through Belgium. This involved the
breach of the Treaty of 1839 and a direct threat to Britain, who
accordingly declared war on Germany on August 4, 1914. Nine
months later Italy, against her treaty commitments, joined the
Franco-British Allies and made war on her ancient enemy, Austria.
Turkey was already committed to the German camp. Before long
Rumania, Greece, Portugal, and (in 1917) the U.S.A. joined the
Allies, Bulgaria the Central Powers. By 1915 Joseph Broz was a
sergeant-major in charge of a platoon of eighty unenthusiastic
Croats fighting Austria's battles up in the Carpathian mountains
against the almost equally unenthusiastic Russians. Their 'employers'
were Germans; their enemies were fellow-Slavs. It was perhaps not
surprising that Croats surrendered a little easily, and their reconnaissance parties were frequently 'lost'; why should they fight to the
death for such a cause? Broz did not seek capture, but he was nevertheless captured—by Russian infantry—severely wounded. For over
a year he was a prisoner-of-war in a camp near Kazan, on the distant
Volga, improving his equipment by learning Russian now, reading
Tolstoy, Turgenev, Dostoievsky, Gogol, Gorky. For a time he was
the 'hired man' of some local kulaks, but soon he was on his travels
again, this time to even more distant Siberia, where he worked on
the railways, and helped in the clerical activities of the Red Cross.
With his background and opinions, it is not surprising that he had a
good deal of contact with grumblers and potential rebels; all Russia
was listening to the rumblings, however faint and confused, of
coming revolt.

At last came March 1917: revolution in Petrograd touched off
sympathetic rebellion all over Russia. Even before the Communist
demand to end the war was accepted, war prisoners were released in
a great surge of enthusiasm. Broz asked no further questions, and
took the long road to Petrograd, where he arrived in time to sympathize and assist in the activities of the extremer Bolshevik elements. When things became too hot for Lenin, in mid-1917, he fled
the few miles over the border to Finland. So did Broz. The chaos of
his own adventures at this time matched the chaos of Russia: he was

arrested, released; he returned to Petrograd, was re-arrested by Kerensky's police, and put on a train for Siberia: but he escaped *en route*. It was the autumn of the most fateful year of modern history. He made his way as well as he could over the empty countryside, on foot, by 'hitch-hike,' by cart, and rail; he at last arrived in Omsk the day after the Bolsheviks had stormed the Winter Palace in Petrograd.

Russia was in confusion. There were areas under the Reds, areas under the Whites (anti-Communists), areas controlled by the partisans, areas in dispute. Civil wars were complicated by the intervention of Western forces, and by the employment of Czech prisoners of war to assist the Whites. Normal communications were everywhere disrupted; brutal atrocities were committed by both sides; in the background constantly lurked the fear of starvation. Omsk itself was in the middle of typical struggles, being held by the Red Guard—which Joseph Broz joined. Omsk then fell to combined White and Czech forces, and Broz went into hiding. He was in fact hidden by a fellow-revolutionary, a fair-haired seventeen-year-old girl who became his wife. But he was denounced to the Whites, and was therefore forced to flee into the surrounding steppe—for all road and rail communications had come under White control. One of the strangest episodes in his adventurous career followed. For months he lived with a tribe of nomadic Kirghiz horsemen, dressing like them, riding with them, breaking horses, hunting wolves, drinking their horses' milk and their powerful kumis, arguing with their mullahs (for the Kirghiz are Muslims), running a flour-mill for their chief, Isaiah, who proved a tough and loyal protector; and no doubt wondering, on moonlit nights amid the birches of the lonely steppe and the tents and horses of his strange companions, what was happening in far Croatia, in the mountains of his homeland. For the war was ending, and Austria, like Russia, had been defeated. Who could doubt that, like Russia, Austria too would see revolution? And who could doubt that Broz wished to be there to play a part in it?

The Red Army prevailed in Russia during 1919, and with the Communist victories Broz emerged from his hiding. He succeeded in finding his wife again—she too had had to go to ground—and they returned home to a new life in a new country, Yugoslavia. He arrived wearing a Russian hat with a red star in it, but he soon learned to adopt a more cautious headgear.

The victorious Allies had made peace at Versailles, and a new map had emerged in Central and Southern Europe. Peace, however, proved to be a relative word. Austria was staggering into bankruptcy; Hungary was under Bela Kun's brief Communist dictatorship, and soon to emerge into the Right-wing dictatorship of Admiral Horthy; Italy was paralysed by strikes and party strife, and in 1922 succumbed to Mussolini; and Yugoslavia, in theory a Parliamentary democratic monarchy, was in fact living under a dictatorship of the Serbs (the 'master race' of the South Slavs). Bread was dear and often scarce; there was a black market in many goods; nine out of ten industrial workers were unemployed; strikes were frequent. Not only was the Government carried on in the interests of the Serbian third of the population—to the intense anger of the Croats and Slovenes—but all extreme Left-wing elements were excluded from public life, and the fifty-three Communist deputies of 1920 were prevented from attending Parliament. On both counts, therefore, Joseph Broz—a Croat and a Communist—had no reason to love the Government of his country, and soon became a vigorous revolutionary and a marked enemy of the State. He was dismissed from his work in 1921 for organizing a strike; and especially after the murder of the Minister of the Interior (Drashkovich) and a subsequent attempt on the life of King Alexander, when the Communists were outlawed, Broz, and men like Broz, were more and more forced to work 'underground.' He was very active in the early 'twenties organizing Communist cells in trade unions—a perilous undertaking that led to his arrest in 1924. (His domestic life at this time was not easy either: his first child was stillborn, his third and fourth died aged two and eight days respectively. Only his second, a son, lived on, later to fight for the Red Army in the Second World War, and to lose an arm at Stalingrad.)

The Communist Party in Yugoslavia in the 'twenties and early 'thirties was hardly an efficient conspiracy. It was riddled by policy differences, and very seriously penetrated by police spies. Later it was dominated by exiles, and was actually led for five years by a traitor. Inside this Party Broz soon became a tough, militant leader. For organizing a strike and distributing pamphlets among the shipyard workers of Kraljevica, where he was employed, he received a seven-months' sentence. Re-employed in a railway-works, he did similar illegal work, and was in 1926 elected secretary of the Croat Metal Workers' Union. Again he was arrested, and this time—as a protest against the brutality of the Serb police—he went on hunger strike. For under the intolerant Serb Government of Belgrade Yugoslavia was by 1928 becoming more and more a 'Police State,' whose only saving grace was its inefficiency. A crisis was reached in 1928–29 in the affairs both of Broz and of Yugoslavia. He was arrested yet again on two occasions in the middle of that year, but was out of prison again in time to take part in the bloody riots and demonstration that followed the sensational murder—inside the Parliament House—of Stefan Radich, the Croat leader, and three of his supporters. After distributing arms to demonstrators, the fiery Broz on one occasion, cornered by the police, escaped them by jumping from a first-floor window; the table he landed on was loaded with pork. However, the police soon arrested him again, discovered bombs in his flat, and interrogated him for eight sleepless days under strong lights with periodic beatings ("Not what you would call torture," explained Tito later, "but my head and chest and arms were all black and blue"). At this period of his life he did not look at all the well-fed, well-dressed, dapper figure of his Tito days. He was still emphatically Joseph Broz, studious-looking, with prominent cheekbones, penetrating eyes behind spectacles; a Communist Cassius, with "a lean and hungry look . . . Such men are dangerous."

In court, after his interrogators had failed to break him, he made a considerable sensation, but at a heavy price. He defied the judge and attacked the court, which had "no validity. . . . I do not recognize any other authority but the Communist Party." For the first time he reached the headlines and the editorials, but the price was a six-year sentence, and, as a result, the break-up of his marriage. Some of his notoriety gathered round his wife—she also was a Communist, with her Russian accent and her striking looks; she too was 'wanted,' and was smuggled back to Russia with her six-year-old son. The marriage was at an end. But there is the possibility that the prison sentence saved Broz's life, for the next year, 1929, King Alexander, backed by the Army, seized dictatorial powers, suspended the constitution, and began to eliminate some of the more dangerous of his enemies; many Communists were quietly murdered by the police, while Broz, a State prisoner, survived. (Communist accounts of his life give lurid stories of his tortures in prison, including an eleven days' hunger strike.)

With him in prison were several of the men later to be in his closest counsels—in particular Pijade (an ex-painter and intellectual, sentenced to fourteen years, who ran a Communist 'school' in prison), and Kardely, later to be Foreign Minister and Tito's deputy. Broz read solidly in the smuggled literature of Pijade's library—Marx's *Das Kapital*, for instance. Such volumes were kept under floorboards, or even camouflaged on shelves. The prison staff's efficiency and loyalty do not seem to have been high; and some of them in fact were themselves enlisted into the Communist study groups.

On his release in 1934 Broz was banished from all Yugoslav *towns*. He was by now, however, an old hand in conspiracy, and organized many secret meetings of 'the Party' in woods and forests, where the greatest danger lay in the 'planted' spy, or *agent provocateur*. Among those he met at this period was Djilas, later to be in turn his colleague and his victim—the man whose forthright criticism of the tyranny of Tito, defiantly smuggled out of prison and printed in America, caused a major sensation over twenty years later.

"Tito" was in fact emerging over these years while Joseph Broz disappeared from the scene. To begin with, it was not "Tito" but other names, many of them assumed and discarded at convenience. For he was in process of becoming a contact man, travelling—always secretly and dangerously—between Yugoslavia and Vienna (where the exiled Yugoslav Communist Party had its headquarters), or to Germany, or Switzerland, or Paris, or wherever the international conspiracy of Communism took him. He grew moustaches and lost them, he dyed his hair and undyed it, he acquired nationalities and abandoned them. He would be a Czech businessman or a German tourist or an Austrian civil servant perhaps: always well-dressed and dapper, with the apparent tastes of a well-fed *bourgeois*. "A white, well-kept hand with a showy ring," he used to say, was always likely to impress the official who inspected your (forged) passport. A well-cut suit, a good-quality overcoat, apart from satisfying your natural desire to look well, gave you a genuine margin of safety—for Reds were notoriously shifty-looking, mackintoshed, and shabby. The other aliases came and went; at last, by 1937, on his return that year from France, he was finally "Tito."

Perhaps his narrowest escape was in 1934 when he was crossing the frontier after the murder of King Alexander (in Marseilles, by Croat gunmen in the pay of Mussolini): a happy accident in a railway-compartment, involving a baby and Tito's smartly creased trousers, amused and confused the frontier guard at the critical moment. Tito was the sort of improbable conspirator who positively *liked* dandling the babies of his fellow-travellers. A month or two later he had the closest of shaves in Vienna. He spent two years from 1935 to 1937 in Moscow at the Communist Party's expense, a picked man receiving intensive training in leadership, and in the theories of Marx and Lenin. It is interesting, in view of later developments, to find him even as early as this critical of the Comintern, in purely Yugoslav Party matters. The Comintern (Communist International Organization) was of course Moscow-dominated, but heavily influenced at this period by the Bulgarian Communist Party; and Bulgarians and Yugoslavs were old rivals and enemies. The great Stalin purges in Russia were only just beginning, and Tito's reputation was high in any case; but afterwards strong evidence was supplied that his enemies—especially his Bulgarian Communist enemies—had tried hard to get him executed. When he was in fact elected Secretary of the Yugoslav Party at this time, the Comintern only assented (so said Tito himself) "hoping I would break my neck."

The nineteen-thirties degenerated slowly from revolution towards war, but in a manner that none foresaw. Ever since Russia went Communist in 1917, and Italy Fascist in 1922, it seemed that a new pattern of modern conflict had developed between the Left and the Right. The democracies of France and Britain seemed decadent and spineless, the U.S.A. seemed distant and detached. In Europe one state after another came under dictatorship and police-rule, and at last Germany, the most influential and powerful of them all, came under the most ruthless and ambitious of all the Fascist dictators, Hitler. A war between the Communist world and the militant Fascist alliance seemed almost inevitable after the Rome-Berlin Axis took shape. (This was when Tito was in Moscow.) Just previously (1936) there broke out in Spain what looked like a prologue to the main event —the Spanish Civil War between the Socialists, Communists, and their supporters on the one side, and the Catholic-Army-Conservative rebels, under General Franco, on the other. Mussolini and Hitler sent troops and arms to Franco's assistance while the Communists sent all the help they could muster to the Spanish Left-wing Government. Both treated the affair as a vital skirmishing- and practice-ground preparatory to the main struggle to come; and Tito was as active as any other Communist secretary organizing the 'underground railway' that sent Red volunteers to fight for the International Brigade in that very grim Spanish war. Many died. Many languished in French prison camps throughout the Second World War. Some, seasoned guerrillas, returned to Yugoslavia to be Tito's lieutenants. In Yugoslavia itself, in the 'thirties, the outlawed Communist Party, like the whole European Communist Movement, was building up its numbers (twelve thousand by 1939 with thirty thousand more in the Youth League), penetrating vital services with its 'cells,' educating its 'cadres' (classes) of leaders, planning for the day when Europe should divide into the Reds versus the Fascists.

Yet this did not happen. The bombshell of the Nazi-Soviet Pact dumbfounded the world in August 1939. Hitler, the arch-Fascist, and Stalin, the arch-Communist, fell into one another's arms. They swallowed up Poland between them. Meanwhile it was the 'decadent' democracies of Britain, France, and the other nations of north-western Europe who were left at war, however unsuccessfully, with Fascist Germany and Italy.

Tito and all loyal Communists were momentarily in confusion. Yet such was the ingrained loyalty and obedience of the movement, such their innate sense that "Moscow knows best," that they were soon—Tito and all—proclaiming the rightness of the Hitler-Stalin pact, which had foiled the Western plan to divert Nazi aggression against Russia.

They defended Stalin, but they continued, very reasonably, to fear Germany and Italy. During 1940 and early 1941 relations between Germany and Russia deteriorated, and by the spring of 1941 Hitler had decided to 'mop up' the Balkans as a preparation for his grand eastward drive. Yugoslavia was an early victim—but when Hitler attacked, with a sudden, devastating bombing of Belgrade, there was a patriotic *coup d'état* by Simovich, which held the Nazis up for longer than they had bargained for. On the eventual collapse of this Yugoslav resistance, Simovich and his Government fled to London, to continue the struggle in exile there, as so many more were doing, and left behind General Mihailovich to lead a Serb guerrilla struggle against the Germans.

Of all the nations of Europe, Yugoslavia suffered most from the war, not excluding Russia or even Poland. Why was this? It was because the war there was not a straight war between two armies, but a complicated war within a war, or even *wars* within a war. To begin with, there was the 'straight' struggle, between the Yugoslav Government and the German Army. Then there was the embittered struggle between the national and religious communities, in particular between Catholic Croat and Orthodox Serb. But above all there was the revolutionary struggle of the guerrilla Partisan armies, led by the Communists, against the double-enemy—the Nazi foreigners and the old-guard Right-wing Government. This last was the war that Tito (and those like him in all the nations of Europe) had always foreseen: the War that was also the Revolution. Guerrilla wars and civil wars are usually the grimmest and bloodiest—and the wars waged inside Yugoslavia from 1941 to 1945 were as horrifying as any fought in those tragic and decisive years. Fitzroy Maclean calls them "a kaleidoscope of heroism and treachery, rivalry and intrigue." Everywhere he saw "the old racial, religious, and political feuds magnified and revitalized by the war, the occupation, and the resistance ... burnt villages, desecrated churches, massacred hostages, and mutilated corpses."

In 1941 the Nazis set up their own Military Government in Belgrade, but in Croatia they supported the rule of one Pavelich, one of the murderers of King Alexander; Pavelich also had the support of the Catholic Church. He was Fascist, clericalist, and anti-Serb. Many Serb peasants fled to the hills to resist him, where they were joined by Communist bands, and the Partisan war had begun. They cut 'phone and power wires; they destroyed bridges, aeroplanes in their hangars, German lorries; they set fire to newspaper offices, for propaganda was a vital aspect of the war; they attacked minor German units but avoided major concentrations. If an area were liberated they set up People's Committees, which they took care to see were always Communist-dominated. If a town were temporarily captured they burned the police-station, the law court, and all tax records and land registers—so that the returning authorities would find the maximum difficulty in governing. Against this kind of fighting, tanks and lorries were not always useful, and their enemies tried the weapon of terror. When, for instance, a train was blown up near Kragujevac, killing about fifty Germans and injuring about a hundred, all the males in the town between fourteen and sixty—nine thousand in all—were machine-gunned. (There were too some schoolmasters over sixty who went voluntarily to their death with their classes.) Any German soldier refusing to fire was also himself shot. The ranks of the Partisans, however, were not thinned by such measures, neither were they by the atrocities of Pavelich's Croatian Ustashe; in fact, the opposite occurred, and the Partisan ranks swelled in revulsion against the barbarity. And the barbarity of this Nazi-Croat State under the puppet Pavelich beggars description. The Catholic Croats were the underdogs of the old Yugoslavia— and now they had their chance to pay off old scores. They massacred Serbs (who were not Catholic but Orthodox), specializing in burning churches with their screaming congregations inside. To please their Nazi masters they killed off any remaining Jews or suspected Communists. Finally, to complicate and heighten the horror, the Bosnian Muslims were enccuraged by Pavelich, by the Nazis, and by the Mufti of Jerusalem to enjoy their own devout massacres of any Orthodox communities that the Ustashe had overlooked.

The Chetniks, the Serb army under Mihailovich representing the Yugoslav Government in London, did, to begin with, fight the Nazis; but already by the end of 1941, and more and more as the war progressed, they saw the Communist-led Partisans as their principal

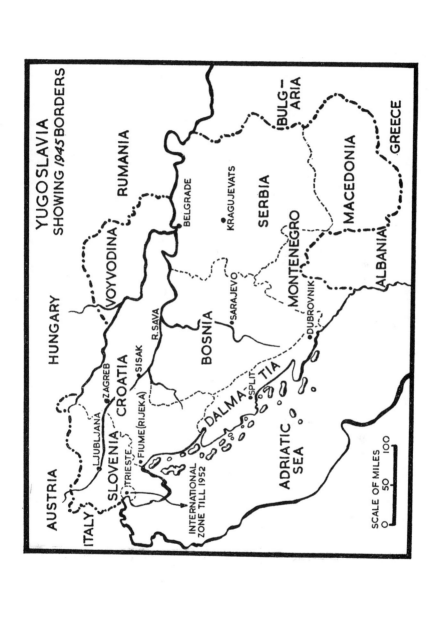

YUGOSLAVIA
SHOWING 1945 BORDERS

AUSTRIA

ITALY

HUNGARY

SLOVENIA

LJUBLJANA

TRIESTE

FIUME (RIJEKA)

INTERNATIONAL
ZONE TILL 1952

SCALE OF MILES
0   50   100

CROATIA

ZAGREB

SISAK

R.SAVA

VOYVODINA

RUMANIA

BELGRADE

KRAGUJEVATS

SERBIA

BOSNIA

SARAJEVO

DALMA-
TIA

SPLIT

DUBROVNIK

MONTENEGRO

BULG-
ARIA

MACEDONIA

ALBANIA

GREECE

ADRIATIC
SEA

enemy, and they ended by being supplied with German arms to carry on the civil war. As for the Partisans, they began with shot-guns and axes, but gradually built up their own armaments of captured German and Italian supplies, until they could fight a two-style war—partly as regular troops fighting from liberated areas, and partly as guerrillas behind the Nazi lines.

Then there was the vexed question of aid from Britain and Russia. Stalin sadly let Tito down, as will appear. As for Britain, anyone who fought the Nazis was Britain's ally, said Churchill, and Britain supplied arms on this principle to Mihailovich's troops throughout 1941 to 1943. Yet more and more it was brought home to Churchill that most of these arms were being used, not against the Nazis, but against the Partisans, and that it was Tito's Partisans who were doing the vital destructive work for the allied cause. From 1943, therefore, Britain began sending assistance to Tito while still maintaining relations with Mihailovich. Brigadier Fitzroy Maclean was dropped by parachute to establish *liaison* with Tito's forces; and, guided by fires in the night, he jumped into this strange country to make friends with Tito's forces.

> In the first field I crossed there was still no one. Then, scrambling through a hedge, I came face to face with a young man in German uniform carrying a sub-machine gun. I hoped the German uniform was second-hand. "Zdravo," I said hopefully. "Ja sam engleski oficir!" At this the young man dropped the sub-machine gun and embraced me, shouting over his shoulder as he did so: "Našao sam generala!"—'I have found the general.' Other Partisans came running up to look at me. They were mostly very young, with high Slav cheek-bones and red stars stitched to their caps, and wearing a strange assortment of civilian clothes and captured enemy uniform and equipment. The red star, sometimes embellished with a hammer-and-sickle, was the only thing common to all of them. Together we walked over towards the fires, which I could now see flickering through the trees. The Partisans chattered excitedly as we went.

By this time they were indeed a severe thorn in the German side. Their organization and the degree of their infiltration into the Nazi machine represented a triumph for Tito and his bold methods. For instance, the Communists' penetration of the official German news agency in Belgrade meant that every day they received a copy of the German confidential bulletin. Further, in 1941 Tito conceived the impudently bold idea of setting up his headquarters in Belgrade, at the heart of things, while his forces concentrated in the country districts. The fanatical devotion of the Partisans to their ideals in this terrible war became legendary. All were volunteers until the very last months—and a quarter of them were women. This meant that their already severe discipline must be severer still. To the strict rules of "no looting, no drinking" must be added the rule of "no love-making"—and in their puritan austerity these dedicated armies remind one of the guerrilla forces of Mao Tse-tung. Nineteen out of every twenty units were officered by the politically faithful, the convinced Communists. And of course the prestige of Communism rose just because it provided the dedicated leaders, so that by the end of the war its numbers had risen to half a million. Even so, they paid a heavy price. Out of the twelve thousand members in 1939, nine thousand were killed, and fifty thousand Yugoslav Communists altogether were killed in the four years of fighting. It was a primitive and barbarous war, fought in the bitter cold of the mountains, for a long time with the wretchedest medical supplies—medieval amputations with the aid of drink and the butcher's knife—troops often near starvation, sometimes suffering from the dreadful hallucinations of those in famine—no 'leaves'—no 'amenities'—no substitute for the weary march when you were already exhausted—no certainty that your wife, your father, your mother, your children were not being tortured back home for your part in these grim proceedings.

Without leadership of the highest order success would have been impossible. Tito himself (the "Old Man") was always in the thick —though still whenever possible immaculate; once a direct-hit bomb stuck unexploded in a beam of the ceiling above him; on another occasion, surprised by Italian troops, he sent the main party in rapid retreat, and stayed himself with a small machine-gun squad to act as rearguard; he also survived a severe parachute onslaught on his headquarters. He was the unquestioned leader, but around him grew a committee of Communist colleagues who were at the end of the war to provide Yugoslavia with a ready-made Cabinet: Kardely, the Slovene, Rankovich, the Serb, Djilas, the Montenegrin. Then there were the girl secretaries—"Zdenka, a strange, pale, fanatical little creature, and Olga, tall and well-built, in her black breeches and boots, with a pistol hanging at her belt, speaking perfect English"; two tough bodyguards, and Tigger, an enormous wolfhound, completed Tito's immediate entourage.

Tito [writes Fitzroy Maclean] stood head and shoulders above the rest.... There were many unexpected things about Tito: his surprisingly broad outlook; his never-failing sense of humour; his unashamed delight in the minor pleasures of life: a natural diffidence in human relationships, giving way to a natural friendliness; a violent temper, flaring up in sudden rages; a considerateness and generosity constantly manifesting themselves in a dozen small ways; a surprising readiness to see two sides of a question.... And yet I did not for a moment forget that I was dealing with a man whose tenets would justify him in going to any lengths of deception or violence to obtain his ends.

Fitzroy Maclean proceeds to list the qualities of the Communist leadership in Yugoslavia that gave it success: singleness of purpose, ruthless determination, merciless discipline, selfless devotion.

> They neither gave nor expected quarter. They endowed the movement with an oracle: the Party line. They brought it a ready-made intelligence system, a well-tried, widespread, old-established underground network. To what had started as a war they gave the character of a revolution. Finally—and this was perhaps their most notable achievement—they succeeded in inducing their followers to forget the old internecine feuds and hatreds, and by throwing together Serbs, Croats, Slovenes, Montenegrins and the rest in the fight against the common enemy, produced within their own ranks a new sense of national unity.

This eventual success came only after disaster had been terrifyingly near. The German Army, forced to take severe action, launched seven separate offensives against the Partisans, who already by 1942 were down to three cartridges apiece. They sent an appeal to Stalin for help; and for weeks Partisans waited in the blizzard and bitter cold of the top of a Montenegrin mountain, waiting for the parachute-drop of supplies that never came. Stalin offered advice on political warfare, advised a less offensive tone towards the Yugoslav Government in London, the 'allies' alike of Britain and Russia, and ignored Tito's protest that this Yugoslav Government's Chetniks were in fact collaborating with the Germans. At last an exasperated Tito radioed, "If you cannot do anything to help us at least stop hindering us." But during the German fourth and fifth offensives of 1943 he was reduced to another desperate appeal. "I entreat you to help us." Typhus was ravaging his forces. Living on their horsemeat, fighting by day, marching by night, they were at their darkest hour, their losses and sufferings fearful. Even after the arrival of the Maclean mission and the collapse of Italy, in 1943, Tito was forced to flee from the mainland to the Adriatic island of Vis, in 1944. Now, however, Anglo-American supplies were coming in—a hundred thousand rifles, fifty thousand sub-machine-guns, one thousand three hundred and eighty mortars, and a good deal else, in 1944. The Royal Air Force too began relieving operations.

Not that Tito trusted Britain or America. Despite his rebuff from Stalin, his faith in Communism and in Russia was still deep and instinctive—and he saw an object lesson in Greece in that year 1944, when Churchill acted swiftly to crush the attempted revolution of the Greek Communist Partisans, and to set up what Tito felt to be a capitalist reactionary Government. Tito perhaps might not have been quite so suspicious had he overheard a conversation that Fitzroy Maclean had about this time with Churchill. They had been comparing the Chetniks and the Partisans, and Maclean had stressed the strong probability that post-war Yugoslavia would be Communist and pro-Russian.

> "Do you intend," Churchill asked, " to make Yugoslavia your home after the war?"
> "No, sir," I replied.
> "Neither do I," he said. "And, that being so, the less you and I worry about the form of government they set up, the better. That is for them to decide. What interests us is, which of them is doing more harm to the Germans?"

In accordance with this line of argument, all aid for Mihailovich's Chetniks was withdrawn in the spring of 1944.

The year 1944–45 was crucial in the history of the world. Germany and Japan were being defeated; in Europe the victorious Russian armies were setting up Communist governments in their wake—in Poland, in Bulgaria, in Rumania, in Hungary, in Eastern Germany; and in China the Communist forces of Mao were more and more advancing the area of their occupation against both the external enemy, Japan, and the internal enemy, Chiang Kai-shek. Churchill prevented Communism in Greece, and Western influence and power prevented it in Italy, France, or Western Germany. Yugoslav Communism, as we have seen, was regarded by Churchill in 1944 as inevitable in any case—though he had argued ineffectively a year or two previously to persuade the Americans to invade that corner of Europe and forestall Russian-backed revolution. Certainly Tito was taking no chances. He point-blank refused Churchill's plea for the return of King Peter, son of the murdered Alexander. Further, the mistake had been made in 1918, he considered, of aiming at "democracy first, Socialism afterwards." Now, in 1945, it was to be "Socialism (Communism) first, democracy afterwards, if possible." He attacked the so-called democracy of the United States, where there were "only two parties, both alike and both run by big business," and set about transforming his war-time hand-to-mouth arrangements into a permanent peace-time constitution based on the dictatorship of the Communist Party—in other words, a People's Democracy. At least it must be admitted that Tito, as a war-time hero and leader of a combined Serb-Croat-Slovene-Montenegrin Army, was more genuinely popular than the Communist leaders of the other so-called people's democracies of East Europe. He proceeded to nationalize 80 per cent. of industry, to confiscate all farms over a hundred and twelve acres, to cut Church lands to twenty-five acres per parish, and to execute, among others, Mihailovich. But he went very slowly indeed with that trickiest of all problems for Communist rulers—the collectivization of farms.

His country was of course devastated and exhausted. Out of its sixteen million inhabitants, one million seven hundred thousand had been killed and an immense number wounded; relief supplies were urgently needed to prevent further epidemics and famine, and aid of all kinds in order to build up shattered farms and industries. This assistance was to some extent provided by the United Nations, which sent Yugoslavia four hundred and twenty million dollars, but bitterness was caused when relief stopped short of aid in building new industries. Seventy per cent. of these relief funds came from America, and when voices were raised there to make the aid conditional on friendly behaviour, Tito reacted strongly. He complained that more aid proportionately was going to defeated Germany than to Yugoslavia, and refused all 'strings' to his dollars. No one was going to 'buy' Tito. The Trieste affair further embittered relations with Britain and America. It *had* been part of the Austrian Empire; it *should* be Yugoslav; but Britain and America were not prepared to allow this (largely Italian) seaport to become a 'Russian' outpost on the Adriatic, and Russia was unable to take the Yugoslav side too openly for fear of offending her numerous Communist supporters in Italy. The breach with U.S.A. was complete after the shooting down of an American plane, and by 1947 Yugoslavia was entirely dependent on the East for her foreign trade.

Tito had quarrelled with the U.S.A.; he was also involved in a bitter dispute with Rome. He accused the Pope of shielding Pavelich and helping his escape to the Argentine. He punished the Ustashe "butchers," some of whom were Catholic priests. He imprisoned Archbishop Stepinac (Stepinats), who was said to have associated with the Ustashe, and who led the whole Catholic priesthood in Yugoslavia in a protest against the Communists' 'war' on the Roman religion.

All these events were much what might have been expected in a world that was split between East and West as it regrettably was by this time. What followed, however, in 1948 was dramatic and totally surprising. The Russians had become used to their own unquestioned supremacy in the Communist world. The Kremlin was to Reds as the Vatican to the Catholics: in matters of faith and high policy it was infallible. Orders which went out from Moscow (even orders to contradict yesterday's orders) were solidly and doggedly obeyed. Moscow's representatives were to be found in every Communist capital giving 'advice' which Moscow assumed would be taken as orders. The whole economy of the Eastern world was planned from the Russian capital; for instance, the Russians were very critical of the Yugoslav plans to build up their own industry; they would have much preferred to supply Yugoslavia with Russian industrial products in return for Yugoslav agricultural products. This assumption of a subservient position did not suit Tito at all. He was no mere puppet set up by Russian armies; he had fought his own battles, and had never received a rifle from Stalin until the struggle was virtually over. In public he still (1947) sang the praises of peace-loving Russia, as against the warmongering West, but he was increasingly worried by Russian arrogance—and most of all by the practice of the Russian secret police in recruiting Yugoslav agents to report direct to Moscow on Yugoslav failings. On his side, Stalin was not only critical of Tito's industrial and agricultural policies, but also resented what he took to be Tito's bid for leadership of the Balkans. In 1946 and 1947 there had been a grandiose scheme for a Yugoslav-Bulgarian federation—and even talk of a still wider grouping to include perhaps Poland, Rumania, and Czechoslovakia. Stalin was not the man to brook rivals—there could only be one Communist Pope. Things became worse when Belgrade was made the centre of the newly established "Cominform"—a postwar version of the old Comintern—and Tito took upon himself the task of publicly chiding some other Communist Parties for failing to be Communist enough. Letters began to flow between Stalin and Tito, containing charge and counter-charge, growing in heat until in March 1948 Tito received from Stalin a veritable rocket. The British writer and politician, K. Zilliacus, reports his conversation with Tito's private secretary, who said that "the really terrifying thing was the honest bewilderment of the Soviet Secretary, a very decent fellow, who simply could not get it into his head that it was possible for a Communist to disagree with the Soviet Union. The very concept was outside his mental range"—and the Soviet Government was honestly indignant at the Yugoslav suggestion that the U.S.S.R. Ambassador should be *merely* an Ambassador, like the representative of any *bourgeois* government! They saw him rather as a sort of proconsul or governor-general. Stalin, at the same time that he sent Tito his rebuke, sent copies of this letter and the previous ones from Stalin (but not Tito's replies) to all the other Communist Parties. Tito was to be made to toe the line with full public infamy, and soon the dutiful children of the Kremlin began passing their resolutions of condemnation. The Cominform itself met in June 1948, and passed an outrageously one-sided and violent motion against the "ambition, arrogance, and conceit" of the Yugoslav "terrorist" Government.

Now the world was awake and rubbing its eyes, and still the wonder grew. For Tito would not eat humble pie. All the old patriotic spirit, all the old war-time pride of achievement, all the new-found unity of the Yugoslav nation, combined to prove stronger even than the immense respect for Russian achievement and enthusiasm for Communist solidarity. Tito told Zilliacus that he was so angry when he heard of the passing of the Cominform resolution that he went out and shot all the frogs in his pond with a ·22 rifle. Moshe Pijade, the old Jewish painter and intellectual who had run the Communist study group with Tito in prison back in the 'thirties, publicly contrasted the conduct of the Yugoslav leaders, who fought and bled in the war, with that of the other Soviet leaders who sat in Moscow smoking their pipes. Tito boldly published the *whole* correspondence between himself and Stalin—an act of 'treason' to all orthodox Communists. The breach was complete.

Stalin could not take this impudent rebellion lying down. He would lift his little finger, and Tito would be no more. Further, he would use the Tito affair as the occasion for ridding all the other Communist lands of potential Titos, 'national' Communists not sufficiently obedient to the crack of the Moscow whip. So in all the other Cominform countries a great series of purges was instituted. Petkov and Kostov in Bulgaria, Rajk in Hungary, Maniu in Rumania, were all tried and shot. Slansky, the Secretary of the Czechoslovak Party, was also liquidated. One-fifth of the Rumanian Party were expelled, and many leaders executed. Certainly the ruthlessness and extent of the Russian Empire was well demonstrated. But in Yugoslavia the essential strength of Tito's position was also demonstrated. After a very few defections the whole country weathered both the psychological and economic shocks, and although the wolf away in the Kremlin huffed and puffed, and all the pack howled in unison, the house did not fall down.

The economic shocks were considerable. Stalin had already been slowing down deliveries from Russia as a means of putting on pressure. But by 1949 all Yugoslav trade with the East was perforce ended; Tito had earlier broken with the U.S.A. Hence many dreams of improvement had to be laid aside, and many belts again tightened. Of necessity, Yugoslavia had to look westward again; yet Tito still took a tough line with the Western Powers when he suspected that they were trying to extract from him a sacrifice of his Communist principles. In fact, Yugoslavia's position in 1948 has parallels with Britain's in 1940. They, like Britain, "stood alone"—and without an English Channel to protect them; and this was perhaps, even more than the war period, Tito's "finest hour." It took something of the same courage, coolness, and sagacity that Churchill showed in 1940 to stand up to the whole world against all the probabilities of success; also a consciousness of the essential rightness of his position.

By 1948 Tito was a world figure. He stood for something: Titoism, independent nationalist Communism; something which it was vital for Stalin (and later Khrushchev) to eradicate; something that at least must not be allowed to spread. Tito in fact survived; he outlasted Stalin, and even had the satisfaction in 1955 of seeing Khrushchev come to Belgrade to make friendly and humble approaches towards burying the hatchet. In a sensational public apology, Khrushchev laid all the blame for the previous attacks on Beria, Stalin's chief of secret police. It was some months later still before he dared launch his even more sensational onslaught on the memory of Stalin himself. It was certainly the memory of 1948, and the acute sense of danger presented to Moscow by Titoism, that helped to produce in 1956 Moscow's violent and ruthless reaction to the revolt in Hungary and the defiance of Poland—the events which followed, so alarmingly for Moscow, Khrushchev's debunking of the Stalin tyranny. The Russians could not afford to allow Gomulka and Nagy, the Polish and Hungarian Communist leaders, to become fresh Titos; and this time they took no chances. They maintained their rule in Hungary by direct bloody intervention. They maintained their paramount influence in Poland by the threat of similar measures. If only the Russian *Army* had been in Belgrade in 1948 direct intervention must have prevailed against Tito; but Yugoslavia reaped the reward of having won her own victories without Russian help. No foreign armies were thus at hand (as they were in all other Eastern countries) to give deadly substance to the Muscovite threat; and Stalin was too shrewd to risk a third world war against a West still with the monopoly of the atomic bomb.

Again Yugoslavia found herself buffeted from the East. In February 1956 Khrushchev had entirely 'blown the gaff' about the earlier Titoist trials in Bulgaria, Hungary, and the other Soviet satellite states, revealing as martyrs, even to Soviet readers, Rajk, Kostov, and the other potential Titos murdered in the purges. In April 1956 the Cominform itself had been dissolved to placate Tito, and

Molotov (the right-hand man of Stalin) dismissed. Tito had even visited Moscow to re-establish formal relations between the two Communist Parties. It was almost like Henry VIII being invited to pay a fraternal call on the Pope. But with the Hungarian revolt of the autumn of 1956, and Tito's criticism of Russia's methods of putting it down, the blast from Moscow became strong and chilly once more. By 1958 a shrill chorus of abuse was being kept up, not only by Moscow, but even more by Peking, against the arch-heretic, Tito. To strengthen his international position he assiduously courted the other rebels against both the big camps—in particular Nasser and Nehru—and in 1959 he undertook a world tour to build up goodwill with 'neutralist' countries of Asia and Africa, with whom he naturally felt a certain affinity. More and more since then he has emerged as one of the leading spokesmen of the unaligned powers.

During the late 'fifties and early 'sixties there was a good deal of talk of increasing liberalization. Trade unions, for instance, in such matters as wage claims and criticism of the social security system, showed a degree of independent activity that would have been impossible in almost any other Communist country. There was a wide-ranging amnesty for political offenders, and much lively public debate of the old issue: should the Government aim at one unitary Yugoslav Socialist State, or a federation of national republics? However, Tito's treatment of Milovan Djilas, formerly his own Vice-President, underlined his regime's fundamental fear of freedom. Djilas, already in disgrace, had smuggled out of prison for American publication his testament of disillusion with Tito's own tyranny—a bold and desperate action for any prisoner. Released later on parole with nearly four years of his sentence still to run, he was rearrested simply for planning the publication *in America* of his documented account of the Tito-Stalin quarrel. The prime villain of the book was bound to be Stalin, not Tito. But after a secret hearing Djilas was recommitted to serve the rest of his original sentence for "hostile propaganda," and five extra years for "disclosing official secrets"; and for yet another five years he was to be barred from appearances on radio, television, or public platforms. Whatever Tito's motives—and it was suggested that one of them might be an anxiety not to impede the latter-day improvement in Russo-Yugoslav relations, and hence a reluctance to rake over old wounds—the second Djilas trial certainly threw a bucket of cold water over Western observers looking for favourable trends in Tito's Yugoslavia.

Of recent years, much thought has been given to a new Constitution. In 1962 Tito was seventy, and still combined the offices of Head of State and head of the Government. Under the new Constitution these positions will be separated—and it is significant that recently Tito has delegated much of his executive power to his *two* Vice-Presidents, Kardely and Rankovic. Each of them, or any of their successors, will be fortunate if he succeeds in commanding half of the authority and prestige of the present holder of both offices. And a bigger question remains. Tito's principal fame lies in his successful maintenance of independence and heresy. Can the Yugoslav type of independent national Communism survive his death?

Table of Events

1848–49.	Failure of Slav revolts against Austrian (Habsburg) domination
1866–67.	Austria defeated by Bismarck's Prussia, loses Venetia, gives equality to Hungary.
1878.	Treaty of Berlin confirms Serbian independence from Turkey.
1892.	Birth of Joseph Broz ("Tito").
1908.	Austria seizes Bosnia and Hercegovina.
1912.	Broz working for Social Democrats.
1914.	"The Black Hand" murder Austrian archduke at Sarajevo.
1916.	Broz a Russian prisoner-of-war.
1917.	Russian Revolution: Broz a Communist.
1918–19.	Austria defeated. End of Habsburg Empire. Yugoslavia created by Versailles Treaty.
1920.	Purge of Communists in Yugoslav Parliament.
1928.	Radich murders in Yugoslav Parliament.
1929.	King Alexander sets up dictatorship.
1929–34.	Broz serves prison sentence.
1934.	Murder of King Alexander.
1936–39.	Spanish Civil War.
1936.	Broz narrowly escapes Moscow Purges.
1941.	Germans invade Yugoslavia. Partisan struggle begins.
1945.	Yugoslavia a federal People's Democracy under Communist domination.
1948.	Break with Stalin and the Cominform powers.
1955.	Khrushchev apologizes for Stalin's treatment of Yugoslavia.
1962.	New Yugoslav Constitution.

11

Gamal Abdel Nasser
(1918–   )

The prime significance of Egypt in antiquity lies in the fact that here civilization began. Here, and in the valleys of the Tigris, the Euphrates, the Indus, and the great rivers of China, arose the first agricultural and urban communities. Here the alphabet was born, and mathematics and geography and astronomy. Here were born the skills that came by devious ways of adaptation and improvement, to Crete, to Phoenicia, to Greece, to Rome, to the Western world.

The significance of Egypt through the centuries since has been twofold. First, it provides a bottleneck between Asia and Africa; second, it offers the shortest of land passages from the Mediterranean Sea to the Red Sea. Beyond the Mediterranean Sea was Europe; beyond the Red Sea was Asia. So Egypt lay at the crossroads between three continents.

Hence to that crossways have come through the centuries a host of conquerors: Alexander the Great, whose name lives on in Alexandria; the Romans, to whom Egypt was a granary, and to some of whom, like Mark Antony, a snare; the Byzantine Greeks who destroyed paganism in the name of Christ and haggled unendingly over their new religion; Omar and his Arabs in the seventh century, who brought the new uncomplicated faith of Islam, and a surprising toleration of the old Coptic Christianity—and who introduced Arabic as the official language; then the Turks, who ruled the land through the agency of the Mamelukes (originally Circassian slaves from the Caucasus); Napoleon, who defeated the Mameluke armies under the shadow of the Pyramids, but lost his fleet to Nelson in Abukir Bay; the Albanian adventurer, Mohammed Ali, who finished off the Mamelukes by inviting four hundred of them to lunch, and massacring them over the dessert, and then built an Egyptian State whose armies even threatened the Sultan in Constantinople; and finally the British, who dominated the country for three-quarters of a century.

The two constant things in this shifting and eventful scene were, first, the Nile itself flowing narrowly between its two deserts, and bearing the life-bringing mud; and, second, the Egyptian peasant, the fellah, toiling under the harsh sun, shivering in the cold nights, struggling to wrest half a living from his few acres, but still making a cheerful best of things, conditioned to subjection by five thousand years of history.

The special position that Egypt holds in the world to-day, especially the Arab world, derives not a little from her uniquely central position, as Rome's did in the Mediterranean world of antiquity. Cairo, not nearly such an 'Arab' city as, say, Damascus, or Baghdad, or even Fez, or Marrakesh, is able to speak to many widely scattered Arab peoples from the Morocco coast in the west to Aden in the south and Baghdad in the east. Cairo lies between Africa and Asia; what better city from which to direct an Afro-Asian alliance of underprivileged peoples? What better people than the Egyptians —the eternal slaves—to symbolize the revolt of the have-nots against their eternal exploiters? What person more fitting than Gamal Abdel Nasser, the son of a humble fellah-turned-postmaster, to direct this defiance?

In one sense the Egyptians are no more Arab than the Welsh are English. The true Arabs were men of the desert oases, with their desert headdress and their pastoral ways, Semites like the Jews and Phoenicians and Assyrians. The Egyptians, on the other hand, had been agriculturalists for three or four thousand years when Omar struck at them across the Sinai peninsula, still a dark-skinned African people for all the mixing of the centuries, familiar to us from the wall-paintings and papyri of the Pyramids. (It is interesting to compare Nasser's profile with that of Queen Hatshepsut's soldiers returning from the wars.) But unity of religion and language has produced a sense of community among Arabs which fights against their multiple and deeply felt differences. It was to fall to Cairo, the most central of the most subjugated, the least Arab of the Arab capitals, to assert this pan-Arab unity; and to Nasser, the Egyptian—and a southern Egyptian at that —to be the man who all over the Middle East, and to some extent Africa, became the figurehead of this Arab nationalism of the underdog. It is relevant to quote Nasser's own definition of an Arab: quite simply, "one who speaks Arabic as his mother tongue."

By 1914 the Arabs had fallen low from the proud position they had once enjoyed. A thousand years before, their civilization, in the days of Harun al-Rashid, had been second to none in the world. In the succeeding centuries their scholars brought Greek science and Hindu numbers to Europe, where they ousted the cumbrous

Roman system. Their doctors laid the foundations of a new study of medicine; their builders raised some of the most delicate marvels of ingenious grace in three continents. But their universities and courts decayed. The infidel Christians proved better at invention, and at the arts of navigation and war. Inside their own Muslim world the subtler Arabs succumbed to the more military Turks, who in their turn lapsed into an incompetent and antiquated tyranny, while Russia, Britain, France, and Italy threatened and conquered the Middle Eastern and North African lands.

By 1914 the Arabs were everywhere poor, backward, subject. Their territories had been overrun by the Turks and the various West European peoples. The dying Turkish Empire still sprawled over the map of the Middle East; no Arab city of note was its own master: Baghdad, Aleppo, Beirut, Damascus, Jerusalem, Mecca, Aden, Cairo, Alexandria, Tripoli, Algiers, Tangier, Fez, Marrakesh —these and all the others were under the foreigner.

During the First World War it became British and French policy to mobilize the desert emirs and sheikhs to take part in the Allied war against the Turks on the understanding that after victory independent Arab kingdoms would be set up under British and French patronage. From Cairo, that centre of British power, the armies set forth that were to liberate Palestine and Syria. T. E. Lawrence—archaeologist, philosopher, and romantic—went to live among the desert armies as a "fellow-Arab," and waged with them a destructive guerrilla war. The Turks were defeated: Iraq, Syria, and Palestine all became 'independent' states more or less under British and French domination. In Cairo and Baghdad there were revolutions against the British; but for another generation the British succeeded in playing their traditional game of giving a little in order to keep much. And the 'much' was all the greater for the immense importance of the oil in which the area (though not Egypt) was so rich. Even the French managed to stay in Syria until the Second World War.

By that time another factor had enormously complicated the Middle Eastern scene. We had promised to father the new Arab states on the collapse of the Turkish Empire; but in 1917 we stood godfather to another infant: a Jewish National Home in Palestine. For years an international Jewish movement known as Zionism had been championing this cause—the return of the Jews to their ancient country—and the persecution of Jews in Eastern Europe had produced much sympathy for the project, both in Europe and America. Nobody, however, had sufficiently bargained for the intense hostility of the newly nationalistic Arabs towards their Semitic cousins. An impossible situation was made worse by Hitler's renewed and horrible persecution. As Jews fled, under British permission, into Palestine, Arabs became refugees from their own country. The British were shown to have undertaken mutually incompatible pledges. When the new independent state of Israel was brought into being in 1948 a foreign body was planted in the centre of the Arab world (as the Arabs saw it, a cancer) which had to be cut away before it had invaded and poisoned the whole. So to anti-Imperialism and the fight against Britain and France was added the fight against Israel; and both these hatreds were focused in the fighting personality of Colonel Nasser.

Nasser is the latest of a series of Egyptian nationalist leaders, and the most important of them, because he is the strongest and most fortunate in the hour of his birth. And where his predecessors were Egyptian in their nationalism, Nasser is pan-Arab. But his predecessors were important, and should be briefly glanced at. The first of them was another colonel who led a revolt of brother-officers—Colonel Arabi Pasha, who staged a rebellion against British influence in 1882. For eighty years, ever since Napoleon's invasion (1798–1801), Egypt had been increasingly open to European influences. Mohammed Ali (in power from 1805 to 1849), himself a European, had done much to modernize the country, introducing the cotton crop and a system of canal irrigation. Under the subsequent rulers (or khedives), Said and Ismail, the country was laid wide open to European exploitation. De Lesseps built his canal, despite British attempts to obstruct it, and under Ismail the country was flooded with ambitious moneymakers anxious for 'concessions.' Ismail treated Egypt like a booming business concern, and flung her doors open for the capitalists and adventurers of Paris and London to come in. So, in the name of free trade Egypt became an open thoroughfare for honest men and swindlers alike. Admittedly the country to some extent benefited; but the shock of being treated like a European estate "ripe for development" produced its own counter: the shock of Arabi's revolt, anti-foreign, nationalist, fanatical—a foretaste of Nasser. But Arabi, unlike Nasser, was defeated by the British—ironically under the Premiership of the anti-imperialist Gladstone; and for forty years (1882–1922) Egypt remained under full British domination. The Khedive remained, but Lord Cromer and Lord Kitchener were the effective rulers of the country for a generation. Again some good was done: railways were built, irrigation systems improved (especially by the first Aswan dam);

banking, administration, and justice all reformed; the cotton crop developed to provide Lancashire with cheap raw material. But as Cromer himself said, "We were popular so long as we bandaged wounds. Nothing can prevail against the fact that we are not Muslims, and that we neither eat, nor drink, nor marry as they do." The war of 1914 came, and with it Britain assumed an official protectorate over the country she had been unofficially ruling for so long. Then the war brought Egypt sudden wealth. There was a great cotton boom. Egyptian war profiteers did very well. Industrialization proceeded rapidly. Communications were drastically improved. In other words, Egypt took a great leap forward in westernization. But Egyptian casualties in 'Britain's War' were high. Students chafed at Kitchener's unimaginative censorship. So war, the midwife of revolution, set off another revolt, led this time by Zaghlul Pasha—a fellah's son, moderate and unfanatical, an ex-Minister of Education. The British banished him to Malta, brought him and his delegation (or Wafd) back to the Versailles peace conference to negotiate, and banished him again—this time to the Seychelles Islands, where they sent Archbishop Makarios of Cyprus on a later occasion. Anti-British rioting continued sporadically in Egypt from 1919 to 1921; but in 1922 Lloyd George's Government recognized Egypt's 'sovereign' independence—severely limited by Britain's still more sovereign strategic requirements. Zaghlul and his Wafd Party provided the Government, no longer under a khedive but a fullblown King.

For thirty years the Wafd Party were Egypt, and ran it somewhat as a Western parliamentary democracy, drawing strength from both peasantry and the new, bustling, prospering middle class; keeping on the right side of the feudal landlords, but sniping constantly at the King; keeping on the right side too of the British, with whom they negotiated a treaty in 1936 by which British troops were to leave all Egyptian soil except the Suez Canal Zone. The Wafd was corrupt; its leaders looked a little too prosperous, and feathered their nests nearly as comfortably as King Faruk himself—but they gave Egypt thirty years in which to grow up. Not the least important reform they made arose out of the 1936 departure of British troops. The Military Academy was henceforth to be open to young men regardless of class or wealth—so the cadets of the Academy, unlike those of Sandhurst, were not to be drawn from the ruling class but from the people of Egypt. How easy was it, therefore, for the Young Officers' Revolt of 1952 to be hailed as a truly popular movement. One such of these cadets of 1936, graduating in 1938, was a certain

Gamal Abdel Nasser, the eager, intelligent son of an Upper Egyptian fellah who had risen eventually to be a post-office employee.

The Second World War brought the British troops back again to Cairo, which was General Headquarters of the Middle Eastern Forces throughout the war, but there was no pretending that the Egyptians wanted them there. Many Egyptians were impressed by Hitler and Mussolini, especially in the early days when they were winning. The devils they did not know were always likely to be more acceptable than the devil they did know—the British. As early as the middle 'thirties Egypt had had her own version of a Fascist militia, the Green Shirts, and young Abdel Nasser, still a schoolboy at Alexandria, had been a member of it: still a schoolboy, but a violently revolutionary one, organizing pupils into a political committee, and petitioning political leaders to "unite the country"; already overflowing with indignation at the British treatment of the Arabs in Palestine and the French brutalities in Syria; looking to Mohammed, to George Washington, to Voltaire, and to Gandhi as heroes—a strange but powerful combination.

Until 1942 the Wafd government was lukewarm when Britain scored a success, but rather less than tepid when she suffered a disaster. The Egyptian army was considered by the British to be so worm-eaten with Axis sympathizers that they seriously considered enforcing its disbandment. Rumours of this reaching Lieutenant Nasser in camp near El Alamein did not lessen his hatred of Englishmen. Similar pro-German elements in Iraq, in 1941, led by Rashid Ali, did in fact stage a *coup d'état*, temporarily successful, and some of Nasser's associates took a plane intending to assist them, but were forced down, and arrested. Others listened to another friend of Nasser, who planned to start guerrilla warfare in the British rear, and actually rented a floating cabaret on the Nile in order to organize methodical eavesdropping from below deck of the British officers dancing on the deck above.

The war in the Western Desert ebbed and flowed. Wavell won his big victory against the Italians, but Rommel's Afrika Korps proved an obstacle that neither he nor subsequent generals could master. In Cairo there were mixed feelings about the war. Some were making fabulous fortunes. There were four hundred Egyptian millionaires by 1944. Foreign capital poured into Egypt. Cotton profits, sugar-refining profits, profits from the pockets of British soldiers anxious to relax from the war and enjoy a good time—these and intensive spending on nearly everything made some Egyptians pray that the war might never end. Others—the majority—watched supplies of bread and fuel get shorter and shorter, and prices rise in the inevitable inflation that accompanied the spending spree, and cursed the British in their hearts.

In February 1942 British troops were forced to surround King Faruk's palace, threaten him with deposition, and forcibly install a pro-British Wafd Government—an action which inflamed still further the resentment of the patriotic young officers. A certain Lieutenant-Colonel Neguib, ten years later to be their figurehead for a space, resigned his commission from an army which was "unable to protect its King." Ten years later that King, with his peculiar mixture of high and low living, did not seem worth protecting. The Wafd, too, from that day, seemed to many critical and bitter Egyptians to be no more than a tool in British hands.

Nasser was shortly after promoted captain, and spent the next four years in military and staff colleges, instructing and lecturing, and sowing the seeds of the revolution to come. These military establishments played much the same rôle in the Egyptian revolution as the officers' academies played in the Young Turk revolution of 1908, and one may even toy with the parallels—Enver Pasha and Neguib, Abdul Hamid and King Faruk, Mustafa Kemal and Abdel Nasser. The differences between Mustafa Kemal and Nasser may be tremendous, but the similarities too are striking—ruthlessness; fanatical hatred of the foreigner, and determination to clear him off the soil of the fatherland; faith in their stars; the politician's flair for the right moment to strike; the overwhelming passion to purge and cleanse their countries of shame and corruption; the dynamic vigour of their leadership; their consuming lust for power. Both promoted army revolts, and both seized power out of the ignominy of national defeat.

This is to move ahead of the year 1942, when Captain Nasser was still a rather timid young officer, not brilliant, but learning to become a good lecturer, fighting to overcome his natural nervousness. On the front Rommel swept dangerously near to Cairo; Churchill visited Egypt; Montgomery took over command; supplies built massively up, until in October the decisive victory of El Alamein was won. The Russians won Stalingrad. Eisenhower landed in North Africa. The Axis for the first time began to face defeat, and the politicians of Cairo tacked and veered in the changing wind. In 1944 they even declared war on Germany and Italy—an expansive gesture which for their Prime Minister was expensive too. He was promptly assassinated.

Egypt was thus one of the 'victors' of 1945. But the end of the war left Egypt ripe for the revolution's picking. The rich grossly rich; the King a pampered creature of a foreign power; corrupt politicians taking their rake-off from deals and contracts; a swollen city population drawn to it as to a magnet by boom trading and industrial conditions; the cost of living soaring above wages; shortages of grain and the paraffin vital to the Egyptian housewife; the sudden cancellation of orders with the onset of peace causing unemployment like that in England after Waterloo; an army seething with nationalist indignation; a Muslim Brotherhood pledged to a puritan revolution; a scapegoat ready at hand in the British, whose soldiers and airmen thronged the streets, and whose wealthy citizens lounged in the hotels and cabarets. It did not need a Marx or a Lenin to diagnose the revolutionary moment; it was a situation as 'classic' as that of France in July 1789 or Petrograd in March 1917.

The fruit was ripe on the tree—but it was another seven years before it dropped into the lap of Neguib and Nasser. Still one more revolutionary factor was added in the interim: national humiliation in the war against Israel. Even this defeat could eventually be blamed directly on to the King and indirectly on to the British. For it was asserted that King Faruk had armed the soldiers with cut-price weapons and pocketed the rake-off for his own expensive tastes, whereas the British were ultimately responsible for the very existence of Israel. Britain had held the League of Nations mandate for Palestine, and had allowed the first immigration of Jews. Britain had permitted the rapid influx of the 'forties. Britain, with the U.S.A. and Russia, sponsored the creation of the republic of Israel in 1947. Britain evacuated her troops altogether from Israel in 1948 while maintaining a considerable force in the Suez Zone. It was conveniently forgotten (or regarded as characteristic hypocrisy) that Britain had also sponsored the creation of the Arab League to promote unity among the Arab peoples.

The idea of a war with Israel was popular with the Army, with the extremist Muslim Brotherhood, with business circles who foresaw the extinction of dangerous Jewish rivals; but it soon involved the rapid defeat of Egypt and the other Arab peoples by a people one-fortieth as numerous. The Jews were few but well-equipped, and fought like tigers for very survival. The Egyptian Army, overwhelmed and humiliated, salved its pride in bitter attacks on the mismanagement and racketeering that surrounded King Faruk. The only Arab state whose military record against the Jews was respect-

able was Jordan, whose Army was largely trained by British officers:
this was rubbing salt into Egyptian wounds.

Nasser himself was promoting the illegal supply of 'volunteers' to
fight Jews even before war was declared. When it came, his original
elation turned somewhat to disillusion when he saw the muddle and
incompetence. His own special brand of romanticism and mistrust
had full play.

> Our hearts remained with our dear fatherland left to the mercy of
> savage beasts. How often I said to myself, "Here we are in the trenches,
> surrounded by the enemy, engaged in a battle for which we were in no
> way prepared. The irony of fate! We were enduring the outcome of ambi-
> tions, plots and passions, here under fire and without ammunition." [This
> was in the trenches at Falluja.] Then I said to myself, "Is not our country
> another Falluja? What we are suffering here is only the reflection of what
> is going on over there in Egypt. Is not our country also being besieged
> by the enemy, a prey to climbers and traitors. . . ?"

He personally distinguished himself, as even more did General
Neguib, and narrowly escaped death when a bullet passed a half-
inch below his heart. Later, like Hitler, he succeeded in seeing in
this narrow deliverance evidence that God was sparing him for a
great destiny. Certainly the Israel war thinned the ranks of his
seniors and rivals in the unfolding of that destiny.

Between the Israel war and the revolution of 1952 there took
place the "battle of the Canal." To begin with, the Wafd Government denounced the Anglo-Egyptian Treaty of 1936. Any Government in Cairo wishing to retain some popularity was forced at this
time to make some such anti-British gesture; and in itself this did
not signify much. Following the denunciation, however, Egyptian
guerrillas started operations against British troops and property in
the Canal Zone which were delightedly written up in the always
more lyrical than accurate Cairo Press. After suffering some dozens
of casualties the British at last, in January 1952, retaliated, and attacked a police barracks, killing about fifty men.

It was the signal for the first chapter of the Egyptian revolution.
Next day rioting in Cairo, starting in a conventional series of anti-
British strikes and demonstrations, mysteriously gathered momentum during the day until by nightfall many of the leading buildings
of the capital were smoking ruins. For this orgy of fire-raising
various groups have been blamed: the Muslim Brotherhood; the
Fascist group calling themselves National Socialists; the Wafd themselves, who at least tolerated the early anti-British stages; the King
and the Army chiefs, who certainly deliberately delayed calling out

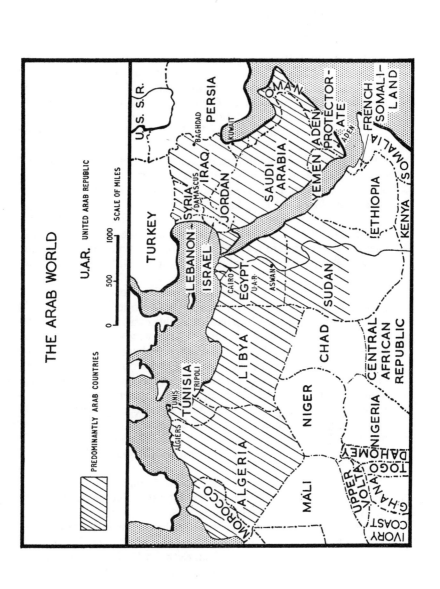

THE ARAB WORLD

PREDOMINANTLY ARAB COUNTRIES

U.A.R. UNITED ARAB REPUBLIC

SCALE OF MILES

0   500   1000

troops to suppress the mob; and of course the Communists, who almost certainly were not responsible, though Nasser himself later blamed them for it. Whoever gave the orders organized gangs of fire-raisers, and (towards the end) the looting rabble of Cairo destroyed or badly damaged between them four hundred properties, valued at £23 million. An unknown number of lives lost included nine Englishmen at the Turf Club, pushed back by the crowd to roast alive, a Canadian diplomat, an Italian opera singer who jumped panic-stricken from the fourth floor of the famous Shepheard's Hotel (her fellow-singers escaped in their underclothes), several Jews, and some dozens of rioters themselves. As a result of this day's work the Wafd Government was further discredited, which temporarily pleased the King; but it had been that day advertised to the world that the Kingdom of Egypt was for sale to any revolutionary group resolute enough to bid boldly for it. Precisely six months later Faruk, lucky to escape with his life, was boarding his yacht at Alexandria to leave Egypt for the last time, and the revolutionary group that emerged was of course Nasser's—the "Free Officers."

King Faruk, the obese great-great grandson of Mohammed Ali, had acquired a reputation of outrageous notoriety. Moving in his luxury yacht between his palace and the casinos and night-clubs of Europe, he was an international figure living under the delighted gaze of all the scandal-sheets of Europe and America. His divorce and remarriage to an already engaged girl; his numerous affairs with the prettier wives of his richer subjects and a carefully chosen international collection of film stars and cabaret singers; the general conviction that all the fun was paid for out of his commission on official appointments and contracts—all this gave the gutter Press good headlines and better pictures; but it gave patriotic Egyptians like Nasser and his companions a consciousness of shame. Worse, Faruk played politics hard, and put his own cronies into key positions—chief of the army staff, head of the political police, and so on. Worst crime of all in the eyes of Nasser and his Free Officers group: Faruk was to blame for the Israel débâcle.

The Free Officers were quite open in their 'conspiracy' for a time, with pamphlets and even a magazine. But as they moved towards action their plans grew more secret. Between 1949 and 1951 some of them had toyed with terrorism—even Nasser himself on one occasion. In his own rather naïve little book he claims to have been too tender-hearted (or perhaps inexperienced) for this kind of work, and after a sleepless night of remorse praying that his victim would not die of his wounds (which he did not) he adhered to methods which were more subtle, less bloody, and more constructive. For this group of officers genuinely wished to be economical of blood; their great desire was to purge the State of corruption and shame.

Since they were mostly officers of junior or middle rank, it was necessary for them to find a figurehead to give their plot substance and respectability, and such a one they eventually found in General Neguib, an honest man, a good soldier, and adequately anti-British —but never one of the inner band of confederates. Since some other senior figures whom they approached refused co-operation, their chances of total secrecy were slight; in fact, the plot had to be advanced four months when they became aware that Faruk's political police knew at least something of what was brewing and might strike at any moment. Originally timed for November 1952, the blow was next to be struck on August 5, but warned by phone of his possible impending arrest, Nasser decided on action at forty-eight hours' notice on July 22. The *coup d'état* was well-planned, and almost bloodless. Neguib assumed power "to purge the Army and set up a clean Government." The black-listed army and police officers were arrested. Foreign embassies were assured that there would be no repetition of the arson and slaughter of six months earlier. Even Faruk, his palace at Alexandria surrounded by Egyptian tanks (ten years earlier it had been British tanks in Cairo), escaped unscathed at the price of abdication. In a few hours it was all over. Faruk apologized for his first, understandably shaky, signature, and signed again. At sunset the royal departure for Capri took place with a certain dignity and even a salute of guns before a huge crowd on the seafront. Neguib, coming to see him off, was delayed by the ecstasy of the crowd surrounding his jeep.

It was Neguib, not Nasser, who took the limelight; in fact, Nasser was hardly noticed in the smoke of general rejoicing. There were of course some who tried to use the smoke as a screen. Two leaders of a Left-wing strike at a cotton-mill where arson had broken out again were hanged; hanged reluctantly by the military committee, Nasser voting against, but hanged nevertheless; and immediately the Communists denounced the revolution—the more so when what began by looking like a spectacular land reform fizzled into a mere partial confiscation of a few of the very largest estates, including the King's. As the months went by it became increasingly obvious that the revolution was still only half over. While Nasser and his young colleagues held revolutionary tribunals in the French Revolutionary manner to eliminate the old guard (by imprisonment rather than death), Neguib was going round the country with his friendly pipe and his charming smile, making friends with everybody, workers, peasants, Muslim Brotherhood (he made the pilgrimage to Mecca), even some of the old politicians. He began talking of free elections. This did not suit the Nasser group, who wished power to remain firmly in the Army's hands, and the seesaw struggle between Neguib and Nasser, veiled at first, came gradually into the open, until some of Nasser's young men forcibly detained a sick and depressed Neguib all day long in his house, and extracted from him a promise to abandon his democratic ideas. Neguib remained for a time as a figurehead President, but from that moment (March 1954) Colonel Nasser was the effective ruler of Egypt.

It is true that in 1956 he introduced a so-called constitution which paid some lip-service to democratic institutions and permitted a popular assembly, but the voting was controlled in such a way as to allow Nasser himself to be elected as president with a 97 per cent. majority, a figure approaching what Hitler and Stalin considered convincing. Censorship and propaganda on Nazi lines were maintained, and any public criticism of the regime inside Egypt became quite impossible, as the Cairo newspaper *El Misr* (*Egypt*) found when it reminded Nasser of his promises to introduce social reforms. *El Misr* was immediately and totally suppressed. The University of Cairo and other educational institutions were thoroughly purged; their academic levels fell as their political cheer-leading advanced, until they provided a tame but noisy Nasserite orthodoxy. In 1959 a compulsory two-hours-a-week study of Arab Nationalism was introduced, on the lines of the Russian compulsory Marxism. The extreme Muslim party, the Muslim Brotherhood with whom Neguib had flirted, were persecuted, especially after an attempt on Nasser's life in October 1954. Those who refused to disband or seal their lips were imprisoned, tortured, and beaten; many were hanged. Nasser's relations with the Communists were more complicated. Undoubtedly he used the Communists in his struggle with Britain and in his championship of the Afro-Asian anti-colonial movement. Many of his actions, in buying arms for instance from Russia and Czechoslovakia, or in importing Russian technicians and accepting Russian financial aid, certainly pleased the Communists and at the same time put Nasser under an obligation to the Soviet Union. Moreover, Russia had never occupied Egypt, unlike Britain; so any benefit of the doubt between West and East would naturally tend to go East. But the odd thing was that however loudly the Egyptian Communists praised their Nasser, he continued to keep large numbers of them in prison. The explanation seems basically simple, however apparently contradictory Nasser's policy: first and last, Nasser was an Egyptian and a dictator (or very nearly so). In other words, Nasser was Egypt and Egypt was Nasser. So long as Communist support served his ends, Communism was tolerable; but a Communism that took orders from Moscow or Peking was another matter. "Thou shalt have no other gods before me." So while Nasser could flirt with Khrushchev to bait the British, he could have nothing but harsh words for him when Communists in Iraq thwarted the expansion of Nasser's Arab 'Empire' in 1959. It should be noted, further, that Communism in Egypt remained paradoxically a creed of the well-to-do literate classes and the educated youth; it made only a small impression on the downtrodden poor. The fellah has as yet hardly heard of it.

Nasser's republic was a khaki republic. Not only did power remain with the Junta, the Twelve—Nasser and his young team—but the whole State became subjugated to the Army as in Bismarck's Prussia. The landlord, the pasha, the merchant, the factory-owner, were taught that they had new masters, masters from the lower or middle class; the colonels refused to share their power with any other group.

This did not mean that the millionaires ceased to be millionaires. Egypt during the 'fifties remained a country where a few enjoyed vast wealth and the many suffered a depressing poverty. There was a little less corruption, perhaps—or at least corruption previously naked and unashamed found it prudent to wear clothes. But very little impact was made on Egypt's basic and sensational poverty. For Egypt was one of the most overcrowded, undernourished, and diseased countries in the world. There were two types of squalor in Egypt, both extreme: the squalor of Cairo, that sucked to itself all that part of the nation's life that was not purely agricultural—the swollen civil service, the few ostentatious rich, the professional classes, the industrial proletariat, the swarming sub-world of one of the world's greatest and dirtiest cities; and the larger squalor of the other, agricultural Egypt, where to cultivate more than half a dozen acres made you a 'middle' fellah, where the expectation of life was under thirty years, and yet the population rose alarmingly by about one per minute, where twenty-five million Egyptians struggled to live in that perilously narrow strip between the deserts, 3 per cent. of the total land area. They ate meat perhaps twice a month. At least four out of every five of them suffered from bilharzia, an endemic disease passing by a parasite from the stinking canal water to the bladder and bowels, and so back to the canals. Over half a million were blind. In the rice area 90 per cent. suffered from malaria. A man was past his prime by twenty-one; four out of five were rejected for military service. Ninety-five per cent. of the fellah class were illiterate. A woman was still her husband's property, despite some half-hearted attempts of the Government to alter things (including giving women the vote); and man-made divorce was easy, so that a woman might well have had two husbands and four children by her twentieth birthday. To fail to have children was shameful for a woman; for a man, they were part of his working capital. So the land that had two-and-a-half million in Napoleon's day, twelve-and-a-half million in 1914, and seventeen million in 1940, now (1963) has twenty-seven million—a figure that must be out of date before these words are read.

It would not be fair to say that Nasser's Government did nothing to tackle these terrifying problems. They did much to secure purer water supplies. They set an upper limit of about two hundred acres to any one holding of land; they set up model agricultural communities and some collective farms; they planned the great project for the Aswan High Dam (of which more later)—but things were improving only slowly throughout the 'fifties for the typical Egyptian —the cultivator knee-deep in his pestiferous mud.

These problems demanded an economic, social, and perhaps religious revolution which the colonels were not—at least, in those days —inclined to promote.[1] How much more exciting and rewarding to raise Egypt's status in the world, her pride in herself, by a vigorous, expansionist foreign policy; to flout the Englishman and the American, to champion the Arab and the African, to raise the name of Nasser to be a banner all over the Middle East!

To begin with, the departure of the British had to be secured. The Egyptian revolution of 1952 had interrupted negotiations but they were resumed immediately after, and conducted very toughly on the Egyptian side, with threats of a resumption of guerrilla warfare. Two issues predominated—the evacuation of the troops themselves from the Zone, and the status of the Sudan. This vast partially Arab country to the south of Egypt had been once part of her territories, but for over half a century, under a nominally joint Anglo-Egyptian rule, the British had governed it as part of their Empire. To Nasser it was important for reasons of history, prestige, and power—and among other considerations was the inescapable geographical fact that Sudan controlled the flood-waters of the Nile: the Nile that was

---

[1] In 1962 Nasser seemed to be grasping some of these nettles; most significantly, he foreshadowed a programme of State-backed birth-control.

Egypt's life-blood. The British Government under Churchill and Eden, forced to give ground over the Suez issue, stood firm over Sudan; they were prepared to give the Sudanese, however backward, self-government, and the right to choose their future status—but they would not sell out a largely non-Arab anti-Egyptian Sudan to Nasser. Nasser could not get his own way here. Despite bribery, intrigue, and high-pressure propaganda tours by various of his Ministers, and although the first elections narrowly favoured Egypt, the new independent Sudan maintained its separation (1954).

In Sudan Britain was beginning a phase of history; in Suez she was ending another. British troops began to leave the Canal Zone they had occupied since 1882; and although it could be well argued that so concentrated a base was hopelessly vulnerable to nuclear weapons and therefore merely a potential death-trap, the world saw the evacuation as the mauled and ageing lion in retreat. In particular, Egypt saw it so, and all the other Arab states. Israel saw it so, fearfully, for the British had served to shield her from Egypt's direct hostility. Back in England the Suez Group of extreme Conservatives saw it so, in shame and impotence. They never ceased to blame Eden (and in some degree Churchill) for allowing it, and were a prime influence in the ill-starred attempt of 1956 to win back by violence the ground lost by negotiation.

Undoubtedly Nasser gained enormously in prestige by the removal of the British base from Suez to Cyprus and elsewhere. Millions of Arabs saw him now as hero and liberator. The Egyptian radio went drunk with joy and malice. The Press was airborne on an odd combination of glee, lyricism, and inaccuracy. The triumphant and gloating ill-will of Cairo was loudspeakered forth, not only into every street of the city itself and every town and village of Egypt, but also into Syria, into Jordan (still under a pro-British King, Hussein), across the Red Sea to Saudi Arabia, to the Yemen, to Aden, to Iraq, to Britain's oil centres of Kuwait and Bahrein, to the Algerians in revolt against the French. The British who had come by power and stayed by cunning were on the move; Suez, the kingpin, was no longer theirs. If only Israel could now be overwhelmed and extinguished, what dreams of Arab greatness suggested themselves, what visions of a Nasserite Empire from the borders of Persia to the shores of far Morocco! Nasser was by this time very far indeed from the shy revolutionary student, the severe young officer of former days. Tall, massively built, with broad athletic shoulders and the look of a tiger ready to spring, he presented an 'image' to conjure with. From countless banners and posters his features looked down, with their powerful jaws and gleaming smile. He *looked* a strong man. When he spoke in public his voice was the voice of a strong man, whom an apt occasion could move to frenzied violence. He swiftly learned the arts of the demagogue. Yet he retained in private a great deal of boyish charm and quiet reasonableness. "What I like about this young man," said Nehru, "is that he is always ready to learn." By 1955 he had certainly learned much: when to shout and when to stay quiet, when to be smooth and when to bite, how to put over the studied lie, how to handle crowds and enemies, journalists and foreign diplomats, how to project himself. Adlai Stevenson, a shrewd American, described him as "the strongest personality of his generation; only the small countries have the luck to find such remarkable rulers."

For it was not only the Arabs who built up the ever-growing image of Nasser. The Americans, chronically susceptible since 1776 to suspicions of British imperialism, regarded him through benevolent eyes. When Secretary of State John Foster Dulles, on a visit to Cairo presented a resplendent Colonel Nasser with a silver-plated pistol, it was perhaps taken to signify more than was intended, but it was a tactless gesture, and threw into relief Dulles's own later change of course. In fact, American policy through these years to 1956 was both irresponsible and confused, and was a major factor producing the sad events of 1956.

From the first the American Government had been friendly to Nasser, seeing possibilities of attracting him into an anti-Russian *bloc* of Middle Eastern states. But in Cairo neutralism is a reflex, and Nasser had no intention of joining any Western group. He merely wanted arms. Some small amount he did get, but powerful Jewish-American interests used their influence to prevent him getting weapons that might well be used against Israel. Nasser therefore turned away from the U.S.A. towards the power that would supply him with arms without any initial conditions—the Soviet Union.

Again American finance was to promote the huge high dam at Aswan, which would cost at least thirteen hundred million dollars, and go far to revolutionize Egyptian agriculture. Little was done until the Russian Minister, Shepilov, visited Egypt, and suggested Russian technical and financial assistance. The Americans immediately bid higher. Then in 1955 Nasser went to the Bandung Conference of Afro-Asian nations, talked with Nehru, officially recognized Communist China, and reacted bitterly against the signing of the Baghdad Pact, which was interpreted in Cairo as an attempt by the pro-British Iraq Government to steal the leadership of the Arab world from Nasser. The recognition of Communist China especially smarted in America, and suddenly the Eisenhower-Dulles Government withdrew its promises of finance for the Aswan Dam, and projected Nasser into his angry reply, the nationalization of the Suez Canal.

Nasser, like Nehru and Tito, was determined to be a 'neutralist' in the East-West struggle. But unlike these others', his neutralism was purely opportunist, and took the form of leaning to one side to extract concessions from the other, and then reversing the process. Fear of Egyptian Communism was used to extract diplomatic support, equipment, and even some arms from the United States. Then, when America shilly-shallied, Russia was approached, and sent Nasser plentiful arms and assistance; Nasser's praise of Russia was profuse. Later, in 1959, when Nasser was alarmed by Communist penetration of Iraq, the contrary cry went up of the evils and dangers of international Communism.

In fairness to the Americans, it must be admitted that Nasser in 1955–56 was being very difficult, and very unprincipled. Perhaps his blackmail—the diplomacy of the pistol-point, whether silver-plated or not—had been a little too successful. By 1956 he had made for himself a powerful group of enemies. He had offended the Americans. He had convinced a rather desperate and angry France that he was at the back of the long and bitter Algerian revolt, whose fighters he was supplying with equipment, and with a barrage of radio encouragement. The Israelis knew very well that he was living for the day when he could launch a war of revenge and annihilation against them. And the British were deeply resentful that he had not matched their willingness to make a fresh start in relations. They had evacuated Suez—to what purpose? Egyptian hostility increased, and a flood of lying propaganda emanated from Cairo to poison the minds of men against Britain all over the Middle East and beyond, even to Kenya. Eden in particular, now Prime Minister, was sensitive to the criticism that he had given away much and gained less than nothing. Like Hitler, Nasser waxed hungry on concessions and demanded more. Indeed, there is evidence from Eden's speeches that the parallel with Hitler and the disastrous 'appeasement' of the 'thirties obsessed him as he faced Nasser in the Suez Canal issue of 1956. One man, and that man Nasser, seemed to be responsible for half the evil of the world. Weakness had been fatal in 1936; let them not be weak in 1956. One must learn from history.

Alas, the lessons of history are not so easily learned. The 'Suez affair,' by the time it was over, cost some hundreds of millions of pounds and some thousands of lives, destroyed Eden, removed the foundations from Britain's position in the Middle East, enabled the unprincipled Nasser to pose simultaneously as bleeding victim and triumphant hero, enormously increased Russia's power in the Middle East, gave a shock to liberal friends of Britain and France the world over, and confirmed the worst opinions of their enemies.

Smarting from the Aswan Dam rebuff, an excited Nasser proclaimed on July 26 the nationalization of the Suez Canal, which had been operating for some eighty years under an international company with headquarters in Paris. This sudden action was promptly condemned by Eden, by Gaitskell, by the French, and other users of the Canal; and at the beginning of August both Britain and France began to take threatening military 'precautions.' Nasser's action (strictly legal) was naturally supported by the Communist countries and by the great mass of the African and Asian nations, who saw him as the David of the underprivileged fighting against the Goliath of Imperialism. While the United Nations debated the issues and the American Government continued its obscure, vacillating, but basically cautious, moves, the British, French, and Israeli Governments moved nearer to grasping the dangerous nettle. Just how much collusion there was between the three Powers was later the subject of bitter argument, but certainly there was a high degree of secret understanding between the Israelis and the French, and between the French and the British—and a deliberate withholding of information from the American Ambassadors. There was a state of extreme tension, very near war, between Israel on the one side and Jordan and Iraq on the other all through October, so that no one was surprised when Israel mobilized her armed forces; but the intensity of the world's attention upon the exciting, and eventually tragic, revolutions in Poland and Hungary somewhat distracted notice from the Middle East. Meanwhile Britain and France concentrated land, see and air forces in North Africa, Malta, Cyprus.

Suddenly, on October 29, Israel declared war on Egypt, and for the second time in a decade utterly humiliated the Egyptian Army —which by 1956 ought to have been moderately strong, for it had received a large quantity of tanks and general equipment from Russia and Czechoslovakia during 1955 and 1956. In the United Nations, to the amazement of the world, Britain and France then vetoed a Security Council resolution calling on Israel to withdraw; Anglo-French air attacks on Egypt began, although another week (a very long week) went by before British and French paratroops began landing on Egyptian soil, and occupying key points in and near Port Said. Before then the three nations attacking Egypt had been condemned in the United Nations Assembly by sixty-four votes to five (their own three votes plus Australia and New Zealand). An incredulous and uncomprehending America was shocked: Eden, above all, had been one of the prime architects of peace. The Russian Government threatened to launch rocket-missiles against London and Paris to force a withdrawal. Nehru, and Indian opinion generally, while refusing to condemn Russia's brutal suppression of the Hungarian revolt (November 1956) on the grounds that 'full information' was lacking, condemned Britain in the bitterest terms: it appeared, after all, that the leopard of imperialism could not change its spots. In Cairo there was an atmosphere of defeat, self-pity, indignation, and impotence—but remarkably little anti-foreign violence. The Egyptian Army was largely behind Israeli barbed-wire; the Israeli forces were approaching the Canal; the British and French had occupied much of its northern stretches, which Nasser blocked with dozens of wrecked ships; bombing raids on Cairo were inflated by the Egyptian Press to hysterical proportions; the considerable casualties in Port Said were multiplied by five for world consumption (just as the British perhaps divided by five), and the 'heroic' Egyptian defence of the town was all the military prowess Nasser could boast about in a sad week for his military reputation.

But seldom has a ruler been able to grasp such advantages from so crushing a defeat. World conscience and the threat of Russian rockets saved him. Eden—a broken, pathetic, sick, but in Britain popular, Eden—went abroad for his health, and soon afterwards resigned. A United Nations force took over from the Anglo-French invaders. The Canal was cleared of its obstacles, and remained, efficient as ever, in Egyptian hands; in fact, by 1959 ten more ships a day were going through the Canal than before Nasser's nationalization. Foreign property and assets in Egypt were seized—though this was to some extent offset by the 'freezing' of Egyptian financial credits in London. Above all Russian influence in the Middle East was immeasurably strengthened. The gamble that was to destroy Nasser merely confirmed his power—though it was now plain that that power was dangerously dependent on Russian support, and that this support was not likely to be continued except at a price.

Nasser's course after the Suez affair continued to show the same reckless improvisation as previously, the same daring somersaults on the high wire. He and his controlled Press continued to be vociferously rude to America in public while remaining shrewdly polite behind the scenes. Khrushchev and the Russians were praised to the skies, and a loan towards the Aswan Dam accepted with maximum publicity, while Communists both inside Egypt and in other Arab countries felt the full force of Nasser's hostility. He pressed every means to overthrow Arab Governments hostile to him. Thus in 1958 King Hussein of Jordan succeeded in maintaining his throne against a Nasserite conspiracy only by a display of great personal courage and initiative, and by the assistance of British troops. In Syria Nasser had an enthusiastic following, and the group of young Syrian officers who had controlled the country since 1956, and whom the West suspected of Communism, decided that they had more to gain from a union with Nasser than from the Communists. Suddenly, therefore, in 1958 Nasser and the Syrian President announced an amalgamation of their two countries—not a federation, but a total union, the United Arab Republic. Nasser thus became at a blow ruler of Syria too, and it soon became plain that he was its not entirely popular dictator. One important consequence of his move was that he now controlled the country through which the great oil pipe-lines flowed from Iraq to the Mediterranean—and after the success of the Canal nationalization, it seemed only a matter of time before oil nationalization should follow.

The sudden proclamation of the United Arab Republic brought an even more hasty counter-move from the bitterly anti-Nasser rulers of Jordan and Iraq. These two young Kings, cousins, King Hussein and King Feisal, both British-educated, and maintaining policies friendly to Britain against the wishes of the majority of their peoples, suddenly announced a federation of their two countries, to which King Saud of Arabia soon adhered. A murderous war of words followed, Nasser attacking "the traitor-kings" who had betrayed the Arab cause, and even asserting that King Saud had plotted to assassinate him.

If this was a routine display of Arab brotherhood, what followed was a little out of the ordinary, even for that bubbling cauldron of the Middle East.

Two compound states now confronted one another—Egypt-Syria on the one hand, and Iraq-Jordan-Saudi Arabia on the other—with a third state in their midst, Israel, to which all of them maintained uncompromising hostility. One of these compound states was dominated by a Nasser passionately pan-Arab and nationalist; the other by the corrupt Iraq Government of Nuri Said, obstinately pro-British, anti-Communist, and anti-Nasser. The Iraq capital of Baghdad, though it was full of Russian sympathizers and Nasser-worshippers, had given its name and its allegiance to the Baghdad Pact, which was roughly the Middle Eastern equivalent of NATO—an alliance of powers lying to the south of the U.S.S.R., forming a British-inspired military alliance against her. Many Iraqis, moreover, had always considered their country a more legitimate leader of Arab nationalism than the upstart and semi-African Egypt. They had the best of the Arab armies; they were, too, a slightly less poverty-stricken country than Egypt, with rich oil assets. There was, in short, a mutual jealousy and resentment between Iraq and Egypt; yet, transcending this, the immense prestige of Colonel Nasser and the strongly felt Arab impulse towards greater unity. Baghdad had been for years a city primed for revolution, but Nuri Said, by a combination of intrigue, ruthlessness, corruption, cunning, and sheer ability, had managed to maintain his unpopular regime until now—even through the shocks of the Suez crisis.

But just two years after that crisis—in the summer of 1958—there was a swift and bloody uprising. The young King, Feisal, was murdered, and so, after escape and hiding, was the old fox, Nuri Said, himself—Nasser's most effective enemy in the whole Arab world. Like Nasser's own revolt, it was a military coup, and after severe mob violence (incited by the rebels' broadcasts), General Kassem emerged as the new ruler of Iraq.

Nasser's support for Kassem, at first enthusiastic, soon turned sour, for Kassem endeavoured to maintain, ever more precariously, an independent line between Communists and Nasserites. Kassem, an unpredictable and slightly crazy autocrat, entirely dependent on his army's loyalty, came at last to live in constant and very reasonable fear of assassination. Cairo Radio constantly enjoined the Iraqis to rise and destroy him; and another round in the prolonged bout was opened when Kassem was overthrown and executed in February 1963. His place was taken by Colonel Aref, originally his deputy-leader and fellow-conspirator of 1958, who had later been condemned to death under Kassem but had remained unexecuted in prison. Aref was a much more enthusiastic Nasserite and pan-Arab than Kassem; and Nasser eventually hailed Kassem's fall with as much enthusiasm as he had originally welcomed his rise. But, in the Middle East, old rivalries such as that between Iraq and Egypt die hard.

The Iraq affair of 1958 had another effect; the end of the honeymoon with Khrushchev—for now the Communists appeared as the most powerful rivals of the Nasserites, and the marriage of convenience between Egypt and Russia, solemnized in 1955, strengthened by the Suez affair, soon showed all the signs to be expected from so cynical a union. The bickerings, previously private and subdued, became increasingly public and unrestrained. Yet it was with the help of Russian finance, Russian bulldozers, Russian technicians, that the grand project of the Aswan High Dam was inaugurated in January 1960. For Nasser must have foreign aid if he is to raise his country out of its deep and ancient poverty. Without aid (and even with it) Nasser, for all his flair and glamour, faces a future full of uncertainty. Although he triumphed for a space on a ruthless opportunism and the rashness of his enemies, his nation cannot live by dreams of glory alone. It must also live by bread.

Knowledge of this economic necessity eventually drove Nasser in 1961 to accelerate moves towards the "Socialist Co-operative Society" to which he had previously paid frequent lip-service. State socialism, however, meant nationalization; and that meant fears among the trading and manufacturing communities of both Egypt and Syria. The Syrians did not wait to be socialized. They gave their enthusiastic backing to an Army revolt which in September severed Syria from Egypt by a swift *coup*. Anti-Egyptian national feeling also played its part. Nasser prepared forceful intervention, thought better of it, and accepted with unaccustomed moderation and dignity the accomplished fact. The union of Syria with Egypt had lasted three years only. Then, the following year, Egypt seceded from the Arab League that she could no longer dominate, though she soon proceeded to give assistance to a pro-Nasser revolution in the Yemen. Probably, however, Nasser's greatest opportunities lie inside his own Egypt. If he could finally rid his land of what he himself calls "feudalists and corrupt capitalists"; if his new schemes of public ownership, workers' profit-sharing, workers' representation on boards of management, limitation of profits and incomes, and so forth are enthusiastically pursued and honestly administered; if the effects of his ambitious plans for public health, for school-building, and for raised production can be made to outpace the still rising rate of population growth, then his ultimate reputation will be secure. And if, on top of these achievements, he contrived to bring about a form of political democracy suitable for Egyptian conditions—his avowed aim—the force of Egypt's example would be immense. One decade of Nasser's revolution is over; the second is likely to provide a different emphasis and a new impetus.

Table of Events

12

Mao Tse-tung
(1893–   )

China has a history of unbroken civilization for five thousand years or so—as long a record as any country's in the world. In that time dynasties have come and gone; invaders have streamed down into the fertile plains, conquered, and become assimilated; at least three great religions have permeated the minds of the Chinese—the Buddhist, the Taoist, and above all the Confucian; the fine and useful arts have flowered, decayed, and flowered again many times over. It would be a rash man who would claim that since 1949 a civilization had grown up in this ancient land that had changed *everything* and destroyed the old venerable ways entirely; but at present (1963) it does seem indeed that the new Communist order there has provided not merely a new 'dynasty,' to take its place duly in the history books alongside the Chin, the Han, the Tang, the Sung, the Ming, and all the rest, but a radically new civilization based on a peasant Communism of a kind that Marx certainly never dreamed of. The Chinese number about 700 million, a quarter of the earth's inhabitants. Soon they are likely to be one-third. It seems undeniable, therefore, that what has happened in China since the Second World War is immeasurably the greatest event in recent history.

Great and settled as Chinese civilization was at its best, the vastnesses of the land always permitted rebellion to flourish in remoter parts. Indeed "China" was a rather vague expression: there is China proper, the land of the great river valleys of the lower Yangtse and Yellow rivers over which a central Government has managed to retain undivided authority for about half of the past twenty centuries or so; and then there were the huge outlying provinces such as Manchuria, Mongolia, Sinkiang, and Tibet, sometimes loosely held, sometimes lost for centuries. Sometimes from the outer regions had come the warriors that had conquered the rich lands of China proper to set up their own dynasties, such as the Mongol or the Manchu, but each in its turn to be absorbed by the civilization they had vanquished—to find the brush mightier than the sword. But all this

great area of the Chinese Empire and its fringe peoples constituted
a world; beyond the world lived the 'barbarians.' It was as though
China was a planet to itself.

An occasional space-traveller to that planet, such as Marco Polo,
came back with his account of it to an incredulous Europe. Then,
during the seventeenth and eighteenth centuries, 'barbarians' from
Britain and the west came to trade, but it was not until the early
nineteenth century that European (and especially British) merchants
made sufficient impact on Chinese life for the imperial Manchu
Government of China to take steps to control this overseas trade,
especially the traffic in opium. All commercial intercourse had to
be through Canton, and was restricted by official regulations intensely irritating to British merchants. The upshot was a succession
of wars by which the British and French forced treaties on the
Chinese giving trading rights, special legal and territorial rights in
the major Chinese ports, shipping rights on the Yangtse, free passage for foreigners throughout China, and protection for Christian
missionaries. This defeat at the hands of the Western barbarians was
the beginning of the end for the Manchu regime. From 1850 rebellion followed rebellion, as the West made its humiliating impact,
and China became more and more a semi-colonial dependency.
Many young Chinese learned now to despise their decrepit Government, to pick up Western ideas of material progress and political
democracy, and to look over the water at the huge strides being
made by a Japan that openly aped Western Europe and in 1895
humiliatingly defeated China in war. Others in hatred of the arrogant foreigner started the Boxer Riots of 1900—murderous attacks
on whites and Chinese Christians, suppressed equally murderously
by European troops. By 1909 provincial assemblies were meeting
—and demanding a national Parliament. The Manchu (Ching)
dynasty was plainly disintegrating, and with it the old China. Many
imperialists in Europe and Japan looked forward to a not-far-
distant day when China might be totally partitioned and colonized
as Africa had been.

Such a crumbling in the old days would have brought forth a new
dynasty, either from China itself or from its border provinces, to
inject the ancient body of Confucian China with new life. But in the
twentieth century everything was changed: China was no longer
a world to itself. The new revolutionaries who became prominent
with the revolt of October 1911 soon destroyed the twin pillars upon
which the two-thousand-year Confucian system had rested—the
monarchy itself, and the civil service examinations that creamed off

the finest scholars to the monarchy's use. Confucian forms and customs lingered till Communism swept them away at the mid-century: but their demise began in 1911–12, when Sun Yat-sen and his followers first attempted the experiment of a democratic republic based largely on Western patterns.

The revolution of 1911–12 would have had a hard enough task in such an enterprise in the most favourable circumstances, given the immensity of the country and the poverty of its inhabitants. India, after obtaining independence in 1947, had a similarly immense task —but India had been given some introduction to democratic forms by her British masters. China had had no such introduction; the tradition was one of a scholars' civil service administering the will of an autocratic emperor. Furthermore, China was a battleground of many rival trading nations and many rival ideas of government— British, American, Russian, Japanese in particular. Her students and intellectuals were wide open to all the winds that were blowing —winds of Nationalism, Liberalism, Socialism, and (soon) of Russian-style Communism. And always in China there was the tradition of the local war-lord who found it easy in times of weakened central authority to build up local peasant armies and defy all comers, like a mighty European baron of the Middle Ages. So that it is hardly surprising that ten years or so after the fall of the Manchu Empire, in 1912, its principal hero, Sun Yat-sen, had very limited authority; war-lords fought it out between themselves over much of China; anti-foreign and anti-Christian movements provoked clashes in the big cities, where a ferment of new ideas bubbled through the universities and educated circles, destroying old ideas of religious observance and marriage custom; and meanwhile the age-old peasant life continued largely undisturbed, except by the bandits (but then they were age-old too), and the eternal enemies took their toll as ever—poverty, disease, famine, flood, war.

Among the enthusiasts for Sun Yat-sen's revolution of 1911–12 had been a certain Mao Tse-tung, then a lean student of eighteen. He had been born in 1893, the son of a fairly well-to-do rice farmer from Hunan. His mother was a Buddhist who hoped he might enter the priesthood, his father a strict Confucian who appears soon to have antagonized his young son. Accordingly, Mao himself said, he "hated Confucius from the age of eight"—and apparently his father too, but this was hardly unusual in a China where most of the young intellectuals were in revolt against Confucianism in any case. An able child, from the age of fourteen he attended a secondary boarding-school fifteen miles from his home, and from here, as a rather lonely and unpopular lad given to long tramps over the countryside and secret nocturnal reading by stolen candle-stumps, he entered college in Changsha a few months before the 1911 uprising. His mind was unformed but impressionable. "I was a pure weathercock. I knew nothing. I simply followed the trend." Before long, first at Hankow, then at Changsha itself, he found himself a soldier of the revolutionary army, and after years of study and political activity he found his way at twenty-five to Peking, where he obtained a position of assistant in the university library. In Peking, although he took little part in political affairs, he was enormously influenced by the climate of thought in the university, and especially by a certain Professor Chen Tu-hsiu, leader of the pro-Western renaissance known as the New Tide, prophet of the new, rejuvenated China, and one of the true founders of Chinese Communism—though one doubts if he would have approved of the paths it eventually took.

Mao did not remain in Peking, but—although he was now married, to another professor's daughter—he lived for some time the life of a wandering scholar, subsisting on very little, moving from Peking to Shanghai and back near home to Changsha, while away in the University of Peking there occurred anti-foreign demonstrations and the famous students' strike of May 4, 1919, from which Mao himself dated the origins of the Communist Party in China. When in 1921 the First Congress of that Party was held in Shanghai Mao was there with the dozen or so others. At almost the same moment a certain Chou En-lai was founding a Chinese Communist Party in France, and still others abroad founded similar groups. Of these early pioneers, some were executed by war-lords; some deserted to Chiang Kai-shek's nationalists; some were executed by Chiang Kai-shek; some were expelled from the Party; only Mao and Chou have survived and flourished.

Sun Yat-sen himself, thwarted of his vision of a unified democratic China, and disappointed by lack of American support, turned towards Russia in these last years of his life. The Chinese Nationalist Party, or Kuomintang, that looked to him as its leader, was reorganized largely on Russian advice; and when Sun Yat-sen propounded the three basic principles of Nationalism, Democracy, and Socialism, these were widely enough defined to allow Communists freely to enter Kuomintang ranks. When Sun died in 1925 he bequeathed to the Kuomintang the legend of his name, a broadly acceptable programme, and a Party organized on a nation-wide basis; and the Kuomintang began its great bid to build a new unified

China. But within the Kuomintang was the virus that was to destroy it, the Communist Party of China.

Chiang Kai-shek himself at this time, having just visited Russia, was full of praise for its achievements, and when he became President of the new Kuomintang Military Academy, in 1924, it was none other than Chou En-lai who was head of its department of political education. When Chiang's army struck northward in 1926, carrying high hopes that it would rid China of the curses of war-lords, bandits, and perhaps even of foreign imperialists, it had Moscow's blessing, as well as some supplies shipped from Vladivostok. In Moscow there was even a new Sun Yat-sen University for Chinese students.

Chiang Kai-shek won big successes. He took Changsha, Wuchang, Hankow, and, in 1927, Shanghai itself, but from the start the Communists were a thorn in his side. They wished to turn the national revolution into a workers' and peasants' revolution, and to hunt down, expel, and destroy all foreign 'imperialists.' In Hankow, Shanghai, Nanking, Canton, and elsewhere they stirred up strikes and anti-foreign incidents like that at Nanking, which provoked American and British gunboats to protect their own nationals by laying down a barrage of protective gunfire. In the country districts of the south (and 90 per cent. of Chinese were peasants) they encouraged bloody agrarian revolts in which unpopular landlords were murdered, and peasant associations temporarily dominated the countryside. All this Chiang Kai-shek disapproved of, and in 1927 he called on the Kuomintang to break with the Communists, and temporarily resigned his command.

Mao Tse-tung was in January 1927 sent from Shanghai to report on the revolts of the peasants in Hunan. His sympathies were entirely with them. Admittedly, he said, they had instituted a reign of terror against landlords, smashing their luxuries before their eyes —their sedan chairs and opium pipes—and dancing on "the ivory beds of their daughters"; admittedly they had robbed and murdered. But revolution was not "a dinner party, nor a poem, nor a painting, nor a piece of pretty embroidery"; and the landlords, he asserted, had committed far worse crimes against the peasants—lynching, torture, mutilation, burning alive.

Mao's 'report' was hardly a set of impartial findings. He had, in fact, had a considerable hand himself in the promotion of these peasants' associations, and in this same year he attempted to lead a revolt, known as the Autumn Harvest Rising, which was severely crushed. Mao had by this time arrived at a conclusion that was to have much significance for the future of China and the world: it was the peasants that must make the revolution. All orthodox Marxists had previously laid stress on the vital rôle to be played in Communist revolutions by the proletariat, the industrial working class, and had thus accepted industrialization as a necessary preliminary to socialist society. But China was a land overwhelmingly of peasants, many of them landless òr nearly so, and therefore the problem of Chinese Communism, considered Mao, was the problem of organizing a mass peasant movement and an agrarian socialist revolution. This movement and this revolution were eventually his unique achievements.

Chiang Kai-shek would have none of this anti-landlord, antiforeign extremism. He acted with brutal energy to purge the Kuomintang of its Communist elements. He struck terror into the rebel peasants whose activities had been so favourably commented upon by Mao; he cleared Canton of its Communist Government; for a time he severed all relations with the U.S.S.R. and seized the Chinese Eastern Railway that Russia had controlled for many years. (Russia, however, restored her hold by direct invasion in 1930.) Mao and his fellow-sympathizers became hunted men. The fateful breach between the Nationalists and the Communists was complete.

Chiang Kai-shek at this time (1927–31) almost, but not quite, succeeded in uniting China under the Kuomintang. He captured Peking, the 'Northern Capital,' though he preferred to set up his own capital at Nanking, nearer to the heart of China; and there was centred the National Government of the Republic of China. There too was built, on Purple Mountain, a grandiose tomb for Sun Yat-sen, who was re-buried in pomp, and deified much as Lenin was in Russia—resting as unsuitably in his great Red Square mausoleum. Children recited Sun's praises, learned his principles, bowed before his portrait, and sang the Kuomintang song. Most of the settled and progressive elements in China approved of the developing regime —industrialists, traders, bankers, intellectuals; European and American Governments approved too. Chiang had recently married a Christian wife; he had himself been baptized into the Methodist persuasion; he, she, and the China they represented were highly regarded abroad. China seemed perhaps to be emerging from the shadows; another decade or so, and perhaps Chiang could rid her of the few remaining war-lords, and of the everlasting bandits that infested her mountains and plains.

There remained, however, two more deadly enemies: the invading Japanese and the Communists. The Japanese were not to undertake full-scale invasion until 1937, but already in 1931 they were chafing at Chiang Kai-shek's increasing mastery of Greater China, and especially of Manchuria. In 1930 it was the Russians who had asserted their power by recapturing the railway that ran through Manchuria. Now, in 1931, the Japanese suddenly pounced. The last thing they wanted to see was a powerful unified China, and within a year they seized the three provinces of Manchuria, and set up the surviving heir of the old Manchu dynasty as a puppet emperor of a new state they called Manchukuo, which they proceeded to industrialize and incorporate in the swelling Japanese Empire. The League of Nations showed itself powerless to intervene.

After the ruthless repression of Communists in 1927, when in Shanghai and other great cities they were suddenly pounced upon, disarmed, shot, and thrown into common graves, Mao Tse-tung had gone to ground in the Changsha district, where he continued to foment peasant disturbances. He was by now undisputed leader, and he even had the official approval of the Communist International (Comintern), which admitted defeat for their policy of urban revolution, and adopted Mao's own line—an agrarian revolution. The centre of Mao's revolt was, to begin with, the Hunan-Kiangsi border, with its pine-forests and foggy mountains, very suitable for guerrilla fighters. The winter of 1927–28 was spent in the captured Buddhist cliff-face monastery of Chinkanshan, which served as headquarters and fortress for a motley army of desperate peasants and bandits, six hundred of whom were recruited on condition that they would accept political indoctrination. Mao made great play with slogans that every one was made to learn and repeat like a multiplication table or religious text:

> When the enemy advances, we retreat,
> When the enemy halts and encamps, we harass him.
> When the enemy seeks to avoid battle, we attack.
> When the enemy retreats, we pursue.

Many men were lost, but new volunteers outnumbered them until the mountain-fortress became overpopulated and faced starvation. On January 1, 1929, therefore, the men of this Red Army, led by Mao and Chu Teh, moved down from their mountain lair towards the hills of Kiangsi. There they faced bitter privations and a bloody defeat when they raided a defended town to gain ammunition. For eighteen months their grim wandering and their reign of terror against the landlords continued; their losses and gains balanced. When they moved against Changsha itself they were defeated, and again they withdrew, this time to the pine-forested hills of Kiangsi to face the winter of 1930–31, hungry, cold, ragged, ill-armed, out-numbered.

For the next three years this pattern of events was several times repeated. The Red guerrillas under Mao developed great skill in the dangerous and desperate game they were playing of long marches, hidden concentrations, sudden strikes, equally sudden vanishings. A factor in their favour, and one which in the long run would prove decisive, was the sympathy they enjoyed of the local peasantry—hardly surprising in view of their rigorous treatment of large or unpopular landlords. As one Kuomintang general put it, "Wherever we go we are in darkness: wherever the Reds go, they are in the light." By 1931 there existed an official Kiangsi Soviet; indeed, that December there met what was ambitiously designated the First All-China Congress of Soviets. The claim was grandiose, but Chiang Kai-shek did not make the mistake of under-estimating his Communist enemies. Five times between 1931 and 1934 he launched 'annihilation campaigns' against them. Four times he failed, and once 35,000 of his men deserted to the enemy. But the fifth time, advised by the German general, von Falkenhayn, he successfully blockaded the Communist area, 'scorched the earth' around it, and threatened to starve out the entire district. The support of the local population wavered. Many of them were put to death—for after the Red terror came the White counter-terror. The Communist Army dwindled from 180,000 to under 100,000, enclosed in a contracting ring drawn by 500,000 well-led and partly mechanized Kuomintang troops. In October 1934 Mao and his fellow-leaders took the famous decision which may be called at once panicky and heroic: to disband the Kiangsi Soviet, escape through the ring, and undertake the Long March which would bring them to the other end of China, six thousand twisting miles away.

Here, in the Yenan district of North Shensi, towards the eastern end of the Great Wall of China another Soviet group was operating, and at long last the remnants from Kiangsi, after two years' wanderings, joined forces with them to continue the struggle. But in 1934 no one knew the destination of these heroic stragglers: certainly not their leaders. They were wandering in search of other Soviet groups wherever they were to be found. The going was almost fantastically hard. Twenty-five thousand perished in the first three weeks. To begin with it rained endlessly as they hid by day and marched by night. Harassed by Kuomintang forces, attacked by the armies of local war-lords, hunted by planes, they fought their way westward, first of all, towards Szechuan, then northward to Shensi.

"There were so very many battles," one survivor said. "Now, when I look back, it seems to be one enormous battle going on for ever." A score of major rivers were crossed, and as many mountain chains. On the borders of Tibet they had to negotiate treacherous gorges, and one particularly nightmarish crossing, under fire, of a swaying half-destroyed bridge three hundred feet above a black torrent. They had to cross the Great Snow Mountain (16,000 feet), where Mao was ill with fever, and half the pack-animals died. Turning north after a month's stay in Szechuan, they suffered worst of all in crossing marshy grasslands where rain, fog, cold, giant mosquitoes, and hostile tribesmen aggravated their already appalling condition. The remaining pack-animals perished, the last medical supplies were lost. The laggards were abandoned, the survivors reduced to chewing wild roots and hides, until the lucky moment when they could barter weapons for the wheat or cattle of the primitive tribesmen—who might well proceed to use their new-won rifles against the intruders as a variant to poisoned arrows. For these Communist soldiers were more than mere soldiers; they were explorers in unknown regions. Mao made notes of new flora, strange trees, unmapped mountains, unknown tribes. It is not surprising that the Long March became a legend, or that modern China abounds in stories, poems, and ballads about the epic journey. Mao himself, though often ill, proved tough enough to survive; he himself claims to have felt "perpetually exhilarated" by the dangers and the ever-renewed wonder of still being alive despite everything. On occasions he would celebrate the wonder in a poem. He was, after all, a scholar and a man of letters. His co-leader, Chu Teh, a man of immense stamina, actually crossed the marsh grasslands three times. Nearly 100,000 strong when they left Kiangsi, the marchers were 20,000 when they reached Shensi, but many of these survivors had enlisted on the way. In October 1935, a year from the starting date, the leading column reached the Yenan district of North Shensi, having come six thousand perilous miles; others arrived later, and it was another year before the last column came in. It is claimed that these tough peasant armies had on their journey, besides fending off incessant Kuomintang attacks, defeated the forces of ten warlords and captured sixty-two towns. The "revolution within a revolution" had been saved—and Mao Tse-tung was now its unquestioned leader.

The withdrawal of the Communists to the remote northern hills pushed one of Chiang Kai-shek's worries, as it were, to the back of the drawer, and although he did go north to plan another 'annihilation campaign,' he found one of his own northern generals so violently opposed to the idea that for a space Chiang was actually arrested by his own subordinate and his life threatened. Strangely enough, he was rescued from this dangerous and humiliating predicament at least partly by Communist intervention. For Chou En-lai was sent by Mao to intervene in the dispute, to negotiate a renewal of the Kuomintang-Communist alliance, and to help create a unified anti-Japanese front. The Red Army was reorganized as the Chinese Eighth Route Army, and the Communists obtained Chiang's recognition as a self-governing Border Administration.

This bargain, after all the horrors of the Long March, might be considered a strange one, but Mao and Chou justified it on the ground that national unity against the Japanese was imperative, and they had at least ensured that Kuomintang forces would now fight the Japanese rather than Chinese Communists. For by now the Japanese threat to China had become full-scale and mortal. Japan itself was by this time completely under the control of aggressive nationalists, with the Army officers enjoying great power and prestige, and by 1937 they were ready to attempt no less than the subjugation of the whole of China. Rapidly annihilating Chiang's small air force, they could bomb the great cities as they pleased, and with their vastly superior mechanization could be sure of victory in pitched battles. They soon captured Shanghai, Nanking, and Hankow—the last two being successive capitals of Chiang's China—and forced him to set up his headquarters at Chungking, far away inland, high on the Yangtse, in Szechuan. Japanese warships could not penetrate so far up the river, and their armies would have to cross a mountainous, railway-less, and largely roadless land to reach him there. As the Communists had already demonstrated—and Chiang already knew to his cost—it was ideal land for unmechanized, or guerrilla, resistance.

Japan, allied with the Axis Powers in Europe, now entered upon her years of greatest triumph. Aiming to build a great south-east Asian "co-prosperity sphere," she exploited the 1940 defeats of Britain, France, and Holland rapidly to overrun their large colonial territories in the area. Gambling on the effects of surprise, she sank much of the American Pacific fleet in Pearl Harbour. By the spring of 1942 her Navy ruled the eastern seas, and her armies were stretched from the Indian border to the islands immediately north of Australia. In China itself she had persuaded a leading Kuomintang politician to head a new puppet regime pledged to collaborate in the "co-prosperity sphere." Meanwhile the Anglo-American

Allies promoted Chiang Kai-shek to a position of extreme respect, accepted China as one of the major 'free' countries, flew in supplies to Chungking from Indian aerodromes (after the Japanese cut the Burma Road), and did everything in their power to save independent China from extinction. Chiang's regime, however, was declining from causes other than his purely military reverses—though these too imposed their own heavy strain. His officials were deplorably corrupt: much United Nations relief and American aid went astray to private destinations, and a bribe came to be the necessary lubricant to make any wheels revolve. His currency became inflated, and eventually collapsed to one three-millionth of its 1937 value. Those among his supporters who used 'police-state' methods gained in power, and the atrocities of his concentration camps became notorious; as an American general officially reported to the President, "secret police operate widely.... People disappear. Students are thrown into jail. No trials and no sentences ... Every one lives with a feeling of fear.... The Kuomintang has become to the Communist revolution what the old, war-lord regimes were to Chiang as he rose to power." In other words, liberals, progressives, and intellectuals were gravitating increasingly towards the Communist ranks. Lacking a true popular backing, he was forced more than ever to rely on the support of the moneyed and official classes. Stalin might proclaim as he did that Chiang, the patriot, was the true leader of all China, and Churchill and Roosevelt might confer with Chiang on equal terms as they did in Cairo in 1943, but by that time his rule was already diseased with the germs that were to destroy it.

The Communists in Yenan, on the other hand, went from strength to strength. By 1945 they controlled an area of 300,000 square miles and a population of 95 million. They had gradually built up an army of over a million men—and an army, moreover, that was not the principal object of the Japanese attacks. It could avoid the heavy casualties attendant on set battles; it could gradually enlarge the north Communist areas, expel landlords and redistribute their land among the peasants, set up village co-operatives, indoctrinate the young in Communist principles, promote the status of women—while still inflicting continual damage on the northern Japanese armies in hundreds of painful pin-prick campaigns. Mao Tse-tung continued to argue for collaboration with the Kuomintang, while remaining free to criticize it. In a series of pamphlets written at this time, he emphasized over and over again that "the people must rule. There is no rule without the people. We must find what the people want, and then satisfy them." Coalition with the Kuomintang would be necessary, and perhaps for a long period, just as capitalism might be necessary for a long period. The great immediate enemies were foreign imperialism, especially that of the Japanese, and feudal landlordism, which extracted from the peasant between 40 and 70 per cent. of his crops. The immediate social need was agrarian reform—for in China between 6 and 9 per cent. of the population (estimates vary) owned 65 per cent. of the land.

By 1945 Mao Tse-tung felt strong enough to demand a coalition between equals; and given such a coalition he felt assured that the Communists' more popular social programme must guarantee them ultimate victory. Chiang Kai-shek was in an almost impossible dilemma: distrusting the Communists (as well he might) he felt unable to co-operate with them fully; but if he were to try once more to annihilate them as he did in the early 'thirties it might well wreck the Kuomintang and his own dominance. In the autumn of 1945, a month or so after American atom bombs had fallen on Hiroshima and Nagasaki, Mao flew southward to meet his old rival and attempt a settlement; but it was only half achieved; the two Chinese armies remained separate and mutually hostile, and the two leaders mutually distrustful. Mao said later, "He treated me like a peasant." The stage was set again for civil war; this time it was to be decisive.

To begin with, Chiang Kai-shek won big successes. The Communists were driven from Yenan and from much of the central plains. By 1947 the Kuomintang appeared to be in control of almost all China. Backed by American aid; accepted in theory by Stalin; possessing a seat on the Big Five of the United Nations Security Council; elected in May 1948 President of China by a National Assembly in Nanking that was to inaugurate a new, democratic, dynamic modern China—Chiang Kai-shek was an outstanding world figure. He announced that he intended to destroy the Communists within six months.

At that very moment the disasters began. A Communist force struck a sudden successful blow at the big town of Kaifeng, in Central China. By the end of 1948 all Chiang's armies in Manchuria had surrendered, and great quantities of American equipment now began to fall into Communist hands, to be used gratefully by them in the task of expelling American imperialism from China. Mao now thundered against the Kuomintang as the creatures of a hated foreign domination. "The particular task of the Chinese Communists," he said at the end of 1948, "is to unite all revolutionary forces within the whole country, to drive out American imperialism.

overthrow the reactionary rule of the Kuomintang, and establish
a unified democratic people's republic in alliance with the Soviet
Union." In Europe the 'cold war' was now on, and no longer was
Stalin likely to support Chiang Kai-shek. In China a new and powerful ally in that war was suddenly appearing—however incalculable
in the long run.

By the beginning of 1949 the avalanche of Red victories was on
the move. The Communist leaders had reason to boast as they did,
"Our army moves among the people as a fish swims in water."
Tientsin fell, and then Peking, after a forty-day siege. Communist
detachments, many of them northern peasants to whom the great
centuries-old capital was a novel mystery, paraded through the town
with bands playing. There was no looting, no molestation of women,
no drunken celebrations; these Communist armies had developed a
puritanical discipline that now stood them in good stead. As a
French observer wrote, "Chinese soldiers who knew how to fight,
who after victory did not pillage the conquered town, who slept on
the pavement instead of invading the houses . . . and who paid for
their tickets in the trams, must really be soldiers from another
planet." The new administrators were often idealistic, sometimes
fanatical, seldom corrupt: a great popular force was sweeping
away the bases of Chiang's power. Whole armies now deserted
to the Communists, with their generals and their fine American
equipment. Nanking fell, Hangchow, Hankow, Shanghai itself (the
heart of foreign imperialism), Foochow, Canton, Chungking. The
Englishman, Peter Townsend, describes the Victory Parade in
Peking:

> Dragon dancers twisted and writhed in the streets. Workers pushed
> mammoth floats of railway engines. A crowd of housewives with brooms
> and brushes rushed to take their place in a procession pursued by de-
> lighted apprentices shouting "Dance! Dance!" And in the evening the
> army passed, well-armed, well-shod, with convoys of American lorries,
> tanks and field guns, an exhibition of an army equipped with captured
> weapons. . . . At midnight they were as many as ever, soaked through,
> singing, peasants from Shantung, Honan, the North-east, peasants almost
> to a man . . .

In an astonishing year the whole of China fell into the hands of the
faction that a year before had been given only six months to live.
The remnants remaining loyal to Chiang Kai-shek succeeded in
escaping over the sea to Formosa. The remaining 600 million were
for the first time for a century under the control of a strong Government whose sway was undisputed over the whole of Greater China.

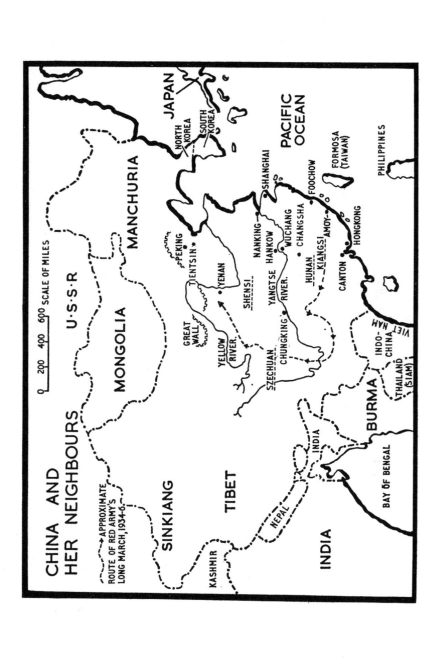

CHINA AND
HER NEIGHBOURS

→ APPROXIMATE
ROUTE OF RED ARMY'S
LONG MARCH, 1934-6.

0 200 400 600 SCALE OF MILES

U·S·S·R

MONGOLIA

MANCHURIA

SINKIANG

TIBET

NEPAL

KASHMIR

INDIA

INDIA

BAY OF BENGAL

BURMA

THAILAND (SIAM)

INDO-CHINA

VIET NAM

JAPAN

NORTH KOREA

SOUTH KOREA

PACIFIC OCEAN

FORMOSA (TAIWAN)

PHILIPPINES

PEKING

TIENTSIN

YENAN

SHENSI

NANKING

SHANGHAI

WUCHANG

HANKOW

CHANGSHA

FOOCHOW

HONGKONG

CANTON

AMOY

KIANGSI

HUNAN

YANGTSE RIVER

CHUNGKING

SZECHUAN

YELLOW RIVER

GREAT WALL

Never before, perhaps, in history, had such vast power fallen so suddenly and sensationally into any leader's hands.

What kind of man was it that wielded this new, huge dominion? Not one that proclaimed himself loudly to the world in general, as Mussolini did, or Hitler, or even Lloyd George, or Roosevelt. A quiet, even secretive, man, standing apart from his fellows; affable with strangers, and courteous, however capable of toughness and decision. One who lived simply, in his blue 'overalls' uniform, with something of Lenin's contempt for luxury; and, again like Lenin, unmistakably an intellectual. In political matters he saw things in black and white, and his political writings, hammering away at their one over-riding 'truth' of the peasant revolution, were hardly subtle or tolerant. But he was bred a scholar and a poet. Even on the Long March he was never without a pocket copy of one of the classical novels of China in his pocket. He wrote much poetry himself in the strict verse discipline of the old writers, without making high claims for himself. He was a strong believer in literature and the arts, but saw them essentially as handmaidens of the revolution; they had no right to an independent existence. Literature was good literature if it reflected and inspired the people's movement. A play was a good play if it dramatized the tyranny of the old world, the promise of the new. This utilitarian philosophy he expressed himself. "Our duty is not to add flowers to the embroidery but to send coal to the snowbound." Physically he was rather tall, with broad shoulders, and a shock of black hair brushed back from a high forehead. Soon the world was to know only too well the features of his now fattening face, for the giant image of this quiet man (as of that other quiet man, Stalin) soon shouted to the world from a thousand processions carrying high a hundred thousand banners—a 'personality cult' carried to monstrous extremes.

The People's Revolution was carried through rapidly and relentlessly, and most fairminded Westerners must see it with mixed feelings of approval, admiration, apprehension, and horror. This strong 'missionary' Government—probably the strongest China has ever known—began an entire reshaping of society. The sort of land reform that the Communists had already introduced in their own areas was extended to the whole of China: landlords' holdings were simply taken, and redistributed among the poor and landless peasants, while in places co-operative and collective farms on the Russian model were instituted. If in the process unpopular landlords were shot or hanged, it must be remembered, as Mao said (though he did discourage the grosser excesses), "Revolution is not like doing embroidery." Murder and terror should not be excused, but they may be explained. Landlords who had caused peasants to rot un-tried in jail for two or three years, or who had organized the torture of peasant 'agitators,' might deserve the mercy of God, but they could hardly expect the mercy of the triumphant people in 1949–50. Less worthy of extenuation were the group executions, where public indignation was systematically fomented, and finally public atten-dance encouraged while "enemies of the people" were liquidated. It is not known how many were put to death during these early months when the revolutionary metal was white-hot; the American authority, Professor Latourette, puts a conservative estimate at three to five million. Communists naturally claim far fewer.

Indoctrination of all classes and age-groups was more thorough and all-pervasive than in any previous society in any country in any century. Children were encouraged to spy on their parents and report "reactionary tendencies." The magazine *Young China* put it thus—"If there are still those among our parents who are not upright, we young must liquidate them in the spirit of the formula which pro-claims: *Liquidate blood relations in the cause of justice. . . .* Your father will even be grateful to you and the People's Government, who have been the instruments of his salvation." Street committees kept similar watch on renegade neighbours. Companies would ask their employees to write down everything they knew of their col-leagues; bank clerks disclosed details of accounts; and then perhaps a year later the victims would be removed for imprisonment and "re-education." An overpowering collective conscience was built up where individual revolt became psychologically almost impossible. The will of the people, as directed by "Chairman Mao" and the Communist authorities, became sovereign and total; refusal to wel-come it came to be accepted as a form of mental disease to be treated in prisons which were also asylums or rehabilitation centres. In these, brain-washing techniques were practised with brilliant success, and in a short space of years propaganda and the collective reforma-tive will had produced an utter transformation in the Chinese scene. The cities that used to house the greatest population of thieves, beggars, opium-addicts, gamblers, and prostitutes in the world soon had none of these. Like the liberal professors, the capitalists, and the diehard Confucians, they were 're-educated' into 'right thinking' —all, that is, who had not committed suicide, fled to Hongkong, or been confined to labour camp. Just as millions of Chinese bodies were re-clothed in the blue boiler-suit-plus-peaked-cap that became universal, so millions of Chinese minds were strait-jacketed into a uniformity that no other civilization has ever paralleled. How should one assess the balance of good and evil in such a transformation? The Chinese Communists abolished beggary, prostitution, capitalism; but they also abolished independent thought. They, in a sense, went near to abolishing 'crime'; but they invented the new crime of "incorrect thinking," and perhaps one Chinese in forty or fifty is still in a labour camp expiating that unforgivable offence.

This total mastery of the collective will had some strange and sensational successes. The regime decided to make war on flies, since these were unhygienic and disease-bearing. Suddenly all China was organized in a frantic competitive campaign to kill flies. Targets were reached, norms fulfilled, the swatter-heroes duly rewarded. The flies had largely gone. Similarly with sparrows: an orgy of socialist exhortation, a fanatical trapping and banging—and the sparrows were no more.

In economic matters Mao's regime made big strides. To begin with, private industry was tolerated, together with the existence of an employer class; but more and more State enterprises were launched under the direction of the Communist Party. In 1952 there was a grand onslaught on the *bourgeoisie*; and fines, confiscations, trials, and 'confessions' completed the downfall of China's industrial employers and merchants. Great public works were inaugurated all over China, and despite some assistance under the Russo-Chinese Treaty of 1950, most of the construction, in view of Chinese industrial backwardness, had to be by hand labour. Symbolic of this new technical achievement was the new road-and-rail bridge over the Yangtse, at Wuhan, over a mile long; it was built overwhelmingly by hand labour, the earth and concrete being shifted by many thousands of men and women, balancing their wicker baskets with their shoulder-poles. There were ambitious schemes of land reclamation, irrigation, and flood prevention, especially on the Yellow River. Russian technicians and advisers, plus unlimited enthusiasm, plus vast manpower resources, achieved much that might have been thought beyond a non-industrialized nation's hopes. But Mao and his advisers were determined that China *should* become industrialized. Inevitably, there followed a five-year plan—later set to be completed in four years. In the late 'fifties they aimed to take the Great Leap Forward into the future, and especially by multiple 'back-yard' furnaces, to catch up with British steel production in ten years; "work hard for a few years," said the placards and the radio, "and live happily for a thousand." One Peking poster in 1959 gaily showed the Chinese people in a dragon boat, skimming the waves under curly clouds, while in the distance an alarmed John Bull, on the deck of a leaky old sailing-vessel, watched their progress through a telescope—the picture being capped by the slogan, "We will overtake Britain in fifteen years," and providing a nice combination of production propaganda and patriotism. By 1960 China could boast an atomic reactor and cyclotron; and factories making cars, aircraft, steamships, electronic tubes, machine tools, power generators, and a hundred other manifestations of the modern age. And although her booming production targets ran far ahead of her published achievements, and these in turn were ahead of subsequently amended figures, still there had been impressive strides towards the industrialization that must come before China could become one of the giant world powers.

Material progress there certainly has been, although it would be unwise to over-estimate it. Unemployment and beggary have been got rid of. The State has kept the value of money stable. It pays its lowest workers better wages than they used to get, and some—in particular Party officials—are tolerably well off. There are many new schools; there are nurseries where working mothers can leave their children. Crime and sexual vice are sensationally diminished. There are no alcohol advertisements or 'public attractions' to lure the citizen to part company with his money or his virtue. Public amusements and sports are cheap, worthy, and popular. For the common man, woman, and child, life is undoubtedly better than in the old days. The old days, however, were very bad indeed, and the average Chinaman still lives in direst poverty. In the villages especially so—and over 500 million live in the villages. Mao Tse-tung himself said in the mid-'fifties, "On account of the teeming population there is a scarcity of cultivated land. . . ." As a result of frequent natural disasters—flood, drought, wind, hail, frost, or insects—and of backward methods of farming, many of the peasants—Mao suggested perhaps 70 per cent.—"are still in difficulties. . . . For them Socialism is the only solution."

This intractable problem of socializing a peasant population (which largely defeated both Stalin and Tito in their day) lay at the core of Mao Tse-tung's problem. He was himself a peasant. He had brought off the remarkable achievement of a peasant 'Communist' revolution. But how was he to communize the Communists? While it was merely a matter of punishing landlords and redistributing their land there were no difficulties. But as collective farms and co-operatives were introduced the old problem raised its beastly

head: the peasants, to quote Mao, were "imbued with Capitalism."
In other words, they were individualists (especially the more prosperous among them), and wished to increase their private holdings.
Eventually Mao's Government attempted an extreme solution:
nothing less than to divide the whole of China up into 'communes.'
In return for labour the workers were to receive food, clothing,
housing quarters, and education for their children, and a small
money wage was to be paid for other requirements until the later
happy day when the State could undertake to provide *everything*,
and money payments could disappear. All adults were to work com-
pulsorily for the community. Mothers were to be 'relieved' of the
task of bringing up their children, who were to be reared from a
tender age by the nurses and teachers of the commune, returning
home one night per week. The family as a unit was to become sub-
sidiary, or even eventually to disappear. Men and women would normally sleep in separate dormitories. All land, of course, was to be
communal property. The opposition to this staggeringly ambitious
plan, however, was so strong that the Chinese Communist Party
announced in December 1958 a slowing-up of the rate of reorganization, and promised that peasants in the communes would be
allowed to keep some personal property, animals, and tools. Collective labour would be limited to twelve hours a day, the dormitory
system modified, and communes for the cities 'temporarily' abandoned. Even in its modified state, however, this attempt of Mao
Tse-tung really to *create Communism*, an entirely new basis of
society, makes Russian Communism sound almost half-hearted,
and Khrushchev a positive reactionary.

The rulers of Russia might well look with mixed feelings towards
Mao and his China of the Great Leap Forward. In 1950 Stalin had
signed the important treaty of friendship and assistance, and the
solidarity of the two great Communist empires remained firm
enough. The only foreigners welcomed in China after 1950 were
Russians, apart from other Communists or specially impressionable
visitors, and the propaganda machines of both countries unceasingly
rammed home the virtues of the anti-imperialist peace-loving powers
in the struggle against the warmongers of Western Europe and
America. China, however, had by 1962 a population of about 700
million, against rather over 200 million in the U.S.S.R.; and every
year the disparity is increased as twelve to fifteen more million are
added to the numbers of the Chinese. In a few more decades—
probably before A.D. 2000—they are likely to number 1000 million.
If their industrial and military strength continues to rise at its

present rate they could well present the U.S.S.R. with a formidable rivalry.

The attitude of Mao Tse-tung's Government towards this bounding population graph has been variable. At times they have appeared to see in it China's most potent weapon, the "big battalions" that have made her a great Power. At others (in 1955, for instance) they promoted talk of birth control, and appeared to be willing to limit the quantity of Chinese to improve the quality of their living standards. Certainly multitudinousness is a double-edged weapon: it gives more arms to work, more fingers on the trigger, but more stomachs to be fed. It presses ever more heavily on a land-hungry country. It takes away with one hand many of the advantages that technical improvements bring with the other.

The Communist landslide of 1949 was much more than a merely Chinese revolution. It gave the signal for general Communist revolt throughout Asia, and for two or three years there appeared to be a real prospect of many more countries being swamped by an anti-colonialist tidal-wave upon which Communist forces might ride to power. In this Far Eastern struggle the Chinese Communists had three great advantages: first, the high prestige of Mao Tse-tung's Chinese revolution, with its successes against corruption and white domination; second, the fact that the Chinese were themselves spread wide through South-East Asia outside their homeland, in such territories as Malaya and Indonesia, Burma and Indo-China— 'missionaries' in many cases of the new Red China; and, third, the extreme poverty of the whole area, which made it ripe for revolution. To counter-balance these advantages there were some drawbacks. First and most important, the people of India, Pakistan, Burma, Ceylon, and Indonesia had already won their independence from the British and Dutch before 1949, and Malaya could by that time see the promised prize within her grasp. Second, the Malays and non-Chinese people tended often to oppose Communism simply because it *was* Chinese-sponsored and therefore foreign. Third, the Western Powers reacted vigorously to Communist pressure. The British organized the extinction of the Malayan jungle guerrillas; the French fought a long and bitter war against the Indo-Chinese Communists (which, however, they lost); and when the Communists in Korea attempted to seize the whole peninsula the American Government and United Nations forces reacted so promptly that General Mac-Arthur was able to defeat their attempt and preserve at least a *South* Korean State free of Communist domination. Fourth, American aid was poured freely upon all friendly or neutral Governments in the area—chief among them Chiang Kai-shek's own refugee Government sheltering in the island of Formosa under the protection of the United States fleet and the ultimate threat of atomic weapons.

To glance briefly at this important clash in Korea—conquered alternately by the Chinese and Japanese in earlier centuries. Korea was a historic battleground, and in 1945 it was a bone of contention between Russia and the U.S.A., the two occupying victor Powers. Each backed a Government which claimed the right to govern the whole country, and in 1950 fighting broke out between the two sides. In the West's view the Korean War was a clear case of aggression by the Russian-inspired North Korean Government. To Mao Tse-tung and the Russians, on the other hand, the South Koreans were American puppets and traitors to the idea of anti-colonialism. When, after early Communist successes, the American and Allied forces, in the name of the United Nations, began pushing the North Koreans back towards the Chinese frontier, and American aircraft began patrolling the Manchurian borders, Mao Tse-tung and his Government were forced to take a crucial decision. The American general, MacArthur, approached the Yalu River—the border—confident that Chinese intervention was not to be feared—indeed perhaps welcoming the chance to settle matters with the Mao regime if after all it should risk such intervention. It did. Chinese 'volunteers' began joining the North Korean forces in November 1950, and India and other ex-colonial Asiatic countries refused in the United Nations to condemn China for aggression. MacArthur wanted to grasp the nettle and bomb the Chinese bases in Manchuria, but President Truman, fearful of a third world war, suddenly dismissed him, and in due course a cease-fire was negotiated in 1953.

Mao's China emerged from the Korean episode with a feeling of confidence and a sense of being leader of the Asiatic anti-imperialist powers. True, a pro-American regime remained south of the 38th parallel in Korea, but Mao had taken a calculated risk in defying the Americo-United Nations forces, and his defiance had succeeded. (So also, in the short run, did a fantastic propaganda story of germ warfare waged from American aircraft.) The U.S.A. stood revealed to most Eastern eyes as a Power which, by its non-recognition of Communist China, refused to accept the realities of the new world situation, and whose policies seemed to point logically—even if not in practice—to a war of reconquest, or a fomented Chinese counter-rebellion, or both. Who, then, asked Chinese, and Indians, and Arabs, and most politically minded non-whites, was the 'aggressor'? But Westerners, even when they deplored the U.S.A.'s non-recognition of China, tended to view her stand against Communism in Korea as a blow struck *against* aggression. At least the days of easy Communist expansion in the Far East were over. The Americans had shown that they meant business, and were prepared to spend money and blood to say, "Thus far and no farther."

By 1954 it seemed that the first missionary phase of the Chinese revolution was over. Chou En-lai, Prime Minister of China (Mao was officially chairman of the State Council and of the Communist Party), met the Indian Prime Minister, Nehru, and first put forward the doctrine of "peaceful coexistence"; and the Bandung Afro-Asian conference of 1955 confirmed the new line. The colonial people of both continents were to reinforce the struggle for independence from their white masters, but the Communists were to work for reform by legal means, not by revolution. The overseas Chinese were to become good citizens of the countries they inhabited.

During the years that followed (1954–57), the prestige of China rose by leaps and bounds throughout Asia. Mao's stand against America and Chiang Kai-shek enabled him to pose as the champion of Asiatic right against colonialist wrong. Moreover, China's material progress impressed everybody—more so perhaps than democratic India's. More in the rice bowl, great works to fight flood and famine, a thriving industrial revolution, great victories in the battle for public health and against illiteracy, an end to corruption, a sensational decline in vice, drunkenness, and crime, and over it all a public enthusiasm genuine enough to rise above the regimented propaganda: all this, performed by Asians for Asians, with only modest help from Russia, and in the teeth of the white man's hostility, was enough to raise the name of Mao Tse-tung and his China high throughout Asia. Few inquired overmuch about any loss of 'liberty' to set against these achievements; few had lived high enough up the scale of material existence for the word to have much meaning. To most, regimentation and rice marked an advance on the liberty to go hungry. The East had always known petty tyrants, cruelty, and injustice; and not many Easterners were as shocked as Westerners at Communist Party tyranny, purges, and 'correct thought' campaigns. A man perhaps requires a degree of protection against plain hunger before he is likely to notice his thirst for freedom.

All this was in the middle 'fifties. Towards the end of the decade, however, China's Asian reputation began somewhat to recede. First, it seemed to be established that the Great Leap Forward was not quite the record long jump that had been claimed for it. The famous backyard foundries turned out a lot of metal—but no high-grade steel. The promised flood of cheap goods for export at prices to suit Asiatic pockets failed to come up to expectations. The grain target was suddenly lowered from 525 million tons to 275 million, the cotton target from 5,200,000 tons to 2,300,000, the steel target from 18 million tons to 12 million. Previously published and accepted figures of major production improvements were questioned. The truthfulness of Chinese statistics was suspect; worse, so was the myth of Communist efficiency. Indians and others began to think that perhaps their less sensational targets were more realistic, their slower democratic methods not so inefficient after all. On top of all this came a sudden slowing-down of the march towards communization, following reports of the bitter hostility with which many Chinese peasants greeted the commune system.

An even more powerful counterweight to enthusiasm about China lay in the growing resentment of her arrogance—imperialism even —towards the peoples and territories surrounding her. The Chinese from earliest times have always regarded themselves, and with some justice, as the natural leaders of their world. 'Civilization' was China; beyond were the barbarians. Historically, these peoples have had reason to view China as a lordly and rather contemptuous giant— and one whose nationals were dangerously scattered over the continent beyond his already vast homeland. In 1956 and subsequently, Mao Tse-tung and Chou En-lai permitted their troops to violate the Burmese frontier (as early as 1939 Mao had described Burma as a Chinese dependent state); a revolt in Tibet produced ruthless suppression by Chinese armies and the flight of the Dalai Lama to India; Chinese pressure was kept up on Laos, one of the new states of Indo-China; an attempt was made to prejudice the Japanese elections against the Right-wing parties; throughout Indonesia and Malaya the large and confident Chinese minorities, now mainly pro-Communist, were increasingly regarded as possible 'Trojan horses'—and distrust was intensified of the successful, hard-working, relatively educated Chinese, who in any case tend to be both feared and envied by the other more retarded nationalities throughout the East, much as Arabs and Indians are in parts of Africa. Then, in 1959, came the Chinese claim to territories along the wild and remote mountain borders with India, which not only angered Indian opinion generally, but at last provoked Nehru, previously a great champion of coexistence and apologist for the new China, to condemn Chinese aggressiveness in downright terms, and prepare military measures to resist it. These border quarrels boiled over in 1962 into undeclared war, with humiliating and far-reaching results for India. At the end of 1962 totalitarian China faced democratic India over the Himalayas in open hostility.[1]

As Mao Tse-tung approaches his seventieth year, he must soon prepare to give way to his successors. Already in 1959 he stepped down from the chairmanship of the Party. No one, not even Lenin, among the subjects of this book has done more to change the world's complexion than he; no one, not even Stalin, has wielded greater power over more people. For good or ill, the new China is one of the great facts of the modern world; and the good and ill are inextricably intermingled. Robert Guillain, the French journalist, in his book *The Blue Ants* (1957), gives a notion of the perturbation of a Westerner faced by this Chinese puzzle. He describes first a monster parade of half a million Chinese in Peking to celebrate the anniversary of the revolution. It lasted five hours as, thousand by thousand, they filed past Mao and his colleagues high up beneath the yellow roof of the Gate of Heavenly Peace—15,000 heroes of labour, 100,000 workers in blue cotton, 5000 peasants in blue cotton, 40,000 office workers in blue cotton, 150,000 schoolchildren, etcetera, etcetera.

> Doubtless to offset the monotony of the blue cotton, the young people had received orders to dress as gaily as possible. They brandished paper flowers, released balloons and doves. When the schoolchildren drew near the Gate of Heavenly Peace, they became delirious. Turning their face towards him they roared, "May President Mao live ten thousand years!" Aloft on the balcony of the great red gate could be seen a tiny President Mao, dressed in grey cloth, above the colossal face of an enormous President Mao hanging on the wall. From time to time he raised his hand to acknowledge the acclamations, and the crowd went mad. . . . An organized but very genuine enthusiasm.

And surely both the achievement and the promise of the new China justified this enthusiasm. But the other side of the picture? "A terrifying uniformity and regimentation," a recital of stock phrases, a scurrying of blue ants. "Was I never to hear a few men and women talking naturally amongst themselves after their work? Should I be able to gossip one evening at my ease with ordinary Chinese, and by these I do not mean Chinese chosen for me by the Information Section of the Ministry for Foreign Affairs." The answer was depressing, and the author bursts forth:

[1] The even more significant quarrel with the U.S.S.R. is dealt with in Chapter 15.

What have they done to them? What in God's name have they done to the Chinese to reduce them to this state? This is the cry of the visitor who knew China and the Chinese of yesterday. It is the question that comes to mind almost at once. For the visitor soon makes a few surprising discoveries, of which these are a few examples: one of the great casualties of the new regime is humour; one of the most noteworthy things to disappear is the intelligent Chinese; and to-day it is almost impossible to find in China a Chinese with any ideas of his own.

It is a harsh note to end on, but the liberal Westerner, however well-disposed, would err if he failed to sound it.

Table of Events

1839.　First Opium War.
1842.　Hongkong ceded to Britain.
　　　　Chinese ports forcibly opened to British trade.
1850–66.　Taiping Rebellion.
1860.　Western treaty rights extended after further war.
1893.　Mao Tse-tung born in Hunan.
1894.　Korea seized by Japan.
c. 1900.　Imperialist powers "scramble for China."
1900.　Boxer (anti-foreign) Riots.
1911.　Revolution led by Sun Yat-sen and the Kuomintang.
1912.　Abdication of last Manchu Emperor.
1921.　First Congress of Chinese Communist Party.
1923.　Co-operation between Kuomintang and Communists.
1925.　Death of Sun Yat-sen.
1926 onward: Drive by Chiang Kai-shek to unify China.
1930–33.　Annihilation campaigns against Communists.
1931.　Japanese invade Manchuria.
1934–36.　The Long March from Kiangsi to North Shensi (Yenan).
1937.　Full-scale Japanese invasion. Renewed agreement between
　　　　　Communists and Kuomintang.
1941–45.　Full alliance between U.S.A., Britain, and China.
1945.　Japan defeated. Renewal of Chinese civil war.
1949.　Triumph of Communist armies. Chiang's forces escape to
　　　　　Formosa.
1950.　Russo-Chinese Treaty.
　　　　Korean War begins.
1955.　Bandung (Afro-Asian) Conference.
1957–58.　Rebellion in Tibet suppressed.
1958–59.　The Great Leap Forward. Commune system introduced,
　　　　　subsequently modified.
1959–61.　Succession of bad harvests brings severe difficulties.
1959 onward: Ideological disputes with U.S.S.R.
1962.　Border war with India.

13

Francisco Franco

(1892-   )

S pain at the end of the nineteenth century was, in the words of
her own Prime Minister, Cánovas, a land where "everything
decays except the race." It was a land of primitive farming,
feeble industry and commerce, fierce religious controversy, and wild
political fluctuation; where hunger and rebellion were chronic, where
medieval superstition and revolutionary idealism rubbed shoulders.
Spain was a place where some had fought for the restoration of the
Inquisition right up to the time when others dreamed of the millennium via the general strike; where the Jesuit, the Liberal, and the
Anarchist could live side by side as it were on different planets,
each nourishing his own dreams and his own intolerance; where
torture and violence were endemic, and each successive government
was certain to be opposed by the great majority. In earlier centuries
it was a country where a high degree of social equality could co-exist
with great differences of wealth (the Spaniard as long ago as the
sixteenth century was accounted by travellers the most egalitarian
of men); where aristocrat and peasant—each being in his own way
a gentleman—could share a contempt for hard work of the sort that
would make a man a successful shopkeeper; a country beneath
whose vital and complex civilization lay, always very near, the
jagged rock of the primitive and the barbarous—as harsh as the
rock and desert which is never far beneath her precarious soils. The
Spaniard was fierce, proud, and independent, at the opposite political
pole from the practical, governable Englishman or the docile, obedient German. The liberty which one Spaniard fought for could only
mean slavery for others: what was meat for one man, one class, one
party, was poison for all the rest. Such a nation was not destined for
smooth progress, for freedom slowly broadening down, but rather
for passion, for visions, and for blood.

The Western European, taking with him his own vocabulary and
preconceptions, finds himself, on crossing into Spain, in a new and
different world, where words tend to mean different things, and where
the mental and emotional climate is liable to changes as sudden

and violent as those of the climate and the landscape. Africa begins at the Pyrenees, some have said: this is a land that the Arab overran in two years and the Christian took eight centuries to reconquer. Certainly, before the stranger to Spanish history can begin to comprehend its patterns and stresses, there are a number of things characteristically Spanish which must be understood.

First, there is the physical nature of the land itself—a poor soil for the most part, much of it barren tableland, two thousand feet on average above sea-level, hot in summer, bitterly cold in winter, a good deal of it lacking water, and some of the best land lacking it most; the whole peninsula carved into strongly independent sections by high mountains and ancient quasi-national traditions. "In what one may call its normal condition," writes Gerald Brenan, "Spain is a collection of small, mutually hostile or indifferent republics held together in a loose federation." Moreover, its central region of Castile, which, if it had been rich and enterprising might have held the outlying regions in its unifying grasp, was in fact among the poorest of lands, barren of soil, and deficient in minerals, industries, and trade. Hence a centrifugal force in Spain was always working towards the assertion of power by the richer, more industrious, more commercial provinces at the periphery, each with its own social and agrarian system—its own costumes, customs, dialects, dances, traditions of every kind. Madrid could answer only with its own trump-cards, geographical centrality and military organization. Thus every war in Spain became (in addition to everything else) a war of secession and a war to impose unity.

The essential poverty of Spain was masked for a time by her sudden acquisition during the sixteenth century of fabulous wealth in the Americas. This encouraged the Spaniard to develop the mentality of the rich investor who lives off his dividends but despises the sweat of clerks and toilers; and easy imports of gold and silver from South America proved fatal to the economic health of Spain. In the words of Hugh Thomas, "all nations are forever scarred by the epoch when they have been great." The Golden Century passed into history, and Spain was left still worrying her ungenerous soil for a living, but still pursued by dreams of grandeur: hence the combination of qualities and circumstances that make Don Quixote and Sancho Panza so quintessentially and immortally Spanish.

Underlying all Spain's troubles was her agrarian poverty. Land systems varied widely, from the great hired-labour estates of Andalusia in the south to the little one-family farms of Galicia, Navarre, and the Basque country in the north; so that no one solution of the peasants' misfortunes presented itself, even in theory. Some areas' troubles seemed to cry aloud for a collectivist remedy—and on many occasions revolutionary peasants, taking temporary control, set up their own village communes. The power of the landlords, and the rift between them and the peasantry, grew greater still after the Liberals in 1837 first effected compulsory purchase of Church estates, and then sold them among their supporters, who were normally speculators interested primarily not in peasants but in profits. Agrarian reform by any means other than revolution became more and more improbable as the parties of the wealthy grew more extreme and the hungry peasantry grew more violent.

Another permanent factor to be taken account of in Spanish history is the Church. For long years it provided the cement in the social fabric. Under the Church the people had ousted the Moors and the Jews. Monks and priests had time and again sided with the peasantry in their struggle against unjust landlords and oppressive taxes. When Napoleon invaded Spain in 1808 it was the Church, in alliance with the common people, that fought tirelessly and savagely against the invader; often the guerrilla bands were led by priests. In the nineteenth century, however, a change came over the scene. The Liberals, those children of the French Revolution, claimed freedom to criticize the Church, its superstitions, and all its works—and especially its principal organ for suppressing heresy, the Inquisition. A bitter century-long struggle developed, in which (broadly speaking) the Army and the Liberals fought on one side, and the Church and its Carlist supporters (followers of the Pretender Don Carlos) on the other. Settled parliamentary government was never possible. A succession of unworthy monarchs discredited the throne; corruption discredited the elections and the Parliaments. The Liberals, by breaking up the Church estates, helped to push the clergy into the arms of the wealthy classes, and a chasm opened between peasants and workers on the one side and the clergy on the other. The Jesuits courted the rich, and indeed even went themselves into big business, owning railways, mines, banks, and shipping-lines. The Church was thrown fatally into the arms of business interests and landowners, while perhaps two-thirds of the population had become either indifferent or opposed to Catholicism by 1914. Immovable in its attitudes, the Church entered the twentieth century in the mood and convictions of a century earlier. In 1821 was founded the Society of the Exterminating Angel, to exterminate all Liberals. Over a century later, in 1927, the fourteenth edition of the Catechism re-listed the Liberal heresies, including freedom of conscience and freedom of education;

it described Liberalism as "a most grievous sin," and rated the sin of voting for a Liberal candidate as "generally mortal." The only Liberal journal whose perusal carried no taint was the *Stock Exchange News*! The Liberals were, of course, a *bourgeois* group; but among the working-class opponents of the Church there were many who despised half-measures, and the burning of churches and nunneries became an ever more common feature of the Spanish scene until the holocaust of the early nineteen-thirties. Just as every Spanish war became a separatist war, so it became also a religious war. The Spanish Civil War of 1936–39 was regarded in the 'thirties as the prototype of the modern war of ideologies—but it was, no less, the last of the wars of the Counter-Reformation, the culminating struggle between the Church and its various enemies, Liberals, Free-masons, Anarchists, Socialists, Communists—'atheists' all.

Of these enemies of the Church, the group that was unique to Spain was that of the Anarchists. These were disciples of the Russian *émigré* Bakunin, who wished to destroy all states and all churches, and substitute free federal societies composed of voluntary unions of small, self-organizing communist groups. "All exercise of authority perverts," wrote Bakunin, "and all submission to authority humiliates." Intensely concerned for the dignity of man, he loved liberty and hated religion with equal passion. Defeated by Marxism everywhere but in Spain, his ideas had in them an extreme radicalism, a generous and wild vision that made a spiritual as well as an economic appeal to many poor Spanish workmen and peasants, by now in the main divorced from Catholicism. The early Anarchists were rich in puritan zeal. They sent missionaries round the countryside to preach the evils of alcohol, tobacco, and adultery; they laboured devotedly to teach the Andalusian poor to read; they propagated the gospel of the new freedom that would dawn when "the last king was strangled with the guts of the last priest." It has been said of the Anarchist movement that it carried an encyclopedia in one hand and a pistol in the other. For many it was an anti-religious religion. In Catalonia and Andalusia especially the Anarchists were strong and fanatical; thousands of them came to see violence as a necessary purifying fire. (The connection between agricultural Andalusia and industrial Barcelona was not chance; for the factory labour of Barcelona was largely recruited from the always half-employed and frequently half-starved hired labour of Andalusia.) By the eighteen-nineties revolutionary processions, strikes, murders, and bomb-outrages were common; Barcelona in particular saw repeated strikes and murderous outbursts, notably in the "Tragic Week" of 1909. The next year at Seville a Confederation was formed of Anarchist trade unions, known as the C.N.T. (National Confederation of Labour); these unions were to use the method of the general strike to defeat the *bourgeoisie* and usher in the reign of liberty—Anarchist collectivism would take the place of private power, and both State and Church would be for ever abolished. This later phase of Anarchism, when the 'syndicate' or trade union was the movement's chosen means of achieving revolution, is normally known as Anarcho-Syndicalism: its C.N.T. was to be one of the key organizations in the revolutionary struggle of the 'thirties. By that time it contained within it a special secret army of terrorists (the F.A.I.—the Iberian Anarchist Federation)—some of them high idealists, some recruits from the criminal classes, all devoted to strikes, to arson, or to murder.

Rivalling the C.N.T. was the U.G.T. (General Union of Labour), a more orthodox confederation of Socialist trade unions, employing paid officials (unlike the C.N.T.) and believing in Parliamentary and municipal action to gain its ends. First and foremost, therefore, the Socialists stood for a purification of the electoral system and an end to the corruption and the boss-management of elections. They were powerful only in the big cities, and especially in Madrid—and thus, in the Spanish manner, since they stood for Madrid rather than Anarchist Barcelona, they stood to some extent also for Castilian centralism against Catalan separatism.

In these few preceding (and over-simplified) pages have been indicated a few of the harsh divisions of Spanish life in existence by the beginning of this century, and some sketchy pointers to their historical and geographical origins. If we now take 1892 as a starting-point, the year of Franco's birth, we shall begin at a moment when the explosive mixture was bubbling with steady menace. That very year there began an epidemic of Anarchist bomb-throwing in Barcelona that lasted for five years. The previous year, four thousand agricultural workmen had marched into Jerez, proclaiming the Revolution to cries of "Long live Anarchy!" The Prime Minister, Cánovas, declared Spain to be practically bankrupt; a few years later, in 1897, after his severe repression of the Barcelona terrorism, he was assassinated. In the colony of Cuba, civil war was once more raging furiously; and in 1898 United States forces finally intervened against Spain. Both in the Caribbean and in the Philippines, by 1900 the Spanish Empire was no more; no bad thing for her economy and manpower, but a major psychological blow.

Morocco remained to her: that is to say, that part of Northern Morocco that lay immediately opposite the southern coast of Spain —to which should be added the barren wastes of the Rio de Oro (Spanish Sahara), Spain's meagre pickings from the general scramble for Africa in the 1880's. In Northern Morocco a Spanish army was engaged through the early years of the twentieth century in 'pacifying' the native Riffs and attempting to consolidate the Spanish position. It was a tough, malarial, thirsty war against the old Muslim enemy, sometimes blazing up into full-scale battle, normally sputtering along, dangerously enough, with guerrilla ambushes and skirmishes at the water-holes. Ever since the heavy casualties (largely from disease) in the Spanish-American War of 1898, there had been a strong wave of pacifism and anti-imperialism in Spain; and this Moroccan war was the most unpopular of all. After a small Spanish setback near Melilla in 1909, and the consequent calling-up of the Catalan reserves—mostly married workers—there was a mutinous uprising, leading to five days of mob rule in Barcelona, some hundreds of casualties and subsequent executions, and the burning of fifty-six churches and convents.

In Morocco Francisco Franco y Bahamonde received his baptism of fire. Born at El Ferrol, Galicia, in the extreme north-western province of Corunna, the son of a naval paymaster, he had himself been intended for the Navy, but had been obliged, by a suspension of the Fleet entrance examination, to transfer his ambitions to the Army. Three years at the Toledo Military Academy had ended in 1910, when he was gazetted second lieutenant. Eighteen months later, a lad of nineteen, he disembarked at Melilla, in Morocco, for a four-year spell of service, in the course of which he was very seriously wounded. He was a model officer, and promotion came quickly: by 1917 he was back in Spain, happy to be alive, and the youngest major in the entire army. He returned to Morocco in 1920 (just before the Spanish disaster at Anual, when the Riffs destroyed a force of 20,000) and served there another seven years with distinction. By 1926 he was, though only thirty-three, a Brigadier, the youngest officer of that rank in Europe. (It should, however, be noted that the Spanish Army had a notoriously high proportion of officers, one in ten, and a very rapid promotion rate.) The Foreign Legion's highly disciplined efficiency, and its eventual success in defeating Abd-el-Krim's Riff tribesmen, were undoubtedly due in considerable part to Franco's organizing ability and tactical prowess: he was in command from 1923, a dedicated professional, eschewing the distractions of wine and women—and mass too, it was said, though he had married a pious Catholic. For all his military brilliance, he was personally cautious: he had little *panache*. Uncommitted in politics, though he was assumed to be vaguely of the Right, he would not have been picked out as one likely to lead a revolution. In appearance, too, he was not at all commanding, being short and fat; his voice was high-pitched, "which caused him to give military commands the note of a prayer." The Spanish Legion had a motto, "Down with Intelligence! Long live Death!" but that particular vein of dark romanticism was not Franco's. He was shrewd and sagacious; physically brave, but a model of sobriety and intelligence.

In 1927 he was appointed head of the General Military Academy at Saragossa, and his inaugural speech was not without a certain conventional eloquence: "Gentlemen cadets . . . the military life is not a road to pleasure and delight. It carries with it great sufferings, hardships, and sacrifices. Glory also, but like the rose it comes forth among thorns. . . ." Present at the ceremony were the dictator of Spain, Primo de Rivera, and the King, Alfonso XIII. Primo de Rivera's dictatorship had begun in 1923 ("My Mussolini!" said Alfonso), to reimpose public order and suppress the political parties —but it had succeeded merely in driving them underground. His one great success was the winding-up of the Moroccan war. Bohemian, garrulous, loose-living, gluttonous, he reminds one more of a sort of good-natured Kemal Atatürk than of Mussolini. Relying on the King, the Army, the Church, and the landlords, he fell foul of the Liberals and many intellectuals (for whom he had total contempt). His censorship was harsh and resented; he constantly promised parliamentary elections which never materialized; and at last he disappeared in the slump of 1930.

The King remained—for a space. But few fully trusted him, and even many in the Church (following the urgings of Pope Pius XI) counselled an evolution towards democracy. Unable at last to resist the demands for elections, he consented in 1931 to hold *municipal* elections. The results were overwhelming: the Monarchists won most of the country districts, but, in every provincial capital but four, Republicans carried the day, and in every great city their majorities were huge. Alfonso would not abdicate, but, when he saw that not a general would lift a finger to save the throne, and even the big landlords and aristocrats wished to get rid of him, he "suspended the use of his royal prerogatives" and left the country. (He was to watch from abroad the cataclysm that his flight was powerless to avert, and to die in exile.) Great was the national joy, and great the general hope, at the inception of the 1931 Republic. National elections for a new Cortes confirmed even more sweepingly the municipal vote. For a month or so the Republic enjoyed its honeymoon.

Its enemies, however, were not quiet for long. The Cardinal-Primate of Spain, the Archbishop of Toledo, launched an uncompromising attack on the Church's "enemies" and advised the faithful to fight like "intrepid warriors." Unsupported by Pope Pius XI, he was removed by the (still moderate) Government; but the fat was already in the fire. Crowds in Madrid had already rioted against Monarchist activities; now worse followed, when in many towns throughout Spain churches and convents were fired, 102 in six big towns alone. Then in Castilblanco villagers overwhelmed a detachment of the quasi-military Civil Guard and fearfully mutilated their corpses. In such an atmosphere moderation became impossible. The Government of Manuel Azaña, proclaiming Spain to be "no longer Catholic," proceeded on a militantly anti-clerical course. The Church was disestablished, the Jesuits expelled; Catholic schools were given a time-limit within which to expire; divorce by consent was to be legalized. All this, moreover, was written into the new Constitution of the country, ensuring the inevitable opposition of good Catholics —even moderate ones—to the young regime. Moreover, by giving the vote to Spanish women for the first time, Azaña's Government accelerated the digging of its own grave, for the female was undoubtedly the devouter sex.

Undeterred by thunder from both the Right and the Left, Azaña pursued his course. Franco's Military Academy at Saragossa was dissolved, and many of the Army's privileges attacked. The Army officers in Spain had always thought of themselves as guardians of order, and had long interpreted their guardianship in a Right-wing sense. In 1917, it was the Army that had crushed the greatest of Spain's many general strikes. It was the Army that had backed Primo de Rivera (and the Army that enforced his notice of dismissal). It was among Army officers that Monarchist plots were brewing in 1932—and, indeed, General Sanjurjo attempted a rising at Seville in that year. It was Sanjurjo, be it noted, not Franco. Franco was still at pains to be 'correct.' Azaña, on his side, certainly meant business: the law was repealed that made all attacks on the Army subject to military law; the supreme military court was abolished, and many senior officers were retired on full pay—there had been *217 generals* alone. As for Franco, he made a carefully weighed speech of farewell to the officers and cadets at Saragossa, lauding the achievements of the Academy's three years' life, asking them "to control their inward sorrow"—but the implications of his dignified rebuke to the Government were not misunderstood. He was transferred first to Corunna, and then, farther out of harm's way, to the Balearic Islands. The Academy became a barracks.

Military reforms were accompanied by an attempt at a social revolution—principally by agrarian reforms in the South and Centre, the country of the great estates, with their hired labour force never far from starvation. The 1932 Agrarian Act in principle confiscated all estates of over fifty-six acres not worked by the owners—with compensation to be paid on the basis of the landlords' *own* previous taxation returns, which had notoriously underestimated values. Partial and modest though the reform was, and ignoring the problems of the North, it was (or might have been) at least a beginning that, given twenty years of orderly transition, might have relieved the extreme poverty of the South. But it was passed in an atmosphere of Anarchist risings, of strikes, murders, and church-burnings. It never had a chance, and was quite abortive. Similarly destined for the scrap-heap were the acts granting independent status to the Catalans and the Basques, and a mass of miscellaneous social legislation, from minimum wages provisions to a statement of female rights.

In 1933 the Left Wing suffered defeat at the elections, and for the next two years Spain had Governments of the Centre and Right, with Gíl Robles, the leader of the Catholic Party, as the dominant political figure—a man who had met Hitler, and was himself not averse to being hailed as *Jefe*—"Leader." The year was, after all, 1933; it was the year of Hitler's rise to power, and Fascism and Nazism were in the air. Over the border in Portugal they were proclaiming Salazar's *Estado Novo*. In Spain it was not only Gil Robles; there was José António Primo de Rivera, the dictator's son and a man of high principles and great charm, who, in the same year, founded the *Falange Española*, a Fascist Party destined later to be Spain's only permitted political party. From November 1933, the date of the elections, Spain slid rapidly down into revolution and war; and when three colleagues of Robles were included in the new Government of October 1934 there was a bloody explosion in many parts. In Madrid the Socialists went on strike, but their leaders were arrested; in Barcelona the Catalan leader Companys proclaimed a Federal Spain, with Barcelona as its provisional headquarters; but he was promptly arrested by the Army. Everywhere else, too, the strikes were crushed, except in Asturias. There the Communist miners (orthodox Communists, as distinct from Anarchists and Socialists, were rare birds in Spain in 1933) proclaimed the Revolution, occupied nearly the whole province and set up a soviet amid much bloodshed and enthusiasm.

The Government, forced to take harsh counter-measures, sent for Generals Goded and Franco. These men had no doubts: the veterans of Morocco, the Foreign Legion, should be brought in to suppress the rebellion. And the Legion did not take long; with the aid of aircraft and Moorish troops, the mining centres of Oviedo and Gijón were taken and desovietized. The rebels had begun by shooting priests, burning convents, raping women; but tenfold revenge was inflicted by the victorious Legion: between 1300 and 5000 were killed (partisan estimates vary), many thousands wounded, and still more imprisoned in makeshift jails. Generals Franco and Goded had "saved the nation"—and all over Europe the Left looked to the miners of Asturias as tragic heroes. For all over Europe men were already taking sides in the great ideological line-up. A few weeks later in Paris there was a big Left-Right clash in the Champs-Elysées. Everywhere in Europe the confused smoke of the Depression era seemed to be clearing to reveal two embattled groups, two mutual hatreds, two ways of thought and life that could know no compromise: the Left (Socialists, Communists, Anarchists, 'workers,' anti-clericals) and the Right (Conservatives, Fascists, 'bourgeois,' Catholics). Those in the middle, Liberals, parliamentarians, and moderates, found themselves ever weaker and ever in danger of being drawn to the popular extremes. Spain was the test case, the perfect illustration, the sacrificial victim, of the Battle of the Thirties, the struggle of Right (or Wrong) with Wrong (or Right). There was much certitude in men's minds, taking sides, either actually or vicariously, in that battle; but as we look back on it from a generation's distance, the outlines of the contestants lose sharpness; the picture is no longer in black and white; and we seem to be on

> . . . a darkling plain
> Swept with confused alarms of struggle and flight,
> Where ignorant armies clash by night.

In the 1936 elections the drift to extremes is clearly seen: the new alliance of the Left, the Popular Front, polled rather more than 4,000,000 votes; the alliance of the Right rather under 4,000,000; the Centre groups a mere 681,000. The Popular Front consequently formed a Government, but had little authority: the militants of both sides were polishing their gun-barrels. General Franco's own attitude is interesting. Although he had assured friends in January 1936 that he had no intention of plotting against the Republic, a month later, just after the Popular Front victory, he was advising the Prime Minister to declare an emergency and prevent the Left from taking office. If that should provoke a revolution, so be it: the Army would see to it that the right side won. But as yet he hatched no plot, even when he was dismissed by the new Azaña Government for his part in the Asturias suppression, and sent off to command the forces in the conveniently distant Canary Islands. It was not Franco but General Mola who over the next few months carefully wove a web of conspiracy from the Canaries to the Pyrenees, from Morocco to Lisbon (where General Sanjurjo was in exile). By June, Mola's plans were complete. He had the support of the imprisoned Falangist leaders, and a handful of leading generals were assigned their objectives. Franco was to fly from the Canaries to Morocco, and there to take command of Spanish Africa. Even so, he made one last move, perhaps to justify to himself the rebellion he now contemplated. He wrote to the new Prime Minister (Azaña having assumed the Presidency), warning him of the "perils involved for the discipline of the Army" in any further dismissals of Right-wing officers. There was no answer. Franco sat down to await July 17, the day fixed by Mola for the revolution.

Meanwhile the Left were not idle. Largo Caballero, the "Spanish Lenin," the secretary of the Socialist General Workers (U.G.T.), was promising imminent revolution, and victory for the proletariat. One of his women supporters, a Socialist deputy, demanded a bigger and more murderous revolution than the Russian (which she appeared to find deficient in bloodshed): "We must have huge flames which can be seen all over the world, and waves of blood to turn the seas red." In wild Estremadura the peasants anticipated the millennium and began parcelling out the land among themselves. In the May Day processions in Madrid, workers with the light of the future in their eyes carried through the streets huge Russian-style portraits of Lenin, Stalin, and Caballero. Political murders were commonplace and unremarkable, until the outrageous assassination of Calvo Sotelo, the leader of the Right-wing opposition, *by the regular police*. He was roused from his bed, driven off in a car, shot in the neck, and dumped with cemetery officials.

July 17, 1936, arrived. Throughout Morocco, rebel forces seized key points, Melilla, Tetuan, Ceuta, Larache. Franco, with his wife and daughter, left Teneriffe for Grand Canary, and from that island broadcast a manifesto promising a New Order for Spain. On July 19, he flew to Morocco in his Dragon Rapide, a fast plane conspiratorially acquired from private sources in England, and took command of the Army in Africa. All over Spain the well-laid plot hatched. In places it was successful, in places not; and within a week, it could be seen that Spain was divided territorially in half, approximately on the lines of the 1936 election voting. Broadly speaking, the East, the South, and the north coast had remained in the hands of the Republican Government; all the North-Centre, a few vital points in the extreme South (such as Cadiz, Cordova, and Seville), and the whole of Spanish Africa was in the hands of the Right-wing rebels.

Franco's rôle in this rising was vital; but it is probable that he rose to the leadership only because of the death of others. Calvo Sotelo had been murdered; Sanjurjo's plane crashed as he left his Lisbon airfield; Goded was killed in an unsuccessful bid to take Barcelona; and Mola, prime organizer of the plot, was at first much less successful than Franco in his military operations, and was in any case eventually killed during the war. Early in the struggle (October 1936), in the throne-room of the Captain-General's Palace at Burgos, Francisco Franco y Bahamonde was solemnly invested with the titles of Generalissimo and Head of the Spanish State.

Before that event, most of the towns and villages in Spain had experienced their own small revolution. It is a savage and tragic story—or rather, many thousands of distinct and savage tragedies piling one upon the other to make a formidable mound of horror. The victors normally shot the vanquished, sometimes simply, often with the grossest and most bestial preliminaries. Squads of prisoners were hurled over cliffs, flung down mine shafts, stoned, bayoneted, shot, burned, and buried alive. Sometimes the foulest horrors were deliberately paraded before the townsfolk (as at Seville), *pour encourager les autres*. An avalanche of hatred thundered down all over Spain during the early months of the war. In many parts, the Left killed priests, monks, and nuns indiscriminately. Most of Barcelona's fifty churches were badly damaged and thirty-two of Madrid's forty: the fatal alliance between the Church and the moneyed classes had brought a fearful retribution. On their side, Franco's Nationalists slaughtered their working-class prisoners with brusque savagery. "All that the Church officially insisted on" [at Seville], writes Hugh Thomas in his fine study of the Civil War, "was that those killed should have the opportunity of confession." And in Majorca the Venerable Brother reported happily (continues Hugh Thomas) that "only ten per cent. of these dear children refused the last sacraments before being despatched by our good officers." All freemasons, trade-unionists, those known to have sympathized with or voted for Left-wing parties, were likely to be arrested, and were in danger of

summary execution. Yet amid all the carnage there was much heroism; there was the exaltation of fraternity as well as murder-lust and
sadism; there were strange puritan visions of idealism and improvement, as in the Andalusian villages which abolished money, private
property, and the drinking of alcohol and coffee as first steps
towards the earthly paradise—or among the Catalonian collective
farms and factories. George Orwell, who went to Barcelona to fight
for the proletariat, and had good reason to come home disillusioned,
could yet write, "I have the most evil memories of Spain, but I have
very few bad memories of Spaniards. . . . They have . . . a generosity, a species of nobility, that does not really belong to the
twentieth century." The Spanish Civil War was indeed a tale of
good and evil, only not quite as its partisan spectators from the
European sidelines saw it: on both sides much good and desperate
evil were inextricably intertwined.

From the beginning Franco received assistance from Mussolini,
Hitler, and to a smaller extent Salazar and the Irish Brigade; and
soon the Left received help from Russia, and to a smaller extent
from France and the international volunteers; and it used to be
thought that the superior weight of the Fascist powers' contribution
was vital to Franco's ultimate victory. That help was certainly very
important; and it is indeed possible that if the British, French, and
American Governments had permitted the Republican Government
to buy arms freely with its large gold reserves, the Republicans
might have been able to win. But it is arguable—even probable—
that Franco would have won even if the Spanish belligerents had
had the field entirely to themselves. Part of the reason lies in Franco
himself; from the start he displayed his solid qualities. Cool, shrewd,
tough, and tireless, he became immediately, and he remained, the
able and undisputed leader of the Nationalists (as his following
came rather inadequately to be called). He took few risks. He seldom
took any part in tactical operations. But as a strategist, planning his
war, allocating his forces, using (but always refusing to be used by)
his powerful foreign friends, slow-moving, and economical of his
troops' lives, he made no major mistake. As head of the Army as
well as head of the State, he could impose a unity on his side that
was altogether lacking on the other. Within six months of the
original rebellion, he had subdued political wrangling among his
supporters—Monarchists, Falangists, Carlists, Catholics of various
political shades. He lacked the fire that burned among the leaders
and devotees of these movements, just as he lacked the dash or
personality of a Sotelo or a Sanjurjo—but he had other less sensa-

tional qualities. In the words of Hugh Thomas, this "dispassionate, duller, greyer, man survived triumphant, as Octavius survived the civil wars of Rome." He survived, and he remained the unchallenged leader of the Army—and the Army was supreme.

On the other side (variously known as the Loyalists, the Government, and the Republic), a contrary situation existed from the start, and deteriorated as time went on. Socialists, Anarchists, Communists, Trotskyists, Catalan separatists, Basque separatists—they were severely and at last desperately divided. At first it gives surprise to find that the Communists were among the more moderate of these groups, advocating an end to the Anarchists' gun-happy executions, and appeasing the peasantry and white-collared workers by guaranteeing property rights. In fact it was the Communists who destroyed the crusading atmosphere of the early days on the Left, substituting their own regimentation, and working to subordinate Spanish revolutionary aims to the European interests of Stalin's regime. Being, moreover, directed by Moscow and the Comintern, the Communists pursued unscrupulously and fanatically their political vendettas against their 'allies'—notably against the so-called Trotskyists of Catalonia, who were characteristically accused of being Fascist agents in the pay of Franco and Hitler, and who were liquidated in the early summer of 1937. (The date is significant: it was the nightmare height of Stalin's great purges.) The Communists were small in number to begin with, but gradually they took control—commissars, political policemen, propagandists, blinkered men of discipline and technique. (The eddies and cross-currents of this turbulence are dark and complicated indeed: many of the Russian leaders in Spain were themselves recalled by Stalin to face purging and death.) At last, in March 1939, after Stalin was writing Spain off in the days following the Munich Pact, and was concentrating on a deal with Hitler, the long-pent-up resentment of the other Left-wing groups exploded against their Communist allies; and both in Barcelona and in heroic Madrid, which had stood against Franco for nearly three years, the Civil War ended for the Left in a paroxysm of mutual destruction, in a last agony of vicious street battles.

As for the famous International Brigades, they too tell a bitter story. Recruited mainly in France from Communists and Left-wing sympathizers of many nations, they counted among their company such tough Stalinists as Ulbricht, Gottwald (of Czechoslovakia), and Gerö (of Hungary)—hardly names that a Westerner associates with the cause of liberty. Others of them were recruited from the unemployed. Some were simply adventurers. But also in the Brigades were men of a different stamp, idealists who were indignant at the insanities and cruelties of Nazism and Fascism, and wished to *do* something (not merely to talk) in the cause of liberty, and equality, and justice. Some of them, like André Malraux, have written of their ideals and disillusionment. Many, like the young English writers John Cornford and Christopher Caudwell, were killed in the undimmed fervour of their convictions. ("I have seen the future, and it works!" said a young American returning from Russia in 1929.) However, the damp hand of the dominant Communist apparatus in Spain quenched most of the flame that Nationalist bullets failed to put out. The Brigades, militarily insignificant, remain indeed a symbol of naïve idealism and altruistic courage. But it was as though St George, setting out to slay the Fascist dragon, awoke with disgust to find himself helplessly astride another dragon, the dragon of Communism. Surviving idealists of the Left emerged older, sadder, angrier, warier—and less romantic. The most outstanding English man of letters to fight in Spain, George Orwell, was not an International Brigade volunteer. He joined the P.O.U.M. (Trotskyist) militia in Barcelona, was wounded, became disillusioned, and wrote two memorable books out of his experiences: one a personal narrative, *Homage to Catalonia*, the other that small satirical masterpiece *Animal Farm*.

The intervention of Mussolini and Hitler in the Civil War was different in one crucial respect from that of Stalin. Stalin, having decided that his vital interests necessitated intervention, gradually and insidiously took over the direction of his side's affairs, through the agency of the international Communist movement and its well-developed propaganda and techniques. The two Fascist dictators, although they sent troops, planes, tanks, technicians, and arms and equipment of all kinds, never made any serious attempt to take over the direction of the war. Throughout Franco was in command of the 50,000 Italian and 10,000 German 'volunteers.' (The figures represent maximum strengths: those of the International Brigades and Russian organizers built up to about 25,000.) Occasionally, it is true, the Germans took the law into their own hands, as on the notorious occasion when German bombers of the Condor Legion destroyed the little Basque town of Guernica and machine-gunned its panic-stricken fugitives, killing and wounding between two and three thousand. Picasso took this piece of wanton savagery as a text for a famous picture that conveyed his condemnation of the horrors of Hitlerian war, as Goya's pictures did for Napoleonic war. Various attempts were made at different times to explain away the incident:

it had not happened, the town had been fired by the Reds, it had happened but was a mistake. Göring and the German Air Force chiefs knew better. The world had to see what the German air power was capable of, said Göring; and he admitted in 1946 that Guernica had been a testing-ground. Live targets plainly made for better practice than dummies. For the Nazis Spain was to serve a double purpose: first, victory there could consolidate the forces of Fascism and turn the flanks of France; second, it could prove an excellent rehearsal area, a proving-ground for men, machines, and military techniques. Von Thoma, commander of the German tank unit fighting under Franco, called Spain "the European Aldershot."

As for the much more numerous Italians, their infantry and tanks were used by Franco strictly as useful extra forces to serve Spanish ends—not by any means as banner bearers of Italian glory. There were some, indeed, on the Spanish Nationalist side who were not sorry in 1937 to see the Italians routed by Madrid's defenders at Guadalajara, a defeat that angered Mussolini so deeply that he childishly announced that no Italians would be allowed to return alive from Spain until they won victory. The Italian air units based on the Balearic Islands formed a rather more independent force; when they delivered repeated and undiscriminating attacks on Barcelona in the spring of 1938, the orders came direct from Mussolini, who was delighted that his brave Italians were matching the Germans in 'frightfulness.' Franco, displeased by foreign reactions, asked for the raids to be discontinued. In general, relations between Franco and his foreign auxiliaries were never good, and at last Mussolini's exasperation was such that, after the Nationalist reverse on the Ebro in the summer of 1938, he said to his son-in-law Ciano, with typical petulance and pomposity, "Put on record in your diary that today, August 29, I prophesy the defeat of Franco. ... The Reds are fighters, Franco is not." For Mussolini, Spain had become a drain upon resources, not a platform for glory; and he decided (not entirely to Franco's regret) upon a partial withdrawal of his Italian 'volunteers.' (The term was always a cynical misnomer; seldom did 'volunteers' go more reluctantly to their graves.)

Franco, Fascist that he was, and deeply committed to the Italo-German cause, was already showing those qualities of wary prudence that stood him in good stead during the coming European war. As the Czech crisis mounted through the late summer of 1938, he was quick to announce that in any European war he would remain neutral: it was enough, wrote Ciano, to make the Italian dead in Spain—there were six thousand of them—turn in their graves. By the time of the Danzig crisis that brought general war at last in 1939, the Spanish Civil War was over. The last offensives had lumbered northwards into the Republican stronghold of Barcelona; the long defence of Madrid had broken at last, and the massive portraits of Lenin and Stalin had been taken down from the Gran Vía and the Calle de Alcalá; some of the embittered remnants of the Left-wing group had fought it out among themselves, while others, ragged and forlorn, stumbled over the Pyrenees into France. Many found their way to Spanish prisons (to stay there long years), many to court-martial and execution. No magnanimity followed this passionate war in which nearly a million had died.

It had been an ugly curtain-raiser to the bigger tragedy ahead. Franco, however, was determined to fend off the greater war from Spanish soil. It is true that he made speeches in plenty praising Hitler and Mussolini; he joined the Anti-Comintern Pact; he afforded Germany air and submarine bases in the early days of the war; he even sent a division, the "Blue Division," 47,000 men in all, to crusade with the Nazis in the Russian campaigns (where its luck-less troops largely froze to death). But he was not forgetful of the geographical and economic ties that linked him with Western Europe and America. He refused reconstruction loans from them, not wishing to be fettered; but he kept open all the diplomatic doors. Especially after Hitler's failure to invade England, Franco's *hábil prudencia* was redoubled. When pressed to join the Axis powers, he stipulated a formidable list of prior Spanish territorial claims, including French Morocco, Oran, and Gibraltar. In vain Hitler tried to pin him down; he was polite, superficially loyal—but evasive. And when Hitler tried out upon him the old magic of his personal magnetism, an interview at Hendaye lasting nine hours (after Franco's siesta had already kept Hitler waiting half an hour) produced from Franco only a damp and vague civility. As well try to strike sparks off a feather pillow; and rather than go through that nine hours again, Hitler told Mussolini (always willing to hear ill of Franco), "he would prefer to have three or four teeth taken out." Franco had played the Spanish game coolly and shrewdly, and Spain maintained her neutrality to the end.

Inside Spain, Franco's Fascism was of a different order from Mussolini's or Hitler's. (It had much more in common with the Portugal of Salazar, with whom an "Iberian Bloc" was formed in 1942.) It is true that one party only was permitted, and that this was the Falange Española, the approximate Spanish equivalent of the Nazi and Fascist parties. It is true too that posters from 1936 onward proclaimed the gospel of "One State, One Country, One Leader," on the Hitler model; that Franco was known as *Caudillo* from that time, the nearest Spanish translation of *Duce* or *Führer*; that Franco from 1936, like Hitler, was Head of State as well as head of the Nationalist Government and the Army; that popular election was rejected, and Franco was accountable "only to God and to history." The Falange, however, never succeeded in permeating Spanish life as the Nazis or Italian Fascists did the life of their countries, or the Communists of theirs. The government of Spain was very far from being monopolized by the Falange, which always had to share power with those two older and stronger forces, the Army and the Church. In any case, the post-1937 Falange was an artificial creation, being an unhappy combination of largely self-cancelling groups: in that year Franco had enforced their 'shotgun wedding,' and the Falange was never again its old fiery self. Franco, moreover, by insisting that all Army officers and non-commissioned officers *automatically* became members of the Falange, so diluted it that any special revolutionary or socially radical qualities it still possessed were soon lost. In parallel manner, the Church and the Falange were thrust together as allies, and the earlier Falangist hostility to religion was necessarily softened. Thus, by one means or another, the Falange became official, tame, and respectable. Franco was no Mussolini, exhorting his Fascists to emulate the ancient pagan glories. Still less did he himself strive to emulate the public image of the Fascist dictator. In power, this short, plump, unheroic man from Galicia behaved exactly as the native of Galicia is proverbially supposed to behave: he was bland and wily at the same time. He drove his four-horse team of Church, Army, Falange, and Big Business unceremoniously and unostentatiously—but there was never any doubt who was in the driving-seat. Even during the Civil War, he had caused the leader of the Falange, Manuel Hedilla, to be arrested for insubordination, and only German intervention had saved him from death. In 1939 he installed his own brother-in-law, Serrano Suñer, a devout Catholic but strong Fascist, at the head of the Falange, and later made him Foreign Minister, a post it was convenient to allow him to occupy during the period when the Fascist powers appeared likely to win the war. When their defeat seemed more and more probable, Serrano Suñer slipped back into insignificance. By 1945 Franco had temporarily rid his Cabinet of Falangists; by 1954 their number had crept back to four out of twelve. So, characteristically, Franco trimmed his sails to meet any prevailing wind.

While the Falange met mixed fortunes, the Church steadily increased its power and influence. The Jesuits were allowed to return (to the chagrin of true Falangists); the law permitting divorce was repealed; religious education was restored in all schools and universities; financial provision for the clergy was once again included in the national budget. As Madariaga writes, "a certain touch of popular and traditional superstition became the fashion." Eventually, in 1953, a new Concordat was signed with the Vatican, and Franco was invested with the rarely bestowed Supreme Order of Christ. A sign of the times was the growth of the Opus Dei movement—a kind of Catholic answer to freemasonry: a privileged non-celibate religious order, rich and influential, whose members live as private citizens and devote themselves to the re-Christianization of Spain. Opus Dei now runs its own university at Pamplona, and grants its own nationally recognized diplomas. To what extent the earlier hatred of the working class for the Church has been lessened it is hard to say, or how far the younger post-civil-war generation has been successfully indoctrinated. A recent estimate gave 10 per cent. of the working-class population of Barcelona as practising Catholics, and 20 per cent. of the population of the city in general. In eight large parishes near Madrid, 14,000 out of 105,000 were found to be practising Catholics; in rural areas, a much larger proportion.[1] It is perhaps significant that Madrid students striking in 1962 named the corrupt influence of Opus Dei as one of the objects of their protest. It is certainly true that Spanish women, now as previously, are much devouter than the men. For the rest, Spain is at least *officially* Catholic; and, although the Church has been far from subservient, it has remained at the right hand of the regime, acting as censor and guardian of public morals.[2] Spain's critics hold that the people remain under the thumb of the priest-hood; that under its ancient trappings the Church is a governmental power, a "top-heavy, semi-police organization." Yet although Liberalism with a capital L is still taboo in Spain, and religious toleration unacceptable, it has frequently, in fact, been from Church

[1] Figures quoted in *Spain and the Defense of the West*, by A. P. Whitaker.
[2] In all sorts of ways. Guide-books to Spain, for instance, contain such useful warnings as these: "It's as well to know that two-piece bathing suits, for women, are not acceptable in Spain; and one-piece bathing-suits must have a skirt. When you emerge from the sea or the swimming-pool, you must cover yourself with a wrap or a cape. For sunbathing, go to the special solarium." In such matters, however, the Church may be doing little more than underline the Spaniard's innate modesty and need of dignity—both liable to be destroyed by public nudity.

circles that pleas have come from time to time for a liberalization of
the regime; many priests, especially in the industrial north, are
radical and dynamic in their interpretation of their religion; and
even the Church hierarchy have more than once come out in favour
of bigger wage increases for the workers, when the officially authorized increases have failed to keep pace with the continuing infla-
tionary rise in prices.

Many thought that the fall of Mussolini and Hitler must mean the
rapid fall of Franco too, and there was much talk of United Nations
pressure, through the Security Council, to secure a democratic Spain.
In 1946 the General Assembly voted to exclude Spain from all
United Nations agencies, and recommended member states to withdraw diplomatic representatives from Madrid. Nothing could have
been better designed to fortify Franco's internal position—not so
much, as has been generally suggested, because foreign meddling
roused Spanish national pride (though it did that too) as because it
rubbed in the lesson to the quarrelsome factions grouped round
Franco that they stood or fell with him. Every time the United
Nations, or foreign Left-wing organizations, passed resolutions
hostile to Franco, his authority in Spain rose. In any case, the Cold
War soon compelled a Western reassessment. Certainly Franco was
anti-democratic, which was bad; but he was undoubtedly anti-
Communist, which was good. He had the support of world-wide
Catholic friends; and even if European powers continued to blackball
him (for had not the Second World War been fought to destroy
Fascism?), the U.S.A., intent on building her anti-Russian power-
system, was more adaptable and less squeamish. By 1951 she was
negotiating for bases in Spain, though the strength of Western
European public opinion made it impracticable for her to press for
Spanish membership of NATO. By 1953 she had secured her agreement, the Pact of Madrid, offering economic aid in return for naval
and air bases. In 1955, at long last, Spain was admitted to the
company of the United Nations; and, though she was still excluded
from NATO, John Foster Dulles, the United States Secretary of
State, paying an official visit to Franco in December 1957 at the
Pardo palace outside Madrid, went out of his way to inform him
personally of the outlines of NATO strategy. President Eisenhower
himself, two years later, officially visited Spain and drove with Franco
in an open car from air base to palace. Adenauer was known to be
in favour of fully accepting Spain into NATO. Gradually other
Western nations took her out of the diplomatic deep-freeze, though
as late as 1961, when Mr R. A. Butler, on a private visit to Spain,

described Spain's exclusion from full West European status as "disgraceful," there was an indignant outcry from Labour politicians. Memories of the Civil War still live, and disgust at Franco's continued imprisonment of considerable numbers of his political enemies is still powerful. Slowly, however, Spain is being drawn into the mainstream of European development. Excluded from the original European Common Market, she later made application to be associated with it, and negotiations began in 1962.

Spain is, of course, still a poor country. At the close of the Civil War in 1939, the whole nation lay bleeding and tattered; and for a further fifteen years or so it crept only slowly out of its wretched state. In fact, between 1945 and 1951 things got worse: the rise in national wages proceeded at about half the rate of the rise of the cost of living, so that the condition of many workers was desperate. Housing was often primitive and unemployment high. Industrial strikes and protest demonstrations were illegal, and liable to very harsh punishment—but that did not prevent, for instance, the workers of Barcelona, 300,000 strong, and 100,000 of the men of the northern industrial towns, from observing a one-day general strike in 1951. At that time also, and on several later occasions, the students of Madrid University went on strike, both as a sign of sympathy with the workers and as a gesture of protest against the intellectual strait-jacket in which the regime placed them. And those old warriors, the miners of Asturias, though without union funds or strike pay, were again fighting in 1962, when their long (and ultimately successful) strike spread rapidly to other industries, sparked off another Madrid student strike, and again elicited protests from intellectuals of the Catholic Left against the refusal of the Government to permit genuine industrial negotiation. ('Syndicates' in Spain are on the Falangist pattern, including representatives of Government, employers, and 'selected' workers; wage rises are governed by productivity and national policy.)

From about 1954, however, the first year in which American aid became effective, there was in general a marked upturn in the Spanish economy. Some of the dollars were earmarked for the purchase of American surplus food production, but the more valuable aid was used for buying heavy industrial equipment. There was a big programme of irrigation, afforestation, chemical-fertilizer manufacture, and colliery modernization; rapid improvements were made in the national hydro-electric grid; many new thermal power stations were built; steel and pig iron production advanced notably after 1957, with important new blast furnaces coming into production at Aviles, in Asturias. Such projects as that near Badajoz to irrigate over 200,000 arid acres of the Estremadura, or the similar Aragón scheme ceremonially inaugurated by Franco in 1958, were among the most important of their kind in Europe. Overseas trade increased; and in particular Franco sedulously courted the Arab countries, whose diplomatic support was valuable in a hostile world, and who (especially Turkey) provided profitable trade. Yet it was Britain, traditionally Spain's foremost overseas market, that still proved the best customer of all. Not least important, there was a big expansion in the tourist industry, until by the end of the 'fifties four millions were coming annually to Spain. Side by side with this very considerable material progress there has been, it must be admitted, a persistent inflation, a stubborn level of unemployment that has led to a steady flow of workers to labour-hungry nations like West Germany, and a chronic shortage of houses. There has been an almost total failure to tackle the basic problem of land tenure—hardly surprising in view of the inevitable offence such agrarian reform would give to the landlords, who are an important prop of the regime. Workers are denied rights that an Englishman or a German would consider elementary. Even so, a Spaniard enjoys some privileges that are new to him, and not to be despised. No worker can be dismissed by the employer alone. Unemployed receive benefit to the extent of 75. per cent. of their basic pay for a period of six months. Spain remains a poor country, but both economically and socially her position is very far from stagnant. An industrial and technical revolution is in progress.

The astute and cautious Franco as long ago as 1943 perceived that 'totalitarian' was an unwise label to wear. In that year he described his regime as an "organic democracy"—a phrase presumably intended, like an advertiser's slogan, to convey a mental association rather than any precise meaning. In that same year the Duce fell. Two years later the Führer was no more. Even the more prudent Caudillo would not last for ever. Very soon, accordingly, he dealt with the problem of what was to happen to Spain after Franco. He was titular head of the Falange, which was anti-Monarchist; but he was supported by the Carlists and other Monarchist groups whose *raison d'être* was a Bourbon restoration. Characteristically, therefore, he played with words and temporized—but moved slowly towards a compromise. By the Law of Succession, approved by referendum in 1947, Spain was declared to be a "traditional, Catholic, social, and representative monarchy" (whatever that might mean). The Franco era was to be treated as an emergency, and as an interlude. The years went by, and Franco himself showed no inclination to die or to retire; neither was he inclined to concede the claims of the Pretender Don Juan de Borbón. But by 1954 he was receiving in audience the Pretender's two sons, Juan Carlos and Alfonso. That year they passed their Spanish state matriculation examination and it was agreed that their education should proceed in Spain. (The Pretender lived in Portugal.) Next year Juan Carlos went as a cadet to Franco's old Military Academy at Saragossa; he went on from there to the Naval Academy. In 1962 he married Princess Sophia of Greece, and it is generally assumed that the pair will become King and Queen of Spain on Franco's death or retirement, or on the Prince's coming-of-age (at thirty) in 1968. At least it can be said of Franco (as it cannot be said of Salazar) that he has made provision for the succession.

History likes to wait longer even than Franco himself before committing herself, and her views on this circumspect dictator are not yet available. Politicians, however, are hastier and more headstrong; and they have already rushed in to denounce him as a Fascist who had neither the courage to repay the 'blood-debt' owed to his European allies in war, nor the magnanimity to pardon his Spanish enemies in his hour of victory; or alternatively they have sung his praises as the 'very perfect gentle knight' of Christendom riding out against atheist Communism. To some he remains a small-minded tyrant, the vindictive enemy of the working-class and the catspaw of superstition. To others he is the bringer of peace—and even, recently, of prosperity—to his tortured country. Certainly it may be argued that only the memory of the Civil War and Spaniards' revulsion from any move that might lead down again to another such abyss of blood has enabled his intolerant regime to survive so long. On the other hand, no judgment that sees him merely in terms of European generalities ("Fascism," "Communism," "democracy") will make much sense. He is a Spaniard attempting to control the uniquely tangled affairs of Spain, that only semi-European land. His own words, spoken at the dedication in 1959 of the imposing Civil War memorial in the Valley of the Fallen, thirty-five miles north-west of Madrid, reveal eloquently both his own view of his historical rôle and the reason why toleration and generosity remain impossible for him:

> The struggle between good and evil never ends, no matter how great the victory. . . . Anti-Spain was beaten and routed, but is not dead. . . . You must maintain with exemplary purity the brotherhood forged in the ranks of the crusade and prevent the enemy, who is always lying in ambush, from infiltrating your ranks.

Even at the ceremony, a voice rang out: "Franco, you are a traitor!" What Franco calls "Anti-Spain" was *half* Spain: there is little reason to think that the fraction has much declined, or that increasing prosperity will in the future necessarily diminish it. Indeed, living standards rising from a very low starting base frequently increase rather than decrease discontent—one of the uncomfortable lessons of history.

Yet it must be reckoned that Franco has shown, if not vision or magnanimity, at least skill and talent: skill in the military handling of the Civil War, in managing his awkward crew in war and peace, in extracting maximum assistance from Hitler and Mussolini for minimum return, in steering his battered craft through the dangerous narrows of the unfriendly post-war world. It was a world where a cool head and a readiness to trim sail were essential. He kept afloat, and in the course of time reached less choppy water. It is over a quarter of a century since he achieved power. At least, as man and as ruler, he shares the talent of the Abbé Sieyès, who, challenged to say what he managed to perform during the turbulent times of the French Revolution, made the immortal reply: "*J'ai vécu.*"

Table of Events

1890's.	Many Anarchist outrages.
1892.	Franco born at El Ferrol.
1898.	Spanish-American War over Cuba.
1909.	Mob rule in Barcelona: the "Tragic Week."
1912–17 1920–27	Franco in Morocco with Foreign Legion.
1923–30.	Dictatorship of Primo de Rivera.
1927.	Franco head of Saragossa Military Academy.
1931.	Fall of monarchy. Far-reaching reforms of Republican Government. Anti-clerical atrocities.
1933.	Right-wing election victory. Foundation of *Falange Española*.
1934.	Foreign Legion subdues Asturias miners.
1936.	Popular Front Government formed.
1936–39.	Civil War. Franco Head of State and Generalissimo.
1940.	Franco resists Hitler's pressure, remains neutral.
1941.	"Blue Division" in Russia.
1942.	Iberian Bloc formed with Portugal.
1945.	Victorious powers 'blackball' Spain.
1947.	Succession Law: Spain a monarchy.
1953.	Concordat with Papacy. Pact of Madrid with U.S.A.
1955.	Spain admitted to United Nations.

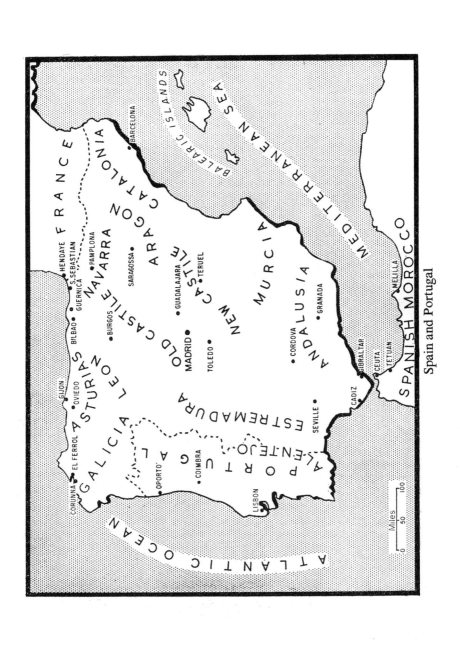

Spain and Portugal

14

António de Oliveira Salazar
(1899-   )

Five and a half centuries ago, in the same year that the English bowmen defeated the French at Agincourt, the Portuguese first ventured overseas to expel the Muslim from Ceuta, on the African side of the Straits of Gibraltar. Back from Ceuta, the half-English Prince Henry, the "Navigator," brought visions of expansion and exploration which during the next century were to take Portuguese sailors further and further southward down the coast of Africa and (rounding the Cape at last) eastward to India and the East Indies; westward too to Brazil and (in the person of the renegade Magellan) along the coasts of South America and over the great ocean back to the Indies, circling the globe. Hence Portugal, a small and poor land, became rich and great by colonial conquest and overseas trade. Seizing the moment when European navigation and armaments were pre-eminent, she sent her ships and soldiers to easy conquests the world over. This minor Iberian kingdom, shut out from the fortunes of the Mediterranean, turned outward to the Atlantic to grasp its ocean destiny; and thus it led the European exploration and conquest of the world.

The centuries moved by, and Portugal, like Spain, did not move with them. Other nations—France, Holland, Britain—left her far behind. A great empire and proud memories remained to her—but she had become a minor power, backward in agriculture, slow in invention and industry, weak in diplomacy and war. The armies of her Napoleonic enemies and her British allies swept over her. More profoundly disruptive, the ideas of the French Revolution—liberty and equality, republicanism and anti-Catholicism—tore her apart for more than a century, making a cleavage between liberals and traditionalists that produced one revolution after another, right up to the age of Salazar. The loss of Brazil in 1822, and its final adoption of a republic in 1889, mocked her impotence and yet further increased her poverty. Portugal entered the twentieth century in financial ruin and political chaos.

While intrigues, party manoeuvres, and the everlasting skirmishing for profit and position discredited the politicians, the standing of the monarchy too was compromised. Republicanism was strong, so an electoral law was introduced to contrive that its supporters were inevitably defeated. Charles I (1889–1908), tied to a decaying system, found himself driven to dictatorial methods, with the result that his unpopularity among the politicians rapidly increased. The Catholic Church, a major force on the side of tradition and conservatism, provoked, as in all strongly Catholic countries, a strong reaction. The country was full of secret anti-religious societies, and there were many anti-clerical outbursts in the larger towns. In 1906 Charles ended pretence, and invited a dictator to assume power. The Parliament (Cortes) was dismissed; municipal corporations that protested were replaced by Government nominees. Critical newspapers were suppressed, and political opponents exiled, without trial, to far Timor. One revolution having been foiled, martial law followed—but the bullets of assassins soon accounted for both Charles I and his heir. His second son, Manuel II, meaning well, was nevertheless powerless to arrest the drift of events. Six Governments followed in two years, until in 1910 the cruiser *Adamastor* shelled the royal palace from the river Tagus, while defecting republican soldiers fought their way to control the city of Lisbon; and Manuel, finding the game up, fled to his long exile in England. The republic was proclaimed. In the University of Coimbra the students, in a frenzy of delight, smashed the furniture, tore up their lecturers' gowns, and riddled the royal portraits with bullets; but a twenty-one-year-old economics student, one António de Oliveira Salazar, continued quietly working for his degree.

The republic provided during the next sixteen years the most sensationally unsuccessful regime in Europe. The elementary precondition of democracy was lacking—an acceptance by all parties of the basic rules of the constitutional game. Instead, the reins of government were fought for by implacable rivals between whom compromise was impossible. For instance, if one Government expelled the religious orders, confiscated their property, closed the convents, permitted priests to marry, and forbade the teaching of religion in schools, all these measures would be revoked by a succeeding conservative Government. When the radical republicans legalized the strike weapon, the workers of Lisbon, Oporto, and the big cities proceeded to an orgy of strikes so violent that a later reaction became inevitable. The Army repeatedly intervened to attempt the overthrow of the regime; and the Navy, much more to the Left than the Army, was so politically active that its warships' magazines were at one time emptied. (This was in time of war, too, and in 1918 enabled a German submarine to sail unmolested up the Tagus!) For sixteen years Portugal suffered an astonishing sequence of revolutions and counter-revolutions, general strikes, bomb-throwings, military revolts, naval mutinies, political assassinations, executions, mass arrests to fill the prisons, mass amnesties to empty them again, interventions by foreign warships to calm things down, and—increasingly as the years went by—a steady and disastrous inflation of the currency. In sixteen years there were 24 revolutions, 44 Governments, 500 Cabinet Ministers, and 158 general strikes. 'Democracy' had never seemed more ineffectual and ludicrous; but in fact the history and temperament of the Portuguese had made them incapable of understanding what democracy involved. They had become the victims of ignorance and poverty, the prey of priests or agitators, of doctrinaires of the Catholic Right or the radical Left. They had become irreconcilable and ungovernable.

The present regime in Portugal had its origins in the revolution of 1926, when General Gomes da Costa proclaimed "the interest of the nation against the parties and the politicians"; in fact, risings continued until 1931—those of 1927 being the bloodiest of all. It was in 1926, however, that the Army took over the Republic and liquidated the old 'democracy.' Da Costa, who had commanded the Portuguese forces that fought with the Western allies in the First World War, assumed power jointly with General Carmona and a civilian. Dismissing the Parliament first, they proceeded to dismiss one another subsequently, until Carmona alone was left. Premier and President to begin with, he was confirmed as President in the plebiscite of 1928, and remained in this office until his death in 1951. Da Costa was invited to retire to the Azores.

It was a country doubly and trebly ruined that Carmona led. Portugal was like a party of drunks rousing stiffly from their overnight brawlings and finding that in their stupor they have broken the windows and smashed all the furniture. And it was a severe wind that blew through those windows in 1926: the country's agriculture was backward, its industry hardly developed, its railways and roads in ill repair, its finances derelict, its armed forces disaffected and ill-equipped, its civil service swollen, its schools few and primitive, its people largely illiterate.

When da Costa was interviewed a few days after his *coup d'état*, he remarked to a journalist, half apologetically, that his Government was the best available in such lean times. The Finance

Minister, for instance: "He is a certain Salazar from Coimbra. They tell me he is a very good man. Do you know him?" The journalist did not. It was not surprising. Nobody knew Dr Salazar, a quiet man from Coimbra, where he taught economics at the University.

António de Oliveira Salazar was born in 1889, the fifth child in a peasant family in the village of Vimieiro, near Coimbra. Intended by his family for the priesthood, like so many children of the poor, he found that he lacked a vocation. But he was a scholarly boy, and managed to proceed from village school to Jesuit seminary, and from seminary to Coimbra University, maintaining himself there by school-teaching. Serious and self-assured, he achieved an excellent degree in economics, and was in 1914 appointed to the teaching staff of the University. His political opinions were never in doubt: Catholic, patriotic, and conservative, he had little use for political parties of any colour. Assuming first a basic devotion to Church, to the family, and to financial sobriety, his views were remarkably close to Alexander Pope's:

> For forms of government let fools contest;
> Whate'er is best administered is best.

In 1919 he had to defend himself against charges that his teaching was anti-republican. Temporarily suspended from his professorship, he was vindicated in the High Court and re-appointed. Elected two years later to the National Assembly, he attended once only, but continued to mingle academic and political activity over the next five years. His speeches proclaim the man: didactic and professorial —preaching always the exaltation of the family and the Church, the necessity of spiritual discipline and the subjection of the State to God. A non-Catholic might well find them high-falutin and platitudinous, but they must be judged against the chaos of the times; certainly Portugal was in need of political sobriety and self-discipline. Liberty, said Salazar, was a fine thing; but man must find "a safeguard against the vagaries of his freedom"; he must discover through God the law that he must obey.

These were exalted sentiments. But Salazar was not just a donnish dreamer philosophizing in his lecture-room. He had cut-and-dried plans for balancing the budget, and it was these that recommended him to the military group who, having taken over the government in 1926, had no idea themselves what to do with it. They had applied to the League of Nations for a £12 million loan to enable Portugal to escape from her chronic bankruptcy (budgets in Portugal had balanced only twice in seventy-four years); but the League's terms were so insulting to Portugal's pride (involving League control of financial administration) that her leaders rejected them and called in instead the professional expert, Salazar, to administer his own severe medicine.

This was a drastic draught. Exploiting his indispensability, he first imposed his own conditions on the Army. These entailed a practical veto on any legislation that appeared too expensive; it was said that Salazar balanced the budget by eliminating expenditure. His was, simply, a budgetary solution: sacrifices, orthodoxy, cutting coat according to cloth. Salazar did indeed succeed in balancing the budget— it was his immediate success—and he continued to do so over the years; but financial uprightness and rigid accountancy did not provide a sufficient policy for people starting from such a low base as the Portuguese. Everything else was subordinated— industrial expansion, agricultural development, social reform, educational advance—so that a Portugal virtuously balancing its small annual budget lagged further and further behind its European neighbours who were climbing quickly ahead in material prosperity.

In 1929, however, what was seen was not the eventual stagnation but the immediate budgetary success, and in the next decade Salazar proceeded systematically to lower the interest charges on the national debt (a large proportion of it owed abroad), to correct the unfavourable balance of payments and build up big gold reserves. Fortified by these, he even attempted to return to the gold standard in 1931, with the gold escudo tied to the gold pound. But 1931 was an unlucky year for such a move: three months after he made it, the gold pound was no more—Britain abandoned the gold standard, and Salazar had to follow suit.

He had achieved enough, however, as financial wonder-worker to enjoy for the time being impregnable prestige in Portugal and high esteem abroad. Already the legend was growing of the quiet, disinterested, devout, shrewd bachelor who shunned publicity as he shunned women; the non-smoking, teetotal, modest, tough man behind the scenes; the back-room dictator. On the rare occasions that he addressed a crowd it was "as if he was talking aloud, alone, and to himself." His own valuation of his mission put him on almost a saintly level: one must not "aspire to power as a right, but accept it as a duty, considering the State as God's ministry for the common good." Here, apparently, was no vulgar, posturing Mussolini-figure, but a lonely, ascetic, dedicated man: one who might have gone into a monastery to save his own soul but instead devoted himself to saving Portugal, "a man of thought transformed into a man of action"; the sort of dictator (in that age of Mussolini and Hitler) that even the English could approve of; quiet, soft-speaking, self-effacing, ironical, practical. Even the word 'dictator' seemed a little harsh, and 'Fascist' conjured up another world altogether.

Undoubtedly this was the image Salazar intended: in his own words, one "who was obliged to abandon the high calling of teaching and to tread a harder path with a heavier cross." There is no doubt, however, either of his relish for power or of the essentially Fascist nature of his political creed. Between 1930 and 1935 the bases were laid of the *Estado Novo*, or New State, a Portuguese regime sharing much of the philosophy and organization of Mussolini's Italy: the "unitary and corporative state." "I do not believe in universal suffrage," said Salazar. "I do not believe in equality but in hierarchy." "I am profoundly anti-parliamentary." His *Estado Novo* demanded absolute loyalty to the *nation,* stressed the primacy of the *family,* the duty of obedience to *authority,* the imperative necessity of religious (*i.e.,* Catholic) *belief,* and acknowledged the *right to work.* As for individual liberty, it was, said Salazar, the greatest of blessings, but just as likely to flourish under dictatorship as under a democracy: all that ordinary men demanded was to be well led. In 1930 a "National Union" was created, the single Salazarian "coalition of men of good will"; no other party was permitted. Striking became a criminal offence, trade unions being in theory merged into "economic corporations" which represented employers and workers. (In fact, Portugal rapidly became an employers' paradise.) These corporations, together with others representing the professions and Catholic organizations, came together to constitute the House of Corporations. The other House, the National Assembly, was from the beginning a farcical affair. Advisory merely, it was solemnly elected from a list prepared by the National Union; 'opposition' lists were allowed, but electoral arrangements ensured the impossibility of their candidates being elected. "The people," Salazar once declared, "has less need of being sovereign than of being governed."

Already Prime Minister by 1932, Salazar presented his new Constitution to a plebiscite in 1933 (without the effective secrecy of the ballot), and won a big vote of national approval. He had, in any case, achieved a notable stabilization of his country's affairs. His Cabinet was a cabinet, not of politicians, but of experts—a lawyer, an engineer, a soldier, and so on: himself the arch-expert, the technocrat-in-chief, remaining until 1940 at the Ministry of Finance.

It must have seemed to Salazar in the mid-thirties that he was swimming with the tide of history. Democracies were collapsing all over Europe, and it must have seemed reasonable to him to forecast, as he did in 1935, that "in twenty years from now, unless there is a setback in political evolution, there will be no more legislative assemblies in Europe." When, in the next year, the Spanish Civil War broke out, there could be no doubt on which side Salazar's sympathies must rest. A Portuguese Legion of 20,000 was raised to assist Franco; the controlled Press was strong for him; material found its way through Portugal for his armies; his agents were given every facility in Lisbon's best hotels; and in the latter part of the war Republican refugees, escaping into Portugal, were rounded up and returned, to face imprisonment or death.

In private Salazar might condemn the "excessively nationalist" youth movements of Italy and Germany, but already Portuguese children at the infant schools were learning to give the Fascist salute and to chant "Salazar, Salazar, Salazar" as a daily routine. Already the well-drilled Press was sedulously conveying to a credulous people the image of the all-wise father who could do no wrong. Already the PIDE, the "International Police for the Defence of the State," was being modelled on the German Gestapo and studying to acquire its techniques. In this their success must be accounted moderate: torture indeed they used, but they were outstandingly unsuccessful in preventing the escape of important political prisoners. The Constitution of 1933 'guaranteed' to all citizens the basic rights: freedom of speech and expression, freedom of worship and association, and freedom from arbitrary arrest; but it also gave the Government the right to override these rights in the cause of order. Hence they were worth, apparently, nothing. In the name of the nation's moral danger, the State could freely commit its own immoralities.

Salazar, whether or not he has any great 'sense of history,' certainly has always had a strong backward-looking sense of national pride (a rather different thing), and gloried in his countrymen's past imperial record. But he has never exalted militarism as Hitler and Mussolini did. He has expounded none of Mussolini's theories of the purifying and ennobling aspects of war. Moreover, Providence had already provided Portugal with vast arenas within which to exercise her mission. "Through the designs of Providence by which the world is ruled," he said in 1934, "Portugal has no need of wars and conquests." No need, certainly, of wars. Her difficulties later would be to escape them. Salazar could not then foresee a time when the very hugeness of Portugal's overseas possessions would ensure her vulnerability to the typical latter-day war—the war of colonial liberation. In 1939, however, there was no doubt of what he should do. His obvious policy, like Franco's, was to tread a path of wary neutrality. There was the ancient alliance with Britain to consider, still commercially important, but hardly sufficient to engender any pro-British belligerence; yet equally the regime's tendency to sympathize with the Fascist powers was not fervid enough to justify any rash Portuguese gestures. Lisbon remained a useful listening-post and headquarters for the spies of all belligerents, and Portugal continued to trade as far as she could with both sides in the war. Her people's sympathies were divided, but Dr Goebbels was happy to note in his diary that "so long as Dr Salazar remains in power nothing really hostile to us will be done." Goebbels was, however, as so often, wrong. In October 1943, Salazar, under pressure from Churchill and Roosevelt, and with the war going against Germany, found himself forced to concede to the Allies bases in the Azores. When the end came in 1945, he reasserted his 'correctness' by conveying his regrets to Hitler's 'successor' upon the Führer's death. Only de Valera of Eire saw fit to act similarly.

Liberals inside Portugal had hoped much of the outcome of Allied success in the (anti-Fascist) Second World War. No sooner was the war over, however, than the (anti-Communist) Cold War began, and in that war Salazar was himself a willing ally. His position inside Portugal, therefore, was in no way weakened, as it might have been, by the concerted disapproval of the victorious democratic powers. Salazar and Franco were indeed odd men out in a democratic Western Europe: but they were both potential collaborators in an anti-Communist bloc. The Americans, in particular, saw them either as possible partners, or—if that seemed to be going too far—at least as potential lessors of air and sea bases vital to a global anti-Communist strategy. And when in fact NATO emerged in 1949 as the crown of that strategy, Portugal was one of its founder members—plainly more respectable than Franco's Spain, whose admission was not tolerable to the Western European democrats. Portugal also found herself one of the original members of the Organization for European Economic Co-operation. Little attention, however, was paid abroad to events inside Portugal itself, where some thousands of hopeful democrats, having signed petitions demanding free elections, a free press, and an amnesty for political prisoners, found that all they had done was to provide the dictatorship with a directory of its enemies.

Other international events of the time carried a portent that the Salazar regime chose to ignore. In August 1947 the British *Raj* in India ended, and the independent Republic of India then became one of the key facts in the new world situation. It was a fact that Salazar turned his back upon. The British had gone from India. The French, slow to face some other colonial facts, faced this one, and followed. The Indian princes either subscribed to the new writ voluntarily, or (as in Hyderabad) were very soon made to bow to it. Only the Portuguese, one of the poorest of European states and, in world terms, a minimal power, clung to its small relic of past grandeur. Goa, with the other small enclaves on the Indian coast, was to be retained out of loyalty to "the greatness of our ancestors" and "as a memorial to Portuguese discoveries." When the Indian Government asked for a discussion of the situation, the Portuguese declined to see any situation. Goa was a part of Portugal. Goans were simply Portuguese—second-class citizens, indeed, and debarred under Salazar's Colonial Act from becoming Army officers and exercising certain other rights, but Portuguese nevertheless—and it is fair to point out that many of them, especially the Goanese Catholics, preferred to remain so. For years Nehru's Government used all the non-military devices open to it—internal subversion, economic blockade, international propaganda—without avail. Salazar not only held on to Goa; he drew on his slender finances to reinforce it. He appealed to the British, his country's ancient ally, and the British Government did what it could to dissuade the Indians from using force—while warning Salazar not to expect British military assistance if they did. For fourteen years they desisted, and when in 1961 they at last ended by invasion what to them seemed an intolerable anomaly, Salazar's Government could do little more than vent its impotent resentment against them—and also against the British, the United States, and the United Nations. Portugal, Salazar announced to his National Assembly, would "surely be among the first" to withdraw from the United Nations. As for the British alliance—that ancient alliance which was an essential ingredient of Portugal's original independence of Spain—he would have to reexamine it to see if it retained any "content."

Prestige is one reason why the great Portuguese overseas empire means so much to the Salazar regime. Another is poverty. Portugal is a poor country, and would be poorer still if she did not take from her African and Asian possessions a sizable fraction of the means of balancing her trade. From Angola and Mozambique, the two biggest of them, come cheap raw cotton, sugar, vegetable oils, coffee, sisal, and other tropical products important to the Portuguese economy. Not only do these provide one-eighth of all imports, but they furnish the basis of more than a quarter of Portugal's exports and re-exports, both to the overseas territories themselves and to the rest of the world.

Despite her colonies, Portugal remains a poor—even a desperately poor—country, and although Salazar's rule has succeeded in doing something, it has hardly done enough to raise living standards. The daily intake of food is probably the lowest in Europe, at about 2400 calories per head; her death rate from tuberculosis (always a good indicator of malnutrition) is the highest in Europe, 51 per 100,000 of the population in 1958; her infant mortality rate (84 per 1000 live births in 1958) is exceeded only by Yugoslavia's; her productivity per head of population, though rising slowly, is only a quarter that of Great Britain. The average Portuguese wage *per day* is roughly equivalent to a Scandinavian wage *per hour*. Under Salazar, in other words, the business-man and the landowner have normally prospered while the worker and the peasant have often gone hungry. Many a poor family dreams of emigration, especially to Brazil; but the fares for the whole family are often prohibitive, and 90 per cent. of the 350,000 who emigrated during the nineteen-fifties were men striking out on their own. Even this flood of refugees from poverty carries away only a third of the natural increase of population; for in Portugal, a Catholic country, birth control is taboo, and the population has now reached nine millions—a hundred of them pressing on every square kilometre. As for Portuguese industries, they are largely in the hands of a small group of monopolists, often foreign. (When the founder of the biggest of these businesses died in 1942 his fortune was accounted the world's sixth greatest.) Strikes are illegal; the profits tax is very low; and no tax may rise above 30 per cent. Salazar himself lives in frugal simplicity, with his two adopted daughters and his old housekeeper—but around him in his Government are representatives of the oligarchs who have benefited most from his regime: bankers, landowners, and industrialists. Despite his economic planning and his absorption in his country's welfare and 'greatness,' it is only too easy to see Salazar's Portugal as the land of the luxury hotel and the slum shack, the Cadillac and the donkey. The agrarian condition of the country is beset by twin evils at opposite extremes. In the north there has been division and subdivision of the available land, until many 'farms' are plots of an acre or two only, only marginally capable of sustaining a peasant family at subsistence level. (Over all Portugal half the holdings do not exceed 2·4 acres.) On the other hand, in the poorer land of the Alentejo, in the south, the smallest holdings are of 7000 acres, and four landowners alone are masters of 235,000 acres. In the north the units are often too small to allow the use of a tractor even if the peasant could afford one; in the south the big landowners have mechanized the cultivation of the more profitable lands and per- mitted the rest to go to waste; and in these southern areas many landless labourers are hired only for seed-time and harvest, and consequently idle much of the year away in enforced unemployment. When in 1946 a novelist published the story of migrant workers of the Alentejo travelling the country in cattle-trucks, looking for work, the authorities banned the book.

Agrarian troubles such as these are typical ills of old and populous countries whose lack of minerals or infertility of soil have held them back from industrialization or easy wealth. (The parallel of Ireland springs to mind.) Salazar, though he was slow to perceive the necessity of planning—being for many years dazzled by his fiscal achievements and obsessed by budget-balancing—did in later years undertake big projects of modernization, school-building, and public works. Public works in particular: some impressive hydro-electric schemes (vital to a coal-less country) have brought water and electricity to many rural areas. A first Development Plan (1953–58) rather belatedly tackled the country's economic backwardness. A second £375 million Six Year Plan (1959-64) is more ambitious, and envisages, among other things, irrigation schemes to bring water to the arid Alentejo, a bridge over the Tagus west of Lisbon, a ship- building yard at Lisbon, a big building programme for both liners and fishing-vessels, further development of electrification and oil- refining, and airports in Madeira and the Azores. Two-thirds of the plan relates to Portugal itself, one-third to the colonies.

Such planning is overdue if Portugal is to keep pace, even at a lagging distance, with the twentieth century. Educational advances, too, are urgent. There has been progress here. Schools have been built, and the rate of illiteracy reduced; for the first time, no Portuguese child today is totally denied schooling; but still two Portuguese in every five or six cannot read. Rural electrification is useless to the peasant who is incapable of understanding it; tractors and new techniques of cultivation may well be lost upon those men whose fixity in old ways is as stubborn as the mules they prefer.

Salazar has not been blind to his country's severe economic

problems, but his proposed solutions have often seemed to belong to a world other than that in which he was living. In a speech long ago in 1936 he ably analysed his country's economic woes: over-population, under-industrialization, lack of capital, lack of fuel and minerals, large areas of arid land, a technically backward people. Portugal *by itself* was not a viable economic proposition. "The logical solution is for the colonies to produce the raw material and to sell it to the Mother Country in exchange for manufactured goods."

It was an eighteenth-century solution to a twentieth-century problem. It presupposed a static world where the Portuguese Empire was a permanency. Even so, it might well be argued, Portugal could hardly hope, in view of her backwardness and lack of resources, to do what a coal-wealthy Britain of much the same population had done a hundred and fifty years previously—thrive and multiply in a small land at the centre of a great trading empire. But the speech well illustrates the basic Salazarian dependence on the colonies.

Interviews with friendly biographers of an earlier epoch show well the trend of his thought concerning the colonies. He could see no threat to them. "Who would covet them?" he asked one such interviewer in 1938. Great Britain? But she was pledged to defend them. France? She had no such ambition. Germany? Herr Hitler had specifically disavowed any claim to them. Italy? Signor Mussolini was perfectly satisfied with Ethiopia. Belgium and Holland? They were out of the question.

> We must put behind us these eternal fears. . . . Let us put the subject aside, because we will not even discuss the question of our sovereign rights. . . . Our sovereignty is our life and we alone can dispose of it. Moreover, our overseas territories were not taken from any other country. They were discovered by us and have always been ours. . . . What country can boast of a colonial record as long as ours?

1938 is a long time ago—another world; and one should not hasten to condemn the misjudgments of 1938 using the hindsight of today. But it plainly did not cross Salazar's mind that the danger lay not in Portugal's fellow-imperialist powers of Europe but among the people of the colonies themselves; that the same current that had borne away Brazil in the nineteenth century might take the African and Asian territories in the twentieth; that nationalism was not destined to be peculiar to Europeans; that the African or Indian natives who had "always" been Portuguese might not wish for ever to be the means of defending the metropolitan Portuguese from starvation.

After the loss of all her New World possessions, Portugal was still left with widely scattered colonies: in India, *Goa* (lost in 1961); in China, *Macao*; in the East Indies, half of *Timor*; in the Gulf of Guinea, the islands of *São Tomé* and *Príncipé* and part of the neighbouring *Guinea* mainland; the *Cape Verde* and *Azores* islands; and —overwhelmingly most important—the two large lands of *Mozambique*, stretching along the Indian Ocean coast for over a thousand miles from Tanganyika to South Africa, and *Angola*, a very large territory on the opposite, Atlantic, coast. These two lands of Angola and Mozambique together constitute an area nearly half the size of India, and since 1951 they, like all the other colonies, have been officially provinces of Portugal; but the legal myth does not provide an escape from the realities of history, geography, and economics. They are vast and primitive, with small white populations (about one per cent.) enjoying privileged status. Flanking as they do South Africa, the Rhodesias, Nyasaland, and the Congo, they are inevitably drawn into those countries' whirlpools of race-consciousness and nationalism. With such practices as forced labour and corporal punishment long-accepted in their economic and legal structure, they are an inevitable target for world condemnation, whether by Communists, by Liberals, or by a United Nations in which the non-white nations are predominant. Some reforms have come recently; but it is useless for Salazar's Government to protest that Angolan affairs are "internal to Portugal." The European-imposed boundaries of Africa seldom have much tribal or national meaning. (The Nyasas, for example, are common to Nyasaland and Mozambique; and the Bakongos to Northern Angola and Southern Congo.) Still less significance attaches to the legal niceties of remote Lisbon.

For long years Portugal has taken her colonizing mission very seriously. In a strict religious sense it was a mission to carry Catholic Christianity to pagan lands. In a more general sense, too, it was the pride of the Portuguese to carry their civilization to primitive peoples. Their attitude was paternal and (until recently) not at all racialist. Un-selfconscious mingling between Portuguese settlers and native women, whether by marriage or concubinage, permitted Brazil to escape the severity of the colour problem that beset the U.S.A.; and similarly in Africa the Catholic Portuguese (the darkest skinned of Europeans) did not develop the abhorrence of mixed blood that obsessed the whiter (and Calvinist) Dutch. Until recently, moreover, it was not very difficult for a black Mozambiquan, by learning Portuguese, by abandoning tribal habits and by possessing an occupation or a little property, to become officially 'assimilated' to Portuguese civilization. (Recently, Salazar has stiffened the qualifications and reduced the numbers of *assimilados* drastically, widening the gulf between 'civilized' and 'uncivilized' citizens.) Until 1959–60, the attitude of the typical 'white' Portuguese to the black natives around him was either paternal and affectionate, or casual and indifferent—or the sort of mixture of the two that came from an unchallenged position of superiority. The Portuguese civil servant in Luanda or bank official in Lourenço Marques was far more likely to be worried about the interfering dictatorship back in Lisbon than the challenging black man on his doorstep. Indeed, many a Portuguese liberal saw the best chance of removing Salazar in making of Angola or Mozambique a new Brazil—a rebel liberating force. (When in 1961 Captain Galvão hi-jacked the *Santa Maria*, it was Angola that he tried, unsuccessfully, to make for.)

The tidal wave of black African nationalism swept away this state of affairs and suddenly transformed the situation—tragically so in Angola. About 1956 the Union of the Peoples of Northern Angola (UPA), a small group with support among the Bakongo people, started operating from Leopoldville, in the Belgian Congo. From the same centre came another group, the People's Movement for the Liberation of Angola (MPLA). Such movements as these, beyond the reach of the Portuguese police, fostered an interest in tribal traditions, languages, and culture—activities superficially blameless—but also encouraged a sabotage of the white man's jurisdiction and property that began with burning of village stores and ended with rape, murder, and the most devilish atrocities—blinding, flaying alive, and mutilation of every beastly kind. As in the neighbouring Congo, tribalism in Angola went suddenly and dangerously mad. The Portuguese reacted in calculable manner: to begin with, by individual reprisals and lynchings; then, as the Army took control, by systematic destruction of entire villages with their inhabitants by machine-gun and napalm bomb, imposing a reign of terror whose casualties in human lives cannot be estimated, but which were certainly heavy. In the words of Salazar, "the work of centuries was destroyed in one month." In the words of his War Minister, addressing troops, "We are going to fight savages. We are going to fight wild beasts... who obey orders from international Communism." An exodus began of white women and children to Portugal or to some relative safety nearer home; but Salazar decreed a veto on all men of military age leaving Angola, himself took over the Ministry of Defence, and dispatched some 25,000 further troops to Angola. To him and his Government it seemed not only dangerous and wicked, but stupid and unreal, to talk (as Africans did) of an "end to colonialism" and "Africanization of the administration." Angola was as unready for what others called 'freedom' as the Congo had been. Under 1 per cent. of the black population was literate; a grand total of about twenty held university degrees. Even if one admitted the *right* of the Angolans to govern themselves, their inability to do so was patent; but Salazar admitted no such right. 'Colonialism' was the catch-phrase of Portugal's enemies (and they were world-wide), but to Salazar Angola was a limb of Portugal itself. Unlike the British, the French, and the other old colonial powers, Salazar would not admit the goal of colonial independence, however distant, even as a principle. Portuguese sovereignty was absolute: "It is impossible for us to accept for our overseas provinces, which make up part of the Nation, a position equivalent to territories under United Nations trusteeship and destined for eventual independence, or to render accounts of how the Portuguese see fit to govern themselves in their own house." United Nations condemnation was flatly rejected as "juridically incorrect." Portugal must "grip the plough in one hand and the sword in the other, as did our forebears throughout the centuries," and in this new task be ready to give dedication, sacrifice, and blood. "That is our destiny; that is the mission of our life. . . ."

It was as though Salazar had awoken to find himself in the twentieth century, had understandably not liked the look of what he saw there, and had willed himself back to sleep, to dream of the conquests of Albuquerque. However, the greatness of Portugal's past, the nobility of her mission, the sense of her destiny, were hardly likely to provide shelter in the nineteen-sixties from the raging winds of change. Salazar seemed on occasions to realize it himself: "Perhaps," he said, "I have lived beyond my time."

Many people in Portugal thought so. There had always been opposition to Salazar; but the Fascist nature of the constitution, the Press censorship, and the secret police had between them kept criticism within bounds until these latter years. The periodic 'election' of a President had always offered some hope to the liberals that a successful candidate would be sufficiently strong and enlightened to dismiss Salazar and introduce free speech and free elections. The Government, however, was not likely to be so caught. In 1949 it proclaimed the opposition candidate a public enemy, gave no guarantees of free elections, and forced his resignation on the eve of the poll. Similarly, in 1951, the next opposition candidate gave up on the day before the election. Anyone who had during the campaign supported these two had disclosed to the police his allegiance, and was therefore liable to arrest and possibly torture. The most important of the enemies of the regime was General Humberto Delgado, the Portuguese representative on NATO, who in 1958 came forward to stand against Salazar's nominee for President, did *not* retire before the Government's threats, toured the country, and spoke to very large and enthusiastic audiences—and was duly declared "not elected" after an almost certainly falsified poll. Even the Bishop of Oporto was moved to write (and to cause to be circulated through the country) a denunciation of Salazar's methods. The 'quiet dictator' was at last provoked into making a public harangue; he appeared angrily on television; he threatened to abolish presidential election by direct suffrage (and later did so); and issued the direst warnings against "agitators"—that is, those publicly disagreeing with Salazar's policies. Delgado was dismissed from his civilian and military posts, and found it prudent to take refuge in the Brazilian Embassy in Lisbon. Only the remarkable tenacity of the Ambassador eventually gained Delgado a safe-conduct to the airport, and thence to Brazil. Salazar, exerting pressure on Brazil, secured the Ambassador's removal, and thus still further lowered his own reputation: Delgado had lost the political, but undoubtedly won the moral, battle. He remained the leader of the liberal revolt from his exile. His friend and supporter Galvão, seizing the moment to escape from his prison hospital under the noses of the secret police (leaving a bolster in his bed), fled to the Argentine Embassy disguised as a delivery man, and also found his way at last into South American exile. After the Delgado incident, signs of unrest and revolt multiplied steadily. There was an unsuccessful military coup in April 1959, and abroad the Liberal exiles built up their funds, their plans, and the good-will of friends—especially in Venezuela and Brazil. The opposition's most spectacular gesture—devoid of practical effect, but providing sensational publicity for anti-Salazarian propaganda—was the piratical seizure of the Portuguese luxury liner *Santa Maria* with her six hundred passengers in a Venezuelan port by a handful of conspirators (largely non-Portuguese) led by Galvão.

This was in January 1961, and it began a bad year for Salazar. In February rebellion broke out in Angola, and increased in horror as the year progressed. At home there was another military revolt in April, small in scale and abortive. Internal resistance mounted steadily. In November, six persons seized a Portuguese air-liner in flight and scattered revolutionary leaflets over Lisbon. Abroad, successive colonial disasters culminated in December with the loss of Goa; and on New Year's Day, 1962, there was yet another unsuccessful coup, an attempt by an Army captain to win over the garrison at Beja, in the poverty-stricken Alentejo.

None of these insurrectionary attempts have been much more than pin-pricks. Salazar is still in command, with the armed forces, it seems, securely loyal. Yet his position, superficially regarded, seems to be more shaky than it has ever been during his long tenure of power. Together with South Africa, his country is treated by the majority of the United Nations as a pariah. The American support which was sustained throughout the Eisenhower-Dulles era flagged notably when Kennedy set out to build in the mind of the Africans and Asians the image of a progressive and liberal U.S.A. British diplomatic support, hitherto 'correct' if unenthusiastic, declined. Inside Portugal itself, there is powerful feeling demanding an amnesty for political prisoners and the dissolution of the secret police. Among intellectuals, and in particular liberal intellectuals, there is a deep longing for freedom of expression and the attainment of such judicial rights as freer Western lands enjoy. The spread of Communism under such a dictatorship is difficult to gauge; but among young students, peasants in the Alentejo, fishermen in the north, and industrial and port workers it is in moderate strength. Moreover, Salazar seems recently to have lost support from certain elements within the Catholic Church.

Looking round the international scene, recognizing the tidal force of the movement against colonialism, contemplating the poverty, corruption, and tyranny inside Portugal, and the dwindling company of the dictator's friends at home and abroad, only a very sympathetic optimist would visualize a calm sea and a prosperous voyage for Salazar's old age. Yet a balanced view, a view in perspective, of Portugal and its leader should not perhaps over-stress these threats, dangers, and defects. Catholic Portugal is not a Western democracy, and never has been. Salazar did not invent poverty, tyranny, or corruption in his country. Indeed, there may well be less of these evils in some respects now than under the nominally 'democratic' Government of forty years ago. There is certainly less disorder and bloodshed. Few Portuguese with long memories would wish to return to the situation that the Salazar regime put an end to. As for poverty, it is serious, and by the standards of an affluent society, intolerable; but most Portuguese have been inured to it for a long time; and it does not appear that a man's contentedness varies in ratio to his wealth. Neither is the ingrained and stable poverty of a peasant people the stuff of which revolutions are normally made.

So Salazar remains, and may well die in his harness. He is seventy-three. Who and what will succeed him? It is the problem that faces all ageing dictatorships. The *Estado Novo* was built around the dominating abilities of a single man, Salazar. When a hereditary monarch dies, one may cry, *"Le roi est mort, vive le roi!"* When a parliamentary Government is defeated, democratic regimes ensure a built-in continuity. Franco has attempted his own monarchical solution of a similar problem in Spain. But when Salazar dies, upon what basis can his regime continue? Has his rule constructed anything that will prevent Portugal from returning to the anarchy that he ended? Or will the Salazar era be considered merely as a lengthy lull in a long story of turbulence?

Table of Events

1386.	First Anglo-Portuguese alliance.
1394–1460.	Henry the Navigator.
1418–86.	Discovery of West Coast of Africa.
1498.	Vasco da Gama reaches India.
1500.	Cabral discovers Brazil.
1808–14.	Peninsular War.
1822.	Independence of Brazil.
1889.	Birth of Salazar.
1908.	Assassination of Charles I and Crown Prince.
1910.	Republic established.
1910–26.	Era of revolutions.
1926.	Army seizes power.
1928.	Salazar Finance Minister.
1932.	Salazar Prime Minister.
1932.	New constitution: the *Estado Novo*.
1936.	Portuguese Legion in Spain.
1939.	Treaty with Franco.
1939–45.	Neutrality in Second World War.
1943.	Allied bases in Azores.
1949.	Portugal joins NATO.
1949, 51.	Opposition candidates forced to withdraw.
1951.	Colonial Act.
1955.	Portugal enters United Nations.
1958.	Delgado stands for President, goes into exile.
1959.	Second Development Plan.
1961.	Angola rebellion.
	Goa occupied by Indian troops.

15

Nikita Khrushchev
(1894-   )

(Chapter 9, on Stalin, provides an essential background for
a reading of this chapter.)

Khrushchev, Nikita Sergeivich, was born April 17, 1894, in a mine-
worker's family in the village of Kalinovka, in the Kursk Province. As
a child he worked as a herdsman and then as a metal-worker in the
factories and mines of the Donbass (Donetz Basin).

There is little to add to the official *Soviet Encyclopedia* account
of Khrushchev's early days. Khrushchev himself says he was
a shepherd at seven, a cowherd later, and finally a miner.
"My parents were muzhiks, poorest of the poor. . . . We went
hungry to bed most nights." "Before I was fifteen I herded cows for
a capitalist." He appears to have been a gregarious, boisterous lad,
ill-educated but intelligent. Although a Ukrainian born, he spoke
Ukrainian only imperfectly. Leaving home at about fifteen, he found
a variety of work in the engineering and mining centre of the
Donetz, in the Southern Ukraine, becoming to some extent involved
in the secret working-class activity of those pre-war years. This
inevitably entailed a degree of conspiracy, yet there seems no sub-
stantiation of accounts of his suffering in the revolutionary cause.
By 1914, as a turner in a locomotive works, he appears to have been
exempt from military conscription. Then came the Russian defeat
and the revolutions, followed by a period of incessant and complicated turmoil—of revolutions, civil wars, foreign intervention; of
general breakdown in industry and transport; of peasants burning
the big houses, workers looting the food depots; hangings, lynchings, atrocities of all kinds; a blighted land peopled by victims—
victims of the wars, of typhus and malaria, of inflation and unemployment, of starvation. These disasters carried off, among about
five million others, Khrushchev's first wife, of whom the records are
silent. The second Mrs Khrushchev, however, in 1959 informed
Western Press correspondents that her predecessor died "in the
famine"; there were two children of this first marriage.

Khrushchev's homeland of the Ukraine became the centre and prey of a variety of armies—Russian, Ukrainian, Polish; of anarchists and bandits; of Whites and Reds; and it is reasonable to suppose that the bitter memory of those years is never far below the rough bonhomie of Khrushchev the modern Soviet leader. Challenged in 1960 by an American television interviewer to say what he thought of Eisenhower's suggestion that there should be a general world plebiscite for or against Communism, Khrushchev retorted, "After the October Revolution, the United States, Britain, Germany, and Japan imposed a civil war on us. That was a national plebiscite. We took a broom and threw them out." It may be thought a poor answer—indeed, no answer at all; but it was a predictable counter-attack, typically indicative of powerful and long-hoarded resentment.

Nikita Khrushchev was luckier or tougher than his wife: in 1918 he joined a regiment of Red Guards, with whom he served for two years. Emerging into a Ukraine in the tightest grip of horrors, he remained a Party member—indeed, became a cell secretary—at the period of the greatest Communist unpopularity, when the Red Terror began to spread out beyond its original class victims to claim its enemies in the midst of the common people. Those who opposed the Bolshevik Government ceased, in fact, to be 'people.' They became instead 'counter-revolutionaries'—and as such earned the death that the secret police forces brought them.

More than ever, at this period of Communist unpopularity, faithful proletarians were needed to be trained in Party action and indoctrinated in Party truth—above all to become future managers of industry and officials of the Party that was to direct and permeate that industry. So Nikita Khrushchev, metal-worker, sometime Red Guard, and Party cell-secretary, got his chance of secondary education in the Yuzovka Adult Workers' Faculty. Here the principal subjects were mathematics, physics, chemistry, Russian, German, and, most important of all, Marxism. It is probable that the basis of Khrushchev's knowledge of the world's history and culture was laid down here. In this oven the clay of his mind was baked; it had already been strawed with harsh years of experience, and the finished brick was tough, serviceable, Marxist unalterably, and little pervious to the influence of other systems or other creeds. The muzhik-turned-metal-worker had received the infallible dogmas of Marx and Lenin and become a believer to whom other doctrines, such as Christianity or liberalism, were strange—or wicked—*bourgeois* gibberish. The mind of the uneducated Khrushchev, an academic desert, had been fertilized and colonized for ever. Political expediency and the necessity to avoid nuclear extinction might well make him later *appear* as one willing to compromise with the capitalist world, a 'soft' Communist and an apparent enemy of the 'dogmatists'; but all reports of his conversations with Western statesmen and journalists show Khrushchev's mind to be firmly set in its original cast. Those who travel abroad tend to see what their education and prejudices predispose them to see; and when, many years later, Khrushchev at last moved out of his Russian world and travelled to Britain, America, and elsewhere, he saw what his education had taught him to see—Governments in the hands of *bourgeois* 'cliques'; these in their turn in the grip of other cliques of capitalist business-men and financiers; trade unionists who were "lackeys of the ruling class"; sham-democratic *bourgeois* elections where one's only choice was between a Gaitskell and a Macmillan, a Rockefeller and a Harriman (both millionaires), a Kennedy and a Nixon. His cocksure confidence in challenging this Western world that he sees so clearly through his Marxist spectacles comes from the supreme dogma of his well-learned creed: the inevitability of socialism; the scientific law that *assures* the death of capitalism; the immutable order of the Marxist-Leninist universe. All this he learned at the Yuzovka Adult Workers' Faculty, and is never likely to unlearn.

He must have worked hard and impressed his teachers, for within little over a year he was appointed Party Secretary of the Institute, with access to the personal record-cards of both students and staff, and the duty of reporting upon their Party reliability. Khrushchev thus arrived within the charmed but dangerous circles of the Party 'apparatus'—only a small man yet, but wielding some power and dispensing some influence at the periphery of the great system at whose centre in the Kremlin there already sat Stalin. The very town where Khrushchev attended his workers' faculty, Yuzovka, was in this year of 1924 renamed Stalino, and it fell suitably to the lot of the new local *apparatchik*, N. S. Khrushchev, to make the first of his innumerable speeches of tribute to the great man. It was at Yuzovka-Stalino in this same year, 1924, that Khrushchev, officially still studying to be a mining engineer, met and married his second wife, Nina Petrovna, a teacher of Marxist theory. In 1925, at the age of thirty-one, having completed his educational course, Khrushchev was appointed to a full-time Party secretaryship in the Stalino district, and he worked there for two more years, controlling factory organization, production, propaganda, and worker-relations, and helping (under his superior, Kaganovich) to make the Ukraine safe for Stalin.

First in Stalino, then in Kiev, next in Moscow, and finally back in the Ukraine, Khrushchev was able to learn, and somewhat to assist in, the regime's techniques of power. Stalin practised and polished these by ruthless control and exploitation of the Party apparatus; by unscrupulous blackening of the character and policies of his opponents; by a continuous process of purging the supporters, or supposed supporters, of those opponents; by temporary alliances with the 'Rightists' to defeat the 'Leftists,' in order to be stronger in due course to turn upon the 'Rightists' too; by an unprecedented use of totalitarian propaganda and a cynical perversion of the meaning of words, so that they became weapons to be turned against the enemy, a sinister code that the faithful understood, the sheepish imitated, and the victims learned to fear. By such devices and by consummate manipulation, in five years from Lenin's death in 1924 Stalin emerged dictator of the U.S.S.R., and in the next decade destroyed all his rivals and potential rivals. The supreme crime was 'deviation,' whether that of Trotsky and the 'Leftists' who wanted policies aiming at immediate world revolution, or of Bukharin and the 'Rightists,' who wanted especially a slower and more humane approach to peasant collectivization.

Khrushchev, as a Party functionary of moderate importance, was during these years inevitably involved in furthering Stalin's policies and destroying his enemies. He faithfully and virulently echoed the current Stalinist catch-phrases and on appropriate public occasions fulsomely sang the praises of Stalin's leadership—and this during a decade when probably not fewer than eight million Soviet citizens were arrested and three million executed. (The figures must necessarily be approximations.) The least charitable interpretation of his actions over this period is that he was scrupulously and cynically ambitious to the exclusion of all other considerations. The most charitable interpretation is that he honestly believed in the necessity for deifying Stalin and extirpating his enemies. But since to see Khrushchev all black is as unprofitable as to see him all white, somewhere between we can perhaps glimpse him, among the murky shadows of that time, caught in a web of intrigue, lies, and sycophancy from which there was no escape but death, and infected, like most Russians of position under Stalin, with the moral insanity that proceeded outward from the Kremlin over the whole Communist world. Moreover, this was a world (it should be remembered) that accepted the Marxist thesis that ends justify means, and that lies and calumnies in a good cause acquire merit.

Both in the Ukraine and Moscow Khrushchev was personally instrumental in carrying through purges of the Party membership (*i.e.*, of 'Leftists' and 'Rightists') as well as "taking steps against rural saboteurs"—Stalinese for liquidating those who failed to collaborate in rural collectivization. In the Moscow region in particular 70 per cent. of the Party membership were purged between 1932 and 1934—that is, *before the main terror began*; and Khrushchev, as Second Secretary of the Moscow City Party Committee at that time, had, with Kaganovich, a principal part in these operations. In his own words of 1934, "We have carried out in our Moscow organization a purge which has still more strengthened the fighting capacity of our ranks." These were now "ideologically united around the Central Committee, and around our genius leader, Comrade Stalin." Khrushchev even demanded, after the already defeated Trotskyites had attempted to propitiate Stalin by handing him a "declaration of submission," that it should not be accepted at its face value, but that the strongest punishment should be meted out to the "incorrigible members of the opposition, regardless of their former merit or position." And a year or two later Khrushchev was publicly demanding that "the organs of the dictatorship of the proletariat" (Stalinese for the secret police) should be made stronger than they already were. In his secret speech of February 1956 denouncing Stalin's tyranny, Khrushchev specifically accused him of originating the concept of "enemy of the people"— a term "which made possible the most cruel repression." Khrushchev, however, made frequent use of this very term himself from 1934 onward, demanding ceaseless "vigilance" against all "wreckers," "Trotskyite degenerates," "traitors to the socialist motherland," "Fascist scum," "spies," and "diversionists"—using the whole catalogue of abuse-categories for those marked down in the Stalin gutter-language for destruction. At least one man so attacked by Khrushchev in 1937, one Gamarnik, who "committed suicide," was posthumously rehabilitated as an honest Communist after the death of Stalin.

These were years of terror, but they were also the years of the first Five Year Plans, and Khrushchev, that indefatigable driver, was in his element organizing and accelerating the construction work on factory sites, and especially on the Moscow underground railway that was one of his principal concerns. It is evident from the reports that both Kaganovich and Khrushchev drove the tunnelling engineers and the shock brigades ruthlessly onward, with the result that the project was completed within six months of its unrealistic time schedule. It is probable that the victory was not achieved without several bad accidents from flooding and subsidence. But this, after all, was in the Russian tradition. This was how Peter the Great built St Petersburg. This was in the military spirit of the Five Year Plan. 'Shock Brigades' expect casualties. The official account of the building of the Moscow Underground—a great prestige achievement for the regime—says, "Comrade N. S. Khrushchev visited the construction sites every day, gave instructions, criticized, checked, encouraged, advised on urgent questions." He drove himself and others with fierce energy; he improvised continually, and took chances (sometimes, it is probable, unreasonable ones); he was tough, and not easily put out. He knew how to lead men, but he knew also how to follow and applaud his own leader, and to walk warily the perilous tight-ropes of Party prudence.

As the tyranny of the 'apparatus' grew ever stronger during the 'thirties, and the tyranny of Stalin himself over the 'apparatus' grew ever more nightmarish, it needed strong nerves and prudent walking to remain on the tight-rope at all. There was no turning back for one who had proceeded as far as Khrushchev; he had either to proceed or to plunge into the chasm with the others. There was no honourable retirement for nervous or dizzy performers. Khrushchev, however, was not nervous or dizzy. He was something of a virtuoso, with a good head for heights. In an era when so many important people were being executed, promotion became ever more rapid for the survivors—and it is calculated that only about 30 per cent. of the middling or upper Party officials did survive the years 1935–38. Lesser men were often sent to prison camps; the bigger fry were executed. Every time a colleague or rival was denounced and dispatched, the stakes were raised. Few rose as quickly as Khrushchev. Here is the list of his chief preferments during the decade after his transfer from Kiev to Moscow in 1929 to study at the J. V. Stalin Academy:

1931, First Party Secretary in two successive Moscow districts;
1932, Second Secretary of the Moscow City Party Committee;
1934, First Secretary of the same, and member of the Party Central Committee;
1937, member of the Supreme Soviet and Foreign Affairs Commission;
1938, a candidate-member of the Politbureau (the supreme Soviet policy-making body, to-day known as the Presidium);
1939, full member of the same.

He was, of course, one of the leaders of the great Stalin orchestra. He played, and played loudly, all the Stalin tunes. It was he who wrote a sickening and hysterical article in *Pravda* in June 1936, during the trials of Kamenev, Zinoviev, and others.

> Miserable dwarfs! They lifted their hands against the greatest of all men, our friend, our wise leader, Comrade Stalin. . . . Damned Fascist degenerates! We promise . . . that Moscow Bolsheviks will sharpen their vigilance still further. They will extirpate what remains of the Trotskyites. . . . They will close ranks . . . around the Central Committee and the Great Stalin!

and a great deal more in the same feverish key. Seven months later it was Khrushchev who "was received with stormy applause" at a mass meeting in Red Square arranged to demonstrate popular approval of the death sentences against Radek and other old Bolsheviks. These veteran revolutionaries were vilified by Khrushchev with all the death-dealing clichés of the current Stalinese: "contemptible nonentities . . . Trotskyite scum . . . lackeys of Fascism . . . traitors . . . murderers . . . *enemies of the people.*" "Stalin," declaimed Khrushchev, "is our hope, he is the beacon which guides all progressive humanity. Stalin is our banner! Stalin is our will! Stalin is our victory!" The whole speech (*Pravda*, January 30, 1937) makes illuminating reading by the side of the same man's denunciations of the dead Stalin in 1956.

Some, morally bolder than Khrushchev, did speak up against Stalin's purges, not in 1956 but *in 1937*. One such was Postyshev, a member of the Politbureau, and Second Party Secretary in the Ukraine, who put his head right into the dragon's mouth by openly expressing anxiety about the purges and doubt about the genuineness of the accused's confession of guilt. He was, of course, in Stalin's good time and Stalin's own manner, first discredited for 'inefficiency' and then shot, together with his First Secretary, Kossior. So the Ukraine needed a new boss, and the Politbureau had another vacancy—and the faithful and efficient Khrushchev was chosen by Stalin for both posts. Thus, at the age of forty-three, Khrushchev returned to his Ukrainian homeland as supreme Party ruler over one-fifth (by population) of the U.S.S.R.

In the preceding score of years, that land—by nature one of the richest in the U.S.S.R.—had experienced tragic suffering. Attempting secession from Russia in 1917, it had been conquered by the Red Army, occupied in 1918 by the Germans, bloodily fought over in a desperate civil war, and reoccupied by the Red Army and Communist police. A grim famine followed. With a non-Russian language and ancient hankerings after nationhood, it was under Lenin first Russified and then partially de-Russified when opposition grew extreme. Under Stalin it felt the full brutality of the forced collectivization—in effect, another war—and saw those of its cultural leaders who showed any deviation from the Stalin line either executed or forced into suicide. Again in 1933 it was faced with a bitter famine. It was in the front line of the Five Year plans, and felt the full rigour of their driving discipline.

All this was prior to 1938, when Khrushchev was sent back there as Stalinist proconsul. Under the Tsars, under Lenin, and now under Stalin, the Ukraine, one might think, had plumbed the depths of misfortune. Another and even more terrible chapter was, however, about to begin. The ruthlessness of Stalin and his Communists was to be matched and even outdone by that of Hitler and the Nazis. The Second World War was to rage and burn over its once fertile fields, and to the old horrors, now repeated, of devastation and guerrilla war was to be added the new savagery of slave labour and mass deportation. This latter part of the Ukrainian story is told later in this chapter. By 1938, the situation was that Khrushchev had arrived in Kiev, charged with the tasks of skimming off any remaining Trotskyite or Bukharinist "scum," suppressing any hopeful relics of Ukrainian nationalism, and Stalinizing the entire area. The Russification drive was inexorably renewed. The "bourgeois-nationalist riff-raff," the "enemies," the "Fascist-Polish-German gangs" were to be extirpated. They were accused in general of trying to detach the Ukraine from the Soviet Union, and in particular of suppressing the Russian language in favour of the Ukrainian. Khrushchev's new broom swept away these "vile spies, monsters and trash of humanity," purged the education departments, 'reformed' the education syllabus, and generally drove home the lesson that the Ukraine was "an inseparable component of the U.S.S.R." In other matters, too, he soon made his bustling presence felt, fulfilling and even exceeding production targets in agriculture and industry.

Soon his administrative and propagandist energies were to be still further extended. In August 1939 there came the Nazi-Soviet Pact, and in September its sequel—the double attack on Poland by Germany and Russia. Now, therefore, large areas of south-eastern Poland were added to Khrushchev's Ukraine, and these areas too were ripe for Stalinization. He was equal to everything. With the Red Army went the Khrushchev propaganda machine, and *Pravda* was kept up to date from Khrushchev's headquarters: "The streets resound with tumultuous joy. . . . Men and women embrace Red Army men with tears in their eyes. Words fail . . ." *et cetera.* Mobile film units, posters by the ton, travelling exhibitions, dance festivals, a barrage from radio and press—Khrushchev and his missionaries had neglected nothing. For a brief space, eastern Poland had been accepted into the Stalin paradise, and Soviet-style elections duly produced their ninety-odd per cent. victories. Defeated remnants of the Polish Army retreating eastward from the Germans into Khrushchev's new territories received dire treatment. In the forest of Katyn there was a great mass murder of Polish officers, which (like the Reichstag fire of 1933) the Communists ascribed to the Nazis, and *vice versa.* The probabilities point to Russian guilt; but the extent of Khrushchev's personal responsibility is unknown. At least he, as the local Communist boss, was in a broad sense responsible for what happened in his area, by this time termed the Western Ukraine. It was not only the Polish officers who suffered and died. Many hundreds of thousands of the *bourgeoisie*, the intelligentsia, political and labour leaders, teachers, Jews, and a host of others considered unreliable or hostile to the new regime were deported in freight trains and truck convoys to the labour camps of the far North and East. Some have put the numbers of the victims of this 'liberation' as high as two million.

As it turned out, the Stalinization of Poland was premature. Hitler attacked the U.S.S.R. in June 1941, and in a week or two, not only Soviet Poland and the Polish Ukraine but also great areas of the Ukrainian S.S.R. itself were drowned beneath the Nazi flood.

Khrushchev's activities during the Second World War are known only in very general terms. In collaboration with the military command, he was responsible for the co-ordination and supervision of guerrilla activities behind the German front, although it does not seem that he himself ever penetrated behind the front. What is certain is that Khrushchev, like all the wretched inhabitants of the Ukraine, and indeed all Russia, "supped full of horrors" during the German war. After the frying-pan of Stalin's forced collectivization, the Ukraine had landed in the fire of Hitler's war and the Nazi conquest. The number of Ukrainian deaths is unknown, but in all Russia deaths amounted to possibly twenty millions, and the Ukraine suffered as usual more than its share. When the Red Army returned to Kiev and Kharkov in 1944 it found only one-fifth of their populations surviving; and the surrounding countryside fared little better. It is true that the rôle of Khrushchev's guerrillas was to keep alive the war, and hence, inevitably, its bitterness—but any hope that the Germans might have had of playing upon a Ukrainian national spirit antagonistic to the U.S.S.R. disappeared in the folly of the Nazi brutalities. Khrushchev, though no soldier, saw this savage war at close quarters. It is not intelligent to consider him as a monster devoid of pity or of indignation, and what he saw during the years 1941–44 can hardly be expected to have prejudiced him in favour of the post-war rearming of a revived Germany. Neither is it necessary to interpret his ravings against Adenauer's Germany as all play-acting and propaganda, though so good a politician does not, of course, neglect these elements.

When the German armies were expelled from the Ukraine in 1944, Khrushchev returned to Kiev as effective ruler. All around was desolation and breakdown, hunger and epidemic disease. It was Khrushchev's task to get the crops sown again and harvested, the towns rebuilt, the water and electricity supplies operating, the people resettled. In this process, well-suited as it was to his abilities, he suffered in 1947 the severe shock of being publicly castigated for shortcomings in the wheat, sugar-beet, and tobacco harvests, and he was temporarily supplanted by Kaganovich in the seat of power. This might well have been the end of him in every sense, but he was lucky; the capricious dictator in the Kremlin had not marked him down. Soon the Khrushchev cork was bobbing on the surface again, and by the beginning of 1950, his twelve-year rule of the Ukraine ending, he was recalled to the centre of affairs in Moscow.

Now he was one of a small group in the immediate Stalin circle— the personal agents and potential heirs of Stalin, drawn by the promise of power, circling like moths round his dangerous but now flickering flame. For Stalin was sick and ageing; his old fears of assassination had reached insane proportions; and, still in possession of total arbitrary power, he was preparing yet another great new series of purges. All men were suspect, but his potential heirs most of all; so it is hardly surprising that they all feared him, or hated him, or both; yet none dared risk offending him. Chief among these men around Stalin were Malenkov, his chief personal assistant and probable successor; Molotov; Beria, head of the secret police; Bulganin, military director; Mikoyan and Kaganovich, economic directors; and Khrushchev, sharing with Malenkov the direction (under Stalin) of the Communist Party.

Suddenly, in January 1953, all these men, and incalculable numbers of others, stood in immediate danger of extinction, when Stalin announced the Doctors' Plot, the tallest of tall stories about an alleged conspiracy by nine Kremlin doctors, all Jews, to poison the high command of the armed forces. Simultaneously began a great new witch-hunt, with the full propaganda treatment against "monsters," spies, traitors, "enemies of the people," "cosmopolitan Jews"—the 1936 atmosphere all over again. It would have been hardly surprising if the men around Stalin had murdered him for the public good and their own safety, but there is no evidence that they did. Stalin officially "died after a grave illness," in March 1953: a mercy too long delayed, but a mercy all the same. With a minimum of ballyhoo, and some few tepid tributes, Stalin's heirs and agents buried him beside Lenin in the Red Square mausoleum, and hastened to form a "collective leadership" which would prevent any one of them taking over supreme power. The nine doctors were rehabilitated and set free: and Beria, Stalin's chief of secret police who had sent unnumbered multitudes to their death, suddenly exuded liberalism and legality. His colleagues in the leadership plainly thought that he was aiming at Stalin's vacant seat by putting himself at the head of a new 'soft' Party line, which would prove highly popular with the repressed peoples not only of the U.S.S.R. but of the satellite states of Eastern Europe. All over the Soviet world men were welcoming the 'thaw,' and daring at last to hope for more freedom and an easier life.

The most dangerous moment for any tyranny is when it begins to relax, and in June 1953 the pent-up resentment of the East German workers did in fact burst out in impatient rebellion in a dozen towns. To the frightened Soviet leadership it looked as if Stalin's death, while it might have saved them personally from becoming victims of his mania, had also uncorked the dangerous imp of liberty (which they called *bourgeois* counter-revolution). They ordered tanks to Berlin, Leipzig, and elsewhere, and smashed the rebellion; and then they turned on Beria. How he was killed is not reliably to be reported—quite possibly by the other members of the leadership themselves. When his death was officially announced *six months later*, it was not difficult to relate the foulest crimes to one so deeply implicated in the Stalin tyranny. With Beria dead, the leadership soldiered on, watching one another like the surviving contestants in a game of musical chairs, but contriving to convey a superficial impression of unity. Stalin had, however, bequeathed them immense problems, and it was not surprising that their unity—even the official pretence of it—did not survive for long.

The whole of Russia was in a ferment. She had lain so long and cruelly in the grip of Stalin that a degree of relaxation was politically inescapable. It was not a case of whether or not there was to be a 'thaw,' but rather of how far the thaw should be allowed to develop. Even under Stalin the first cracks in the ice had begun to show, with some desperate strikes in the labour camps. ('Show' is perhaps the wrong word, for not a word leaked out till the 'rehabilitated' camp survivors crept back two or three years later.) The tyrant's death allowed to be vocal what previously had had to be expressed in whispers: the feeling that there must be less regimentation of thought, less terror from the secret police, more consumer goods in the shops, more and better houses, more and better food, some escape from the siege atmosphere that had persisted for as long as even ageing men could remember—through the First War, the Revolution, the post-revolutionary wars, the famines, the Plans, the collectivization, the purges, the Second War, the epidemics, the shortages, the Cold War, the threat of yet more and greater purges. A new spirit was in the air from 1953. The Kremlin itself was now opened to the public—a symbolic move. Many political prisoners were released, and the powers and numbers of the political police were much reduced. A spate of poems and novels began openly to criticize and satirize Soviet civilization—even the Party itself; and when the flow was checked, it flooded over again a year or so later. Hundreds of thousands of educated Russians of the post-Revolution era had grown up into important posts in industry, agriculture, the armed forces, education, the arts and sciences; and not all of them were devoted Party members. They constituted what the West would call a middle class—words hateful to the proletarian ear, but signifying men and women with a respect for ease and comfort, with some educational training, with views of their own problems and the world's problems that were Communist indeed, but different from the views of Stalin and the severer Party dogmatists. Russia, in short, though it remained in part the slow-moving and primitive giant, was at the same time a modern technological society. Its engineers and officials, its scientists and technicians, were likely to have desires not totally alien from those of their opposite numbers in America, Germany, or Britain. Furthermore, if such a society in the mid-twentieth century bred (for example) teenage hooligans and the quest for status-symbols in the West, it appeared to do similar things to some degree too in the East. Differences were vast, but similarities were obstinate, and not to be brushed away by propaganda against '*bourgeois* values.'

There were those among Stalin's close circle who had for some time been advocating a more lenient policy, at home and abroad.

The two chief of them were Malenkov and Beria. It is probable that just after Stalin's death there was a real chance of a bargain between East and West, that might have permitted a Russian withdrawal from East Germany (considered by Malenkov and Beria a millstone round Russia's neck) in return for a similar Western withdrawal to the Rhine. On both sides, unfortunately, the sceptics prevailed, and no such relief came about. The 'Stalinists' (Molotov, Kaganovich, and very probably Khrushchev at this time) won over a majority of the Presidium to the conviction that if East Germany defected from the Soviet bloc, others might go with her, and counter-revolutionary disorder might spread all over Eastern Europe—conceivably even to Russia itself. Then came the suppression of the East German rising, and the defeat and killing of Beria. The moment for a bargain had passed; the Cold War and the arms race continued.

The struggle over foreign policy was in part an outcome of another struggle concerning policies in Russia—which may perhaps be described as whether to abide by Stalin's "jam the day after to-morrow" or move towards "jam to-morrow, and even a little jam to-day." For long years Russians had lived under conditions of extreme, even brutal, austerity. Housing standards had not risen much above the average of one room per family. Consumer-goods industries had been wholly subordinated to the heavy industries that produced the tools of war and the capital goods of peacetime reconstruction. Clothing, boots and shoes, and household utensils were dear and often of shoddy quality. Rationing was universal, but for a long time only the permitted free market (a kind of licensed black market) had rendered life tolerable for the ordinary Russian. By Western standards it was indeed *not* tolerable—except for the privileged classes, such as Army officers and Party officials, who enjoyed special rations in special shops, as well as much-higher-than-average incomes. Worst of all, Soviet farming was in a state of even more severe crisis than usual—and agricultural shortcomings have always been (and remain still) the heaviest of internal Russian problems. And agriculture was the department of Soviet policy most closely affecting Khrushchev. He had himself been almost extinguished (as we have seen) in 1947 by his agricultural failures in the Ukraine. In the last few years of the Stalin regime, however, he had become the principal Kremlin spokesman on farming policy, and was particularly the advocate of a major scheme for amalgamating collective farms into very big units and integrating the villages into large settlements ("agro-cities"). At the same time the farmers' private plots were to have been limited to about a third of an acre, since part of the trouble had been that Russian farmers had spent too great a proportion of their time and labour tilling them. Stalin's enemy, the stubborn peasant, was still fighting! The "agro-city" policy had been initiated in 1950, but met popular resistance and opposition, too, within the Presidium from Malenkov. In 1951 it was dropped. There remained many stresses and short-falls in Soviet farm production, but the principal deficiency lay in livestock production; and actually in 1953 the cattle population of the U.S.S.R. was two million lower than it had been in the last year of Tsarist rule, 1916, the human population having advanced since that time by about 36 million. In Khrushchev's anti-Stalin speech in 1956 this failure in meat and dairy production was one of many laid at the door of the dead dictator, but Khrushchev's own share in framing agricultural policy—although he plainly could not always get his own way—had been considerable.

Malenkov remained, after Beria's extinction, the leader of the group within the Presidium who felt most strongly that there must be new policies to lighten the almost intolerable load on the Soviet citizen's back. Even in 1940, he pointed out, two-fifths of Soviet production had been of consumer goods, but by 1953 the fraction had declined to three-tenths. Morale was low, criticism mounting; the time had arrived for a bigger cut of the cake. Khrushchev, however, in this matter as in foreign policy, threw his weight with Molotov and the rest upon the Stalinist side. In a barely disguised attack on Malenkov in *Pravda* at the end of 1954, he dismissed any idea of relaxation. In a hostile anti-Communist world, heavy industry (and of course farming) must have absolute priority; and two months later Malenkov modestly announced that he was retiring from the Premiership because of "inexperience." All smiles and urbanity, this able, plump, quick-thinking, ex-right-hand of Stalin was demoted to the Ministry of Electric Power Stations. Unlike the sinister Beria, Stalin's other hand, he stayed alive. He even kept a seat on the Presidium, and turned up in Britain the following year, still smiling, to reconnoitre the land for the forthcoming visit of his nominal successor as Premier, Bulganin, and his real successor as the most powerful man in Russia, Khrushchev. But politically, from the beginning of 1955, Malenkov and his policies were dead ducks: greater intellectual freedom, more consumer goods, public admission of the suicidal folly of war (suicide for Communism as well as Capitalism), a compromise settlement of the German question and an end to the Cold War—at least for a time, these were too much for the trainees of Stalin and devotees of Lenin to swallow.

Not relaxation, but imaginative hardship, was Khrushchev's line: a new agricultural scheme that was big enough to take one's breath away. In 1954–55, he planned, 31 million acres of virgin land in Siberia, the Urals, the Volga region, and Kazakhstan must be ploughed up: eventually, 90 million acres, an area over half the size of Western Europe. At the same time new goals were set for the tractor plants, whose output had remained surprisingly and miserably low. To do all this, there must be a grand campaign to elicit enthusiasm and self-sacrifice, and the Party orchestra began to play the tune to good effect. Young people could combine hard work, adventure, and patriotism in tapping riches latent since the beginning of things. Volunteers went, Army units went, some peasants themselves went from collective farms; the huts and tents sprang up in the bitter cold and burning heat of the hitherto untrodden steppe: pioneers, in a virgin setting, of the "agro-cities" that had foundered amid the scorn of Malenkov five years earlier.

Khrushchev's whole soul went into his attempts to expand and modernize Soviet farming. He spent his boundless energies upon them—and still does—for success here is vital to his dream of a great, prosperous, well-fed Russia marching in seven-league boots into the future, with the dwindling capitalist world left far behind. Wherever he goes throughout the length and breadth of his vast country, he, the ex-muzhik, the son of the soil and as earthy as his audience, is to be found expounding informally to groups of peasants the virtues of scientific farming, and exposing the follies of their out-of-date habits. For Russian farming is still by Western standards primitive; in parts the ideas of its peasants are medieval. To produce less than the United States it employs a labour force nearly seven times as numerous. Khrushchev is never more himself than when giving an impromptu talk to collective farmers on how to fatten pigs, why they should grow maize, the proper method of milking cows, how to get the best out of potato crops, why beet and beans are better than clover and leys—homilies, lectures, reproof, encouragement—all spiced with racy stories, salted with politics, gritty with sense. On a different level he is liable to explode into some high official's account of his agricultural stewardship with the most indecorous contradiction and correction, like a tetchy schoolmaster admonishing his ignorant or perhaps dishonest class—and all the pupils know that there is in the cupboard a cane that he can apply very hard. It has proved easier, however, to train technologists than farmers, easier to orbit the earth in a space-craft than to reach the grain target. Sputniks that do not answer back have proved simpler to guide than peasants who neglect the collective interest to concentrate on their private allotments. Despite all the effort and all the propaganda, farming remains the weakest part of the Soviet economy.

Malenkov's successor as Prime Minister was Marshal Bulganin, and between September 1954 and May 1956 Khrushchev and he— that is, the leader of the Party and the nominal leader of the Government—made a series of foreign tours: first to China; then to Yugoslavia, where Khrushchev tried rather lamely to lay the blame for Stalin's break with Tito upon "imperialist agents and spies" such as Beria. (Tito stopped the interpreter in mid-translation and left nobody in doubt about his feelings; but at least a first awkward move had been made towards healing old wounds.) Next at Geneva there was a meeting of heads of Governments, and much display of 'Geneva spirit,' but little achievement. At the end of the year the oddly assorted pair—the ebullient, vulgar Khrushchev and the professorial Bulganin—flew off to India to be fêted and garlanded as never before, but to overshoot the mark somewhat with some wild anti-British propaganda. On the whole, however, 1955 was a year of relative reasonableness and good temper; and in May 1956 the two globetrotters came to Britain itself, to be received by the Queen, to visit Oxford and elsewhere, to have a famous row with some members of the Labour Party who asked awkward questions, to face British pressmen and television cameras. The deferential Bulganin was hardly noticed; Khrushchev was plainly top man— expansive, incisive, effervescent, extrovert, hugely self-approving: a 'card.'

Beria had been liquidated and Malenkov demoted, and the first headlong enthusiasm of the Thaw had been checked by 1955. Writers were no longer free to say just what they pleased about the bad old days and the bad old styles; beneath the surface the ferment was still there; behind the cupboard door the skeleton still stood. Stalin was a name less frequently mentioned than of old, and the collective leaders were determinedly hostile to "the cult of personality"; nobody, however, had had the temerity frontally to attack the dead dictator's memory. Then came the Twentieth Party Congress in 1956 and the toppling of the giant. It came about in an obscure manner. Thirteen hundred Party delegates met in the Kremlin in February 1956, with several hundred foreign guest-delegates, and Khrushchev delivered the seven-hour opening speech, of routine dimensions and content. Stalin was barely mentioned. Then came Mikoyan, the shrewd Armenian, with a sharp attack on the idolization of Stalin and his disregard for democratic processes within the Party. The thing was sensational, novel, and popular. For thirty years Stalin had been a god, and any whisper against him had struck the blasphemer dead. The congress buzzed with excitement. But what followed was of stunning effect: Khrushchev delivered, in secret session, a *second* speech which amounted to a full-scale attack on the political terror and military incompetence of the man he had so long served and praised. The sequence of events at the meeting and an analysis of the language and content of this second Khrushchev speech appear to lend credibility to the theory that this was a sudden change of tactics on his part: if you cannot hold criticism in check, it is perhaps well to lead it. It is even possible that it was only 'his' speech in the sense that he uttered it. It gave voice to a long document, carefully prepared; and it is quite possible that Khrushchev took over the public delivery of a script that the Presidium had earlier considered and rejected. It will be a long time before the hidden history of these events is fully known. That Khrushchev stood self-condemned by many of his condemnations was a matter to be decently neglected; the impact of the speech—'secret,' but soon fully reported at thousands of Party meetings, and published verbatim throughout the non-Soviet world—was tremendous. The sorcerer's apprentice certainly had found the formula, and the flood-waters of the Thaw rose so rapidly that soon Khrushchev and all the Soviet leaders were in some panic to find the spell for undoing the magic. It was not so easy to find. Khrushchev worked hard later to make some reparation to Stalin's (and thus in some sense his own previous) reputation; and he found it prudent to wait five years before publishing *openly*, for all in the Soviet Union to read, the full tale of Stalin's wickedness. It was not till 1961 that his corpse was removed from its Red Square mausoleum, and the names of towns, streets, and institutions throughout the U.S.S.R. were de-Stalinized—but the step, once taken, of the Twentieth Congress speech of 1956 was irretraceable, for Russia and for Khrushchev himself. From that day he sided against the men like Molotov, Kaganovich, and Voroshilov—the "Stalinists." He had demonstrated to men within the U.S.S.R., and confirmed to all outside, that Party propaganda for a generation had been based on lies, and government based on injustice and terror. The whole of Communist history had henceforth to be rewritten. Facts became 'unfacts.' The past was remoulded. Encyclopedias, school textbooks, thousands of names and titles, whole ways of thought, had to be unmade or remade. Bad words became good words, enemies of the people became wronged victims, falsehood became truth. It was confusing, shocking, for some even unnerving.

Following the sensational speech came stirring and tragic events in the Soviet empire. First Tito, the prototype Communist rebel, was received in Moscow. Then Molotov was dismissed from the Foreign Ministership. In Poland the prospect of de-Stalinization raised nation-wide hope and enthusiasm, among both Communists and non-Communists. In Hungary the brutal tyranny of the Rakosi government looked suddenly to be vulnerable after all, despite the grip of his secret police. "Let us say it openly," wrote one fatally bold young author, typical of his hour, "what we have in mind is full, unrestricted freedom." (The whole trouble in Hungary, Khrushchev said later, arose from the dangerous liberty given to such novelists and poets: if they had only been executed in good time, the subsequent revolution would not have happened. In similar circumstances his own "hands would not tremble.") In Poland, Gomulka, the leading "Titoist"—that is, independent national Communist—was released from prison while the whole nation stirred with optimism. In June there were riots in the Polish city of Poznan. A little later, Khrushchev, Mikoyan, Molotov, and Kaganovich flew hurriedly to Warsaw in an attempt to check the rising flood of revolt, but were forced to accept Gomulka as the only alternative to full-scale Russian intervention. At least Gomulka was a Communist, and would not be a tool of the Western powers. He did manage, however, to maintain his own 'national' line; and this success of Gomulka's was to be emulated and fatally outdone by his southern neighbours, the Hungarians, who swept Imre Nagy (the Gomulka-Tito of Hungary) into power at the head of a broad-based popular coalition. Even that the Russians might have tolerated: Nagy too was a Communist. But the Hungarian revolutionaries went further, and were plainly about to detach Hungary from the Soviet system. Budapest went wild with joy; political prisoners were released from the jails; the giant statue of Stalin bit the dust; and the patriotic triumph appeared to be complete. All over the Western world there was elation, mingled with a fear that the news was too good to be finally true. It was. In Moscow the Presidium met several times and took its crucial decision: Red Army tanks rumbled into Budapest. Those patriots who could not escape were rounded up, and many of them herded off to detention in the U.S.S.R. An exclusively Communist regime was restored, Nagy kidnapped and later murdered, and his patriotic supporters (practically all Hungary) written off by the Soviet propaganda machine as a few *bourgeois* counter-revolutionaries exploited by capitalists, landlords, and Western imperialists. The position of Khrushchev, the debunker of Stalin, was clear: "when it comes to fighting imperialists we are *all* Stalinists."

Khrushchev had survived his worst moments, though many blamed him for unleashing the whirlwind by his original speech. In June 1957 he met a still tougher moment. A coalition of his ousted rivals—Molotov, Kaganovich, Malenkov, Bulganin, and others— came together in the Presidium to vote him out of his First Secretaryship of the Party. He has himself (over drinks later in Bucharest) told the story, Bulganin said, "Well, we are seven and you are four." "In mathematics," answered Khrushchev, "two and two are four indeed, but politics are different." He would not be deposed. Instead, he secured the alliance of Marshal Zhukov, brought in hundreds of his supporters from far and wide, and routed his enemies at a full session of the Central Committee. Triumphant now, this master of political judo turned on his late attackers, ejected them from the Presidium, labelled them the "anti-Party group" (a more potent expression than the "anti-Khrushchev coalition"), and dominated a new and enlarged Presidium. A little later he turned on his temporary ally, Zhukov, and dismissed him too. The era of collective leadership was over: Khrushchev, the undoubted successor of Stalin, had over-topped all his rivals. In March 1958 he became Premier as well as chief Party leader, Bulganin retiring with the customary rituals of self-accusation. Yet if Khrushchev was in the saddle, he was not a dictator in the Stalin sense. His defeated and demoted colleagues, the "anti-Party group," in particular Molotov, were still important enough to earn denunciation in press and radio right up to 1962. (Khrushchev himself said to Averell Harriman, "We must respect Molotov. . . . He has firm opinions and he sticks to them.")

Khrushchev was once a poor boy in a poor country. He had by industry, ambition, cunning, and ability become an immensely powerful man in a country that had grown immensely powerful too. As a Marxist he could not fail to detest and despise the civilization of the capitalist West, but as the once-poor peasant of once-backward Russia, he could hardly fail to see the riches of America to some degree in an envious light. America was corrupt, malevolent, and doomed to inevitable defeat, so his ideology assured him. Yet American industrial power, agricultural plenty, technological sophistication, and personal luxury were plain to see. The greatest of triumphs for the poor boy from Kalinovka would be to go as the representative of his own great country to sit in the gilded seats of the enemy and talk straight-sense-and-no-flattery to the capitalist millionaires. The supreme moment for the U.S.S.R. would be when it could confront the capitalists with the visible proofs that the socialist civilization had leaped ahead of the capitalist, that socialist power was mightier than capitalist. Khrushchev, the ill-educated ex-miner, the mannerless upstart, the mentally imprisoned Marxist, the Russian jingo, was, during the months that followed his attainment of full power, to taste—for himself and his country—some of these delightful sweets of achievement. As he characteristically put it after his American visit:

> We are being respected and hailed because we are strong. While I was standing on the airfield in Washington—and it is a tremendous honour for a man to represent a country like ours—and saying goodbye to America, the band played the Soviet Anthem, and then the guns fired 21 salutes. So I said to myself: "That first salute is for Karl Marx, and the second salute for Friedrich Engels, and the third salute for Vladimir Ilyich Lenin, and the fourth salute for His Majesty the Working Class, and so on—salutes for our country, for its various peoples. Not bad, comrades, really not bad at all!"

It was the sputniks in 1957 that first symbolized for Khrushchev and Russia this pride of achievement, this sense of having out-matched the West, despite its initial advantages of wealth, scientific tradition, and technological efficiency. Russian scientists were first to launch an earth-orbiting missile, first to send a missile round the moon, and first to send a man in a space-craft round the earth—and Khrushchev's transparent delight in these achievements arose only partly from their reassuring military implications. In all his public appearances and utterances amid these triumphant events there was manifest a certain childish glee. His gestures betrayed the naïve satisfaction of the under-dog who has become a top dog at last, the office-boy-turned-tycoon, the self-made man at the head of the self-made nation circling the globe and outstripping its rivals.

With the demonstrations of the sputniks behind him, and a series of rocket-rattling speeches to rub home the lessons of Soviet power, Khrushchev faced the West in a posture of defiant strength. If his actions were to prove as hostile as his words, the world faced extinction, for each side could now annihilate the other. Khrushchev's foreign policy, however, though it proved tough and at times seemed capricious, at least appeared to accept that the ultimate disaster of mutual annihilation must be avoided. As a good Lenin-ist yet firm realist, he faced a difficult contradiction. As a Leninist he believed that the capitalist-imperialist world intended to make war on the U.S.S.R., and that war was therefore inevitable. Yet as a man of sense he knew that nuclear war was mutual suicide, and therefore unthinkable. How does a Leninist resolve such a contradiction? Perhaps by honestly declaring (as he did on one blasphemous occasion to the Chinese) that Lenin needed bringing up to date. More normally and less shockingly, by denying the existence of any contradiction at all, by "interpreting" Lenin differently (with the aid of further well-chosen texts), and asserting that "true" Leninism means Khrushchev's policy of coexistence. In a very similar manner Christians have seldom found difficulty in discovering a wide range of Biblical texts to support any policy they hold it necessary to pursue.

Khrushchev, fortified by Russian technological and industrial triumphs, proceeded to lay down the new orthodoxy: peaceful, competitive coexistence. Communism was so strong, so successful, that in a generation it would have defeated capitalism without a war. By 1970 the U.S.S.R. would "catch up and outstrip the United States' industrial output. . . ." Capitalism was "incapable of freeing itself from the death grip of its own contradictions." Or—to put the same doctrine more tersely—"*We will bury you.*"

Burial of the capitalist U.S.A. was a long-term aim; a more immediate object in 1959 was to visit it. During that year 'Summitry' was much in the air. First Macmillan flew to Moscow, and was roughly handled by Khrushchev, who bluntly declared in a public speech (with Macmillan present) that the Western proposals under discussion were designed to waste time, and that what was necessary was a Summit meeting to prepare for a German peace treaty. After a good deal more skirmishing, Khrushchev flew to America in September 1959, conferred amicably with Eisenhower at Camp David, and secured his agreement that "the specific Berlin question should be re-opened." Politics apart, he ranged over the American scene with the *élan* and tact of a young rhinoceros: preaching peace and coexistence; proposing *complete* disarmament in an address to the United Nations; touring far and wide; admiring the modernity and productivity of the farms of Idaho; sitting through a Hollywood 'can-can' show as pained as a Presbyterian at Mass; slapping Uncle Sam on the back and telling him that he was pretty good but had a lot to learn; getting in return a mainly polite, but not enthusiastic, welcome.

The way had been prepared for the Summit, in Paris, in May 1960, in which Khrushchev's chief aims would be to obtain a 'free city' of West Berlin and to end its occupation by the Western Powers. Expressed in terms of Western fears, this meant squeezing the Allies out of Berlin and jettisoning the liberty of two and a half million Berliners, in exchange for a dubious internationalization of the city. Behind the Summit lay the threat: if the Western Powers refused to sign a peace treaty with Communist East Germany (which none of them wished to recognize), the U.S.S.R. would herself sign one with her without them, and leave Berlin, and the Allies in it, islanded in the middle of a sovereign Communist Germany.

A fortnight before the Paris Summit meeting, an American U2 reconnaissance plane was shot down over Soviet territory and its pilot captured as a spy. A high level of indignation was maintained by the Russians, especially after Eisenhower's Government admitted the flight, and its purpose of espionage, and Eisenhower personally failed to accept Khrushchev's 'invitation' to dissociate himself from it. Khrushchev nevertheless travelled to Paris, as did the other Summit leaders. Once there, he refused to proceed unless Eisenhower admitted American guilt and punished the guilty—and he withdrew the invitation already issued for Eisenhower to visit Russia. Proposing a long postponement of the conference, he then gave an angry Press conference at the street corner and left for a sight-seeing tour in the country! The President of the United States had been humiliated and the Summit torpedoed. It may be a long time before anybody knows precisely why Khrushchev acted as he did. It may be that, under pressure from Stalinists, both Russian and Chinese, he fairly suddenly decided against the settlement he had long favoured. It may be that he calculated that the West was not in a compromising mood, and that, if the conference was to be broken up, this was the best way to do it—with the maximum of propaganda advantage to Russia and an enjoyable public insult to the insolent U.S.A. and its President. If he was acting, then he is a good actor: his pudgy fists pounding the air, his stubby forefinger hammering out his indignation and anger, seemed rather to betoken a genuine emotion, however complicated its motivation.

Russian foreign policy after May 1960 oscillated between ultimatum and concession. Khrushchev still appeared to hanker after another Summit meeting and an accommodation with the West over Berlin, and several times he announced a deadline for such an accommodation, failing which he would sign a treaty with the East Germans and hand over full powers to them. Each time, however, when the Western Powers refused to negotiate under an ultimatum, he withdrew his insistence on a date. He did briefly meet President Kennedy in Vienna in June 1961, but a few hours' conversation merely revealed the width of the chasm between the two men's worlds. Very probably Khrushchev wished (like Malenkov) to go down in history as the Russian who lightened the load of armament and apprehension upon the backs of his people; but at not too severe a risk. Nuclear bomb tests—even atmospheric tests on a gigantic scale—must be continued, to keep the technical lead over the Americans. Any projected system of internationally supervising a suspension of warlike atomic activity collided heavily with his siege mentality, the deep-bred Leninist conviction that all Westerners, being capitalists, were potential counter-revolutionaries and spies. So, for all the genuine desire to lighten the load, the two sides— each fearing that to give an inch might mean to give a mile— continued to pile up ever more massive, deadly, and unusable weapons. All over the shifting and crumbling world, each side manoeuvred and intrigued to secure its ideological foothold. Wherever there was a Fidel Castro to be hugged—a gift from Heaven on the enemy's doorstep—Khrushchev would be there hugging with calculated zest. Wherever there was a platform from which to denounce imperialism Khrushchev would be on that platform thumping home his advantages. Wherever there was some Left-wing movement to exploit, some landlords' government to undermine, some thin edge of a Communist wedge to drive further home, in the countries of the Middle East, or of South-East Asia, or of South America, Khrushchev and the international Communist movement would be diligent and untiring. Wherever the dark-skinned man was struggling under the shadow of the white, or only recently emerged therefrom, and especially all over the African continent, Khrushchev's U.S.S.R. would be competing for his allegiance, with 'scholarships' tenable in Moscow, technical aid, financial aid, and all available devices of propaganda. Sometimes, it is true, Khrushchev would overplay his hand, as at the 1960 United Nations Assembly, where he attended personally, played a little too patently upon Afro-Asian prejudices, and clowned too truculently and crudely for the general taste, with much playing to the gallery and banging of desks—even with his boots removed for the purpose. During 1961, indeed, it appeared that Khrushchev's policies were deliberately aimed at destroying a United Nations that he could not control. Again, his vicious personal attacks on its Secretary, Hammarskjöld, were much resented, by Afro-Asians as well as Westerners. Certainly Khrushchev never failed to hold the initiative. Sometimes he heated the international pot to boiling-point, sometimes he clearly aimed to cool it down. His immediate motives were not always plain, but his objectives were constant enough. Enemy positions must be probed and weaknesses exploited. Every device *except general war* must be employed to hasten the natural processes of degeneration and collapse within the capitalist world and to promote the advance of universal socialism. This is what Khrushchev means by peaceful, competitive coexistence.

He played to the limit upon fears resulting from Western Europe's extreme vulnerability to nuclear war and her peoples' understand-able reluctance to 'die for Berlin.' He utilized every stratagem that would divide Britain, France, Italy, and West Germany from one another, or collectively from the United States. These West European states Khrushchev amiably described as his "hostages": two or three dozen of his best bombs could obliterate all four of them: and this appalling fact he sought to make use of, at worst in order to paralyse the policies of their 'protector' the U.S.A., and at best to persuade them into neutralism.

Khrushchev to Western eyes might appear jingoistic and un-scrupulous, a tough player of the rough game of power politics. To the Chinese Communists, however, he seemed to be the arch-'deviationist,' dangerously ready to compromise with the West, and in so doing to depart from Leninism and the true faith; and from 1959 onward a steadily more bitter doctrinal battle was fought out between the two Communist giants. Solidarity and mutual trust were repeatedly proclaimed, and the neutral observer might some-times suppose that the whole argument was being conducted in a code intelligible only to the protagonists; but behind the façade of sober words, the quoting and quoting-back of texts from Lenin, tempers were obviously high and vital issues in dispute. Chief among these was Khrushchev's heresy that peace with the capitalist world was possible. In Peking in 1959 he said, "We must do everything possible to preclude war as a means of settling outstanding questions, which must be settled by negotiations." The Chinese replied (for example, in *People's Daily* in April 1960), "Socialist countries should not be afraid of war, since a third world war would not annihilate mankind." Capitalist systems would *not* crumble from their own contradictions; they must be overthrown by prole-tarian revolutions. Acrimony increased through 1961, with China openly challenging Russia's interpretations of the gospel, and publicly supporting Khrushchev's principal Stalinist opponent in satellite Europe, Hoxha, the dictator of Albania. Chinese-supported

Hoxha was almost as embarrassing for Khrushchev as Russian-supported Castro was for the White House; and by 1962 an open Russo-Chinese breach looked increasingly probable. It was plain that among the things that China's rulers feared was exactly what moderate men the world over sighed for: a relaxation of tension between the United States (in Chinese eyes the concentration of all evil) and the U.S.S.R. That would be "deviation" indeed! And if the relaxation led to a measure of disarmament and an end of the Cold War, Khrushchev would go down in Chinese history, as Stalin went down in Trotsky's, as "the betrayer of the Revolution." These Chinese fears were reinforced by the outcome of the Cuban crisis of late 1962, when the nuclear rocket bases which Khrushchev had set up, with Castro's blessing, in Cuba provoked an ultimatum from President Kennedy demanding their removal. Khrushchev judged it better to retreat before the Americans and lose a diplomatic battle than to run a real risk of nuclear war. The world has some reason to be thankful that, beneath the rumbustious aggressiveness of Khrushchev's manner, there lies a rich vein of realism and a strong intention to survive.

Table of Events

1894.	Khrushchev born at Kalinovka.
1917.	The Russian Revolution.
1918–21.	Civil wars, Wars of Intervention, famines.
1922–25.	Khrushchev at Yuzovka Adult Workers' Faculty.
1924–29.	Stalin builds up his dictatorship.
1925–29.	Khrushchev a Party functionary in the Ukraine.
1931–38.	Khrushchev moves up the Party ladder in Moscow.
1936–38.	The great purges.
1938.	Khrushchev in Politbureau, returns to rule the Ukraine.
1939–41.	He 'Stalinizes' the Polish Ukraine.
1941–44.	In charge of guerrilla activities against Nazis.
1944–48.	Soviet satellite empire established.
1947.	Khrushchev's agricultural shortcomings publicized.
1950.	"Agro-cities" experiment.
1953.	"Doctors' Plot," death of Stalin, beginnings of 'thaw.' East German revolt, death of Beria.
1954.	Virgin lands scheme.
1955.	Fall of Malenkov.
1956.	Twentieth Party Congress: Khrushchev attacks Stalin. Risings in Poland and Hungary.
1957.	Khrushchev defeats "anti-Party" group. First sputniks.
1959 onward:	Growing rift with China.
1960.	Abortive Paris Summit meeting. Khrushchev at United Nations.
1961.	Russian astronauts orbit the earth.

16

Charles de Gaulle
(1890-   )

J'étais la France." So said de Gaulle to a news conference in 1954.
He said it simply, and without arrogance, as one stating a fact
not open to argument; and in fact none of the journalists present
challenged the proud, and by then half-wistful, statement. This
man had escaped in a small aeroplane from his defeated and totter-
ing country in 1940, carrying with him, as Churchill wrote, the
honour of France. Never has anyone in recent times been so utterly
certain that in his own person he embodied his country's reputation,
her past glories, her precarious present, her hopeful future. "When
General de Gaulle wants to consult a map of France he looks in a
mirror." Some exasperated admirers nicknamed him, in jest, the
Symbol.

"*J'étais la France.*" There were times when it seemed to be so.
Certainly when in August 1944 he came back to a Paris that was
weeping tears of joy and triumph, certainly then, as his towering,
informal figure strolled majestically among the throng, this man
was France. That was a moment of unanimous emotion, and it has
entered French legend, as the little ships of Dunkirk and the Spitfire
pilots of 1940 have entered the British legend. But, except at such
rare moments of a union of hearts, de Gaulle's identification of himself with his country ignores some basic realities. For there are
many Frances, and de Gaulle has represented only some of them—
Catholic, traditionalist France, the France that was "the elder
sister of the Church"; patriotic, revolutionary France, the France
of the barricades and the *Marseillaise*, the never-say-die France of
Valmy and Verdun, of Gambetta and Clemenceau; the suffering,
tragic France of Joan of Arc and the Unknown Warrior; the
triumphant France of Austerlitz and the Liberation of 1944.

Yet it is rash to generalize about the soul of a nation—most of
all a nation so individualist and diverse, so critical and divided, as
France. There were, and there are, many other Frances than these
—not many of them breathing the same spiritual atmosphere as the
General. Even now, in 1963, when he has become politically indis-

pensable, most Frenchmen would probably dissent from his basic attitudes. His almost mystical patriotism is certainly not characteristic of the modern Frenchman, especially the modern French townsman, who is predominantly Left-wing in politics and anti-Catholic in religion. The paradox of de Gaulle is that this military man of the Right, who was restored to power by a Right-wing *coup d'état*, has emerged as the best hope for democracy that France possesses, and its principal shield against a military dictatorship. Hence, even though only a minority of Frenchmen will take the General at his own valuation, a majority of them are likely to give him their support.

De Gaulle's account of his parents is in the key of his own later life. Both father and mother were descended from 'good' Catholic families, and his father had abandoned an Army career to become a teacher of philosophy, mathematics, and literature in a Jesuit college in Paris:

> a thoughtful, cultivated, traditional man, imbued with the feeling of the dignity of France. He made me aware of her history. My mother had an uncompromising passion for her country, equal to her religious piety.... As a young native of Lille living in Paris, nothing struck me more than the symbols of our glories: night falling over Notre-Dame, the majesty of the evening at Versailles, the Arc de Triomphe in the sun, conquered colours shuddering in the vault of the Invalides.

It is page one of his Memoirs: all the ingredients of de Gaulle and de Gaulle's France seem here to be laid out. Life proceeded to mix them. He was a thoughtful, intelligent, rather precocious boy, already (so he writes) "saddened" by the misfortunes of France at that time —the surrender to the British at Fashoda, the Dreyfus case, social and religious conflicts. He left school to enter the military college of Saint-Cyr; and Pétain, soon to be the hero of Verdun, was his first colonel. Young de Gaulle made few friends, worked hard, and passed out in 1912 among the first ten of the seven hundred cadets. The Army was "one of the greatest things in the world," and before long both it and Lieutenant de Gaulle were to be sternly tested. The war came, and twice in the first eight months he was wounded; then in 1916 near Verdun he was again wounded in the course of bloody hand-to-hand fighting, and captured unconscious; for his part in rallying his men he was mentioned in dispatches by Pétain, and made a Chevalier of the Legion of Honour. After four attempts to escape (in which his great height, six feet four, proved a handicap) he spent the rest of the war in the grim fortress of Ingolstadt; even from here he attempted one more escape. "If I had not remembered my Greek poetry," he said later, "I think I should have died."

A sick de Gaulle eventually returned to a sick France—a nation victorious indeed, but exhausted. De Gaulle puts it with his own characteristic emphasis: the nation was "exhausted from losses and devastation, with her social structure and moral balance overthrown . . . while the regime rejected greatness and returned to confusion." France had won the war, but at such terrible cost (1,358,000 dead, over 4,000,000 wounded, and her north-eastern provinces ravaged) that she remained dominated by her fears and her memories of horror until the Second War was upon her.

This state of mind closely affected the French theory of military defence. At great cost, a system of defensive fortifications was constructed—the Maginot Line—which was considered to be all but impregnable. French soil must be safeguarded and French lives spared; the terrible toll of 1914–18, especially in offensive warfare, must never be exacted again. This defensive theory of the war of the future de Gaulle thought to be futile and defeatist: it handed the whole initiative to the enemy. France, he argued, must have a hundred-thousand-strong army of manoeuvre and attack, mechanized, armoured, composed of picked regulars and supported by its own aircraft, to range deep behind the enemy's lines and to disorganize his supply system and rear areas. His book of 1934 putting forward these theories sold barely a hundred copies in France; but a German translation did much better! Hitler had it read to him, and listened carefully to the very similar ideas of Guderian, von Seeckt, and Nehring: that same year (November 1934) the first three German armoured divisions were created. By the next year their accompanying dive-bombers were being built. The weapons that sliced through France in 1940 were being created while the French political and military chiefs clung to the theory of static defence and pooh-poohed de Gaulle and his solitary important champion, Paul Reynaud.

It is not surprising that by this time de Gaulle had a poor view of politicians, though it might well be thought that his principal complaint should have been against his military chiefs. It can hardly be claimed that during this period of the 'twenties and 'thirties the politicians showed up well. There was a swift succession of weak Governments until the arrival of Léon Blum's Popular Front Government in 1936; de Gaulle himself, as Secretary-General of National Defence, served *fourteen* administrations between 1932 and 1937. The many small and splintered parties argued furiously and bargained cynically, their leaders, as de Gaulle said, often talented men, but consumed and paralysed by the game of politics. There was a continuing tradition of corruption in high places, which came to the surface with the scandals and riots of 1934. French foreign policy hovered between pressing home upon Germany the lessons of her defeat, as Poincaré attempted when France invaded the Ruhr in 1923, and conciliating her, as Briand attempted at Locarno in 1925. The governmental weakness coincided with a declining birth-rate; a corrupt Press; a population robbed of its best young men by the First World War and ready to accept cynical, defeatist, or extreme counsels; financial crises, and a great industrial depression after 1930 to raise political tempers higher and encourage the growth of both Communist and Fascist groups; a reaction to the rise of Hitler that combined fear, horror, and contempt—or alternatively, with some, even envy: the pro-Nazi, anti-Semitic, anti-British paper *Gringoire* reached a circulation of 700,000. All this made of France by the nineteen-thirties a nation into whose framework the worm had eaten.

On the side of the politicians, it should be remembered that the moderates' room for manoeuvre was small. On each side they were menaced by powerful groups who regarded the Third Republic with contempt: on the one side the Communists, dedicated to revolution and dancing to Stalin's tune, and on the other, the royalist *Action Française* and a wide variety of 'patriotic' leagues aping Mussolini's Fascists and aiming at a Right-wing dictatorship. The professional Army, de Gaulle among them, harboured little but contempt for the professional politicians; and many of these officers—but emphatically not de Gaulle—went further and more or less openly expressed the view: Rather Fascism than the Popular Front, *rather Hitler than Blum*. The democratic 'centre' was narrow, and subject to almost intolerable pressures. As for the ordinary Frenchmen and Frenchwomen, many of these were dominated by a profound pacifism; most of them shrugged their shoulders at the politicians; almost all grasped readily at the promise of protection offered by the Maginot Line—often forgetting that in any case it was not extended along the Belgian frontier. Perhaps they gave Hitler and Mussolini reason for thinking them 'soft'; they certainly wanted to be left alone to live in peace. The French Governments of those days were fleeting, insubstantial shadows; other shadows, more powerful ghosts, really governed France—the great host of the dead of 1914–18 mustered below the long, straight lines of wooden crosses.

One of the great French heroes of the First World War had been Pétain; Pétain of Verdun, where so many of those crosses had been earned; Pétain, whose *Ils ne passeront pas* was the proudest of French wartime boasts. Ironically, de Gaulle was a Pétain protégé. He served under him on the Verdun sector. He named his son Philippe after him; he had held several Staff posts under him during the 'twenties; and it was Pétain and Weygand who sponsored de Gaulle as Secretary-General for Defence in 1932. Pétain, however, had little use for de Gaulle's ideas on armour. What would be the use of a great mass of enemy tanks arriving in the region of Paris? he asked in 1934; lorry-borne troops and a few armoured cars would be quite enough to deal with them. And four years later, in 1938, he wrote, "The Maginot Line has given Europe a new stability. As for tanks . . . their failure is startling." A small concession, however, was made to de Gaulle's ideas: in December 1938, two armoured divisions were belatedly decided upon (later increased to four); they were to have 120 tanks each instead of his recommended 500, two artillery groups instead of his seven, one lorry-borne infantry battalion instead of his seven caterpillar-tracked battalions; and these divisions were not to be independently operating units. Even so, it was one of these relatively weak armoured divisions, under de Gaulle himself (recently promoted to Major-General), that launched almost the only successful counter-attack against the Germans, at Abbeville, in May 1940, when the Panzers and dive-bombers were tearing their way through Northern France to the Channel, isolating the British and Belgians around Dunkirk and preparing to sweep round Paris to the south and east, before taking the humiliated and useless Maginot Line in the rear.

By this time Paul Reynaud was French Premier—the only prominent politician who had consistently supported de Gaulle—and in the midst of the defeat and confusion Reynaud appointed de Gaulle Under-Secretary at the Ministry of Defence. Through the arguments and intrigues of the desperate June of 1940 de Gaulle strove repeatedly to stiffen Reynaud's will to resist to the end. However, to save the city, Paris was surrendered without a fight, against de Gaulle's advice. Bordeaux was briefly and hectically the capital of the dissolving official resistance, though de Gaulle had advocated making instead a defensive "redoubt" of Brittany. De Gaulle flew to London to see Churchill: a fighter, he decided, who would not flinch—"equal to the rudest task, provided it had also grandeur." Then Churchill flew to Tours (just before the retreat to Bordeaux) to plead with Reynaud, as de Gaulle also pleaded, to continue the fight, if necessary from Algiers and from the high seas still domin-ated by the Anglo-French navies. For the second time in a week, de Gaulle went to London, and received from Eden the first news of the dramatic, imaginative, but desperate offer that Churchill was about to make, of the total union, military and economic, of Britain and France. By the time de Gaulle was back in Bordeaux that same evening, a battered and exhausted Reynaud had resigned. There was to be no flight to Algiers (as he had promised de Gaulle there would be). The new Premier was the aged and by now defeatist Marshal Pétain, who described Churchill's proposed union of France with Britain as "fusion with a corpse." The new Minister of Defence was General Weygand. These were men, and they were surrounded by men, who were profoundly distrustful of the British, and had no will to continue the struggle. In de Gaulle's words, Pétain, "too proud for intrigue, too forceful for mediocrity, too ambitious to be a time-server, nourishing in his solitude a passion for domination," now, suddenly in the extreme winter of his life, had his chance so long awaited—but at a price: "that he should accept disaster as his elevation's scutcheon and should adorn it with his glory."

The Battle of France, that had lasted only a month, was over; in a few days came capitulation. Before that happened, however, de Gaulle took the historic step that was to take him at last, after many trials and misfortunes, to the leadership of his country. Bordeaux already seemed enemy territory to him, and he himself was now a suspect character; so he compounded a plot with General Spears, the chief British liaison officer in France, to escape with him from Bordeaux airport. Appearing to be officially bidding fare-well to Spears, he shook hands with him, waited for the gangway to be pulled away, and at the very last minute leaped for the door, leaving police and officials gaping. He had already given his wife the word to make her own subterfuges and to get away to England with their children. Mercifully, her car was delayed; if it had not been, she would have left Brest on the afternoon boat, which was torpedoed and sunk, with great loss of life. The night boat that she took safely arrived, as did Spears' and de Gaulle's plane. De Gaulle was interviewed by Churchill at the very moment that Pétain was asking for an armistice, the most humiliating armistice in French history—that cut France in two, surrendering the North and West (including Paris and all the coast) to the Germans, and permitting a Pétain-led 'independent' Government for the South-east to survive at Vichy. After such a surrender—and Pétain seemed to embrace it like a religious experience—Churchill had no need to hesitate. He

accepted de Gaulle as the leader of the Free French, and agreed that
he should broadcast from London an appeal to all Frenchmen to
continue the fight. This de Gaulle did on June 18 and 19, 1940; "I,
General de Gaulle, assume the right to speak in the name of France."
He spoke as one who had taken up the mandate of Heaven; by
Divine Right, under the Providence that guards the affairs of France,
he, Charles de Gaulle, as 'legitimate' as any Bourbon, now spoke
for his suffering and betrayed country. France, he proclaimed, had
lost a battle, but had not lost the war. "For France is not alone.
She is not alone. . . ." She had Britain still with her (Pétain's
"corpse," Weygand's "chicken" whose neck was due to be wrung
in three weeks). She had access to the U.S.A. She had her navy.
She had her vast empire. The flame of French resistance must never,
would never, be extinguished. It was brave talk, and as things
turned out it had great potential significance; but few in France
or elsewhere thought in June 1940 that there was much truth in it.
There was not much "flame" left in France—only a few smoking
embers. Most leading Frenchmen were Pétainist—churchmen, civil
servants, Army officers, intellectuals, as well as humbler folk. After
a few weeks the number of Frenchmen who had rallied to the Free
French (with their symbol, the double-barred Cross of Lorraine)
was a mere seven thousand; and recruitment was further hindered
by the wave of anti-British feeling that followed the Royal Navy's
attack on the French fleet at Oran (Mers-el-Kebir) to prevent it
falling into German hands.

Neither was de Gaulle's cause assisted by his first major enterprise, the attempt to take control of Dakar, in French Senegal—a
sad Franco-British muddle and a blow to de Gaulle's prestige,
however little his own responsibility for the failure. Although he
did succeed in establishing himself in French Equatorial Africa
(chief centre Brazzaville), the French Empire in general, bolstered
as it was by tough Vichy-French representatives, by no means
rushed to his support. The British Government, too, had strong
reservations about him. They noted especially the intrigues within
his organization; in particular, that his naval chief, Admiral
Muselier, behaved more like a rival than a subordinate, accusing
him of being an "apprentice-dictator." Churchill certainly distrusted
the security precautions of the Free French, and thought it more
prudent secretly to attack the French colony of Madagascar with
British forces—a bombshell for de Gaulle. Then, after allied Free
French and British troops had invaded Syria—where the Germans
had been using the airfields, and 30,000 Vichy French troops put

up very tough resistance—de Gaulle was hit, and badly hurt, by a second bombshell: the Vichy representatives in Syria concluded an armistice with *British* authorities, de Gaulle being ignored. He had hoped to enlist Syria and the Lebanon freely into the war; he had promised them independence as a prize; but now he felt that his sovereignty and his prestige had been cut from under him. He, de Gaulle—which was to say France—had been treated like a subaltern. He protested proudly and sourly to the British his *intransigent* attachment to the rights of France. *Intransigence* was in those days the great de Gaulle word. "Our greatness and our strength consists only in our intransigence. . . . We shall have need of that intransigence right to the banks of the Rhine." A few months later he could prove that famous intransigence of his to another power, the U.S.A., whose Government had a much poorer view of him than Churchill's. Churchill did admire de Gaulle, though he found him prickly. He did admire his greatness of heart, and his intensity of vision, even while he was complaining that the heaviest of the crosses he had to bear was the Cross of Lorraine. Roosevelt, however (and even more his Secretary of State, Cordell Hull), thought de Gaulle a puffed-up and sulky nonentity; Hull positively hated him, and strongly opposed the next move that the Free French mooted: the seizure of Saint-Pierre and Miquelon, the French West Indian islands. Churchill supported de Gaulle; the islands were seized by Admiral Muselier's Free French forces, despite the U.S.A.; and de Gaulle in the subsequent referendum received an overwhelming vote in his favour—98 per cent. De Gaulle had the immediate laugh here, but the hostility of Roosevelt's Government was confirmed, and much trouble was later to stem from this circumstance.

By the end of 1941 Germany's troubles were beginning, and in France the mood of accepting defeat—the Pétain phase—was passing. Not only had the Germans failed to invade Britain, but they had begun to run into trouble in Russia—and the Free French became increasingly a factor in the struggle as the Nazi war remained unwon. The broadcasts from London and the B.B.C.'s *Les Français Parlent aux Français* won an immense audience. After Hitler attacked Russia, the French Communists—and there were several millions of them—suddenly discovered the war to be a righteous war after all. The factory worker, the little shopkeeper, the farmer, the winegrower, all those Frenchmen who would have voted for ending the war in 1940, now began to consider the possibility of the impossible. And who but de Gaulle had promised this incredible victory all along? By the end of 1941 he could provide a legend that was no longer laughable, and a hope that was, if still faint, at least not ridiculous. The "Resistance" inside France was not yet strong. Apart from a few daring groups who ran clandestine news-sheets, the most that 'resistance' had amounted to in most places during the early days was, perhaps, for a shop assistant to sell a German soldier a poor article, or for a traveller in the Métro to direct him to a station miles out of his way. At least such actions argued a mental refusal to collaborate. But, as hopes of German defeat began to dawn, real resistance groups of every kind began to proliferate all over France, both Occupied and Unoccupied. Some respected de Gaulle's leadership; many did not, thinking him (how mistakenly!) a tool of the British, or even an "apprentice-dictator" himself. In the forests and mountains of the South a guerrilla army grew up known as the *Maquis*: and when the Compulsory Labour Force was introduced, many tens of thousands preferred to desert to the Maquis rather than slave for the enemy. The Communists had their own underground, and the Socialists theirs. There was an important Left-wing Catholic group which early on declared for de Gaulle. There was a small group led by a priest who specialized in the rescue of Jewish children. All these and a host of others, large and small, represented many shades and even conflicts of opinion, and took a great deal of uniting, even approximately, into one force; yet often the resisters transcended both party and class loyalties: the Communist signalman planned his sabotage with the Catholic booking-clerk; the village labourer went off to the Maquis with the young medical student or the bank cashier; the anti-Catholic journalist and the *curé* plotted the prisoners' escape-route together. There was a comradeship of shared danger, of shared disgust, and increasingly of shared hope. As the war progressed, the Resistance lived more and more under the shadow of torture and death; constantly they had to fear betrayal by enemy agents who honeycombed their movement—French agents mainly, acting from conviction or greed. Neither was there a shortage of such Frenchmen, or of recruits for the French S.S. (the *Milice*). The German Gestapo was itself matched by the French. Altogether about 30,000 men and women of the Resistance were shot, and of the 112,000 deported to German concentration camps, only 35,000 returned to tell their story—many of them physically or mentally crippled.

Most of this Resistance story, however, belongs to the second half of the war. Before that phase, de Gaulle had first to suffer the greatest of his indignities at the hands of the Anglo-Americans, and then to score his first major triumph—full Anglo-American recognition. In November 1942 (at the time of the battle of Stalingrad, and just after the British victory at Alamein), Anglo-American forces under Eisenhower landed at Casablanca, Algiers, and Oran—but the Free French forces were not invited to take part, and de Gaulle himself was patently snubbed. At first it appeared to him that the most loyal policy was to swallow his pride, and he urged French North Africans to welcome this invasion. However, Pétain ordered resistance. Despite this, the Americans were able to do a deal with his representative in North Africa, Admiral Darlan—who went over to them, but before long was assassinated. The Americans then proceeded to back an escaped general, Giraud, as ready-made leader—a 'safe' man, without de Gaulle's awkward illusions of grandeur, and one likely to appeal to the Algerian 'establishment' and all those now anxious to prove their patriotism by jumping on the Allied bandwagon. De Gaulle's contempt and anger exploded. "Mr President," he wrote to Roosevelt, "you may buy treachery from traitors, but you will never pay for it with the honour of France." A difficult man indeed. As for Churchill, he attempted to justify matters to de Gaulle: the Americans were having the major share of the fighting, therefore their decision must stand; nevertheless ("showing signs of emotion," as de Gaulle writes) Churchill assured him, "We shall not abandon you." But then de Gaulle did not forget that over earlier matters of disagreement Churchill had once growled to him, "My conscience is a good girl. I can always come to terms with her." De Gaulle could admire Churchill and appreciate his difficulties, but never really trust him; for Churchill was always, in de Gaulle's view, the chief representative of a rival power, France's ancient adversary who was always aiming to steal her territory, always intriguing against her rights. Indeed at this time Churchill, for his part, so resented de Gaulle's suspicious and arrogant behaviour that he was very willing to agree with Roosevelt that Giraud should be given his chance. Gradually during 1943, however, Roosevelt, Eisenhower, and their advisers came to realize what Churchill already knew—that de Gaulle might be resented, but not ignored. His hands, unlike Darlan's, were clean of collaboration with the Germans; he alone had been present at the birth of the Resistance; all over North Africa his name counted; Giraud's did not. The crowds in Algiers and Oran shouted *Vive de Gaulle* when Giraud appeared; the Cross of Lorraine materialized wherever there were walls to paint on; the Algiers crowds on May Day 1943 marched to the rhythm of *We want de Gaulle*. Inside France, thanks to the unifying work of Jean Moulin (before the Gestapo captured and killed him), the secret National Council of the Resistance was formed, and immediately demanded the presidency of de Gaulle. After a brief period of power shared between the two generals, Giraud accepted the popular judgment, and retired. "Do you know," Eden remarked to de Gaulle, "you have caused us more trouble than all our other European allies put together?" "I don't doubt it," replied de Gaulle. "France is a great power."

Even now, however, Roosevelt would not really consider France as one of the great powers, or de Gaulle as likely to last as a peacetime leader of his country. The four nations that were to lead the world after the defeat of Germany and Japan were, in Roosevelt's view, the U.S.A., the U.S.S.R., China, and Britain. Furthermore, de Gaulle, like Churchill (Roosevelt considered), had out-of-date notions of the imperial greatness of his country, and by this time Roosevelt was envisaging America as the champion of the North African Arabs in their forthcoming liberation from France. The Sultan of Morocco, for instance, had already been promised American support for his independence. Even when Allied forces landed in Normandy in June 1944 and began the reconquest of France, de Gaulle had to struggle hard to be treated as head of a major power returning legitimately to his rightful jurisdiction. The Americans long delayed full recognition. "For the moment," said Roosevelt to de Gaulle, "you are there. But will you be there at the end of the act?"

At least de Gaulle did manage to persuade the Americans to allow Frenchmen to dominate the big moment of the next scene of the drama, the liberation of Paris. Ever since "D" Day Frenchmen had played a considerable part in freeing their country: the Resistance went into action everywhere and succeeded in capturing control of twenty-eight *départements* in the first two months; hundreds of miles of railway track were torn up, thousands of locomotives and trucks damaged or derailed; General Leclerc's Free French Armoured Division fought its way eastward from Normandy under Eisenhower's command; and then in August the Parisians of the poorer quarters rose against the hated Germans. They put up barricades of overturned cars and old furniture— pathetic as barricades, but at least symbolic of the spirit of revolutionary Paris; they brought out the secretly stored old rifles and pistols ("*A chacun son boche*"), and at last were able to bring into use the home-made anti-tank grenades. In this irregular warfare perhaps 1500 Frenchmen were killed. Fortunately the German commander, a civilized man, disobeyed Hitler's orders and did not destroy Paris as he retreated, and on August 25 one of the great days in modern history arrived. Leclerc's Division led the advance into Paris, and de Gaulle followed, to taste the sweetest of all his triumphs. Visiting his old office at the Ministry of War, he found everything as he had left it in 1940, with even the same names on the call buttons. "Nothing was missing," he wrote, "except the State. It was my duty to restore it." He publicly rejected Bidault's request that he should proclaim the Republic from the Hotel de Ville: "The Republic has never ceased to exist," he said. "I myself am President of the Government of the Republic. Why then should I proclaim it?" The next day, as the firing died away, the streets burst into joyful celebration; the crowds danced in them and wept for joy. At 3 p.m. de Gaulle rekindled the Eternal Flame at the Arc de Triomphe, and walked at the head of an informal procession of his chief aides and supporters down the Champs Elysées, through the Place de la Concorde towards the great cathedral of Notre-Dame; past "the children—so pale but dancing and screaming for joy; the women—bearing so many sorrows but now smiling and cheering; the men—flooded with a long forgotten pride, shouting their gratitude; the old—doing me the honour of their tears." As his towering figure moved majestically but almost casually along the delirious streets, on several occasions shots rang out (nobody ever established from whom). Unmoved, as the crowds rushed for cover, he crossed the square before Notre-Dame and proceeded into the cathedral to hear Mass. Even during the service, shots continued to be fired from the galleries. De Gaulle serenely ignored them, full of his "sacred emotions."

A chacun son boche was all very well; but it was a Communist slogan, and the fifty thousand Parisians of the Resistance who rose against the Germans were largely Communist too. Hence the first thing de Gaulle had to do was to make sure that there was no Resistance-fighters' coup against his regime. Two days after the Liberation march he ordered the disbanding of all the Paris groups and transferred the seat of his Government from Algeria to Paris. There was no attempted coup; instead the anti-climax of a meatless, fuel-less, taxi-less, black-marketeer sort of peace that brought the city back to a grey normality after its few days of high drama. De Gaulle was no economist; and at this time he failed to support the one man in his Government whose proposed monetary reforms might have checked inflation—Mendès-France. The chance was missed; Mendès-France resigned; the franc slid downward again and the black marketeer soared upward. It proved easier and more enjoyable to try traitors than to risk the harsh surgery of financial reform.

Many Frenchmen in the winter of 1944–45 had little enough bread; but they had a regular supply of 'circuses' in the trials of those who had collaborated with the enemy. Some of these had been summarily humiliated or executed immediately following the Liberation: women who had consorted with the Germans were paraded with shaved heads, and some of the more notorious French propagandists for the Nazis were shot by Resistance men. Perhaps there were, in all, as many as 10,000 summary executions. Next came the official trials of offenders of middling importance, and finally the trials of the principals, Pétain and Laval. The senile Marshal's death sentence was commuted to life imprisonment, but the trial of Laval, Pétain's principal Minister, before a jury that shouted him down and insulted him, was a disgraceful affair. After he had attempted suicide, he was revived in order to be hastily and sordidly dispatched. Altogether forty thousand collaborators were sentenced by 1946.

De Gaulle and his supporters promised the *renovation* of France; the Communists, very strong after their great part in the Resistance, wanted something much more revolutionary. Yet after the Liberation, under the lead of Thorez, they at first accepted de Gaulle as the President of the Government and worked with the other parties under him; and during this period (1944–45) some notable reforms were achieved: the nationalization of the Bank of France, of the "Big Four" deposit banks, of the larger insurance houses, of gas and electricity undertakings, of coal-mining, and of those large concerns whose managements had collaborated with the Germans—notably the great Renault works. Women were given the vote for the first time in France. To supplant the old French Empire a new "French Union" was initiated, though it was destined not to weather the anti-colonial hurricane of the next decade. All of this was a great deal, but not enough for the Communists, who saw Big Business, the Church, and the Army still entrenched in their old strong positions. Emerging from the 1945 election as the biggest single party, the Communists played their hand high, and demanded the three key Ministries of War, Foreign Affairs, and Home Affairs. De Gaulle had no hesitation in refusing to hand over such a concentration of power; but even so, Communists at one time headed five (mainly economic) Ministries, which many Frenchmen thought dangerous enough. For the Cold War was already launched, and the Communists under Thorez were increasingly seen as the 'foreign' party—not as the tricoloured patriots of 1941–45. So long as Russia had been the great war-time ally and co-victor over Hitler, Frenchmen could forget (for instance) that Thorez had spent the duration of the war in Moscow. At the end of 1944 de Gaulle himself had gone to Moscow and signed a Franco-Soviet Pact. Even in 1945, while de Gaulle was attempting to hold a balance between East and West and visualizing France as a "middle power" between the two, Communism in France was still almost respectable. (It has in any case always been *more* respectable in France than in either Britain or the U.S.A.) De Gaulle was far too hurt by the Americans' excluding him from the Yalta and Potsdam conferences, far too angry with the British for forcing the withdrawal of French troops from Syria as they did in 1945, to consider taking any Western side against the Russians. Throughout 1945 he pursued his rôle of the inveterate odd man out. In fact it was not till 1947, a year or so after de Gaulle's first retirement, that France became finally exasperated and rebuffed by the persistent hostility of Stalin and Molotov, and reluctantly joined the Western camp in the Cold War. Already, however, by the end of 1945 de Gaulle and the Communists had repeatedly quarrelled. In fact all the old party squabbling and intrigue seemed to be beginning all over again— transformed a good deal by the War, the Resistance, the Inflation, and the Black Market—but basically continuing the old French party dog-fight. And both the political atmosphere and the scent of corruption were as thick as ever. Out of a working population of nineteen million, something like four million were living, wholly or in part, on a wide variety of unproductive rackets. The France of *les trafiquants* had arrived—the racketeers. It is said that, in the Paris night clubs, among every six people present, there were five black marketeers and one foreigner. As for the social justice that Liberation was to bring, the gap between rich and poor was wider than ever (it was one reason for the continuing high Communist vote—about five millions); there was even, the following year, in the tradition of the Third Republic, a "wine scandal" involving racketeering among the Prime Minister's staff. Altogether it was a cheerless and disgruntled atmosphere that had followed so swiftly on the elation of August 1944. France was disillusioned, and so was de Gaulle. Suddenly, without notice, in January 1946, he announced to his Cabinet his "final and irrevocable" decision to resign. Getting up from his chair, he walked out without another word or a sideways glance. Thorez spoke: "There is a departure that does not lack greatness."

That year of 1946 the new Constitution came into force, and with it the Fourth Republic. Designed to prevent the dictatorship of just such a man as de Gaulle, it ended by repeating all the old weaknesses of the Third Republic, and under its operation France was governed by twelve Ministries in five years, twenty in a decade. Not until the premiership of Guy Mollet in 1956 did any Government last a full year, and it became almost habitual for Bidault, the French Foreign Minister in many of these Cabinets, to have to go home in the middle of an international conference because his Government had just fallen. (Once he returned three days later as Premier *and* Foreign Minister.) Several times an international crisis (the beginning of the Indo-China War and the Korea affair are two examples) caught the French with no Government at all. It was not really enough for the apologists to explain that over eight years France had only two Foreign Ministers, Bidault and Schuman: in one decade of the Fourth Republic, France was *without a Government at all* for a cumulative total of 241 days.

When de Gaulle went into retirement in 1946, France was facing her worst years—so bad that some, not altogether in irony, wrote letters to the papers sighing for the days of the German occupation! Prices were rising two or three times as fast as wages; strikes promoted by the Communist-dominated trade unions were widespread, serious, and at times violent; the bread ration had to be cut to miserable proportions; and in the midst of everything came the showdown between the Communists and their late allies in the party coalition. Even a third world war did not seem improbable as Europe froze into two bitterly opposed blocs.

In this crisis atmosphere de Gaulle launched his Rally of the French People (RPF). This was an attempt to unite patriotic Frenchmen across existing parties, to "re-establish the unanimity of France." Its programme, like most of the General's phrases, was of a calculated and grandiose vagueness, but there were, at least, the strongest of suggestions that the Communists should be outlawed, the powers of trade unions limited, and a new Constitution worked out which would give France a strong President and freedom from the eternal party crises. As bad luck would have it, there was no general election due for four years, but in the municipal elections of that year (1947), the Gaullist Rally scored sensational successes, polling over 38 per cent. of the total vote—8 per cent. more than the Communists, and over double the percentage of any other party.

Had de Gaulle really been ambitious to be a Fascist dictator—of which he was being freely accused—this would have been the moment to strike; and, certainly, some in France and abroad expected civil war at that time. De Gaulle himself addressed on Vincennes racecourse the largest crowd ever to attend a political meeting in Paris, half a million strong. As he attacked the Communists and demanded the immediate dissolution of Parliament, the excited crowds shouted and shouted again, *"De Gaulle au pouvoir!"* However, the excitement was followed by anti-climax. There was no revolution, no civil war. The Socialist Home Secretary, Jules Moch, broke the strikes by strong-arm methods, and the trade unions split into Communist and non-Communist groups. De Gaulle sat patiently in the wings, waiting for his call to come upon the stage, "to guide the country in the direction of salvation and greatness." No call came. With American aid flowing in to a now safely anti-Communist France, economic conditions steadily improved. The black marketeers began to find it more profitable to get honest jobs. Governments still came and went, and the foreign and colonial situation remained in chronic crisis—but Frenchmen, like others, grew used to these things. The Fourth Republic staggered on its way for another decade, and de Gaulle continued to await the nation's call. His Rally, the RPF, had gone up like a rocket in 1947; it came down gently, and with few sparks, over the next six years. Occasionally the General would make an explosive speech, as when in 1951 he spoke in vaguely revolutionary terms of "a rendezvous on the Champs Elysées"—but more often he would confine himself to imprecise and generalized condemnation of the "sterile games" of the party politicians and the wasteful manoeuvres of the trade unions, combined with lofty but cryptic observations upon France's destiny to lead Europe and the necessity for all who were not 'separatists' (*i.e.* Communists) to rally to the flag—and a good deal more that the French *bourgeois* could interpret, each to his own pleasure. But revolutions are not made by such sonorous platitudes or majestic ambiguities—and de Gaulle by 1952 appeared to many as the dictator who had lost his chance. As one of the most distinguished Gaullists, André Malraux, wrote, "De Gaulle marched us full speed to the Rubicon, and then told us to get out our fishing-rods." By 1953 the Gaullist Rally had disintegrated.

There are certain intellectual and political parallels to be noticed between those temperamentally very different characters, Churchill and de Gaulle. Both possessed a romantic view of their country's history, glorying in the poetry of its greatness. Both were destined to personify that greatness at a dark hour, and later both wrote memorably of their own rôle. Both clung tenaciously (and critics would say over-long) to the idea of their country's prestige. Churchill, by virtue of his electoral defeat in 1945, and his greater age, was to some extent spared what de Gaulle was not spared, the fate of accepting the inevitable decline of that imperial position, both in Asia and Africa. At first glance there is an air of grandiose anachronism about them both—yet a closer examination would contradict such an easy generalization. Both refuse to be type-cast. Both had the knack of surprise, the capacity to dismay friends and delight enemies. Both, too, had a stubborn ambition to rise to the top of the political "greasy pole," and persevered in climbing when few would have given much for their chances. Both Churchill and de Gaulle, moreover, suffered a period of partial eclipse, when it became customary to talk of them in the past tense, as of men whose effective careers were over: for Churchill the nineteen-thirties, for de Gaulle the middle nineteen-fifties. But both were to be summoned from prospective decline into obscurity to meet the challenge of a national crisis.

Before that day came for de Gaulle in 1958, he lived a life of semi-retirement at his modest country house in Colombey-les-deux-Eglises, with his devoted, self-effacing wife and (until her death in 1948) his invalid daughter. Here in a small turret study he wrote his War Memoirs, a detailed and often eloquent three-volume work. From here he made his weekly journeys to Paris to keep in touch with the centre of events; occasionally he undertook a more publicized sortie to make a big speech or give a Press conference—for it was emphatically a *semi*-retirement. Always he held himself in readiness for the day when the nation should demand that he, its natural leader, like Cincinnatus of old, should emerge from rusticity to 'renovate' the State.

It could hardly be denied that it was in need of renovation. On one major issue after another France was borne along by events that were too strong for her. There was, for instance, the necessity for Western Europe to unite her military defences against Russia. On this issue de Gaulle was against a fully international and integrated European Army, but he favoured participation by a strongly reinforced *French* Army in a Western alliance. France, having been rescued to some extent by American economic aid, inevitably had become one of the Western bloc, but the prospect of co-operating with a similarly rescued and rearmed Western Germany made agonizing demands upon a people that had thrice in a lifetime been invaded by the *boches*. The idea of a European Defence Community with a fully integrated European Army—the American solution— was debated through long months of political frustration, bitterness, and indecision. It was Mendès-France, eventually, who had the courage to thrust upon the Assembly and the nation the moment of truth. Compromises, formulas, safeguards—all these had kept the politicians busy for years; but when Mendès-France forced at last a Parliamentary vote, the Government could not persuade the Assembly. A piqued John Foster Dulles thereupon threatened to withdraw American military support from Western Europe, but instead proceeded with the other Western powers to build up the German army within NATO whether France liked it or not—and eventually France *had* to like it. Her vote against the European Defence Community represented more a confused cry of protest than an effective policy.

In colonial affairs, similarly, France was far from being mistress of events. With the second greatest overseas empire in the world, her imperial position was exposed and precarious—the more so after Britain had set the trend by granting independence after the war to India, Pakistan, Burma, and Ceylon. Even before those events (in fact, from the very day after Japan surrendered), Ho Chi Minh emerged from his underground activities into the open to proclaim himself President of a "free and independent Vietnam" (part of the old Indo-China), and by 1946 a war had developed between the French and their Vietnamese subjects that was to last eight years, cost very heavy casualties, drain away much money and military manpower, stamp France as a diehard colonialist power, dig deeper than ever the gulf between Left and Right in France, and result in the end in bitter and total defeat—a defeat, moreover, that was a stimulus to new revolts of other major French colonies in North Africa. The last tragedy in a long sequence in Indo-China came at Dien Bien Phu, a French-held fortress that was overwhelmed by Ho Chi Minh's Communist forces in May 1954. As with the European Army, it was to be the dynamic Jewish Radical, Mendès-France, who provided the moment of decision. He had throughout opposed the Indo-China war; now he gave himself and his new Government a deadline for ending it: July 20, a month from his taking office. France had not seen such energy, realism, and decision from a Government for a long time. But, of course, he made countless enemies, and within eight months he too had been ousted from the Premiership.

De Gaulle's imperial conceptions, though grandiose, were not illiberal. His *Union Française* was an attempt to move with the twentieth century; but he, like most Frenchmen of his sort, patriotic and prestige-minded, was always at least one jump behind practicable policies for African or Asian colonies hungry for independence. As a rueful French expert wrote in 1951, "The English manage to leave at the right time, and are discovered later to be still there—unofficially—and as influential as they ever were. The French have confidence only in written documents and continue to cling to them even when the world has changed." Clinging to French Indo-China, they lost all. Trying to retain their protectorates of Tunisia and Morocco in a French Union, they were forced to concede complete independence, even though formal acknowledgment was made of 'interdependence.' The trouble was that French Governments repeatedly failed to come to terms with the moderate Muslim nationalists when agreement might still have been possible; affairs then proceeded beyond the point of crisis, and negotiations with such moderates became impossible. It is also true that French Governments of the Fourth Republic were too weak to carry through policies of peaceful colonial transition towards independence even where they wanted to. They were constantly thwarted by local administrators, by white settlers, and by the 'colonial lobby' in the French Chamber.

By the time Morocco and Tunisia had achieved independence (1956), nearly half a million French soldiers were fighting a grim war in Algeria against Muslim nationalists. The Arab land of Algeria had been French territory since 1830, and had long sent deputies to the French Parliament. It was four times the size of France, and its French inhabitants numbered considerably over a million, some of them third or fourth generation settlers. It had recently been found to contain valuable oil deposits in its Saharan territories. A decade ago all Frenchmen would have agreed that Algeria was, and must remain, French. But that thesis soon had to be argued for and fought for with ever-increasing desperation; and the events of the late 'fifties made it in fact certain that in the old sense *Algérie Française* could not survive. French influence might remain —or even a French enclave in a partitioned Algeria—but as for the old settler-dominated Algeria, de Gaulle himself said of it, "*Algérie de papa* is stone dead."

Algeria was the issue that unmade the Fourth Republic in 1958, and brought de Gaulle at last his long-awaited call. It was the issue upon which de Gaulle, and with him the Fifth Republic, stood or fell—for Algeria usurped the position held between 1789 and 1870 by Paris—the natural centre for hatching of revolutions and overturning of regimes. But the Algerian issue was more significant still. This protracted and deadly war did more than anything else to rob France of her potential place in international affairs, and to force her into rash and intransigent postures. It was a direct cause of the French intervention (and eventual humiliation) at Suez, in order to overthrow a Nasser whose anti-French propaganda was, in the French view, poisoning the North African air. It was for years a millstone round the neck of the Atlantic Alliance, weakening NATO and France herself by locking up most of the French Army away from Europe, and embarrassing France's associates, who saw themselves to some extent as allies involved in French conduct and policy that they could not approve. It poisoned relations between France and her newly independent ex-colonies, Tunisia and Morocco, neighbours of Algeria and sympathizing with the Arab rebels. And it largely destroyed mutual respect between a hostile United Nations and a resentful France. Most important of all, it was a prolonged human tragedy of great dimensions, involving a constant draining of French and Arab blood (including much Arab blood spilt by other Arabs), mutual and despicable atrocities, and a heartrending refugee problem.

Syria, Indo-China, Tunisia, Morocco, Suez—everywhere since the Second World War France had been forced to accept defeat and withdrawal. For the Army all this, coming on top of the humiliations of the Second World War itself, produced a sense of intolerable anger and frustration; and these feelings were inevitably vented against the politicians who, after all the soldiers' blood and suffering, appeared to have 'betrayed' them. Thus the professional soldiers entered the Algerian war determined that there should be no more weakness. Their country had been kicked around enough. This time they would fight as tough a war as was necessary—and win it.

The story of Algeria proceeded to illustrate once again the inability of the politicians in France to govern. It was not the French Governments so much as three other groups who, right up to 1958, determined French policy in Algeria: the local administrators, the white settlers, and above all the professional Army. When the Socialist Prime Minister, Guy Mollet, visited Algeria in 1956 he was met with a riot, because it was considered by local French opinion that he was preparing yet another 'sell-out.' He returned to France a shaken man. It was the settlers, not the Army, that rioted, but very soon the two elements were to be allies in overthrowing the regime and bringing de Gaulle to power. In particular it was the 'poor whites' (in Algeria as in the Southern States of America) who were the most frightened and therefore violent opponents of racial equality. From then on, no French Government dared make concessions or risk open political negotiation. Even conscripts were now sent to Algeria. The Army and its Right-wing allies were determined upon total French victory at all costs, by whatever means. Some of those means were scrupulous and conscientious, for French colonialism at its paternal best was very good indeed. Some of the means were worthy of the Nazis: sometimes guerrilla terrorism was met with counter-terrorism and torture of prisoners so disgraceful that it exposed the nerve of liberal consciences both in France and abroad.

The fury and the frustration of the Algerian affair spread inevitably to France itself. The impotence of Ministers was repeatedly demonstrated as one weak and divided Cabinet followed another. The reputation of the politicians sank below zero. Right-wing thugs broke up meetings demanding peace in Algeria. The Algerian community in France became honeycombed with rebel elements. The Paris police, constantly involved in quelling violence, demonstrated one day in front of the Assembly building, demanding danger-money, but also chanting anti-parliamentary and anti-Jewish slogans. France, the despair of her friends, seemed to many to be sliding into chaos. Yet a degree of chaos was so endemic to France that no one could certainly foretell revolution. After all, the Third Republic had suffered endless crises—Panama and Dreyfus affairs, corruption scandals, dictatorship scares and Fascist riots—and yet it had lasted seventy years. Why should the Fourth Republic live any less long? We are faced with one of the many paradoxes of modern France. *Everything* had happened to France many times over, defeat, triumph, foreign occupation, inflation, recovery—and as for revolution, it was an old acquaintance. Life, however, had proceeded with obstinate resilience. The Christmas shopping receipts were not affected. The summer week-end holiday traffic continued to grow. Indeed, during the Whitsun week-end of 1958 when the de Gaulle revolution was in full swing, the roads were choked with Parisians off to the races or to the country. Industrial production and consumer goods sales both leaped upward in the late 'fifties. Frenchmen had never been so prosperous. The birth-rate, once the lowest in Europe, turned smartly and optimistically upward. Revolutions were something the French could take in their stride; the situation, as often before, was 'desperate but not serious.'

The 1958 revolution was triggered off by Algerian-French indignation at the shooting of three soldiers by the Tunisians. (Relations with Tunisia were very difficult—a little earlier there had been a French Army reprisal-bombardment over the Tunisian border, flatly against the instructions of the French Government.) The French settlers and the Army were convinced that the latest French Ministry was about to make a settlement with the rebels. The civilian settlers (a considerable proportion of them teenagers) went on to stage a revolt in Algiers against the authority in Paris. The Army, uncertain at first, did not suppress the revolt, and then, after a day or so, threw in its lot with the rebels—seizing Corsica as an earnest of its intentions. The revolution was then conducted by telephone. The Algiers generals, led by Salan, demanded the recall to power of de Gaulle. Behind the subsequent phonings, conferences, comings and goings, lay the threat that the politicians in Paris well understood. It was simply that if they did not themselves wind up the Government and the Fourth Republic, the parachute troops would occupy France and make them. France was almost undefended and at the mercy of *les paras*—or so at least it seemed to enough people to make the threat decisive.

A few months before, de Gaulle had said, "I had hoped that I should be called last year. Now I begin to fear it is too late." His hour, however, was arriving. The Algiers rebels declared for him. Back in France, it was realized that he was the only alternative to a military dictatorship. Now, therefore, there came to Colombey a procession of politicians to interview the General upon his intentions. These, it appeared, were impeccable. "I am a man who belongs to no one and to everyone . . . . I hold myself at the disposal of my country." He would insist on democratic forms. A dictatorship was abhorrent to him. Of course, the Fourth Republic was abhorrent to him too, and he would insist on special powers. The General, it seemed, was capable of satisfying even his old opponents, the Socialists. (Mollet led them to vote convincingly for accepting him.) In Algeria the Army wanted de Gaulle because he would silence the politicians and act to win the war. In France the politicians wanted de Gaulle because he would have the authority to rule the rebellious Army. De Gaulle thus came to power as almost everybody's choice and in support of a bundle of conflicting causes. In May 1958 he pleased almost everybody except the Communists; only a few demonstrators paraded with placards—"*Le girafe au zoo!*" ; and probably even some Communists voted for him on the quiet. Ambitious as he was, he had the further advantage of not having plotted the revolution. Greatness had this time truly been thrust upon him. Cincinnatus had come up from the country. He was older, fatter-faced; he wore strong glasses; he seemed milder and mellower. The phrases, however, had a familiar ring: "I wish to give courage and vigour to Frenchmen who want national unity."

De Gaulle came to power legally and has since ruled (one might say reigned) with scrupulous legality. It is true that he was so completely indispensable that he could insist on his own terms, which included a new Constitution giving much greater power to the President and his Government, and much less to the Assembly; and it is true that he has demanded and received special near-dictatorial powers for a limited space; but fears that he would become a totalitarian dictator proved groundless. The elected Assembly retained ample powers to get rid of him if it dared. The simple fact was, and is likely to be for the duration of his active life, that it did not dare: the General has become irreplaceable. The strange situation has arisen that de Gaulle, the bogey-man of democrats for many a long year, has become the indispensable guardian of democratic forms.

He had such authority, this saviour of the State, that he could afford in some spheres to act toughly. After the massive popular vote approving his new Constitution, he was permitted four months' supreme power, during which three hundred ordinances and decrees reformed almost every aspect of French life. During this period, his Ministers devalued the franc by $17\frac{1}{2}$ per cent. to enable France to compete better in Common Market trade. Prices were held steady, and the economic situation improved remarkably. From England, many looked wryly over the Channel at the buoyant condition of a France they were so recently pitying or patronizing.

In European and world affairs de Gaulle lived up to his reputation as odd man out. Others wished for a Summit meeting: not de Gaulle. Others wished to negotiate on Berlin: de Gaulle only after eloquent hesitation and with strong reservations. Others suspended nuclear tests: de Gaulle proceeded with France's in the Sahara—amid not very serious *domestic* opposition, but to violent protests from surrounding African countries. De Gaulle showed notable coolness towards NATO, and something near contempt for the United Nations, dominated as it was by Afro-Asian powers bitterly critical of France. Everywhere and always his paramount motive, as of old, was to assert the great-power status of France and to pursue her national interest with single-minded passion. Thus he was mistrustful of an Americo-Russian deal at Europe's expense (remembering, perhaps, Roosevelt at Yalta); and of any scheme of close European federation which might submerge the sovereignty of France. He pursued friendship with West Germany and such Common Market policies as would further France's interests. If Britain wished to enter that market, it must be on terms that were not destructive of its principles or of France's advantage. As during the War, he continued to give the impression of a man fighting two wars, one against his enemies (the Nazis, the collaborators, the Communists) and another against his allies (the Americans, the British, the other members of the "Six"), those "difficult allies" who did not always perceive the paramountcy of France.

In colonial affairs the shock of the revolution enabled de Gaulle to make a new start, with a gesture of imagination. Picking up such pieces of the French Empire and the French Union as remained, he gave all the remaining French colonies a choice between immediate secession and continued association with France in her new French Community (with even then the right ultimately to claim independence if they chose). Only Guinea voted to secede, and promptly did so. Thus de Gaulle at one step brought French colonial policy in line with the most liberal twentieth-century conceptions.

There remained Algeria. Here he "bought time with ambiguity." He was pragmatical and wily. In speeches full of mellifluous but sibylline phrases, he consummately displayed the art of saying everything and nothing, and contrived to bolster the most contradictory hopes. As the months went by, however—and still outright French victory was not coming any nearer—the suspicion began to grow among the Army and the Algerian settlers that this de Gaulle whom they had brought to power was, like all the earlier politicians, preparing to sell out. He was aiming his appeal at the *Muslims*; he attacked racial discrimination and poverty; he quietly posted Salan away from Algiers and began purging the Army; he reprieved terrorists under sentence of death; he discussed the possibility of negotiations with the rebels; at last he gave guarded approval to self-determination. The Right and the Army took fright. They had thought to put in power an intransigent patriot, or, better still, to enthrone a symbol while they themselves wielded effective influence. They had not reckoned upon an enlightened liberal who was also a crafty politician; the General was a horse of a colour they had not bargained for. When Massu, the general of the *paras*, violently attacked de Gaulle and was therefore recalled, a second Algiers revolt took place (January 1960), while the *paras* stood inactive by. De Gaulle was firm and impressive. He broadcast an emotional yet reasoned appeal to the Army (having little need to appeal to France) —and triumphed. The revolt collapsed; the insurgents were arrested. There was another military plot against de Gaulle in April 1961, led by General Challe, but this too collapsed, mainly because the *conscripts* would not support the rising. The next month, peace talks ("unthinkable" but inevitable) began at last. "We must accept history. *We must negotiate*," said de Gaulle. Long after it had ceased to be safe for him to do so, he returned to Algiers, with that casually worn personal courage of his, to assert the decisions and underline the sovereign authority of the Fifth Republic, and of de Gaulle, its President. While the long-drawn-out, secret, and often interrupted peace-talks continued, gangs of French hooligans in Algiers and elsewhere freely murdered Muslims, and sometimes Muslims murderously retaliated. In France itself, General Salan's own "Secret Army," the O.A.S., an extreme organization of Right-wing desperadoes, planted their plastic bombs and several times made attempts on the life of the man whom a few years earlier they had helped to bring to power. Salan himself, arrested in Algiers and brought to France for trial, was fortunate to escape the death penalty. Meanwhile, while hundreds of thousands of its apprehensive white population fled to France, Algeria reached independence.

It is safe to say that nobody but de Gaulle could have seen France through this most painful operation. Laconic and imperturbable in the midst of assassination attempts, he continued on his majestic and calculated way. In France itself, he continued consistently to ignore the frequently hostile criticism of Press and politicians, and to plan a referendum to ensure his successor's election by direct popular vote. As for the newly emerging Europe, a triumphant tour of West Germany in September 1962 flood-lighted the new edifice that was arising as the dust of ancient battles settled. Many were critical and suspicious of his apparent intention to build this new Europe on a too dominantly Franco-German foundation. He showed a minimum of enthusiasm for British entry into the European Community, and continued to ridicule the plans of those Frenchmen and others who wished to plan a fully federal Western Europe. To such a one as de Gaulle, who had devoted his whole life to reminding the world that France—despite everything—was a great power, it would indeed be inconceivable that France should be "merged in Europe." Rather Europe must be built around its historic and natural centre—a France happily and magnanimously reconciled to the old German enemy.

In January 1963 de Gaulle set the seal on this reconciliation by signing with Adenauer the Franco-German Treaty. At the same moment, however, he caused consternation among his five partners in the Common Market (including the Germans), and some indignation in Britain, by brusquely vetoing the British application to join it. In his view, Britain would seek to transform the Market into a large, nebulous free-trade area; French agriculture would suffer; the promise of French hegemony in Europe would be threatened. And, once admitted, the British would strengthen the European link with the U.S.A. that de Gaulle wished to weaken. Macmillan had underlined British dependence on the U.S.A. when, by the Nassau agreement, he accepted Polaris missiles; de Gaulle would do no such thing. The French nuclear force must be French; and Europe must be European, a strictly continental confederacy shorn of "Anglo-Saxon" influence.

The mysteries of this stubborn man's logic are, like most mysteries, not arguable: de Gaulle is France, France is Europe, Europe is civilization. He may not eventually carry Europe with him. But meanwhile he does not fail to display those qualities he himself long ago postulated for a great leader: *égotisme, orgueil, éloignement, ruse*.

Table of Events

1890.	De Gaulle born at Lille.
1914–18.	Serves in First World War.
1934.	De Gaulle's book on the Army of the Future.
1940.	France defeated; de Gaulle flies to London to continue resistance.
1940–44.	France under Nazis and Vichy regime; the "Resistance."
1942.	Allied forces land in North Africa.
1944.	Allies reconquer France; de Gaulle re-enters Paris.
1944–46.	De Gaulle's first period of office.
1946.	Fourth Republic established.
1946–54.	War in Indo-China.
1947.	De Gaulle forms the RPF (Gaullist Rally).
1954.	France rejects E.D.C. (European Army).
	Outbreak of Algerian Revolt.
1956.	Independence of Morocco and Tunisia.
1958.	E.E.C. (The Common Market) comes into force.
	Revolt in Algeria brings de Gaulle to power.
	Fifth Republic established.
1962.	Independence of Algeria.
1963.	Treaty with Germany; veto on British entry to E.E.C.

17

Jawaharlal Nehru

(1889-   )

(Chapter 4, on Mahatma Gandhi, is necessary background
for a reading of this chapter.)

The two men who more than any others have made modern
India—Gandhi and Nehru—although they both served
passionately the same cause of Indian nationhood, were in
many respects at opposite poles. Gandhi, for all his Western education, was an oriental, a simple-lifer, a man of the people, of the
ancient village ways, a spirit of profound sensibility and humility.
Nehru, by contrast, is the modern man, scientific, sceptical, urban,
Westernized. Where Gandhi was intuitive, Nehru was rational.
Where Gandhi burned with a quiet flame, Nehru blazed with
indignation. Nehru, for all his yoga exercises and his devotion
to his beloved master's non-violence, found constant difficulty
in turning the other cheek and taming his pride and rage.
While Gandhi sat quietly listening to God's still small voice, Nehru
would consider it more profitable to study the lessons of Soviet
planning. Where Gandhi stood for the archaic spinning-wheel, Nehru
(though he did his stint of hand-spinning in his time) stands for the
fertilizer factory and the steel mill. Where Gandhi squatted in his
loin-cloth and shawl, and made history fasting in his jail, Nehru
(though he too knew many years of prison) stands upright, a natural
emperor of men. Gandhi, shrewd and successful revolutionary that
he was, was also a symbol of the age-old India that the West had at
once left behind, exploited, and misunderstood. Nehru is a symbol
of the potential India that is trying to be born amid five-year plans
and ambitious schemes of modernization. "These," said Nehru a
year or two ago as he pushed the button to inaugurate a great new
power dam, "these are our temples." The natural horizons of
Gandhi, cosmopolitan though he was in his contacts and his
intellectual interests, were essentially Indian. Nehru, Indian nationalist though he was and is, is essentially a figure more than Indian, a
champion of such movements as non-alignment and Afro-Asian

solidarity, a world statesman. The two men represented opposite sides of the coin of Indian independence—but it was one coin. They differed frequently over issues and policies, but never quarrelled personally, for Gandhi trusted and valued Nehru even when he thought him dangerously impetuous. He reasoned with him as a son with whom he had had a difference, and he saw in him increasingly, under the trial of events, his natural heir. Nehru was "one who is more than a comrade, and whom no amount of political differences will ever separate from me. . . . He is courage personified. . . . He has an indomitable faith in his mission." And again: "Jawaharlal says that he does not understand my language, and that he speaks a language foreign to me. This may or may not be true. But language is no bar to a union of hearts. And I know this, that when I am gone, he will speak my language." As for Nehru, his repeated impatience with Gandhi was more than matched by his vast respect and love. When Gandhi was "fasting unto death" in 1933 Nehru was shocked by what he took to be primitive and irrational tactics, but he wrote to him, "I feel lost in a country where you are the only familiar landmark, and I try to grope my way in the dark. . . . Whatever happens, my love and thoughts will be with you." His little world, he said, shook and tottered when he contemplated it without Gandhi. To whom should he go for advice when in doubt, or for comfort when in sorrow? And few who heard it will forget the grief in his voice when, upon the Mahatma's assassination in 1948, he spoke impromptu to the Delhi crowd to tell them, "The light has gone out of our lives, and there is darkness everywhere." It was the voice of a son who had lost his father.

Nehru was born in 1889 at Allahabad—in the same year as Hitler, when Gandhi was already twenty years old—and the circumstances of his birth were indeed princely. His father, Motilal Nehru, was an extremely rich lawyer and a Kashmiri Brahmin, a member of the highest of Hindu castes. The young Jawaharlal was as privileged in his upbringing as any son of a Whig grandee or American millionaire. He was healthy, wealthy, and intelligent, and surrounded by adoring parents, numerous servants, private tutors, opportunities to play cricket and tennis and to ride and swim: there were two swimming-pools, one indoors and one out, in the luxurious mansion that the Nehru family moved to when Jawaharlal was ten years old. The tutors were mainly English, as was much of the distinguished company that was entertained at the Nehru house, and as was the motor-car that Motilal imported—the very first in India. It was inevitable that the young Nehru should imbibe English ways of thought, English manners and habits, long before he was sent to Harrow and Cambridge. English, indeed, was his parents' and teachers' tongue, and therefore his. Only as a second language and with some effort did he come to speak Urdu. He read Keats and Kipling, Lewis Carroll and Conan Doyle, Scott, Dickens and Thackeray. Gandhi himself later said of him, "He is more English than Indian in his thoughts and make-up," and a jail companion once complained that he dreamed in English. But he did not fail to notice, and to resent, that in crowded railway trains Englishmen always had carriages to themselves, or that in public parks there were always benches reserved for them alone. He mixed much with adults and little with children of his own age, but was not unhappy. Religion—that is, Hinduism—seemed to be a woman's affair, and sometimes he would go with his mother or aunt to take a dip in the Ganges, but mostly it seemed more manly to imitate his father and shrug the whole thing off as unaccountable or outrageous. As the mature Jawaharlal said later, he agreed with the Buddha: "This life is enough for me; and when you don't know about something, why talk about it?"

From 1905 to 1907 Nehru attended Harrow, and from there proceeded to Trinity College, Cambridge, where he took second class honours in Natural Sciences. His school and university career certainly did not reveal him as a future leader of men and opinion. He spoke infrequently and haltingly in public, being terrified of an audience; he achieved no particular academic distinction. Nietzsche and Bernard Shaw he dabbled in, in an undergraduate, fashionable sort of way; socialists and suffragettes he noted with mild interest. Indian nationalism he quietly approved of; but none of this cut very deep. He lived well on his ample allowance, dressing and behaving much as other young Edwardian aristocrats. And when he abandoned science for his father's profession of the law, and entered the Inner Temple in 1910, he appeared to have emerged into manhood as the conventional rich young-man-about-town, patterned by Harrow, Trinity, and Bond Street—as he himself put it later, "a bit of a prig with little to commend me." Back in India, he practised law for a short space, dabbled a little in politics, and was married amid regal splendour and expense in 1916. Few would have prophesied any unusual distinctions, except those naturally attending his social position, for this likeable and debonair young man. His was a youthful career, in its different way, not unlike that of the young Franklin Roosevelt.

Two men may be said to have blown his latent fires into flame.

One was the British General Dyer, who ordered his troops to fire on the demonstrating crowds in Amritsar, and in a few minutes killed 379 and wounded 1200 Indians. The other was Gandhi, whose revolutionary techniques of passive resistance and civil disobedience seemed to provide the politically practical and morally perfect answer to the British. It was as if Nehru was seeing this British assumption of superiority, this divine right of theirs to govern lesser breeds, for the first time. "I realized then, more vividly than I had ever done before, how brutal and immoral imperialism was, and how it had eaten into the souls of the British upper-classes." Realization of the sins and narrowness of India's rulers was accompanied by a realization of his own shortcomings:

> I was filled with shame and sorrow—shame at my own easygoing and comfortable life and our petty politics of the city which ignored this vast multitude of semi-naked sons and daughters of India, sorrow at the degradation and overwhelming poverty of India. A new picture of India seemed to rise before me, naked, starving, crushed, and utterly miserable. I listened to their innumerable tales of sorrow, their crushing and ever-growing burden of rent, illegal exactions, ejectments from land and mud-hut, beatings; surrounded on all sides by vultures who preyed on them—zamindar's [tax-collector's] agents, money-lenders, police. . . .

He never felt moved, as Gandhi did, to dress like these naked masses or follow their way of life. He never pretended to see anything ennobling in physical squalor. He was no St Francis: "I hate poverty," he said. However, Kashmiri Brahmin though he was, and *bourgeois* inescapably, from the hungry masses he took new strength. He found his tongue in talking to them; they acted on him like a tonic and gave him a sense of power. He was thirty years old now, a new Nehru—and his new militancy was powerfully reinforced when his formidable and majestic father, Motilal Nehru, announced his own conversion to the Mahatma's policies and methods. ("There were sixteen horses in the stable one day, and none the next.") *Satyagraha* had arrived for the Nehru family. It was to dominate their lives for a long time—all of them, including Jawaharlal's old mother, his tubercular wife, and his young sisters. It was to take them to many scenes of riot and bloodshed (though by the nature of their movement, the violence was not theirs), to the inside of a considerable number of prisons, and at last to the splendid triumph, the independence of their country.

The cause, the sacrifices it demanded, the leader and the devotion he so readily won, all combined to give a sense of elation and exaltation. Nehru would go to prison "willingly and joyfully . . . one feels almost lonely outside." Prison had become "a place of pilgrimage." He marvelled at his double good fortune, to serve India and to serve her under a leader of the quality of Gandhi. Between 1921 and 1945, Nehru spent altogether nine years of his life in ten different prisons, serving nine separate sentences. As an important political prisoner he was often given, it is true, special conditions of leniency, with books, newspapers, visitors, and supplemented food, and sometimes he enjoyed caste privileges, too, proper to a Brahmin. But prison is prison, nevertheless, and exaltation does not normally last for long at a time. His was often a dreary and frustrating existence, especially during those times when differences within the Congress leadership were acute. On the occasions when he felt he was being ill-treated in prison, his health was strong and his nerves well-equipped to stand strain. "My body has served me well," he wrote. When, however (more frequently), he was being well-treated, the realization of his privileges sometimes aroused a sense of guilt, and he would force himself to work hard to expiate it, perhaps by spinning or weaving, perhaps by household work, or by writing—for in jail he eventually wrote three considerable books, including his *Glimpses of World History*, a stimulating Asian view of history and a useful corrective to the orthodox Europe-centred story. It is written in the form, unusual for a history book, of letters to his young daughter Indira.

The ups and downs of the Congress in its struggle against British rule have been earlier outlined in the chapter on Mahatma Gandhi. Inevitably in such a wide movement with such vast tasks there were strong differences over tactics and a great deal of hard-hitting dispute. In all this the younger Nehru came to be accepted as the leader of the radical wing against the "Old Guard," who frequently had the sympathy of the Mahatma himself. Perhaps the word 'radical' may mislead. Gandhi had a tremendous *moral* radicalism, and his non-violent techniques were in one sense radical, even extreme; it would have seemed laughable to an Englishman of the period to hear Gandhi described as a conservative; but he was politically more cautious than Nehru. Furthermore, he distrusted Nehru's socialist ideas; he clung to many of the ancient forms of Hinduism; he was offended by any intention to draw India along a road parallel to Soviet Communism. Nehru, on the other hand, had progressed very far down that road from his correct young aristocrat's position of a few years earlier. He had discovered 'the masses.' He had shed his expensive clothes and taken to getting about Allahabad in a bullock cart—to his father's horror. He had become confirmed in his rejection of religion. On a visit to Europe in 1926–

27, undertaken primarily for the health of his wife (who had developed the lung tuberculosis that was eventually to kill her) he had been deeply impressed by what he understood to be the achievements of Soviet Russia: its sense of purpose, its social and educational reforms, its lack of racial arrogance, its leadership in the anti-imperialist struggle. Later experience caused him to have some second thoughts but never to turn right-about on this subject. His earlier rather uncritical acceptance of Russian socialism had necessarily, in the light of Stalin's tyranny, to be hedged round with later reservations; but he remained, and remains, a man of the Left, eager to apply—with the modifications necessary to suit India's peculiarities—the lessons of planning and socialism. In his European journeyings of 1927, Nehru also met many of the Left-wing intellectuals of Western Europe (as well as Frank Buchman, of "Moral Rearmament," who horrified him)—and attended a significant Anti-Imperialist Congress at Brussels, together with other potential Asian rebels. The dream was growing of an Asia free of Western shackles, and in Nehru's mind the seed was sown of an Asian brotherhood, or perhaps even an Afro-Asian brotherhood, of nations liberated from their colonial masters. One day in 1955 the Bandung Conference was to give a firmer outline to that idea.

Gandhi could approve Nehru's anti-imperialist zeal, and his diatribes against British exploitation, but not the Marxist phrases that now flowed so readily from his lips, not his championing a "republican army," not his impetuous demand for immediate independence of British rule. Gandhi wanted one thing at a time, and that one thing to be practicable: Dominion status, for instance, before total independence. He thought Nehru was unwittingly encouraging mischief-makers and hooligans. "I love you too well to restrain my pen when I feel I must write. You are going too fast." And he even proposed that since a break between them was inevitable, they should publish a full correspondence between them in *Young India*, setting out their respective positions. Nehru did not accept, for he was too full of reverence for his master, not sufficiently converted to Communism, too convinced a believer in non-violence. The socialist and anti-religious speeches continued, and the hard-hitting attacks on the British (including the "sanctimonious and canting humbugs" of the Labour Party); but he went so far as to concede that on the day that Britain cast away her empire, India would be ready to co-operate with her. He hardly made it appear that he expected any such act of generosity.

In 1924 Nehru had been elected General Secretary of the Congress

Party. Five years later, at the age of forty, he was elected President at the Lahore Congress. The honour, however, did not impress him at the time so much as the humiliation in the manner of his being chosen. For he was not the Congress's first choice, and it was only the surprising insistence of Gandhi himself that secured his election. As Nehru put it, he was made, as it were, to appear on the platform "suddenly by a trapdoor." For Gandhi knew his man, and he knew his Congress. Jawaharlal Nehru was just radical enough to keep the wildest radicals and Communists in check; he was young and dynamic; responsibility would, moreover, tame him; and above all, he was "pure as crystal, truthful beyond suspicion. . . . The nation is safe in his hands." Yet Nehru's presidential address showed certainly no signs of any tameness; it was a trumpet-call, and one that played all the old fanfares unrepentantly. "Before us is the conquest of power. . . . We cannot command success. But success often comes to those who dare and act."

Events were indeed set for action: the years 1930–32 were to see the climax of the Gandhian movement in India between the wars. Nehru might be President of the Congress, but every one recognized who was the real leader of the movement: the unpredictable Mahatma—unpredictable, and to Nehru and the radicals more than a little unreliable and disappointing on occasions. No one else could have so quickened the pulse of Indians or focused the eyes of the watching world as Gandhi did when he announced the great march from Ahmedabad to the coast, illegally and symbolically to collect salt on Dandi beach. The simple, single, but prolonged gesture of defiant pilgrimage at once silenced his Indian critics and produced a sort of political hush over the land—a hush in which one might almost hear the synchronized hearts of Indians beating. All the confusion and disarray was concentrated into an act of simple and eloquent drama.

Nehru, like everybody else, was bowled over by the wonderful little man whose tactics only so short a time before had seemed timid and hesitant. While the Mahatma with his seventy-eight disciples was still marching along the road to the coast, Nehru had written in almost biblical tones of admiration, as one whose breath had been caught, "The fire of a great resolve is in him and surpassing love of his miserable countrymen. And love of truth that scorches, and love of freedom that inspires. And none that passes him can escape the spell. . . ."

After the hush came the explosion, and Nehru was one of the first to be arrested for breaking the Salt Law, as all over India men proceeded to do. He was in fact taken into custody three weeks before Gandhi himself, and after serving a six months' sentence was rearrested after only a week, and served a further three months. Indeed, over a period of nearly five and a half years between April 1930 and September 1935, a total of exactly four years was spent in serving four separate sentences. The only prolonged period out of custody was in 1931, the year of the London Round Table Conference, when there was a truce—the "Delhi Pact"—in the battle between the Congress and the British.

It was not only Jawaharlal in the Nehru family who went into battle. His ailing wife Kamala threw herself into the struggle, helping to organize the women of Allahabad in the boycott of British cloth and alcoholic liquor; she too was eventually imprisoned, and rejoiced that she was able to show Jawaharlal (who by his own admission had taken her very much for granted) that she too could fight and suffer in the cause. In 1932, to Jawaharlal's extreme anger, his aged mother was injured in a Congress procession in Allahabad, when the police charged to break up a *satyagraha* demonstration. His sister Mrs Pandit and her husband were both deeply engaged in the non-violent fight: the latter eventually died in prison in 1944. And Nehru's father Motilal, having donated his mansion and estate to the Congress, first succeeded his son as (acting) Congress President and then followed him to Naini Jail. Stricken by cancer, he was released, rearrested, and again released; he died in Lucknow in 1931, and was cremated there by the side of the sacred river, as impressively as he had lived, in the presence of many thousands.

The great civil disobedience campaign against the British Raj had in fact already failed by 1932, though the dwindling struggle continued until 1934. Again in these years Nehru had occasion to differ strongly from Gandhi and his tactics. The great fast against Untouchability in 1933, for instance, Nehru considered to be from all points of view a mistake. First, it was a red herring: the main issue was Indian independence, and he considered that to introduce a side-issue, even if a morally important one, at a critical stage of the struggle for independence—and, moreover, at a time when Congress fortunes were low—was ill-considered. Besides, the whole business of fasting for self-purification struck him as smacking of primitive magic; he never could understand or sympathize with it. Sometimes, indeed, Gandhi's archaic religious approach to events provoked Nehru to throw up his hands in despair: the Bihar earthquake, that huge disaster, Gandhi thought might well be God's judgment upon Indian iniquities, particularly for permitting the sin of Untouchability. This to Nehru was mere superstition, and hard to bear. Harder still, a few months later, at a dark period of his life, facing from prison political failure and domestic worry (his wife was ill again—the disease was gaining), was Gandhi's decision to terminate civil disobedience. Hardest of all to stomach was Gandhi's public criticism of Nehru himself on the grounds that he was more interested in his "private studies" than his "allotted task": it is understandable that this wounded him. The cords binding him to Gandhi had for a time, he felt, snapped. Even non-violence itself he came temporarily to question: independence *with* violence would surely be preferable to continued subjection with non-violence? He returned to the fold, however, for he could never break with a man who meant as much to him as Gandhi. But in the depression induced by prison life, amid the Congress doldrums of 1934 and the nagging news of his wife's health, he was liable on occasions to lean towards Lenin's way and away from Gandhi's. His own health showed sufficient signs of wear for the authorities to move him from Calcutta to Dehra Dun, in the hills, where he was lodged in an adapted cattle-shed, tantalizingly cut off by a high wall from the magnificent mountain view. Here he found some help from his tension in writing his *Autobiography*, a book fitting to be put beside his *Glimpses of World History*. As for Gandhi, he did his best to heal Nehru's wounds with calm and friendly words, and showed that he still backed him for the Congress Presidency. The British authorities, knowing his wife's grave state of health, offered to release him if he would undertake to refrain from political agitation, but he refused— with her approval. However, they did transfer him so that he could be near her, and did later release him on compassionate grounds to join her: she had already gone to Europe in search of a cure. Early in 1936 the end came in a Swiss resort. Nehru flew back home to throw himself once more into the turmoil of politics, and was soon at Lucknow re-elected to the Presidency of the Congress. He was still fiery and extreme in his public speeches, and lashed the new Government of India Act of 1935 (which gave the Indian provinces internal self-government) in almost Marxist terms. But it was not only the British with whom he lost patience. His own Right-wing colleagues on the Congress Working Committee were soon offering to resign because of his policies and his manner of arguing them: a manner, they considered, compounded of impatience, irritability, arrogance, and self-righteousness. Again it was Gandhi who, more in sorrow than anger, put his finger on the exact spot of criticism which many others have felt for Nehru before and since, both in

India and in Europe and America. "Your colleagues," wrote Gandhi, "have chafed under your rebukes and magisterial manner, and above all your infallibility and superior knowledge." The Mahatma never minced his words.

Preoccupied as he was with the problems of how to win independence and how to mitigate the poverty of India's exploited millions, Nehru in these days seriously underestimated the difficulties of another basic problem—the latent hostility between the various religious communities, and especially between Hindu and Muslim. Having himself little use for purely Hindu nationalism, perhaps he rated too high the reasonableness and patriotism of the common Hindu or Muslim. The murderous religious feuds of communalism, which had appeared in ugly shape in the early 1920's and recurred spasmodically since, he thought would die down with time. Given the common passion of a quest for unity and independence, the nation would not—could not—be so lunatic as to sever its own limbs by such follies. As late as 1936, when under Nehru's leadership the Congress Party won a great victory in the provincial elections that followed the Government of India Act, the Muslim League (which was fighting for a separate Muslim state) won fewer than one in twenty even of Muslim votes. In the years that followed, however, intercommunal bitterness and fear increased rapidly. Nehru himself might be only a lukewarm Hindu, however exalted his Brahmin origins; but the Congress undoubtedly had many Hindu politicians who could hardly claim Nehru's objectivity. Jinnah's Muslim League complained of Congress arrogance, Hindu favouritism, Hindu attempts to wipe out Muslim culture (for example, by making Hindi the future official language rather than Urdu), even of downright Hindu persecution. By the time the Second World War broke out there was a wide, and as it turned out unbridgeable, chasm between the two major communities. The seeds of Pakistan and partition had germinated and grown fast. During the War, with the Congress Party leaders in prison and its funds confiscated as a consequence of its rebellious attitude to the British Government, the Muslim League raced ahead, increasing its membership to two millions. "No power on earth," Jinnah boasted, "can prevent Pakistan."

The Second World War presented Nehru with a complicated set of conflicting loyalties, dangers, and opportunities. For years he had been a passionate anti-Fascist and anti-Nazi. He had declined to meet Mussolini while passing through Rome in 1936 after his wife's death. He had strongly championed the Spanish Government against

Franco, and retained vivid memories of a 1938 visit to besieged Barcelona. (He remembered also five huddled days in a Chungking dug-out in 1939 sheltering from Japanese bombs.) As for Hitler, he was an affront to human decency and dignity. Hence, when the European War came, Nehru would have gladly thrown non-violence overboard to associate India with a just and necessary war against Germany—if only the English would abandon imperialism and give India unconditional independence. But she would not: with a Conservative-dominated Government and with the most wooden of Viceroys, Lord Linlithgow, Britain failed to make any imaginative gesture. Even when her position grew grave with Hitler's 1940 triumphs, and then desperate with the Japanese triumphs of 1941 and 1942, the farthest that Britain would go was to promise Dominion status *on the war's successful conclusion.* Already Nehru had received a sentence of four years' rigorous imprisonment for sedition, in October 1940—which even Churchill—no friend— thought a bit stiff: and although he served only fourteen months of his term and immediately upon his release made a statement sympa- thizing with the "progressive forces of the world" (represented by the United States, Britain, Russia, and China), Nehru, and the majority of Congress with him, were not prepared to co-operate with a Britain that would not grant full freedom till after the War. Indeed, they had perhaps some reason to be suspicious of British intentions when Churchill, their old enemy, had recently remarked, "I have not become His Majesty's first Minister to preside over the liquidation of the British Empire." To many in 1942 it appeared that, perhaps, willy-nilly, the British Empire was already in liquida- tion. Hongkong, Malaya, Singapore, and much of Burma had all fallen to the Japanese—and many Indians did not know whether or not to allow pleasure in the discomfiture of their old imperial masters to outweigh fear at the imminence of the invasion of new and perhaps more ruthless ones. True, the Japanese were fellow-Asians, but Nehru and most humane Indians had been appalled at their brutality. For a time he was in favour of organizing guerrilla war against them if they invaded—but returned to the Gandhian fold of passive resistance very soon.

So once again civil disobedience came to India, and for the last time Nehru went to prison, as did all the prominent Congress leaders; and the Government of India now undertook the task of breaking the rebellion at home while the Army fended off the enemy abroad. Very severe measures were taken—for the authori- ties, expecting a mass rebellion, thought it well to nip it in the bud.

During the last few months of 1942 riot casualties numbered at the very least four thousand—probably more—while one hundred thousand nationalists were imprisoned. Then these events were succeeded and dwarfed by a disastrous famine in Bengal that either killed or caused severe suffering to at least six million. Far off, in his Bombay prison, Nehru wrote in moving tones of this grisly tragedy in the last of his three books written in prison, the *Discovery of India*: "Men were dying all over the world and killing each other in battle; usually a quick death, often a brave death, death for a cause. . . . But here death had no purpose, no logic, no necessity; it was the result of man's incompetence and callousness. . . ."

With the end of the War and a Labour Government in Britain there came for the first time the prospect of a genuine all-Indian Government, with an Indian Prime Minister at last. Who was it to be? Sardar Patel, a strong Hindu nationalist and anti-socialist, and a brisk, practical, party man without the vision of either Gandhi or Nehru, was the choice of four-fifths of the local party committees. Gandhi, however, who was both in the battle and above it, and was of course not himself a candidate, once again used his influence and prestige to secure the choice of Nehru, rather than Patel, though in fact the two men shared the reins of government as colleagues and rivals until 1950. "I told Jawaharlal that he must wear the crown of thorns for the sake of the nation and he has agreed." He did agree —for who could refuse? But it was a solemn moment, considering (as he said) the five thousand years of Indian history. "All that past crowds upon me and exhilarates me, and at the same time oppresses me. Am I worthy of that past? . . . Standing on the sword's edge of the present between the mighty past and the mightier future, I tremble a little. . . ."

He had reason to. After the near-rebellion of 1942 and the famine of 1944 came the savage communal strife of 1947, involving the murder of half a million Indians: slaughter and counter-slaughter of Hindu and Muslim in Calcutta, East Bengal, Bihar, and the United Provinces.[1] It became increasingly plain that a single independent India of all communities was not a practicable proposition: a Muslim state became inevitable; and Nehru himself, while bitterly deploring it, was resigned to its inevitability. (Not so Gandhi.)

As for Attlee's statement fixing a firm date for independence, Nehru considered it "a brave and definite statement"—contrasting vividly with the depreciating comments of his fellow Old Harrovian, Churchill, a diehard to the last in matters Indian, who spoke of

[1] See Chapter 4.

Nehru and his like as "men of straw" and of the Attlee policy as "a shameful flight, a premature, hurried scuffle." When the Punjab broke into vicious flame in the spring of 1947 many thought Churchill might have been right. Temporarily, however, the fire of religious hatred was damped down; Independence Day came (August 15, 1947); the crowds danced and sang in the streets and cheered themselves hoarse; the fireworks spouted and crackled; the new flags were hoisted; a great and complicated act of statesmanship had been accomplished; and Nehru, first Premier of a free India, made his solemn speech of dedication in the Delhi Parliament:

> At the stroke of the midnight hour, when the world sleeps, India will awake to life and freedom. . . . It is fitting that at this solemn moment we take the pledge of dedication to the service of India and her people and to the still larger cause of humanity. . . . We end today a period of ill-fortune and India discovers herself again. . . .

Ill-fortune was not ended: Nehru had been too sanguine. The worst was yet to be, with the huge and appalling explosion of murder, panic, looting, arson, flight of refugees out of India into Pakistan and out of Pakistan into India—and in the Punjab full-scale civil war. In all, perhaps ten million Indians were terrorized, uprooted, or killed—ill-fortune indeed, and a bitter pill for all sane Indians to swallow. It was especially bitter for Nehru, who had been partly responsible for the acceptance of partition. Yet in the perspective of history, his words were just and measured. It was a giant stage ahead in the story of a substantial fraction of the world's people. It was a tribute to the reasonableness of the leaders of two great nations. For all the savagery that preceded and followed it, it was a great day in the history of the world. It is not so easy peacefully to liquidate an empire.

Nehru, a man now of fifty-eight, had been both personally and politically courageous during the rioting. Driven by disgust and rage, he had rushed into the middle of an ugly armed mob at the height of the Delhi killings to try to restrain its blood-lust; and he, a Hindu, had ordered Hindu looters to be shot. Now, no sooner had some calm been restored to the communal scene (very largely by the two-way mass flight of the survivors), than two more disasters struck: the outbreak of war in Nehru's own ancestral Kashmir and the assassination of Gandhi. For Gandhi he wept true tears—tears of shock, of shame at his own possible responsibility as Premier for the old man's security, tears of grief at the passing of "that man with the divine fire," the greatest of modern Indians, a fellow-fighter, Nehru's own sternest critic and truest friend. His own speeches in praise of the dead leader were as far from the usual obituary platitudes as sincerity, emotion, and eloquence could take them. "How can we praise him, how can we who have been children of his? . . . A glory has departed . . . and we shiver in the cold and the dark."

The killings in the Punjab had spilled over into neighbouring Kashmir, where in the south Hindus were freely murdering their Muslim neighbours. Kashmir, beautiful and poverty-stricken, was one of the six hundred princely states, some of whose rulers were anxious, once the British had gone, to retain their own partial independence. (Hyderabad was another, but Nehru's new India employed force against its ruler, the Nizam, and within four days engulfed his dominions.) Hari Singh, Maharaja of Kashmir, a Hindu ruling a state where the majority of the people was Muslim, eventually, after fatal indecision, applied to join the Republic of India, but only when Pathan tribesmen, invading his territories with some 'unofficial' Pakistan support, had savaged their way to within five miles of the capital, Srinagar. Nehru's Government, regarding this invasion as Pakistan aggression, then decided to fly troops to save Srinagar, which they did. Nehru deplored the murder by Hindus in Southern Kashmir, but claimed that the tribesmen's invasion was simply a plot to seize Kashmir for Pakistan. So began the dispute between India and Pakistan which has poisoned relations between them ever since, involving them first in actual war and then in the constant mutual threat of war, and exhausting an absurd proportion of their ill-filled treasuries in military preparations. India referred the dispute to the United Nations, whose Security Council sent teams to report, and in due course to supervise a cease-fire in January 1949. In effect, Kashmir, the land whence came Nehru's own forebears, and whose beauty he deeply loved, has lain bisected ever since. Nehru early on conceded the principle of a plebiscite but steadily refused to allow the plebiscite to take place—ostensibly because it would cause such an upheaval as to bring the whole area once again into communal, and perhaps international, bloodshed. If (as would be a strong possibility) a majority voted for Pakistan, Nehru considered that he would be powerless to hold back the Indian demand for war against Pakistan. Kashmir remained a matter on which his mind was made up—some would say closed. To him Kashmir was Indian. In his view, Pakistan provoked an aggression and remained uncondemned by the United Nations (unlike, as he pointed out, North Korea in 1951). The deep bitterness remaining from this unhappy aftermath of partition has poisoned more than Indo-Pakistan relations. When Pakistan joined the Baghdad Pact (later CENTO) and accepted American military aid, it was only too easy for Indians to imagine that some of this aid might be turned against them. Britain, too, was frequently accused of being too sympathetic with Pakistan's position on Kashmir. It has been a sad, stubborn, and so far (1963) deadlocked story.

Continuing bitterness between Hindus and Muslims occasioned yet another serious outbreak of communal violence in 1950, when many thousands of Hindus were expelled or fled from the East Bengal area of Pakistan. This last great mass migration (perhaps a million people were involved altogether) served also to bring to a head inner conflicts within the Congress Party that eventually led to a showdown and a total victory for Nehru. Sardar Patel, Nehru's most important colleague and rival, was anxious, like many Right-wing Hindu extremists, to expel ten Muslims from India for every one Hindu fleeing from Pakistan, and so to whittle down the Muslim content of the new India, which still stood at the considerable figure of forty million. They wanted, in short, a Hindu state in the sense that Pakistan is a Muslim state, or Burma a Buddhist state. Nehru would have none of it. His India was to be 'secular.' No exclusive religion was to dominate it. Christians, Muslims, Sikhs, Parsees, Buddhists, Jews, atheists, tribal animists (there were twenty million of these last)—all were to be of equal status. Discrimination against any man by virtue of religion, race, or caste should be expressly forbidden (and in fact was forbidden in India's eventual Constitution of 1950). On other matters, too, Nehru was between 1947 and 1951 under attack from the Patel right wing. Nehru openly favoured planning and was not afraid to be called, in general terms, a socialist. He laid stress on social reforms (especially on land reform, education, and women's rights), and on industrialization. His policy was as his philosophy: a Western blend of socialism, liberalism, and secularism; a denial of fanaticism and extreme nationalism; a sane moderation. This moderation had even enabled him to accept membership of the Commonwealth, and, although India was herself a Republic, to admit the British monarch as symbolic head of the free association of Commonwealth peoples. When anti-British extremists protested and quoted his earlier speeches at him, he denied inconsistency; by giving India equal status and full independence, Britain had merited in return, as he had always said she would, full co-operation. Inside his own Congress Party, however, there were strong immoderate elements, and furthermore many flagrantly corrupt politicians. Nehru did battle against them uncompromisingly. Then, at the height of the struggle, Patel died—which undoubtedly strengthened Nehru's position. In any case, he always had his trump-card: his popularity with the masses, he, the old campaigner, Gandhi's favourite son, the scourge of corrupt pocket-liners, the aristocrat who was the idol of the common people. The Patel wing was brushed aside, and the elections of 1951–52 secured a double success: success for the Congress Party, despite its bickerings and corruption, and success for its now undoubted leader and master, Jawaharlal Nehru.

It was in all ways a remarkable landmark, this election. For one thing it was the biggest election that had ever been held in any country. No less than 105 million voted, four-fifths of them illiterate; and they voted soberly, with a 60 per cent. poll, all over the infinitely various Indian scene, in 133,000 polling stations. There was no violence; and the illiterate villagers were perhaps even more serious and conscientious than the townsmen. In 1957, the same percentage of an even larger electorate (193 million) voted, again peacefully, in India's second general election. These were India's first successful demonstrations of large-scale democracy. The competition of other forms of government, notably in Communist China, made them of key significance; for if democracy should fail in India, it might well be that totalitarian Communism would win a grand slam throughout Asia. At the moment there is no prospect of that, although too rosy a picture should not be painted. There *has* been some corruption and nepotism in India. The Congress Party in particular has perhaps been living on its past and putting on a sort of spiritual fat that Gandhi would have scorned. Its Ministers have often flaunted the trappings of power, with a limousine much larger than their sense of responsibility. Even Nehru himself lives in a palace. Victories at the elections have come too easily to prevent a certain rank-and-file lethargy and complacence. After all, it was the Congress that won freedom for India; the prestige and power that arose therefrom have been regarded by too many politicians as a cake to be shared. Periodic castigations by Nehru failed to rekindle the old enthusiasm, and it is at least arguable that British-style democracy may persist only as long as Nehru himself, its champion. The Indian Communists, once derided by Nehru as "the most stupid party among the Communist parties of the world," emerged from the 1957 election as the Congress Party's principal opposition, and for a time held power in the state of Kerala. But the expansionism of Red China and its challenge to Indians' view of their rightful northern borders have caused Communism to be for an Indian an unpatriotic creed, despite the fact that the Indian Communist Party eventually supported Nehru's stand against the Chinese. On the whole it seems probable that at present a greater *immediate* challenge to democracy comes not from the Left but from the Right—from conservative Hindu extremism. Nehru's supreme triumph would be to keep alight after his death his moderation and his love of liberty.

Two purely internal affairs caused much conflict in India during the 'fifties: the language controversy and the reorganization of the Indian states. What was to be the official language of a politically united India still divided into at least fourteen major language areas? "Hindustani," a compound of Hindi and Urdu, got no further than Esperanto in Europe. If Hindi were to be adopted, there was the supreme objection that it could not be understood by Southerners. In fact, the greatest of its champions in the Parliamentary debates on the issues spoke (like most of the others) in English—simply, as he explained, because he wished to be *understood*. That English itself should be adopted was regarded as an admission of failure and a perpetuation of imperialist influence. No other language commanded sufficient numerical support. Eventually English was accepted as a temporary second-best; but it was to be succeeded by Hindi in 1965. It has proved, however, quite impossible for a transition to take place so early, and educated Indians are likely to be long destined to continue speaking the language of their former imperial masters—as long, say, as those masters themselves seem likely to continue driving on the wrong side of the road, and for very similar reasons.

The language disputes, though heated, at least did not provoke bloodshed, as the reorganization of the states of India did. In Bombay, in Orissa, Bihar, and Bengal, and in the Punjab, very severe clashes arose when the attempt was made to reorganize the antique muddle of states large and small into sixteen modern units based predominantly on language and culture groups. In Bombay the rioting was especially bloody, and in the Punjab, as late as 1961, five years after the reorganization, there was an uncompleted 'fast-unto-death' by the Sikh leader, Master Tara Singh, in the cause of a separate Sikh state. Earlier, Nehru had shown considerable vacillation on various state issues; this time he loftily and consistently proposed to let the old man starve if necessary. The Master remains alive, and the Sikhs unsatisfied.

During the first few years after Independence, in the fluid and tense situation that existed, and held somewhat in check by the necessity of working with Patel and the Hindu conservatives, Nehru was unable to launch any sizable scheme of socialist planning such as he had always advocated. Meanwhile, growing unemployment, inflation, and profiteering all produced a mood of disillusion and discontent. Moreover, partition had dislocated the economy, artificially separating raw material areas, for instance in cotton, from their corresponding areas of manufacture, and cutting off natural granaries like West Punjab from the centres they customarily fed. Even without these troubles, the chronic problems of India seemed dauntingly huge and entrenched: a population rising by five millions every year, and already the poorest in the world, with an average annual income of under £20, and an expectation of life of about thirty years; a varied but everywhere medieval system of land tenure, with the peasantry crippled by tax payments and debts owed to the eternal money-lender; many scores of millions of tiny fragmented farmholdings, cultivated by ignorant farmers obstructive to new ideas, and in any case lacking capital to utilize them; less than a third of the land under crops, with great areas of wasteful fallow and "cultivable waste"; housing at the mud-hut level, and fuel at the cow-dung level, for perhaps three-quarters of all Indians; a great host of forty million landless labourers side by side with extensive rich men's estates; primitive methods of tillage and disease-ridden beasts; a period of up to eight months in the year when the climate enforces idleness on the mass of the peasantry (hence, partly, the Gandhian insistence on hand spinning and the need for cottage industries); a social system hidebound by its stubbornly lingering caste divisions, and still, despite all Gandhi's campaigns and all official denunciations, containing nearly fifty million Untouchables; most industries at the infant stage or non-existent altogether (though communications by Asiatic standards were good, thanks to British railways and ports); not a steel mill in the whole of India; great towns stinking with poverty, beggary, and destitution, while many business-men and speculators lived in opulence; an illiteracy rate of over 80 per cent., and under 10 per cent. enjoying any form of secondary education. Nehru's approach to these immense economic difficulties was gingerly. Nationalization was reserved at first mainly for those industries that in 1950 hardly existed—such as iron and steel, coal-mining, aircraft- and ship-building, with the addition of railways and armaments. In 1951, a First Five Year Plan was announced that was also a little unambitious, many thought. Private industry was left to rule the roost. The Indian tortoise, many considered, could not compare with the Chinese hare. The principal object of the first Plan was to ensure that improvements in agriculture overtook the rise in population, by the construction of a great fertilizer plant, irrigation works and flood control, hydroelectric schemes, and so on. It was a modest success: while population rose by 6 per cent., production rose by 18 per cent. Moreover, the most ambitious and fundamental of all India's projects was inaugurated during this era; it was Nehru's own favourite child, and with good reason. Known as the Community Project, it was an attack on Indian poverty at its roots, the village communities. These hundreds of thousands of villages of India were too small to form economic or enterprising units. Hence the Project proposed gradually to develop them into co-operatives of perhaps a hundred villages, and in each of these rural super-units to assign teams of educators and experts to stimulate and advise. They would have better methods of tillage to demonstrate, better rotations, better seeds, better ideas on drainage and irrigation. They would try to jerk the farmer out of his ancient conservatism, to enlist his enthusiasm for a new road, perhaps, a local school, a village council, a health clinic, even perhaps a centre for teaching adults to read. This to Nehru was "sacred work"; but it also has been slow work. The flame has been lit and is spreading, though not all of rural India has been swept yet with illumination. This is the most basic of all the revolutions that India needs, for even an 'industrialized' India will remain four-fifths, or even nine-tenths, agricultural. As Nehru knows, this revolution *must* succeed. Some of his critics have insisted that it will not, or will not fully, unless he is willing to grasp more firmly the nettle of land reform, to tackle more radically the absentee landlords, the rent system, and the multiple complications of Indian land tenure. One typically Indian approach to this land problem has been the 'village-gift' (*gramdan*) movement of the Gandhi-like figure Vinoba Bhave, who walks from village to village preaching his message of sacrifice and co-operation, and seeking, through the voluntary relinquishment of private land, a collectivization of farms by peaceful means. His successes have been considerable and impressive—yet they remain small against the vastness of the problem.

The Second Five Year Plan (1956–61), a considerably bolder venture than the first, ran into the heavy successive difficulties of flood, of drought, and of financial crisis. From the last of these, Nehru's Government sought refuge in severer taxation at home and increased foreign assistance, especially from the U.S.A. This American aid, though it was granted, was granted not quite ungrudgingly—

for Nehru never bothered to conceal his contempt for the more materialistic aspects of "the American way of life," and always (like Tito and Nasser), refused—even passionately refused—to have any 'strings' to his aid; and hence on their side many Americans were irritated by a man who, they thought, was 'soft' with the Russians, and morally 'superior' with themselves. Under the Second Plan, despite its setbacks, India has been developing heavy industries as well as agriculture. Three great steel plants have been built, each with the assistance of a separate foreign power—Britain, the U.S.S.R., and Germany; and the machine-tool, coal, electric power, heavy chemical, and oil industries are among the many other developments. By the end of her first decade of planning, India can claim an 18 per cent. rise in the national income per head. Her Third Plan is again ambitious.

And what of caste, the hobble round the legs of the new India? Complex, habitual, universal, potent, it has been part of India too long to be legislated away in a decade, or probably in a century. Caste declares these truths to be self-evident, that men are born unequal and that those outside the castes are born, and must live, unclean. It is a total denial of democracy. Moreover, it makes nonsense of any attempt to turn India into a mobile, industrial society. Working, say, as a bus conductor, or on a factory conveyor belt, a man can hardly spend all his time avoiding his fellow's shadow, or take time off to dip in the sacred Ganges in order to wash off the contamination of contact with an Untouchable. Nehru's Government has done what it can. Untouchability has been abolished in law; civil marriage is now permissible between members of any caste; and it is an offence to enforce any disability on the grounds of Untouchability. Right of access to temples, to rivers, tanks, and wells, and to public vehicles is secured to all Indians. It is easy to see that changes such as these are easier to promote in the town than in the village, where tradition and superstition die hard, and to see too how such socially revolutionary changes (together with others denying some of the ancient Hindu laws of marriage and enforcing monogamy) are regarded with suspicion by extreme Hindus. But the old high-caste Brahmin ascendancy is dying. Brahmins may still be 'top people,' but, squeezed out of many of their old privileged positions in Church, State, and countryside, many of them now turn to engineering, technology, or planning: still 'top people,' but of a different sort, building a different India, which will have less and less use for the old hierarchy, and the old caste prestige. It is said that even the Communist Party, that won control of Kerala, in the South, largely by attacking inequality and caste privilege, *was led by Brahmins*. But it is also true that the old cords tug hard: the Brahmin who deprecates caste conventions in public by day may still as he undresses in the privacy of his bedroom reveal the Sacred Thread of the Brahmin round his chest. Great changes are taking place too in women's status. Where in the old days it would be unthinkable for a girl to marry other than by the parentally arranged match within her sub-caste, now the girl herself may have some choice in the matter, and the man need not always be of her sub-caste—though it remains strongly probable that he will be. In every way Western ideas of equality, democracy, and emancipation of women, together with technology and industrialization, begin to permeate Hindu society and thought. And it must presumably be in the long run by the emancipation of its women that India will tackle one of the most controversial of its problems, its teeming population. At present there is death control (the expectation of life has advanced to thirty-seven years); but Nehru has (at least until recently) somewhat shied away from an unequivocal campaign in favour of birth control. Properly farmed, Indian land could, he thinks, fill many more mouths than even teeming India has at present.

In the domain of foreign policy, Nehru's primary principles since 1947 have been non-alignment in the Cold War and coexistence between rival ideologies; anti-colonialism; championship of the ex-colonial or Afro-Asian countries' status in the world; and hence a passionate attack on all forms of discrimination by white peoples against coloured or black. Nehru is often, and rightly, described as a man of reason: the pose of being above the battle, or at least above all but the righteous battles, comes to him with perhaps irritating ease. Yet no man, least of all an independent Indian, is independent of his emotions and history—and Nehru, however rational and moderate, is patently, to a fair extent, the creature of both. Russia never colonized India; Britain did. So when Russia invaded Hungary in 1956 she received from Nehru, and his spokesman, Krishna Menon, calm words and an extreme reluctance to assign blame. When at the same time Britain and France attacked Suez, they received immediate, excited, and outraged condemnation. (There was another point to consider, of course. If a United Nations commission were allowed to interfere in Hungary, might that not set a precedent for Kashmir?—and over Kashmir Nehru's emotions were positively passionate.) Again, although Nehru did finally condemn Communist North Korean aggression in 1950, he managed, then too, to convey an extreme sense of reluctance, and judiciously maintained that none of the parties concerned was wholly free from blame; but America's motives in resisting North Korean and Chinese forces received less charitable treatment. Certainly Nehru was emotionally predisposed to think well of the U.S.S.R. and the new Communist China. He was not himself a Communist, but he had long and openly professed admiration of a good deal in the Soviet way of life. There was a tendency too to regard these powers as fellow ex-underdogs, while the Americans (despite 1776) were demonstrably not so. Nehru, Harrovian and intellectual though he is, can no more escape his colonial memories than can Nasser or Nkrumah or Kenyatta. Indeed, being an old Harrovian of his particular era might positively accentuate his instinctive distrust of rich and upstart Americans. Thus SEATO, the attempt to link South East Asian states against Communist penetration, was seen by him and his Government simply as a device by which the Western powers could strengthen or re-establish their domination. The Baghdad Pact (later CENTO) was seen similarly as veiled British neo-imperialism to maintain a hold over the Middle East. Worse still, the only Asian state to belong to both these organizations was *Pakistan*—already, since the Kashmir struggle, regarded with hostility and suspicion.

Nehru does not approve of the word 'neutralism.' He likes instead to think of creating "an area of peace." "With us," he says, "peace is a passion"; and it is (within his own definitions) true. There is a genuine and reasonable hatred of the Cold War. The black-and-white view of politics so prevalent in the U.S.A. and among such movements as Moral Rearmament is offensive to him, as are such misused and overworked phrases as "the free world" or "freedom-loving nations." The only black-and-white world for him is where virtuous anti-colonialists face wicked colonialists, or where wicked Afrikaners or Southern Whites oppress virtuous Bantu or American Negroes. Colonialism apart, Nehru does not see international politics as a game of cops and robbers: such a view is altogether too brash and crude. It breeds too a sort of moral jingoism which is dangerous and could destroy the whole world. And unlike the Chinese Communists, Nehru has never been under the illusion that his country could survive a global nuclear cataclysm. There is also in Nehru's attitudes a strong legacy from Gandhian principles of pacifism, however watered down or modified by Nehru and the majority of his party. Surely, if there were not, the old Portuguese colony of Goa would not have lasted as long as it did; militarily it long lay at the mercy of India, before the final take-over at the end of 1961. And never was Nehru happier than when building up the Five Principles of Coexistence with Chou En-lai and the Chinese Communists—principles based on ideas such as equality, non-interference in one another's affairs, and commercial co-operation. Never was he so visibly nettled and shaken as when Chou En-lai's Government disregarded those principles and, having overrun Tibet, proceeded to lay claims upon frontier territories that all Indians regard as undoubtedly Indian. Over this treason of the Chinese against the ways of peace an angry Nehru at last—pressed hard by a violent domestic jingoism of his own followers—announced that if necessary India would go to war. They were words that did not lightly pass the lips of one brought up under the Mahatma.

Nehru's disillusionment with the aggressive foreign policies of China was especially severe since he had always championed the new China against foreign calumny, and seen in her the other great reborn Asian giant. The friendship of India and China, however different their political systems, was basic both to the "area of peace" policy and also to the concept of a renascent Asia freed from the chains of colonialism. This was the idea whose seed was sown in the Brussels conference of 1927. This was the healthy young growth that was shown to the world at the Bandung Conference of 1955. At Bandung, Chou En-lai's display of reasonableness impressed everybody, and many thought it partly due to Nehru's private influence; certainly the Americans and the European colonial powers were made to appear imperialist leopards whose spots were black and unchanging, while the Asiatic doves cooed in unison.

In the early 'fifties, however, China conquered Tibet, a land she had never ceased to claim, even when lacking the strength to hold it; and thus Chinese troops came to the very limits of India. Along this Himalayan border, however, Indian maps had always shown one frontier, dating from the heyday of British imperial power; and Chinese maps had always claimed territory well to the south of this demarcation, in particular at two points: high in remote Ladakh, in northern Kashmir, and in the North-East Frontier Agency, to the north of Assam. From 1959 onward increasingly angry words flew between Peking and Delhi over the roof of the world, where Chinese and Indian patrols probed and occasionally skirmished. In the wildernesses of Ladakh the Chinese had even been able to build, inside 'Indian' territory, a vital link in their system of strategic roads. Nehru and his Defence Minister, Krishna Menon, both favourably disposed towards the new China, still could not believe that its Government meant war. The Indians were committed to non-alignment in the Cold War; and—once Goa was taken—they threatened none, save perhaps, eventually, the Pakistanis in Kashmir. They relied to some extent on their very unaggressiveness to protect them. Hence, when in October 1962 the Chinese forces suddenly struck in the North-East Frontier Agency and Ladakh and swiftly routed the Indians, Nehru's policy was in shreds. Non-alignment and virtue were, after all, not enough.

A contrite and disillusioned Nehru publicly admitted his own responsibility. As for Menon, even Nehru's friendship could not save him; popular indignation forced his dismissal. And then, as the Chinese drove on south towards the Brahmaputra—and less swiftly in Ladakh—Nehru took a step whose full consequences are still far from certain: he appealed to Britain and the United States for massive aid. At this moment the Chinese unexpectedly announced a cease-fire which was also something of an ultimatum—for the terms laid down involved the cession of the vital Ladakh area.

One casualty of the frontier humiliation was what was left of the Gandhi spirit: a wave of militant patriotism swept India as its troops were overwhelmed in the North-east. Even if Nehru had wished to win peace by concession, it was unlikely that the mood of the country would have allowed him to.

It is a measure of Nehru's prestige in India that, amid the accompanying anger, humiliation, and recrimination, and in the face of the failure of his Chinese policy, his personal dominance does not appear to be endangered. Few other great national leaders have sat in the seat of power so long, or enjoyed such undisputed supremacy; perhaps, even now, few combine so many impressive qualities. In an intolerant and ranting world, his, on the whole, has been the cool voice of sanity. He offended many by his seizure of Goa, his stubbornness over Kashmir, his 'double-standards' over Suez and Hungary, his occasional airs of censorious rectitude. But his virtues are formidable: courage, intelligence, idealism, imagination, tolerance, moderation, magnanimity. He will need them all to cope with the equally formidable tasks that at present beset him.

Table of Events

(See also under Gandhi, pages 94–95)

1889.	Nehru born at Allahabad.
1905–10.	Nehru at Harrow and Cambridge.
1919.	Amritsar Massacre. Nehru joins Gandhian movement.
1921–45.	Serves nine prison sentences.
1924.	General Secretary of Congress Party.
1929.	President of Congress Party.
1947.	Independence of India, Pakistan, and Ceylon.
1946–50.	Inter-communal violence.
1947.	Kashmir conflict begins.
1947–51.	Duumvirate of Patel and Nehru.
1948.	Assassination of Gandhi.
1950.	New Constitution of India.
1951.	First Five-Year Plan.
1952, 1957, 1962:	General elections confirm Nehru in power.
1955.	Bandung Conference.
1956.	Second Five-Year Plan.
	Hungarian and Suez Crises.
1959 onward:	Indo-Chinese relations embittered.
1961.	Third Five-Year Plan. India occupies Goa.
1962.	India defeated in border war with China.
	Nehru turns to West for aid.

Some Recommended Books

General Books, Historical Atlases, etc.

BOYD, A.: *An Atlas of World Affairs* (Praeger, 1959).

CONNELL-SMITH, G.: *Pattern of the Post-war World* (Penguin Books, 1957).

ELLIOTT, F., and SUMMERSKILL, M.: *A Dictionary of Politics* (Penguin Books, 1957).

GUNTHER, J.: *Inside Europe Today* (Harper, 1961).

JACKSON, J. HAMPDEN: *The Between-war World* (Gollancz, 1947).

— *The Post-war Decade* (Gollancz, 1955).

MOWAT, C. L.: *Britain between the Wars, 1918–40* (Methuen, 1955).

RICHARDS, I., GOODSON, J. B., and MORRIS, J. A.: *Sketch-map History of the Great War and After 1914–39* (Harrap, 4th ed., 1961).

THOMSON, D.: *World History from 1914 to 1950* (O.U.P. 1954).

THOMSON, I.: *The Rise of Modern Asia* (Pitman, 1958).

WARD, B.: *Five Ideas that Change the World* (Norton, 1959).

Kemal Atatürk

ARMSTRONG, H. C.: *Grey Wolf: Mustafa Kemal* (Methuen, 1932; Penguin Books, 1937).

LEWIS, G. L.: *Turkey* (Benn, 1955).

ORGA, I.: *Phoenix Ascendant* (Hale, 1958).

ORGA, I. and M.: *Atatürk* (Joseph, 1962).

Lloyd George and Churchill

CHURCHILL, W. S.: *Into Battle: Speeches of the Hon. Winston S. Churchill* (Cassell, 1941).

COWLES, V.: *Winston Churchill* (Grosset, 1960).

EADE, C. (Ed.): *Churchill: by his Contemporaries* (Hutchinson, 1953).

JONES, T.:*Lloyd George* (O.U.P., 1951).

KIERNAN, R. H.: *Lloyd George* (Harrap, 1940).

MOOREHEAD, A.: *Gallipoli* (Harper, 1956).

OWEN, F.: *Tempestuous Journey: Lloyd George, his Life and Times* (Hutchinson, 1954).

SCOTLAND, A. (Ed.): *Sir Winston Churchill's "The Second World War"* (Cassell, 1960).
THOMSON, M.: *David Lloyd George* (Hutchinson, 1948).

Lenin, Stalin, and Khrushchev

CHARQUES, R. D.: *Short History of Russia* (Dutton, 1956).
CONQUEST, R.: *Common Sense about Russia* (Macmillan, 1960).
CRANKSHAW, E.: *Khrushchev's Russia* (Penguin Books, 1959).
DEUTSCHER, I.: *Stalin* (O.U.P., 1949).
GUNTHER, J.: *Inside Russia Today* (Harper, 1958).
HILL, C.: *Lenin and the Russian Revolution* (E.U.P., 1947).
KELLEN, K.: *Khrushchev, a Political Portrait* (Praeger, 1961).
KOESTLER, A.: *Darkness at Noon* (Macmillan, 1940).
LEONHARD, W.: *Child of the Revolution* (Collins, 1957).
MOOREHEAD, A.: *The Russian Revolution* (Harper, 1958).
ORWELL, G.: *Animal Farm* (Harcourt, Brace, 1954).
PALOCZI-HORVATH, G.: *Khrushchev: The Making of a Dictator* (Little, Brown, 1960).
PARES, B.: *History of Russia* (Knopf, 1953).
PISTRAK, L.: *The Grand Tactician: Khrushchev's Rise to Power* (Praeger, 1961).
REED, J.: *Ten Days that Shook the World* (Vintage, 1960).
TROTSKY, L.: *Stalin* (Grosset, 1958).
— *The Revolution Betrayed* (Faber and Faber, 1937).
— *The Russian Revolution,* ed. by F. W. Dupee (Doubleday, 1959).

Gandhi and Nehru

BRECHER, M.: *Nehru, a Political Biography* (O.U.P., 1959).
FISCHER, L.: *Life of Mahatma Gandhi* (Harper, 1950).
NANDA, B. R.: *Mahatma Gandhi* (Beacon, 1958).
— *The Nehrus* (Allen and Unwin, 1962).
NEHRU, J.: *An Autobiography* (John Lane the Bodley Head, 1936).
PANIKKAR, K. M.: *Common Sense about India* (Macmillan, 1960).
POLAK, H. L. S., BRAILSFORD, H. N., and LORD PETHICK-LAWRENCE: *Mahatma Gandhi* (Odhams, 1949).
ROLLAND, R.: *Mahatma Gandhi* (Allen and Unwin, 1935).
SCHMID, P.: *India: Mirage and Reality* (Putnam, 1961).
SHEEAN, V.: *Nehru, the Years of Power* (Random House, 1959).
ZINKIN, T.: *Caste Today* (O.U.P., 1962).

Mussolini and Hitler

ALFIERI, D.: *Dictators Face to Face* (Elek, 1954).
BULLOCK, A.: *Hitler, A Study in Tyranny* (Harper, 1960).

HIBBERT, C.: *Il Duce: The Life of Benito Mussolini* (Little, Brown, 1962).

KERSTEN, F.: *Kersten Memoirs* (Hutchinson, 1956).

LEBER, A.: *Conscience in Revolt* (Vallentine, 1956).

MANVELL, R. and FRAENKEL, H.: *Dr. Goebbels* (Simon and Schuster, 1960).

MANVELL, R., and FRAENKEL, H.: *Goering* (Simon and Schuster, 1962).

MONELLI, P.: *Mussolini* (Thames and Hudson, 1953).

MUGGERIDGE, M. (Ed.): *Ciano's Diary* (1) 1937–39 and (2) 1939–43 (Heinemann, 1947).

PAPEN, F. VON: *Memoirs* (Deutsch, 1952).

ROTHFELS, H.: *The German Opposition to Hitler* (Wolff, 1961).

SMITH, D. MACK: *Mussolini, Artist in Propaganda* (History To-day, April 1959).

TREVOR-ROPER, H. R.: *The Last Days of Hitler* (Macmillan, 1947).

WHEELER-BENNETT, J. W.: *The Nemesis of Power: the Germany Army in Politics 1918–45* (Macmillan, 1953).

YOUNG, D.: *Rommel: The Desert Fox* (Harper, 1951).

Roosevelt and Modern U.S.A.

BRAGDON, H. W., and McCUTCHEN, S. P.: *History of a Free People* (Macmillan, 1956).

BURNS, J. M.: *Roosevelt: the Lion and the Fox* (Harcourt, Brace, 1956).

EINAUDI, M.: *The Roosevelt Revolution* (Harcourt, Brace, 1959).

GUNTHER, J.: *Roosevelt in Retrospect* (Harper, 1950).

NYE, R. B. and MORPURGO, J. E.: *History of the U.S.A.*, Vol. 2 (Penguin Books, 1955).

PERKINS, F.: *The Roosevelt I Knew* (Viking, 1946).

ROSENMAN, S. I.: *Working with Roosevelt* (Harper, 1952).

Tito

MACLEAN, F.: *Eastern Approaches* (Cape, 1949).

ZILLIACUS, K.: *Tito of Yugoslavia* (Joseph, 1952).

Nasser and the Arab World

ATIYAH, E.: *The Arabs* (Penguin Books, 1955).

CHILDERS, E.: *Common Sense about the Arab World* (Macmillan, 1960).

JOESTEN, J.: *Nasser: the Rise to Power* (Odhams, 1960).

LACOUTURE, J. and S.: *Egypt in Transition* (Criterion, 1958).

STEWART, D.: *Young Egypt* (Wingate, 1958).

WINT, G., and CALVOCORESSI, P.: *Middle East Crisis* (Penguin Books, 1957).

De Gaulle

ASHCROFT, E.: *De Gaulle* (Transatlantic, 1962).
BROGAN, D. W.: *Development of Modern France (1870–1939)* (Hamilton, 1940).
DE GAULLE, C.: *Call to Honor* (Simon and Schuster, 1958).
— *Unity* (Simon and Schuster, 1959).
— *Salvation* (Simon and Schuster, 1960).
PICKLES, D.: *France: The Fourth Republic* (Barnes & Noble, 1955).
— *The Fifth French Republic* (Praeger, 1960).
SCHOENBRUN, D.: *As France Goes* (Harper, 1957).
WERTH, A.: *France, 1940–55* (Hale, 1956).
— *The De Gaulle Revolution* (International Publications Service, 1960).
WILLIAMS, P. M., and HARRISON, M.: *De Gaulle's Republic* (Longmans, 1960).

Franco and Salazar

ATKINSON, W. C.: *A History of Spain and Portugal* (Penguin Books, 1960).
AUBIER, D., and DE LARA, M. T.: *Spain* (Viking, 1960).
BRENAN, G.: *The Spanish Labyrinth* (C.U.P., 1943).
FIGUEIREDO, A. DE: *Portugal and its Empire: the Truth* (Gollancz, 1961).
FRYER, P. and PINHEIRO, McG.: *Oldest Ally: Salazar's Portugal* (Hillary, 1961).
HEMINGWAY, E.: *For Whom the Bell Tolls* (Scribner, 1940; Penguin, 1955).
MADARIAGA, S. DE: *Spain* (Praeger, 1958).
ORWELL, G.: *Homage to Catalonia* (Beacon, 1955).
THOMAS, H.: *The Spanish Civil War* (Harper, 1961).
WHITAKER, A. P.: *Spain and the Defense of the West* (Harper, 1961).

Mao Tse-tung and Modern China

CARTIER-BRESSON, H.: *China in Transition* (Thames and Hudson, 1956).
GUILLAIN, R.: *The Blue Ants* (Secker and Warburg, 1957).
LATOURETTE, K. S.: *History of Modern China* (Penguin Books, 1956).
PALOCZI-HORVATH, G.: *Mao Tse-tung, Emperor of the Blue Ants* (Secker and Warburg, 1962).
PAYNE, R.: *Mao Tse-tung* (Secker and Warburg, 1951).

PING-CHIA KUO: *China: New Age and New Outlook* (Penguin Books, 1960).
SCHMID, P.: *New Face of China* (Harrap, 1958).
TOWNSEND, P.: *China Phoenix* (Cape, 1955).
WINT, G.: *Spotlight on Asia* (Penguin Books, 1955).
— *Dragon and Sickle* (Pall Mall Press, 1959).
— *Common Sense about China* (Macmillan, 1960).
WOLLASTON, N.: *China in the Morning* (Roy Publishers, 1960).

Index

DATE DUE

NOV 29 '65			
APR 12 '66			
APR 26 '66			
NOV 30 '67			
MAR 26 '68			
APR 22 '68			
MAY 8 '68			
FEB 4 '75			
FEB 20 '75			
MAR 7 '75			
NO 8 '82			
MAR 4 '86			
GAYLORD			PRINTED IN U.S.A.